Business Accounting

Business
ACCOUNTING

Rob Jones

Causeway Press

Acknowledgements

Educational and accounting consultant
Shaun Urwin, Head of Accounting, St Mary's College, Blackburn.

Accounting consultant
Chris Sawyer, FCCA of Sawyer, Quine & Co, Ormskirk.

The author and publisher would also like to thank the following people for their help and guidance in writing this book.
Jim Barr, Kate May, Helen Trusch and Ray Wooding.

All errors are the responsibility of the author and publisher. Any errors or omissions brought to the notice of the publisher will be corrected in subsequent printings.

Cover design, page design and typesetting by Caroline Waring-Collins
Additional typesetting by Anneli Jameson
Proofreading by Heather Doyle and Tony Barnes
Edited by Jim Nettleship and Dave Gray
Cover photograph: Telegraph Colour Library

British Library Cataloguing in Publication Data
A catalogue record for this book is available from the British Library.

ISBN 1 902796 41 1

Causeway Press Ltd
PO Box 13, Ormskirk, Lancashire, L39 5HP
© Rob Jones
1st impression, 2002

Typesetting by Waring-Collins Ltd
Printed and bound by Legoprint, Italy

Contents

What is accounting?

unit**objectives**

To understand:
- the nature of business transactions;
- the accounting process;
- who produces accounts;
- who uses accounting information;
- the role of an accounts department.

Business transactions

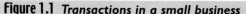

Business activity involves purchasing resources, such as raw materials, labour and machinery, and selling goods or services that have been produced using these resources. The purchase of resources from suppliers and the sale of products to customers are examples of BUSINESS TRANSACTIONS. Other examples include borrowing money from the bank and the payment of taxes.

Figure 1.1 shows examples of business transactions that might take place in a small business, such as a restaurant. The business needs to keep records of all its transactions. The value of sales is likely to be recorded on a till roll. The value of purchases might be written in a BOOK. During the year, a small business such as a restaurant might be involved in several thousand individual transactions.

By contrast, a large telecommunications business such as Orange might make billions of transactions each year. Every telephone call made using the Orange network is recorded as a separate transaction. Such transactions are recorded electronically and their value is calculated by computer. Orange's customers receive regular statements summarising these transactions. Orange must also record details of its expenditure, such as payments to its employees and purchases of telecommunications equipment.

Figure 1.1 *Transactions in a small business*

The purchase of potatoes from a wholesaler for £250.

The sale of a chicken salad to a customer for £7.90.

The sale of fish and chips to a customer for £5.30.

The payment of £120 wages to an employee.

The accounting process

ACCOUNTING is a process that involves recording, classifying and summarising business transactions. The aim is to generate financial information that can be communicated to a range of people and institutions who will then make use of this information.

The stages of the accounting process are shown in Figure 1.2 (and are described in more detail in unit 2). The first stage is the identification and recording of business transactions. For example, a business such as a restaurant will identify the value of its sales to customers and its purchases of raw materials

QUESTION 1

Karren Engstrom makes wax candles and models for gift shops in Devon and Cornwall. She employs three other staff and operates her business from a waxworks in Exeter. On 11 December 2000, the following business transactions were recorded.

1. Sold candles to Lizard Gifts for £156.
2. Paid £450 wages to employees.
3. Bought materials from a supplier for £210.
4. Sold wax models to The Bude Gift Shop for £279.
5. Sold candles to a local church for £90.

(a) Classify each transaction made by Karren Engstrom.
(b) How might the transactions be summarised?
(c) Suggest why Karren might keep records of such transactions.

such as potatoes and fish. The second stage in the accounting process is the classification and summary of these business transactions. They must be placed into various categories and totalled for a particular trading period. In the example of the restaurant, the transactions could be categorised in the following way:

- the purchase of potatoes from a wholesaler for £250: **purchases**;
- the sale of fish and chips to a customer for £5.30: **sales**;
- the sale of a chicken salad to a customer for £7.90: **sales**;
- the payment of £120 to an employee: **wages**.

The categories used in the above example are typical of those used in accounting. **Purchases** are transactions that involve buying raw materials or goods intended for resale. **Sales** are transactions that involve selling goods or services to customers. **Wages** are payments to employees. Other examples of categories that could be used are rent, motor expenses, bank charges, heating and lighting and advertising. When transactions have been classified in this way it is usual to summarise them. This might involve adding up the totals every week. Business transactions are summarised so that large numbers of transactions can be handled more easily.

At the end of an accounting period, the overall totals in each category are calculated. So, for example, a business will add up total sales and total purchases. By measuring these totals a business can generate useful financial information. This includes the amount of PROFIT or LOSS that the business has made. A business will make a profit if its sales revenue is greater than its costs. If costs are greater than revenue, a loss is made.

The last stage in the accounting process is to communicate information in a suitable format to people and institutions who will use it. Certain types of business are legally obliged to publish an annual report which contains their **final accounts** (see unit 17). Some of the information is required within a business. For instance, managers might need information to help them make decisions. The owners will want to know how the business is performing and will also be interested in the level of profit. The Inland Revenue will base its tax assessment on this profit.

Figure 1.2 *The accounting process*

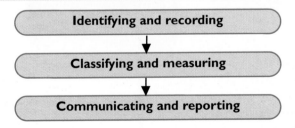

Who produces accounts?

The first stages of the accounting process, ie those aspects concerned with identifying and recording data, are known as BOOKKEEPING. Bookkeepers keep and maintain records of business transactions. The bookkeeping information is used by **accountants** to produce and then interpret accounts. There are different types of accountants, as shown in Figure 1.3.

Figure 1.3 *Types of accountants*

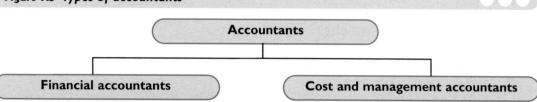

FINANCIAL ACCOUNTANTS are mainly concerned with past transactions. Their role is to supervise the bookkeeping process, produce final accounts and interpret financial information. Some financial accountants are employed directly by businesses. They supervise the bookkeeping process in their own accounts department and prepare the final accounts and other accounting information for the organisation that employs them. Some financial accountants are taxation specialists. Their role is to ensure that the business minimises the tax paid to the government.

Some accountants are employed in specialist accountancy firms. The work carried out by these **private practice accountants** can involve the following tasks.

- Preparing final accounts for businesses which do not employ their own specialist accountants.
- AUDITING business accounts. This involves checking the authenticity of bookkeeping records and final accounts. The auditors need to check that the accounts produced by a business are '**true and fair**'. It is a legal requirement for most large companies to have their accounts checked by an independent firm of accountants and registered auditors.
- Advising businesses on tax issues. Businesses often employ accountants to help reduce their tax liability.
- Consultancy work. This might involve giving advice to business owners, such as how to raise more finance or how to improve financial control in the organisation.
- Specialist work, such as the administration of trusts or dealing with insolvent businesses (see unit 20).

COST and MANAGEMENT ACCOUNTANTS are concerned with providing information to help the decision making process in business. They might also be involved in forecasting, controlling and evaluating costs. **Management accountants** are often qualified in financial accounting but also have training in economics and management science. They play an increasingly important role in the planning and running of business organisations.

Cost accountants are specialists who provide cost information. For instance, they might be involved in calculating the production cost of products or of contract work that a business has taken on. It is important to be able to work out the costs of production. This allows a business to decide

QUESTION 2

The role of accountants in business has grown in recent years. In particular they are getting more involved in decision making and planning. The salaries and benefits that accountants receive reflect the value that they provide. Figure 1.4 shows a job advert for an accountant placed by a leading electronics company.

(a) What type of accountant is AIWA trying to recruit? Explain your answer.
(b) Describe the type of work that the successful applicant might be expected to undertake.

Source: adapted from the *Financial Times*.

Figure 1.4 *A job advert for an accountant*

European Finance Manager

AIWA is known throughout the world for high quality audio visual products. Turnover within the European market is continuing to grow through increasing market share and new product categories. European Headquarters are located in the UK, with distributors throughout Western and Eastern Europe.

c£45,000 + Benefits

Your responsibilities will include:
- control and analysis of European cash management systems
- development and implementation of Risk Management Strategy
- provision of financial control and analysis on key strategic projects
- review, analysis and production of a consolidated European budget.

West London

Ideally, candidates will have a recognised accountancy qualification, preferably with three years post qualification experience, and previous experience of a fast moving and dynamic organisation. They will be able to demonstrate a flexible and proactive approach, while adding value to a rapidly growing business. Previous experience in financial markets and banking relationships would also be advantageous.

what price to charge in order to cover costs or to make a profit. Cost accountants might also calculate other costs such as the cost of moving premises, the cost of making a number of staff redundant or the cost of installing some new plant. Cost accountants often provide information for management accountants and therefore a strong link exists between the two.

The users of accounting information

Accounting information is of interest to a wide variety of users. Some of the most important users are shown in Figure 1.5.

Figure 1.5 *Main users of financial information*

The individuals and organisations that have an interest in the accounts of a particular business are sometimes called STAKEHOLDERS. These need accounting information for different reasons.

- **Owners** - to assess the profitability of the business and to judge the performance of managers.
- **Managers** - to help make decisions and plans for the business and to exercise control.
- **Government** - to assess how much tax the business should pay and, in some cases, to decide whether financial support is needed.
- **Suppliers** - to assess whether the business can afford to pay for the goods and services supplied.
- **Customers** - to assess whether the business is able to continue in business and to meet the needs of customers.
- **Lenders** - to assess the ability of the business to repay its debts and to pay any interest owed.
- **Employees** - to assess whether the business can continue to provide employment and to pay higher wages.
- **Competitors** - to assess how well the rival business is performing.
- **Community groups** - to assess the business's impact on the community and the wider environment. Social accounting is covered in unit 46.
- **Investment analysts** - to assess the possible risks and rewards of investing in the business.

The accounts department

Large businesses often have an accounts department. Within this department a number of bookkeeping and accounting tasks will be undertaken. An example of the structure of an accounts department is shown in Figure 1.6. The diagram shows the chain of command, ie to whom different people are responsible.

Figure 1.6 *An example of an accounts department*

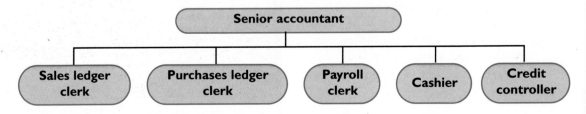

- The head of the accounts department is the **senior accountant** who will be responsible for its running. This person will be accountable to the owners of the business or a more senior executive. The senior accountant might be responsible for recruiting the department's staff, handling the department's **budget** and reporting to the senior management team. He or she is likely to be a management accountant and will be involved in decision making.
- The **sales ledger clerk** is responsible for dealing with customer accounts. This person will record all transactions relating to the firm's sales and will deal with enquiries on customer accounts.
- The **purchases ledger clerk** is responsible for dealing with supplier accounts (see unit 10). This person's job is to record all transactions relating to the firm's purchases of resources. The work will also involve dealing with enquiries on supplier accounts.
- The **payroll clerk** is responsible for the calculation of employees' wages and salaries. This might involve calculating gross pay, by adding overtime payments to the basic wage, and then calculating net pay by subtracting deductions such as tax, National Insurance and pension contributions.
- The **cashier** is responsible for all banking and cash transactions. This person's work involves checking bank statements to see if they agree with entries in the bookkeeping system, ensuring that cheques are sent to suppliers and, possibly, managing the **petty cash** system (see unit 13).
- The **credit controller** has the task of ensuring that customers pay for goods and services when payment becomes due. This person might also be involved in assessing whether new customers are creditworthy, collecting overdue payments and making decisions regarding **bad debts** (see unit 20). The credit controller will work closely with the sales ledger clerk because both deal directly with customers.

QUESTION 3

West Point Cycles is a medium-sized manufacturer of mountain bikes. It employs 76 staff and is based in Bristol. The accounts department is organised in the same way as the one illustrated in Figure 1.6. The staff employed in the department are:

    Sherwin - senior accountant
    Ruth - credit controller and cashier
    Pauline - sales ledger clerk
    Ron - purchases ledger clerk
    Beth - payroll clerk.

One morning, when the accounts staff arrive at the office, the following tasks have to be dealt with urgently.

1. A customer telephones to make an enquiry regarding a possible error on his account.
2. A supplier who is waiting in reception requires a cheque payment.
3. Nine purchases need to be entered into the bookkeeping system.
4. An employee has a query on her wages slip.

(a) Explain which members of the accounts department would deal with the above tasks.
(b) Explain Sherwin's role in the department.
(c) Suggest how the owners of West Point Cycles might make use of the information generated by the accounting department.

key terms

Accounting - a process that involves recording, classifying and summarising business transactions to generate useful financial information that can be communicated to a range of users.

Auditing - checking by accountants that the accounts produced by a business are 'true and fair'.

Book - a financial record of transactions.

Bookkeeping - the process of recording all the details of business transactions.

Business transaction - an event that affects the finances of a business, for example the purchase of resources from suppliers and the sale of products to customers.

Cost accountant - a specialist that calculates the cost of specific business activities.

Financial accountant - an accountant involved in the preparation of final accounts from bookkeeping records.

Loss - the amount by which business costs are greater than sales revenue in a given trading period.

Management accountant - an accountant involved in the preparation of financial reports, statements and other data for use in decision making.

Profit - the amount of business income left over after all business costs have been met for a trading period.

Stakeholders - the individuals and organisations that have an interest in the accounts of a particular business.

UNIT ASSESSMENT   QUESTION 1

Atherton and Jenkins manufactures catering equipment for hotels, restaurants and other caterers. The company employs 60 staff. The main role of its accounts department is to keep accurate records of all business transactions, provide monthly accounts for the management team and ensure that customers are paying for what they have bought.

MEMO

TO: Accounts
FROM: C. Jones (marketing)
DATE: 23.2.00
SUBJECT: Customer complaint

I have just spoken to an angry customer (P. Collins & Co.) who complain that they have received an invoice for a payment which they actually made three weeks ago. The amount is £456 for goods they purchased on 12.11.00.
Can you deal with this please?

There are three staff in the department:
- Jenny - a financial accountant in charge of the department;
- Maxine - a bookkeeper responsible for keeping records;
- Tariq - a bookkeeper responsible for wages, chasing customer payments and writing out cheques to suppliers.

On 23 March 2000 the memo shown below was received by the accounts department.

(a) **Which member of the accounts department is most likely to have recorded the transaction that was conducted on 12 November 2000?**

(b) **Assuming that the customer had made the payment, who might be to blame for the error? Explain your answer.**

(c) **Outline the reasons why a company like Atherton and Jenkins has an accounts department.**

summary questions

1. Give four examples of business transactions.
2. How might a small business keep records of its sales?
3. What are the main stages in the accounting process?
4. In what stages in the accounting process is a bookkeeper involved?
5. What is the difference between a management accountant and a financial accountant?
6. Suggest two tasks that a cost accountant might undertake.
7. State three services that an accountant in private practice might offer.
8. What is a stakeholder in a business?
9. State two users of accounting information.
10. Briefly describe the roles of (i) a payroll clerk; (ii) a sales ledger clerk; (iii) a purchases ledger clerk.

UNIT ASSESSMENT   QUESTION 2

Crawley Aerials is owned by Linda and David Ashton. The business specialises in selling, fitting and servicing TV satellite systems for customers in mid-Sussex. Most of the work is carried out by the owners. However, they do employ an apprentice and two part-time fitters who both work for three days per week.

The business is run from a shop which was bought using money borrowed from a mortgage lender. Recently, Crawley Aerials won a contract from a local education authority to upgrade and maintain the satellite systems in its secondary schools. This required the business to buy a second van which it did using a bank loan.

The Ashtons keep their own bookkeeping records and employ a firm of accountants to prepare their end-of-year accounts. In 2000, the business had sales of £98,000 and a profit before tax of £12,500.

(a) **Which users of financial information will be most directly interested in the amount of profit made by Crawley Aerials?**
(b) **Suggest which other 'stakeholders' might be interested in the financial performance of Crawley Aerials. Explain why they would be interested.**

unit 2

Stages in the accounting process

unit objectives

To understand:
- the stages in the accounting process;
- the relationship between source documents, books of prime entry, ledger accounts and final accounts.

The accounting process

Figure 2.1 shows in detail the stages that take place in the accounting process. The term **bookkeeping** is used to describe the first stages of the process, ie those concerned with identifying and recording transactions.

Identifying transactions When business transactions occur, it is usual for SOURCE DOCUMENTS to be produced. Examples include **receipts**, **paying-in slips** and **invoices** (see units 3 and 4). Source documents are generally retained for a number of years so that businesses can verify that particular transactions have occurred. This might be important if a dispute arises with a customer or supplier, or if the Inland Revenue investigates the affairs of the business.

Figure 2.1 *Stages in the accounting process*

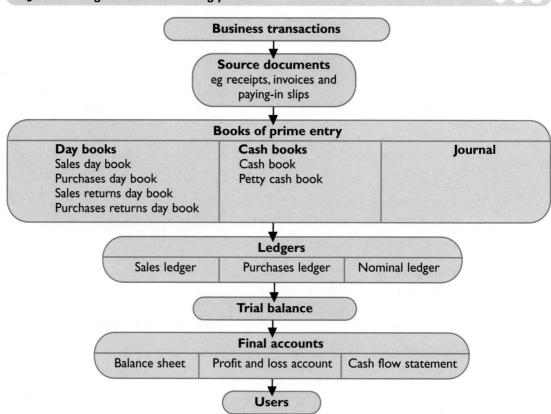

Recording transactions Over a period of time, most businesses generate large numbers of source documents. The details from these documents are summarised and recorded in BOOKS OF PRIME ENTRY. These are also known as **books of original entry** or **primary accounting records**. By summarising the details in this way, the process of bookkeeping is made quicker and more efficient. For example, it is easier to check past transactions by looking at the books of prime entry than by sorting through large numbers of source documents.

Many small business owners record their own transactions. However, some businesses employ a bookkeeper who is responsible for recording the details. Large business organisations are likely to have their own accounts departments where bookkeepers work under the supervision of accountants.

The books of prime entry were at one time actual books into which the details of transactions were recorded manually. Today computers are increasingly used and the books of prime entry are simply computer files. Nevertheless, they retain their original name and purpose.

Businesses generally keep separate books for different types of transaction. So, for example, sales are entered in one book, and purchases in another. The books which many businesses use are summarised below.

- **Sales day book** or sales journal (see unit 9) records details of sales made to customers. Most businesses record credit sales, where the customer is given a period of time to pay, in the sales day book and use the cash book for cash sales, where payment is immediate.
- **Purchases day book** or purchases journal (see unit 10) records details of the credit purchases made from suppliers. Most businesses record cash purchases in the cash book.
- **Sales returns day book** or returns inwards journal (see unit 11) records returns of goods that have been sold, ie details of goods returned to the business by customers.
- **Purchases returns day book** or returns outwards journal (see unit 11) records details of goods returned by the business to suppliers.
- **Cash book** (see unit 12) records the money received and paid out by a business. This book is normally reserved for bank transactions and is therefore a record of money paid into and out of a bank account.
- **Petty cash book** (see unit 13) records small or minor cash transactions in which notes and coins are used for payment.
- **Journal** or general journal, or journal proper (see unit 14) records transfers of money between accounts, or those transactions not recorded elsewhere. The journal is a diary for recording less common transactions or adjustments, such as the correction of errors in accounts.

Classifying and summarising transactions At the end of each day, week or month, batches of transactions are totalled and POSTED, ie transferred, from the books of prime entry to LEDGERS. A system of bookkeeping known as **double entry** is used in the ledger accounts (see unit 8). By using the books of prime entry to summarise the information from source documents, fewer details need to be posted to the ledger accounts. This speeds up the process and therefore improves efficiency. However, the distinction between the books of prime entry and ledger accounts is not clear cut in the case of cash books. These fulfil both the roles of books of prime entry and of double entry accounts. This is explained in more detail in unit 12.

Ledgers are vital to any bookkeeping system. They contain summarised information regarding individual ACCOUNTS. An account holds details of transactions that are similar in type. For example, a customer's account might contain information such as the value of goods bought and payments made.

Historically, the ledger was a leather bound book, subdivided into three main sections:

- **Sales ledger** - this contains all of the customer accounts. It shows details of sales and how much is owed by customers. The accounts in the purchase and sales ledgers are all **personal accounts** and are given the names of suppliers and customers.
- **Purchases ledger** - this contains all of the supplier accounts. It shows how much a business has purchased and what is owed to each supplier.
- **Nominal or general ledger** - this contains **impersonal accounts** such as wages, rent and bank charges, and **real accounts** such as machinery and buildings.

Today, these ledgers are often in the form of computer files.

Checking transactions An important stage in the accounting process is the preparation of a trial balance (see unit 16). A trial balance is a summary of information contained in the ledger accounts. It is used to check the arithmetic accuracy of bookkeeping.

Communicating useful accounting information The final stage in the accounting process is to present the financial information contained in ledgers in a meaningful and useful form. In the UK, businesses that are incorporated as companies (see unit 33), are legally obliged to publish an ANNUAL REPORT which includes the **final accounts**. These are the PROFIT AND LOSS ACCOUNT, the BALANCE SHEET and the CASH FLOW STATEMENT (see unit 38).

- The **profit and loss account** shows the income and expenditure of a business over a trading period. It is used to calculate the amount of profit the business makes.

- The **balance sheet** shows the value of resources owned by a business and the sources of finance, ie money raised by borrowing and from the owners. It represents a 'snapshot' of the business's financial circumstances at a particular point in time.
- The **cash flow statement** shows sources and uses of cash over a trading period.

key terms

Account - details of transactions that are similar in type, such as those in connection with a named supplier.

Annual Report and Accounts - a formal company report containing financial and other performance information that is produced for the owners of the business once a year.

Balance sheet - a statement showing the value of resources, sources of finance and financial circumstances of a business. It represents a 'snapshot' of the business's affairs at a particular moment in time.

Books of prime entry (or books of original entry, or primary accounting records) - the books in which details from source documents are first recorded.

Cash flow statement - a statement showing the sources and uses of cash for a trading period.

Ledger - a collection of accounts of a similar type.

Post - a term used to describe the transfer of information from the books of prime entry to the ledgers.

Profit and loss account - a summary of business income and expenditure used to calculate the profit (or loss) made in an accounting period.

Source documents - documents issued by businesses in the course of transactions.

UNIT ASSESSMENT QUESTION 1

Andrew McGowan owns a fish farm in the Scottish Highlands. He sells fish to wholesalers and to a large supermarket chain. His business has flourished in recent years even though the price of fish has fallen. On the 12 June 2000, the following business transactions were recorded by Andrew.

1. Fish sold to A. Parkin (fish merchant) for £260.
2. Fish food purchased from D. McBride for £78.
3. Boat maintenance expenses paid £100.
4. Fish sold to S. Walters (fish merchant) for £200.
5. Equipment purchased for £280.

(a) Distinguish between personal and impersonal accounts in the above transactions.
(b) How might the transactions be verified?
(c) Why is it important to verify such transactions?

summary questions

1. Why are source documents required by businesses?
2. Which are the main books of prime entry?
3. What is the difference between a sales day book and a purchases day book?
4. What is the difference between a cash book and a petty cash book?
5. What happens to the information that is summarised in the books of prime entry?
6. Where is the double entry system of accounting used?
7. Give two examples of accounts that might be found in the nominal ledger.
8. What is a trial balance used for?
9. What are the final accounts of a business?
10. What is the difference between the profit and loss account and the balance sheet?

UNIT ASSESSMENT QUESTION 2

Trevor Anderson runs a printing business. He specialises in greetings cards such as birthday cards, Christmas cards and cards for special occasions. He employs three other staff and operates from rented premises in Sheffield. Trevor used to employ a bookkeeper but in order to cut costs he has decided to record all business transactions himself at the end of the week. Trevor's accountant has suggested that if he keeps careful records the accountancy fees charged at the end of the year will be lower. Trevor uses a manual system that consists of day books, a cash book, a purchases ledger, a sales ledger and a nominal ledger. When he first started, Trevor was uncertain how to record the transactions listed below.

1. The payment of annual rent of £5,000.
2. The purchase of printing paper from a supplier £400.
3. The payment of wages to staff £600.
4. The sale of wedding cards for £100.

(a) In which ledgers should the transactions be recorded? Explain your answer.
(b) Suggest why accountancy fees might be lower if Trevor keeps careful records.
(c) What might be the consequences if Trevor makes a mistake when recording transactions?

unit**objectives**

To understand:
- the nature and purpose of source documents;
- the stages in a business transaction;
- which documents are used in a business transaction.

What are source documents?

Businesses usually ensure that transactions are verified by source documents. These documents:
- provide evidence that a transaction has taken place;
- provide detailed information about the nature of the transaction. This is particularly important for CREDIT TRANSACTIONS. In such cases, goods are sold but payment is made at a later date, unlike cash transactions where payment is immediate (see units 9 and 10);
- help to ensure that the right goods are sent to the right place, at the right time;
- provide a means of checking that deliveries of goods match those that have been ordered;
- can be used to clarify misunderstandings if disputes occur.

If a business, or one of its employees, cannot show that a transaction has taken place because there is no source document, it might create difficulties. For instance, if a sales representative buys £35 of petrol for a company car and does not retain a record of the transaction, he or she might not be able to claim the money back from the company. If a business cannot prove to the Inland Revenue that a particular transaction has taken place, the tax bill could be higher than it might otherwise have been.

Most large businesses are required to have an **audit**, or independent examination, of their accounts. Part of this process involves checking source documents against transactions that have been recorded. Businesses generally keep source documents for at least six years before throwing them away. This is because, in the UK, a court action relating to a contract cannot begin more than six years after the contract was made. Therefore source documents are only required for this period.

QUESTION 1

Willis, Brockhurst & Protheroe is a firm of chartered accountants in Cardiff. One of its clients, Henry Johnson, operates an import agency shipping carpets and rugs from Morocco. Walter Willis is working on the preparation of Henry Johnson's accounts and he is having problems. A number of ledger entries cannot be verified by source documents. They appear to be missing from the records. One transaction in particular is causing difficulty. The cash payment by Henry Johnson of £5,000 for a valuable antique carpet is not supported by any written documentation.

(a) Write a letter to Henry Johnson to explain the purpose of source documents and the problems that might be encountered if they cannot be provided.

Source documents used when buying and selling

Businesses often have documentation systems to deal with transactions that involve buying and selling. These systems are likely to vary. They depend on the type of good or service that is being traded and the types of business organisation involved (see unit 33). For example, a street vendor is not likely to use much documentation when selling newspapers to pedestrians. However, a large car manufacturer will use a comprehensive system of documentation when buying components or supplying vehicles. Figure 3.1 shows the different stages that might be involved in a **credit transaction**. At each stage in the process, a document is likely to be used.

Figure 3.1 *Stages in a business transaction involving buying goods and services*

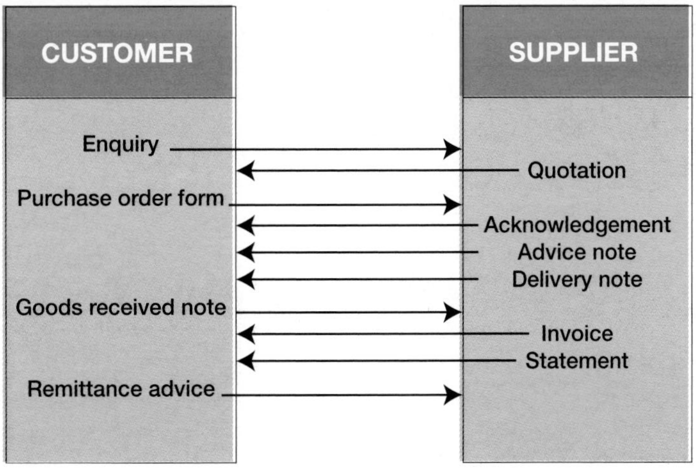

The transaction might start with an enquiry from a purchaser. This enquiry could be done over the telephone or by sending a LETTER OF ENQUIRY using the post or email. A supplier might respond to a letter of enquiry with a QUOTATION, which gives the price and details of what can be offered. Once a buyer has decided which supplier to use, it might place an order. Details of the order are listed on a PURCHASE ORDER FORM, which is sent to the supplier. The supplier might acknowledge the customer order by sending an ACKNOWLEDGEMENT or a SALES ORDER RECEIVED NOTE.

Before the supplier dispatches the goods, an ADVICE NOTE might be sent to advise the buyer when the goods will arrive. When the goods arrive, they are accompanied by a DELIVERY NOTE that describes the goods that have been sent. This is signed by the customer and, usually, one copy is returned to the supplier. It might then act as a GOODS RECEIVED NOTE, ie proof that the goods have been delivered.

Shortly after a delivery, the buyer receives an INVOICE from the supplier. This document tells the buyer how much is owed to the supplier. If a customer makes regular purchases from an established supplier, a STATEMENT OF ACCOUNT might also be sent to the customer. This summarises all the transactions for a particular trading period and shows the total amount outstanding. Finally, the buyer sends a cheque (or other form of payment) to the supplier with a REMITTANCE ADVICE. This shows how much is being paid to the supplier.

A letter of enquiry

When a purchaser wishes to buy a good or service, a letter of enquiry might be used to investigate what various suppliers have to offer. A letter, fax, or email might be sent to enquire about the specifications, prices, terms of payment, delivery times and quality guarantees which each supplier can offer. Some businesses use standard forms for this. An example is shown in Figure 3.2. Bedford Low Voltage Systems Ltd has sent the enquiry to Cornfield Fabrications, a Bradford-based supplier. The buyer is asking for a quotation to supply different quantities of metal parts. A description of the parts, the part specifications, the quantity required and a stock reference number are all shown on the enquiry form. The names and addresses of both the buyer and the supplier are shown and the date by which the quotation is required is also stated (14 August, 2000). The person making the enquiry is John Clarke, the purchase manager.

Figure 3.2 An example of a letter of enquiry using a standard form

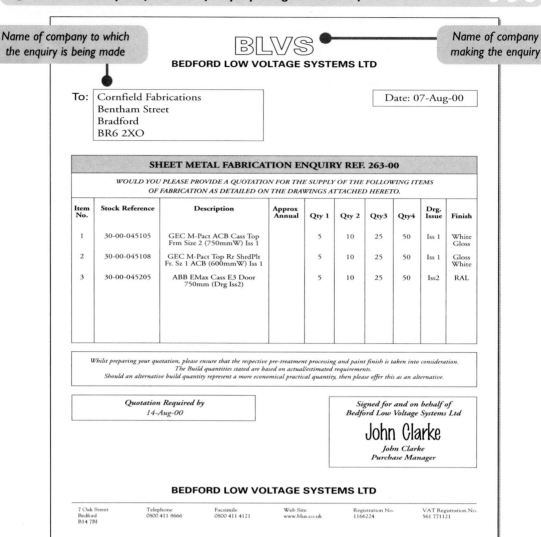

A quotation

When a business receives a letter of enquiry from a potential customer, it will normally try to reply as quickly as possible with details of what it can offer. It might reply by sending:

- a price list;
- an illustrated leaflet or catalogue;
- a quotation letter.

Some firms have detailed price lists of all the products they sell. These can be dispatched quickly by post, fax or email. Many businesses send prospective customers a brochure containing the products they supply. The brochure might describe the products and give other relevant details, such as price and delivery time. Sometimes, when a business does not produce standard products, price lists and illustrated catalogues are not appropriate. In this case a business might send a prospective customer a quotation. This is a letter which explains the terms, such as price and delivery times, under which goods or services can be supplied.

Sometimes businesses are invited to TENDER for contracts. This is a request by a purchaser for interested suppliers to provide a quotation for a particular good or service. Local authorities and government agencies often use this system by placing notices in newspapers or trade magazines. The main advantage of using tenders is that they create competition between the firms that place the tenders. Therefore terms should be more favourable for the purchaser. Also, the amount of resources used in searching for a suitable supplier might be reduced. This is because, once the notice has been placed, the purchaser simply waits for the tenders to be submitted by the deadline date.

QUESTION 2

Figure 3.3

(a) Who is the purchaser in the notice on the right?
(b) What is the purpose of the notice?
(c) Describe the advantages to Sefton Council of using such a method.

✠ Sefton Council

SOUTHPORT PIER

Tenders are invited for the provision and operation of the tram service and pavilion on Southport Pier.
• Available as separate lots or one lot.
• Offered on a sub-lease for a term of 25 years less one day.
• Operator(s) to provide the tram and 'fit out' the pavilion for proposed use.

Information pack, including tender details, lease terms and specifications available at a cost of £25 from Property Management Group, Sefton Technical Services, Balliol House, Bootle L20 3NJ.

Closing date for receipt of tenders 12 noon Friday 29th September 2000.

Source: adapted from the *Southport Midweek Visitor*.

An order form

When a buyer has chosen a suitable supplier for particular goods or services, an order form is sent to request delivery. An example of an order form is shown in Figure 3.4. The order has been requested by AMRO Engineering Ltd and the supplier is Monmouth Abrasives. The addresses of both businesses are shown on the form. The form also shows the following information:

• a description of the goods (50 GRINDING DISC NORTON);
• the price per unit (25p) and the number required (200);
• the purchase order number (303515);
• a reference number for Amro's order (XDISC 50G 100X16F228);
• the date the order was placed (8.8.00);
• the date the goods are required (9.8.00);
• the price (£50) and amount due (£58.75), the difference being VAT (£8.75);
• the name and signature of the person authorising the order (Amanda Davies);
• a list of special instructions (such as payment terms);
• the company registration number (816700) and VAT registration number (714 6411 81).

This order might have been sent by fax or email and verbally agreed by telephone because the date of the order is only one day before the goods are required.

Figure 3.4 *An example of an order form*

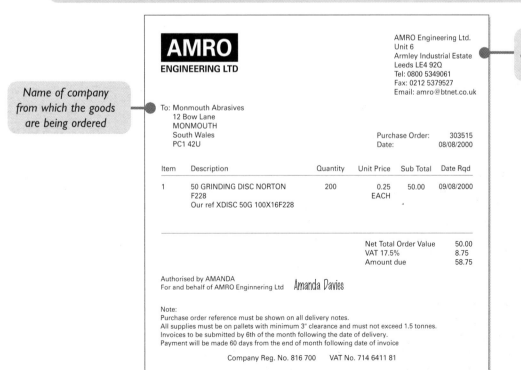

Name of company from which the goods are being ordered

Name of company wanting the order

AMRO ENGINEERING LTD

AMRO Engineering Ltd.
Unit 6
Armley Industrial Estate
Leeds LE4 9ZQ
Tel: 0800 5349061
Fax: 0212 5379527
Email: amro@btnet.co.uk

To: Monmouth Abrasives
12 Bow Lane
MONMOUTH
South Wales
PC1 42U

Purchase Order: 303515
Date: 08/08/2000

Item	Description	Quantity	Unit Price	Sub Total	Date Rqd
1	50 GRINDING DISC NORTON F228 Our ref XDISC 50G 100X16F228	200	0.25 EACH	50.00	09/08/2000

Net Total Order Value 50.00
VAT 17.5% 8.75
Amount due 58.75

Authorised by AMANDA
For and behalf of AMRO Enginnering Ltd   *Amanda Davies*

Note:
Purchase order reference must be shown on all delivery notes.
All supplies must be on pallets with minimum 3" clearance and must not exceed 1.5 tonnes.
Invoices to be submitted by 6th of the month following the date of delivery.
Payment will be made 60 days from the end of month following date of invoice

Company Reg. No. 816 700   VAT No. 714 6411 81

An acknowledgement note

Often a supplier will send a customer an acknowledgement note, or a **sales order received note**, to confirm that an order has been received. It also acts as confirmation that the goods can be supplied. The acknowledgement note will usually state the expected delivery date for the order. An example of an acknowledgement note is shown in Figure 3.5. Cedric Jones, the supplier, is confirming that 4 Victorian Chandeliers can be supplied to the customer, F. Robertson, and will be delivered on 21 July 2000.

Figure 3.5 *An example of an acknowledgement note*

ORDER ACKNOWLEDGEMENT

Cedric Jones & Co ●—— *Name of supplier*
12 Turley Street
Oxford
OX1 6SF
Tel 01865 235518
Fax 01865 241563

Date: 12.7.00

VAT Reg. No. 213 76541 98

Co. Reg. No. 2187 46531

Mr F. Robertson ●—— *Name of customer*
23 Bemrose Street
Compton
Shropshire

Account No. FR/12901

Order No. 002451

Ref. No.	Date ordered	Description	Qty	Unit price
219/a	9.7.01	Victorian chandeliers	4	£1,280

Delivery date: 21.7.00

A delivery note

A delivery note, sometimes called a **dispatch note**, is sent with the goods to a customer. When the goods arrive, the customer can check that the goods which are delivered match those listed on the delivery note. If they do, then the customer signs the delivery note and keeps a copy as a record. A copy is returned to the supplier and acts as a **goods received note**. It provides proof that the customer has taken delivery of the goods should a dispute occur. An example of a delivery note is shown in Figure 3.6. It shows the details of a delivery from a book wholesaler, Lion Books International plc to a bookshop in Chorley, Lancashire.

The terms of trade (30 days) are stated on the delivery note. This means that when the invoice is sent, the purchaser has 30 days in which to pay the invoice total.

Figure 3.6 *An example of a delivery note*

LION BOOKS INTERNATIONAL PLC ●━━ *Name of supplier*
51 Hampton Road, Teddington, Middlesex TW1 3JL
Tel: 020 8192 5577 Fax: 020 8192 6551

DELIVERY NOTE
Page 1 of 2
VAT No. 390 6127 54

INVOICE ADDRESS:
As delivery

DELIVERY ADDRESS:
Chorley Books ●━━ *Name of customer*
53 Steely Lane
Chorley
Lancashire PR6 1RJ

Dispatch No.	Dispatch Date	Account No.	Customer Order Ref.	Terms
02989	24/08/01	300	23/08/01	30 days

Quantity ordered	Title	Price
1	Native Americans, The	£12.99

Terms and conditions
Non delivery of goods and all shortages/damages must be reported.
Goods remain the property of Lion International plc until such time as they are paid for in full.
Please sign botttom copy and return to Lion Books International plc.

An invoice

An invoice is one of the most important source documents. This is because bookkeepers usually transfer details of transactions from invoices onto their bookkeeping system. An invoice is a demand for payment, ie it is a bill that sets out what is owed. When issued by a supplier, it is known as a **sales invoice**. When received by a customer, it is known as a **purchase invoice**.

Figure 3.7 is an example of an invoice. It was issued by Greenfens, a car dealer and service centre, to Mrs Sharples, a customer. It describes the work done on her car and how much the customer owes (£122.91).

Invoices usually contain the following details.

- **Addresses** - the supplier's address, the customer's address and the delivery address, if different from the customer's address.
- **Reference numbers** - the invoice number and customer account number are included to help the supplier cross reference the documents for the transaction. A customer order number might also be included. This helps the customer check the invoice against the order.
- **Dates** - it is usual to record the order date and the delivery, or dispatch, date on an invoice. The date is important because it is the tax point, ie the official date of the transaction for VAT (see unit 26) purposes.
- **Description of goods** - these are details about the goods. They usually include the quantity, a stock or catalogue number, a brief description, the unit price and the total price (quantity × unit price).
- **Amount owed and VAT** - the total amount of money owed by the customer is stated at the bottom of the invoice. The amount includes a payment for VAT which is shown separately. Accounting for VAT is covered in unit 26.
- **Terms** - the terms of trade, or payment, are stated on an invoice. For example, it might state how long the customer has to pay or what discount the customer is allowed. If the expression 28 days net, or similar, is printed on the invoice it means that full payment is due within 28 days. The 'net' amount is the payment due after any discount is deducted.

Figure 3.7 *An example of an invoice*

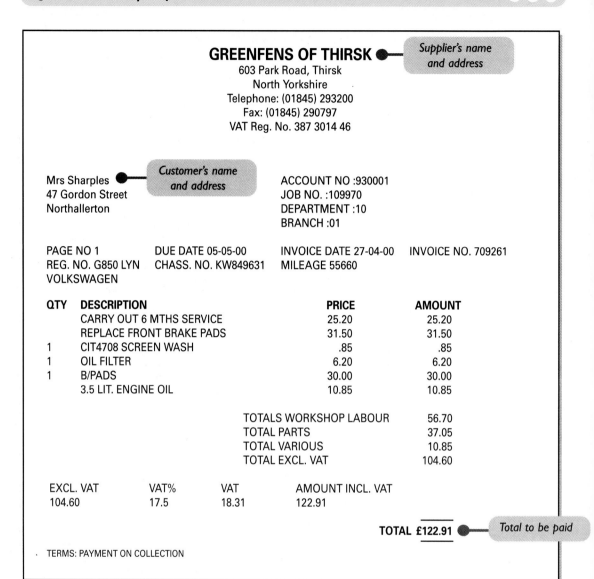

GREENFENS OF THIRSK
Supplier's name and address

603 Park Road, Thirsk
North Yorkshire
Telephone: (01845) 293200
Fax: (01845) 290797
VAT Reg. No. 387 3014 46

Mrs Sharples *Customer's name and address*
47 Gordon Street
Northallerton

ACCOUNT NO :930001
JOB NO. :109970
DEPARTMENT :10
BRANCH :01

PAGE NO 1   DUE DATE 05-05-00   INVOICE DATE 27-04-00   INVOICE NO. 709261
REG. NO. G850 LYN   CHASS. NO. KW849631   MILEAGE 55660
VOLKSWAGEN

QTY	DESCRIPTION	PRICE	AMOUNT
	CARRY OUT 6 MTHS SERVICE	25.20	25.20
	REPLACE FRONT BRAKE PADS	31.50	31.50
1	CIT4708 SCREEN WASH	.85	.85
1	OIL FILTER	6.20	6.20
1	B/PADS	30.00	30.00
	3.5 LIT. ENGINE OIL	10.85	10.85

TOTALS WORKSHOP LABOUR	56.70
TOTAL PARTS	37.05
TOTAL VARIOUS	10.85
TOTAL EXCL. VAT	104.60

EXCL. VAT	VAT%	VAT	AMOUNT INCL. VAT
104.60	17.5	18.31	122.91

TOTAL £122.91 *Total to be paid*

TERMS: PAYMENT ON COLLECTION

If the term **carriage paid** appears on an invoice it means that the price of the goods also includes the cost of delivery. On some invoices, the term **E & OE** is printed. This stands for errors and omissions excepted. It means that if there is a genuine error, eg something is missed off the invoice by mistake, the supplier claims the right to correct the error at a later date.

An invoice is not necessarily a demand for immediate payment. When customers make regular and numerous purchases during a short trading period, they might pay several invoices all at the same time, for example at the end of a month.

QUESTION 3

Figure 3.8 *An invoice issued by Delpoint Screenprint Company*

Delpoint Sceenprint Company
211 Morgan Street, Romford
Essex RM6 4AX
Telephone: 020 8143 8080 Fax: 020 8143 8100

To: McClelland Ltd
     411 Kingston Road
     London

INVOICE

Invoice Number	2411
Invoice Date	18.07.00
Your Order Number	62
Method of Dispatch	TNT
Date of Dispatch	12.07.00

Quantity	Description	Unit Cost	Goods Total	VAT Rate	VAT Amount
50	Screenprinting CCU Size 2 posters	£1.50	£75.00	17.5%	
60	CCU Size 3 posters	£1.60	£96.00	"	
1000	White dispatch labels		£30.00	"	
1000	Green dispatch labels		£35.00	"	
1000	Yellow dispatch labels		£35.00	"	
	Sub totals		£271.00		£47.43
	VAT		£47.43		
	Invoice Total		**£318.43**		

Terms: Strictly 28 days net from date of invoice.
VAT Reg. No. 306 888927
All Goods remain the property of DSC unitil full payment is received

(a) Name the buyer and the seller.
(b) Outline the purpose of the invoice.
(c) (i) How much does McClelland Ltd owe the Delpoint Screenprint Company? (ii) What are the terms of payment?
(d) Why is the invoice date (18.07.00) important?

A statement of account

Some businesses have regular suppliers and conduct many transactions during a short trading period. One common way of informing customers how much is owed at the end of the period, such as one month, is to send a statement of account. This document lists all the transactions for the time period and also includes details of any payments and refunds that have been made.

Some statements list transactions in two columns. The **debit** column lists invoices relating to goods bought by the customer. The **credit** column shows details of payments made by the customer and any refunds made to them due to goods being returned. Finally, the statement shows the total amount outstanding. Figure 3.9 shows an example of a statement of account sent out by Crawfords Ltd, a fabric supplier to one of its customers, Raja Singh. All transactions are identified by invoice numbers. Raja Singh made a payment on account for £800 on the 16 March 2001. The amount outstanding at the end of the month was £834.

Figure 3.9 *An example of a statement of account*

STATEMENT OF ACCOUNT

CRAWFORDS LTD
2760 Wantage Road
Swindon
Wiltshire
SW3 98D

Supplier's name and address

Tel: 01235 288715
Fax: 01235 276519
VAT Reg. No. 129 871716519

Raja Singh
32 Walton Street
Cheltenham
Gloucester
GL52 2NF

Customer's name and address

Account No. 2311

Statement No. 310

Date	Reference	Debit (£)	Credit (£)	Balance (£)
1.03.01	Balance b/f			120.10
3.03.01	Invoice No. P2176	235.00		355.10
10.03.01	Invoice No. P2190	341.50		696.60
15.03.01	Invoice No. P2203	290.00		986.60
16.03.01	Payment (thank you)		800.00	186.60
26.03.01	Invoice No. P2238	321.90		508.50
29.03.01	Invoice No. P2247	288.00		796.50
30.03.01	Invoice No. P2257	37.50		834.00

Amount outstanding **834.00**

A remittance advice

When an invoice or statement is sent to a customer, it sometimes has a detachable slip, known as a remittance advice note or remittance slip. It can be torn off by the customer and enclosed with a cheque, for example. The purpose of a remittance slip is to match payment with a particular invoice or statement and is therefore a help with record keeping. Figure 3.10 shows an example of an invoice with an attached remittance slip that has been sent by the Royal Mail to a mail order company in Oldham.

Figure 3.10 *An example of an invoice with attached remittance slip*

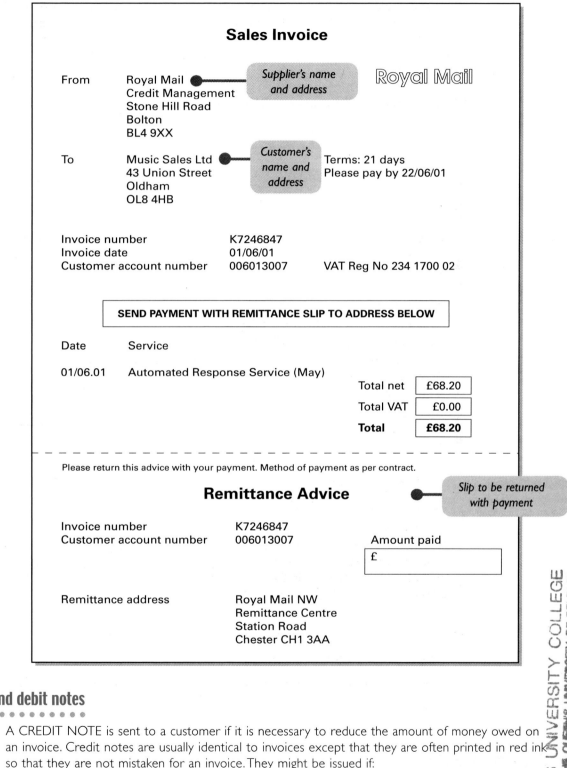

Credit and debit notes

A CREDIT NOTE is sent to a customer if it is necessary to reduce the amount of money owed on an invoice. Credit notes are usually identical to invoices except that they are often printed in red ink so that they are not mistaken for an invoice. They might be issued if:

- a mistake has been made when entering details on the invoice;
- goods have been damaged in transit or lost;
- insufficient goods have been delivered;
- goods are returned by the customer, with the supplier's agreement, for whatever reason.

A credit note is used to set against the value of future purchases, ie it reduces the amount the customer pays in the future.

A DEBIT NOTE might be issued if a mistake on an invoice results in the customer underpaying the

J. Docherty is a clockmaker based in Bath. One of his customers, Mary Tench, owns a shop in Colchester where she sells a range of gifts. On the 25 May 2000 J. Docherty sent Mary Tench the credit note shown in Figure 3.11.

Figure 3.11 *A credit note sent by J. Docherty Ltd*

CREDIT NOTE				No. 3211

J. Docherty Ltd ●— *Name of supplier*			
87 Princes Terrace	VAT Reg. No.	215 5673 45	
Bath	Registered No.	1630056	
BA1 2PH	Tel:	01225 938325	

Mary Tench ●— *Name of customer*	Invoice No.	21309
68 West Street	Invoice date:	13/05/00
Colchester	Credit note date:	25/05/00
Essex CO2 5IA		

Qty	Cat.No.	Description	Unit price	Amount
1	44/2	Carriage clock	£408	£408.00
			VAT	£71.40
			TOTAL	**£479.40**

Reason for credit:
Hand missing from clock face.

(a) **What is the purpose of the document shown in Figure 3.11?**
(b) **Why has the credit note been raised?**
(c) **Suggest how the £479.40 might be refunded.**
(d) **Under what circumstances might J. Docherty send a debit note to a customer?**

supplier. The debit note will show the customer how much more needs to be paid and why the underpayment occurred.

Other source documents

In addition to the source documents described in this unit, there is a number of other source documents which bookkeepers use. They include cheque counterfoils, paying-in slips, bank statements, till rolls and petty cash vouchers. These are mainly concerned with payment systems which are described in Unit 4.

key terms

Acknowledgement or sales order received note - a response from a supplier stating that a customer order has been received and is being dealt with.

Advice note - a document from a supplier saying when goods are to be delivered.

Credit transactions - the exchange of goods where payment is deferred, ie where payment is made several weeks or months after goods have been bought.

Credit note - a document used to confirm that a customer has been overcharged, stating the allowance due to the customer and the reason for the overcharging.

Debit note - a document used to notify a customer of an undercharging stating the amount outstanding and the reason for the undercharging.

Delivery note - a document that describes the goods that have been delivered by a supplier.

Goods received note - normally a copy of a delivery note that has been signed to confirm that the correct goods have been delivered.

Invoice - a document that tells a customer how much is owed for goods that have been purchased.

Letter of enquiry - a letter sent to a supplier to investigate what the supplier has to offer.

Purchase order form - a document requesting specified goods to be sent.

Quotation - a response to a letter of enquiry from a supplier quoting the price and other details of goods and services on offer.

Remittance advice - a document showing how much a purchaser is paying a supplier.

Statement of account - a document sent to a customer showing a summary of recent transactions and the total amount owing.

Tender - an offer to supply specified goods or services at a particular price.

summary questions

1. State four reasons for using source documents.
2. State four pieces of information that you would expect to find on a source document.
3. Why do businesses normally keep documents for a number of years?
4. Why would a business issue (i) a letter of enquiry, (ii) a quotation?
5. State four pieces of information that might appear on an order form.
6. Why would a business issue an acknowledgement note?
7. What does the signing of a delivery note by a customer indicate?
8. Why is an invoice an important source document?
9. When is a statement of account used by a business?
10. What is the difference between a credit note and a debit note?

UNIT ASSESSMENT QUESTION 1

MTS provides a parts and fitting service to motorists. It specialises in the supply and fitting of parts such as exhausts, batteries and tyres. It is a national company with branches all over the country. The document shown in Figure 3.12 was issued at its Widnes branch to Mr Brown, a prospective customer. He arrived at the MTS garage in his car and made an enquiry about the supply of exhaust parts.

Figure 3.12 ***A document issued by MTS for a prospective customer***

MTS **MTS NORTH WESTERN LIMITED**

Tanhouse Lane
Widnes
WA8 6RD

Telephone: 0151-424 8011
VAT Reg. No. 145 1666 69

Customer: Mr Brown

SALES QUOTATION

Number: 101422
Date: 08-DEC-00

Reference	Description	Qty	Total Ex. VAT	Total Inc. VAT
EXVW219M	EXHAUST PART NO VW219M	1	90.02	105.77
NSCLAMP	CLAMPS/BRACKETS/MOUNTINGS	1	3.33	3.91
SEEXSD	ENVIRONMENT DISPOSAL - EXHAUST	1	0.60	0.71
EXVW218P	EXHAUST PART NO VW218P	1	58.56	68.81

This quotation is valid for SEVEN days.

All sales or supplies are subject to our current terms and conditions of trading, a copy of which is available on request.

(a) What is the document shown in Figure 3.12 called?
(b) What is the purpose of the document?
(c) How much would Mr Brown be charged in total for the parts listed?
(d) If the transaction described in the document went ahead, what might be the next document issued by MTS? Explain your answer.
(e) Explain why reference numbers are used on such documents.

UNIT ASSESSMENT   QUESTION 2

Susan James Ltd is a supplier of sports equipment to retailers and other organisations such as schools and athletics clubs. The company specialises in the supply of athletics equipment and operates a wholesaling operation in Leicester. All the products sold by Susan James Ltd are listed in a catalogue.

On the 23 March 2001 an order form (No. 4612) was received from Andrea Mitton, Head of PE, King Charles I High School, Worcester Rd, Birmingham. The following goods were requested:

- 6 Javelins Cat. No. 443/2 @ £18 each;
- 6 Tape measures Cat. No.12/9 @ £8 each;
- 10 Discus Cat. No. 446/3 @ £12 each;
- 4 High jump bars Cat. No. 312/2 @ £16 each;
- 2 Stop watches Cat. No. 78/1 @ £28 each. (All prices exclude VAT.)

Figure 3.13 *Invoice for Susan James Ltd*

SUSAN JAMES LTD
SPORTS EQUIPMENT SUPPLIER

46 Camford Avenue, Leicester, LE4 5EA

Tel: 0116 934 2727   Fax: 0116 934 2800

VAT REG. No. 876 239987 98

To

Invoice No.   0244
Order Ref. No.   _____
Invoice date: _____

Qty	Cat. No.	Description	Unit price	Amount	VAT	Total

Terms: 90 days from invoice date

Total payment due: _____

(a) **Using a copy of the Susan James Ltd invoice (see Figure 3.13), complete the invoice for the goods being ordered. Assume that all the items are in stock, they are available for delivery, and the invoice date is 29 March 2001.**
(b) **Calculate the total amount that the customer owes (assuming that VAT at 17.5% will be charged) and show this total on the invoice.**
(c) **Describe the purpose of the document that is likely to accompany the goods when they are sent to the school.**
(d) **Why might a remittance note be returned with the school's payment?**
(e) **Under what circumstances might Susan James Ltd use a debit note?**

Payment systems

Making payments

The method of payment that businesses and customers use largely depends on the type of good or service that is being bought and on the value of the transaction. For example, a business that buys a machine for £500,000 is not likely to use bank notes as a means of payment. It would not want to hold so much cash and take the risk that it could be lost. However, the business might use cash to pay for low value items such as milk, tea and coffee used by its office staff.

The ways that customers make payments affect bookkeepers and accountants. This is because transactions are recorded differently and generate different types of documents depending on the payment method that is used. For example, the documents used for CHEQUE payments are likely to be different from those used when payments are made by notes and coins.

Cheques

A cheque is a document that instructs a bank to transfer money from one bank account to another. The money is transferred from the DRAWER'S bank account to the PAYEE'S account when the cheque is presented at a bank. The drawer is the person or business making the payment and the payee is the person or business receiving the payment.

Cheques are a flexible method of payment because different amounts can be paid using the same standard document. They also have the advantage of providing proof of payment because the transaction is recorded on a **bank statement**. In addition, security problems are reduced because unauthorised personnel cannot easily cash cheques.

One disadvantage of cheques compared with cash is that the payee cannot be certain that a cheque will be **honoured** by the bank. This means that a bank might refuse to transfer money from the drawer's account to the payee's account, probably because there is insufficient money in the drawer's account. The cheque will then be returned to the drawer. Another disadvantage of cheques is that they take a minimum of three working days to 'clear'. In other words, it takes time for the funds to be transferred between accounts.

An example of a cheque is shown in Figure 4.1. The cheque contains the following details.

- The **drawer** is Weston Ltd, which means that money will be transferred from Weston Ltd's bank account.
- The cheque is signed by R. Simpson, the authorised signatory, on behalf of Weston Ltd. Sometimes, to protect against fraud, a business cheque must be signed by two staff.
- The payee is Horsely Catering Ltd. This is the business receiving payment. The money will be transferred into its account.
- The **drawee** is the NorthWest Bank. This is where Weston Ltd has its bank account. The money will be transferred from Weston's account at the NorthWest Bank to Horsely Catering Ltd's bank.
- The amount, £450, is written in both words and figures for security and clarity.
- The cheque has a counterfoil which is retained by the drawer as a record of the cheque details. This is also called a **cheque stub**.
- All cheques should be dated with the current date by the drawer. A bank might not honour a cheque if it is postdated, ie is given a future date. The date is useful for bookkeepers when tracing specific payments.

- Since 1992, all UK cheques have been printed **crossed**, ie they have two parallel lines drawn across their face. This means that they must be paid into a bank account. Previously, when banks issued uncrossed cheques, there was no need to pay such a cheque into an account. It could be cashed over the bank counter. A crossed cheque can be 'endorsed' - it can be signed on the back by the payee and then paid into someone else's bank account. However, many cheques also contain the words 'account payee' or 'A/C payee only' between the parallel lines. This means that the cheque can only be paid into the payee's bank account.
- There is a series of numbers on every cheque. In this case, 016659 is the cheque number. All cheque books are serially numbered and each number helps to identify the payment for the drawer. The second number on the bottom of the cheque, 10-65-21, is the sort code. This identifies the branch of the drawee, ie the NorthWest Bank's branch in King Street, Newcastle (this number is also shown in the top right-hand corner). The third number, 02556789, is the drawer's bank account number.

Figure 4.1 *An example of a cheque*

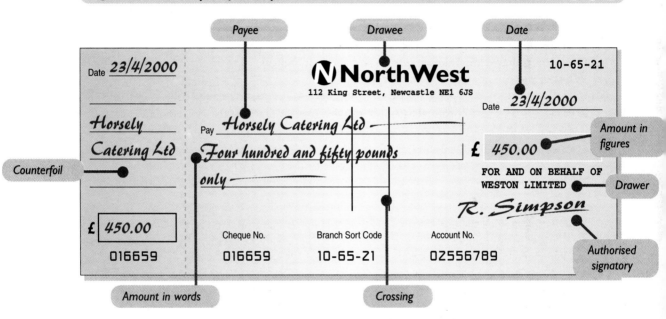

As a safeguard against fraud, banks suggest that all the writing on a cheque should be in ink, any alterations should be initialled or signed by the drawer, and a line should be drawn through any blank spaces where the amount is written.

Banks send their account holders bank statements, usually at the end of each month. They provide the account holder with a record of transactions over a given time period. They show the date of transactions such as withdrawals of cash, payments made by cheques and details of money paid in. The overall balance is also shown. An example of a bank statement is shown in Figure 4.8. At regular intervals it is important for bookkeepers or accountants to crosscheck their bookkeeping entries against their bank statements. This process is known as **reconciliation** (see unit 25). It provides a safeguard against mistakes and fraud.

Cheque cards

CHEQUE CARDS are used to improve the security of cheque payments. A small plastic cheque card acts as a guarantee that a cheque will be honoured by a bank up to a certain limit, usually £50 or £100. However, there are certain conditions. Generally, banks will only guarantee payment if the:

- card number is written on the back of the cheque;
- cheque bears the same name, code number and signature as the card;
- cheque is signed before the expiry date on the card;
- card has not been damaged or defaced;
- drawer is not a limited company (see unit 33).

Cheque cards encourage the use of cheques because businesses feel happier about accepting

QUESTION 1

Figure 4.2 *A cheque used in a transaction*

(a) Name the: (i) drawer; (ii) drawee; (iii) payee.
(b) Describe the two mistakes made in the above cheque.
(c) What is the purpose of the counterfoil?
(d) In the case of Great Barr Timber Ltd, suggest what security measures might be taken to protect the company against fraud when cheques are written.

them, knowing that banks will guarantee to honour the payment. Also, fraud is more difficult because a thief needs both the card and cheque book to take money from an account.

Cash

Most businesses still use CASH when conducting certain transactions. This is despite the growing number of alternative methods of payment that are available. Cash, in this context, refers to payments made using notes and coins. Advantages of using cash include:

- it is a speedy way of settling bills;
- it limits purchases to the value of cash held and therefore helps to avoid overspending;
- some customers might wish to settle bills in cash because they do not have any other means of payment;
- cash is a secure form of payment for a supplier compared with a cheque which might not be honoured if it is not supported by a cheque card.

However, there is a number of disadvantages of using cash:

- cash transactions must be supported by documents - otherwise bookkeepers and accountants will have difficulty in keeping accurate records;
- it is unsuitable for large payments because it is bulky;
- it can be lost and stolen and, unlike a cheque, it cannot be 'stopped'. This happens if a drawer instructs the bank to stop payment of a cheque;
- cash receipts might build up and pose security problems. This might increase the need for more journeys to deposit cash in the bank, and thus impose extra costs.

Petty cash

Many businesses operate a PETTY CASH system. Petty cash is the cash used by a business to pay for small items such as stationery, stamps and coffee in the office. It might also be used to make refunds to staff if they have used their own money for business purposes. For example, an employee might have paid for a taxi on a business trip using personal cash. This can be refunded from petty cash. To operate a petty cash system a business needs a stock of petty cash vouchers, a **petty cash book** to record all transactions (see unit 13), a cash float and a secure cash box. A **petty cashier** is usually responsible for operating the system.

When a cash payment is made using petty cash, the petty cashier usually carries out the following tasks:

- obtains a RECEIPT showing that payment has been made;
- completes a petty cash voucher (an example is shown in Figure 4.3) noting the date of the payment, details of the purchase and the amount;
- obtains the signature of the claimant;
- obtains the signature of the person authorising the payment;
- attaches the receipt to the voucher;
- enters the details into the petty cash book;
- issues the cash to the claimant.

Figure 4.3 shows a completed petty cash voucher. It was issued on 23 June 2000 and £11.75 was given to M. Jenkins in payment for some stationery. Of this £1.75 was for VAT. The payment was authorised by Helen Jones, the petty cashier.

Figure 4.3 *A petty cash voucher*

```
                                              No. 107
     Petty Cash Voucher      Date  23.6.00

        For what required              Amount

     Stationery                     £10  00



                            VAT      £1   75

                        Total £     £11   75

     Signature  M. Jenkins
     Authorised by  Helen Jones
```

Some businesses use an IMPREST SYSTEM to organise their petty cash (see Figure 4.4). This involves putting a certain amount of money in the cash box, say £100, at the beginning of a specific time period such as a week. The £100 is called the imprest amount. During the week the amount of cash remaining in the cash box falls as payments are made. In Figure 4.4, £37 is left at the end of the week. The difference between the imprest amount and what is left in the box is paid in by the main cashier at the beginning of the next week. In this case it is £63 (£100 - £37 = £63).

Figure 4.4 *The imprest system*

	£
Imprest amount at start of week	100.00
Total payments during week	63.00
Cash remaining at end of week	37.00
Cash paid in by cashier	63.00
Imprest amount at start of new week	100.00

Credit cards

An increasing number of businesses use CREDIT CARDS for making and receiving payments. The plastic card contains certain information. On the front there is:

- a 16 digit number;
- the date from which the card is valid and the expiry date;
- the name of the cardholder, ie the buyer;
- the name of the credit card company, eg MasterCard/EuroCard or Visa;
- the name of the agent/card issuer, eg Alliance and Leicester or Lloyds TSB.

QUESTION 2

Oakwell Ltd makes paper in its mill which is based in Settle, North Yorkshire. The company uses the imprest system to manage its petty cash and the imprest amount is £200. At the end of one week (on 18 August 2000) the amount of money left in the cash box was £41.50. The only person who can authorise payments from petty cash is the petty cashier.

(a) How much cash will have to be introduced at the beginning of the next week, ie the week following 18 August 2000?
(b) Mark Harrison, an employee, claims £18.75 for posting two parcels of samples by special delivery. What proof might Mark produce when making his claim and suggest how he might go about making his claim.
(c) What might determine the size of the imprest amount that Oakwell Ltd uses?

On the back there is a magnetic strip which contains the information listed above in a computer readable format and a copy of the cardholder's signature. Some new style and foreign credit cards use a small computer chip embedded in the card rather than a magnetic strip. This provides greater security against fraud.

All credit card transactions use documents to record payments. The most common way to administer credit card transactions involves computer technology. When receiving a payment the vendor, ie supplier, 'swipes' the credit card through a computerised credit card reader which records the card details. The computerised till then issues a duplicate itemised voucher and an authorisation document for the cardholder to sign. One copy is given to the customer and the other is retained by the vendor.

The vendor receives money from the credit card company to cover the cardholder's payment. This takes a few days and is generally paid automatically into the vendor's bank account. The credit card company charges the vendor, typically between 2 - 5 per cent of the transaction value. The cardholder is sent a monthly statement which summarises all transactions involving the credit card. If the cardholder pays the amount outstanding within a certain time, usually 28 days, there is no charge for the credit. However, if the bill is not settled, interest is charged on the outstanding balance until it is eventually paid.

Credit cards have a number of advantages when making payments.

- They are very convenient, eg they are easy to carry and they avoid the need to carry large amounts of cash.
- They are flexible, payments can be made for any amount up to the limit granted by the issuer of the card.
- Credit card limits are generally higher than the limits on cheque guarantee cards.
- They can be used to make payments over the telephone and over the internet.
- They can be used to obtain cash from banks and cash dispensers, although a charge is often made for this.
- Goods can be bought on credit.
- There is no interest charge for the credit if the cardholder settles the bill within the time period.
- The credit card company will reimburse the purchaser's money if the goods or services are not supplied.

Some businesses issue company credit cards to employees, such as sales representatives, directors and executives. These cards can be used to pay for hotels, meals and travel. Credit cards can also be used abroad and can reduce the need for exchanging and carrying large amounts of foreign currency.

One relatively recent innovation is the use of STORE CARDS. These are credit cards which can only be used to buy goods or services from the card issuer. Large retailers such as Debenhams and Marks & Spencer are examples of companies that issue store cards.

Debit cards

These cards, such as Switch or Delta, act in the same way as cheques. Money from a customer's bank account is automatically transferred to the vendor's bank account when a transaction is made.

Debit cards can also be used, like credit cards, to make payments over the telephone and the internet. They are a convenient system of payment because they avoid the need to carry cash and a cheque book. Banks prefer their customers to use this method of payment because administration costs are lower than for handling cheques. Increasingly, debit cards are combined with cheque guarantee cards so that one card carries out both functions.

The system of **Electronic Data Interchange (EDI)**, which transfers funds from one account to another, is called EFTPOS (Electronic Funds Transfer at Point of Sale). When a debit or credit card is 'swiped', a computer link between the vendor's till and the EFTPOS processing centre is activated. The system checks whether a customer has sufficient funds to cover the payment, in the case of a debit card, or whether the customer is within his or her credit limit, in the case of a credit card. Once the check has been made, the transaction can be authorised. EFTPOS improves efficiency, cuts queuing time at checkouts, reduces the amount of cash handling and guarantees payment to the seller.

For transactions by debit card or credit card that are carried out in person, sellers need to check that the cardholder's signature matches that on the card. They must also check the expiry date on the card. Purchasers need to check that the amount on the paper voucher they sign is the same as the amount agreed. For transactions that are carried out by telephone or mail order, there is less security because the vendor cannot check the cardholder's signature.

Standing order and direct debit

These methods of payment involve the electronic transfer of money directly from one bank account to another. They require prior arrangement between the buyer and the seller and involve the use of information technology. In the UK, the electronic transfer of funds is carried out by an organisation known as Bankers Automated Clearing System (BACS). This system is also used by some employers to pay wages directly into employees' bank accounts.

- A STANDING ORDER is mostly used for making regular payments of the same amount, such as a loan repayment or an insurance premium.
- A DIRECT DEBIT is used when payments vary, both in amount and regularity. With a direct debit it is the recipient who administers the payment and not the payer. Examples of payments made using a direct debit might include water or gas bills, subscriptions and annual insurance premiums.

The main advantages of these methods are convenience, administrative efficiency and, therefore, reduced costs. Although these systems use computer technology to transfer money, some documentation is still required. It is necessary for the payer to complete a standing order or direct debit mandate. This is an instruction to the payer's bank to authorise these types of payment. The mandate will include:

- the name of the payee;
- the payer's bank details such as name, address, account number and sort code;
- the amount to be paid;
- the date and frequency of payment;
- the signature of the payer.

Bank giro credit

A BANK GIRO CREDIT is a document that enables money to be paid into a bank account. Businesses sometimes attach a giro credit slip to statements or invoices which they send to customers. An example of a bank giro credit slip is shown in Figure 4.5. This is issued by a telephone company for customers to use when paying their telephone bills. The slip can be sent with a cheque payment by post. Alternatively it can be presented at a bank or post office, in which case a clerk will stamp the counterfoil as proof of payment. The system reduces the chance of payments going astray because the slip matches payments to particular invoices and also contains preprinted details of the payee's bank account.

As shown in Figure 4.5 a bank giro slip contains the following important information:

- the bank details (HSBC 44-67-63) of the payee;
- the payer's signature and customer number;
- the amount and date of the payment.

Figure 4.5 *An example of a bank giro credit slip*

```
Your Customer No.   LC 2084 3249                    Bank Giro Credit

Total amount due              £      58.49

Payment slip        Dear Customer
                    • Please fill in parts 1 to 3 and insert a total
Cashier's stamp and initials     next to the £ sign below.
                    • Details of how to pay are shown overleaf.
                    • Please do not send cash by post.

                          1 Signature _____    3 Cash _____
                    Bank details
                    HSBC Bank plc
                    Head Office Collection Acct.   2 Date _____   or cheques
                    44-67-63
                                                                       £
No. cheques   Fee
                    Please do not fold, pin or staple this slip or write below this line.

        03   LC   20843249   Q046    SQ              58.49

        <3LC20843249Q046<   446763+<   73    X
```

Receipts and till rolls

Most retailers and other businesses that sell goods and services to consumers issue receipts. A RECEIPT is a document that acknowledges payment. It normally states:

- the name of the vendor or supplier;
- the amount of money received from the customer;
- the date the money is received;
- a description of the goods sold.

Different businesses include different information on their receipts. For example, some show the time of the transaction, the name of the sales person, the company's VAT registration number, the method of payment, the address of the company and the amount of change given, if it is a cash transaction.

Customers are usually advised to keep their receipts. If there is a query regarding a transaction, a receipt proves when and where the goods were bought. Receipts are particularly important if a payment is made in cash. This is because the customer is unlikely to have any other documentation to confirm that the transaction has occurred.

QUESTION 3

A branch of Office Supplies is situated in Liverpool. It sells a wide range of office equipment and computers. On the 17.4.00 a new computer printer was sold to Valerie James. She runs a small business that specialises in providing domestic cleaning services. Valerie wanted the printer so that she could produce leaflets for potential customers. She was issued with the receipt shown in Figure 4.6.

(a) How was the payment made by Valerie?

(b) What was purchased and why might it be helpful to have details of the item printed on the receipt for the buyer and the seller?

(c) On 29 April, 2000, Valerie found that the printer's ink cartridge was leaking. She returned the printer to the store. Explain why the receipt would have been important when taking this action.

Figure 4.6 *A receipt issued by Office Supplies*

```
*************************
    OFFICE SUPPLIES
          50: Liverpool
**** Telephone: 0151-130-0369 *****

Receipt 50:087734          17/04/00
Salesperson: 06        Darren Small

Elite 1212 printer
             Qty 1 x        699.00


Total amount due:           699.00
includes VAT of:            104.11
At the rate of: 17.50%

Paid by Mcard/Visa          699.00

***** VAT Reg No: 581 2759 15 *****

*************************
```

A TILL ROLL is usually a carbon copy of a receipt. It is retained in a retailer's till or cash register as a record of transactions and it provides a total of daily, weekly or monthly sales. As such, it provides important information for bookkeepers and accountants.

Paying-in slips

Businesses that receive money in the form of cash and cheques need to deposit their takings in a bank. To record the value of cheques and the amount of cash that is being paid in, a PAYING-IN SLIP is used. In most banks this is a bank giro credit similar to the document described earlier. Together with their counterfoils, these documents provide a record of money paid into a bank account. They show the date the payment is made, the amount, the details of cheques and notes and coins being paid in, the name of the person paying in and the bank details. An example of a paying-in slip is shown in Figure 4.7.

Figure 4.7 An example of a paying-in slip

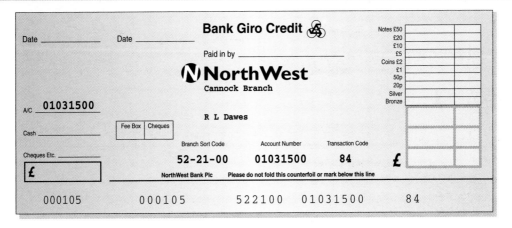

How do businesses choose methods of payment?

Many factors influence businesses when deciding between different methods of making and receiving payments.

Cost As with many decisions in business, cost is an important influence. Businesses prefer those methods which minimise transactions costs. For example, some small retailers do not accept credit cards because of the charge made by credit card companies and the need to invest in an electronic till. Similarly, they might refuse to accept cheques for small amounts because bank charges can be as much as fifty pence per cheque. On the other hand, handling cash and cheques can be time consuming and expensive. The electronic transfer of money is often cheaper.

Convenience For very small transactions, such as buying a newspaper or paying a bus fare, cash is used. This is because it is more convenient for both the purchaser and the vendor. Credit cards are convenient for larger payments such as meals in restaurants, hotel bills and buying consumer durables. They can also be used abroad, and for transactions over the telephone, internet and by mail order. For large and regular payments, electronic methods, such as standing orders and direct debits are often preferred.

Competitive pressure Some businesses are forced to use particular methods of payment because their rivals do. For example, most petrol stations accept credit and debit cards. If one did not, customers might go elsewhere. Some businesses offer a wide range of different payment methods as a marketing strategy to encourage sales.

Technology The development of new technology has influenced payment systems quite significantly, mainly because technology tends to reduce transaction costs. For example, computer links between tills and banks have encouraged more retailers to accept credit and debit cards. This cuts the amount of cash and cheques to be handled. Most transactions over the internet also require credit and debit cards.

Security The need to control and monitor the flow of money into and out of a business might influence the method of payment. Cash is the least secure form of payment because it is vulnerable to theft. For this reason businesses often prefer other methods of payment.

UNIT ASSESSMENT QUESTION 1

Paula Bloxham runs a small model shop in Earlsdon, Coventry. She sells a range of model boats, planes and trains to children and model enthusiasts. She banks with the NorthWest Bank and a copy of a recent bank statement is shown in Figure 4.8.

Figure 4.8 A bank statement for Paula Bloxham

```
233 Wright Street        (N) NorthWest
Earlsdon
Coventry                 Current account
CV2 9PP                  Ms Paula Bloxham              Sheet No.342

STATEMENT DATE 27.06.01              Account No. 09876226

Date     Payment details              Payments    Receipts   Balance (£)
                                                              349.80
2 Jun    Direct Debit   BRITISH GAS     36.00                 313.80
4 Jun    Cheque         014432         191.00                 122.80
5 Jun    Cheque         014433          12.60                 110.20
9 Jun    Credit         001049                      651.99    762.19
9 Jun    Direct Debit   CC COUNCIL      86.00                 676.19
11 Jun   Standing Order LloydsTSB      532.70                 143.49
15 Jun   Cheque         014434           9.99                 133.50
17 Jun   Direct Debit   SCOT AM 23      23.50                 110.00
19 Jun   Cheque         014436         219.65                 109.65 o/d
24 Jun   Credit         001050                      699.54    589.89
27 Jun   Balance carried forward to sheet number 343          589.89

Ms Paula Bloxham
The Model Shop
13 Renshaw Street
Earlsdon
Coventry CV2 5HE
```

(a) What is the purpose of the statement shown in Figure 4.8?
(b) What happened to the bank balance on 19 June and why is it important for Paula to know this information?
(c) On 20 June, Paula paid a supplier £98 by cheque. What effect would this have on the balance carried forward if the cheque had been included on the statement?
(d) Why might the cheque described in (c) not be included on this statement?

summary questions

1. Explain the difference between the drawer, the drawee and the payee on a cheque.
2. Why is the amount on a cheque written in words and in figures?
3. What is the purpose of a cheque counterfoil?
4. What is an advantage of using a cheque card?
5. From a bookkeeper's point of view, what are the disadvantages of using cash to make payments?
6. Why do businesses operate a petty cash system?
7. Why might someone use a credit card rather than a debit card?
8. Which payment systems involve the electronic transfer of funds?
9. What is the difference between a till roll and a receipt?
10. What factors influence businesses when choosing payment systems?

key terms

Bank giro credit - a system of payment which allows a payer to pay money directly into a payee's bank account.

Cash - notes and coins used to make payments.

Cheque - a document that instructs a bank to transfer money from one bank account to another.

Cheque card - a plastic card that acts as a guarantee that a cheque will be honoured by a bank provided certain conditions are met.

Credit card - a plastic card that allows a buyer to obtain goods on credit.

Debit card - a plastic card that is used to transfer money from one bank account to another.

Direct debit - an electronic method of transferring money from one bank account to another where the responsibility for administering the transfer lies with the payee.

Drawer - the person or business making a payment by cheque.

Imprest system - a method of operating petty cash that involves starting with the same amount of money, the imprest amount, in the cash box every week or other set period.

Payee - the person or business receiving a payment by cheque.

Paying-in slip - a document that records the amount being paid into a bank account.

Petty cash - notes and coins used by businesses to make small cash payments.

Receipt - a document which confirms that payment has been made by a customer.

Standing order - an electronic method of transferring a set amount of money at regular intervals from one account to another.

Store card - a credit or debit card for use in a particular shop or chain of shops.

Till roll - a document that records sales on a till or cash register. Generally it is a copy of the receipts that have been issued.

UNIT ASSESSMENT QUESTION 2

Celandine Press is a small publishing company that issues its staff with a company credit card. The staff use this card for items of expenditure such as rail fares and hotel conference bills.

On 4 September, 2000, one of Celandine's staff, Jeremy Newton, booked a return rail ticket from London to Manchester on the telephone. He used the company credit card and booked direct with Virgin Rail. On the phone, Jeremy had to quote the card number and expiry date, and to confirm the company address to which the tickets would be sent. The fare was £134.50 and this was the amount shown on the credit card voucher which arrived with his tickets.

After his return from Manchester, Jeremy mistakenly threw away his used rail ticket and the credit card voucher.

(a) **Outline the advantages to Celandine Press and Jeremy Newton of using a credit card to pay for the rail tickets.**

(b) **Given that he had thrown the tickets and voucher away, would there be any supporting documentary evidence that Jeremy had used the company credit card to pay for the rail tickets? Explain your answer.**

(c) **If Jeremy had bought the tickets at Euston Station using the credit card, what additional security measures could have been taken to ensure that no fraud was involved?**

unit 5

The accounting equation

unit objectives

To understand:
- the accounting equation;
- the effects of business transactions on the accounting equation;
- the link between the accounting equation and the balance sheet;
- the effects of business transactions on the balance sheet;
- the effects of revenue, expenses and drawings on the accounting equation;
- the accounting equation and the profit and loss account.

The accounting equation

One of the most important concepts in accounting is the relationship between the value of a business's assets, its capital and its liabilities. The relationship is called the ACCOUNTING EQUATION. For any business:

Assets = Capital + Liabilities

ASSETS are the resources that a business uses in the production of goods and services. Assets include machinery, land, buildings and stocks of raw materials. They also include cash in hand and money in a bank account. Money that is owed to a business by TRADE DEBTORS, ie customers who have not yet paid for goods, is also classed as an asset.

CAPITAL is the money introduced by the owners of a business. It is used to purchase assets. LIABILITIES are the debts of a business, ie what it **owes** to other businesses, individuals and institutions. Liabilities, like capital, are a source of funds for a business. They might be short term, like a bank overdraft, or long term, such as a mortgage. Liabilities also include the money owed to TRADE CREDITORS, ie suppliers of goods and raw materials.

The accounting equation states that the value of all the resources owned by a business, ie the assets, must equal the value of all the money introduced into or owed by the business, ie the capital plus the liabilities. The two sides of the equation will always equal each other. This is because any money introduced in the business or owed by the business, shown on the right hand side of the equation, must have the same value as the resources bought with that money, shown on the left hand side of the equation.

The following example illustrates the accounting equation. On 1 June 2000, Rita Miah set up a business producing computer software for musicians. She provided £2,000 capital from her savings and persuaded a bank to lend her business £1,000 for two years. With the money, she bought a computer for £2,700 and deposited the remaining £300 in the bank. For the first month she worked from home and did not undertake any other transactions. At the end of the month the financial position of Rita's business can be shown using the accounting equation.

Assets	=	Capital	+	Liabilities
Computer (£2,700)	=	Rita's savings (£2,000)	+	Loan (£1,000)
Money in bank (£300)				

Rita's business has two assets, the computer which was bought for £2,700 and a bank deposit of £300. Therefore the total value of assets is £3,000. The £3,000 spent on assets comes from the £2,000 capital introduced by Rita and the £1,000 bank loan, which is a liability. Therefore the value of assets for Rita's business (£3,000) is exactly the same as the value of capital and liabilities added together (£2,000 + £1,000 = £3,000).

The accounting equation will always **balance**. Any change in the value of assets will be matched by a change in the total value of capital and liabilities. And, any change in the value of capital and liabilities will have an equal effect on the value of assets. Such changes are explored later in this unit.

QUESTION 1

Tomkinsons is a travel company based at Stourbridge in the West Midlands. It is owned by Jeremy Tomkinson who used £25,000 of his own money to set up the business in 1997. The company runs day trips for senior citizens and once a month there is a weekend excursion to destinations such as Torquay, Ilfracombe and South Wales. The following information is also known:

- two coaches are owned by the company;
- a portakabin, which was bought second-hand when the business was set up, is used as an office; it is located in a yard that the company owns;
- the company owns a storage tank which contains 2,000 litres of diesel fuel;
- there is £439 in Tomkinsons' bank account;
- £500 is owed to a local mechanic for repairs to one of the coaches;
- £10,400 is owed to Barclays Bank.

(a) Which of the above items are Tomkinsons' assets?
(b) What is the value of Tomkinsons' liabilities?
(c) Use the accounting equation to calculate the value of Tomkinson's assets.

By rearranging the accounting equation, it can be expressed as:

Capital = Assets - Liabilities

So, in the case of Rita's business:

Capital (£2,000) = Assets (£2,700 + £300) - Liabilities (£1,000)

This is an alternative way of representing the financial position of Rita's business using the accounting equation. It is useful when preparing the balance sheet of a business, as described later in the unit.

What effect will transactions have on the accounting equation?

Business transactions affect both sides of the accounting equation. To illustrate the impact of a single transaction, consider what would happen if Rita Miah, in the earlier example, introduced another £1,500 into the business and deposited it in the bank during July. The effect of this transaction on the business would be:
- an increase of capital by £1,500, from £2,000 to £3,500;
- an increase in assets by £1,500, from £3,000 to £4,500, because the money deposited at the bank has risen from £300 to £1,800.

The accounting equation now becomes:

Assets	=	Capital	+	Liabilities
Computer (£2,700)	=	Rita (£3,500)	+	Loan (£1,000)
Money in bank (£1,800)				
£4,500	**=**	**£3,500**	**+**	**£1,000**

This transaction illustrates another very important concept in accounting. It is that **any transaction will have two effects**. This is called DUALITY or DUAL ASPECT. In the example above, capital has risen on one side of the equation and assets have risen on the other. Some more examples illustrating duality are shown in Figure 5.1.

Figure 5.1 shows how the values of assets, capital and liabilities change following a transaction. For example, when a shop buys goods from a wholesaler on credit, the shop takes ownership of the new stock, so there is an increase in assets, but arranges to pay at a later date. This creates a liability because money is now owed to a trade creditor, ie the wholesaler.

Although all transactions can be considered as having a dual aspect, in some cases the overall balance of the accounting equation is unchanged. For example, if Rita Miah buys a car for her business costing £850 in July, the total value of assets, capital and liabilities does not change. What happens is that one asset falls in value because she has less money in the bank, and another rises by the same amount because she now owns a car. The transaction still has a dual aspect but one

Figure 5.1 *The dual aspect of transactions on the accounting equation*

Transaction	Effect on accounting equation
Stocks of goods are bought on credit from suppliers	1 Increase in liabilities (more owed to trade creditors) 2 Increase in assets (more stocks)
Owner withdraws cash from the business	1 Decrease in capital 2 Decrease in assets (less money in the bank)
Loan repaid to the bank	1 Decrease in liabilities (less owed to the bank) 2 Decrease in assets (less money in the bank)
Payment made to supplier (for goods bought on credit)	1 Decrease in liabilities (less owed to trade creditors) 2 Decrease in assets (less money in the bank)

cancels out the other. The effect on the accounting equation is shown below. This is the position on 31 July 2000.

Assets	=	Capital	+	Liabilities
Computer (£2,700)	=	Rita (£3,500)	+	Loan (£1,000)
Car (£850)				
Money in bank (£950)				
£4,500	**=**	**£3,500**	**+**	**£1,000**

A similar effect occurs if goods are sold by a business. Consider, for example, what happens if a manufacturer sells one of its products to a customer on credit. The customer takes delivery and arranges to make payment at a later date. The transaction causes a decrease in assets for the manufacturer, because its stock of goods has fallen. However, there is a matching increase in assets because the customer, ie trade debtor, owes money to the manufacturer.

The accounting equation and the balance sheet

The accounting equation shows the value of resources owned by a business and the sources of finance, ie capital and liabilities, used to acquire these resources. The same information forms the basis of a financial statement known as a BALANCE SHEET (see unit 17). This sets out the value of a business's assets, capital and liabilities on a particular date.

QUESTION 2

Walton Business Supplies operates from a warehouse in Nuneaton. It is a mail order company which sells stationery and other office equipment. Some financial information on the company is provided below.

- Value of buildings owned by Walton Business Supplies: £70,000.
- Value of vehicles owned: £33,300.
- Value of stock: £170,000.
- Trade debtors (ie money owed by customers): £9,800.
- Money at bank: £14,000.
- Owner's capital: £260,500.
- Trade creditors (ie money owed to suppliers): £32,000.
- Money owed to Inland Revenue: £4,600.

(a) **Use the accounting equation to show that the value of assets is the same as the total value of capital and liabilities.**

(b) **Show the effect on the accounting equation if the company pays a supplier £3,100 by cheque for goods that have been bought on credit.**

(c) **Show the effect on the accounting equation if the company then sells £2,300 of stock for cash.**

A balance sheet for Rita Miah's business, described earlier in this unit, is shown in Figure 5.2. It states the assets, liabilities and capital of her business at 31 July 2000. Like the accounting equation, a balance sheet must always balance. In this example, the value of assets less the value of liabilities (£4,500 - £1,000 = £3,500) is shown to be equal to the value of capital (£3,500).

Figure 5.2 *Balance sheet for Rita Miah's business on 31 July 2000*

Figure 5.3 *Balance sheet for Rita Miah's business on 31 August 2000*

The use of 'as at' in the heading of the balance sheet emphasises that it is describing the financial position of the business on a particular date.

Rita Miah
Balance Sheet as at 31.7.00

	£
Assets	
Computer	2,700
Car	850
Money in bank	950
	4,500
Less liabilities	
Loan	1,000
	3,500
Financed by	
Capital	3,500
	3,500

Rita Miah
Balance Sheet as at 31.8.00

	£	£
Assets		
Computer		2,700
Office equipment		400
Car		850
Money in bank		950
		4,900
Less liabilities		
Loan	1,000	
Creditor	400	
		1,400
		3,500
Financed by		
Capital		3,500
		3,500

Note that the liabilities are listed in a left hand column and the subtotal is entered on the right.

In the same way that business transactions affect the accounting equation, they also affect the balance sheet. For example, if Rita bought some office equipment on credit for £400 during August 2000, the total of assets and liabilities would change. This is shown in the new balance sheet in Figure 5.3. The total assets have increased by £400 due to the acquisition of a new asset, the office equipment. The total of liabilities has also risen because £400 is owed to the office equipment supplier who is therefore a creditor. The overall totals on the balance sheet have not changed. This is because the increase in assets from £4,500 to £4,900 has been offset by an increase in liabilities from £1,000 to £1,400.

QUESTION 3

Michael King trades as a clothes retailer. He leases a shop in Halifax and sells clothes and fashion accessories to the 15 - 21 age group. When he opened the shop he invested his savings in buying stock and in making the shop interior look attractive. He also bought an electronic till. The value of his business assets is shown in the balance sheet (Figure 5.4).

(a) Use the information on Michael King's balance sheet to draw up the accounting equation for his business. Explain the connection between the accounting equation and the balance sheet.

(b) On 1 November 2000 Michael paid a creditor £470 and withdrew £500 of his capital. Redraw the balance sheet showing the effect of these two transactions.

Figure 5.4 *Balance sheet for Michael King's business*

Michael King
Balance Sheet as at 31.10.00

	£	£
Assets		
Equipment		2,350
Fixtures and fittings		3,400
Stock		12,450
Money at bank		2,900
		21,100
Less liabilities		
Creditors	4,660	
Bank loan	5,000	
		9,660
		11,440
Financed by		
Capital		11,440
		11,440

The expanded accounting equation

So far, when looking at the accounting equation, only assets, capital and liabilities have been taken into account. However, the effect of transactions on revenue, expenses and drawings must also be considered.

- REVENUE is the money that businesses receive when selling their goods or services to customers.
- EXPENSES are the costs incurred in running a business. They include the cost of buying goods that are later sold (these goods are known as PURCHASES) and other expenses such as payments for wages, electricity, insurance and transport.
- DRAWINGS refers to money taken out of a business by the owner(s) for personal use. The effect of drawings is to reduce capital.

The accounting equation can be expanded to include revenue, expenses and drawings:

Assets = Capital + Liabilities + Revenue - Expenses - Drawings

Expressed in words, this means that the total resources owned by a business **(assets)**:
equals
- the money introduced from owners and creditors (**capital and liabilities**);
- plus the money received from selling goods or services (**revenue**).

less
- the money spent on resources (**expenses**);
- and the money taken out by the owner for personal use (**drawings**).

To illustrate the impact of changes in revenue and expenses, consider the previous example of Rita Miah. Suppose that during September 2000, Rita sells some computer software to a musician, banking a cheque for £740, and that she pays £230 by cheque to a newspaper for placing an advert. Taking the totals of assets, capital and liabilities in Figure 5.3 as a starting point, the effect is shown below. This is the position of the business on 30 September 2000.

Assets	=	Capital + Liabilities + Revenue - Expenses - Drawings
£4,900 + (£740 - £230)	=	£3,500 + £1,400 + £740 - £230 - 0
£4,900 + £510	=	£3,500 + £1,400 + £740 - £230
£5,410	**=**	**£5,410**

On the left hand side of the equation the total assets have risen by £510. This is due to an increase in the bank balance as a result of the two transactions. The right hand side has also increased by £510. The sale of computer software to a musician has increased revenue by £740, but this is offset by the £230 expense of the newspaper advert.

The accounting equation and the profit and loss account

A PROFIT AND LOSS ACCOUNT is a statement of the profit, or loss, of a business over a period of time (see unit 17). It is constructed using some information from the expanded accounting equation, ie the revenue and expenses of a business. If revenue is greater than expenses, the business makes a **profit**. However, if revenue is less than expenses, the business makes a **loss**. This can be expressed as an equation:

Revenue - Expenses = Profit (loss)

Note that this equation can be substituted in the expanded accounting equation to give:

Assets = Capital + Liabilities + Profit (loss) - Drawings

Figure 5.5 illustrates how the two transactions of Rita Miah in September 2000 can be shown in a simplified profit and loss account. The expenses, ie the expenditure of £230 on a newspaper advert, are subtracted from the revenue, ie the sale of computer software worth £740, to give the profit of £510.

Figure 5.6 illustrates the effect of the two transactions involving revenue and expenses on the balance sheet. The £510 profit resulting from the transactions is added to capital which now amounts to £4,010 (£3,500 + £510). This is because profit belongs to the business owner. The assets of the business, in this case money in the bank, have also risen by £510.

Figure 5.5 *Profit and loss account for Rita Miah for the month ended 30 September 2000*

Figure 5.6 *Balance sheet for Rita Miah on 30 September 2000*

Note 'month ended' in the heading of the profit and loss account. This emphasises that it is describing the financial position of the business over a period of time.

Rita Miah
Profit and Loss Account
for the month ended 30.9.00

	£
Revenue	740
Less	
Expenses	230
Profit	510

Rita Miah
Balance Sheet as at 30.9.00

	£	£
Assets		
Computer		2,700
Office equipment		400
Car		850
Cash		1,460
		5,410
Less liabilities		
Loan	1,000	
Trade creditors	400	
		1,400
		4,010
Financed by		
Capital		
Original capital		3,500
Add profit		510
		4,010

key terms

Accounting equation - the relationship between a business's assets, capital and liabilities which states that Assets = Capital + Liabilities.

Assets - resources that are used by a business.

Balance sheet - a statement that shows the assets, capital and liabilities of a business on a particular date.

Capital - the money provided by owners to set up and run a business.

Drawings - money taken from the business by the owner for personal use. It has the effect of reducing capital.

Duality (or dual aspect) - the idea that a transaction has two effects on the accounting equation.

Expenses - payments for resources that businesses use when producing goods and services.

Liability - money owed by a business or individual.

Profit and loss account - a statement of the profit (or loss) made by a business over a period of time.

Purchases - goods that are bought for resale, or raw materials and components that are made into goods for sale.

Revenue - money received by a business for selling its output.

Trade creditors - suppliers who are owed money by a business (classed as a liability).

Trade debtors - money owed to a business by customers (classed as an asset).

summary questions

1. List three assets that a retail business might own.
2. What is capital used for?
3. Give two examples of business liabilities.
4. If the value of a business's assets is £86,000 and its capital is £42,000, what is the value of its liabilities?
5. If the value of a business's capital is £4.5m and its liabilities are £1.7m, what is the value of its assets?
6. If a retailer buys some stock for cash, what effect will this have on the accounting equation?
8. How do transactions involving revenue and expenses affect the balance sheet?
9. Explain why profit is added to owner's capital.
10. What is the difference between the accounting equation and the expanded accounting equation?

UNIT ASSESSMENT   QUESTION 1

In October 2000 Adrian Stilgoe graduated from Coventry University with a degree in Art and Design. His parents gave him £5,000 to clear his student loan but Adrian decided to use the money to set up in business as an interior designer. He also borrowed £3,000 from a bank.

Adrian decided that he needed an office from which to run his business. Fortunately, a friend who had a large spare room over a high street shop was keen to help. It was agreed that Adrian could use the room as an office, rent free for the first year.

By the end of October Adrian had bought a computer for £900, some design software for £1,100, a car for £3,500 and some office furniture for £1,760. He set up a bank account for the business in which he deposited the rest of his money.

(a) With reference to Adrian Stilgoe's business, explain what is meant by assets, liabilities and capital.
(b) Use the accounting equation to work out the bank balance, ie the amount of money deposited in the bank, for Adrian's business at the end of October.
(c) Draw up a balance sheet to show the financial position of Adrian's business on 31.10.00.

UNIT ASSESSMENT   QUESTION 2

Lorna Hignett has a garden maintenance business. She specialises in redesigning and landscaping people's gardens in south Manchester. During her first month of trading, Lorna concentrated on obtaining transport, tools and equipment. At the end of the month, on 30 September 2000, she was able to provide the following financial information:

Van	£2,400
Trade creditor	£350
Gardening tools and equipment	£350
Cash in hand and at bank	£300
Lorna's capital	£2,700

(a) Use the accounting equation to show that the assets equal capital plus liabilities of the business.
(b) Draw up a simple balance sheet for Lorna's business as at 30 September 2000.
(c) In October Lorna won a contract for two weeks' work, clearing and replanting the overgrown garden of a large Victorian house. She was paid £400 by cheque for her work. During the same month Lorna paid £50 cash for the hire of a chainsaw. Show the effect of this transaction on the expanded version of the accounting equation:

Assets = Capital + Liabilities + Revenue - Expenses - Drawings.

(d) Draw up a simple profit and loss account to show the profit made by Lorna's business during October. Assume that she had no other transactions.
(e) Redraw the balance sheet to include the two October transactions.

unit 6

Capital and revenue expenditure

unitobjectives

To understand:
- the difference between capital and revenue expenditure;
- why the distinction between capital expenditure and revenue expenditure is important;
- the difference between revenue and capital income.

What is capital expenditure?

Spending on the purchase, alteration or improvement of FIXED ASSETS is called CAPITAL EXPENDITURE. Fixed assets are those assets of a business that are intended for repeated and continued use. They are not intended for resale. Examples include buildings, machinery, computers and vehicles. A fixed asset is normally expected to have a life span of more than one year.

An example of capital expenditure is the purchase of a shop by a clothes retailer. Any money spent on obtaining or improving the asset, by adding to its value, is also included. So, the following are all classed as capital expenditure:

- the legal and other fees associated with the purchase of the shop;
- the installation of new windows;
- the building of an extension to the shop for use as a stock room;
- the carriage of raw materials used to construct the extension.

What is revenue expenditure?

Money spent on the running expenses of a business is called REVENUE EXPENDITURE. Examples are spending on raw materials, fuel, advertising and stationery. These resources are generally used up in less than one year. Revenue expenditure also includes the maintenance and repair of fixed assets. In the case of a shop, the following are all classed as revenue expenditure:

- the maintenance of the shop, such as window cleaning;
- repairs to the shop, such as replacing a broken drainpipe;
- redecoration, such as painting the interior.

Wages that are paid to employees who are engaged in producing goods and services are also classed as revenue expenditure. So, in the case of a shop, the pay of the sales staff, warehouse staff and clerical staff is included. Figure 6.1 shows typical items of capital and revenue expenditure that take place in many businesses.

Figure 6.1 Examples of capital and revenue expenditure

EXAMPLE	CAPITAL EXPENDITURE	REVENUE EXPENDITURE
Delivery van	Purchase and delivery cost Modifications to the van Painting of company logo on van	Road tax Insurance Fuel Servicing, repairs and MOT Driver's wages
Machinery	Purchase and delivery cost Installation and testing Initial staff training	Fuel/power costs Insurance Maintenance and servicing Repairs and replacement of worn out parts Operating costs including wages

QUESTION 1

Katie MacDougal runs a successful dry cleaning business in Aberdeen. Her shop is located in the city centre and she employs six part-time staff. Recently she spent some time analysing the weekly expenditure of the business. She was alarmed by the high levels of expenditure for the week and wondered if she was beginning to lose control of costs. Her weekly operating costs are normally between £1,100 to £1,300. The following items of expenditure were recorded by Katie's business for the week:

- staff wages £800;
- upgrade for one of the dryers to increase its efficiency £210;
- cleaning fluids and materials £110;
- a new printer for the office computer £250;
- rent £150;
- telephone bill £96;
- stationery £34.

(a) Using examples from Katie MacDougal's business, explain the difference between capital expenditure and revenue expenditure.
(b) Calculate the amount of capital expenditure and revenue expenditure for Katie's business for the week in question.
(c) In your view, are Katie's business costs a problem? Explain your answer.

Problems distinguishing between capital and revenue expenditure

Sometimes the distinction between capital and revenue expenditure is not clear. This is particularly true if an item of expenditure falls into both categories. For example, a business might pay £19,000 to a builder for work carried out on premises. If £12,000 of this expenditure is for repairing damaged roofing, and £7,000 is for improving the external appearance of the building, the expenditure must be split. The £12,000 for roof repairs is classified as revenue expenditure because it is maintaining the value of a fixed asset. However, the £7,000 for improving the appearance is capital expenditure because it is adding value to the premises.

Another difficulty might occur if a business uses its own employees to carry out work that is classified as capital expenditure. For example, consider a farmer who organises two of his workers to build a new storage unit. Assume that the employees take four weeks to build the unit and are each paid their normal wages of £200 per week. The total labour costs will be £1,600 (2 x 4 x £200). If the materials cost a further £4,100 then the total construction expenditure for the storage unit is £5,700. All of this should be treated as capital expenditure. Note that the £1,600 wage bill is not classed as revenue expenditure because it is not part of the farm's normal running costs.

Capital expenditure can be expensive. For example, the purchase of a new articulated lorry might cost a business £60,000. An alternative way of acquiring the lorry is to LEASE it from a leasing company. This involves hiring the lorry for an agreed period of time and avoids having to raise the entire £60,000. The leasing charges are classed as revenue expenditure because the business does not own the asset. This type of arrangement is called an **operating lease** (see Figure 6.2). A different form of arrangement where a business eventually pays the full cost of an asset is called a **finance lease**. In the case of a finance lease, the payments are treated as capital expenditure.

Figure 6.2 *The difference between an operating lease and a finance lease*

A business wishes to acquire a new lorry	
Operating lease	*Finance lease*
The lorry is hired for an agreed period of time. The business does not own the lorry. Spending is classed as **revenue expenditure**.	Payments eventually cover the full cost of the lorry. The business is considered to own the lorry. Spending is classed as **capital expenditure**.

Rutherford and Sons manufactures concrete products such as fence posts, paving slabs and lamp posts. It operates from a small factory in Burslem, Stoke-on-Trent. Recent success has meant that the company has had to expand its premises to increase production. Some of the expenditure incurred in the last financial year is listed below:

- £52,000 paid to a builder to construct a new extension;
- £3,000 legal fees paid to secure planning permission for the extension;
- £3,200 interest paid on a loan to fund the extension;
- £5,000 wages paid to Rutherford's own employees to construct a new loading bay, plus a further £4,000 for materials;
- £11,800 paid to the builder for work on the existing premises (£2,900 for repairing broken drainage, £4,200 for installing double glazing in the office and £4,700 for installing a new heating system).

(a) Explain whether the £5,000 wages should be treated as capital expenditure or as revenue expenditure.

(b) Calculate the total amount of capital expenditure and revenue expenditure for Rutherford and Sons.

(c) After incurring the development expenditure, Rutherford and Sons experienced a shortage of funds. In view of this it arranged an operating lease for a new machine costing £300 a month rather than purchasing it outright for £22,000. Explain how this expenditure is classified.

If a business uses its own funds to buy a fixed asset, this is capital expenditure. However, many businesses use borrowed money for this purpose. For example, a business might take out a mortgage to purchase some premises. The interest payments on the borrowed money are usually classed as revenue expenditure. This is because the interest is not a cost of acquiring the asset, but a cost of financing the acquisition.

Capital expenditure, revenue expenditure and final accounts

Accountants treat capital expenditure and revenue expenditure in different ways in the final accounts of businesses. Capital expenditure is shown on the **balance sheet** and revenue expenditure is shown on the **profit and loss account** (see unit 17). If expenditure is not classified correctly, the result is that the final accounts will be inaccurate and misleading.

Consider, for example, the purchase of a machine for £12,000. This represents an increase in a business's assets. Since the balance sheet lists all of the assets owned by a business, capital expenditure must be included on this statement. Failure to do so results in the business's assets being undervalued. As a result, the value of the business will also be understated.

Revenue expenditure, on the other hand, is treated as an expense in the profit and loss account. It is subtracted from the revenue to calculate profit. If revenue expenditure is understated, profit is overstated, and vice versa. For example, if a business purchases some raw materials for £2,000 and incorrectly classifies this as capital expenditure, revenue expenditure and expenses will be understated. As a result, profit will be overstated.

Figure 6.3 shows a balance sheet for A. C. Clarke, an ice cream manufacturer, and illustrates how capital expenditure is included. Figure 6.4 shows the profit and loss account for A. C Clarke and illustrates how revenue expenditure is included.

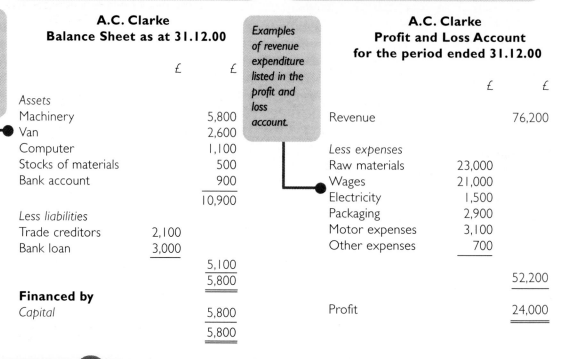

Figure 6.3 *Balance sheet for A. C. Clarke illustrating how accountants deal with capital expenditure*

Examples of capital expenditure listed in the balance sheet.

A.C. Clarke
Balance Sheet as at 31.12.00

	£	£
Assets		
Machinery		5,800
Van		2,600
Computer		1,100
Stocks of materials		500
Bank account		900
		10,900
Less liabilities		
Trade creditors	2,100	
Bank loan	3,000	
		5,100
		5,800
Financed by		
Capital		5,800
		5,800

Figure 6.4 *Profit and loss account for A. C. Clarke showing how accountants deal with revenue expenditure*

Examples of revenue expenditure listed in the profit and loss account.

A.C. Clarke
Profit and Loss Account
for the period ended 31.12.00

	£	£
Revenue		76,200
Less expenses		
Raw materials	23,000	
Wages	21,000	
Electricity	1,500	
Packaging	2,900	
Motor expenses	3,100	
Other expenses	700	
		52,200
Profit		24,000

QUESTION 3

Lorraine Day runs a shop selling mobile phones and mobile phone accessories in Southampton. She started on 1 January 1999 and within two years she had successfully grown the business. Even in her first year she made a profit and in the second year she expected to double it. She employs two part-time staff and the revenue for the second year was £112,500. A list of her business expenditure for the same year, ended 31 December 2000, is shown below.

- stock for resale £65,400;
- wages £23,000;
- heat and light £760;
- electronic till £1,400;
- repairs to heating system £430;
- installation of new fixtures and fittings £2,600;
- interest on bank loan £960;
- other operating expenses £3,400.

(a) Distinguish between capital expenditure and revenue expenditure in the above list.
(b) Using the information provided, draw up a simple profit and loss account for Lorraine Day's business for the year ended 31 December 2000, and calculate how much profit she made.
(c) Where will the capital expenditure that you have identified be shown in the final accounts of the business?

The impact of errors in classification

If capital expenditure is treated as revenue expenditure by mistake, there will be an impact on the profit and loss account and on the balance sheet. For example, if the computer bought for £1,100 by A. C. Clarke (see Figure 6.3) is incorrectly treated as revenue expenditure, the following errors will occur:

- The amount of profit will be understated by £1,100. This is because the £1,100 will be listed as an expense in the profit and loss account, and so total expenses will rise by £1,100 to £53,300

QUESTION 4

Sami Hajaig runs a fast food restaurant specialising in kebabs and pitta breads. His outlet is situated in the centre of Cirencester. A copy of his profit and loss account for the year ended 31 July 2000 is shown in Figure 6.5. The account contains an error.

(a) **Identify the error in the profit and loss account for Sami Hajaig.**
(b) **What effect will this error have on the profit of the business?**
(c) **Explain how the error should be corrected.**

Figure 6.5 *Profit and loss account for Sami Hajaig*

Sami Hajaig
Profit and Loss Account for the year ended 31.7.00

	£	£
Revenue		131,900
Less expenses		
Wages	47,000	
Materials	31,040	
Heat and light	6,220	
Refrigerator	4,000	
Advertising	450	
Leasing charges	3,200	
Telephone	780	
Other expenses	2,910	
		95,600
Profit		36,300

(£1,100 + £52,200). Thus, when total expenses are subtracted from revenue, profit is reduced to £22,900 (£76,200 - £53,300).

- The total of assets will be understated by £1,100. This is because the computer, bought for £1,100, will not appear in the list of assets. Thus, the assets will only be £9,800 (£10,900 - £1,100). Since the total of assets is understated, the value of the business is also understated.

The opposite effects will occur if revenue expenditure is treated as capital expenditure by mistake. Profit and fixed assets will be overstated.

A problem that arises from these errors is that the owner of a business will be misinformed about its performance and value. Another difficulty is that the amount of tax paid will be incorrect. This is because tax is linked to the level of profit that a business makes.

Capital and revenue income

Most business income is generated from the sale of goods and services. It is called REVENUE INCOME and is entered in the profit and loss account. However, a business might receive income from other sources, such as renting out a flat above its premises, or interest paid on its bank deposit. This is also classed as revenue income but is usually recorded separately, for example as 'other revenue'. On the other hand, if a business receives income when a fixed asset is sold it is called CAPITAL INCOME.

key terms

Capital expenditure - expenditure on the purchase, alteration or improvement of fixed assets.
Capital income - money received from the sale of fixed assets.
Fixed assets - those assets of a business that are intended for long-term, continuing use. They are not intended for resale.
Leasing - the hiring of fixed assets for a period of time.
Revenue expenditure - money spent on the running expenses of a business including expenditure on resources that will generally be used up in less than one year.
Revenue income - money received from the sale of goods and services by a business and also any income from other sources, such as interest payments but excluding the sale of fixed assets.

summary questions

1. Give three examples of capital expenditure.
2. Give three examples of revenue expenditure.
3. How are capital expenditure and revenue expenditure treated in the final accounts of a business?
4. What will happen to the amount of profit if capital expenditure is treated as revenue expenditure by mistake?
5. What will happen to the total of assets if revenue expenditure is treated as capital expenditure by mistake?
6. What is the difference between capital income and revenue income?

UNIT ASSESSMENT QUESTION 1

Eric Gustafson trades as a financial adviser in Woking. He rents an office in the town centre and employs three full-time staff. He advises clients on how to manage their savings, investments and pension funds. Eric decided that he needed a new computer system for the business in order to improve efficiency. The following expenditure was incurred when the new system was purchased:

- Cost of computer £1,900;
- Paper, ink cartridges and other consumables £110;
- Cost of colour laser printer £450;
- Installation and testing costs £200;
- Staff training on the new system £500;
- Annual insurance against theft and breakdowns £90;
- Cost of rewiring to accommodate new computer £340;
- Annual maintenance agreement £99.

(a) Calculate the total of capital expenditure incurred by Eric Gustafson's business when acquiring the computer system.
(b) To what extent would the business's profits have been reduced by the expenditure listed?
(c) Suggest two items of revenue expenditure incurred by Eric Gustafson's business that are not included on the list.
(d) If Eric had borrowed £3,000 to pay for the new computer system, how would the interest payments on the loan have affected the business's revenue expenditure and profit?

UNIT ASSESSMENT QUESTION 2

Colin Walters runs a wine bar called The Bar Zone in Liverpool. In 1999, Colin had to pay £320 to an engineer for repairs to two of his refrigerated storage and display units. In the following year the display units again malfunctioned and Colin realised that they both needed to be replaced. The cost of buying them outright would be £4,000. The leasing cost for the units, on an operating lease, would be £100 per month.

(a) Would the £320 repair costs paid by Colin be classed as capital or revenue expenditure? Explain your answer.
(b) What would be the effect on Colin's annual profit figure if he decided to lease the display units?
(c) Colin eventually decided to buy the units because he thought they would last at least 10 years and this would be the cheapest option in the long run. However, the expenditure was entered on the profit and loss account as an expense. Explain the effect of this mistake on: (i) profit; (ii) the value of business assets.
(d) If Colin sold his old refrigeration units for a scrap value of £100, how might this income be classified? Explain your answer.

Accounting concepts

unitobjectives

To understand:
- the need for accounting concepts;
- the meaning of accounting concepts;
- that accounting concepts sometimes conflict with each other.

Why are accounting concepts needed?

The accounts of a business should reflect a 'true and fair' view of its financial position. To achieve this, accountants apply a series of 'rules' or ACCOUNTING CONCEPTS. These are also known as **conventions** or **principles**. In the USA, and increasingly in the UK, the expression GAAP is used to refer to 'generally accepted accounting principles'.

By using agreed concepts when analysing and presenting financial information, accountants can avoid confusion and inconsistency. There is also less scope for presenting misleading financial information and the accounts of different businesses can be compared more easily.

The concepts or principles have developed over time as a framework within which accountants operate. In the UK, the Accounting Standards Committee (ASC) was established in the 1970s. This committee issued a number of **Statements of Standard Accounting Practice (SSAPs)**. The ASC described four 'fundamental accounting concepts' in its Statements of Standard Accounting Practice (SSAP 2). These are the:

- going concern concept;
- consistency concept;
- prudence concept;
- accruals or matching concept.

Since 1990, the regulation of accounting in the UK has passed over to the Accounting Standards Board (ASB) (see unit 45). SSAPs still exist but any new standards are now called **Financial Reporting Standards (FRSs)**. During 2001, the Financial Reporting Standard *Accounting policies* (FRS 18) came into force and superseded SSAP 2. It requires that businesses should use those accounting policies that are 'most appropriate to their particular circumstances' for the purpose of giving a true and fair view. Policies should be judged against the objectives of:

- relevance;
- reliability;
- comparability;
- understandability.

FRS 18 states that a business should regularly review its accounting policies to ensure that they remain the most appropriate to the business's particular circumstances. Specific disclosure about the policies used, and any changes to the policies, must be made.

In addition to the fundamental concepts listed above, a number of others are generally accepted. These include the concepts of:

- objectivity;
- business entity;
- money measurement;
- historical cost;
- dual aspect;
- realisation;
- materiality.

Objectivity concept

As far as possible, accounts should be based on verifiable evidence rather than on personal opinion. In other words, they should be OBJECTIVE rather than SUBJECTIVE. So, for example, accountants should value a transaction on the evidence of an invoice rather than on their own personal opinions. This avoids bias. Consider what might happen if two accountants were asked their opinion on the value of a particular transaction, for example the purchase of new premises. They might disagree because value can be measured in many different ways. However, if they were asked to value the transaction according to the invoice, they would be likely to record the same value.

Business entity concept

The BUSINESS ENTITY concept states that the financial affairs of a business should be completely separate from those of the owner. The business is treated as a **separate entity**. This means that personal transactions must not be confused with business transactions. Difficulties can arise, however, if resources are used both by a business and by its owner. Suppose, for example, that a van is used during the week for business purposes and at the weekend for personal use. From an accounting point of view, the costs associated with the van must be divided between the business and the owner. One approach might be to split the costs so that 5/7 (ie five days out of seven) of the van's costs are charged to the business and 2/7 to the owner.

The business entity concept does not conform with the legal position of sole traders and partnerships (see unit 33). In these cases, the law does not distinguish between a business and its owners. So, for example, a sole trader is liable, ie responsible, for all the debts of the business. However, in the case of limited companies, there is a separation of identity between the owners and the business itself. The owners are not liable for the debts of the business. They have **limited liability**. For accounting purposes, these legal distinctions are not relevant. In all cases, a business and its owners are treated as separate entities.

QUESTION 1

Paul Whitehouse runs a management information service from an office which he has at home. He writes specialist reports on the economic state of African countries. These reports are commissioned by large multinational companies.

Paul's business assets include a computer that he bought for £2,400. Paul uses his computer during five days of the week for an average of six hours per day. However, during the evening and at weekends, the computer is used by his children for doing their homework and for games. They use the computer for, on average, ten hours per week.

(a) With reference to Paul Whitehouse's business, explain what is meant by the business entity concept.

(b) Suggest what proportion of the computer cost should be attributed to Paul's business.

(c) Suggest two other costs that might have to be split between Paul's business and his personal use.

Money measurement concept

The MONEY MEASUREMENT concept states that financial records, including the value of transactions, assets, liabilities and capital, should be expressed in monetary terms. The main reasons for recording financial information in this way are that:

- most transactions have an agreed monetary value and are expressed in monetary terms; few transactions are carried out by barter or 'swapping', ie with no money involved;
- the different values of products and assets can be more easily compared in money terms; for example, the relative value of two buildings that cost £50,000 and £250,000 is more clearly expressed in monetary terms than in descriptive terms such as 'medium price' and 'high price'.

However, the use of money to record financial information does have some limitations. One problem is that information which cannot be recorded in monetary terms might be ignored. As a result, accounts might not always reflect a 'true and fair' view of a business's financial position. For example, a business might have a workforce that is poorly managed, with high rates of absenteeism. This information cannot easily be expressed in monetary terms. However, clearly it is important and, when taken into account, would have an impact on the financial position of the business.

Historical cost concept

This concept states that accounting should be based on the original costs incurred in a transaction. So, for example, assets such as machinery should be valued at their HISTORICAL COST, ie the cost when purchased. The historical cost of an asset can be verified by documentary evidence such as an invoice (see unit 3). This should allow the valuation to be objective.

There are some disadvantages of using historical cost as the basis for valuation. The price of some assets, such as property and land, can rise or fall. For example, in the early 1990s, the value of many business properties fell sharply when the economy suffered a recession. A business that bought a building for £100,000 in 1989 might have found that it was worth only £80,000 in 1991. This would mean that the value of the asset would be overstated.

INFLATION has the opposite effect. It is defined as a general and persistent rise in prices. Because it causes land and property prices to rise, the historical cost of these assets is likely to be less than their current value. For this reason, businesses sometimes arrange for a professional revaluation of these assets in order to reflect a true and fair view of what they are worth.

A further problem with inflation is that money becomes unreliable as a measure of value when prices are rising rapidly in the economy. Over the past decades, inflation has caused a rise in the monetary value of most assets. For example, the average price of a house in Britain in 1970 was just over £5,000. By 2000, this had risen to almost £100,000. So, care must be taken when comparing monetary values in different time periods.

Using the historical cost concept might also lead to difficulties when valuing stock. The Statement of Standard Accounting Practice *Stocks and work-in-progress* (SSAP 9) states that a business should value its stock at the 'lower of historical cost or **net realisable value**' (see unit 24). Net realisable value is the sales value of stock, ie what it is worth when sold, less any costs incurred in selling the stock. So, if it is likely that stock can only be sold for less than its historical cost, it is the lower valuation that must be used.

Dual aspect concept

The DUAL ASPECT concept states that every transaction has two effects on a business's accounts (see unit 5). Suppose, for example, that a business buys some goods on credit. Assets increase, because stocks increase, and liabilities also increase because money is owed to a trade creditor. Similarly, if the business repays a loan of £1,000 to a bank, there is a dual aspect. Liabilities decrease,

---

QUESTION 2

The Avon Tanker Company (ATC) is owned by Charles Hunter and operates from a site in Bristol. The company owns three road tankers and transports oil from a terminal to depots in the South West. In its 1999 accounts, the company showed a profit of £123,000 and in 2000 this profit rose to £126,000.

In 1991, Charles had purchased an old warehouse. He uses this as a garage for his tankers. He discovered in 1999 that a similar sized, nearby warehouse was up for sale. Thinking that this might be an opportunity to expand his business, Charles contacted the estate agent to ask the price. He was surprised when the agent said that the warehouse was on sale for 'offers over £90,000'. According to the Avon Tanker Company's financial records, its own warehouse was valued at just £22,000.

(a) With reference to the Avon Tanker Company, outline an advantage and disadvantage of using historical cost as the basis of valuing assets.

(b) Between 1999 and 2000 the rate of inflation in the UK was 3 per cent. To what extent did the company's actual £3,000 increase in profits give a true and fair view of its financial position?

because the loan is repaid, and assets decrease because the business has less money.

In accordance with the dual aspect concept, each transaction is recorded twice by bookkeepers. This is the basis of the **double entry system** of bookkeeping (see unit 8).

Realisation concept

The REALISATION concept states that revenue should not be recognised until the exchange of goods or services has taken place. In other words, revenue should not be recorded until it has been **realised**. For example, if a retailer supplies £300 of goods on a 'sale or return' basis, the customer might return some, or all, of the goods at a later date. According to the realisation concept, the £300 should not be recorded as revenue at the time that the goods are supplied. If the customer returns £230 of the goods two months later and buys the remainder, revenue of £70 would only then be recorded.

Materiality concept

According to the concept of MATERIALITY, accountants should not spend time trying to record accurately any items that are trivial or immaterial. Information is considered **material** if its omission from a financial statement could be misleading. An example of applying the concept occurs when business expenses are classified. Most are grouped under headings such as 'heating and lighting' or 'insurance'. However, in the case of inexpensive items, a heading of 'sundry expenses' is often used. This avoids spending time in categorising trivial expenditure.

The concept of materiality is particularly relevant when distinguishing between capital expenditure and revenue expenditure. Capital expenditure is shown as an increase in a business's fixed assets on the balance sheet. Revenue expenditure is shown as an expense on the profit and loss account. Therefore, if expenditure is wrongly classified, there is an effect on the balance sheet and the profit and loss account. However, under certain circumstances, the materiality concept states that it is acceptable to treat some capital expenditure as revenue expenditure.

For example, a business might purchase a waste paper bin for £2.50. The bin will be used repeatedly over a period of time so, technically, it is a fixed asset and its purchase is capital expenditure. As such, it should be included on the business's balance sheet. However, according to the materiality concept, it is acceptable to treat the £2.50 as revenue expenditure and as an expense on the profit and loss account. This avoids cluttering the balance sheet with trivial items.

Unfortunately, the concept does not provide clear guidelines to help businesses decide which transactions are material. Businesses therefore use a variety of arbitrary methods to determine materiality. A small business might decide to treat all capital expenditure under £50 as revenue expenditure. On the other hand, a larger business might use £500 as the limit.

QUESTION 3

Ingrid Kalnins recently set up a retail business selling cameras and other photographic equipment. She leases a shop in Bournemouth and caters for photography enthusiasts. When she set up the business the following resources were purchased:

- fixtures and fittings £1,700;
- secure display cabinets £2,100;
- electronic till £220;
- calculator £5.99;
- stapler £8.50;
- broom £3.95.

All of these resources are expected to be in use for many years. However, Ingrid is not sure whether some or all of this expenditure should be treated as capital expenditure.

(a) Using the materiality concept, suggest which of the resources might be listed as fixed assets.
(b) Suggest a method that Ingrid might use to classify future spending as revenue expenditure or capital expenditure.

Going concern concept

The GOING CONCERN concept assumes that a business will carry on trading for the foreseeable future. In other words, it is not expected to close down or to be sold. This concept affects the way that assets are valued. For a going concern, it is reasonable to value assets at their historical cost. However, if the business is about to close down, assets should be revalued at their 'break-up' value. This is the amount that they would sell for if the business closed and the assets were sold off. Under most circumstances it is likely that the break-up value of assets such as machinery and stock, ie their second-hand value, will be lower than their historical cost. However, in the case of property and land, the opposite might be true and on the break up of a business these assets might be sold for more than their historical cost.

QUESTION 4

Marcus Rogers initially set up in business in rented premises. He purchased some specialist machinery and equipment and began producing high quality, Belgian style chocolates. The business started well and in the first six months of trading, which included the Christmas period, Marcus made a small profit. Unfortunately the novelty of his products wore off and trade dwindled. After poor summer sales, Marcus was considering whether the business might have to close down. He had some ideas for a new business which he might be able to finance by selling assets from his old business. The balance sheet for his business at the end of his first year of trading is shown in Figure 7.1.

Figure 7.1 *Balance sheet for Marcus Rogers*

Marcus Rogers
Balance Sheet as at 31.10.00

	£	£
Assets		
Machinery		3,500
Packaging equipment		1,700
Van		1,500
Stocks		1,400
Money at bank		150
		8,250
Less liabilities		
Bank loan	4,000	
Trade creditors	1,900	
		5,900
		2,350
Financed by		
Capital		2,350
		2,350

(a) Explain how an accountant might have valued Marcus Rogers' fixed assets if the business was a going concern.

(b) If Marcus did decide to close down, what factors might have affected the value of his fixed assets and his stock of chocolates?

Consistency concept

The CONSISTENCY concept states that the accounts of a business should be prepared on the same basis every year. In other words, there should be consistent treatment of similar items within each accounting period and from one period to the next. This allows the accounts to be compared over time. If accountants are not consistent in their policies, it is unclear whether changes in reported profits or the value of assets are the result of changes in business conditions or of changes in accounting practice. For example, changes in the policy of stock valuation (see unit 24) can lead to changes in the profit made by a business. The result is that the accounts create a misleading impression about the performance of the business.

The consistency concept does not mean that a business can never change its accounting policies. However, if it decides to adopt a new policy, it is normal for the business to report this in its final accounts. Sometimes a business might change its accounting policies deliberately to convey a false impression. The practice of manipulating accounts is known as 'window dressing' (see unit 45).

Prudence concept

The PRUDENCE concept states that accountants should be cautious when reporting the financial position of a business. It is therefore better to understate profits or the value of assets than to overstate them. In general, when accountants apply the concept of prudence they should:

- not record revenue or profit until it is certain, ie realised;
- anticipate all possible losses and record them as soon as they are known;
- choose the lowest value when faced with a choice of revenue or asset valuations:
- choose the highest value when faced with different estimates of costs.

For example, if a business buys a commercial vehicle at an auction for a bargain price of £2,800, and then discovers that it is actually worth £3,500, the lower value should be listed in the balance sheet. This is a cautious, or 'conservative', valuation and also conforms to the historical cost concept.

A similarly prudent approach should be adopted with bad debts. If goods have been sold on credit and the customer goes bankrupt, it is not likely that payment will be received. The money owed is classed as a 'bad debt' and should be recorded immediately. In accounting terms, introducing a 'provision for bad debts' is treated as an expense on the profit and loss account.

Accruals and matching concepts

These two concepts have slightly different meanings, but their effect is similar so they are generally considered together.

The ACCRUALS concept states that revenue should be recognised when it is earned and not when the money is received. This distinction can be illustrated by considering a business transaction in which goods are sold on credit. Suppose the business sells the goods to a customer in December and receives payment in the following March. Even though the payment is not received until March, it should still be recorded as revenue in December. The same principle applies to purchases made by a business. Costs should be recognised when they are incurred and not when the money is paid. For example, if a business buys components from a supplier on credit, the transaction should be recorded as an expense when the items are received, not when payment is made.

The MATCHING concept states that, in calculating profit, revenue should be matched against the expenditure incurred in earning it. To illustrate this, consider a confectioner who buys 100 chocolate bars for 20p each in May. During the month, 70 of these chocolate bars are sold for 25p each. According to the matching concept, the profit in May is determined by calculating the cost of buying 70 chocolate bars and offsetting this expense against the revenue generated from their sale. This is shown as follows:

	£
Revenue (70 x £0.25)	17.50
Less	
Expenses (70 x £0.20)	14.00
Profit (for May)	3.50

Only the cost of acquiring the 70 bars that are sold should be matched with the sales revenue. The 30 unsold chocolate bars are treated as an asset and not as an expense. If they are eventually sold, the profit would be calculated by subtracting the purchase cost of the 30 bars from the revenue raised when selling them.

In practice, it is not always possible to match precisely the revenue and costs for every item sold. This is particularly the case in manufacturing where a wide range of raw materials and components are used to produce different products. It is for this reason that most accountants take the view that revenue and costs should be matched 'so far as these costs are material and identifiable'.

Conflicts between accounting concepts

Accounting concepts provide a framework within which accountants can operate. However, there are occasions when the concepts conflict. Under these circumstances, a choice has to be made as to which concept is most important. For example, the going concern concept states that the value of assets should be based on their historical cost. However, the prudence concept states that the valuation should be based on the lowest possible estimate. This might be their value if the business closed down and the assets were sold off. In this case, accountants generally take the view that the going concern concept is more important than the prudence concept.

Another conflict can arise between the materiality concept and the objectivity concept. Decisions on whether something is material or not are subjective because they are based on opinion. In this case, accountants accept that they cannot be entirely objective and therefore the materiality concept takes precedence.

key terms

Accounting concepts (also known as accounting principles or conventions) - rules or guidelines that accountants follow when drawing up accounts.

Accruals - an accounting concept that distinguishes between the exchange of goods in one time period and the payment for those goods in another.

Business entity - an accounting concept which states that the financial affairs of a business should be completely separate from those of the owner. An entity is a business organisation.

Consistency - an accounting concept that requires accountants, when faced with a choice between different accounting techniques, not to change policies without good reason.

Dual aspect - the idea that every transaction has two effects on the accounts.

Going concern - an accounting concept that assumes a business will continue to trade in the foreseeable future.

Historical cost - the cost of an asset when purchased.

Inflation - a general and persistent rise in prices in the economy.

Matching - an accounting concept that ensures revenues are associated with their relevant expenses.

Materiality - an accounting concept which states that accountants should not spend time trying to record accurately items that are trivial or immaterial.

Money measurement - an accounting concept which states that all transactions recorded by businesses should be expressed in money terms.

Net realisable value - the amount at which any asset could be sold for, less any direct selling costs.

Objective - (in accounting) the concept that accountants should adopt standard practices rather than base their work on personal preferences or their own, ie subjective, opinions.

Prudence - an accounting concept that requires accountants to recognise revenue or profit only when they are realised.

Realisation - an accounting concept which states that revenue should be recognised when the exchange of goods or services takes place.

Subjective - an opinion that is based on personal preference.

summary questions

1. What are accounting concepts?
2. Explain why objectivity is important in accountancy.
3. What is the relevance of the business entity concept for a sole trader?
4. Why might the money measurement concept create a misleading impression of how a business is doing?
5. Explain the difference between historical cost and net realisable value.
6. How might inflation undermine the historical cost concept?
7. From an accountant's point of view, what is material when considering business transactions?
8. How might assets be valued if a business is about to close down?
9. What is the likely effect of the prudence concept on the profit and loss account of a business?
10. At what stage in a transaction should revenue be recognised?

UNIT ASSESSMENT QUESTION 1

Janet Chang and Paul Roberts operate as estate agents in the London suburb of Hillingdon. Janet handles the financial side of the business but at first was not responsible for bookkeeping. When their bookkeeper retired, Janet decided to take over responsibility. While updating records, Janet was unsure about how to treat a number of transactions.

1. One month before the end of the financial year, Janet had sent a cheque to the landlord for £6,000. This was to cover the payment of rent for the next 12 months. Janet decided not to record this payment because most of it was for the following financial year.
2. A new computer had cost £1,400. Paul said to Janet two months after the purchase that he had seen exactly the same system advertised in the newspaper for £650. Janet was not sure which value to record.
3. One of their clients sent a cheque for £3,200 by mistake when paying fees. The amount due was £2,300. Janet is not sure which figure to enter.

(a) **Explain how Janet should treat each of the above transactions according to the appropriate accounting concepts.**
(b) **In the role of Janet's accountant, write her a memo explaining why she should adopt accounting concepts when doing her bookkeeping.**

UNIT ASSESSMENT QUESTION 2

Simon Parker runs a property development company in Cornwall. He owns a number of cottages and other holiday homes that he rents out. Most are let on a short-term basis to holiday-makers. However, he does have some properties that are occupied by permanent residents. In January he purchased a large property in Helston for £100,000. It was in need of restoration and modernisation. Simon decided to split the property into two luxury holiday apartments and invested a further £60,000 into the development. By June the apartments were complete. Almost immediately Simon was offered £130,000 for one of the apartments which he accepted. The other apartment was also valued at £130,000 but Simon decided to keep it for renting.

(a) **What valuation should be placed on the unsold apartment in Simon's balance sheet? Explain your answer with reference to the relevant accounting concepts.**
(b) **One of Simon's long-term tenants fell behind with her rent. At the end of April she owed two months rent, a total of £600 (2 x £300). Simon was not sure how to record the situation. Since he had not received any money, he decided that he should not enter the two months rent for that tenant as revenue. Explain how Simon should have dealt with the unpaid rent, applying the accruals concept.**
(c) **If Simon had decided that the tenant must be evicted and there was no prospect of receiving any more rent, explain how the unpaid rent should have been treated?**

Double entry bookkeeping

unit**objectives**

To understand:
• double entry bookkeeping;
• how to record transactions in T accounts.

What is meant by double entry?

All business transactions have a **dual aspect**. For example, if a business pays cash for some goods, the value of goods in stock increases but, at the same time, there is a decrease in the amount of cash it holds. The system of bookkeeping that is used to record the two aspects is called the DOUBLE ENTRY SYSTEM.

Details of transactions are normally first recorded in the books of prime entry using evidence from source documents. For example, information from an invoice is recorded in a sales day book (see unit 9). The details are then **posted**, ie transferred, by bookkeepers to ledgers. A ledger is a big book, or computer file, containing a collection of accounts. It is in ledgers that the double entry system is used.

The double entry bookkeeping system requires that each business transaction is entered in two ledger accounts. These are known as T ACCOUNTS (see Figure 8.1). A T account provides a standard layout for recording business transactions and its T shaped appearance explains its name. Each account contains two sides.
• On the left-hand side of the account, DEBIT (Dr) entries are made.
• On the right-hand side of the account, CREDIT (Cr) entries are made.
• On top of the account is its name.

Figure 8.1 *T account*

Dr (Debit)	Account Name	Cr (Credit)
	£	£
Date	Date	

The **fundamental principle** of double entry bookkeeping is that for every debit entry, there must be an equivalent credit entry.

Note that the words debit and credit are not used here in their everyday sense. In T accounts, debit simply means the left-hand side and credit means the right hand side. It is important not to confuse these terms with the use of the same words in expressions such as 'debit card' or 'credit transaction'.

How are transactions posted to ledger accounts?

There are two important issues when posting transactions to ledger accounts.
• In which accounts should a transaction be recorded?
• Which part of the dual aspect should be a credit entry and which should be a debit entry?

There is no standardised system for deciding which accounts a business should use for recording transactions. In practice, different businesses use a variety of accounts. It is a matter of judgment and experience to know which account is appropriate.

In this unit, a limited number of accounts are used to illustrate particular transactions. Note that they are all transactions in which payment is made immediately. Transactions which involve the sale or purchase of goods on **credit**, ie when payment is made at a later date, are described in units 9 and 10.

There are two main approaches when deciding whether an entry is a debit or a credit. Both are described in this unit. The first approach is based on a set of 'rules' which relate to how transactions affect assets, expenses, drawings, capital, revenue or liabilities. The second approach is based on whether **value** is **given** or **received** in a transaction.

The 'rules' of double entry bookkeeping

Every transaction gives rise to two accounting entries, one is a debit and the other a credit. It is possible to apply a set of rules to determine whether an entry in the accounts is a debit or a credit. These rules relate to the impact that a transaction has on the assets, expenses, drawings, capital, revenue and liabilities of a business. So:
- an **increase** in assets, expenses and drawings is a debit:
- a **decrease** in assets, expenses and drawings is a credit;
- an **increase** in capital, revenue and liabilities is a credit;
- a **decrease** in capital, revenue and liabilities is a debit.

The rules are illustrated in Figure 8.2.

Figure 8.2 The 'rules' for posting transactions

	DEBIT		CREDIT
increase	ASSETS EXPENSES DRAWINGS	**increase**	CAPITAL REVENUE LIABILITIES
decrease	CAPITAL REVENUE LIABILITIES	**decrease**	ASSETS EXPENSES DRAWINGS

Assets are the resources owned by a business, eg fixed assets such as buildings, or current assets such as money in the bank.
Expenses are the costs incurred in running a business, eg wages, rent, raw materials.
Drawings are the amount of money taken out of a business by its owner.
Capital is the money introduced into a business by its owner.
Revenue is the money received from selling goods and services.
Liabilities are the debts of a business, eg current liabilities such as a bank overdraft, or long-term liabilities such as a mortgage.

How is a transaction recorded in the accounts?

To illustrate how a transaction might be recorded in two T accounts, consider what happens when a wholesaler sells £50 of goods to a retailer. Assume, in this case, that payment is by cash, ie notes and coins. This money is an asset. It is recorded in the wholesaler's **cash account** and is a debit entry because the asset has increased. If the payment had been by cheque, it would be recorded as a debit in the wholesaler's bank account.

The sale of goods earns revenue for the wholesaler. This is recorded in the **sales account**. It is a credit entry because revenue has increased. Figure 8.3 shows how a bookkeeper would record this transaction.

Figure 8.3 T accounts for a sales transaction

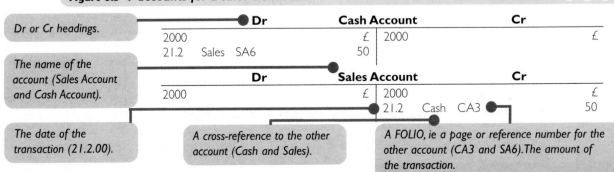

Dr or Cr headings.			

	Dr	Cash Account	Cr
2000		£	2000	£
21.2	Sales SA6	50		

	Dr	Sales Account	Cr
2000		£	2000	£
			21.2 Cash CA3	50

The name of the account (Sales Account and Cash Account).

The date of the transaction (21.2.00).

A cross-reference to the other account (Cash and Sales).

A FOLIO, ie a page or reference number for the other account (CA3 and SA6). The amount of the transaction.

It has already been pointed out that in double entry bookkeeping the terms debit and credit simply mean the left-hand and the righthand side of a T account. Confusion can arise because the terms credit and debit are sometimes used on bank statements. Here they mean precisely the opposite to what they mean on T accounts. For example, a 'credit' on a bank customer's statement means that the amount in the customer's account has increased. According to the principles of double entry bookkeeping, this should be a debit because the money in the account, which is an asset, has increased. The explanation is that the bank statement is written from the bank's point of view. From this perspective, the flow of money from the bank to the customer is considered a credit because the bank's assets have decreased.

Another source of confusion is the use of the term 'bank account'. In double entry bookkeeping, a bank account is simply one of the ledger accounts that a business will use to record transactions. It is not the same as a bank account that a bank provides and which is used by individuals and businesses for writing cheques or receiving payments.

QUESTION 1

Graham Perkins is a boat builder based in Hampshire. He repairs and manufactures small craft suitable for amateur sailing enthusiasts. Most of his boats are built to order and he employs one part-time member of staff to help with some of the heavier work. In January 2000, Graham made two sales. Details of the two transactions are as follows:

- a small dinghy was repaired on 11 January for £150;
- a replacement mast was sold for £80 on 25 January.

(a) Record the transactions in two appropriate T accounts using the double entry system. Assume that payments were made in notes and coin, and ignore the folio entry.
(b) Using one of the transactions as an example, explain the difference between a debit entry and a credit entry.

Recording a number of transactions in the accounts

In order to illustrate how transactions are recorded in different accounts, consider the following example. Kieran Malone set up in business in October 2000. He invested £3,000 of his own money as capital and received a £1,000 loan to help establish the business. He planned to buy a van, lease some tools and then trade as a mobile mechanic in Worcester. In his first week of trading, six transactions were recorded. They are outlined below.

Each of the transactions is posted to two ledger accounts (see Figure 8.4). In this example, one of the accounts is always the bank account. The other account is the relevant ledger account. Note that if the bank account is debited, the other account must be credited, and vice versa. By first considering whether an entry in the bank account is a **debit**, ie **money in**, or a **credit**, ie **money out**, it makes it easier to decide what happens in the other account.

1. October 3: £3,000 capital is deposited in the business's bank account.
An increase of money in the bank is an increase in assets, so the bank account is debited.
There is an increase in capital, so the capital account is credited.
2. October 3: A loan of £1,000 is paid into the bank account.
An increase of money in the bank is an increase in assets, so the bank account is debited.
The loan causes an increase in liabilities because money is owed to the lender, so the loan account is credited.
3. October 4: A van is purchased and paid for by cheque £1,200.
A decrease of money in the bank as a result of the cheque is a decrease in assets, so the bank account is credited. The van is an asset so, because assets have increased, the van account is debited.
4. October 5: A leasing charge for tools is paid by cheque £200.
A decrease of money in the bank is a decrease in assets, so the bank account is credited.
Money spent on a lease is an expense so, because expenses have increased, the leasing account is debited.

5. October 7: A £120 cheque is received as payment from a customer for car repairs.
An increase of money in the bank is an increase in assets, so the bank account is debited.
Money received from a customer is revenue so, because revenue has increased, the sales account is credited.

6. October 9: £100 is withdrawn from the bank for personal use.
A decrease of money in the bank is a decrease in assets, so the bank account is credited.
Drawings increase, so the drawings account is debited.

Figure 8.4 *T accounts showing six transactions*

Dr		Bank Account		Cr	
2000	£	2000			£
3.10 Capital	3,000	4.10 Van			1,200
3.10 Loan	1,000	5.10 Leasing			200
7.10 Sales	120	9.10 Drawings			100

Dr		Capital Account		Cr	
2000	£	2000			£
		3.10 Bank			3,000

Dr		Loan Account		Cr	
2000	£	2000			£
		3.10 Bank			1,000

Dr		Van Account		Cr	
2000	£	2000			£
4.10 Bank	1,200				

Dr		Leasing Account		Cr	
2000	£	2000			£
5.10 Bank	200				

Dr		Sales Account		Cr	
2000	£	2000			£
		7.10 Bank			120

Dr		Drawings Account		Cr	
2000	£	2000			£
9.10 Bank	100				

Capital expenditure, expenses and purchases

Business expenditure can be classified as capital expenditure or revenue expenditure. Capital expenditure is spending on fixed assets, such as the purchase of the van in the example above. In bookkeeping, it is usual for important fixed assets such as vehicles or machinery to have their own ledger account.

Revenue expenditure is spending on the running expenses of a business. These expenses are normally classified into:
- **purchases** which are goods that are bought for resale, or raw materials and components that are made into goods for sale;
- other expenses such as wages, rent, fuel and insurance.

Bookkeepers generally keep separate ledger accounts for purchases and other expenses. So for example, in an engineering business there might be a single ledger account for purchases of raw materials and separate accounts for wages, fuel and all the other major expenses.

To illustrate how these different types of expenditure might be posted to ledger accounts, consider the following example. For simplicity, it is assumed that all the payments are made by cheque. Dawkins Ltd is a specialist manufacturer of electronic temperature gauges. During one month, it had the following transactions:
- July 10 bought electrical components for £1,300;

- July 13 bought a delivery van for £9,800;
- July 14 paid wages of £5,400;
- July 21 paid insurance premium of £250.

These transactions are recorded in Figure 8.5.

Figure 8.5 *T accounts for Dawkins Ltd*

The purchase of components and the other expenses represent an increase in expenses so are entered on the debit side of their respective accounts.

Entries in each account are made in chronological order.

Money in the bank (an asset) has decreased so the payments are entered on the credit side of the bank account.

Each transaction is entered twice, once on the credit side and once on the debit side.

Dr	Bank Account		Cr
2000	£	2000	£
		10.7 Purchases	1,300
		13.7 Vehicle	9,800
		14.7 Wages	5,400
		21.7 Insurance	250

Entries are cross referenced.

Dr	Purchases Account		Cr
2000	£	2000	£
10.7 Bank	1,300		

The purchase of the van represents an increase in assets so it is entered on the debit side of the vehicle account.

Dr	Vehicle Account		Cr
2000	£	2000	£
13.7 Bank	9,800		

Dr	Wages Account		Cr
2000	£	2000	£
14.7 Bank	5,400		

Dr	Insurance Account		Cr
2000	£	2000	£
21.7 Bank	250		

An alternative approach to T accounts – receiving and giving value

When deciding if a particular transaction should be recorded as a debit or as a credit, an alternative method can be used. This is to consider whether value is received or given. If an account **receives** value, ie there is an inflow of goods, services or money, it is a debit entry. If an account gives value, ie there is an outflow of goods, services or money, it is a credit entry. This is illustrated in Figure 8.6.

QUESTION 2

Pauline O'Grady took voluntary redundancy from her design job when the company in which she worked was taken over. She invested £20,000 redundancy money in a design business which she set up in June 2000. Pauline rented an office in her home town of Swindon and bought a computer. She intended to design seating fabrics for cars using a computer aided design software package. In her first week she undertook the following business transactions.

1. June 3 Paid £20,000 capital into the business bank account.
2. June 5 Bought a computer for £2,700 and paid by cheque.
3. June 6 Paid £500 rent to a landlord by cheque.
4. June 9 Received a cheque for £1,000 from a customer for preliminary work on new designs.

(a) **For each transaction, state whether the business's assets, expenses, drawings, capital, revenue or liabilities were affected.**
(b) **Record the transactions in the appropriate T accounts.**

Figure 8.6 *Receiving and giving value*

DEBIT	CREDIT
VALUE RECEIVED	VALUE GIVEN

The six transactions outlined in Figure 8.4 can be posted using this principle.

1. £3,000 capital is deposited in the business's bank account.
Money is being provided to the business from the capital account, ie value is being given, so the capital account is credited with £3,000. The bank account is receiving value, so it is debited.

2. The loan of £1,000 is paid into the bank account.
Money is being provided from the loan account, ie value is being given, so the loan account is credited with £1,000. The bank account is receiving value so it is debited.

3. A van is purchased and paid for by cheque £1,200.
The van account is debited because value is being received, in the form of the van. The bank account is credited because value is being given, ie money is paid for the van.

4. A leasing charge for tools is paid by cheque £200.
The leasing account is debited because value is being received, ie the use of the tools. The bank account is credited because value is being given, ie money is paid to the leasing company.

5. A £120 cheque is received as payment from a customer for car repairs.
The sales account is credited because value is being given, ie a service is provided for a customer. The bank account is debited because value is being received, ie money is paid by the customer.

6. £100 is withdrawn from the bank for personal use.
Money is taken out of the bank account, ie value is being given, so it is credited. The drawings account is debited because value is being received, ie money is received by the owner.

QUESTION 3

The Moorcroft Tool Company sells a range of tools and equipment from its large store located on the Cowley Industrial Estate near Oxford. Most sales are to traders such as builders, decorators, mechanics and engineers. The store is also open to the public. During May 2000 the following transactions occurred:

1. May 22 A fork lift truck was purchased for £4,000 (by cheque).
2. May 22 A £400 bill for roof repairs was paid (by cheque).
3. May 23 £11,700 of tools were purchased by Moorcroft from a manufacturer (by cheque).
4. May 24 A customer bought cutting tools for £85 (paid by cash).
5. May 25 Julian Moorcroft withdrew £50 cash from the business for personal use.
6. May 25 A customer paid £1,340 for scaffolding (by cheque).
7. May 26 Staff wages of £2,500 were paid (by cheque).

(a) (i) Suggest in which ledger accounts each of the transactions should be recorded and
   (ii) in each case, state whether the account receives or gives value.
(b) Record the transactions in appropriate T accounts using the double entry system.

key terms

Credit - an entry on the right-hand side of a T account.
Debit - an entry on the left-hand side of a T account.
Double entry system - the method used by bookkeepers when recording business transactions; it involves recording all transactions twice.
Folio - a page or reference number listed in an account to help trace the other entry for the transaction.
T account - a standard layout for recording business transactions with debit entries on the left-hand side and credit entries on the right-hand side.

summary questions

1. What is the fundamental principle of double entry bookkeeping?
2. What is a ledger?
3. What information is entered in a T account when a transaction is recorded?
4. Explain the difference between a debit and a credit entry.
5. If cash is paid to a business, is this a debit or credit in the cash account?
6. What are the 'rules' of double entry bookkeeping when considering assets, expenses and drawings?
7. What are the 'rules' of double entry bookkeeping when considering capital, revenue and liabilities?
8. What is the difference between purchases and other business expenses?
9. If an account receives value, is the entry a debit or a credit?
10. If a capital account has a credit entry, has the capital account received or given value?

UNIT ASSESSMENT   QUESTION 1

Sarah Marshall put £8,000 of her own capital into a business and borrowed another £4,000 from a bank. She set up an employment agency in Leeds specialising in the provision of teaching staff for schools facing teacher shortages. For each teacher she supplies, she earns a commission from the school. Figure 8.7 shows an extract from her financial records.

Figure 8.7 *Entries in the bank account of Sarah Marshall's business*

Dr			Bank Account		Cr
2000		£	2000		£
28.8	Capital	8,000	28.8	Office equipment	1,400
29.8	Loan	4,000	30.8	Computer	1,700
7.9	Commission	500	1.9	Advertising	900
			3.9	Stationery	85

(a) Using the information in Figure 8.7, complete the double entry by recording the transactions in the appropriate accounts.

(b) Which of the accounts relate to (i) assets; (ii) expenses; (iii) revenue; (iv) liabilities?

UNIT ASSESSMENT   QUESTION 2

Sorrell and Son began trading in November 2000. The company produces metal products such as hinges, brackets, locks, door fasteners and bolts. It leases a factory unit from the local council in Tipton, in the West Midlands, and uses a range of machinery which it bought at auction for £3,200. Two staff are employed to operate the machinery. Details of some of the company's transactions are listed below. All payments were made by cheque.

1. November 6 Owners paid £6,000 capital into the business's bank account.
2. November 13 Paid £3,200 at an auction for machinery.
3. November 15 Paid £200 leasing charge to the council.
4. November 16 Purchased £700 of steel from a local stockist.
5. November 24 Paid £400 wages to staff.

(a) For each transaction, state whether the business's assets, expenses, drawings, capital, revenue or liabilities were affected.

(b) Record the transactions for Sorrell and Son in the appropriate T accounts.

Recording credit sales

unit**objectives**

To understand:
- credit sales;
- the system used to record credit sales in a sales day book;
- how credit sales are posted to ledgers;
- the difference between trade discount and cash discount.

Credit sales

When businesses sell goods and services they sometimes allow a period of time before payment is due. This type of transaction is known as a CREDIT SALE. The length of time between the date on which an invoice is issued and when payment is due is known as the **trade credit** period. It is typically between 30 and 90 days. Because there is a time lag between the invoice date and eventual payment, it is important to keep careful records of what is owed.

How are credit sales recorded in the sales day book?

When a credit sale is made by a business, it normally sends a sales invoice to the customer and retains a copy for its own records. The invoice is a **source document**. Details of the transaction are then entered into the SALES DAY BOOK or SALES JOURNAL. The sales day book is a **book of prime entry**. It is used to record credit transactions before details are posted to the **ledgers**. It is in the ledgers that the double entry system of bookkeeping is used.

The reason for entering credit transactions in a day book is to avoid overfilling the ledgers. If details from every transaction were put through the double entry system, the ledgers would contain an unmanageable amount of information. It is therefore easier to transfer daily or weekly totals from the sales day book to the ledgers.

The information recorded in a sales day book typically includes:
- date of the transaction;
- name of the customer;
- invoice number;
- folio, ie a reference to the relevant ledger;
- price of goods, ie the price excluding VAT;
- amount of VAT (see unit 26);
- total price of goods, ie the price plus VAT.

When recording information from an invoice, only the totals are entered into the sales day book. It is not common practice to record descriptions of goods. If this detailed information is required, it is necessary to refer back to the invoice.

To illustrate how a transaction is recorded in a sales day book, consider the information contained on the sales invoice in Figure 9.1. D.H. Oliver & Co, a supplier of pine furniture, issued the invoice to P. Tanner, a customer. Information from the invoice is recorded in D. H. Oliver & Co's sales day book in Figure 9.2.

As the example over shows, the entry in the sales day book is a summary of the transaction. The folio shown in Figure 9.2, SL6, is a reference number that helps trace where the entry is posted in the ledgers.

During a trading period, the transaction would be one of many recorded in the sales day book. At the end of each day, or perhaps week, the three columns containing monetary values would be totalled. D. H. Oliver & Co would then know the total value of sales and also the total VAT charged.

QUESTION 1

Maureen Casey supplies packaging products such as polythene film, shrink wrap, adhesive tape, bubble film, loose fill chips and corrugated rolls. The business operates from a warehouse/store in Bedford. Details of credit sales are recorded in a sales day book at the end of each day. A list of credit sales made on 18 September 2000 is shown below:

- T. Jones (01299) £100;
- A. Thompson (01300) £260;
- B. Reynolds (01301) £210;
- M. Khan (01302) £90;
- C. Button & Son (01303) £120;
- L. Bennett (01304) £50;
- A. Ng (01305) £100.

The transaction values do not include VAT @ 17.5%. The invoice number is shown in brackets.

(a) Record the credit sales for Maureen Casey in the sales day book. You will need to calculate the VAT charged and the price including VAT. The folios have been ignored.

(b) Calculate the overall totals of sales, VAT and sales plus VAT.

(c) Explain how the sales day book might be helpful to Maureen.

Figure 9.1 *An invoice issued by D. H. Oliver & Co to P. Tanner*   ● ● ●

D.H. OLIVER & Co

PINE FURNITURE SUPPLIER

13 James Street, Corby, NN18 9TS
Tel: 01865 867270   Fax: 01865 867288
VAT REG. No. 906 293927 41

INVOICE

To:
P. Tanner
Unit 6
Saxon Way East
Corby NN20 6TQ

Invoice No.   003881

Invoice date: 12 - 07 - 00

Qty	Description	Catalogue	Unit price	Amount	VAT	Total
			£	£	£	£
2	Wardrobes	W112	200.00	400.00	70.00	470.00
1	Double bed	DB02	670.00	670.00	117.25	787.25
4	Coffee tables	CT11	45.00	180.00	31.50	211.50
6	Armchairs	AC04	120.00	720.00	126.00	846.00
				Total 1,970.00	**344.75**	**2,314.75**

Terms: 30 days from invoice date

Figure 9.2 *An extract from the sales day book of D.H. Oliver & Co*   ● ● ●

SALES DAY BOOK 2000						(page 31)
Date	Customer	Invoice no.	Folio	Total	VAT	Price
				£	£	£
12.7	P. Tanner	003881	SL6	2,314.75	344.75	1,970.00

How are credit sales recorded in ledgers?

The next stage in recording credit sales is to post information from the sales day book to ledgers. The double entry system of bookkeeping is used. Businesses normally have a SALES LEDGER, a purchases ledger and a NOMINAL LEDGER or GENERAL LEDGER. Two of these, the sales ledger and the nominal ledgers are used to record credit sales. The sales ledger contains customer accounts. These **personal accounts** summarise credit sales made to particular customers. The nominal ledger contains **impersonal accounts** such as wages or rent and, as in this case, the sales account. In a manual system of bookkeeping, ie where books are used rather than computers, each account is likely to be on a separate page. Figure 9.3 shows the stages in transferring information from invoices via the sales day book to the ledgers.

Figure 9.3 *Stages in recording credit sales*

```
                    ┌─────────────────────┐
                    │      INVOICES       │
                    └──────────┬──────────┘
                               ↓
                    ┌─────────────────────┐
                    │   SALES DAY BOOK    │
                    └──────────┬──────────┘
              ┌────────────────┴────────────────┐
              ↓                                  ↓
   ┌─────────────────────┐        ┌─────────────────────────┐
   │    SALES LEDGER     │        │    NOMINAL LEDGER       │
   │ Debit customer      │        │  (GENERAL LEDGER)       │
   │ account             │        │  Credit sales account   │
   └─────────────────────┘        └─────────────────────────┘
```

To illustrate how information is posted to ledgers, consider the example of Pemrose Engineering. This is a business that specialises in selling reconditioned engines. Figure 9.4 shows an extract from the company's sales day book. One day's credit sales have been entered and totalled. Details have then been posted to the relevant ledger accounts. In order to simplify the example, VAT has been ignored. The treatment of VAT when posting credit sales to the ledgers is explained in unit 26.

Figure 9.4 *Posting credit sales from the sales day book to the ledgers of Pemrose Engineering*

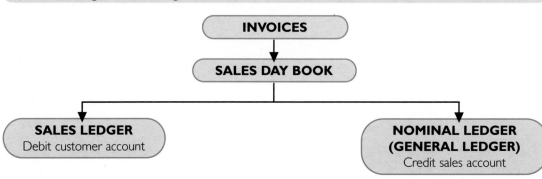

SALES DAY BOOK 2000 (page 54)

Date	Customer	Invoice no.	Folio	Amount £
6.2	P. Collins	0221	SL3	170
6.2	B. Sanchez	0222	SL56	230
6.2	Dolland & Sons	0223	SL25	90
6.2	Bexley Motors	0224	SL19	278
6.2	Transferred to Sales Account		NL42	768

SALES LEDGER

Dr   **P. Collins** (page 3)   Cr

		£		£
6.2 Sales SDB54		170		

Dr   **B. Sanchez** (page 56)   Cr

		£		£
6.2 Sales SDB54		230		

Dr   **Dolland & Sons** (page 25)   Cr

		£		£
6.2 Sales SDB54		90		

Dr   **Bexley Motors** (page 19)   Cr

		£		£
6.2 Sales SDB54		278		

NOMINAL LEDGER

Dr   **Sales Account** (page 42)   Cr

	£		£
		6.2 Credit sales SDB54	768

Figure 9.4 shows how credit sales are posted.

- Each credit sale in the sales day book is posted to the relevant customer account in the sales ledger. For example, the P. Collins account is debited with £170.
- From Pemrose's point of view, the debt, ie the money owed by P. Collins, represents an increase in assets and is therefore a debit entry (see unit 8 for the 'rules' on posting transactions).
- Because the sales ledger contains the accounts of debtors, ie customers who buy on credit, it is sometimes called the **debtors ledger** and the individual accounts are called **debtors accounts**.
- The total value of credit sales for the day is posted to the sales account in the nominal ledger. This is a credit entry because the £768 represents an increase in revenue for Pemrose Engineering.

Note that in Figure 9.4, the folio entries provide a cross reference between the pages of the various accounts. By looking at the folio in one entry, it is relatively easy to find the matching entry in the corresponding ledger. So, for example, the folio entries in the sales ledger and nominal ledger (SDB54) refer to page 54 of the sales day book.

It is usual to post details to the customer accounts in the sales ledger soon after each entry is made in the sales day book. The frequency of posting to the sales account in the nominal ledger depends on the nature of the business. In some cases, the totals might be transferred weekly or even monthly rather than daily as in the example above. In practice, the daily number of credit sales is likely to be much higher than shown in Figure 9.4. However, most businesses, whether their bookkeeping systems are computerised or manual, use the method of recording credit sales explained here.

QUESTION 2

F. Bannerman & Co. is a wholesale butcher and manufacturer of meat pies in its Wigan factory. It employs 4 staff and distributes pies to retailers, restaurants, public houses, hotels and schools in the North West. All sales are on credit. On the 31 October 2000, Bannerman's sales day book contained three entries. These are shown in Figure 9.5.

Figure 9.5 *Sales day book for F. Bannerman & Co.*

SALES DAY BOOK 2000				(page 197)
Date	**Customer**	**Invoice no.**	**Folio**	**Amount** £
31.10	Bolton College	0188	SL12	310
31.10	The Red Cow	0189	SL34	260
31.10	B. Naughton	0190	SL56	150
31.10	Transferred to Sales Account		NL22	720

(a) **Draw up appropriate accounts in the sales ledger and the nominal ledger and then post the information contained in Bannerman's sales day book to these accounts.**

(b) **Explain why folio entries and invoice numbers might be useful for Bannerman's bookkeeping.**

The use of control accounts

The system of bookkeeping described in this unit might typically be used by a small business. The number of customer accounts in the sales ledger is not likely to be large and it is relatively easy to calculate the total amount of money owed. In a computerised system, this total is normally generated automatically.

In businesses that have a large number of customer accounts, it is less convenient to keep a record of the total amount owed in the sales ledger. For this reason, many businesses use a SALES LEDGER CONTROL ACCOUNT, or **total debtors account**, in the nominal ledger. This summarises the customer accounts and is a convenient means of checking how much is owed. The system avoids having to add up all the totals in the individual customer accounts whenever an overall total is required.

Where a sales ledger control account is used, the sales totals are entered as debits to match the credits in the sales account. The customer accounts in the sales ledger are now treated as subsidiary or **memorandum accounts**. They do not form part of the double entry system. Figure 9.6 shows how the sales ledger control account fits into the bookkeeping system. The use of control accounts is described in more detail in unit 27.

Figure 9.6 *Sales ledger control account in the bookkeeping system*

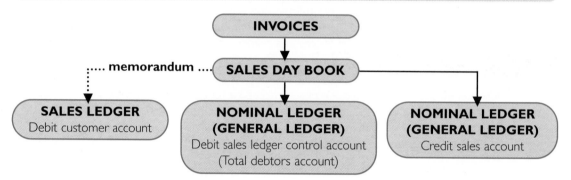

How do trade discounts affect the recording of credit sales?

Some businesses publish a **list price** of goods for sale but charge certain groups of customers less than this. For example, a timber merchant might sell products at a lower price to traders such as builders and joiners, ie trade customers, than to members of the public. The reduction in the list price is called a TRADE DISCOUNT. The simplest form of trade discount is to have a two tier pricing system. For example there might be the list price for the general public and a 10% discount for traders who buy in bulk. Sometimes the discount is related to the value of purchases with higher discounts on offer to those who spend the most.

When recording credit sales, any trade discount is shown on the sales invoice. An example is given in Figure 9.7 for Wilson's Fish Market. This invoice was issued to a trade customer, the Fresh Fish Shop, and a 20 per cent discount was given. When entering the credit sale in the sales day book for Wilson's Fish Market, it is the **net** figure of £84 that is entered. This is the actual selling price, ie after the discount has been applied. The effect of the trade discount is simply to reduce the value of the

Figure 9.7 *A sales invoice issued by Wilson's Fish Market*

WILSON'S FISH MARKET
87 Wellington Lane, London EC1P 5AV
Tel: 020 7977 7112   Fax: 020 7977 7830
VAT REG. No. 482 4829647 91

To: Invoice Number 7312
The Fresh Fish Shop
112 Bell Street
Sidcup
DA14 7JB   Invoice date: 18/02/00

Qty	Description	Price per kilo	Amount	Discount	Net
		£	£	%	£
20 kilos	Cod fillets	1.50	30.00	20	24.00
30 kilos	Salmon	1.00	30.00	20	24.00
20 kilos	Haddock	1.00	20.00	20	16.00
5 kilos	Lobster	3.00	15.00	20	12.00
10 kilos	Whiting	1.00	10.00	20	8.00

Terms: 30 days   **Total 105.00**   **84.00**

sale. Other adjustments in the bookkeeping system are not required. When the entry is posted from the sales day book to Wilson's ledgers, the nominal ledger is credited with £84 because there is an increase in revenue. The Fresh Fish Shop account in the sales ledger is debited with £84 because there is an increase in debts, which are assets.

How do cash discounts affect the recording of credit sales?

Some businesses give CASH DISCOUNTS to customers if they settle their bills early. An example might be a 5% discount, ie a reduction in the amount due, if payment is made within seven days. Unlike trade discounts, cash discounts are recorded separately in their own ledger accounts. The method used is explained in unit 12.

UNIT ASSESSMENT QUESTION 1

Dawlish Books is a small publishing company that specialises in the local history of Devon and Cornwall. It supplies book shops throughout the South West and it also has a number of regular private customers. The book shops are given a 15% trade discount. The private customers are not given a discount, but they are allowed to buy on credit terms. Figure 9.8 shows the two sales invoices issued by Dawlish Books on 26 February 2000. P. Collingwood is a private customer. No VAT is charged on books in the UK.

(a) Enter details from the two invoices in the sales day book of Dawlish Books.
(b) Post the relevant items from the sales day book to the appropriate accounts in the sales ledger and the nominal ledger. Ignore folio entries.
(c) Suggest why Dawlish Books offers a trade discount to book shops only.

Figure 9.8 *Extracts from two sales invoices issued by Dawlish Books*

Dawlish Books
Unit 14, The Trading Estate, Dawlish, Devon

To: P. Collingwood			Invoice No. 0428 Invoice date: 26 - 02 - 00		
Qty	Description	Unit price	Amount	Discount	Net
		£	£	%	£
1	Mining on Bodmin Moor	15.50	15.50	nil	15.50

Terms: 30 days from invoice date   **Total to pay 15.50**

Dawlish Books
Unit 14, The Trading Estate, Dawlish, Devon

To: Lizard Book shop			Invoice No. 0429 Invoice date: 26 - 02 - 00		
Qty	Description	Unit price	Amount	Discount	Net
		£	£	%	£
10	The Pirate Coves of Cornwall	10.50	105.00	15	89.25
10	China Clay	12.50	125.00	15	106.25
6	Cornish Fishermens' Tales	7.50	45.00	15	38.25
2	Shipwrecks and Rescues	12.50	25.00	15	21.25

Terms: 30 days from invoice date   **Total to pay 255.00**

UNIT ASSESSMENT — QUESTION 2

The Southend Catering Centre sells a wide range of cooking and refrigeration equipment from its showroom in Southend. It also offers a design, planning and installation service. A list of credit sales for 2 April 2000 is shown below (VAT is ignored).

- A. Killin (invoice: 02488) £1,200;
- The Welford Hotel (invoice: 02489) £760;
- B. Collins (invoice: 02490) £210;
- The Bulldog Inn (invoice: 02491) £320;
- W. Thomas (invoice: 02492) £540.

(a) Enter the transactions in the sales day book for the Southend Catering Centre.

(b) Post the appropriate information from the sales day book to the sales ledger and the sales account in the nominal ledger. Ignore folio entries.

key terms

Cash discount - a price reduction given to customers who pay before the end of the trade credit period.

Credit sales - sales in which payment is made at an agreed later date.

Nominal ledger or general ledger - a ledger which contains all impersonal accounts, ie those that are neither customer or supplier accounts.

Sales day book or sales journal - a book of prime entry in which credit sales are entered. It is sometimes also called the sold day book.

Sales ledger - a ledger which contains customer accounts and is used to record credit sales.

Sales ledger control account or total debtors account - an account in the nominal ledger that shows the total amount owed by customers.

Trade discount - a reduction in the list price of goods, generally given to trade customers.

summary questions

1. What is meant by a credit sale?
2. What is the typical trade credit period?
3. What information is recorded in a sales day book?
4. What is the source of the information that is recorded in a sales day book?
5. On which side of the sales ledger are credit sales entered?
6. What information is transferred to the nominal ledger from the sales day book?
7. Why do businesses not transfer information directly from invoices into the ledgers when recording credit sales?
8. In which part of recording credit sales is the double entry system used?
9. What is the difference between a trade discount and a cash discount?
10. How does a trade discount affect the recording of credit sales?

Recording credit purchases

unitobjectives

To understand:
- the system used to record credit purchases in a purchases day book;
- how credit purchases are posted to ledgers;
- the use of analysed day books.

Credit purchases

Businesses often buy goods from a supplier and pay for them at a later date. These are CREDIT PURCHASES. When goods are bought on credit by a business, a sales invoice is sent by the supplier. This **source document** contains a description of the goods, the date of the transaction and the price. It also states the period of credit, ie the date by which payment should be made. When the invoice is received by the business which is buying the goods, it is referred to as a **purchase invoice**.

In accounting, the term PURCHASES is used for goods that are intended for resale, or raw materials and components that are made into goods for sale. For example, when a supermarket buys supplies from a producer, these goods are classed as purchases. If a clothing manufacturer buys fabric, zips and buttons, these components are also classified as purchases. The details of such credit purchases are transferred from the purchase invoice into the PURCHASES DAY BOOK (or PURCHASES JOURNAL). This is a **book of prime entry**.

How are credit purchases recorded in the purchases day book?

The purchases day book summarises information on the invoices received by a business and is used to avoid overfilling the ledgers. The information recorded typically includes:
- date of the transaction;
- name of the supplier;
- invoice number;
- folio, ie a reference to the relevant ledger;
- price of goods, ie price excluding VAT;
- amount of VAT;
- total price of goods bought, ie price plus VAT.

To illustrate how a credit purchase by a business is recorded in a purchases day book, consider the purchase invoice shown in Figure 10.1. It was received by T. Rolfe, the owner of a pet shop, and issued by G. Atkinson, a supplier of pet foods and related goods. Information from the purchase invoice is recorded in the purchases day book for T. Rolfe shown in Figure 10.2.

As with the recording of credit sales in a sales day book, it is not common practice to record descriptions of goods in the purchases day book. Provided the invoice number is shown, the invoice can be traced if details need to be checked. The folio is PL3. This shows where the transaction can be traced in the ledgers. In this case, it is page 3 in the PURCHASES LEDGER. Note that in the purchases day book the transaction is split into the price, the VAT and the total amount including VAT.

At regular intervals, the amounts in each of the columns are totalled. The transfer of these totals to ledger accounts is described later in the unit.

How are credit purchases recorded in ledgers?

The stages in the bookkeeping process are illustrated in Figure 10.3. Information is first transferred from purchase invoices to the purchases day book. This is not part of the double entry system because only one entry for each transaction is recorded. Details in the purchases day book are then

Figure 10.1 *A purchase invoice received by T. Rolfe*

G. Atkinson
27 Thames Crescent
Bromley-by-Bow
London E3 4NR
Telephone: 020 7987 2380

To:
T. Rolfe
65 Brunell Road
Canning Town
London E16 1QD

Invoice Number 0166
Invoice date: 19.05.00

Qty	Description	Unit cost	Goods total	VAT
		£	£	£
12	Leather dog collars	4.50	54.00	9.45
10	Dog chains	6.00	60.00	10.50
5	Std dog kennels	25.00	125.00	21.87
10	Rubber dog bones	2.00	20.00	3.50

Sub totals   £259.00
VAT   £45.32
Invoice Total £304.32

Terms: Strictly 28 days from date of invoice.
VAT Reg. No. 106 7679 23

Figure 10.2 *Purchases day book for T. Rolfe*

PURCHASES DAY BOOK 2000   (page 56)

Date	Supplier	Invoice no.	Folio	Total	VAT	Price
				£	£	£
19.5	G. Atkinson	0166	PL3	304.32	45.32	259.00

transferred to the ledgers where the double entry system of bookkeeping is used. The diagram shows that details of transactions are posted to the supplier accounts in the purchases ledger and to the purchases account in the nominal ledger. The nominal ledger contains all the **impersonal accounts**, ie those that are neither supplier accounts nor customer accounts.

Because the purchases ledger contains the accounts of creditors, ie suppliers who sell goods on credit, it is sometimes known as the **creditors ledger** and the individual accounts are known as **creditors accounts**.

QUESTION 1

Westmore Electrical Factors is an independent wholesaler of electrical products. It sells light fittings, plugs, electric wires, lights, sockets, burglar alarms and many other items. The company is located in Braintree, Essex. It employs 4 full-time staff and 9 part-time staff. On 3 January 2000, the following credit purchases were made by the store manager from suppliers:

- Malden Electrics (1458) £600;
- TLD Ltd (01332) £550;
- ELCO (0231) £1,400;
- Herrod Alarms (6241) £3,200;
- Massey Wright & Co (0944) £1,200.

The prices exclude VAT which is charged at the rate of 17.5%. The numbers in brackets are invoice numbers.

(a) Record the credit purchases in the purchases day book of Westmore Electrical Factors. You will need to calculate the VAT and the prices including VAT. Ignore folio entries.

(b) Calculate the overall totals of purchases, VAT and purchases plus VAT.

Figure 10.3 *Stages in recording credit purchases*

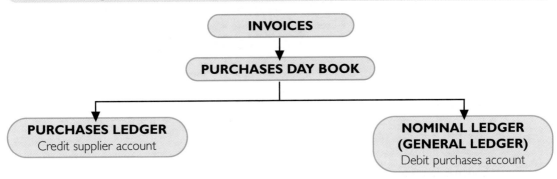

To illustrate how information is transferred from the purchases day book to the ledgers, consider the example of Watkins Metals, a steel merchant based in Northampton. Figure 10.4 shows a page from the purchases day book of Watkins Metals and extracts from the purchases ledger and the nominal ledger. Four credit purchases are recorded in the purchases day book and the total for the day is £4,950. Note that, in order to simplify this example, VAT is ignored. The treatment of VAT when posting credit purchases from the purchases day book to the ledgers is explained in unit 26.

Figure 10.4 *Posting credit purchases from the purchases day book to the ledgers*

PURCHASES DAY BOOK 2000 (page 101)

Date	Supplier	Invoice no.	Folio	Amount £
17.5	Bolden & Sons	1556	PL12	800
17.5	Pressed Steel	0342	PL31	1,200
17.5	Cartwrights	1123	PL9	450
17.5	Tyrell & Co	9117	PL75	2,500
17.5	Transferred to Purchases Account		NL34	4,950

PURCHASES LEDGER

Dr **Bolden & Sons** (page 12) **Cr**

£		£
	17.5 Purchases PDB101	800

Dr **Pressed Steel** (page 31) **Cr**

£		£
	17.5 Purchases PDB101	1,200

Dr **Cartwrights** (page 9) **Cr**

£		£
	17.5 Purchases PDB101	450

Dr **Tyrell & Co** (page 75) **Cr**

£		£
	17.5 Purchases PDB101	2,500

NOMINAL LEDGER

Dr **Purchases Account** (page 34) **Cr**

£		£
17.5 Credit purchases PDB101	4,950	

- In Figure 10.4, every purchase recorded in the purchases day book is posted as a credit entry to the relevant supplier account in the purchases ledger. For example, the supplier account for Bolden & Sons is credited with £800. It is a credit entry because it represents an increase in Watkins Metals' liabilities. The business has bought the goods on credit and therefore owes the money to Bolden & Sons.
- The folio in the purchases day book for the entry relating to Bolden & Sons is PL12. This shows that the purchase amount of £800 is posted to Bolden & Sons' account which is on page 12 of the purchases ledger. Similarly, in the supplier accounts in the purchases ledger, the folio entries (PDB101) provide a cross reference to the relevant page in the purchases day book.
- The total of credit purchases for the day is £4,950. This total is posted to the purchases account in the nominal ledger and is recorded as a debit entry. It is a debit because the new stock represents an increase in the assets of Watkins Metals. Note that the folio entry in the purchases day book provides a cross reference with the purchases account in the nominal ledger.

It is usual to post details to the supplier accounts in the purchases ledger after each entry is made in the purchases day book. The frequency of posting to the purchases account in the nominal ledger depends on the nature of the business and on the number of transactions that occur. In some cases, the totals might be transferred weekly or even monthly.

QUESTION 2

Alex McGuinness is a locksmith who runs KeySafe in Norwich. The business has two divisions. There is a shop which stocks an extensive range of locks for doors, patios, safes, garages and warehouses. There is also a locksmith emergency service for people and businesses who lose keys and need assistance. On 25 February 2000, the purchases day book of KeySafe showed three purchases of goods intended for resale. They are shown in Figure 10.5. Note that, in this question, VAT is ignored.

Figure 10.5 *Purchases day book for KeySafe*

PURCHASES DAY BOOK 2000				(page 56)
Date	Supplier	Invoice no.	Folio	Amount £
25.2	Britten & Co	1870	PL21	459
25.2	Lockworld	2233	PL45	490
25.2	Keys & Co	3166	PL34	90
25.2	Transferred to purchases account		NL94	1,039

(a) What is the likely source of the information that is recorded in the purchases day book?

(b) Transfer the information from the purchases day book to the purchases ledger and the nominal ledger.

The use of control accounts

As in unit 9 on credit sales, the system of bookkeeping described in this unit might typically be used by a small business. The number of supplier accounts in the purchases ledger is not likely to be large and it is relatively easy to calculate the total amount of money owed. In a computerised system, this total is normally generated automatically.

In businesses that have a large number of supplier accounts, it is less convenient to keep a record of the total amount owed in the purchases ledger. For this reason, many businesses use a PURCHASES LEDGER CONTROL ACCOUNT, or **total creditors account**, in the nominal ledger. This summarises the supplier accounts and is a convenient means of checking how much is owed by the business. The system avoids having to add up all the totals in the individual supplier accounts whenever an overall total is required.

Where a purchases ledger control account is used, the purchases totals are entered as credits to match the debits in the purchases account. The supplier accounts in the purchases ledger are now treated as subsidiary or **memorandum accounts**. They do not form part of the double entry system. Figure 10.6 shows how the purchases ledger control account fits into the bookkeeping system. The use of control accounts is described in more detail in unit 27.

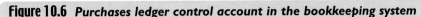

Figure 10.6 *Purchases ledger control account in the bookkeeping system*

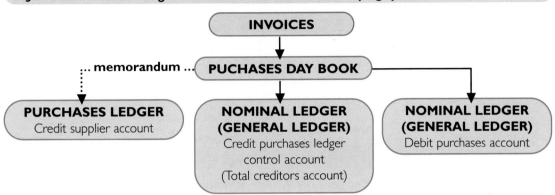

How do trade discounts affect the recording of credit purchases?

The treatment of trade discounts when recording credit purchases is the same as for credit sales. Bookkeepers simply record the net price, ie the price after the discount has been subtracted. For example, suppose a business buys £500 of goods on credit and there is a 20% trade discount. This discount is £100 (ie £500 × 20 ÷ 100). The price recorded is £500 - £100 = £400.

The effect of the trade discount is simply to reduce the price of the purchase and this is shown as the net price on the invoice. As long as the net price is recorded in the purchases day book, no other adjustments are necessary in the bookkeeping.

How do cash discounts affect the recording of credit purchases?

Sometimes a supplier might state on an invoice that a cash discount is available for prompt payment. For example, the invoice total might be £1,000 and there is a cash discount of 5% if payment is made immediately. If the business making the purchase chooses to take the discount, the amount to be paid is £950 (ie £1,000 less 5%). Unlike trade discounts, cash discounts are recorded separately in the bookkeeping system. The method used is described in unit 12.

How are analysed day books used?

Sometimes businesses find it convenient to classify transactions into different categories. One way of doing this is to use ANALYSED DAY BOOKS. Sales day books, purchases day books and cash books are examples of books that might be in this format. An analysed purchases day book has several columns in which different types of expenditure are recorded. The advantage of using an analysed day book is that spending in different areas or departments is more easily monitored.

Figure 10.7 shows the analysed purchases day book of a clothes retailer. Purchases are divided into just three categories:
- women's wear;
- men's wear;
- children's wear (zero rated for VAT).

Figure 10.7 *An extract from an analysed purchases day book (folio entries are ignored)*

PURCHASES DAY BOOK 2000								(page 100)
Date	Supplier	Invoice	Total £	VAT £	Price £	Womens £	Mens £	Childrens £
31.1	Drexel Ltd	78346	3,525.00	525.00	3,000.00	3,000.00		
3.2	Dales	674	94.00	14.00	80.00		80.00	
3.2	Garment World	56439	150.00		150.00			150.00
4.2	Gate Fashions	4593	250.00		250.00			250.00
	Weekly total		4,019.00	539.00	3,480.00	3,000.00	80.00	400.00

key terms

Analysed day book - a day book in which transactions are classified into different categories.
Credit purchases - expenditure on goods with an arrangement to pay for the goods at a later date.
Purchases - expenditure on goods intended for resale or on materials and components that are used directly in the production of the finished goods.
Purchases day book or purchases journal - a book of prime entry in which credit purchases are first recorded. It is also known as the bought day book.
Purchases ledger - the ledger which contains the accounts of suppliers that supply goods on credit.
Purchases ledger control account or total creditors account - an account in the nominal ledger that shows the total amount owed to suppliers.

UNIT ASSESSMENT QUESTION 1

Robinson's Textiles manufactures linen products in a Rochdale mill. The company produces bed linen, tablecloths, tea towels and napkins. Jenny Robinson is responsible for bookkeeping and accounts. One of her jobs is to record all transactions in the day books and then transfer information to the ledgers. The transactions listed below are the credit purchases made in May 2000. Invoice numbers are shown in brackets and, for the purpose of this question, VAT is ignored.

- 3.5.00   Betty Collins & Co. (871) £460;
- 10.5.00 Wilson Cotton (2339) £4,900;
- 12.5.00 Jones Bros. (4453) £650;
- 22.5.00 Oldham Cotton Supplies (3321) £2,500;
- 26.5.00 Birmingham Dyes (0911) £800.

(a) **Enter the transactions into the purchases day book.**
(b) **Calculate the total of credit purchases for May 2000.**
(c) **Post the appropriate information from the purchases day book to the purchases ledger and the nominal ledger.**
(d) **Jenny transfers information from the purchases day book to the nominal ledger at the end of each month. Some businesses do this weekly or even daily. Suggest why businesses might record this information at different time intervals.**

UNIT ASSESSMENT QUESTION 2

Charles Zacharias is a wholesale food merchant who specialises in organic fruit and vegetables. He sells mainly to restaurants, off-licences and hotels but has recently set up an e-commerce business using the internet. Details of his credit purchases for the second week of June 2000 are entered in the purchases day book shown in Figure 10.8. Food is zero rated for VAT which means that VAT is not payable.

(a) Post the appropriate information from the purchases day book to the supplier accounts in the purchases ledger and the purchases account in the nominal ledger.

(b) The bookkeeper for Charles Zacharias' business is leaving and a new person is about to be employed. Produce a flow chart that outlines how the system for recording credit sales and credit purchases works. Show the stages in the process from issuing or receiving an invoice to posting details in the ledger accounts. Explain in your diagram which are credit entries and which are debit entries.

Figure 10.8 *Purchases day book for Charles Zacharias*

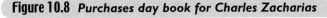

PURCHASES DAY BOOK 2000				(page 71)
Date	Supplier	Invoice no.	Folio	Amount £
8.6	Wade Food Supplies	192	PL32	245
9.6	Winters Farm Products	01334	PL34	260
11.6	Manninghams	2199	PL23	100
11.6	S.A. Wholefood	1100	PL28	160
14.6	Lindemans Herbs	2119	PL20	210

summary questions

1. Explain what is meant by credit purchases.
2. What is the main source document used when recording credit purchases?
3. What information is recorded in the purchases day book?
4. What information would not normally be transferred from a purchase invoice into the purchases day book?
5. On which side of the purchases account are credit purchases entered?
6. What information is transferred to the nominal ledger from the purchases day book?
7. At which stage in the recording of credit purchases is the double entry system used?
8. Why is information recorded in the purchases day book before being transferred to the ledgers?
9. What is a purchases ledger control account used for?
10. Why are the accounts in the purchases ledger also known as creditors accounts?

Recording returns

unit**objectives**

To understand:
- the meaning of returns inwards and returns outwards;
- how returns are entered in the returns day books;
- how information is posted from the returns day books to the ledgers.

What are returns?

In bookkeeping, when goods are returned to a supplier from a customer, they are called RETURNS INWARDS, or SALES RETURNS, in the accounts of the supplier. They are called RETURNS OUTWARDS, or PURCHASES RETURNS, in the accounts of the business that ordered the goods.

When goods are returned, the supplier issues a **credit note**. This reduces the amount of money owed by the customer. The credit note gives the date of issue and the price of the goods, ie the total to be **credited** in the customer's account. It might also state the reason for returning the goods. This could be because:

- the goods are damaged or faulty;
- the wrong goods have been sent;
- the customer has purchased too many by mistake.

How are returns inwards recorded in the returns inwards day book?

When a supplier issues a credit note, details are transferred from the credit note to the supplier's **returns inwards day book**. This is also known as a **sales returns day book** although the term 'journal' is sometimes used instead of day book. The credit note is a **source document** and the returns inwards day book is a **book of prime entry**. The returns inwards day book is useful for businesses because it provides a summary of the returns received and the credit notes issued.

The returns inwards day book is not part of the double entry system because only one entry is made for each return. However, information is posted from the returns inwards day book to the supplier's ledger accounts. It is here that the double entry system is used.

An entry in a returns inwards day book is shown in Figure 11.1. The example relates to T. Francis Ltd which makes children's clothes. On 16 August 2000 the company sent out a credit note (No. 016) to Kids Clothes. This customer had returned £210 of goods because the stitching was faulty. The entry is made in the returns inwards day book of T. Francis Ltd. There is no VAT because it is not charged on children's clothes.

The information recorded in the returns inwards day book includes:

- the date;
- the customer's name;
- a credit note number to trace details of the goods returned;
- a folio to trace the entry in the ledger. In this case the entry is posted to page 12 in the sales ledger;
- the amount, ie the total price of the goods returned.

How are returns inwards recorded in the ledgers?

The procedure that a supplier uses for recording goods that have been returned by a customer, ie returns inwards, is summarised in Figure 11.3. Details from a credit note are recorded in the returns inwards day book. Later they are posted to the ledgers. The customer account in the sales ledger is credited and the returns inwards account in the nominal ledger is debited.

Figure 11.1 *A credit note and extract from the returns inwards day book of T. Francis Ltd.*

CREDIT NOTE No: 016

T. Francis Ltd
Unit 23
Saxon Industrial Estate
Milton Keynes MK2 3HS
Telephone: 01908 296100

Kids Clothes	Invoice No. 5724
310 Saffron Street	Invoice date 10/08/00
Telford	
TF1 4MN	Credit note date 16/08/00

Qty	Description	Unit price £	Amount £
20	Coats	10.50	210.00

Reason for credit: Faulty stitching

RETURNS INWARDS DAY BOOK 2000 (page 23)

Date	Customer	Credit note no.	Folio	Amount £
16.8	Kids Clothes	016	SL12	210.00

QUESTION 1

Pearson & Son is a fruit and vegetable wholesaler in Brighton. The firm supplies greengrocers, hotels, pubs and restaurants in the local area. It usually receives orders over the telephone and delivers goods to customers who buy on credit. On 28 September 2000 Pearson & Son sent out a credit note when goods were returned by a customer. Instead of delivering mixed vegetables to a pub restaurant called The Hop Pole as requested, Pearson & Son had sent out 10 cases of bananas by mistake.

Figure 11.2 *A credit note issued by Pearson & Son*

CREDIT NOTE No: 57

Pearson & Son
13 Pool Terrace
Brighton BN1 6PK
Telephone: 01273 992599

The Hop Pole	Invoice No. 309
68 West Street	Invoice date 23/09/00
Hove	
BN3 1QA	Credit note date 28/09/00

Qty	Description	Unit price £	Amount £
10	Boxes of bananas	12.00	120.00

Reason for credit: Incorrect goods delivered.

(a) Enter the details from the credit note in a copy of the returns inwards day book of Pearson & Son. Ignore the folio entry.

(b) What is the purpose of the credit note issued to The Hop Pole?

Figure 11.3 *The procedure for recording returns inwards*

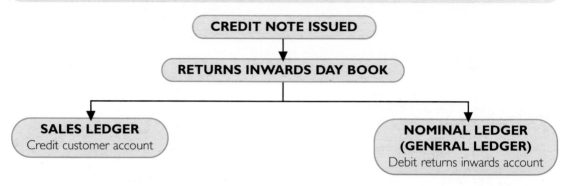

Figure 11.4 shows how information is posted from the returns inwards day book to the ledgers of R. G. Edwards Ltd, a supplier of toys. Returns from three customers were received during one week. Details from the credit notes issued are entered in the returns inwards day book. VAT has been ignored in this example.

Figure 11.4 *Posting sales returns from the returns inwards day book to the ledgers*

RETURNS INWARDS DAY BOOK 2000 (page 45)

Date	Customer	Credit note no.	Folio	Amount
				£
2.4	L. Perkins & Co	0223	SL91	200
7.4	Wheatly Toy Shop	0224	SL99	45
8.4	Peters Toys	0225	SL92	240
9.4	Transferred to Returns Inwards Account		NL43	485

SALES LEDGER

Dr　　　　　**L. Perkins & Co** (page 91)　　　　　Cr

£				£
	2.4	Returns inwards	RIDB45	200

Dr　　　　　**Wheatly Toy Shop** (page 99)　　　　　Cr

£				£
	7.4	Returns inwards	RIDB45	45

Dr　　　　　**Peters Toys** (page 92)　　　　　Cr

£				£
	8.4	Returns inwards	RIDB45	240

NOMINAL LEDGER

Dr　　　　　**Returns Inwards Account** (page 43)　　　　　Cr

		£	£
9.4	Returns RIDB45	485	

- The total amount of returns for the week, £485, is posted to the returns inwards account in the nominal ledger. It is a **debit** entry. This is because the £485 represents a decrease in revenue. The 'rules' for posting transactions are outlined in unit 8.
- The folio in the returns inwards account is RIDB45. This shows that the figure comes from page 45 in the returns inwards day book. The folio in the returns inwards day book is NL43. This shows that the amount is posted to page 43 in the nominal ledger.
- The amount credited to each customer is posted to the customer accounts in the sales ledger. For example, the account of L. Perkins & Co is credited with £200. It is a **credit** entry because it

represents a decrease in the assets of R.G. Edwards Ltd. This is because the debtor, ie the customer, now owes less money. The folios in the sales ledger and the returns inwards day book again provide a cross reference so that entries can be traced.

It is usual to post entries to the customer accounts soon after each credit note is issued. The entries to the returns inwards account in the nominal ledger tend to be made less frequently, perhaps weekly or even monthly. Businesses that issue credit notes to large numbers of customers often post the totals more frequently than those which issue few credit notes.

QUESTION 2

Jayasuriya is a business that supplies Asian restaurants in the West Midlands with a wide range of spices. The firm owns a warehouse in Birmingham which acts as the main storage and distribution centre. All sales are on credit. In early June, Jayasuriya issued three credit notes to customers who had sent goods back. These returns are entered in the returns inwards day book in Figure 11.5. VAT is not charged on food.

Figure 11.5 *Returns inwards day book for Jayasuriya*

RETURNS INWARDS DAY BOOK 2000				(page 27)
Date	Customer	Credit note no.	Folio	Amount £
3.6	Sanjay's Balti House	6410	SL34	120
6.6	Bay of Bengal	6411	SL12	96
9.6	Gate of India	6412	SL23	56
10.6	Transferred to Returns Inwards Account		NL18	272

(a) Transfer the appropriate information from the returns inwards day book of Jayasuriya to the appropriate ledgers.

(b) The bookkeeper for Jayasuriya suggests that it would be simpler if totals were transferred to the nominal ledger monthly rather than weekly. What factors might be considered when making this decision?

How are returns outwards recorded in the returns outwards day book?

The procedure for recording returns outwards is very similar to the procedure for recording returns inwards. The first stage involves the receipt of a credit note after goods have been returned to a supplier. Details from the credit note are then recorded in the **returns outwards day book**. This is also known as a **purchases returns day book**. As with other day books, the term journal might also be used.

To illustrate how information is entered in the returns outwards day book, consider the example of Colt Computer Supplies. This company sells computers from a shop in Newark. In May 2000, Colt returned ten computer monitors that had been damaged in transit. The supplier, CCIT, sent Colt a credit note to confirm the returns. Details from the credit note were entered in the returns outwards day book shown in Figure 11.6. The information recorded includes the date, the supplier's name, the credit note number and the amount. Also included is a folio entry which refers to the page in the purchases ledger which contains CCIT's account.

Figure 11.6 *An extract from the returns outwards day book of Colt Computer Supplies*

RETURNS OUTWARDS DAY BOOK 2000				(page 3)
Date	Supplier	Credit note no.	Folio	Amount £
31.5	CCIT	9112	PL9	670

How are returns outwards recorded in the ledgers?

The procedure for recording returns outwards is summarised in Figure 11.7. Details from a credit note are recorded in the returns outwards day book. Later they are posted to the ledgers. The supplier account in the purchases ledger is debited and the returns outwards account in the nominal ledger is credited.

Figure 11.7 *The procedure for recording returns outwards*

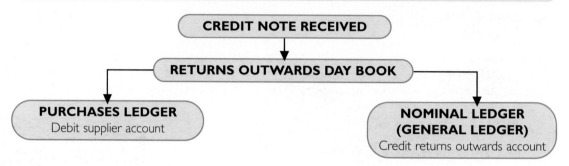

Figure 11.8 shows how information is transferred from the returns outwards day book to the ledgers of P. Tempest & Co, a manufacturer of industrial sewing machines. The double entry system of bookkeeping is used. The returns outwards day book shows that goods were returned to three suppliers. The total amount of purchases returns for the week is shown as £1,554. VAT is ignored.

Figure 11.8 *Posting from the returns outwards day book to the ledgers*

RETURNS OUTWARDS DAY BOOK 2000 (page 4)

Date	Supplier	Credit note no.	Folio	Amount
				£
25.9	H. Thomas	3320	PL32	234
27.9	NGP Steel	1009	PL28	1,200
29.9	B. Minton Ltd	2117	PL21	120
30.9	Transferred to Returns Outwards Account		NL41	1,554

PURCHASES LEDGER

Dr	H. Thomas (page 32)	Cr
	£	£
25.9 Returns outwards RODB4	234	

Dr	NGP Steel (page 28)	Cr
	£	£
27.9 Returns outwards RODB4	1,200	

Dr	B. Minton Ltd (page 21)	Cr
	£	£
29.9 Returns outwards RODB4	120	

NOMINAL LEDGER

Dr	Returns Outwards Account (page 41)	Cr
£		£
	30.9 Returns RODB4	1,554

- The supplier accounts in the purchases ledger are each debited with the price of the goods returned. For example, the supplier account of H. Thomas is debited with £234. It is a **debit** entry because there is a decrease in the liabilities of P. Tempest & Co. In other words, the supplier, H. Thomas, is owed less money. The folios provide a cross-reference between the day book and the accounts.
- The total amount of returns outwards for the week, £1,554, is posted to the returns outwards account in the nominal ledger. It is a **credit** entry. This is because it represents a decrease in the expenses of P. Tempest & Co.

QUESTION 3

Carters is a small chain of greengrocers in South Wales. Where possible, it buys fruit and vegetables direct from local farmers but, sometimes, the quality of goods delivered does not match the necessary specifications. When this happens, the goods are returned. The list of returns below relates to the first week in May 2000.

- 2.5 C. Bartlett (credit note 1200) £45;
- 4.5 D. Perkins (credit note 0332) £120;
- 6.5 C. Bartlett (credit note 1203) £45;
- 7.5 C. Bartlett (credit note 1205) £90;
- 7.5 D. Perkins (credit note 0335) £70.

(a) Enter the returns in the returns outwards day book of Carters. Ignore folio entries.
(b) Post the appropriate information from the returns outwards day book to the purchases ledger and to the returns outwards account in the nominal ledger.

The use of control accounts

In those businesses which use control accounts as summaries of the supplier and customer accounts, the system of recording returns is slightly more complex. For instance, if a customer returns goods, in addition to crediting the customer account in the sales ledger, the sales ledger control account in the nominal ledger is also credited. Under these circumstances, the customer account is not part of the double entry system and is treated as a **memorandum account**. Figure 11.9 shows how the system works.

Figure 11.9 *Recording returns inwards in a control account*

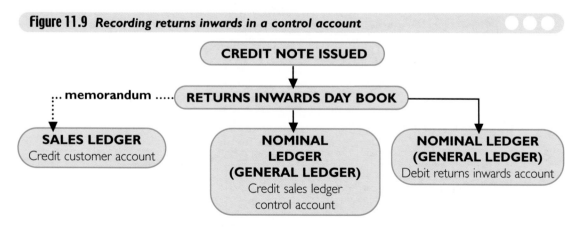

The recording of returns outwards in a purchases ledger control account follows a similar pattern. When goods are returned to a supplier, in addition to debiting the supplier account in the purchases ledger, the purchases ledger control account in the nominal ledger is also debited. This is shown in Figure 11.10.

Figure 11.10 *Recording returns outwards in a control account*

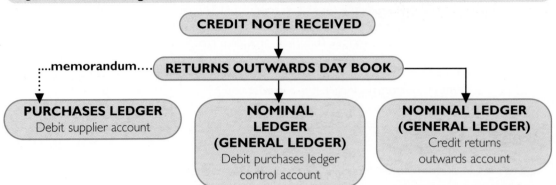

CREDIT NOTE RECEIVED

....memorandum.... → RETURNS OUTWARDS DAY BOOK

PURCHASES LEDGER
Debit supplier account

NOMINAL LEDGER (GENERAL LEDGER)
Debit purchases ledger control account

NOMINAL LEDGER (GENERAL LEDGER)
Credit returns outwards account

summary questions

1. State three reasons why goods might be returned.
2. What is the purpose of a credit note?
3. In which book of prime entry are returns inwards recorded.
4. If a credit note is received, in which day book would the details be recorded?
5. State four pieces of information that might be recorded in a returns inwards day book.
6. At which stage in the recording of returns is the double entry system used?
7. In which account in the nominal ledger is the total of returns inwards recorded?
8. On which side of the customer account in the sales ledger are returns inwards entered?
9. In which account in the nominal ledger is the total of returns outwards recorded?
10. On which side of the supplier account in the purchases ledger are returns outwards entered?

UNIT ASSESSMENT QUESTION 1

Apex Promotional Products makes and supplies promotional goods such as mugs, coasters, pin badges, umbrellas and T shirts. Figure 11.11 shows two accounts contained in the ledgers of Apex. The accounts show all credit transactions for October 2000.

Figure 11.11 *Two accounts in the ledgers of Apex Promotional Products*

Dr	A. Maxwell (page 19)			Cr	
		£			£
4.10 Credit sales SDB35		980	12.10 Returns inwards RIDB23		450
7.10 Credit sales SDB35		780			
19.10 Credit sales SDB36		1,010			

Dr	Rochdale Textiles (page 32)			Cr	
		£			£
5.10 Returns outwards RODB11		200	1.10 Credit purchases PDB15		870
9.10 Returns outwards RODB11		400	7.10 Credit purchases PDB15		850
19.10 Returns outwards RODB12		750	17.10 Credit purchases PDB17		750

(a) In which ledgers would the two accounts be contained?

(b) Explain what the entry in the A. Maxwell account on the 12.10.00 represents.

(c) As a result of the transactions shown in the A. Maxwell account, how much did A. Maxwell owe to Apex at the end of October?

(d) In the Rochdale Textiles account, what does the folio RODB11 mean?

(e) At the end of October, Apex ceased trading with Rochdale Textiles. What reasons for this are suggested in the accounts?

UNIT ASSESSMENT QUESTION 2

Anil Mustaq manufactures jewellery in Hockley, Birmingham. He buys stones and precious metals from specialist suppliers. Sometimes it is necessary to return gems and metals if incorrect goods are supplied. Following a return to one supplier, Anil Mustaq received the credit note shown in Figure 11.12. VAT is ignored.

Figure 11.12 *A credit note received from Alvin Gem Supplies*

CREDIT NOTE

Alvin Gem Supplies
Unit 15 Handley Estate
Birmingham B3 6EQ

Anil Mustaq   Credit note number 046
31 Vose Street
Hockley
Birmingham B18 9GD   Credit note date 04/08/00

Qty	Description	Amount
		£
100	Semi-precious stones	600.00

Reason for credit:
Colour not as requested.

(a) **What effect will the credit note have on the amount that Anil Mustaq owes Alvin Gem Supplies?**

(b) **Use the credit note to record the returns to Alvin Gem Supplies in the returns outwards day book of Anil Mustaq. Ignore folio page numbers.**

(c) **Post the appropriate information from the returns outwards day book to the purchases ledger and nominal ledger.**

key terms

Returns inwards or sales returns - goods that are sent back by customers.
Returns outwards or purchases returns - goods that are sent back to suppliers.

unit objectives

To understand:
- the role of the cash book in bookkeeping;
- how to post entries from the cash book to other ledgers;
- the purpose of contra entries in the cash book;
- how to treat cash discounts allowed and cash discounts received.

What is the cash book?

The CASH BOOK is used to record transactions that involve the payment and receipt of money. These payments and receipts can be in the form of **cash**, ie notes and coins, or **cheques** and other **bank transfers**, such as direct debits or standing orders. Some businesses only record transactions involving cheques or bank transfers in the cash book. They record transactions involving notes and coins in a petty cash book (see unit 13). However, in this unit, examples of transactions involving cash, cheques and bank transactions are all shown in the cash book.

The cash book is a **book of prime entry** in which details from source documents are recorded. It is also a **ledger** in which the double entry system is used. This is explained in detail later in the unit.

Most cash books contain two accounts, the **cash account** and the **bank account**. The cash account records details of all payments and receipts made in cash. The bank account records details of payments and receipts by cheque and bank transfers. The person who supervises the recording of transactions in the cash book is called the CASHIER. Responsibilities of a cashier generally include:

- recording the details of all transactions involving the cash account and the bank account in the cash book;
- paying cash and cheques into the bank;
- supervising and authorising payments to suppliers using cash, cheques and other methods such as bank transfers;
- ensuring the security of cash on the business premises;
- issuing cash to the petty cashier;
- checking the accuracy of entries in the cash and bank accounts at regular intervals;
- maintaining the confidentiality of certain payments and receipts, such as salary payments.

The two column cash book

A variety of cash book layouts is used by businesses. The two column format is relatively simple (see Figure 12.1). It is set out like a T account, with a left-hand, debit side and a right-hand, credit side. The 'two columns' refer to:

1 the cash account;
2 the bank account;

which appear on both the credit and debit side. The receipt of money is a debit because it represents an increase in assets. It is entered on the left. The payment of money is a credit because it represents a decrease in assets. It is entered on the right. The details column in the cash book refers to the other account in which the double entry is recorded. The folio refers to the page number and ledger in which this other account is contained. In Figure 12.1 there are no columns for VAT. In order to simplify the explanation, VAT is ignored in this unit. It is dealt with in detail in unit 26.

How are transactions recorded in the cash book?

Information that is recorded in the cash book comes from **source documents**. On the debit side, information relating to receipts might come from:

- copies of receipts given to customers;

Figure 12.1 *A two column cash book*

Debit					CASH BOOK			Credit		
Date	Details	Folio	Cash	Bank	Date	Details	Folio	Cash	Bank
			£	£				£	£
	RECEIPTS						**PAYMENTS**		

- cheques received;
- bank giro credits received;
- paying-in slips;
- BACS payments documents;
- bank statements (containing details of interest received);
- credit card vouchers from sales.

On the credit side of the cash book, information regarding payments might come from:

- receipts from suppliers;
- cheque book counterfoils;
- bank statements (containing details of standing order and direct debit payments, bank charges and interest paid).

In order to illustrate how transactions are recorded in the cash book, consider Malcolm Matthews, a cereal farmer in Essex. In the first week of November 2000, the following transactions took place:

- 2.11.00 £1,200 cheque (no. 012288) paid for tractor repairs;
- 3.11.00 £4,000 cheque received from the Eastern Brewing Company for barley sold on credit 30 days ago;
- 5.11.00 £580 wages paid in cash;
- 6.11.00 £500 cash received for cash sales;
- 6.11.00 £2,000 cheque (no. 012289) paid to W. Giles for seed supplies bought on credit.

Malcolm Matthews keeps a two column cash book with a cash account and a bank account. The transactions are entered in the cash book shown in Figure 12.2.

Figure 12.2 *The cash book of Malcolm Matthews*

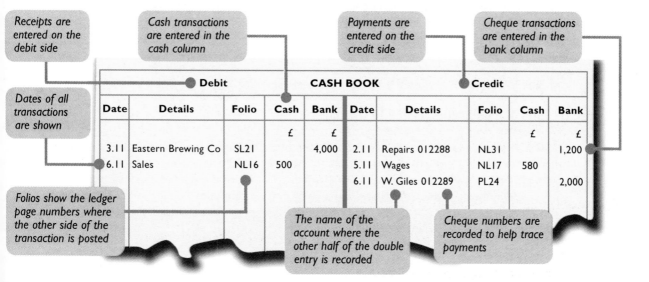

Receipts are entered on the debit side

Cash transactions are entered in the cash column

Payments are entered on the credit side

Cheque transactions are entered in the bank column

Dates of all transactions are shown

Debit					CASH BOOK			Credit		
Date	Details	Folio	Cash	Bank	Date	Details	Folio	Cash	Bank
			£	£				£	£
3.11	Eastern Brewing Co	SL21		4,000	2.11	Repairs 012288	NL31		1,200
6.11	Sales	NL16	500		5.11	Wages	NL17	580	
					6.11	W. Giles 012289	PL24		2,000

Folios show the ledger page numbers where the other side of the transaction is posted

The name of the account where the other half of the double entry is recorded

Cheque numbers are recorded to help trace payments

QUESTION 1

East Coast Motor Parts is a supplier of vehicle parts. It trades from a large depot in Grimsby, supplying local mechanics, garages and some private buyers. Trade customers have accounts with East Coast Motor Parts and buy parts on credit. However, private customers normally pay over the counter by cash or cheque. The transactions for 12 April 2000 are listed below (discounts and VAT are ignored):

- paid £2,850 to Ford Motors (cheque no. 012339) for motor parts;
- received a cheque from Cleethorpes Motors for goods supplied on credit £1,300;
- paid £1,200 wages to part-time staff in cash;
- received £120 cash for parts sold over the counter to a private customer;
- paid £350 to Newcastle Insurance (cheque no. 012340);
- received a cheque from P. Linton for goods supplied on credit £450;
- paid £280 to Grimsby Weekly for advertising (cheque no. 012341).

(a) What source documents might have been used to record the first two transactions?
(b) Record the transactions in a cash book of East Coast Motor Parts (ignore folio entries).

Analysed cash books

Some businesses use analysed cash books to record different types of payment or receipt. For example, a business might wish to divide its payments into the different categories shown in Figure 12.3. In this example, only the payments side of the cash book is shown. When the columns are totalled at the end of a trading period, a business can see how much it has paid in each category. This is helpful when trying to monitor and control costs.

Figure 12.3 An analysed cash book (payments only)

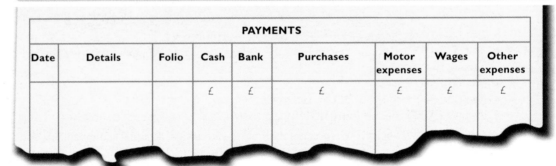

					PAYMENTS			
Date	Details	Folio	Cash	Bank	Purchases	Motor expenses	Wages	Other expenses
			£	£	£	£	£	£

A similar layout is used to record receipts in different categories. For example, a business might wish to keep a record of sales in different geographical regions. In this case the headings in the analysed cash book would be these regions. Alternatively, receipts could be divided according to the types of good sold. For example, a clothes retailer might subdivide its receipts into categories such as men's, women's and children's garments. In practice there are many different formats for analysed cash books. Businesses choose the format that best suits their needs.

How are receipts and payments posted to the ledgers?

Figure 12.4 shows the role of the cash book in the bookkeeping system. The cash book is a book of prime entry because it is where details from source documents are first recorded. Unlike other books of prime entry, such as day books or journals, it is part of the double entry system. Every entry made in the cash book must have a matching entry in the sales, nominal or purchases ledger. Note that the cash book is itself also a ledger because it contains accounts, in this case the cash account and the bank account.

Figure 12.4 *The cash book in the bookkeeping system*

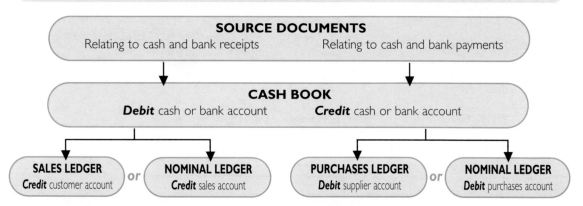

Receiving payments The receipt of money is shown on the left-hand side of Figure 12.4. When a business receives payment for goods and services, the amount is entered as a **debit** in the cash book. Payments made by cash are recorded in the cash account and payments made by cheque or bank transfer are recorded in the bank account. To complete the double entry, details are posted as a **credit** in the nominal ledger or the sales ledger.

In a sale where a customer pays immediately for goods or services (ie it is a 'cash' transaction), the money received is recorded as a **debit** in the cash book and as a **credit** in the sales account in the nominal ledger. This is illustrated in Figure 12.5.

Figure 12.5 *Posting a 'cash' sale to the ledger accounts*

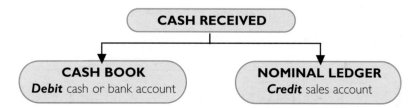

- In a credit transaction, goods and services are paid for at a later date. When the transaction takes place, it is recorded as a **debit** in the customer account in the sales ledger and as a **credit** in the sales account in the nominal ledger.
- When payment is received from the customer, it is recorded as a **debit** in the cash book and as a **credit** in the customer account in the sales ledger.
- The two entries in the customer account cancel each other out. This indicates that the debt has been paid. The entries in the cash book and sales account are then the same as if it had been a 'cash' transaction. This is illustrated in Figure 12.6.

Figure 12.6 *Posting a credit sale and receipt of payment to the ledger accounts*

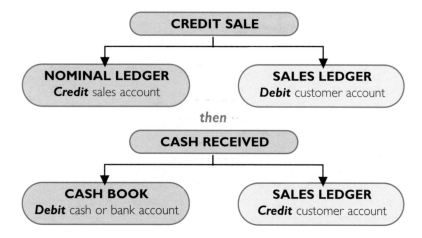

Making payments The payments made by a business for its purchases are shown on the right-hand side of Figure 12.4. A payment is recorded as a **credit** in the cash book. If the payment is by cash it is recorded in the cash account and if it is by cheque or bank transfer, it is recorded in the bank account. To complete the double entry, details are posted as a **debit** in the purchases account in the nominal ledger or in the supplier account in the purchases ledger.

If payment is immediate (ie it is a 'cash' purchase), the purchases account in the nominal ledger is **debited** and the cash book is **credited**. This is illustrated in Figure 12.7.

Figure 12.7 *Posting a 'cash' purchase to the ledger accounts*

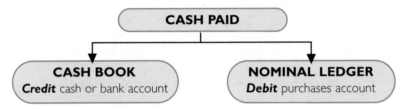

- In a credit purchase, the amount to be paid is first recorded as a **credit** in the supplier account in the purchases ledger and as a **debit** in the purchases account in the nominal ledger.
- When payment is actually made, it is recorded as a **credit** in the cash book and as a **debit** in the supplier account in the purchases ledger.
- The two entries in the supplier account cancel each other showing that the debt is paid. The entries in the cash book and the purchases account are the same as if there had been a 'cash' purchase. This is illustrated in Figure 12.8.

Figure 12.8 *Posting a credit purchase and payment to the ledger accounts*

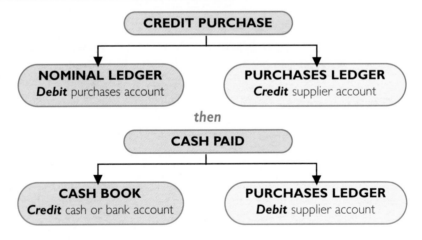

Posting transactions

To illustrate how transactions are posted, consider the example of Malcolm Matthews, the cereal farmer whose cash book is shown in Figure 12.2. Extracts from his cash book and his ledgers are reproduced in Figure 12.9.

- The £4,000 received from the Eastern Brewing Company for goods sold on credit is posted to the customer account in the sales ledger. It is a credit entry because it represents a decrease in an asset of Malcolm Matthews, ie the amount owed to him is reduced. The folio CB9 in the sales ledger shows that the entry is posted from page 9 in the cash book.
- The cash sale for £500 is posted to the sales account in the nominal ledger. It is a credit entry because it represents an increase in revenue.
- The cheque payment of £1,200 for tractor repairs is posted to the tractor repairs account in the nominal ledger. It is a debit because it is an increase in expenses.
- The payment of £580 wages is posted to the wages account in the nominal ledger. It is a debit because it represents an increase in expenses.

- The payment of £2,000 to a supplier, W. Giles, for goods bought on credit, is posted to the supplier account in the purchases ledger. It is a debit because it represents a decrease in the liabilities of Malcolm Matthews, ie the amount owed is reduced.
- Note that the payment made to W. Giles and the payments made for tractor repairs and wages are treated differently in the ledgers. The goods bought from the supplier W. Giles are bought on credit and are purchases, ie they are goods intended for resale. The payment is therefore posted to the purchases ledger (see unit 10). The tractor repairs and wages are expenses and, in this case, are both 'cash' transactions. They are therefore posted to the relevant accounts in the nominal ledger.

Figure 12.9 *Posting transactions from the cash book to the ledgers*

		Debit			**CASH BOOK (page 9)**			Credit		
Date	Details	Folio	Cash	Bank	Date	Details	Folio	Cash	Bank
			£	£				£	£
3.11	Eastern Brewing Co	SL21		4,000	2.11	Tractor repairs 012288	NL31		1,200
6.11	Sales	NL16	500		5.11	Wages	NL17	580	
					6.11	W. Giles 0122289	PL24		2,000

SALES LEDGER

Dr   **Eastern Brewing Company** (page 21)   Cr

	£		£
		3.11 Bank CB9	4,000

PURCHASES LEDGER

Dr   **W. Giles** (page 24)   Cr

	£		£
6.11 Bank CB9	2,000		

NOMINAL LEDGER

Dr   **Sales Account** (page 16)   Cr

	£		£
		6.11 Cash account CB9	500

Dr   **Tractor Repairs Account** (page 31)   Cr

	£		£
2.11 Bank CB9	1,200		

Dr   **Wages Account** (page 17)   Cr

	£		£
5.11 Cash CB9	580		

What are contra entries in the cash book?

Sometimes businesses need to transfer money between the cash account and the bank account in the cash book. For example, a retailer might record and keep daily cash receipts and then pay the takings into the bank at the end of each week. This involves a transfer from the cash account to the bank account. The business might also withdraw money from the bank so that it has cash in hand, for example if it needs petty cash. This involves a transfer from the bank account to the cash account. Transfers between accounts in the cash book are called CONTRA ENTRIES. Contra means 'opposite' in Latin. The folio 'C' is used to show a contra entry.

In order to illustrate how movements of money between the cash account and the bank account are recorded, consider the example of two unrelated businesses (see Figure 12.10):
- Sarah Watson, a newsagent, pays £1,200 cash receipts into a bank account on 23 September;
- Peter Nelson, a printer, withdraws £100 from the bank to use as petty cash on 26 September.

The bank account of Sarah Watson shows a debit entry of £1,200 because there has been an increase in an asset, ie an increase of money in the bank. The cash account shows a credit entry because there has been a decrease in an asset, ie a decrease in the amount of cash held by Sarah's business.

The £100 withdrawal by Peter Nelson is shown as a credit entry in the bank account because there has been a decrease in an asset, ie there is less money in the bank. The cash account shows a debit entry because there has been an increase in an asset, ie more cash is held.

Figure 12.10 *Cash books of Sarah Watson and Peter Nelson*

	Debit				CASH BOOK (Sarah Watson)			Credit		
Date	Details	Folio	Cash	Bank	Date	Details	Folio	Cash	Bank	
			£	£				£	£	
23.9	Cash	C		1,200	23.9	Bank	C	1,200		

	Debit				CASH BOOK (Peter Nelson)			Credit		
Date	Details	Folio	Cash	Bank	Date	Details	Folio	Cash	Bank	
			£	£				£	£	
26.9	Bank	C	100		26.9	Cash	C		100	

QUESTION 2

Helen Waterfield owns a small manufacturing company in Guildford. The company designs and makes clothes for young children. Nearly all the company's sales are made on credit and customers generally pay by cheque. Most purchases are on credit and are paid for by cheque. However, sometimes the company makes payments for relatively small items using cash. An extract from the company's cash book is shown in Figure 12.11.

Figure 12.11 *An extract from the company's cash book*

	Debit				CASH BOOK (page 12)			Credit		
Date	Details	Folio	Cash	Bank	Date	Details	Folio	Cash	Bank
			£	£				£	£
12.8	W. Simpkins	SL9		1,110	16.8	Rent 002990	NL23		1,000
15.8	Bentham's	SL7		1,780	18.8	W. B. Jones 002991	PL41		3,450
					20.8	Motor expenses	NL18	26	

(a) **Enter the payments and receipts in the appropriate ledger accounts. Show the folios.**
(b) **Explain how it is possible from the entry in the cash book to know that the sale of goods to W. Simpkins was a credit transaction.**
(c) **If the sale to W. Simpkins had been a 'cash' transaction (ie payment was received immediately), how would this have affected the ledger accounts?**

Recording cash discounts: the three column cash book

A CASH DISCOUNT is a reduction in price given to customers who pay their bills promptly whether by cash, cheque or other means. For example, a customer might be given a 5% cash discount if payment is made within seven days.

A **three column cash book** is used to record cash discounts as in Figure 12.12. This is similar to the two column cash book described earlier except that there is an extra column on each side to show discounts. On the debit side, the column heading is DISCOUNTS ALLOWED. This records cash discounts given to customers who pay their bills promptly. On the credit side, the column is DISCOUNTS RECEIVED. This records cash discounts received from suppliers who reward prompt payment.

Figure 12.12 *The layout of a three column cash book*

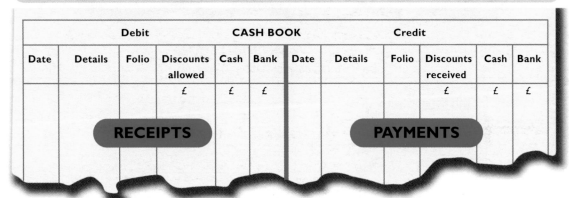

Unlike the entries in the cash and bank columns of the cash book, the entries in the discount columns in the cash book are not part of the double entry system. They are known as **memorandum entries**. Their purpose is to keep a record of how much discount has been allowed or received. In this respect, the cash book is being used in the same way as the other books of prime entry, such as the sales day book.

Details are posted from the discounts column in the cash book to the other ledgers (see Figure 12.13). For instance, the discounts allowed are posted to customer accounts in the sales ledger. Discounts received are posted to the supplier accounts in the purchases ledger. At regular intervals, such as weekly or monthly, the discounts are totalled. These totals are then posted to the nominal ledger, which contains the accounts of discounts allowed and discounts received.

Figure 12.13 *Recording discounts in the ledgers*

Posting discounts

To illustrate how discounts are recorded, consider the example of Derek Wilkes, a meat wholesaler. He allows and receives cash discounts at a rate of 5 per cent on each transaction if prompt payment is made. The cash book in Figure 12.14 shows a mixture of receipts and payments. The ledger accounts show where entries are posted.

Figure 12.14 *Cash book and ledgers of Derek Wilkes*

Debit					CASH BOOK (page 54)					Credit	
Date	Details	Folio	Discounts allowed	Cash	Bank	Date	Details	Folio	Discounts received	Cash	Bank
			£	£	£				£	£	£
15.1	B. Collins	SL4	20		380	15. 1	B. Middleton	PL21	30		570
20.1	S. Lucas	SL9	50		950	19.1	Carter Bros	PL6	15		285
21.1		NL7	70			21.1		NL8	45		

NOMINAL LEDGER

Dr   **Discounts Allowed Account** (page 7)   **Cr**

	£		£
21.1 Cash book CB54	70		

Dr   **Discounts Received Account** (page 8)   **Cr**

	£		£
		21.1 Cash book CB54	45

SALES LEDGER

Dr   **B. Collins** (page 4)   **Cr**

	£		£
		15.1 Bank CB54	380
		15.1 Discount CB54	20

Dr   **S. Lucas** (page 9)   **Cr**

	£		£
		20.1 Bank CB54	950
		20.1 Discount CB54	50

PURCHASES LEDGER

Dr   **B. Middleton** (page 21)   **Cr**

	£		£
15.1 Bank CB54	570		
15.1 Discount CB54	30		

Dr   **Carter Bros** (page 6)   **Cr**

	£		£
19.1 Bank CB54	285		
19.1 Discount CB54	15		

- In Figure 12.14, the total discounts allowed, £70, is posted to the discounts allowed account in the nominal ledger. It is a debit entry. This is because, in bookkeeping, a discount allowed is treated as an increase in expenses.
- The customer accounts in the sales ledger are credited with both the money received in payment and the discount allowed. These are credit entries because they represent a decrease in assets. There is a reduction in the amount owed to Derek Wilkes.
- The total discounts received, £45, is posted to the discounts received account in the nominal ledger. It is a credit entry. This is because the discount received is treated as an increase in revenue.
- The supplier accounts in the purchases ledger are debited with both the amount paid to them and the discount received. They are debit entries because they represent a reduction in the liabilities of Derek Wilkes.

QUESTION 3

Dave Smith is a carpet fitter in the West Midlands. His business has a contract with a large carpet retailer, Halesowen Carpets, and fits all the carpets sold by them. Dave allows Halesowen Carpets a 5% discount if it pays his bills within a month of the carpet fitting. Dave's business purchases gripper rods and other supplies from P. Hunter Ltd. This company allows a 5% cash discount for prompt payment. In one week of trading, the following transactions occurred:

- 5 December Received a cheque for £475 from Halesowen Carpets, a £25 cash discount was allowed for prompt payment on a bill of £500;
- 6 December Paid P. Hunter Ltd £190 by cheque (no. 002220), the amount owing was £200 but Dave's business received £10 cash discount;
- 8 December Withdrew £100 cash from the bank to use as petty cash.

(a) Enter the transactions in a three column cash book (ignore folios).
(b) With reference to the transaction on 8.12, explain what is meant by a contra entry.

UNIT ASSESSMENT QUESTION 1

Melissa Holmes owns and runs a catering company in Edinburgh. She provides ready-made meals for corporate lunches and meetings. Her company operates from a unit on an industrial estate where it has a kitchen and storage area. Melissa allows cash discounts to contract customers and also receives discounts from some of her suppliers. Two transactions recorded in the cash book are shown in Figure 12.15.

Figure 12.15 Cash book of Melissa Holmes' business

Date	Details	Folio	Discounts allowed	Cash	Bank	Date	Details	Folio	Discounts received	Cash	Bank
			£	£	£				£	£	£
13.3	A. McDonald	SL31	25		475	17.3	W. Willis	PL42	10		90
18.3		NL21	25			18.3		NL22	10		

Debit — CASH BOOK (page 102) — **Credit**

(a) Calculate the percentage cash discount that Melissa gave to her customer and received from her supplier.
(b) Enter the payments and discounts in the appropriate ledger accounts.

UNIT ASSESSMENT QUESTION 2

Miller & King is a wholesaling business that deals in toys, games, sports equipment and bicycles. Goods are bought direct from manufacturers and sold to retailers in the UK. Most of these transactions are on credit. An extract from Miller & King's cash book is shown in Figure 12.16. The page contains records of cash and cheque transactions for the last week in October.

Figure 12.16 Cash book of Miller & King

Date	Details	Folio	Discounts allowed	Cash	Bank	Date	Details	Folio	Discounts received	Cash	Bank
			£	£	£				£	£	£
24.10	Watkins Toys	SL16	20		380	25.10	Olton Racers	PL6	40		760
27.10	Forest Cycles	SL23	100		1,900	28.10	Smith & Son	PL51	35		665
						29.10	Motor expenses	NL2		54	
30.10		NL3	120			30.10		NL4	75		

Debit | *CASH BOOK (page 41)* | *Credit*

(a) **Post the payments, receipts and discounts shown in Miller & King's cash book to the appropriate ledger accounts.**

(b) **Explain how the transaction recorded on 29 October is different from the other payments.**

summary questions

1. What types of transactions are recorded in the cash book?
2. Which two accounts are shown in the cash book?
3. Which transactions are recorded on the (i) debit side and (ii) credit side of the cash book?
4. Describe the advantages of using an analysed cash book.
5. Explain how the cash book is part of the double entry system.
6. What information is entered in the cash book when recording payments?
7. Suggest two nominal ledger accounts that might be used when posting cash book (i) receipts and (ii) payments?
8. When might a contra entry be made in the cash book?
9. Under what circumstances might a supplier allow a cash discount?
10. Explain the difference between a two column and a three column cash book.

key terms

Cash book - a book used to record payments and receipts of money. It combines the cash account and the bank account.

Cash discount - a reduction in price to customers who pay bills promptly.

Cashier - a person who supervises the receipt and payment of money and the recording of these transactions.

Contra entry - an entry for the same amount made on opposite sides of the same book or account.

Discounts allowed - cash discounts given to customers who pay their bills promptly.

Discounts received - cash discounts received from suppliers who reward prompt payment.

Recording petty cash transactions

unit**objectives**

To understand:
- the purpose of the petty cash book;
- the layout of the petty cash book;
- how to record transactions in the petty cash book;
- how to post petty cash transactions to the ledgers.

What is the petty cash book?

Many businesses operate a **petty cash system** to pay for small items such as stationery and stamps. A common method is to keep a certain sum of cash (a **float** or **imprest**) in a cash box to use for 'petty' expenditure. At regular intervals, cash is withdrawn from the bank and paid into the cash box to bring it back to the imprest amount.

A PETTY CASH BOOK is used to record all the payments and receipts that are made in the petty cash system. Although such transactions are sometimes recorded in the cash book, there are advantages in having a separate book for petty expenditure.

- If trivial and small cash transactions are recorded in the main cash book, it is necessary to post a large number of entries to other ledgers. This is time consuming and inefficient. By using a petty cash book, only the periodic totals need be posted to the ledgers.
- In large organisations, the responsibility for recording petty cash transactions can be delegated to a junior member of staff. This allows the cashier to focus on more important tasks.

Figure 13.1 shows how petty cash transactions are recorded. The double entry system is used which means that, like the cash book, the petty cash book is both a **book of prime entry** and a **ledger**. A number of steps take place when recording petty cash transactions.

- Money is taken from the bank and placed in the petty cash box. Then the bank account in the cash book is credited and the petty cash book is debited.
- The source documents that are used for verifying payments from petty cash are petty cash vouchers and receipts. For each payment, a voucher that sets out the details is completed. The person claiming the petty cash then attaches a receipt to the voucher.
- At regular intervals, perhaps weekly or monthly, payments in the petty cash book are totalled, and posted either to expenses accounts in the nominal ledger or to supplier accounts in the purchases ledger.

These procedures are explained in more detail later in the unit.

Figure 13.1 *The system for recording petty cash transactions*

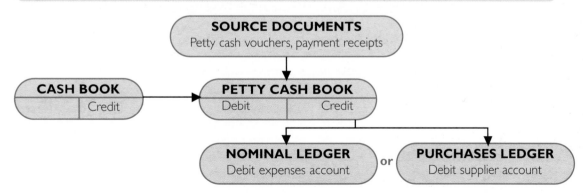

What is the layout of the petty cash book?

Many businesses use an **analysed** book for recording petty cash transactions (see Figure 13.2). It is in the form of a T account with a debit side to record receipts and a credit side to record payments. Note that the date column is used for both debits and credits. The receipts side in an analysed book is usually smaller than the payments side because it contains less information. Receipts are transfers of cash from the bank to the petty cash box. Payments, on the other hand, are for a wide variety of goods and services. By classifying payments into a number of categories, the task of posting details to ledger accounts is made easier.

Figure 13.2 *An example of an analysed petty cash book*

					PETTY CASH BOOK							
Receipts	Folio	Date	Details	Voucher no.	Total payments	Petrol	Postage	Cleaning	Sundry expenses	Stationery	Folio	Ledger account
£					£	£	£	£	£	£		£

The debit side of the petty cash book has:

- a column to record receipts;
- a folio column to show the page in the cash book where the credit entry is made.

On the credit side of the petty cash book, expenditure is broken into different categories:

- SUNDRY EXPENSES are 'one-off' payments for items such as a replacement light bulb or a new waste basket. Such infrequent expenses do not require a column of their own;
- the voucher number refers to the petty cash voucher on which the details of the payment are recorded;
- the ledger account column is used to record any payments made from petty cash to a regular supplier. Such a payment is posted to that supplier's account in the purchases ledger and the adjacent folio column is used to show where the payment is recorded.

How are petty cash transactions recorded?

To illustrate how transactions are entered in the petty cash book, consider the example of Geraldine Richmond who owns a garden centre in Dorset. To simplify the explanation, VAT is ignored (see unit 26). A list of the garden centre's petty cash transactions for a 6 day period in January 2000 is shown below:

- 10.1.00 Geraldine cashed a £200 cheque for the petty cash box;
- 10.1.00 paid £4.50 to a window cleaner (voucher no. 25);
- 12.1.00 paid £8.50 for stamps (voucher no. 26);
- 12.1.00 paid £20 to an employee for petrol expenses (voucher no. 27);
- 13.1.00 paid £4.70 for computer printer paper (voucher no. 28);
- 14.1.00 paid £8 for a special delivery charge (voucher no. 29);
- 15.1.00 paid £40 for petrol (voucher no. 30).

These transactions are recorded in the petty cash book (see Figure 13.3). The first transaction is a receipt of £200 into petty cash. It is entered on the debit side of the petty cash book because it represents an increase in petty cash assets. The cash is a transfer from money held in the bank. The bank account in the cash book is credited with £200 because it represents a decrease in the asset of money in the bank. The folio in the cash book, PCB19, shows where the entry is posted, ie to page 19 of the petty cash book. The folio in the petty cash book, CB87, shows that the matching entry is on page 87 in the cash book.

The list of payments made from petty cash are recorded on the credit side of the petty cash book. The amounts are recorded in the total payments column and also in the relevant column in the analysed section. For example, the payment of £4.50 to the window cleaner is recorded in the total payments column and in the cleaning column. The date and the petty cash voucher number are also entered. At the end of the week, for example, the columns in the petty cash book might be totalled to give the overall amounts spent in each category. The sum of the totals in the different categories equals the sum of the total column (£60.00 + £8.50 + £4.50 + £8.00 + £4.70 = £85.70). This addition is a useful means of checking that no errors have been made when recording the payments.

Figure 13.3 *Entering transactions into the petty cash book*

Debit					CASH BOOK (page 87)				Credit	
Date	Details	Folio	Cash £	Bank £	Date	Details	Folio	Cash £	Bank £	
					10.1		PCB19		200.00	

Receipts £	Folio	Date	Details	Voucher no.	Total payments £	Petrol £	Postage £	Cleaning £	Sundry expenses £	Stationery £	Folio	Ledger account £
200.00	CB87	10.1	Window cleaner	25	4.50				4.50			
		12.1	Stamps	26	8.50		8.50					
		12.1	Petrol	27	20.00	20.00						
		13.1	Paper	28	4.70					4.70		
		14.1	Special delivery	29	8.00				8.00			
		15.1	Petrol	30	40.00	40.00						
200.00		15.1			85.70	60.00	8.50	4.50	8.00	4.70		

PETTY CASH BOOK (page 19)

QUESTION 1

Trudy Hampton owns a veterinary practice in Surrey. Her office manager operates a petty cash system and during a week in June 2000 the following petty cash transactions were recorded (VAT is ignored):

- 12.6 £100 is withdrawn from the bank and paid into the petty cash box;
- 12.6 £5.40 is paid for stamps (voucher no. 87);
- 13.6 £48 is paid for petrol (voucher no. 88);
- 14.6 £5 donation is made to a local charity (voucher no. 89);
- 14.6 £35 is paid to repair a broken office window (voucher no. 90);
- 15.6 £100 is withdrawn from the bank and paid into the petty cash box;
- 16.6 £8.50 is paid for envelopes (voucher no. 91);
- 16.6 £18 is paid for office cleaning materials (voucher no. 92).

(a) Draw up a suitable petty cash book with analysis columns to show expenditure on the above items.

(b) Record the transactions in the petty cash book.

How are payments in the petty cash book posted to other ledgers?

To illustrate how payments are posted to the other ledgers, consider the example of Ahmed Hussain who sells spare parts for domestic appliances. Figure 13.4 shows a page from his business's analysed petty cash book.

The payments side shows expenditure by the business for a number of transactions. The totals of various purchases and expenses are posted to accounts in the nominal ledger or in the purchases ledger. They are all debit entries because they represent an increase in expenses. The folio entries provide a cross-reference between the petty cash book and the other ledgers.

- £60.50 is debited to the petrol account in the nominal ledger;
- £6.60 is debited to the sundry expenses account in the nominal ledger;
- £19.00 is debited to the stationery account in the nominal ledger;
- £18.60 is debited to the supplier account, R. Brookes & Son, in the purchases ledger. This is different from the other postings which are to expenses accounts in the nominal ledger. The reason is that R. Brookes & Son is a supplier of goods intended for resale. These **purchases** are posted to the purchases ledger. Such a payment using petty cash is not likely to occur frequently, but might happen for a relatively inexpensive item that is bought over the counter.

Figure 13.4 *Posting information from the petty cash book to other ledgers*

PETTY CASH BOOK (page 32)

Receipts	Folio	Date	Details	Voucher no.	Total payments	Petrol	Sundry expenses	Stationery	Folio	Ledger account
£					£	£	£	£		£
200.00	CB12	21.8	Petrol	11	25.00	25.00				
		22.8	Paper	12	15.60			15.60		
		23.8	R. Brookes & Son	13	18.60				PL2	18.60
		24.8	Petrol	14	20.00	20.00				
		24.8	Milk	15	1.60		1.60			
		25.8	Envelopes	16	3.40			3.40		
		26.8	Charity raffle	17	5.00		5.00			
		28.8	Petrol	18	15.50	15.50				
200.00		28.8			104.70	60.50	6.60	19.00		18.60
						NL21	NL24	NL25		

NOMINAL LEDGER

Dr   **Petrol Account** (page 21)   **Cr**

	£		£
28.8 Petty cash PCB32	60.50		

Dr   **Sundry Expenses Account** (page 24)   **Cr**

	£		£
28.8 Petty cash PCB32	6.60		

Dr   **Stationery Account** (page 25)   **Cr**

	£		£
28.8 Petty cash PCB32	19.00		

PURCHASES LEDGER

Dr   **R. Brookes & Son** (page 2)   **Cr**

	£		£
28.8 Petty cash PCB32	18.60		

QUESTION 2

Hopkins Ltd manufactures Christmas decorations in its Nottingham factory. The company employs 18 full-time staff, one of whom is responsible for the petty cash system. An extract from the petty cash book is shown in Figure 13.5. B. Milton & Co is a supplier of crepe paper that is used in the decorations.

(a) Explain (i) the £300 debit entry and (ii) the £22 credit entry in the petty cash book.
(b) Add up the columns in the petty cash book and enter the totals for 17 March.
(c) Post the petty cash payments to the appropriate ledger accounts of Hopkins Ltd.

Figure 13.5 *An extract from the petty cash book for Hopkins Ltd*

PETTY CASH BOOK (page 28)

Receipts	Folio	Date	Details	Voucher no.	Total payments	Travel expenses	Cleaning	Sundry expenses	Stationery	Folio	Ledger account
£					£	£	£	£	£		£
300.00	CB7	12.3									
		14.3	Train fare	65	54.80	54.80					
		14.3	Pens, pencils	66	4.90				4.90		
		15.3	Taxi fare	67	11.00	11.00					
		16.3	B. Milton & Co	68	22.00					PL16	22.00
		17.3	Cleaning fluids	69	25.00		25.00				
		17.3	Padlock	70	12.50			12.50			
		17.3	Ink cartridge	71	13.80				13.80		
						NL19	NL8	NL21	NL32		

key terms

Petty cash book - the book in which relatively small cash payments and receipts are recorded.
Sundry expenses - small or infrequent items of expenditure that do not fit into any other named category of expenses.

summary questions

1. State three examples of expenditure that might be paid from petty cash.
2. Explain why the cash book might not be used to record all cash payments.
3. Which source documents are used to record petty cash transactions?
4. Why is the debit side of the analysed petty cash book smaller than the credit side?
5. Explain how the petty cash book is both part of the double entry system and also a book of prime entry.
6. State two examples of sundry expenses.
7. Where are the debit entries in the petty cash book also posted?
8. Where are the total credits in the petty cash book also posted?

UNIT ASSESSMENT QUESTION 1

J. Follows Printing Services (JFPS) is located in Stafford. The business produces a wide range of printed documents such as letterheads, business cards, invitations, menus and brochures. During the first two weeks of October 2000, the following petty cash transactions occurred:

- 2.10 £100 cash withdrawn from the bank for petty cash;
- 3.10 £3.50 paid to register a letter at the Post Office (voucher no. 43);
- 5.10 £12.00 paid for petrol (voucher no. 44);
- 10.10 £32.80 paid for assorted stationery (voucher no. 45);
- 11.10 £21.00 paid for taxi fare (voucher no. 46);
- 12.10 £13.00 paid to window cleaner (voucher no. 47);
- 12.10 £100 cash withdrawn from the bank for petty cash;
- 13.10 £50.00 paid to a landscape gardener for tidying grounds (voucher no. 48);
- 15.10 £20.00 paid for cleaning materials (voucher no. 49).

(a) **Explain the advantage to JFPS of using a petty cash book.**
(b) (i) **Draw up a suitable petty cash book with analysis columns to show expenditure on the above items; (ii) enter the transactions in the petty cash book and total the columns.**

UNIT ASSESSMENT QUESTION 2

Acorn Shopfitters is owned by Ann and Bob Bremner. They employ 8 fitters and have an office in Stoke-on-Trent. Ann Bremner is the office manager and she is also responsible for keeping financial records. Acorn Shopfitters operates a petty cash system and an extract from the petty cash book is shown in Figure 13.6.

Figure 13.6 *An extract from the petty cash book for Acorn Shopfitters*

PETTY CASH BOOK (page 9)

Receipts	Folio	Date	Details	Voucher no.	Total payments	Motor expenses	Sundry expenses	Stationery	Folio	Ledger account
£					£	£	£	£		£
100.00	CB31	10.7								
		10.7	Envelopes	22	6.80			6.80		
		11.7	Petrol	23	25.00	25.00				
		11.7	Tea and coffee	24	8.50		8.50			
		12.7	Milk bill	25	18.30		18.30			
		13.7	Petrol	26	34.00	34.00				
100.00	CB31	14.7								
		14.7	T. Burton Ltd	27	23.50				PL6	23.50
		14.7	Meal with client	28	29.80		29.80			
						NL12	NL18	NL17		

(a) **Complete the double entry for the receipts of cash on 10.7 and 14.7.**
(b) **Calculate the column totals in the petty cash book.**
(c) **Post the petty cash payments to the appropriate ledgers of Acorn Shopfitters.**

Recording journal transactions

unitobjectives

To understand:
- the purpose of the journal;
- how to record transactions in the journal;
- how to post journal entries to the ledgers.

What is the journal?

The JOURNAL is a **book of prime entry**. It is used to record details of non-routine transactions that are not entered in the cash book or in other day books. Sometimes the journal is also known as the **journal proper** or **general journal**. When transactions are recorded in the journal, a **narrative** is written which describes the details. This acts as a diary of events and is useful as a means of tracing and checking transactions.

A number of different types of transaction might be recorded in the journal. They are likely to be one-off or non-routine transactions which do not occur on a regular basis.

- **Opening entries** These relate to the start of a business. A common example is the recording of how much capital an owner introduces into the business when it is set up.
- **Closing entries** These are made at the end of a financial year when the profit or loss of a business is determined. At this time, accounts in the nominal ledger are **closed off** and the balances are transferred to the **trading and profit and loss account** (see unit 17). A journal entry is made to record this transfer.
- **Purchase of fixed assets on credit** Some businesses record expenditure on fixed assets, such as vehicles or computers, in the journal.
- **Sale of fixed assets** Sometimes businesses sell fixed assets if they are no longer required (see unit 21). The details of the sale are recorded in the journal.
- **Correction of errors** When recording transactions, mistakes can occur. For example, a bookkeeper might only record the debit side of a transaction or an entry might be posted to the wrong account. The journal is used to record the correction of such errors.
- **Adjustments** At the end of a financial year it is sometimes necessary to make adjustments to certain figures. For example, a business might sell goods on credit to a customer who then fails to pay. The journal is used to record this adjustment as a bad debt (see unit 20). Other adjustments include the provision for depreciation (a fall in value of a fixed asset - see unit 22), accruals (amounts still due at the end of the accounting period) and prepayments (advance payments for resources not yet used - see unit 19).
- **Other transactions** Examples of other non-routine transactions that might be recorded in the journal include the receipt and repayment of bank loans. Also included are 'expenses charged to owner's drawings'. These might arise if, for example, a business owner uses business facilities, such as a car, for private reasons. The proportion of car usage that is private is charged to the owner as drawings and is recorded in the journal. The remainder is treated as a business expense.

The layout of the journal

The layout of the journal is different from other day books. Figure 14.1 shows an example of a layout with five columns. The following information is included:
- the date of the journal entry;
- the name of the account to be debited and the amount;
- the name of the account to be credited and the amount;
- the folio for each account;
- a description of the transaction (or narrative) which might include reference to the relevant source document.

In this example, the name of the account to be debited is written on the first line and the name of the account to be credited on the second line. Many bookkeepers indent the second line to emphasise the distinction between debit and credit. Because each journal entry stands alone as a record of a transaction, it is ruled off to separate it from the next entry.

Figure 14.1 *Layout of the journal*

	JOURNAL			
Date	**Details**	**Folio**	**Debit**	**Credit**
			£	£
	Name of the account to be debited			
	Name of the account to be credited			
	Narrative description of the transaction			

QUESTION 1

Creely Signs, based in West London, makes and supplies signs for businesses. Examples of the products which the company sells to its customers include shop signs, perspex lettering, plastic menu cards and commercial vehicle graphics. The business has recently employed a part-time bookkeeper to reduce the burden of work on the owner, Nicholas Creely. During December, the following transactions occurred.

1. Van bought on credit for £7,800 (1.12).
2. Signs sold to a customer on credit for £850 (5.12).
3. £457 paid to a regular supplier for sheets of perspex bought on credit (15.12).
4. £46 damaged perspex returned to the supplier (17.12).
5. Error correction, £340 posted to the B. James customer account instead of the R. James account (18.12).
6. £500 payment to bank in settlement of outstanding loan (20.12).
7. Cash sale of 50 menu cards (21.12).

(a) Which of the listed transactions might be recorded in the journal?
(b) In which books of prime entry should the other transactions be entered?

Recording and posting journal transactions

Figure 14.2 shows the role of the journal in the bookkeeping process. Entries are made using information from source documents such as invoices. Sometimes a memo or a letter might be the source document if, for example, someone writes to the bookkeeper pointing out an error.

There is a debit and a credit entry for each transaction. However, the journal is **not** itself part of the double entry system. Entries shown on the **debit** side of the journal are posted to the **debit** side of accounts in the ledgers or the cash book. Similarly, entries shown on the **credit** side of the journal are posted to the **credit** side of accounts in the ledgers or the cash book.

Recording and posting an opening entry

In order to illustrate how information is recorded in the journal, consider the example of Steven Butterworth who has set up a plumbing business in Kent. On 1 March 2000 he introduced £3,000 of capital into the business. £2,900 was placed in a business bank account and £100 was held in cash. The journal entries for this transaction are shown in Figure 14.3.

- The date of the transaction is shown in the date column.
- In the details column, the names of the accounts to be debited and credited are written. In this case, two accounts are debited. This is because some of the capital introduced by Steven was held

Figure 14.2 *Journal transactions*

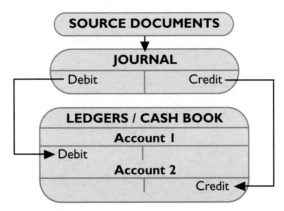

as cash and the rest was paid into the bank. Therefore, the cash account is debited with £100 and the bank account is debited with £2,900. They are debit entries because they refer to an increase in assets.

- The capital account is credited with £3,000. It is a credit entry because the owner has introduced £3,000 capital.
- The folios show where the journal entries are posted. Both debit entries are posted to page 1 in the cash book. The credit entry is posted to page 2 in the nominal ledger.
- The narrative, shown in italics, explains that the journal entry relates to the value of assets and liabilities of the business on the 1 March 2000. It is an opening entry.
- It is usual to total and underline an opening entry.

Figure 14.3 *Journal and ledger entries for S. Butterworth*

	JOURNAL			
Date	**Details**	**Folio**	**Debit**	**Credit**
2000			£	£
1.3	Cash	CB1	100	
	Bank	CB1	2,900	
	Capital	NL2		3,000
	Assets and liabilities at		3,000	3,000
	the start of business			

	Debit		CASH BOOK (page 1)				Credit		
Date	**Details**	**Folio**	**Cash**	**Bank**	**Date**	**Details**	**Folio**	**Cash**	**Bank**
2000			£	£				£	£
1.3	Capital	NL2		2,900					
1.3	Capital	NL2	100						

NOMINAL LEDGER

Dr Capital Account (page 2) **Cr**

	£		£
		1.3 Bank CB1	3,000

QUESTION 2

Jenny Moss has set up a manufacturing business that specialises in high quality women's underwear. She trades as Moss Garments. Figure 14.4 is the opening journal entry for Moss Garments. It shows that Jenny introduced £5,000 of her own money as capital. She deposited the whole amount in the bank.

Figure 14.4 *Journal entry for Moss Garments*

JOURNAL				
Date	Details	Folio	Debit	Credit
			£	£
10.6	Bank	CB1	5,000	
	Capital	NL2		5,000
	Assets and liabilities at the start of business		5,000	5,000

(a) Explain why the entry in the cash book is a debit.
(b) Post the journal items to the appropriate accounts in the cash book and the nominal ledger.

Recording and posting the purchase of fixed assets

Robinsons Tyres is a tyre wholesaler in Swansea. On 25 May, the company purchased a secondhand delivery van for £2,950. The van, registration number HYG 299E, was bought on credit from P. Jenkins, a local dealer. The journal and ledger entries for this transaction are shown in Figure 14.5.
- The date of the transaction is shown in the date column.
- The van account of Robinsons Tyres is debited with £2,950. It is a debit entry because it represents an increase in assets, ie a van.
- The P. Jenkins account is credited with £2,950. It is a credit entry because there is an increase in a liability, ie £2,950 is owed to the supplier, P. Jenkins.
- The folios show that the debit entry is posted to page 34 of the nominal ledger. The credit entry is posted to page 29 of the nominal ledger. Note that in this example the business posts the credit purchase of a fixed asset to a supplier account in the nominal ledger. It reserves the purchases ledger for the accounts of **trade creditors**, ie suppliers of goods intended for resale.
- The narrative explains that the journal transaction relates to the purchase of a van for the business. The van registration is included so there is no uncertainty as to which vehicle the entry refers.
- The journal entry is ruled off to separate it from the next entry.

QUESTION 3

Laura Johnson has set up a fast food business. She sells food from a van which she has converted into a mobile kitchen. On 14 August 2000 she introduced £4,000 capital into the business. She placed £2,000 in the bank and held £2,000 in cash. The next day, 15 August, she purchased an old van on credit from a commercial vehicle dealer, Watford Van Sales. The cost was £1,350, payable in one month's time.

(a) Record in the journal the opening entries for Laura on 14 August 2000. (Omit page numbers in the folio entries.)
(b) Make a journal entry for the purchase of the van on 15 August.

Figure 14.5 *Journal and ledger entries for Robinsons Tyres*

JOURNAL				
Date	Details	Folio	Debit	Credit
2000			£	£
25.5	Van	NL34	2,950	
	P. Jenkins	NL29		2,950
	Purchase of delivery van			
	reg. no. HYG 299E			

NOMINAL LEDGER

Dr	Van Account (page 34)		Cr	
		£		£
25.5 P. Jenkins NL29		2,950		

Dr	P. Jenkins (page 29)		Cr	
		£		£
			25.5 Van NL34	2,950

Recording and posting the correction of errors

Many different types of error can be made when recording business transactions. The correction of such errors is explained in unit 28. To illustrate how a relatively simple, **misposting** error is corrected, consider the example of Roberts Engineering. This is a small manufacturing company that makes equipment for dentists. On 4 May 2000 the bookkeeper noticed that an entry had been debited to the wrong account by mistake. Following a credit sale, the account of L. Simmonds should have been debited with £49.50. But, due to an error, the account of J. Simmons was debited. So, according to the ledger accounts, it appeared that J. Simmons owed the money rather than L. Simmonds. The journal entries required to correct this error are shown in Figure 14.6.

Figure 14.6 *Journal and ledger entries for Roberts Engineering*

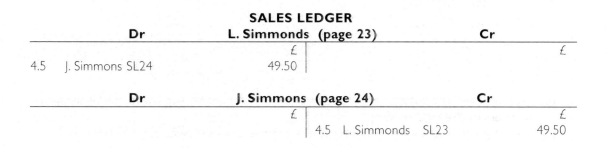

JOURNAL				
Date	Details	Folio	Debit	Credit
			£	£
4.5	L. Simmonds	SL23	49.50	
	J. Simmons	SL24		49.50
	Correction of mispost			
	invoice 00956			

SALES LEDGER

Dr	L. Simmonds (page 23)		Cr	
		£		£
4.5 J. Simmons SL24		49.50		

Dr	J. Simmons (page 24)		Cr	
		£		£
			4.5 L. Simmonds SL23	49.50

- The date of the correction is written in the date column.
- The name of the account to be debited is L. Simmonds. The purpose of this entry is to show that it was L. Simmonds who bought goods and owes money to Roberts Engineering.
- The name of the account to be credited is J. Simmons. The purpose of this entry is to cancel the debit entry made in error, ie to show that J. Simmons does not owe £49.50.
- The folios show that the debit entry is posted to page 23 in the sales ledger and the credit entry is posted to page 24 in the sales ledger.
- The narrative explains that the journal entry is made to correct a posting error.

summary questions

1. What is the role of the journal in the bookkeeping process?
2. State four types of transaction that might be recorded in the journal.
3. Suggest three reasons why the journal is useful?
4. Describe the layout of the journal.
5. What is recorded in the details column of the journal?
6. What is the purpose of the narrative written in the journal?
7. On which side of ledger accounts are debit entries in the journal posted?
8. Give an example of a journal entry that might be posted to the cash book.
9. In which ledger would the account of a fixed asset such as a van be found?
10. In which ledger(s) might the account of a supplier of a fixed asset be found?

UNIT ASSESSMENT QUESTION 1

Weston Skip Hire is based in Oxfordshire. In addition to hiring out waste skips, the business undertakes contract work, site clearance and recycling. Below are described two events which required journal entries.

- Weston Skip Hire bought a new computer on credit for £2,500 from Kidlington Computers. This transaction took place on 23 March 2000 and the computer model number was DS99747.
- The bookkeeper noticed that an error in posting had been made. The account of P. Johnson had been debited with £350 by mistake. The amount was actually owed by T. Jackson. The error was corrected on 27 March 2000.

(a) **Make the necessary journal entries for the two transactions. (Omit page numbers in the folio entries.)**
(b) **Explain the reasons why a journal entry was necessary on 27 March 2000.**

UNIT ASSESSMENT QUESTION 2

Carla Moretti owns a cafe in Scarborough. In February 2001, she made two journal entries. They are shown in Figure 14.7. One relates to a bank loan which was used to fund repairs to the cafe roof. The other relates to a new oven which was bought on credit from the Cooker Warehouse.

Figure 14.7 *Journal entries for Carla Moretti's bakery*

	JOURNAL			
Date	Details	Folio	Debit	Credit
2001			£	£
21.2	Bank	CB12	3,000	
	Loan account	NL28		3,000
	Loan to pay for roof repairs			
25.2	Oven	NL10	1,450	
	Cooker Warehouse	NL15		1,450
	Purchase of new oven			

(a) **Post the journal items to the relevant accounts in the ledgers and the cash book.**

(b) **Explain why the information contained in the journal is useful for Carla's business.**

key terms

Journal - the book of prime entry that is used to record details of non-routine transactions that are not entered in the cash book or other day books.

unit 15

Balancing accounts

unitobjectives

To understand:
- why accounts are balanced;
- how ledger accounts are balanced;
- how the cash books are balanced.

Why are accounts balanced?

Periodically, all the accounts contained in the double entry system are BALANCED or BALANCED OFF. Balancing the accounts ensures that the totals of the credits and debits are equal. This process involves adding up the debits and the credits in the T accounts. If the totals are not the same, a BALANCE is inserted to make them equal.

Balancing the accounts is a vital part of the bookkeeping process. The balances in the ledgers and cash books are used by accountants to produce the **trial balance** (see unit 16). This provides a check on the arithmetic accuracy of the bookkeeping. It is also an important stage in the production of the **profit and loss account** and the **balance sheet** (see unit 17).

Another reason for balancing the cash books is to check that the balances match the actual cash in hand and the balance on the bank statement. This helps prevent fraud and is a useful means of keeping control over cash transactions. A process known as **bank reconciliation** (see unit 18) is used to cross-check the balance on the bank account in the cash book with the balance on the bank statement. In practice it is unlikely that these balances will be exactly the same because of delays in processing payments through the banking system.

Balancing ledger accounts where debits and credits are equal

Figure 15.1 shows the account of a customer, S. Phillips, in the sales ledger of a wholesaler, A. Martin & Co. It shows that S. Phillips made three purchases on credit from A. Martin & Co in September. It also shows that S. Phillips paid A. Martin & Co £440 at the end of the month to settle the account.

Figure 15.1 *The account of S. Phillips, a customer of A. Martin & Co*

SALES LEDGER

Dr			S. Phillips		Cr
		£			£
10.9	Sales	98	30.9	Bank	440
19.9	Sales	210			
26.9	Sales	132			
		440			440

The total debits and credits are equal in this account. Therefore the following steps are taken to balance the account.
- The debits are added together and the total, £440, is written below.
- The credit total, £440, is written on the same line as the debit total.
- Both totals are written with a single line above and a double underline below.

Sometimes there might be just one entry on each side of an account. If the two entries are equal, it is common practice to double underline the entries on both sides in order to show that the account is balanced. An example is given in Figure 15.2. It is the account of a customer, Bolland & Son, in a sales ledger. On 23 September Bolland & Son bought goods on credit for £230 and paid for them on 30 September.

Figure 15.2 *The balanced account of Bolland & Son*

SALES LEDGER

Dr		Bolland & Son		Cr	
		£			£
13.9 Sales		230	30.9 Bank		230

QUESTION 1

Body Beautiful is a business that supplies a range of equipment for health clubs and gyms. Most of its sales are on credit and customers settle their accounts every month. Two customer accounts are shown in Figure 15.3.

Figure 15.3 *Customer accounts of Body Beautiful*

SALES LEDGER

Dr		Roberts Gymnasium		Cr	
		£			£
3.4 Sales		220	30.4 Bank		836
10.4 Sales		187			
16.4 Sales		199			
23.4 Sales		230			

Dr		Kendal Beauty Centre		Cr	
		£			£
17.4 Sales		228	30.4 Bank		228

(a) Balance the two customer accounts.
(b) Explain why the procedure is different for the two accounts.

Balancing ledger accounts where debits and credits are not equal – sales ledger accounts

Often the totals of debits and credits in accounts are not equal. For example, Figure 15.4 shows the sales ledger account of G. Carpenter, a customer of A. Martin & Co. In this account, the debit total is greater than the credit total.

Figure 15.4 *The account of G. Carpenter, a customer of A. Martin & Co*

SALES LEDGER

Dr		G. Carpenter		Cr	
		£			£
2.9 Sales		332	25.9 Bank		500
10.9 Sales		219			
27.9 Sales		281			

Figure 15.5 *The balanced account of G. Carpenter*

SALES LEDGER

Dr		£		Cr	£
2.9	Sales	332	25.9 Bank		500
10.9	Sales	219			
27.9	Sales	281	30.9 Balance c/d		332
		832			832
1.10	Balance b/d	332			

G. Carpenter

In order to balance the account, the steps shown in Figure 15.5 are taken.
- The debits and credits are added up. The larger total, £832, is written on both sides of the account and is double underlined.
- The smaller total is subtracted from the larger total to find the balance. In this account it is £332 (£832 - £500). The balance is entered on the side with the smallest total. In this case it is included on the credit side. The term BALANCE C/D is written next to it. Note that c/d is an abbreviation for 'carried down'. The date of the entry is the last day of the period, in this case the last day of September.
- The balance c/d is added to the credit entries in the account.
- The balancing procedure is completed by entering the balance underneath the total on the opposite side to the balance c/d. The term BALANCE B/D is written next to it. Note that b/d is an abbreviation for 'brought down'. It is a **debit balance** because it is on the **debit side** of the account. The date of this entry is the first day of the next period, in this case October 1.

The balance in Figure 15.5 is a debit balance because the total of debits is greater than the total of credits. It shows that, at the start of the next period, the customer G. Carpenter is a **trade debtor**, owing £332 to A. Martin & Co. The balance b/d is the first entry on the debit side in the account for October. Debit balances are typical of customer accounts in the sales ledger because goods are purchased on credit and generally there will be unpaid invoices outstanding.

If there is no balance b/d, it means that the customer has settled the account in full during the period in question. A credit balance on a customer account in the sales ledger is unlikely but not impossible. It could occur, for instance, if a customer returns some goods after payment is made. If this happens, the credit note would be entered on the credit side of the customer account and so cause the credit total to be greater than the debit total.

QUESTION 2

The Tile Warehouse in Gateshead sells a wide range of tiles for floors, kitchens and bathrooms. One of the Warehouse's trade customers is Benny Dodds. An extract from his account is shown in Figure 15.6.

Figure 15.6 *Benny Dodds' account, a customer of the Tile Warehouse*

SALES LEDGER

Dr		£		Cr	£
1.7	Sales	280	18.7 Bank		500
4.7	Sales	230	28.7 Bank		450
9.7	Sales	389			
19.7	Sales	261			

Benny Dodds

(a) Balance the account of Benny Dodds.
(b) Explain what 'balance b/d' in the Benny Dodds account means.

Balancing ledger accounts where debits and credits are not equal – purchases ledger accounts

The procedure for balancing supplier accounts in the purchases ledger is similar to that used for customer accounts in the sales ledger. Consider the example of Jackson Bros, a supplier of goods to the wholesaler A. Martin & Co. The account with this supplier is shown in Figure 15.7. It shows that:

- the balance b/d was £140 meaning that, at the beginning of the trading period, A. Martin & Co owed £140 to Jackson Bros; in other words, Jackson Bros was a **trade creditor**;
- A. Martin & Co made two credit purchases during the month for £250 and £420;
- A. Martin & Co paid Jackson Bros £570 on 29 March;
- A. Martin & Co received a cash discount of £30 on the payment.

Figure 15.7 *Jackson Bros account, a supplier to A. Martin & Co*

PURCHASES LEGER

Dr		£		Jackson Bros	Cr	£
29.3	Bank	570	1.3	Balance b/d		140
29.3	Discount received	30	18.3	Purchases		250
			27.3	Purchases		420

In order to balance the account:

- the balance between the total debits and the total credits is calculated. In this case it is a credit balance of £210 (£810 - £600) because total credits are greater than total debits;
- the balance is entered as 'Balance c/d' on the side of the account with the lowest total, ie the debit side, to make the totals balance. The entry date is the end of the month, ie 31 March;
- the totals are entered and double underlined;
- the 'Balance b/d' is entered on the credit side of the account underneath the totals. It becomes
- the first credit entry at the start of the next trading period, ie 1 April.

The balanced account is shown in Figure 15.8.

Figure 15.8 *The balanced Jackson Bros account*

PURCHASES LEDGER

Dr		£		Jackson Bros	Cr	£
29.3	Bank	570	1.3	Balance b/d		140
29.3	Discount received	30	18.3	Purchases		250
31.3	Balance c/d	210	27.3	Purchases		420
		810				810
			1.4	Balance b/d		210

It is likely that most supplier accounts in the purchases ledger will have **credit balances**. This is because suppliers provide goods on credit and are therefore generally owed money by their customers.

If there is no balance b/d in a purchases ledger account it means that the business has paid everything owed to the particular supplier. A debit balance on a supplier account is unlikely to occur, but might happen if some goods are returned to the supplier after payment is made. Under these circumstances, the credit note would be entered as a debit in the supplier account and would cause the debit total to be greater than the credit total.

Balancing ledger accounts where debits and credits are not equal – nominal ledger accounts

The procedure for balancing accounts in the nominal ledger is similar to that for the sales and purchases ledgers. The balances b/d might be debit or credit balances depending on the nature of the account. Accounts for assets, expenses and drawings generally have debit balances at the end of a trading period. Accounts for capital, revenue and liabilities generally have credit balances.

To illustrate how accounts in the nominal ledger are balanced, consider the example of an account of an asset that belongs to A. Martin & Co (see Figure 15.9). It contains details of just one transaction, the purchase of an asset, in this case a delivery van. Note that the balance c/d is written on the same line as the debit entry. There is a debit balance on this account. It shows that A. Martin & Co owns a van that cost £9,860.

Figure 15.9 *A debit balance on an asset account*

NOMINAL LEDGER

Dr		Van Account		Cr	
			£		£
10.3	Bank		9,860	31.3 Balance c/d	9,860
1.4	Balance b/d		9,860		

Figure 15.10 is an account of a liability. It shows that A. Martin & Co owes £2,980 to a bank. At the start of the month in question, a credit balance of £3,320 was brought down. In other words, this was the outstanding bank loan. During the month, £340 of the loan was repaid and this is shown by the debit entry. The credit balance b/d represents that part of the loan still unpaid.

Figure 15.10 *A credit balance on a liabilities account*

NOMINAL LEDGER

Dr		Loan Account		Cr	
			£		£
24.3	Bank		340	1.3 Balance b/d	3,320
31.3	Balance c/d		2,980		
			3,320		3,320
				1.4 Balance b/d	2,980

QUESTION 3

Gerald and Ruby Armstrong run a guest house in Settle, North Yorkshire. Most of their guests pay by cash but they do allow some business customers 30 days credit. Figure 15.11 shows three nominal ledger accounts for their business.

Figure 15.11 *Three accounts from the nominal ledger of Gerald and Ruby Armstrong*

NOMINAL LEDGER

Dr		Property Repairs Account		Cr	
			£		£
12.2	Bank		2,500		

Dr		Sales Account		Cr	
			£		£
		1.2	Balance b/d		2,100
		14.2	Cash sales		990
		26.2	Credit sales		430

Dr		Capital Account		Cr	
			£		£
		1.2	Balance b/d		132,210
		4.2	Bank		2,000

(a) Balance the three accounts.
(b) Explain what the balances mean.

Balancing the cash book

The cash book contains a business's cash account and bank account. To illustrate how the cash book is balanced, consider the example in Figure 15.12. This is an extract from the two column cash book of A. Martin & Co. It lists payments and receipts for one month. Folios are ignored. The debit balances b/d from the previous trading period are £320 on the cash account and £1,980 on the bank account. On the debit side of the cash book there are entries showing both cash receipts and cheque receipts. On the credit side there is a range of expenses and payments to suppliers.

The process of balancing the accounts in the cash book is exactly the same as in the ledger accounts. The debits and the credits are totalled and the balances are entered on the side with the lowest total. In this case, a cash balance of £125 and a bank balance of £1,427 are entered on the credit side. The debit balances b/d on 1 August mean that A. Martin & Co's business had £125 cash in hand and £1,427 in the bank. Note that, in other circumstances, the bank balance b/d could occur on the credit side. This would indicate that the bank account was overdrawn.

Figure 15.12 *A page from the cash book of A. Martin & Co*

Date	Details	Cash £	Bank £	Date	Details	Cash £	Bank £
1.7	Balances b/d	320	1,980	1.7	Rent		500
4.7	Sales	120		1.7	Petty cash	200	
5.7	S. Phillips		219	5.7	Carl Traders		218
10.7	Sales	135		24.7	Loan account		340
25.7	Bolland & Son		310	25.7	Jackson Bros		540
27.7	L. Ostenstad		265	27.7	Wages	250	
28.7	G. Carpenter		251	31.7	Balances c/d	125	1,427
		575	3,025			575	3,025
1.8	Balances b/d	125	1,427				

QUESTION 4

Holgate Sports supplies a range of sports equipment and accessories to independent retailers in the East Midlands. Most customers buy goods on credit but there are some occasional cash sales. A page from the cash book of Holgate Sports is shown in Figure 15.13.

Figure 15.13 *Cash book of Holgate Sports*

Date	Details	Cash £	Bank £	Date	Details	Cash £	Bank £
1.5	Balances b/d	120	320	1.5	T. Winters		320
5.5	Sales	150		4.5	Eastern Electricity		145
11.5	B. Gall		730	12.5	Soccer Supplies		250
18.5	Terry Sports		520	16.5	Petty cash	200	
22.5	Sales	90		22.5	Royal Insurance		129
28.5	B. Foster		510	23.5	Fullers Footwear		340
31.5	T. Wells		488	31.5	Wages		1,000
				31.5	Buttermead Sports		241

(a) Balance the cash account and the bank account for Holgate Sports.
(b) Explain what the balances mean.

Balancing the petty cash book

Like the cash book, the petty cash book is part of the double entry system and is balanced periodically. A page from the analysed cash book of A. Martin & Co is shown in Figure 15.14. The business operates an imprest system. The imprest amount is £200 and this is brought down from the previous trading period. To balance the petty cash book the following steps are taken.

- A line is drawn across all the columns containing payments, including the total column.
- All the payments columns are totalled, including the total column.
- The overall total in the total column (£153.80) is checked against the sum of the totals in the analysed columns (£71.00 + £50.00 + £9.70 + £8.30 + £14.80 = £153.80).
- A double underline is drawn across all the payments columns except the total column.
- Because £153.80 has been used from petty cash, this amount needs to be replaced so that the imprest amount is replenished. The entry in the petty cash book in the receipts column for £153.80 on 30 September shows this transaction.
- The entries in the receipts column are added together and the total is entered. In this case it is £353.80. It is double underlined.
- The balance c/d is entered. This is the imprest amount (£200) and the entry is the last in the trading period, ie on 30 September.
- The balance c/d is added to the total in the total column. This overall total, £353.80 (£153.80 + £200) is then written in the total column and double underlined.
- The balance b/d (£200) is written in the receipts column against the start date of the next trading period, 1 October.

Figure 15.14 *A page from the petty cash book of A. Martin & Co*

PETTY CASH BOOK

Receipts	Date	Details	Vou.	Total	Petrol	Cleaning	Stationery	Sundries	Folio	Ledger
£				£	£	£	£	£		£
200.00	1.9	Balance b/d								
	2.9	Stamps	23	5.20				5.20		
	5.9	Cleaning	24	30.00		30.00				
	11.9	Petrol	25	30.00	30.00					
	12.9	Window cleaner	26	20.00		20.00				
	19.9	Petrol	27	16.00	16.00					
	23.9	T. Jones	28	14.80					PL12	14.80
	24.9	Coffee	29	3.10				3.10		
	29.9	Envelopes	30	9.70			9.70			
	30.9	Petrol	31	25.00	25.00					
				153.80	71.00	50.00	9.70	8.30		14.80
153.80	30.9	Cash								
	30.9	Balance c/d		200.00						
353.80				353.80						
200.00	1.10	Balance b/d								

UNIT ASSESSMENT   QUESTION 1

Freshpack Food operates from a factory unit in Nantwich, Cheshire. The business supplies supermarkets and large retailers with pre-packed salads and fresh vegetables. The produce is either bought from local farms or imported from Mediterranean countries. Figure 15.15 shows some accounts from Freshpack Food's purchases ledger and nominal ledger.

Figure 15.15 *Accounts from Freshpack Food's ledgers*

PURCHASES LEDGER

Dr		Rode Heath Farm			Cr	
		£				£
13.6	Bank	1,000	1.6	Balance b/d		1,760
15.6	Purchases returns	180	6.6	Purchases		345
27.6	Bank	500	18.6	Purchases		480

Dr		Prenton Farm			Cr	
		£				£
30.6	Bank	1,340	1.6	Balance b/d		1,340
			19.6	Purchases		1,490

Dr		San Pedro Foods			Cr	
		£				£
17.6	Bank	2,000	1.6	Balance b/d		1,970
28.6	Bank	2,000	9.6	Purchases		1,870
			18.6	Purchases		1,540

NOMINAL LEDGER

Dr		Telephone Account			Cr	
		£				£
1.6	Balance b/d	231				
23.6	Bank	278				

Dr		Insurance Account			Cr	
		£				£
26.6	Bank	1,270				

Dr		Loan Account			Cr	
		£				£
12.6	Bank	5,500	1.6	Balance b/d		5,500

(a) Balance the ledger accounts (on the last day of the month in question).
(b) How are the balances likely to be used by the business?

key terms

Balance - the difference between the total credits and total debits in an account.
Balance b/d - the balance entered under the total on the opposite side of the account to the balance c/d, at the start of a new time period in the account.
Balance c/d - the balance entered on the side of the account with the lowest total to ensure it equals the greater total.
Balancing the accounts - the process of working out the balance between debits and credits and entering the balance c/d and the balance b/d. The process is also known as **balancing off**.

UNIT ASSESSMENT QUESTION 2

North Quay Recoveries is based in Torquay and is owned by Larry Miles. The business has a contract with a national provider of breakdown services to provide cover in the South West. North Quay Recoveries uses a cash book to record receipts and payments and it also operates a petty cash system. The cash books are balanced every week. Figure 15.16 shows an extract from the cash book and petty cash book.

Figure 15.16 *Cash book and petty cash book for North Quay Recoveries*

	Debit			CASH BOOK		Credit		
Date	Details	Cash	Bank	Date	Details	Cash	Bank
		£	£			£	£
2.1	Balances b/d	150	3,490	3.1	Devon CC		890
3.1	Sales	230	650	4.1	CD Motors	124	
4.1	L. Jones		258	4.1	Bensons		320
4.1	Sales	165	440	6.1	Devon Cars	87	
5.1	National Recovery		1,800	6.1	Wages		2,490
7.1	Sales	120	750	6.1	Petty cash	135	

Receipts	Date	Details	Vou.	Total	Drawings	Carriage	Stationery	Sundries	Folio	Ledger
£				£	£	£	£	£		£
200.00	2.1	Balance b/d								
	2.1	Paper	15	21.50			21.50			
	2.1	L. Miles	16	20.00	20.00					
	3.1	Coffee	17	2.70				2.70		
	3.1	Carriage	18	12.00		12.00				
	4.1	L. Miles	19	30.00	30.00					
	5.1	T. Peel	20	11.50					PL5	11.50
	6.1	Carriage	21	12.30		12.30				
	6.1	L. Miles	22	20.00	20.00					
	6.1	Milk	23	5.00				5.00		
135.00	6.1	Cash								

(PETTY CASH BOOK)

(a) **Balance the cash book.**
(b) **Balance the petty cash book.**
(c) **Explain why it is useful for North Quay Recoveries to balance the cash books.**

summary questions

1. Describe the action required to balance an account when debits equal credits.
2. What action is required if a T account contains one equal entry on either side of the account?
3. What action is required to balance an account when debits and credits are not equal?
4. Where is the balance b/d entered?
5. Against what date is the balance b/d written?
6. Explain why the balance b/d in the sales ledger is likely to be a debit balance.
7. Explain why the balance b/d in the purchases ledger is likely to be a credit balance.
8. Under what circumstances might the balance b/d in the nominal ledger be a debit balance?
9. What does a credit balance in the cash book show?
10. Describe the action required to balance the petty cash book.

unit 16

The trial balance

unit objectives

To understand:
- the nature and importance of the trial balance;
- the reasons for producing a trial balance;
- how to construct a trial balance;
- how to carry out checks when the trial balance does not balance;
- that errors might exist even when the trial balance does balance.

What is the trial balance?

The TRIAL BALANCE consists of two columns of figures listed under the headings debits and credits. The figures are balances extracted from a business's ledger accounts. Debit entries represent a business's assets, expenses or drawings. Credit entries represent its revenue, liabilities or capital.

The most important feature of a trial balance is that the total of debits should be the same as the total of credits, ie they should **balance**. This results from the double entry system of bookkeeping in which every transaction is recorded twice, once as a debit and again as a credit. For example, if a business sells some goods for £100, the sale is recorded as a credit and the money received is recorded as a debit.

An example of a trial balance is shown in Figure 16.1. This trial balance is for Manning's Petcare Centre, a business which operates a boarding kennel and cattery. The total of debits, £123,607 is equal to the total of credits, £123,607. An example of a debit entry in the trial balance is premises, £48,000. This is an asset. The total of Manning's Petcare Centre's trade creditors on 31 December 2000 is £3,432. This is a credit entry and is a liability.

Figure 16.1 *Trial balance for Manning's Petcare Centre* ● ● ●

Manning's Petcare Centre
Trial Balance as at 31.12.00

The heading should always have the name of the business and the date on which the trial balance is drawn.

	Debit £	Credit £
Sales		73,991
Purchases	11,880	
Wages	15,020	
Motor expenses	3,400	
Advertising	1,299	
Premises	48,000	
Equipment	12,564	
Trade debtors	2,001	
Bank deposit	6,443	
Trade creditors		3,432
Bank loan		10,000
Capital		36,184
Drawings	23,000	
	123,607	123,607

Debit and credit are sometimes abbreviated to Dr and Cr.

Debit and credit balances extracted from the ledger accounts.

When the account balances, the total credits equal the total debits. These are double underlined.

What are the reasons for producing a trial balance?

In accounting the trial balance has a number of purposes.

Checking accuracy The trial balance 'tests' the arithmetic accuracy of a business's bookkeeping. When balances are extracted from ledger accounts, the total of all the debit entries should be equal to the total of all the credit entries. If they are different then an error must have been made. For example, a transaction might have been entered on the debit side but omitted on the credit side. In this case, the trial balance would not balance because the total value of debits would be greater than the total value of credits.

Identifying important accounting information For a given accounting period, the trial balance shows the totals for key accounting data. For example, the trial balance for Manning's Petcare Centre, in Figure 16.1, shows the following totals on the debit side:
- bank - the business has £6,443 in the bank;
- equipment - the business has bought equipment costing £12,564;
- trade debtors - the business is owed £2,001 by customers.

On the credit side of the trial balance, some examples are:
- sales - the total value of sales for the year was £73,991;
- trade creditors - the business owes £3,432 to its suppliers;
- bank loan - the business owes £10,000 to a bank.

Preparing final accounts Accountants use the trial balance to produce the final accounts, ie the profit and loss account and the balance sheet (see unit 17). The trial balance is a link between the bookkeeping process and the final accounts.

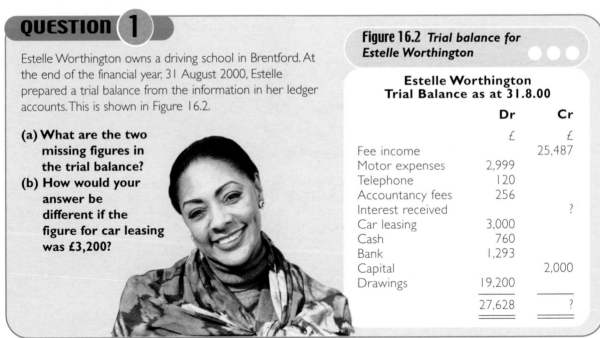

QUESTION 1

Estelle Worthington owns a driving school in Brentford. At the end of the financial year, 31 August 2000, Estelle prepared a trial balance from the information in her ledger accounts. This is shown in Figure 16.2.

(a) What are the two missing figures in the trial balance?

(b) How would your answer be different if the figure for car leasing was £3,200?

Figure 16.2 *Trial balance for Estelle Worthington*

Estelle Worthington
Trial Balance as at 31.8.00

	Dr	Cr
	£	£
Fee income		25,487
Motor expenses	2,999	
Telephone	120	
Accountancy fees	256	
Interest received		?
Car leasing	3,000	
Cash	760	
Bank	1,293	
Capital		2,000
Drawings	19,200	
	27,628	?

How is the trial balance constructed?

The trial balance is extracted from the accounting records of a business. Businesses often produce a trial balance at the end of a period such as six months, or at the end of the financial year. To demonstrate how a trial balance is extracted from ledger accounts, consider the following example.

Rachel Watson sets up a business on 1 May 2000 to provide specialist floral decorations for important functions. A list of her transactions for the first trading month is given below:

May 1   Business start-up capital deposited in the bank £5,000;
May 1   Loan of £1,000 from Rachel's mother deposited in the bank;
May 1   Paid rent to estate agent by cheque £1,000;
May 2   Bought cut flowers from a supplier on credit for £300;
May 2   Bought ribbon and other floral accessories for £200 and paid by cheque;

May 7   Sold goods on credit for £650;
May 21   Bought cut flowers from a supplier for £400 on credit;
May 23   Sold goods on credit for £600;
May 31   Paid wages by cheque £900;
May 31   Loan of £1,000 repaid to Rachel's mother by cheque.

Before a trial balance can be extracted it is necessary to draw up the ledger accounts and balance them. Rachel's balanced accounts on 31 May 2000 are presented below and on the next page.

Figure 16.3 *Balanced ledger accounts for Rachel Watson's business*

Dr	Bank Account		Cr	
		£		£
1.5 Capital		5,000	1.5 Rent	1,000
1.5 Loan received		1,000	2.5 Purchases	200
			31.5 Wages	900
			31.5 Loan repaid	1,000
			31.5 Balance c/d	2,900
		6,000		6,000
1.6 Balance b/d		2,900		

Dr	Capital Account		Cr	
		£		£
31.5 Balance c/d		5,000	1.5 Bank	5,000
			1.6 Balance b/d	5,000

Dr	Rent Account		Cr	
		£		£
1.5 Bank		1,000	31.5 Balance c/d	1,000
1.6 Balance b/d		1,000		

Dr	Loan Account		Cr	
		£		£
31.5 Bank		1,000	1.5 Bank	1,000

Dr	Purchases Account		Cr	
		£		£
2.5 Trade creditors		300	31.5 Balance c/d	900
2.5 Bank		200		
21.5 Trade creditors		400		
		900		900
1.6 Balance b/d		900		

Dr	Trade Creditors Account		Cr	
		£		£
31.5 Balance c/d		700	2.5 Purchases	300
			21.5 Purchases	400
		700		700
			1.6 Balance b/d	700

Dr	Sales Account		Cr	
		£		£
31.5 Balance c/d		1,250	7.5 Trade debtors	650
			23.5 Trade debtors	600
		1,250		1,250
			1.6 Balance b/d	1,250

Figure 16.3 continued

Dr	Trade Debtors Account		Cr	
	£			£
7.5 Sales	650	31.5 Balance c/d		1,250
23.5 Sales	600			
	1,250			1,250
1.6 Balance b/d	1,250			

Dr	Wages Account		Cr	
	£			£
31.5 Bank	900	31.5 Balance c/d		900
1.6 Balance b/d	900			

From these ledger accounts, Rachel can construct a trial balance by listing all the debit balances and all the credit balances (see Figure 16.4). In this example, the trial balance is written in the same order as the ledger accounts.

If the trial balance is correct, the total value of debits will be equal to the total value of credits. In the case of Rachel's business, the totals are both £6,950. Note that if any ledger accounts show a nil balance, the account is not included in the trial balance. For example, the two sides of the loan account are equal and there is no balance to be brought down, so there is a nil balance.

Figure 16.4 *Trial balance for Rachel Watson*

Rachel Watson
Trial Balance as at 31.5.00

	Debit	Credit
	£	£
Bank	2,900	
Capital		5,000
Rent	1,000	
Purchases	900	
Trade creditors		700
Sales		1,250
Trade debtors	1,250	
Wages	900	
	6,950	6,950

QUESTION 2

After leaving Walsall Sixth Form College, James Ashworth set up a small business making personalised mouse mats for computers. He prints designs onto mouse mats for private and commercial customers. During his first month of trading he recorded the following transactions.

June 2	Business start-up capital deposited in bank £2,000;
June 9	Bought printing machine for £1,000, paid by cheque;
June 16	Bought materials on credit from a supplier for £200;
June 21	Sold goods for £250, customer paid by cheque;
June 25	Sold goods on credit for £300;
June 30	Bought ink cartridges for £100, paid by cheque.

(a) Draw up the accounts for the above transactions.
(b) Balance the accounts.
(c) Prepare a trial balance for James Ashworth as at 30 June.

Constructing a trial balance from a list of ledger balances

The source of information for Rachel Watson's trial balance was a list of transactions. These were used to draw up a series of ledger accounts. The balances were then extracted from the accounts to construct the trial balance. In cases where only the balances are provided, it is necessary to distinguish between debit balances and credit balances before they are listed in the trial balance. Consider the example of Bristol Fabrications Ltd, a steel fabricator. This company had the following ledger balances for the year ended 31 December 2000.

Purchases £325,450, sales £985,000, wages £120,000, office expenses £34,000, interest received £54,000, rent £24,000, trade debtors £98,000, trade creditors £23,450, bank deposit £650,000, cash £1,200 and capital £190,200.

To produce the trial balance for Bristol Fabrications Ltd it is necessary to separate the balances into debits or credits. The assets and expenses are debits. Liabilities, capital or revenue items are credits. So, for example, office expenses are a debit, and sales revenue is a credit. Note that a bank balance can be either a credit or a debit. In this case it is a debit because a bank deposit is an asset. A bank loan or overdraft is a liability, so would be classed as a credit. Once ledger balances have been classified into credits and debits, the trial balance can be drawn. This is shown in Figure 16.5.

Figure 16.5 *Trial balance for Bristol Fabrications Ltd*

Bristol Fabrications Ltd
Trial Balance as at 31.12.00

	Debit £	Credit £
Purchases	325,450	
Sales		985,000
Wages	120,000	
Office expenses	34,000	
Interest received		54,000
Rent	24,000	
Trade debtors	98,000	
Trade creditors		23,450
Bank deposit	650,000	
Cash	1,200	
Capital		190,200
	1,252,650	1,252,650

QUESTION 3

Castleford Bearings Ltd manufactures a range of bearings for the motor industry. At the end of the financial year (30 June 2000) the following balances were extracted from the ledgers of the company.

Sales £5,466,891, purchases, £4,070,615, staff wages £981,990, directors' wages £400,000, factory overheads £127,098, bank charges £3,422, bank interest paid £24,870, machinery £300,000, sundry expenses £12,000, trade debtors £143,222, trade creditors £345,887, bank deposit £23,561, bank loan £224,000 and capital £50,000.

Prepare a trial balance for Castleford Bearings Ltd as at 30 June 2000.

What happens if the trial balance does not balance?

It is possible that the trial balance will not balance. This might be due to errors in the following areas:
- in extracting balances from ledgers, for example the balance might be copied incorrectly;
- in addition of the trial balance (errors of addition are sometimes called CASTING errors);
- in bookkeeping, for example a transaction might be recorded as a single entry - either on the credit or debit side of the accounts, rather than on both sides which is required for double entry.

Measures that can be taken to find an error in the trial balance include:
- checking the additions of the two columns;
- checking that the ledger balances are entered under the correct heading (Dr or Cr);
- checking that all figures have been included in the trial balance;
- checking if the trial balance is out by a value that is divisible by nine, then the error might result from figures being transposed (a TRANSPOSITION error), for example if a value is written as £67 instead of £76.

If the error is not found after these checks have been made then the error might have resulted from a bookkeeping mistake in the ledger accounts. The following checks can be made to find this error.
- Check that the balances on the accounts have been calculated correctly.
- Look for a figure in the accounts that has the same value as the error.
- Look for a figure in the accounts that is half the value of the error.
- If the error is a round number such as £100 or £1,000, it is likely to be found in the calculation of the balances on the accounts.

If the trial balance still does not balance after all of these checks, the bookkeeping entries must be checked against the primary sources, such as invoices and bank statements.

Limitations of the trial balance

Even if the trial balance does balance, some errors might still have been made. These errors which are not revealed by the trial balance can include the following.

Errors of omission If a transaction has not been recorded at all in the bookkeeping process the trial balance will still balance. For example, a business might pay £500 for some goods from a supplier. The normal bookkeeping procedure is to debit the purchases account and credit the bank account. However, if the transaction is omitted, both the debit total and the credit total will be understated by £500. Such an error is more likely to occur in a small business, when an invoice gets lost for example. If documents are numbered serially this type of error is less likely to occur. Computerised accounting systems (see unit 47) are also less likely to produce this type of error

Errors of commission This type of error, also known as MISPOSTING, occurs when a correct amount is POSTED, ie entered, to the right type of account but to the wrong name. For example, a sale of goods to P. Harding Ltd for £1,200 might be posted to the account of G. Hardman Ltd instead. This will result in the correct figure for sales, but no error in the trial balance. The error might only come to light when G. Hardman Ltd complains that it is being billed for goods that it has not received.

Errors of principle This type of error occurs when a transaction is recorded in the wrong type of account. For example, the purchase of a new computer for £1,500 might be posted to the computer maintenance account instead of the fixed assets account. The trial balance will still balance but computer maintenance expenses will be overstated by £1,500 and fixed assets understated by £1,500.

Compensating errors The trial balance will balance if there is a mistake of equal value on both the debit side and the credit side of the accounts. For example, if both the debit and the credit sides are overstated due to addition errors of £1,000 each, the trial balance will still balance.

Reversal of entries This type of mistake occurs when a transaction is listed in the right accounts but on the wrong side. For example, if the cash account is credited and the sales account debited following a cash sale, the trial balance will still balance. However, both the cash account and the sales account will be incorrect by twice the value of the transaction.

An error of original entry This is where the wrong amount for a transaction is entered correctly in the bookkeeping system. For example, a cash sale of £345 might be entered as £34.50. The trial balance will balance but the sales ledger and the cash book will be wrong.

Note that the trial balance only shows recorded transactions. It needs to be adjusted for items such as bad debts, prepayments and provision for depreciation. These issues, and the correction of errors in the accounts are covered in units 28 and 29.

QUESTION 4

Robert Blackburn runs a mini-mart in Brighton. He keeps careful records of his business transactions. At the end of each financial year he produces a trial balance, an example of which is shown in Figure 16.6. Unfortunately the trial balance does **not** balance. However, Robert is convinced that the error(s) is not in his bookkeeping. The extracted ledger balances as at 31 January 2000 are listed below.

Sales £98,321, casual labour £4,600, motor expenses £1,210, telephone £190, advertising £250, sundry expenses £410, purchases £87,991, trade debtors £651, trade creditors £783, bank overdraft £711, cash in hand £299, capital account £12,322 and drawings £16,536.

(a) Find the errors in the trial balance.
(b) Explain how the errors might have arisen.

Figure 16.6 *Trial balance for Robert Blackburn*

Robert Blackburn
Trial Balance as at 31.1.00

	Dr	Cr
	£	£
Sales		98,231
Casual labour	4,600	
Motor expenses	1,210	
Telephone	190	
Advertising	250	
Sundry expenses	410	
Purchases	97,991	
Trade debtors	651	
Trade creditors		783
Bank overdraft		711
Cash in hand	299	
Capital		12,322
Drawings	16,536	
	122,137	112,047

key terms

Casting - another term for adding.
Misposting - entering transactions in the wrong account.
Posting - entering transactions in an account.
Transposition - a change in the order or position of numbers.
Trial balance - a listing of all the debit balances and credit balances extracted from the ledgers. When each list is added the total debits should be equal to the total credits.

summary questions

1. Why should a trial balance balance?
2. Explain the purposes of a trial balance.
3. What are the likely sources of information for a trial balance?
4. If there are no errors in the bookkeeping, why might the trial balance not balance?
5. Describe the nature of the following errors: (i) error of omission; (ii) error of commission; (iii) error of principle; (iv) compensating error; (v) reversal of entries; (vi) error of original entry.
6. What do all of the errors in question 5 have in common?
7. If a business has a bank overdraft, on which side of the trial balance will it appear?
8. If the value of sales is undercast, what effect will this have on the trial balance?
9. Give four examples of credit entries in the trial balance.
10. If a business forgets to enter discounts received in the trial balance, what effect will this have?

UNIT ASSESSMENT   QUESTION 1

On the 1 March 2001 Julian Arranovic and Barry Cairns set up a car repair business in Gillingham, Kent. They were quickly successful in securing a contract with a local taxi firm to service and maintain all of its 46 cabs. It was agreed that Julian would be responsible for recording business transactions since he had studied business accounts at college. A list of transactions for the first month of trading is shown below.

1.3.01   Deposited £10,000 capital in bank.
1.3.01   Paid quarterly rent by cheque £1,000.
3.3.01   Bought £2,000 of materials on credit from a supplier.
5.3.01   Completed work on credit for Kent Taxis £190.
8.3.01   Received a cheque for £320 for work done (on a friend's car).
14.3.01 Completed work on credit for Kent Taxis £560.
20.3.01 Bought supplies on credit from a supplier £450.
30.3.01 Paid leasing charge of £200 by cheque.
30.3.01 Received cheque payment from Kent Taxis £500.

(a) Draw up the accounts to show the transactions.
(b) Balance the accounts.
(c) Prepare a trial balance for Julian Arranovic and Barry Cairns as at 30 March 2001.
(d) Consider the following two errors made by Julian when doing the books at the end of the month:
  - **on 8 March 2001 the work completed for £320 was not entered at all in the system;**
  - **on the 20 March 2001 the transaction listed was entered on the wrong side of the accounts.**
  What types of errors are those listed above?
(e) Explain why such errors will not prevent the trial balance from balancing.
(f) Show the effect of the errors on the trial balance.

UNIT ASSESSMENT   QUESTION 2

Slimwear Ltd is a mail order company that specialises in the manufacture and distribution of women's clothes. Its owner is Rachel Morgan. The end of the trading year extracts from the ledgers are listed in Figure 16.7.

(a) Prepare a trial balance for Slimwear Ltd as at 31 January 2000.
(b) Describe the initial checks that an accountant might make if the above trial balance fails to balance.
(c) (i) After some routine checking of the Slimwear books it was discovered that sundry expenses should have been £3,991 and sales should have been £342,998. Explain why these errors might not have been detected when the trial balance was drawn up.
   (ii) What will be the effect on the trial balance when the corrections are made?

Figure 16.7 Extracts from the ledgers of Slimwear Ltd as at 31 January 2000

	£
Sales	341,998
Purchases	223,900
Purchase returns	21,001
Postage & packaging	23,776
Advertising	65,990
Wages	87,990
Rent & rates	12,900
Trade debtors	54,000
Trade creditors	32,771
Interest paid	4,553
Sundry expenses	2,991
Bank overdraft	13,330
Bank loan	119,000
Director's salary	40,000
Motor car	10,000
Taxation paid	12,000
Capital	10,000

unit 17

The final accounts

unit**objectives**

To understand:
- the nature and purpose of final accounts;
- the trading account;
- the profit and loss account;
- the appropriation account;
- the balance sheet.

What are the final accounts?

The stages in the bookkeeping and accounting process are shown in Figure 17.1. The process begins with the transfer of information from source documents, such as invoices, into the books of prime entry. The information is then posted to ledgers from which the trial balance is constructed. The trial balance is used to produce the final accounts. These include the **profit and loss account** which incorporates the trading account, the **balance sheet** and the **cash flow statement**.

Figure 17.1 *Stages in the bookkeeping and accounting process*

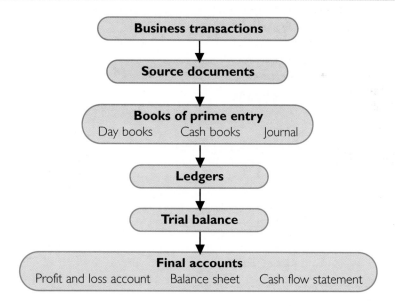

This unit focuses on the profit and loss account and the balance sheet of sole traders. These are small businesses owned by a single person. The accounts of partnerships and companies are described in units 36 and 38.

Profit and loss accounts and balance sheets are produced at the end of each financial year. However, some businesses produce them more regularly, perhaps every six months. Final accounts give an indication of how well a business is performing. For example, the profit and loss account shows how much profit the business has made and the balance sheet shows how much the business is worth.

The profit and loss account is divided into three parts:
- the trading account;
- the profit and loss account;
- the appropriation account.

The trading account

The TRADING ACCOUNT is used to calculate GROSS PROFIT. The gross profit of a business is its sales revenue less its cost of sales. This is illustrated in Figure 17.2 which shows a trading account for the Solihull Golf Centre, a retailer of golf clubs and accessories. The business is owned by Dave Charnock who is a sole trader. The trading account is prepared for the year ended 31 March 2001 and shows three columns of figures. The figures on the right-hand side are the key figures in the account. The figures on the left-hand side show calculations. Note that some accounts might have more than three columns, for example to represent totals for previous years. The number of columns used depends on the style of presentation preferred by a business.

Figure 17.2 *Trading account for Solihull Golf Centre, year ended 31 March 2001*

Solihull Golf Centre
Trading Account for the year ended 31.3.01

	£	£	£
Sales		211,980	
Less returns inwards		2,120	
			209,860
Opening stock (1.4.00)		23,640	
Add			
Purchases	115,500		
Carriage in	11,400		
Less returns outwards	5,670		
Net purchases		121,230	
		144,870	
Less closing stock (31.3.01)		25,710	
Cost of sales			119,160
Gross profit			90,700

The first entry in the trading account is SALES or TURNOVER. This is the total revenue received for goods sold by the Solihull Golf Centre during the year. It excludes VAT. Any returns inwards, ie sales returns made by customers, are then subtracted. The total of sales for the Solihull Golf Centre was £211,980. However, £2,120 was subtracted from this because some goods were returned during the year. The resulting total of £209,860 is sometimes known as **net sales**.

The next key figure in the trading account is the COST OF SALES or **cost of goods sold**. For a retailer this is the cost of the stock that is bought by the business and which is then resold. For a manufacturer it is the **direct costs** of production such as the cost of raw materials and the wages paid to production workers (see unit 48). The cost of sales must be **adjusted for stock movements** in the trading account. This is because the value of stock at the beginning of the trading period is not likely to be exactly the same as the value at the end of the period. To adjust the cost of sales for stock movements at the Solihull Golf Centre, the following information is required.

- **The value of opening stock** This is the value of stock which the business had at the start of the trading year. It is exactly the same as the closing stock for the previous year. On 1 April, the value of opening stock for the Solihull Golf Centre was £23,640. This is shown in the account in Figure 17.2.

- **The total amount spent on purchases** For the Solihull Golf Centre, the cost of golfing equipment and accessories purchased from suppliers during the year was £115,500. The cost of 'carriage in', £11,400, is added to this figure. It relates to delivery costs that the Golf Centre had to pay. Returns outwards, ie purchases returns, £5,670, made to suppliers are subtracted. For the Solihull Golf Centre, purchases for the year, including carriage in and excluding returns outwards, was £121,230. This figure is sometimes known as **net purchases**. The combined total of net purchases and opening stock, £144,870, represents the total amount of stock that the business could potentially sell during the year.

- **The value of closing stock** This is the value of unsold stock at the end of the trading period. A business must carry out a STOCKTAKE to determine this figure. For the Solihull Golf Centre, the value of stock on 31 March was £25,710. This is subtracted from £144,870 in the trading account to obtain the cost of sales for the year.

Figure 17.2 shows that the cost of sales for the Solihull Golf Centre was £119,160. It is entered in the right hand column of the account.

The final figure in the account is gross profit. This is calculated by subtracting the cost of sales from sales.

Gross profit = sales - cost of sales

The Solihull Golf Centre made a gross profit of £90,700 during the year. However, if the cost of sales for a business was greater than its sales revenue, the gross profit would be negative. This is called a gross loss.

QUESTION 1

Figure 17.3 *Trading account for Good Food, year ended 31 July 2001*

Good Food
Trading Account for the year ended 31.7.01

	Dr	Cr
	£	£
Sales	129,010	
Less returns inwards	1,090	
		127,920
Opening stock (1.8.00)	16,490	
Add purchases	61,230	
	77,720	
Less closing stock (31.7.01)	15,310	
Cost of sales		******
Gross profit		******

Tracy Graham runs a chain of sandwich bars called Good Food. The trading account for Good Food is shown in Figure 17.3.

(a) Calculate (i) the cost of sales; (ii) the gross profit for Good Food. Assume that there were no returns outwards or payments for carriage in.

(b) Calculate (i) the cost of sales; (ii) the gross profit if the closing stock was £17,290 and not £15,310.

(c) Explain why the returns outwards must be subtracted from purchases.

The profit and loss account

The profit and loss account is used to calculate NET PROFIT. The net profit of a business is its sales revenue minus all its expenses. These include the cost of sales and all other costs involved in running the business. In practice, the profit and loss account is a continuation of the trading account and is drawn up below it. Figure 17.4 shows both the trading account and the profit and loss account for the Solihull Golf Centre.

The first entry in the profit and loss account is the gross profit of £90,700 from the trading account. At this stage in the account it is usual to show any discounts received from suppliers. In this example, the Solihull Golf Centre received £400. Any other income that the business receives is then added. This is income that is not directly related to the business's normal trading activities. It is sometimes called NON-OPERATING INCOME. For example, the Solihull Golf Centre has a flat above the shop which is let out for £2,000 per annum. The total income before expenses was £93,100.

The next section in the account shows the **expenses**, or **overheads**, that the business incurs during the year. They are shown in a list in the central column of the account. These expenses are then totalled and subtracted from the total income of the business. The list of expenses for the Solihull Golf Centre, such as wages, heat and light, and rates are typical of those incurred by a business. The total expenses incurred by the Solihull Golf Centre was £32,280.

At the end of the profit and loss account, the net profit is calculated. Net profit is given by:

Net profit = gross profit (plus discounts received and any non-operating income) - expenses

The net profit made by the Solihull Golf Centre was £60,820. This is the amount of profit available to the owner. If the total of expenses was greater than gross profit, a loss would be made.

Figure 17.4 *Trading and profit and loss account for the Solihull Golf Centre*

Solihull Golf Centre
Trading and Profit and Loss Account
for the year ended 31.3.01

	£	£	£	
Sales		211,980		
Less returns inwards		2,120		
			209,860	Trading account
Opening stock (1.4.00)		23,640		
Add				
Purchases	115,500			
Carriage in	11,400			
Less returns outwards	5,670			
Net purchases		121,230		
		144,870		
Less closing stock (31.3.01)		25,710		
Cost of sales			119,160	
Gross profit			90,700	
Add discount received			400	
Rent received			2,000	
			93,100	
Less expenses				
Wages		25,000		
Heat and light		760		
Rates		2,670		Profit and loss account
Cleaning		1,290		
Insurance		750		
Telephone		590		
Sundry expenses		1,220		
			32,280	
Net profit			60,820	

The appropriation account

For partnerships and companies, an APPROPRIATION ACCOUNT is used to show how net profit is shared between the owners of the business. It also shows how much profit is retained by the business and, in the case of companies, how much is paid in corporation tax. However, in the case of sole traders, it is not conventional to have an appropriation account. This is because, in effect, all the net profit belongs to one owner. The appropriation accounts for partnerships and limited companies are described in units 36 and 38.

QUESTION 2

Erdington Pet Supplies is a pet shop owned by Steve Dawson. The shop sells a wide range of pet foods and accessories such as rabbit hutches, dog kennels, bird cages and aquariums. The trading account and profit and loss account for the business is shown in Figure 17.5.

(a) What is the total of (i) purchases; (ii) net profit for Erdington Pet Supplies? Assume that there were no charges for carriage in and there were no returns outwards.

(b) When the account was produced, £430 of returns inwards, ie sales returns, were completely omitted. How would the value of net profit be affected by this?

Figure 17.5 *Trading account and profit and loss account for Erdington Pet Supplies*

Erdington Pet Supplies
Trading and Profit and Loss Account
for the year ended 31 August 2001

	£	£
Sales		176,890
Opening stock	17,340	
Add purchases	******	
	84,640	
Less closing stock	19,010	
Cost of sales		65,630
Gross profit		111,260
Add discounts received		1,200
		112,460
Less expenses		
Wages	22,000	
Rent and rates	25,000	
Advertising	2,190	
Electricity	1,450	
Telephone	430	
Motor expenses	3,210	
Sundry expenses	2,530	
		56,810
Net profit		******

The balance sheet

The balance sheet provides a summary of a business's assets, liabilities and capital. It is sometimes described as a 'snapshot' of a business's financial position at a particular point in time. This means that the totals of assets, liabilities and capital shown in the balance sheet are only accurate for the day on which the balance sheet is published. The very next day, some of the amounts in the balance sheet will change. This is because the business continues trading. For example, the total of cash at the bank will rise and the total owed by debtors will fall when a customer pays for some goods bought on credit. The balance sheet for the Solihull Golf Centre is shown in Figure 17.6.

The details in the balance sheet are as follows.

- **Fixed assets** These are the long term resources owned by a business. In this case, the business owns its premises, fixtures and fittings such as shelving, display units and lighting, and a range of other equipment. The total value of fixed assets for the Solihull Golf Centre was £186,990.
- **Current assets** CURRENT ASSETS are resources that are likely to be converted into cash within one year. They are also known as **liquid assets**. They include stocks of goods, debtors, ie money owed by credit customers, cash at the bank and cash in hand. Three such assets are shown for the Solihull Golf Centre and their total value was £39,820. Note that the £25,710 stock value is the closing stock for the business that is also included in the trading account.
- **Current liabilities** The total of CURRENT LIABILITIES for the Solihull Golf Centre is £20,700. This is money that is owed by the business and is due to be repaid within one year. In this case the examples include money owed to trade creditors, ie to suppliers of golf clubs and accessories bought on credit, and a short term bank loan.
- **Working capital** By subtracting current liabilities from current assets, a business can calculate its WORKING CAPITAL. This is the amount of resources that a business has available to fund day to day business activity. It is an important indicator of the financial position of a business. This is

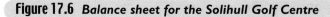

Figure 17.6 *Balance sheet for the Solihull Golf Centre*

Solihull Golf Centre
Balance Sheet as at 31.3.01

	£	£	£
Fixed assets			
Premises			150,000
Fixtures and fittings			21,500
Equipment			15,490
			186,990
Current assets			
Stocks		25,710	
Cash at bank		12,100	
Cash in hand		2,010	
		39,820	
Less current liabilities			
Trade creditors	17,200		
Short-term bank loan	3,500		
		20,700	
Working capital			19,120
			206,110
Less long-term liabilities			
Mortgage			80,000
Net assets			126,110
Financed by			
Opening capital			91,200
Add net profit			60,820
			152,020
Less drawings			25,910
Capital employed			126,110

explained in unit 44. The amount of working capital for the Solihull Golf Centre was £19,120. It is added to fixed assets in the balance sheet to give a subtotal of £206,110. Working capital is sometimes called **net current assets** in the balance sheet.

- **Long term liabilities** LONG TERM LIABILITIES are amounts of money owed by a business that are not due to be repaid for at least a year. In some cases the money might not be repaid for up to 25 or 30 years. In this case, the Solihull Golf Centre had one such liability. It has a mortgage, ie a long term loan of £80,000 to buy property.
- **Net assets** NET ASSETS is the total of all the business's assets less all its liabilities. It provides a rough guide to the value of the business. It is also one of the two balancing figures in the balance sheet. Solihull Golf Centre had net assets of £126,110.
- **Capital** The bottom section in the balance sheet shows the capital of the business. This is the money introduced or contributed to the business by its owner. The first figure in this section is the opening capital. This is the same as the closing capital in the previous year's balance sheet. For the Solihull Golf Centre, it was £91,200. The next figure is the net profit made during the year, £60,820. This was calculated in the profit and loss account and is added to the opening capital in the balance sheet. It gives a total of £152,020 from which the drawings are subtracted. During the year, the owner drew £25,910 from the business for personal use. This reduced the closing capital to £126,110 which was, in effect, how much the Solihull Golf Centre owed its owner on 31 March, 2001. It is also the second balancing total in the balance sheet. The total of capital in the balance sheet, sometimes called CAPITAL EMPLOYED, is the same as the total of net assets.

QUESTION 3

Bishops is a supplier of sailing equipment in Portsmouth. The balance sheet for the business is shown in Figure 17.7.

(a) What was the total of (i) net assets; (ii) opening capital for Bishops?

(b) What evidence is there in the balance sheet to suggest that Bishops rents its premises?

(c) What will be the total of opening capital for Bishops in the next financial year?

(d) What is the amount of Bishops' total liabilities?

Figure 17.7 Balance sheet for Bishops

Bishops
Balance Sheet as at 31.12.01

	£	£	£
Fixed assets			
Fixtures and fittings			129,300
Motor vehicles			23,100
			152,400
Current assets			
Stocks		131,210	
Debtors		31,390	
Cash at bank and in hand		10,070	
		172,670	
Less current liabilities			
Trade creditors	45,790		
Loan	12,000		
		57,790	
Working capital			114,880
Net assets			*******
Financed by			
Opening capital			*******
Add net profit			110,010
			300,030
Less drawings			32,750
Capital employed			267,280

Formats for final accounts

The final accounts in this unit have been presented in a VERTICAL FORMAT. This means that the information is presented as a list with one section following underneath the other. The sections also follow a particular order. For example, in the balance sheet the order is:

- fixed assets;
- current assets;
- current liabilities;
- net current assets, ie working capital;
- long term liabilities;
- net assets;
- capital.

Most UK accountants adopt this method of presentation. It is useful if the presentation of final accounts is standardised because it is easier to make comparisons between different companies, for example. However, even though the vast majority of UK businesses use the vertical format, differences in style and terminology exist. Variations in style and terminology occur because business have different trading circumstances. Also, their legal status might not be the same. Such differences will become apparent in later units when the accounts of different types of business organisations are explained.

An alternative approach in presenting final accounts is to use a HORIZONTAL FORMAT. This involves presenting information in two sections side by side rather like a T account. The trading

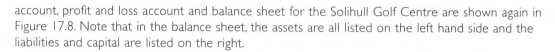

account, profit and loss account and balance sheet for the Solihull Golf Centre are shown again in Figure 17.8. Note that in the balance sheet, the assets are all listed on the left hand side and the liabilities and capital are listed on the right.

Figure 17.8 *Final accounts for the Solihull Golf Centre - presented in horizontal format*

Solihull Golf Centre
Trading Account for the year ended 31.3.01

	£		£
Opening stock (1.4.00)	23,640	Sales	211,980
Purchases (net)	121,230	Less returns inwards	2,120
	144,870		
Less closing stock (31.3.01)	25,710		
Cost of sales	119,160		
Gross profit c/d	90,700		
	209,860		209,860

Solihull Golf Centre
Profit and Loss Account for the year ended 31.3.01

	£		£
Wages	25,000	Gross profit b/d	90,700
Heat and light	760	Rent received	2,400
Rates	2,670		
Cleaning	1,290		
Insurance	750		
Telephone	590		
Sundry expenses	1,220		
Net profit	60,820		
	93,100		93,100

Solihull Golf Centre
Balance Sheet as at 31.3.01

	£	£		£	£
Fixed assets			*Capital*		
Premises		150,000	Opening capital		91,200
Fixtures and fittings		21,500	*Add* net profit		60,820
Equipment		15,490			152,020
		186,990	*Less* drawings		25,910
					126,110
Current assets			*Less long-term liabilities*		
Stocks	25,710		Mortgage		80,000
Cash at bank	12,100				206,110
Cash in hand	2,010		*Current liabilities*		
		39,820	Trade creditors	17,200	
			Short-term bank loan	3,500	
					20,700
		226,810			226,810

The purposes of final accounts

Final accounts provide useful information for the various stakeholders in a business. For example, the owners of a business can use them to see how well the business has performed during the year. Creditors might use them to see how easily the business can pay its debts.

The profit and loss account can be used for the following purposes.

- Business owners are interested to see how much profit they have made at the end of the trading year. The size of profit is a guide to how well a business has performed. Owners often compare this year's profit with profit from previous years. Final accounts will usually show two years figures in the statements so an immediate comparison can be made with the previous year. It also might be possible to compare the profit with that made by a similar business such as a competitor.
- A business needs to prepare a profit and loss account for tax purposes. The Inland Revenue will require copies or summaries of profit and loss accounts to verify the amount of tax to be paid.
- A business can use the profit and loss account to help measure its growth. This is indicated by changes in sales revenue over time.
- The account can be used to see how well the business has controlled its overheads and other costs.

The balance sheet is used for the following purposes.

- It provides a summary and valuation of a business's assets, liabilities and capital.
- It can also provide a guide to the overall value of a business. Generally, the total of net assets (total assets - total liabilities) represents the value of a business. For example, according to the balance sheet in Figure 17.6, the Solihull Golf Centre was worth £126,110. However, sometimes the total of net assets is not a very good guide to the value of a business. For example, net assets might undervalue a business if intangible assets such as trade marks or goodwill are valuable.
- The balance sheet shows the working capital (current assets - current liabilities) of the business. This is an important financial indicator. It helps to tell whether a business has enough liquid resources to meet its immediate debts. The value of working capital for the Solihull Golf Centre was £19,120.
- The balance sheet shows the sources of funds that a business has used, ie how much money has been raised by loans and how much has been contributed by the owners. The balance of loans and capital is often important. For example, if the value of loans is higher than the value of capital, the business might be in danger of becoming overburdened with debt. The different sources of funds that a business uses is often called the CAPITAL STRUCTURE.

summary questions

1. What is meant by the final accounts?
2. How is gross profit calculated?
3. Explain how the cost of sales is adjusted for stock movements in the trading account.
4. Give two examples of non-operating income.
5. How is net profit calculated?
6. What is the difference between current assets and fixed assets?
7. Explain the difference between the vertical format and the horizontal format when presenting accounts.
8. How is net assets calculated in the balance sheet?
9. State three uses of a profit and loss account to a business.
10. State three uses of a balance sheet to a business.

key terms

Appropriation account - the third part of the profit and loss account which shows what happens to the net profit that is made by a business.

Capital employed - the total of capital in the balance sheet. It is equal to the total of net assets.

Capital structure - the different sources of funds that a business uses.

Cost of sales - the total of purchases made during the year adjusted for stock.

Current assets - resources that are likely to be converted into cash within twelve months.

Current liabilities - money owed by a business that must be repaid within twelve months.

Gross profit - the difference between sales and cost of sales.

Horizontal format - a method of presenting accounts, side by side.

Long term liabilities - money owed by a business but not due for repayment for at least one year.

Net assets - the total of all assets less all liabilities.

Net profit - the gross profit plus any non-operating income less overhead expenses.

Non-operating income - business income from sources other than normal trading activities.

Sales (or turnover)- the revenue earned by selling goods or services during a trading period.

Stocktake - a process in which the value of stock is determined.

Trading account - that part of the profit and loss account used to calculate gross profit.

Vertical format - a method of presenting accounts, with information listed vertically.

Working capital - the amount of liquid resources that a business owns, calculated by subtracting current liabilities from current assets. It is sometimes called net current assets.

UNIT ASSESSMENT QUESTION 1

Tom Brookes & Son is a business that imports bicycles and bicycle parts. Most sales are by mail order from adverts placed in specialist cycling magazines. The following financial information was taken from the books at the end of December 2001.

- Sales   £187,210
- Purchases   £96,340
- Returns outwards   £610
- Carriage in   £50
- Opening stock   £13,890
- Closing stock   £15,120

(a) Produce a trading account for Tom Brookes & Son for the year ended 31.12.01.

(b) During the year, the business incurred total overhead expenses of £41,020. Calculate the net profit.

(c) Explain why the profit and loss account might be useful to the owners of this business.

UNIT ASSESSMENT QUESTION 2

Plantworld supplies floral displays for conferences, weddings, hotels, reception areas and exhibitions. The balance sheet for Plantworld is shown in Figure 17.9.

(a) **What does the total of net assets in the balance sheet tell you about Plantworld?**
(b) **Explain why the total capital employed is lower than the total of opening capital for Plantworld.**
(c) **On 31.8.01 the owner put £8,000 of her own money into Plantworld's bank account. Redraw the balance sheet showing the effect of this transaction.**

Figure 17.9 *Balance sheet for Plantworld as at 31.8.01*

Plantworld
Balance Sheet as at 31.8.01

	£	£	£
Fixed assets			
Premises			120,000
Van			3,200
Equipment			2,100
			125,300
Current assets			
Stocks		4,200	
Debtors		12,800	
Cash in hand		250	
		17,250	
Less current liabilities			
Trade creditors	4,610		
Bank overdraft	3,450		
		8,060	
Working capital			9,190
			134,490
Less long-term liabilities			
Mortgage			56,000
Net assets			78,490
Financed by			
Opening capital			89,210
Add net profit			21,700
			110,910
Less drawings			32,420
Capital employed			78,490

unit 18

The preparation of final accounts

unit objectives

To understand:
- how to prepare a profit and loss account from a trial balance;
- how to prepare a balance sheet from a trial balance;
- the final accounts of service providers;
- the final accounts and double entry bookkeeping.

Preparing a profit and loss account from the trial balance

The information generated by the double entry bookkeeping system enables businesses to prepare a trial balance. This is a list of ledger balances relating to items such as assets, expenses and drawings (debits) and revenue, liabilities and capital (credits). The trial balance is then used to produce the final accounts of the business.

In order to illustrate the steps involved in the preparation of the trading and profit and loss account, consider the example of EuroPop, a retailer of CDs. The trial balance for EuroPop as at 31 August 2001 is shown in Figure 18.1. The notes on the right do not form part of the trial balance but are used to indicate in which part of the trading and profit and loss account the items appear. The unmarked items relating to assets, liabilities, capital and drawings are discussed later in the unit in the section on the balance sheet.

Figure 18.1 *Trial balance for EuroPop as at 31.8.01*

EuroPop
Trial Balance as at 31.8.01

	Debit £	Credit £	Notes
Sales		190,010	*Trading account (revenue)*
Discounts received		2,190	*Profit and loss account (income)*
Opening stock 1.9.00	27,980		*Trading account (stock, ie previous purchases)*
Purchases	121,230		*Trading account (purchases)*
Wages	23,100		*Profit and loss account (expense)*
Telephone	1,230		*Profit and loss account (expense)*
Motor expenses	2,190		*Profit and loss account (expense)*
Rent	3,000		*Profit and loss account (expense)*
Insurance	540		*Profit and loss account (expense)*
Light and heat	1,870		*Profit and loss account (expense)*
Bank charges	120		*Profit and loss account (expense)*
Sundry expenses	2,320		*Profit and loss account (expense)*
Van	5,930		
Cash at bank	2,450		
Trade creditors		16,820	
Capital		20,100	
Drawings	37,160		
	229,120	229,120	

Additional information: the value of closing stock on 31.8.01 was £29,100.

The value of the **opening stock** at the start of the trading year is shown in the trial balance as a debit. The value of **closing stock** is also required before the final accounts can be completed. However, the value of closing stock does not usually appear in the trial balance. This is because closing stock is valued at the very end of the accounting period. For EuroPop, the value of closing stock on 31 August 2001 was £29,100.

The trading and profit and loss account for EuroPop is shown in Figure 18.3. The steps required to produce the account are described below.

- Write the name of the business and the date at the top of the trading and profit and loss account.
- Go through the entries in the trial balance and decide whether each entry relates to the trading account or the profit and loss account. Items relating to sales, purchases and stock are recorded in the trading account. Discounts received and expenses are recorded in the profit and loss account.
- Enter the sales total, £190,010, at the top of the trading account in the right-hand column. When an item is transferred from the trial balance to the account, it is helpful to tick the figure in the trial balance. This acts as a check. If there are any unticked items at the end of the process, a mistake will have been made.
- Enter the opening stock in the left-hand column of the account so that the cost of sales can be calculated. The value of opening stock for EuroPop is shown as a debit entry in the trial balance. It is £27,980.
- Enter the total of purchases, £121,230, in the left-hand column of the account. This is added to opening stock to obtain the total of potential goods for resale. It is £149,210 in this case.
- Enter the closing stock in the account. This is given as additional information and is not normally shown in the trial balance. It is £29,100 in this case.
- The closing stock is subtracted from the opening stock and purchases to calculate the cost of sales. The figure, £120,110 (£149,210 - £29,100), is entered in the account in the right-hand column.
- The gross profit is calculated by subtracting the cost of sales from sales. This is £69,900 (£190,010 - £120,110). It is entered in the account in the right-hand column.
- EuroPop received £2,190 as discounts from suppliers. This is classed as income and is added to gross profit to give a total of £72,090 (£69,900 + £2,190).
- The remaining expenses, or overheads, are entered in the left-hand column. They are totalled to give the total expenses for the year. The figure is £34,370 and is entered in the right-hand column.
- The final entry in the account is net profit. This is calculated by subtracting the total expenses for the year from the gross profit. The net profit for EuroPop is £37,720 (£72,090 - £34,370) and is entered in the right-hand column and double underlined.

The entries that have not been labelled in the trial balance are used later in the unit to produce the balance sheet.

QUESTION 1

Heather Davies runs a general store and newsagents in Waterloo, Merseyside. The business has struggled in recent years due to intense competition from supermarkets and the growing trend in petrol stations selling groceries and newspapers. However, she has responded by offering special delivery services, opening 24 hours and diversifying the range of stock. The trial balance for her business is shown in Figure 18.2.

(a) **Identify the items in the trial balance that relate to the trading account and those that relate to the profit and loss account.**
(b) **Produce a trading and profit and loss account for Heather Davies.**

Figure 18.2 *Trial balance for Heather Davies*

Heather Davies
Trial Balance as at 31.12.01

	Dr £	Cr £
Sales		110,050
Purchases	72,990	
Opening stock	9,100	
Wages	6,300	
Telephone	430	
Motor expenses	590	
Light and heat	320	
Rates	670	
Sundry expenses	420	
Premises	46,000	
Fixtures and fittings	1,280	
Van	3,650	
Cash in hand	390	
Trade creditors		3,890
Bank overdraft		430
Capital		39,770
Drawings	12,000	
	154,140	154,140

Additional information: the value of closing stock on 31.12.01 was £10,320.

Figure 18.3 *Trading and profit and loss account for EuroPop*

EuroPop
Trading and Profit and Loss Account
for the year ended 31.8.01

	£	£
Sales		190,010
Opening stock	27,980	
Purchases	121,230	
	149,210	
Less closing stock	29,100	
Cost of sales		120,110
Gross profit		69,900
Add discounts received		2,190
		72,090
Less expenses		
Wages	23,100	
Telephone	1,230	
Motor expenses	2,190	
Rent	3,000	
Insurance	540	
Light and heat	1,870	
Bank charges	120	
Sundry expenses	2,320	
		34,370
Net profit		37,720

Preparing the balance sheet from the trial balance

To illustrate how a balance sheet is compiled from a trial balance, consider again the example of EuroPop. In Figure 18.4, the items relating to the balance sheet are marked and are classified according to whether they are assets, liabilities, capital or drawings.

Figure 18.4 *Trial balance for EuroPop as at 31.8.01*

EuroPop
Trial Balance as at 31.8.01

	Debit £	Credit £	Notes
Sales		190,010 ✓	
Discounts received		2,190 ✓	
Opening stock 1.9.00	27,980 ✓		
Purchases	121,230 ✓		
Wages	23,100 ✓		
Telephone	1,230 ✓		
Motor expenses	2,190 ✓		
Rent	3,000 ✓		
Insurance	540 ✓		
Light and heat	1,870 ✓		
Bank charges	120 ✓		
Sundry expenses	2,320 ✓		
Van	5,930		*Balance sheet (asset)*
Cash at bank	2,450		*Balance sheet (asset)*
Trade creditors		16,820	*Balance sheet (liability)*
Capital account		20,100	*Balance sheet (capital)*
Drawings	37,160		*Balance sheet (drawings)*
	229,120	229,120	

Additional information: the value of closing stock on 31 August 2001 was £29,100.

The following steps are taken when preparing the balance sheet.
- Look at the unticked entries in the trial balance and decide whether they are assets, liabilities, capital or drawings. Debit balances will be assets or drawings, and credit balances will be liabilities or capital.
- Write the name of the business and date at the top of the balance sheet (see Figure 18.5).
- First list the fixed assets in the balance sheet. EuroPop only has one fixed asset, this is the van valued at £5,930. If there is more than one fixed asset, add up the total.
- List the current assets. Place them in order of liquidity with the least liquid first. The least liquid is stock. It is the closing stock of £29,100 that is entered in the balance sheet, not the trial balance opening stock figure. The other current asset of EuroPop is cash at bank £2,450. The total for current assets is therefore £31,550.
- List the current liabilities and add them up. However, in this example there is only one, trade creditors, and the total is £16,820.
- Enter the total of working capital. This is calculated by subtracting current liabilities from current assets. For EuroPop, working capital is £14,730 (£31,550 - £16,820).
- Add the total of working capital to the total fixed assets. This gives a subtotal which is sometimes called 'total assets less current liabilities'. For EuroPop the amount is £20,660.
- Enter any long-term liabilities. The total is subtracted from total assets less current liabilities. However, EuroPop does not have any long-term liabilities so there is no entry in this example.
- Since there are no long-term liabilities to subtract, the amount of total assets less current liabilities is also the total of net assets. For EuroPop, net assets is equal to £20,660.

Figure 18.5 *Balance sheet for EuroPop as at 31.8.01*

EuroPop
Balance Sheet as at 31.8.01

	£	£
Fixed assets		
Van		5,930
Current assets		
Stock	29,100	
Cash at bank	2,450	
	31,550	
Current liabilities		
Trade creditors	16,820	
Working capital		14,730
Net assets		20,660
Financed by		
Opening capital		20,100
Add net profit		37,720
		57,820
Less drawings		37,160
Capital employed		20,660

The lower part of the balance sheet shows the capital account. It is customary to write 'Financed by' before entering the details.
- First enter the opening capital. This is £20,100 for EuroPop and is shown as a credit balance in the trial balance.
- Enter the net profit for the year and add to the opening capital. The net profit comes from the profit and loss account for EuroPop. This is shown in Figure 18.2 and is £37,720. When added to opening capital, the total is £57,820.
- The amount of drawings is then subtracted from the total above. Drawings for EuroPop is £37,160 and is shown as a debit entry in the trial balance.

- When drawings has been subtracted, the total of capital employed is obtained. It is £20,660 for EuroPop and is the same as net assets. This shows that the balance sheet balances and that the total of assets less liabilities is the same as the total of capital for the business (see the accounting equation in unit 5). Since the net assets equals capital employed, this also indicates that no mistakes were made when constructing the profit and loss account in Figure 18.2.

QUESTION 2

Use the information and trial balance for Heather Davies in Question 1 to answer the following questions.

(a) Label the entries in the trial balance that relate to the balance sheet as assets, liabilities, drawings or capital.
(b) Produce the balance sheet for Heather Davies.
(c) Suggest a value for Heather's business.

Preparing final accounts for service providers

Service providers are businesses which operate in the tertiary sector. They sell services rather than goods to customers. Examples of such businesses include solicitors, driving instructors, travel agents, hairdressers, private tutors, advertising agencies, garden designers and employment agencies. The final accounts for such businesses are slightly different from those described so far. The main difference is that there is **no trading account**. This is because these businesses do not buy goods for resale nor raw materials for processing. Therefore, there is no cost of sales and, consequently, no gross profit. In order to illustrate this, consider the business run by Clare Russell, a driving instructor. The trial balance for her business is shown in Figure 18.6.

Figure 18.6 *Trial balance for Clare Russell*

Clare Russell
Trial Balance as at 31.10.01

	Debit £	Credit £	Account
Fee income		19,230	P&L
Motor expenses	3,100		P&L
Telephone	190		P&L
Advertising	540		P&L
Sundry expenses	430		P&L
Bank interest	710		P&L
Motor car	6,500		BS
Cash at bank	980		BS
Cash in hand	170		BS
Sundry creditors		670	BS
Bank loan (5 years)		5,000	BS
Capital		5,000	BS
Drawings	17,280		BS
	29,900	29,900	

Note: items are marked with P&L to indicate that they relate to the profit and loss account and BS to indicate they relate to the balance sheet.

To prepare the profit and loss account for Clare Russell's business, the following steps are taken.
- Go through the trial balance and identify the entries as relating to the profit and loss account or the balance sheet. This has been done in Figure 18.6.
- Write the name of the business and the date at the top of the account (see Figure 18.7).
- Enter fee income, £19,230, at the top of the account. This is equivalent to sales revenue. It is called fee income because of the nature of the business. The business does not sell goods, it provides a service for which a fee is charged.

- Since there is no cost of sales, there is no gross profit to calculate. Thus, the next step is to list the expenses and add them up. The total comes to £4,970.
- Subtract the total expenses from fee income to obtain net profit. The net profit for Clare Russell's business is £14,260 (£19,230 - £4,970).

Figure 18.7 *Profit and loss account for Clare Russell's business*

Clare Russell
Profit and Loss Account
for the year ended 31.10.01

	£	£
Fee income		19,230
Less expenses:		
Motor expenses	3,100	
Telephone	190	
Advertising	540	
Sundry expenses	430	
Bank interest	710	
		4,970
Net profit		14,260

The balance sheet for Clare Russell's business can also be prepared from the trial balance. It is shown in Figure 18.8. There is no important difference between this balance sheet and that of a retailer or manufacturer. The structure is the same. However, there might be differences in the types of assets employed by the businesses. For example, a business selling furniture will have a substantial amount of stock listed in the balance sheet. Most service providers do not hold much, if any, stock. Note also that the balance sheet in this case has a section below working capital that is labelled 'long-term liabilities'. This is where the five year bank loan is entered. The amount is subtracted from the working capital to give the net assets.

Figure 18.8 *Balance sheet for Clare Russell as at 31.10.01*

Clare Russell
Balance Sheet as at 31.10.01

	£	£
Fixed assets		
Motor car		6,500
Current assets		
Cash at bank	980	
Cash in hand	170	
	1,150	
Current liabilities		
Sundry creditors	670	
Working capital		480
		6,980
Less long-term liabilities		
Bank loan (5 years)		5,000
Net assets		1,980
Financed by		
Opening capital		5,000
Add net profit		14,260
		19,260
Less drawings		17,280
Capital employed		1,980

QUESTION 3

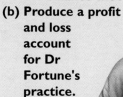

Doctor Brenda Fortune is a medical consultant. She is a skin specialist with a practice in Oxford. She treats both private and NHS patients. The trial balance for Dr Fortune's practice is shown in Figure 18.9.

(a) Identify the items in the trial balance that relate to the profit and loss account and the balance sheet.

(b) Produce a profit and loss account for Dr Fortune's practice.

(c) Produce a balance sheet for Dr Fortune's practice.

Figure 18.9 *Trial balance for Doctor Brenda Fortune as at 31.12.01*

Dr Brenda Fortune
Trial Balance as at 31.12.01

	Dr	Cr
	£	£
Fees		132,800
Secretary's wages	16,340	
Telephone	780	
Motor and travel expenses	4,200	
Lecture trip expenses	3,210	
Rates	890	
Insurance	1,290	
Subscriptions	410	
Light and heat	1,200	
Bank charges	210	
Freehold surgery and office	159,000	
Fixtures and fittings	11,910	
Motor vehicle	27,500	
Debtors	2,190	
Cash at bank	2,100	
Sundry creditors		1,270
Mortgage		105,000
Capital		21,040
Drawings	28,880	
	260,110	260,110

Final accounts and double entry bookkeeping

The trading account and the profit and loss account are part of the double entry system. This means that every entry in these accounts has an equal and opposite entry somewhere else in the bookkeeping system. For example:

- a credit entry for sales in the trading account will have an equivalent debit entry in the sales account in the nominal ledger;
- a debit entry for purchases in the trading account will have an equivalent credit entry in the purchases account in the nominal ledger;
- a debit entry for wages in the profit and loss account will have an equivalent credit entry in the wages account in the nominal ledger.

To illustrate the link between the profit and loss account and other accounts in the bookkeeping system, consider the rent account and profit and loss account for the Dalton Bookshop, a book retailer. The rent account and an extract from the profit and loss account are shown in Figure 18.10. The rent account shows that rent is paid quarterly and that a total of £6,000 rent is debited to the profit and loss account at the end of the year. This process is repeated for all expense accounts in the nominal ledger. In this example, the profit and loss account for the Dalton Bookshop only shows the one expense, rent. There will obviously be others and the total will be offset against the gross profit of £81,910 on the credit side of the account. When the account is balanced, the balance c/d is equivalent to net profit.

By contrast to the profit and loss account, the balance sheet is not part of the double entry system. When preparing the balance sheet, entries are not made into other accounts. The totals of assets, liabilities and capital are simply listed on the balance sheet.

Figure 18.10 *Rent account and an extract from the profit and loss account for the Dalton Bookshop*

NOMINAL LEDGER

	Dr	Rent Account		Cr	
2001		£	2001		£
1.1	Bank	1,500	31.12	Balance c/d	6,000
1.4	Bank	1,500			
1.7	Bank	1,500			
1.10	Bank	1,500			
		6,000			6,000
31.12	Balance b/d	6,000	31.12	Profit and loss	6,000

	Dr	Profit and Loss Account		Cr	
2001		£	2001		£
31.12	Rent	6,000	31.12	Gross profit	81,910

UNIT ASSESSMENT · QUESTION 1

Evans Fabrics is a soft furnishings shop in Swansea. It supplies curtains, blinds, loose covers, cushions and tracks and poles. A trial balance for the business is shown in Figure 18.11.

(a) Prepare the trading and profit and loss account for Evans Fabrics.

(b) Prepare the balance sheet for Evans Fabrics.

Figure 18.11 *Trial balance for Evans Fabrics, year ended 30.4.01*

Evans Fabrics
Trial Balance as at 30.4.01

	Dr	Cr
	£	£
Sales		181,400
Discounts received		2,410
Purchases	121,020	
Opening stock	25,610	
Wages	21,890	
Motor expenses	4,120	
Rent and rates	7,210	
Insurance	650	
Heat and light	1,650	
Sundry expenses	2,190	
Fixtures and fittings	3,500	
Motor vehicle	5,900	
Cash at bank	2,530	
Cash in hand	670	
Trade creditors		15,070
Capital		43,200
Drawings	45,140	
	242,080	242,080

Additional information: the value of closing stock for the business is £28,560.

UNIT ASSESSMENT QUESTION 2

Simon Parker runs a garden design business in Tunbridge Wells. He visits the homes of clients, discusses their needs and requirements, takes measurements and returns one week later with computer generated garden designs. The concept has proved very successful for Simon. A trial balance for the business is shown in Figure 18.12.

(a) Prepare the profit and loss account for the business.
(b) Prepare a balance sheet for the business.
(c) Suggest why gross profit is not shown in the profit and loss account for Simon's business.

Figure 18.12 *Trial balance for Simon Parker's business*

Simon Parker
Trial Balance as at 31.3.01

	Dr	Cr
	£	£
Fees		42,810
Office rent	3,000	
Motor expenses	1,780	
Telephone	450	
Insurance	740	
Light and heat	680	
Rates	1,200	
Fixtures and fittings	1,870	
Motor vehicle	18,600	
Computer	2,600	
Debtors	2,840	
Cash at bank	3,100	
Sundry creditors		810
Bank loan (3 years)		3,500
Capital		6,500
Drawings	16,760	
	53,620	53,620

summary questions

1. How are the (i) debit entries; (ii) credit entries in the trial balance recorded in the final accounts?
2. What might be added to sales in the trading account?
3. Explain how the cost of sales is adjusted for stock.
4. State three types of business activity that would not require a trading account.
5. What is the trading account used to calculate?
6. Explain how carriage is treated in the final accounts.
7. How is net profit calculated in the profit and loss account?
8. State three examples of current assets.
9. How is capital employed calculated in the balance sheet?
10. How are net assets calculated in the balance sheet?

Accruals and prepayments

What are adjustments?

Before the **final accounts** of a business are prepared it is often necessary to make ADJUSTMENTS to the trial balance. Adjustments might be required because some transactions have not yet been taken into account. For example, a business might not have calculated the depreciation on its assets (see unit 22). Also, some of the transactions recorded might relate to a different accounting period. For example, a rent payment made near the end of the trading year might relate partly to the current year and partly to the next year. If this happens it is necessary to calculate the fraction of the payment that relates to the current year.

The main adjustments that are made to the trial balance are:
- accrued expenses owed by the business;
- accrued receipts owed to the business;
- prepayments;
- provision for bad and doubtful debts (see unit 20);
- provision for discounts (see unit 12);
- depreciation of certain assets;
- drawings (see unit 18).

The purpose of making adjustments is to produce a set of accounts that provide 'a true and fair view' of a firm's financial circumstances. Details of adjustments are entered in the **journal** and might also be included as footnotes to the **trial balance**. This unit focuses on two of these adjustments, accruals and prepayments. Later units look at other adjustments.

What are accruals?

An ACCRUAL is an estimate of money that is owed, but which is not supported by an invoice at the time the trial balance is prepared.

Accrued expenses Sometimes a business might use a resource during the current trading year and still owe money for it at the end of the year. For example, a business might hire a van near the end of the trading year and not receive the invoice until the next year. This is an example of an ACCRUED EXPENSE. It is important for a business to include this expense in the current year's accounts even though payment has not been made.

Another example of an accrued expense is when a business receives a bill that partly relates to the previous trading year. For example, a £600 quarterly bill for December, January and February will relate to the previous trading year if the year end is December 31st. Accountants need to calculate the proportion of the £600 bill that should be attributed to the previous year. In this case it would be £200 ($\frac{1}{3}$ × £600). This is because one month of the quarterly bill (ie one third) relates to December and two months (ie two thirds) relates to January and February in the next year.

Accrued revenue This is money owed to a business at the end of the trading year, but where no invoice has been issued. Examples of ACCRUED REVENUE include interest receivable from banks, rent that is due and commission owed from selling another firm's goods. Such revenues tend to be quite small in comparison with the sales revenue that a business receives.

QUESTION 1

Edward Hodges owns a river transport company called Eastern Promise. It operates barges on the River Thames from a warehouse in Tilbury, Essex. Part of the warehouse is rented out to another business, Tideway Packaging, for £1,800 a quarter. The following financial information relates to 31 December 2000 which was the end of year for Eastern Promise.

- Eastern Promise owed an advertising agency £300 for an advert taken out in a magazine in November 2000. The amount was not paid until January 2001 when the invoice was received.
- A quarterly electricity bill was received at the end of January 2001, two months of which related to the previous year. The bill was £450.
- Eastern Promise owed one of its regular suppliers £3,500 for goods bought in December 2000.
- Tideway Packaging had fallen behind with rent payments and owed a full quarter's rent.
- On 31 January 2001 Eastern Promise received bank interest of £600 for the period 1 August 2000 to 31 January 2001.

(a) **Which of the above amounts is not an accrual? Explain why.**
(b) **Calculate the value of accrued expenses for Eastern Promise.**
(c) **Calculate the value of accrued income for Eastern Promise.**

Adjustments for accruals do not include money owed for credit sales and credit purchases. Although this money might be outstanding at the end of a trading period, it is already accounted for in the debtors accounts in the sales ledger and the creditors accounts in the purchases ledger.

Accounting for accruals

The **accruals concept** (see unit 7) states that revenue and costs should be recognised when they are earned or incurred, not when the money is received or paid. So, any money that is owed by a business in the current year **must be added to expenses**. Similarly, any money owed to the business **must be added to revenue**.

In order to illustrate how adjustments for accruals are dealt with in bookkeeping, consider the example of Ben McDonald who runs a restaurant called Cafe Noir in Nottingham. Above the restaurant is a flat which is rented out for £1,000 per quarter. The rent is classed as part of the business's income. At the end of the financial year, which fell on 31 December 2000, the trial balance for Cafe Noir indicated the following.

- The amount paid for gas was £980. However, this did not include the bill for the last quarter's gas which had not yet been paid. The bill was for £330, all of which related to the trading year which ended on 31 December 2000.
- The amount of rent received for the year was £3,000. Ben's tenant still owed £1,000 for the period up to 31 December 2000.

An extract from the trial balance, before adjustments, is shown in Figure 19.1. It must be adjusted before it can be used to prepare the final accounts.

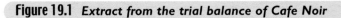

Figure 19.1 *Extract from the trial balance of Cafe Noir*

Cafe Noir
Trial Balance as at 31.12.00

	Dr	Cr
	£	£
Gas	980	
Rent receivable		3,000

Accounting for an accrued expense The accrued expense in this case is the unpaid gas bill. The gas account for Cafe Noir is shown in Figure 19.2. This account was balanced on 31 December 2000 and £980 was transferred to the trial balance as shown in Figure 19.1. However, £330 was still owed by Cafe Noir for the current year's consumption of gas. This amount must be accounted for in the gas account.

Figure 19.2 *Gas account for Cafe Noir*

NOMINAL LEDGER

Dr		Gas Account		Cr	
2000		£	2000		£
3.3	Bank	290	Balance c/d		980
10.7	Bank	340			
6.10	Bank	350			
		980			980
31.12	Balance b/d	980	31.12	Profit and loss	1,310
31.12	Balance c/d (accrual)	330			
		1,310			1,310
			2001		
			1.1	Balance b/d	330

- The payments for gas on 3 March, 10 July and 6 October represent quarterly payments already made. Their total is the amount transferred to the trial balance in Figure 19.1.
- The amount still owed must be added to the total and therefore the gas account is debited with £330. This is done by writing in the entry 'Balance c/d (accrual) £330' on 31.12.00. The account now shows that a total expense of £1,310 was incurred for gas in the current trading year.
- £1,310 is posted as a credit and is transferred to the profit and loss account where it is treated as an expense.
- The credit balance on 1 January 2001 shows that Cafe Noir still owed £330 for gas at the beginning of the next trading year. In the balance sheet, this is shown as an accrual under the heading of current liabilities, ie it is money owed in the short term.
- After the adjustment for accruals has been made, the gas account can be redrawn as in Figure 19.3. Note that the £330 credit balance b/d on 1 January will form the opening balance for the account in the next accounting period.

Figure 19.3 *Redrawn gas account for Cafe Noir*

NOMINAL LEDGER

Dr		Gas Account		Cr	
2000		£	2000		£
3.3	Bank	290	31.12	Profit and loss	1,310
10.7	Bank	340			
6.10	Bank	350			
31.12	Balance c/d (accrual)	330			
		1,310			1,310
			2001		
			1.1	Balance b/d	330

Accounting for accrued revenue The accrued revenue in the case of Cafe Noir is for rent that is owed but not yet received. The rent received account is shown in Figure 19.4. This account was balanced on 31 December 2000.

- The £3,000 received as rent was transferred to the trial balance as shown in Figure 19.1. However, £1,000 was still owing from the tenant in respect of the current year's occupancy. This should be added to the total rent received and therefore the rent received account should be credited with another £1,000. This is done by writing 'Balance c/d (accrual) £1,000' on 31 December 2000.
- The account now shows a total rent received of £4,000 for the current year. This amount is posted to the profit and loss account. There is a £1,000 debit balance on the rent received account which is listed on 1 January 2001. This means that Cafe Noir was owed £1,000 by the tenant at the beginning of the next trading year. In the balance sheet, this amount is shown as a current asset.

Figure 19.4 *Rent received account for Cafe Noir*

NOMINAL LEDGER

	Dr		**Rent Received Account**		**Cr**	
2000		£	2000			£
31.12 Balance c/d		3,000	2.1	Bank		1,000
			1.4	Bank		1,000
			5.7	Bank		1,000
		3,000				3,000
31.12 Profit and loss		4,000	31.12 Balance b/d			3,000
			31.12 Balance c/d (accrual)			1,000
		4,000				4,000
2001						
1.1 Balance b/d		1,000				

The rent received account can be redrawn to show the effect of the adjustment (see Figure 19.5). Note that the £1,000 debit balance b/d on 1 January will form the opening balance for the account in the next accounting period.

Figure 19.5 *Redrawn rent received account for Cafe Noir*

NOMINAL LEDGER

	Dr		**Rent Received Account**		**Cr**	
2000		£	2000			£
31.12 Profit and loss		4,000	2.1	Bank		1,000
			1.4	Bank		1,000
			5.7	Bank		1,000
			31.12 Balance c/d (accrual)			1,000
		4,000				4,000
2001						
1.1 Balance b/d		1,000				

Adjusting the trial balance The adjustments for accrued expenses and accrued income can be included in the trial balance. A new trial balance extract for Cafe Noir is shown in Figure 19.6. The debit balance on the gas account has increased to £1,310 to show the effect of the accrued expense. A new balance for £330 is listed for gas accrued. This shows that Cafe Noir owes £330 for gas. It is a credit balance because it is a liability. The credit balance on the rent received account has risen to £4,000 to show the effect of the accrued revenue. A new balance for £1,000 is listed for rent accrued which shows that £1,000 of the rent total is still owed to Cafe Noir. It is a debit balance because it is a current asset, ie it is expected to be received in the short term.

Figure 19.6 *An extract from the trial balance of Cafe Noir showing the adjustments for accruals*

Cafe Noir
Trial Balance as at 31.12.00

	Dr £	Cr £
Gas	1,310	
Gas accrued		330
Rent receivable		4,000
Rent accrued	1,000	

QUESTION 2

Adrian Hughes runs a health centre called Muscles in Swansea. The centre was created by converting an old squash club that had closed down. Adrian keeps up to date records of financial transactions and two accounts are shown in Figure 19.7. Both accounts are balanced and the balances have been transferred to a trial balance. The trading year for Muscles ends on 31 December.

Figure 19.7 *Telephone and interest received accounts for Muscles*

NOMINAL LEDGER

Telephone Account

Dr		£	Cr		£
2000			2000		
1.3	Bank	231	31.12	Balance c/d	752
6.6	Bank	310			
8.9	Bank	211			
		752			752
31.12 Balance b/d		752			

Interest Received Account

Dr		£	Cr		£
2000			2000		
31.12 Balance c/d		312	2.7	Bank	312
			31.12	Balance b/d	312

After the trial balance had been prepared for Muscles, two adjustments were required to the accounts shown in Figure 19.7.
- A telephone bill for the final quarter of the year had not been paid. This was received on 30 December 2000 and £278 was owed on the account.
- Interest of £349 received from the bank on 2 January 2001 had not been accounted for. This interest was for the period 1 July 2000 to 31 December 2000.

(a) **Adjust the telephone account shown in Figure 19.7 to account for the accrued telephone charge.**
(b) **Adjust the interest received account in Figure 19.7 to account for the accrued interest received.**
(c) **Draw up a new trial balance extract to show the effects of the adjustments.**

What are prepayments?

A PREPAYMENT is a payment made in advance of the accounting period to which it refers. For example, a business might pay an annual insurance premium in advance of receiving the cover. Sometimes a prepayment is received by a business in advance of a transaction. For instance, a customer might pay a builder a deposit or advance payment before work begins.

If a prepayment is made, an adjustment to the trial balance is required. The first stage is to calculate how much of the prepayment relates to the current trading year. For example, if a business paid an annual motor insurance premium of £450 on the 1 July 2000, and the trading year ended on 31 December 2000, only six months of the premium would relate to the current trading year. Therefore, half of the premium (£225) must be subtracted from the insurance expenses for that year in order to give a 'true and fair view' of the firm's financial circumstances.

Accounting for prepayments

In order to illustrate how prepayments are accounted for, consider the example of Hornchurch Metal Products (HMP), a company that makes metal ornaments for gift shops and other retailers. At the end of a trading year, on 31 December 2000, the trial balance for HMP showed that total insurance expenses were £1,200 (see Figure 19.8). However, the insurance premium was paid on 1 February 2000 for one year's cover. Therefore one month of the total premium was for the next trading period, ie for January 2001. So, there had been a prepayment of £100.

Figure 19.8 *An extract from the trial balance of HMP at 31.12.00*

Hornchurch Metal Products
Trial Balance as at 31.12.00

	Dr	Cr
	£	£
Insurance	1,200	

Figure 19.9 is the insurance account for HMP. It shows that £1,200 was paid for insurance on 1 February 2000. The account was balanced on 31 December 2000 and £1,200 was transferred to the trial balance on 31 December 2000 as shown in Figure 19.8. However, the account must be adjusted to show the prepayment for £100. The total charge for insurance must be reduced by £100 to £1,100. This total charge is then posted to the profit and loss account. The prepayment is shown by writing 'Balance c/d (prepayment) £100' on the credit side of the insurance account. The date of this entry is 31 December 2000. To complete the bookkeeping, the prepayment is shown as a debit balance on 1 January 2001. It is, in effect, the opening balance for the next trading period. This means that HMP had already paid some of that year's insurance premium. It is treated as a current asset in the balance sheet.

Figure 19.9 *The insurance account for HMP*

NOMINAL LEDGER
Insurance Account

Dr			Cr	
2000		£	2000	£
1.2 Bank		1,200	31.12 Balance c/d	1,200
31.12 Balance b/d		1,200	31.12 Profit and loss	1,100
			31.12 Balance c/d (prepayment)	100
		1,200		1,200
2001				
1.1 Balance b/d		100		

A new trial balance extract can be drawn up to show the effect of this adjustment. It is shown in Figure 19.10. The debit balance on the insurance account has decreased to £1,100 to show the effect of the £100 prepayment. A new debit balance of £100 is written in the trial balance to show the prepayment following the adjustment.

Figure 19.10 *An extract from the trial balance of HMP at 31 December 2000 showing the prepayment*

Hornchurch Metal Products
Trial Balance as at 31.12.00

	Dr	Cr
	£	£
Insurance	1,100	
Prepayment:		
insurance	100	

QUESTION 3

Bletchley Camera Equipment makes camera equipment for specialist photographers. It sells its products throughout the UK. The end of a financial year for the business is on 31 December. Figure 19.11 shows an extract from the rent account and the insurance account for Bletchley Camera Equipment.

Figure 19.11 *Rent account and insurance account for Bletchley Camera Equipment*

NOMINAL LEDGER

Dr	Rent Account		Cr
2000	£	2000	£
2.2 Bank	4,000	31.12 Balance c/d	13,000
2.5 Bank	3,000		
3.8 Bank	3,000		
1.11 Bank	3,000		
	13,000		13,000
31.12 Balance b/d	13,000		

Dr	Insurance Account		Cr
2000	£	2000	£
1.3 Bank	600	31.12 Balance c/d	600
31.12 Balance b/d	600		

After the trial balance had been prepared for Bletchley Camera Equipment, two adjustments were necessary to take into account prepayments on the rent and insurance accounts.
- The fourth rent payment made on 1 November 2000 was for a three month period up to and including January 2001.
- The annual insurance payment made on 1 March 2000 included the period up to 28 February 2001.

(a) Calculate the amount of the rent and insurance prepayments.
(b) Adjust the rent account to show the prepayment.
(c) Adjust the insurance account to show the prepayment.

summary questions

1. Why are adjustments necessary?
2. Give two examples of accrued expenses.
3. Give two examples of accrued revenue.
4. Under what heading is an accrued expense shown in the balance sheet?
5. Give an example of accrued revenue that would be shown as an asset in the balance sheet.
6. Give two examples of prepayments.
7. Explain why a prepayment of an insurance premium is an asset.
8. Will a prepayment appear as a debit or a credit on the trial balance?
9. What effect will a prepayment have on an expense for the year?
10. If an accrued expense is ignored, what effect does this have on profit for the year?

UNIT ASSESSMENT QUESTION 1

Stellios Panopoulos runs an insurance agency that sells insurance policies for holidays, homes and contents. At the end of the financial year, on 31 December 2000, the business rates account and electricity account were balanced. The two accounts were then adjusted to account for a prepayment of business rates and an accrued expense that related to a quarterly electricity bill which was received on 31 January 2001 for £180. These two accounts are shown in Figure 19.12.

Figure 19.12 *Rates and electricity accounts for Stellios Panopoulos's business*

NOMINAL LEDGER

Business Rates Account

Dr		£			Cr £
2000		£	2000		£
2.4	Bank	2,400	31.12	Balance c/d	2,400
31.12	Balance b/d	2,400	31.12	Profit & loss	1,800
			31.12	Balance c/d (accrual)	600
		2,400			2,400
2001					
1.1	Balance b/d	600			

Electricity Account

Dr		£			Cr £
2000		£	2000		£
2.5	Bank	145	31.12	Balance c/d	540
4.8	Bank	195			
1.11	Bank	200			
		540			540
31.12	Balance b/d	540	31.12	Profit & loss	660
31.12	Balance c/d (accrual)	120			
		660			660
			2001		
			1.1	Balance b/d	120

(a) Suggest how the £600 business rates prepayment was calculated.
(b) Suggest how the £120 accrual for electricity was calculated.
(c) Explain what effect the prepayment and the accrued expenses had on total business rates and electricity expenses for the year.
(d) Prepare an extract from the trial balance for the business showing business rates, electricity, prepayments and accruals.
(e) Explain why the prepayment is a debit balance in the trial balance.
(f) Explain why the accrued expense is a credit balance in the trial balance.

UNIT ASSESSMENT QUESTION 2

Claire and Thomas James own Hallatrow Farm in Somerset. They have a herd of dairy cows and produce milk for local cheese makers. The farm has a large cottage which is rented out for £600 per month.

At the end of the financial year, on 30 June 2001, three adjustments were necessary before the final accounts could be produced. They related to the following accruals and prepayment:

- A vet's bill for £240 relating to work done in June was expected to arrive in July.
- The tenant living in the cottage still owed rent for April and May.
- An equipment leasing charge for £900 relating to the period 1 June 2001 to 31 August 2001 was paid on 2 June 2001.

The business accounts relating to the income and expenses listed above are shown in Figure 19.13. The accounts only show the balances b/d on 30 June 2001.

Figure 19.13 *Three accounts for Hallatrow Farm*

NOMINAL LEDGER

Veterinary Fees Account

Dr			Cr	
2001		£		£
30.6	Balance b/d	4,390		

Rent Received Account

Dr			Cr	
		£	2001	£
			30.6 Balance b/d	6,000

Equipment Leasing Account

Dr			Cr	
2001		£		£
30.6	Balance b/d	3,100		

(a) Make the necessary entries in the veterinary fees account to adjust for the accrued expense.

(b) Make the necessary entries in the rent received account to adjust for the accrued revenue.

(c) Make the necessary entries in the equipment leasing account to adjust for the prepayment.

(d) Prepare a trial balance extract for Hallatrow Farm to show the adjustments on all three accounts.

key terms

Accrual - an estimate of money still owing that is not supported by an invoice at the time the accounts are prepared.

Accrued expenses - money still owed by a business at the end of the trading year for resources that have been used.

Accrued revenue - money owed to a business (not for goods sold) at the end of the trading year.

Adjustments - changes made to accounts or the trial balance before using them in the final accounts.

Prepayment - advance payments or receipts of money.

Bad and doubtful debts

What is a bad debt?

Many businesses sell goods on credit. This means that customers are given a period of time before payment has to be made. By allowing customers to 'buy now and pay later', a business takes a risk that a customer might not pay at all. If this happens, and the business is unable to recover payment, the unpaid debt is known as a BAD DEBT. Bad debts are **written off** in the accounts and an entry in the **journal** is made to record this.

Bad debts occur for a number of reasons.

- One of the most common causes of bad debts is that a customer becomes INSOLVENT. This inability to pay debts can arise for many reasons, such as the failure of the customer's business. For an individual, insolvency can lead to **bankruptcy** and in the case of a company it can lead to **liquidation**. In both cases it is unlikely that the money owed will be recovered.
- Sometimes a trading dispute can cause a bad debt. For example, a customer might claim that an order was not delivered. If the customer refuses to pay, the debt might be written off. A trading dispute might be resolved by a customer paying part of what is owed and the rest being written off. The proportion written off is then treated as a bad debt.
- If a business has a poor CREDIT CONTROL system, bad debts might occur. For example, a business might not be able to recover a debt if it fails to keep track of what is owed or does not send out reminders. Credit control is discussed in more detail at the end of this unit.
- A business might write off a long standing debt if it considers that the cost of enforcing payment is greater than the debt itself.
- A bad debt might occur because a business is the victim of fraud. For example, a new customer might take delivery of goods on credit and then move address. If the customer cannot be traced, recovery of the debt is unlikely.

Accounting for bad debts

Bad debts are treated as an expense in accounting. They are listed in the profit and loss account with other expenses such as stationery, rent and motor expenses. Judgment is required in deciding if and when a particular debt is to be written off. The **concept of prudence** suggests that bad debts should be recognised as they arise. However, depending on the circumstances of the business, the decision to write off debts might be left until the end of the trading period.

In order to show the bookkeeping entries needed to write off a bad debt, consider the example of Dawson's Denim Products, a company that makes jeans, jackets and skirts. At the end of the trading year, 31 December, two of Dawson's customers owed money for goods bought on credit. Both of these customers had ceased trading in November and the money owing was not likely to be recovered. Details of their accounts in the sales ledger are shown in Figure 20.1. The account for BJ Fashions shows that goods for £341 were bought in May and paid for in August. However, goods bought in September for £287 had not been paid for. Similarly, the Lucy Bennett account shows that £740 was owed for goods that were bought in October.

Figure 20.1 *Sales ledger accounts for BJ Fashions and Lucy Bennett*

SALES LEDGER

Dr		BJ Fashions		Cr	
		£			£
21.5	Sales	341	20.8 Bank		341
12.9	Sales	287			

Dr		Lucy Bennett		Cr	
		£			£
4.10	Sales	740			

To write off the amounts owed by these two customers, the following actions are required. They are shown in Figure 20.2.

- The amount owed by each customer has to be identified. This is the difference between the total credits and total debits in each account. In this case, BJ Fashions owed £287 and Lucy Bennett owed £740.
- The account of each customer is credited with the amount of the bad debt. This is done by writing 'Bad debt £287' for BJ Fashions and 'Bad debt £740' for Lucy Bennett. If this is done at the end of the trading year, the date of the entries is 31 December. However, if the debts were recognised as being bad at an earlier date, then the bad debt should be written against this date.
- The two customer accounts are then balanced. These two accounts are now considered closed by Dawson's Denim Products. Both totals for each account are double-underlined. There is no balance b/d.
- The amounts written off are debited to the bad debts account in the nominal ledger. This is also sometimes called the 'bad debts written off account'. The name of the bad debtor and the amount written off are entered on the debit side of the account. This is because the bad debts are treated as an expense. The dates of these entries are the dates on which the debts are written off. In this case, it is at the end of the financial year, ie 31 December. The total of bad debts for the year, £1,027, is posted to the profit and loss account. The effect is to reduce the amount of profit for the year.

Figure 20.2 *Sales ledger accounts and bad debts account for Dawson's Denim Products*

SALES LEDGER

Dr		BJ Fashions		Cr	
		£			£
21.5	Sales	341	20.8 Bank		341
12.9	Sales	287	31.12 Bad debts		287
		628			628

Dr		Lucy Bennett		Cr	
		£			£
4.10	Sales	740	31.12 Bad debts		740

NOMINAL LEDGER

Dr		Bad Debts Account		Cr	
		£			£
31.12	BJ Fashions	287	31.12 Profit and loss		1,027
31.12	Lucy Bennett	740			
		1,027			1,027

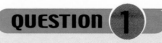

Anthony Fernandes runs an office supplies business. He sells stationery, office equipment and furniture to companies in the Luton area. Anthony allows customers to buy goods on credit and he gives them 30 days to settle their accounts. During the trading year ending on 31 December, Anthony's business suffered two bad debts.

- One related to a consignment of furniture that was delivered to a customer in Bedford. The invoice total of the goods was £800. However, T. Walters, the customer, claimed that the goods were damaged in transit. He paid £500 but refused to pay the rest. After a lengthy dispute, Anthony decided to write off the remaining £300 as a bad debt.
- One of Anthony's regular customers, Gregsons, ceased trading in September leaving £110 unpaid on the account. This was written off.

Figure 20.3 *Customer accounts for T. Walters and Gregsons*

SALES LEDGER

Dr		T. Walters		Cr	
		£			£
23.5 Sales		800	12.11 Bank		500

Dr		Gregsons		Cr	
		£			£
6.1 Sales		178	4.5 Bank		178
12.3 Sales		291	12.7 Bank		291
26.8 Sales		110			

(a) Complete the bookkeeping entries required to write off the bad debts in the customer accounts of Anthony Fernandes' business.

(b) Draw up the bad debts account of Anthony's business.

(c) Explain the effect these bad debts will have had on profit for the year.

Provision for doubtful debts

In addition to writing off bad debts, a business might make a provision for DOUBTFUL DEBTS. These are debts that the business believes are unlikely to be paid and will therefore become bad debts. A PROVISION is an amount set aside in the accounts to cover a known liability. In this case, the provision is to cover the possible non-payment of a debt, which is an asset. This provision is also sometimes known as a provision for bad debts.

When a business makes a provision for doubtful debts, it is acting in accordance with the prudence concept. It is recognising that profits might not be as high as would otherwise be stated. However, there is a problem in deciding which debts to class as being doubtful. A number of methods are used.

- Accountants might try to identify specific doubtful debts by looking at the AGED DEBTORS SCHEDULE. This is a list of customers that shows the size and 'age' of their debts. Figure 20.4 is an example of an aged debtors schedule. It shows the name and account number of each customer and the total balance outstanding on the account.
- The balance is subdivided into columns according to the length of time the money has been owed. For example, Blakemores has a balance on its account of £720. This is the total amount owed. Of this total, £300 relates to the most recent trade credit period of 30 days, and £420 relates to a period of between 30 and 60 days. Doubtful debts are likely to be those in the final column which indicates that a debt has been outstanding for more than 120 days. For example, Eagle Bros. has owed £419 for more than 120 days. A **specific provision** might be made for this doubtful debt.

Figure 20.4 *An example of an aged debtors schedule*

Account	Customer	Balance	Current	30+days	60+days	90+days	120+days
		£	£	£	£	£	£
SL01	Blakemores	720	300	420			
SL02	Eagle Bros.	419					419
SL03	Goulden K.	455	455				
SL04	Harris M.	322	100	122	100		
SL05	Miles Cars	450		450			
Totals		2,366	855	992	100		419

- Sometimes, rather than spending time in trying to identify specific doubtful debts, a business might estimate an overall percentage of doubtful debts. For example, a business might know from several years' experience that, on average, 2.5% of its total customer debts will not be paid. Therefore, if the value of total debtors at the end of a particular trading year is £67,000, the provision for doubtful debts will be £1,675 (ie £67,000 × 2.5%). This is known as a **general provision** for doubtful debts.
- A third method of estimating the size of doubtful debts is to make a general provision using the aged debtors list. This is done by weighting the provision towards those debts which have been outstanding the longest. Previous experience is used in estimating the likelihood of payment. Figure 20.5 shows how this might work using the total debts listed in the aged debtors schedule from Figure 20.4. Those debts that have been outstanding for the longest period of time are the ones that are most likely to be unpaid. For example, debts outstanding for more than 120 days are most likely to be bad. Therefore, 20% of the total debt in this period is estimated to be bad, ie £83.80 (20% × £419). On the other hand, the most recent debts are more likely to be paid. Therefore, only 1% of the total is estimated to be bad, ie £8.55 (1% × £855). Using this weighting system, the total provision for doubtful debts in this example is £151.95.

Figure 20.5 *Calculating a general provision for doubtful debts using a weighting system*

Duration of debt	Amount	Estimated percentage doubtful	Provision
	£		£
Current	855.00	1	8.55
31-60 days	992.00	5	49.60
61-90 days	100.00	10	10.00
91-120 days	-	15	-
120+days	419.00	20	83.80
Total	2,366.00		151.95

Accounting for doubtful debts

Once the size of doubtful debts has been estimated, a provision can be made in the accounts. In order to illustrate the bookkeeping entries, consider the example of C. Watkins, a furniture manufacturer. At the end of the trading year, 31 December 2000, C. Watkins made a general provision for doubtful debts. This was £400 which represented 2% of £20,000 outstanding debts. Two bookkeeping entries are required. These are shown in Figure 20.6.

- The profit and loss account of C. Watkins' business is debited with £400 because it represents an increase in expenses. Profit is reduced by the amount of the provision. The provision for doubtful debts is treated like any other expense when listed in the profit and loss account.
- The provision for doubtful debts account is credited with £400. It is a credit because it represents a decrease in assets, ie fewer debts are likely to be paid. As the account shows in Figure 20.6, the provision for doubtful debts is not identified with any particular customer.

In the balance sheet, the provision for doubtful debts is subtracted from the total value of debtors. This helps to give a 'true and fair view' of total debtors for the year.

Figure 20.6 *The bookkeeping entries required to account for the doubtful debt provision of C. Watkins' business*

NOMINAL LEDGER

Dr	Profit and Loss Account	£	Cr	£
2000				
31.12 Provision for doubtful debts		400		

Dr	Provision for Doubtful Debts	£	Cr	£
			2000	
			31.12 Profit and loss	400

QUESTION 2

Warwick Motors is a garage just outside Coventry. It carries out car repairs and MOTs for mainly local customers. Many of these customers have accounts and are given 30 days credit. Bill Rogers, the owner of the business, appreciates the risk involved in this practice and regularly incurs bad debts. However, since he charges premium rates for all of his services he believes the practice is to his advantage. On 31 May 2000, the end of year for Warwick Motors, the total amount of money owed by credit customers was £12,500.

At the end of the trading year, Bill decided to introduce a provision for doubtful debts. His approach was to make a general provision equal to 3% of total debts.

(a) Suggest a reason why Bill Rogers would make a general provision for doubtful debts rather than a specific provision.
(b) Calculate the provision for doubtful debts for Warwick Motors.
(c) Show the bookkeeping entries required to provide for doubtful debts.
(d) What effect will the doubtful debt provision have on profit for Warwick Motors?

How might the provision for doubtful debts be increased or decreased?

At the end of each year it is likely that a business will want to change or revise the provision for doubtful debts. A revision is necessary under the following circumstances.

- **If the value of total debtors changes** This is almost certain to happen. For example, if a business grows, credit sales are likely to increase. Therefore the value of debtors is likely to rise.
- **If the likelihood of bad debts rises or falls** For example, during a recession bad debts are more likely to occur. Therefore, a business might decide to raise its provision for doubtful debts from 3% to 5% of total debtors.

Increasing the provision In order to illustrate the bookkeeping entries needed to increase a provision for doubtful debts, consider the earlier example of C. Watkins. At the end of the trading year, 31 December 2000, a £400 provision for doubtful debts was made. Suppose that during the following year, debtors rose to £25,000 as a result of more credit sales. Based on the 2% general provision used in the example, the provision for doubtful debts would need to be increased from £400 to £500 (ie 2% x £25,000) in 2001. This requires an adjustment to the provision. An increase of £100 is needed. The bookkeeping entries are shown in Figure 20.7.

- The profit and loss account of C. Watkins' business in 2001 is debited with the increase in the provision, ie £100. This reduces the amount of profit by £100 in that year.
- In the provision for doubtful debts account, the existing provision of £400 is brought down. To account for the increase in the provision, a credit entry of £100 is required. The total provision for doubtful debts is now raised to £500.

Figure 20.7 *Bookkeeping entries required to increase the provision for doubtful debts for C. Watkins' business (2001)*

NOMINAL LEDGER

Dr	Profit and Loss Account		Cr	
2001		£	£	
31.12 Provision for doubtful debts		100		

Dr	Provision for Doubtful Debts		Cr	
2000		£	2000	£
31.12 Balance c/d		400	31.12 Profit and loss	400
			2001	
			1.1 Balance b/d	400
			31.12 Profit and loss	100
			(increase in provision)	

Decreasing the provision In order to illustrate the bookkeeping entries needed to reduce a provision for doubtful debts, consider again the example of C. Watkins. Suppose that, at the end of the trading year 2002, total debtors fell to £22,000. Based on the 2% general provision used previously, the provision for doubtful debts is reduced from £500 to £440 (ie 2% x £22,000). This requires a decrease of £60 in the provision. The bookkeeping entries are shown in Figure 20.8.

- The profit and loss account is credited with the decrease in the provision, ie with £60. This increases the amount of profit by £60.
- In the provision for doubtful debts account, the existing provision of £500 is brought down. To account for the decrease in the provision, a debit entry of £60 is required. The total provision for doubtful debts is now reduced to £440 (ie £500 - £60). This is the amount brought down at the start of the next year.

Figure 20.8 *Bookkeeping entries required to decrease the provision for doubtful debts for C. Watkins' business (2002)*

NOMINAL LEDGER

Dr		Profit and Loss Account		Cr	
	£	2002			£
		31.12 Provision for doubtful debts			60

Dr		Provision for Doubtful Debts		Cr	
2000	£	**2000**			£
31.12 Balance c/d	400	31.12 Profit and loss			400
2001		**2001**			
31.12 Balance c/d	500	1.1 Balance b/d			400
		31.12 Profit and loss			100
		(increase in provision)			
	500				500
2002		**2002**			
31.12 Profit and loss	60	1.1 Balance b/d			500
(decrease in provision)					
31.12 Balance c/d	440				
	500				500
		2003			
		1.1 Balance b/d			440

QUESTION 3

Whitman & Co. manufactures glassware in a small factory in Glasgow. It makes glass ornaments, bowls and kitchenware. The company sells to retailers in Scotland and the north of England giving customers 60 days credit. At the end of the trading year, 31 December 2001, £1,400 of bad debts were written off. This left a total of remaining debtors of £38,000. In the previous year, Whitman & Co. had made a general provision for doubtful debts of £900. The company's policy is to classify 3% of debts (after writing off bad debts) as doubtful. The provision for doubtful debts account of Whitman & Co.'s business is shown in Figure 20.9.

Figure 20.9 *Provision for doubtful debts account of Whitman & Co.*

NOMINAL LEDGER

Dr		Provision for Doubtful Debts		Cr	
2000	£	**2000**			£
31.12 Balance c/d	900	31.12 Profit and loss			900
		2001			
		1.1 Balance b/d			900

(a) Calculate the provision for doubtful debts in 2001 for Whitman & Co.
(b) Calculate the change in provision that is needed for 2001.
(c) Show the entries needed in the provision for doubtful debts account for the change in provision.
(d) Show the adjustment necessary in the profit and loss account to change the provision.

Recovering a bad debt

Sometimes a business might write off a bad debt and then receive payment from the customer unexpectedly. In order to illustrate how the recovery of a bad debt is accounted for, consider the example of Roy Simmonds, a supplier of corporate uniforms. At the end of the trading year, 31 December 2000, his business wrote off a £450 debt that was owed by E. Hemmings. However, on 12 May 2001 the customer paid the debt in full. The bookkeeping entries for this transaction are shown in Figure 20.10.

- The customer's account in the sales ledger is debited with £450. This is to show that E. Hemmings has, in effect, honoured the debt and the original sales transaction has taken place.
- The matching entry is in the bad debts recovered account in the nominal ledger. This account is credited with £450. At the end of the trading year, the £450 credit balance on the bad debts recovered account will be transferred either to the bad debts account or directly to the profit and loss account. The effect is the same because the bad debts account is itself transferred to the profit and loss account at the end of the year.
- The payment made by E. Hemmings is shown by debiting the bank account and crediting the customer's account with £450.

Figure 20.10 *Bookkeeping entries to show the recovery of Roy Simmonds' bad debt from E. Hemmings*

SALES LEDGER

Dr			E. Hemmings		Cr	
2001		£	2001			£
12.5	Bad debts recovered	450	12.5	Bank		450

NOMINAL LEDGER

Dr		Bad Debts Recovered Account		Cr	
		£	2001		£
			12.5	E. Hemmings	450

Dr		Bank Account		Cr	
2001		£			£
12.5	E. Hemmings	450			

Credit control

Most businesses that sell goods on credit are likely to have some form of credit control. The purpose of credit control is to monitor customer payments. In particular, it is to ensure that customers pay what they owe when payment is due. An example of a credit control system is shown in Figure 20.11. It illustrates the procedure a business might follow when selling to customers on credit.

Figure 20.11 *An example of a credit control system*

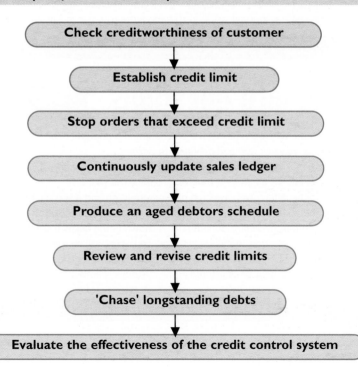

Check creditworthiness of customer
↓
Establish credit limit
↓
Stop orders that exceed credit limit
↓
Continuously update sales ledger
↓
Produce an aged debtors schedule
↓
Review and revise credit limits
↓
'Chase' longstanding debts
↓
Evaluate the effectiveness of the credit control system

- The first step in the credit control procedure is to check the creditworthiness of a potential customer. A business would be taking a risk if it sold goods on credit to a new customer without checking on the customer's ability to pay. This might be done by requesting references from other suppliers, from the customer's bank and possibly from a specialist credit rating agency. Once it is confirmed that a new customer is creditworthy, a business must decide how much credit to allow. The information collected when checking on creditworthiness might be used to help decide on the credit limit.

- If a customer makes an order that exceeds the established credit limit, action has to be taken. The result might be to place a 'stop' on the order until any outstanding debt is cleared. It is important to maintain up to date records of all customer purchases and payments. Failure to keep a track of all customer transactions could result in credit limits being exceeded.

- Many businesses produce an aged debtors schedule (see Figure 20.4). This is produced on a regular basis, for example monthly. It helps to keep track of the amounts that customers owe and how long they have owed the money.

- The credit control department is responsible for ensuring that all debts are paid. In the case of debts that are outstanding for a long period, urgent action might have to be taken. A copy of the statement of account might be sent, followed by a letter to 'chase' the debt, then a reminder. If a customer still fails to pay, a telephone call might be made to enquire on the reason for non-payment. Finally, if all else fails, a business might threaten to take legal action to recover the debt. However, this is expensive and could cost more than the amount of the outstanding debt. There is also the consideration that legal action would damage relations with the customer. It is therefore only likely to be used as a last resort.

- It is useful for businesses to evaluate the performance of their credit control department. This might be done at the end of the trading year. For example, a business might calculate the number of days on average it takes customers to pay or calculate the proportion of bad debts to overall debts.

key terms

Aged debtors schedule - a list of credit customers showing the 'age' of their debts.
Bad debt - money owed by a customer that is unlikely to be paid and is therefore 'written off' by a business.
Credit control - the monitoring and collection of customer payments.
Doubtful debt - a debt that might become a bad debt.
Insolvent - when a business is no longer able to meet its debts and is likely to cease trading.
Provision - an amount set aside in the accounts to cover a known liability.

summary questions

1. Explain the difference between a bad debt and a doubtful debt.
2. Give four reasons why bad debts might occur.
3. What bookkeeping entries are required to account for a bad debt?
4. What effect will a bad debt have on profit for the year?
5. Explain the difference between a general provision and a specific provision for doubtful debts.
6. What bookkeeping entries are required to account for a provision for doubtful debts?
7. How is the provision for doubtful debts shown in the balance sheet?
8. If the provision for doubtful debts is reduced, what will be the effect on profit?
9. Describe the bookkeeping entries needed to account for the recovery of a bad debt.
10. Why should a debt be reinstated in the customer's account if it is recovered?

UNIT ASSESSMENT QUESTION 1

Angus Dalglish owns a fish processing plant in Ullapool, Scotland. He buys fresh fish from local fisherman and produces canned fish, fish paste and pet food. The business, called Ullapool Fish Processing, sells to wholesalers and supermarkets. All of the sales are on credit.

At the end of the trading year, 31 August 2001, Angus wrote off two bad debts. Peter Collins, a wholesale fish merchant in Glasgow, ceased trading in September 2000 owing £890. Another customer, Fishmart of Carlisle, refused to pay £120 claiming that a delivery had contained some rotting fish. Although Angus disputed the claim, he decided not to use legal action to recover the debt because of the adverse publicity the case might attract. The customer accounts of Peter Collins and Fishmart are shown in Figure 20.12.

Figure 20.12 *Customer accounts for Ullapool Fish Processing*

SALES LEDGER

Dr	Peter Collins		Cr
2000	£	2000	£
10.9 Sales	890		

Dr	Fishmart		Cr
2000	£	2000 £	
6.9 Sales	228	4.12 Bank	228
2001		2001	
12.1 Sales	333	12.4 Bank	333
26.5 Sales	120		

(a) **Complete the bookkeeping entries required to write off the bad debts in the customer accounts.**

(b) **Draw up the bad debts account for Ullapool Fish Processing.**

(c) **On 21 November 2001 Ullapool Fish Processing unexpectedly received a cheque for £890 from Peter Collins. This customer had managed to raise new capital and was now trading again. Show the bookkeeping entries needed to record the recovery of the bad debt in the customer account, the bank account and the bad debts recovered account.**

UNIT ASSESSMENT QUESTION 2

Devon Plant Hire, based in Paignton, leases plant and equipment such as cranes, excavators, bulldozers, generators and heavy vehicles. Last year the business decided to make a general provision for doubtful debts using the aged debtors schedule. The provision was weighted towards debts that had been outstanding the longest. Figure 20.13 shows the estimated percentage of doubtful debts and the aged debtors schedule of Devon Plant Hire at the year end, 31 December.

Figure 20.13 *Aged debtors schedule of Devon Plant Hire and the estimated percentage of bad debts for different time periods*

Account	Customer	Balance £	Current £	30+days £	60+days £	90+days £
EN11	Ensor	230	230			
BL16	Blacks	870	370	300	200	
ER29	Eric Jones	340				340
TA65	Taunton KVB	2,890	1,690	1,200		
LI57	Lister Bros	300		300		
VA49	VA Builders	2,800	1,200	1,200		400
WI10	Wilson	980	400	280	300	

Duration of debt	Estimated percentage doubtful
Current	1
31-60 days	3
61-90 days	5
91+ days	10

(a) Calculate the provision for doubtful debts for Devon Plant Hire.

(b) Show the bookkeeping entries required to provide for the doubtful debts.

(c) Suggest how Devon Plant Hire might have arrived at the estimates of percentage doubtful debts shown in the table.

(d) Explain why the method used by Devon Plant Hire to calculate its doubtful debts provision might be better than providing a provision of, say, 4% of total debtors.

(e) Explain why a change in the provision for doubtful debts might be necessary in the next trading year.

(f) During the last three years, Devon Plant Hire has seen bad debts rise quite significantly. Explain how a credit control system might help the company.

unit 21

Fixed assets

unit objectives

To understand:
- the difference between fixed and current assets;
- the difference between tangible and intangible assets;
- the use of a fixed assets register.

Fixed and current assets

Assets are the resources that a business uses to produce goods or services. Their value is included on the balance sheet where they are classified as either FIXED ASSETS or CURRENT ASSETS.

Fixed assets These are assets intended for repeated and continued use. They can be divided into TANGIBLE ASSETS, such as vehicles and buildings, and INTANGIBLE ASSETS, such as the brand names of products. Fixed assets generally have a life span of at least one year, but might be used by a business for a much longer period of time. For example, a manufacturer could use a factory for many years. Spending on fixed assets is known as **capital expenditure**.

Fixed assets are often expensive to purchase and have to be maintained in order to be effective. For example, an articulated lorry might cost a haulage company over £50,000 to buy. The lorry will be used by the business to generate income by charging customers for carrying their freight. The lorry will have to be serviced regularly so that it remains reliable. Even so, it will suffer wear and tear and, eventually, its value will be 'used up'. In accounting, it is recognised that the cost of a fixed asset is gradually consumed as the asset wears out. The measure of **consumption** or any other reduction in the useful economic life of a fixed asset is known as DEPRECIATION (see unit 22).

Current assets Current assets, or circulating assets, are resources that have a relatively short life span, generally less than one year. Examples include stocks of raw materials and finished goods. Cash, debtors and prepayments are also classed as current assets.

Tangible assets

Tangible assets are fixed assets that have a physical substance and can be 'touched'. They include the following categories.

Land and buildings Property, such as land and buildings which is owned outright by a business, is known as **freehold property**. The value of freehold property in the UK has tended to rise over time. This is because of inflation and the long-term rise in property values during the last 50 years. Some businesses choose to **revalue** their property at regular intervals to show the rise in value on their balance sheet. Others prefer to value the property at its historical cost, ie its purchase price. The approach that is chosen depends on the accounting policy of the business.

Even though freehold buildings might be revalued from time to time, businesses and accountants recognise that the fabric of a building does eventually wear out. To conform with the **matching concept**, a depreciation charge is usually made in the accounts. However, in the case of freehold land, many businesses take the view that depreciation does not occur.

Leasehold property A lease is a contract between the owner of an asset and another person or business. When a business acquires the lease of a property, it buys the right to use that property for a fixed number of years. The way in which a business treats the depreciation of leasehold property depends upon the length of the lease. In the case of land that is held on a long lease such as 99 years, for example, most businesses take the view that depreciation does not occur. However, in the case of shorter term leases, the property will soon revert to the owner. Under these circumstances, it is generally accepted that depreciation does occur. In the UK, the term **amortisation** is often used to refer to depreciation in the context of leases and intangible assets. However, in the USA, amortisation and depreciation are usually taken to mean the same thing.

Machinery, vehicles and other equipment Most businesses use some fixed assets other than land and buildings. For example, manufacturing companies use machinery and tools, shops use fixtures and fittings such as counters and tills, and offices use computers and specialist furniture. Often businesses use vehicles such as delivery vans or company cars. In all cases, these items suffer from wear and tear and are therefore subject to depreciation. The rate of depreciation and the way this is accounted for is described in unit 23.

Tangible assets and the balance sheet

The tangible assets of a business are shown in the balance sheet at their NET BOOK VALUE (NBV) or WRITTEN-DOWN VALUE (WDV). The net book value of an asset is calculated as:

Net book value = historical cost - depreciation

The historical cost is the amount of money paid for an asset when it is purchased. Depreciation is defined as the measure of consumption of a fixed asset.

QUESTION 1

Below is an extract from the Annual Report and Accounts (2000) of J. Sainsbury plc.

Figure 21.1 *The net book value of the fixed assets of J. Sainsbury plc*

TANGIBLE FIXED ASSETS	Properties	Fixtures, equipment and vehicles
	£m	£m
Cost or valuation at 1 April 2000	5,968	3,664
Depreciation at 1 April 2000	904	2,165

(a) **Calculate the net book values of Sainsbury's properties and its fixtures, equipment and vehicles on 1 April 2000.**
(b) **Give four examples of tangible fixed assets that might be owned by J. Sainsbury plc.**
(c) **Explain why the assets in (b) are (i) tangible and (ii) fixed.**

Intangible assets

Intangible assets are non-physical fixed assets such as goodwill, patents and trademarks.

Goodwill In accounting, GOODWILL is defined as the difference in value between the **net assets** of a business and what the whole business could be sold for. Net assets are equal to total assets (excluding goodwill) less total liabilities. For example, if the net assets of a restaurant excluding goodwill were valued at £54,000 and the restaurant was then sold for £100,000, the value of goodwill would be £46,000 (ie £100,000 - £54,000). This goodwill is sometimes described as the 'premium paid for the acquisition of a business as a going concern'. Goodwill is created when a successful business builds up a relationship with its customers and develops a reputation for quality and service.

The accounting standard FRS10 *Goodwill and intangible assets* states that the value of **purchased** goodwill should be shown in the balance sheet and then depreciated (or amortised) over its expected useful economic life. The reason for this is that goodwill eventually 'wears off' unless there is new investment to maintain and improve customer relations. In the case of businesses which have not been sold, the value of goodwill is omitted from the balance sheet. This is because, in practice, it is extremely difficult to place an objective value on the goodwill that has been built up by a business. Only when an offer has been made by a buyer and accepted by a seller will a business have an idea of its value.

Patents, copyright and trademarks If a business or an individual invents or develops a new product or technique, a patent can be obtained from the Patent Office. A patent grants exclusive rights to exploit the invention and it prevents other firms from copying it for 20 years. To protect an invention abroad, patents have to be applied for in other countries. Patents can be of great value. For instance, in 1965, a patent was obtained for the ring-pull used to open cans. This generated a financial benefit of £49 million for the owner of the patent.

Copyright is the exclusive legal right to reproduce 'intellectual property'. This is the work of authors, composers, artists, software writers and other creative people. It prevents the re-use of this material without the author's consent. The ownership of copyright can be valuable. For example, it was reported that Michael Jackson paid nearly £30 million for a back catalogue of 250 Beatles' songs, outbidding former Beatle Paul McCartney. As the copyright holder, he is entitled to royalty payments if, for example, the songs are played on the radio or used in television advertising.

A trademark is a distinctive symbol, logo or name that represents a company or product. An example is the 'golden arches' m-shaped symbol that appears on McDonald's restaurants. Once it has been registered at the Register of Trade Marks, a trademark cannot be used or copied by another business without the consent of the owner.

It is usual for businesses to **capitalise** the cost of acquiring trademarks, copyright and patents. This means that, if they have been purchased, their value is included as an intangible asset on the balance sheet. They are then depreciated or amortised over a period of time.

Research and Development Large companies, particularly those in the pharmaceuticals industry, spend millions of pounds on researching and developing new products. The accounting standard SSAP13 *Accounting for research and development* states that businesses must write off research expenditure in the period during which it occurs. This means that the spending must be treated as an expense in the profit and loss account. However, in the case of development expenditure, businesses are allowed to capitalise the amount spent in certain strictly defined circumstances. Development spending is shown as an intangible asset on the balance sheet and is depreciated (or amortised) in the same way as purchased trademarks and goodwill.

Brand names Many companies own successful BRAND NAMES. These are the names which are used in advertising to build up brand loyalty. Examples include Kellogg's Corn Flakes, Heinz, Virgin and the Big Mac. Brand names can be extremely valuable to a business. For instance, Interbrand, a New York based brand valuation consultant, estimates that the value of the Coca-Cola brand name is worth more than 95 per cent of all the company's corporate assets.

In the UK, the accounting standard FRS10 *Goodwill and intangible assets* applies to the valuation of brands. As with goodwill, only purchased brands can be capitalised and shown on the balance sheet. For example, in the early 1990s, Nestlé bought the UK company Rowntree and in doing so, purchased brand names such as Kit Kat, Smarties, Polo, Black Magic and Rolo. Nestlé's Annual Report and Accounts (2000) states that:

...the excess of the cost of an acquisition over the fair value of the net tangible assets is capitalised. This value comprises intangible assets acquired including brand names.....Intangible assets are amortised over a period not exceeding 20 years.

The reasons why the value of non-purchased brand names are not included on the balance sheet are the same as those that relate to goodwill.

- It is very difficult to place a value on a brand name until it is sold. Only then, when an offer has been accepted from a buyer, can an objective valuation be obtained. Because of this difficulty, the prudence concept suggests that the value of non-purchased brand names should be omitted from the balance sheet, even though this might not give a 'true and fair' value of the business.
- The value of brand names can change quite sharply. For example, a business with a successful brand name could see its value fall rapidly if a rival launched a more popular brand or if the public lost faith in a brand. For example, in the mid-1990s, the source of Perrier water was found to be contaminated. The problem was quickly resolved but, for a time, the brand name was virtually worthless.

ASSET SALES

During the 1980s and the 1990s, the UK government raised in excess of £40 billion by selling off state assets. These included British Steel, British Telecom, the electricity distribution companies, British Rail and council houses. They were sold to a range of buyers in the private sector in a large-scale privatisation programme.

Attention has now switched to the sale of intangible assets. In 2000, the government auctioned off five mobile telephone licences to telecommunications companies for £20 billion. These licenses allow the owners the right to use particular mobile phone frequencies for a period of 20 years.

Another example is the BBC's plan to raise up to £4 billion by selling some of its online assets. The BBC has developed some impressive web sites with strong content and brand identities around programmes such as Top Gear and Gardener's World. If these web sites were developed into genuine commerce sites, through partnerships with private investors, the Corporation could raise a large sum which it could plough back into programme making.

The government might also consider selling information it holds on databases. For example, the Driver Vehicle Licensing Centre holds details on all UK cars and drivers. This information, which could be sold in aggregate form so that personal details could not be extracted, would be of interest to global car manufacturers.

Source: adapted from the *Financial Times* 10.4.2000.

(a) With reference to examples in the article, explain the difference between tangible and intangible assets.

(b) Using examples from the article, explain how a value might be placed on intangible assets.

Investments

In the context of business accounts, INVESTMENTS are defined as financial assets owned by a business. They are classed as fixed assets if they are expected to be held for at least one year. Examples include **shares** in other companies (see unit 34), **bonds** and **debentures** (see unit 35). Shares are issued by limited companies to raise capital. Shareholders who hold ordinary shares are the part-owners of the business and are entitled to a share in the profit. Bonds and debentures are IOUs that are issued by businesses and other institutions in order to raise money.

If a business owns more than 50 per cent of the ordinary shares in another company, it becomes the owner. It is known as a HOLDING or parent company. The company that is owned is said to be a SUBSIDIARY. Owning a majority of shares gives the holding company complete control and therefore it can directly influence the operating activities of its subsidiary. This might happen if, for example, a business buys a main supplier so that it can exercise control over the quality and delivery of components. If 100 per cent of the shares are owned, the company is said to be a **wholly owned subsidiary**.

Investments are generally listed in the balance sheet either at historical cost or at their current market value. The method that is used depends upon the accounting policies of the business. Investments are not subject to depreciation.

Fixed assets register

Businesses that own a large number of fixed assets generally keep a detailed record in a FIXED ASSETS REGISTER. This is not part of the double entry system, but is used for memorandum and control purposes. A fixed asset register might contain the following information:

- a description of the asset;
- an identification number, for example a serial number;
- the date of purchase;
- the purchase price of the asset;

- the invoice number;
- the physical location of the asset in the business;
- the method of depreciation used (see unit 22);
- the estimated useful life of the asset;
- the estimated scrap value;
- the accumulated depreciation to date;
- the net book value of the asset;
- the disposal date of the asset, if it has been sold or scrapped, and authorisation;
- the proceeds from disposal.

   The layout of a fixed assets register will vary from one business to another. One method of recording information is to have a separate page for each individual asset. Another approach is to enter the information on a spreadsheet or on a computer database. An extract from a fixed assets register is shown in Figure 21.2.

Figure 21.2 *An extract from a fixed assets register*

Description	Apple Performa Computer 6400
Serial number	CK6471918
Invoice number	104863
Date of purchase	27 June 1997
Cost	£1,292.50
Location	Print workshop
Accumulated depreciation	£1,292.50
Depreciation %	25%
Depreciation period	4 years
Depreciation method	Straight line
Date of disposal	3 July 2001
Sale proceeds	£0.00

   For a fixed asset register to be useful it must be kept up to date. Its main purpose is for monitoring the fixed assets that a business owns. This is particularly important if the assets are expensive. The register can be used to make physical checks on the location of specific fixed assets. It can also be used to **reconcile** information in the register with the fixed asset accounts in the nominal ledger. This will ensure that the information in the two records matches. If there are any discrepancies as a result of the check, then an investigation can be carried out to find reasons for the differences. If businesses do not make such checks, valuable fixed assets might be stolen or might go missing.

summary questions

1. Explain the difference between fixed and current assets.
2. Give five examples of tangible assets that might be owned by a manufacturing company.
3. Explain the difference between tangible and intangible assets.
4. Explain why it is difficult to place a value on internally generated intangible assets.
5. Give three examples of intangible assets other than goodwill.
6. Under what circumstances might the value of intangible assets be listed on a balance sheet?
7. Explain what it means when the value of an intangible asset is capitalised.
8. How is the term amortisation generally used in the UK?
9. What is the difference between a subsidiary and a wholly owned subsidiary?
10. State six pieces of information that might be recorded in a fixed assets register.

key terms

Brand name - the name given by a business to one or more of its products; it is classed as an intangible asset.

Current assets (or *circulating assets*) - resources used by a business that have a relatively short life span, generally less than one year.

Depreciation - the measure of wearing out, consumption or other reduction in the useful economic life of a fixed asset.

Fixed assets - resources that are intended for repeated and continued use. They generally have a life span of at least one year.

Fixed assets register - a detailed list of the fixed assets owned by a business.

Goodwill - the value that is placed on good customer relationships and a business's reputation for quality and service. It is an intangible asset. In accounting it is defined as the difference in value between the **net assets** of a business and what the whole business could be sold for. In this context, net assets equal total assets (excluding goodwill) less total liabilities.

Holding company (or *parent company*) - a company that owns more than 50 per cent of the shares in another company.

Intangible assets - non-physical assets.

Investments (as shown on balance sheets) - financial assets, such as shares, owned by a business.

Net book value (or *written-down value*) - the value of an asset shown on a balance sheet calculated by subtracting depreciation from the historical cost of the asset.

Subsidiary - a company that is controlled by a holding company because more than 50 per cent of its shares are owned by the holding company.

Tangible assets - physical assets that can be seen and touched.

UNIT ASSESSMENT   QUESTION 1

Nestlé is a multinational company that manufactures beverages, confectionery and foodstuffs. Its brand names include Nescafé, Buitoni, Kit Kat and Smarties. In 2000, its worldwide total sales revenue was over £30bn and its stock of fixed assets was valued at almost £15bn. Figure 21.3 shows the proportion of its fixed assets in six main categories.

Figure 21.3 *Fixed assets owned by Nestlé*

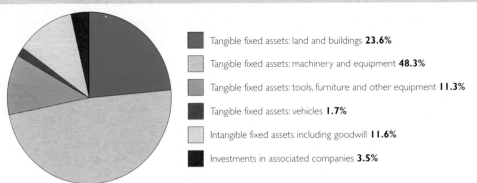

Tangible fixed assets: land and buildings **23.6%**

Tangible fixed assets: machinery and equipment **48.3%**

Tangible fixed assets: tools, furniture and other equipment **11.3%**

Tangible fixed assets: vehicles **1.7%**

Intangible fixed assets including goodwill **11.6%**

Investments in associated companies **3.5%**

Source: adapted from *Nestlé Management Report*, 2000.

(a) **Approximately what monetary value did Nestlé's intangible assets have in 2000?.**

(b) **Why are intangible assets important to Nestlé?**

(c) **Explain what might happen to the value of Nestlé's intangible assets if a competitor launched successful new products into the same markets.**

(d) **What type of investments might Nestlé own? Explain your answer.**

UNIT ASSESSMENT · QUESTION 2

The Clarence Hotel is located in central London. It is a large, privately owned hotel with 55 rooms, a restaurant, a bar, a small swimming pool and a sauna. The hotel maintains a fixed assets register, extracts from which are shown in Figure 21.4. Recently a national hotel chain has made an offer to buy the hotel and this offer has been accepted by the owner.

Figure 21.4 *Extracts from the fixed assets register of the Clarence Hotel*

Description	Pine wardrobe	Transit van	Television	Toshiba computer
Serial number	N/A	M112 UTR	XA/2771	CD1776/8
Invoice number	RT9012	A1999	Q1911	SS554
Date of purchase	11.2.96	1.4.97	21.5.97	15.3.98
Cost	£200.00	£12,000.00	£240.00	£2,000.00
Location	Room 21	Garage	Room 19	Reception
Accumulated depn.	£60.00	£9,408.00	£80.00	£1,200.00
Date of disposal		3.3.01		
Sale proceeds		£2,200.00		

(a) **Explain how a fixed assets register might be used at the Clarence Hotel.**

(b) **Which of the assets in the register is no longer owned by the hotel? Explain your answer.**

(c) **The tangible net assets of the hotel are valued at £2,600,000. The agreed selling price of the hotel is £3,000,000. What does the difference between these amounts represent?**

(d) **How might the Clarence Hotel increase the value of its goodwill?**

Calculating depreciation

What causes depreciation?

During the production process, the fixed assets of a business are 'used up' or CONSUMED. For example, premises and machinery wear out over time and equipment becomes outdated. **Depreciation** is the measure of this consumption over a particular period.

Suppose a business buys a machine for £15,000 and estimates that depreciation is £3,500 in the first year. This £3,500 is in effect the cost of the fixed asset that has been consumed by the business during that period.

According to the **matching concept** (see unit 7), the cost of consuming an asset must be matched in the accounts against the income earned by the asset in a particular time period. So, in the example above, the £3,500 depreciation must be listed in the business's profit and loss account as an expense. It is known as a **provision for depreciation** and its effect is to reduce profits. However, unlike most other expenses, no actual money is paid out.

It is a common misconception that depreciation involves putting money 'on one side' in order to pay for the replacement of a fixed asset at a later date. This is not the case. Depreciation represents an attempt to spread the cost of a fixed asset over its useful life. This must be calculated whether or not the asset is to be replaced.

Fixed assets are consumed over a period of time for a number of reasons.

- **Wear and tear** Fixed assets that are mechanical will have moving parts that wear out the more they are used. Even non-mechanical assets such as fixtures and fittings will eventually wear out. This is because they become damaged and worn. The more frequently that fixed assets are used, the faster they will depreciate from wear and tear. For example, if a haulage company buys a lorry and uses it for 12 hours a day and 7 days a week, it will wear out more quickly than if a hire company uses the same lorry for, say, 5 hours a day, just 3 days a week.
- **Erosion and decay** Some fixed assets deteriorate physically if they are exposed to the natural elements. For example, assets such as vehicles and machines that are made from steel will eventually rust when exposed to damp. Assets such as wooden boats and buildings will eventually rot.
- **Economic obsolescence** Some assets depreciate because they become out of date or OBSOLETE. This means that, although they still work, they need replacing because they are not as effective as newer models. Assets are most likely to become obsolete in businesses where technology develops rapidly. For example, a computer used for graphic design might become obsolete because its memory is too small, even though it still works perfectly well. An asset might also become obsolete if there is a change in consumer demand. For instance, machines that produce vinyl albums are no longer required in large numbers now that CDs are the main music format.
- **Inadequacy** Sometimes assets depreciate because they are no longer able to perform the function for which they were bought. They are therefore inadequate and have to be replaced. For example, a hotel might find that its telephone switchboard can no longer cope with demand. Therefore it has to be replaced by one with a greater capacity. The old switchboard is not worn out, but is of little or no use.
- **Depletion** Some fixed assets depreciate because their resources are used up. Such assets are sometimes called **wasting assets**. Examples include mines, quarries and oil wells.
- **Passage of time** Some assets have a lifespan which is fixed by law or by contract. Examples include patents and leases on buildings. Depreciation occurs as the expiry date on a patent or lease gets closer.

How is depreciation calculated?

A precise figure for depreciation can only be determined when a fixed asset is sold. For example, if a business buys a machine for £13,000 and disposes of it five years later for £3,000, the total depreciation **charge** or **allowance** for the entire life of the asset is £10,000 (ie £13,000 - £3,000). However, in most businesses, when an asset is purchased it is not certain for how long it will be used nor what its disposal value will be. Therefore accountants have to make an estimate. To do this they need to know the historical cost of an asset (ie its purchase price), its expected useful life and the estimated disposal value. The disposal value is also known as the NET RESIDUAL VALUE or scrap value. This is the value of the asset at the end of its useful life.

There is a number of ways in which the annual depreciation of fixed assets can be calculated. The accounting standard FRS15 *Tangible fixed assets* does not specify a particular method. However, it states that, whichever method is chosen, it should be 'appropriate' and should be applied in a systematic and consistent fashion. Any change in the method of depreciation must be explained in a note in the final accounts.

Straight line method of depreciation

One of the most common methods used for calculating depreciation is called the STRAIGHT LINE METHOD. It is also sometimes known as the fixed instalment method. It involves depreciating the value of an asset by exactly the same amount each year. To calculate the annual depreciation charge, the following formula is used:

$$\text{Annual depreciation charge} = \frac{\text{Historical cost - Net residual value}}{\text{Estimated life of asset}}$$

To illustrate how this method is used, consider the example of a packing machine costing £17,000. The machine is expected to be useful for 5 years before having to be replaced. Its estimated net residual value is £2,000.

$$\text{Annual depreciation charge} = \frac{£17,000 - £2,000}{5 \text{ years}}$$

$$= \frac{£15,000}{5}$$

$$= £3,000 \text{ per year}$$

When calculating depreciation, it is sometimes helpful to draw up a table to show how an asset is **written off**, ie depreciated, over its lifetime. Figure 22.1 shows the annual depreciation charge which is recorded in the profit and loss account, and the **net book value** which is recorded in the balance sheet. The net book value is the historical cost of an asset less the accumulated depreciation charge. For example, at the end of year 3, the annual depreciation charge is £3,000 and the net book value of the machine is £8,000.

Since the depreciation charge is the same every year, it is sometimes expressed as a percentage of the historical cost of the asset. So, in the above example, the annual depreciation charge is approximately 17.6% of the cost (ie 17.65% of £17,000 = £3,000).

Figure 22.1 *The annual depreciation charge and the net book value of the packing machine using the straight line method*

Year	Cost of machine	Annual depreciation charge	Accumulated depreciation	Net book value
	£	£	£	£
1	17,000	3,000	3,000	14,000
2		3,000	6,000	11,000
3		3,000	9,000	8,000
4		3,000	12,000	5,000
5		3,000	15,000	2,000

There are two main advantages of the straight line method of depreciation.
- It is simple to understand and easy to use. Little calculation is required and exactly the same amount is charged for depreciation each year.
- It is an appropriate method for an asset such as a property lease, where the income or benefits arising from the asset are likely to be fairly constant over time.

The straight line method gets its name from the shape of the graph when the net book value is plotted against the life of the asset, as in Figure 22.2.

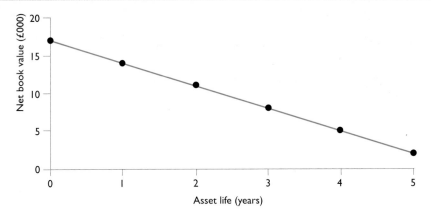

Figure 22.2 *The net book value of the packing machine using the straight line method*

QUESTION 1

Debbie Prince owns an opticians in Wrexham. When she started her business in 1997, £20,000 was spent on fixtures and fittings. Her accountant decided to make an annual charge for depreciation of the fixtures and fittings by using the straight line method. It was estimated that the fixtures and fittings would have a useful life of 5 years and no residual value.

(a) Calculate the annual depreciation charge for the fixtures and fittings using the straight line method.
(b) What is the annual depreciation charge as a percentage of the purchase price?
(c) Draw up a table to show how the fixtures and fittings are written off over their useful life.
(d) Suggest two factors that are likely to affect the rate of depreciation of fixtures and fittings in Debbie's business.

Reducing balance method of depreciation

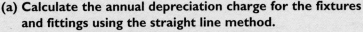

The REDUCING BALANCE METHOD calculates the annual depreciation charge as a fixed percentage of the net book value of an asset. The outcome is that the charge is higher in the early years of an asset's life than in the later years. To illustrate this method, consider again the example of the packing machine that was purchased for £17,000. Assume that the machine depreciates by 40 per cent of the net book value each year for five years. Figure 22.3 shows the annual charge and the net book value at the end of each year. The charge is calculated by taking 40% of the previous year's net book value. So, for example, in year 2 the depreciation charge is £4,080 which is 40% of £10,200. This is much higher than the charge in year 5, which is only £881. It is shown graphically in Figure 22.4.

Figure 22.3 *The annual depreciation charge and the net book value of the packing machine using the reducing balance method (numbers are rounded to the nearest £)*

Year	Cost of machine £	Annual depreciation charge £	Accumulated depreciation £	Net book value £
1	17,000	6,800 (17,000 × 40%)	6,800	10,200
2		4,080 (10,200 × 40%)	10,880	6,120
3		2,448 (6,120 × 40%)	13,328	3,672
4		1,469 (3,672 × 40%)	14,797	2,203
5		881 (2,203 × 40%)	15,678	1,322

Figure 22.4 *The net book value of the packing machine using the reducing balance method*

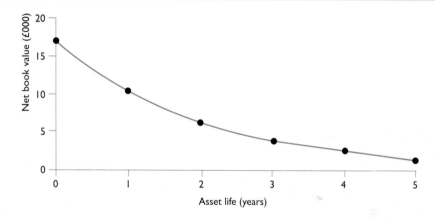

In Figure 22.3, the 40% rate of depreciation is given. However, it is sometimes necessary to calculate this percentage if, for instance, only the historical cost, the expected life span and the net residual value of an asset are known. So, if a machine had a purchase price of £17,000, assuming a net residual value of £1,322 and a 5 year lifespan:

$$\text{Percentage depreciation rate} = \left(1 - \sqrt[n]{\frac{s}{c}}\right) \times 100$$

Where:

c = historical cost
s = net residual value
n = lifespan

So:

$$\text{Percentage depreciation rate} = \left(1 - \sqrt[5]{\frac{1,322}{17,000}}\right) \times 100$$

$$= \left(1 - \sqrt[5]{0.08}\right) \times 100$$

$$= (1 - 0.6) \times 100$$

$$= 40\%$$

The reducing balance method of calculating depreciation has two main advantages.

- It takes into account that some assets, such as vehicles, lose far more value in the first year than they do, say, in the fifth year. Consequently, the net book value of such an asset more accurately reflects the actual value.
- It conforms to the matching concept when spreading the total expense of using certain fixed assets. This is because, for many assets, maintenance and repair costs rise as the depreciation charge falls. For example, at the end of year 1, the depreciation charge for a vehicle might be £5,000 with only a £500 maintenance charge. In year 5, the depreciation charge might have fallen to £1,700 but repairs and maintenance might have risen to £3,200. The two totals for expenses

are almost the same (year 1 = £5,500 and year 5 = £4,900). This gives a fairer reflection of the actual costs of using the vehicle than if the straight line method was used.

The reducing balance and straight line methods compared

The reducing balance method and the straight line method of calculating depreciation have different effects on a business's profits and balance sheet. In the long term, the two methods make little difference to the overall level of profits or the value of assets. This is because the total charge for depreciation is virtually the same no matter which method is used. However, in the short term, the reducing balance method creates a much higher depreciation charge than the straight line method in the first year or two. Because depreciation is treated as a business expense, this has the effect of reducing profits.

In the example of the packing machine, in Figure 22.3, the depreciation charge using the reducing balance method at the end of year 1 is £6,800 and the net book value of the asset is £10,200. However, if the straight line method is used, as shown in Figure 22.1, the depreciation charge at the end of year 1 is £3,000 and the net book value is £14,000. So, depreciation is higher and profits in year 1 are lower by £3,800 (ie £6,800 - £3,000) if the reducing balance method is used. On the balance sheet, the value of fixed assets is lower, again by £3,800 (ie £14,000 - £10,200) if the reducing balance method is used.

Over the whole 5 year period, the reducing balance method gives a total depreciation charge of £15,678. The straight line method gives a similar total of £15,000. Therefore the level of profits over the period is only different by £678. Similarly, after 5 years the net book value is £1,322 using the reducing balance method and £2,000 with the straight line method. The difference of £678 is much less than the difference after one year (£3,800).

QUESTION 2

Jennifer Widows is a self-employed taxi driver based in Tenby, Wales. Her main fixed asset is the car that she bought new for £12,000 in 2001. Jennifer has been a taxi driver for 20 years and she replaces her car every four years. Her accountant recommends that the new car should be written off using the reducing balance method at a rate of 40 per cent per year.

(a) Draw up a table to show the annual depreciation allowance and the net book value at the end of each year for Jennifer's car.
(b) To what extent is the reducing balance method more appropriate than the straight line method of calculating depreciation for Jennifer's business?

Sum-of-the-year's digits method of depreciation

In the UK, the straight line and the reducing balance methods of calculating depreciation are the most widely used. However, a number of other methods are also in use. One of these is the SUM-OF-THE-YEAR'S DIGITS (or sum-of-the-digits) METHOD. It is similar to the reducing balance method in that assets are shown to depreciate more quickly in the early years. To illustrate how this method is applied, consider again the example of the packing machine that was purchased for £17,000. Assume that it has an expected life of 5 years and a net residual value of £2,000. Taking the 5 year lifespan, the sum of the year's digits is 15 (ie 5 + 4 + 3 + 2 + 1 = 15). The depreciation charge for the first year is $\frac{5}{15}$ of the total amount to be written off, ie the historical cost less the net residual value (£17,000 - £2,000 = £15,000). For the second year it is $\frac{4}{15}$ of the total amount to be written off, and so on. The annual depreciation charge and the net book value at the end of each year is shown in Figure 22.5.

Figure 22.5 *The annual depreciation charge and the net book value of the packing machine using the sum-of-the-year's digits method*

Year	Cost of machine	Annual depreciation charge	Accumulated depreciation	Net book value
	£	£	£	£
1	17,000	5,000 (15,000 × 5/15)	5,000	12,000
2		4,000 (15,000 × 4/15)	9,000	8,000
3		3,000 (15,000 × 3/15)	12,000	5,000
4		2,000 (15,000 × 2/15)	14,000	3,000
5		1,000 (15,000 × 1/15)	15,000	2,000

Depletion method of depreciation

The DEPLETION METHOD is most often used for wasting assets such as quarries or mines. Depreciation is calculated according to the rate of depletion of the resource. For example, suppose a coal mine that contained an estimated 500,000 tonnes of coal was bought for £10 million. If 40,000 tonnes of coal was extracted each year, the annual depreciation charge would be:

$$\text{Annual depreciation charge} = \text{Historical cost} \times \frac{\text{Quantity of material extracted}}{\text{Estimated total contents of asset}}$$

$$= £10,000,000 \times \frac{40,000}{500,000}$$

$$= £10,000,000 \times 0.08$$

$$= £800,000 \text{ per year}$$

Usage methods of depreciation

Usage methods of depreciation relate to the rate at which fixed assets are used by a business. They take into account that the useful life of many assets is affected by how often they are used.

The MACHINE HOUR METHOD calculates depreciation according to how many hours a machine is used per year. To illustrate this method, consider the example of the packing machine bought for £17,000. It has an expected net residual value of £2,000. Suppose that the machine is used for 2,000 hours in a particular year, and the machine has an expected operating life of 12,000 hours. The annual depreciation charge is:

$$\text{Annual depreciation charge} = (\text{Historical cost - net residual value}) \times \frac{\text{Number of hours used in a year}}{\text{Estimated operating life}}$$

$$= (£17,000 - £2,000) \times \frac{2,000}{12,000}$$

$$= £2,500 \text{ per year}$$

A second approach is called the UNITS OF OUTPUT METHOD. This calculates the depreciation charge according to how much output a machine produces. Taking the same packing machine as in the example above, if the machine packs 50,000 bags of potatoes in a year and the machine is expected to pack 200,000 bags in its life, the annual depreciation charge is:

$$\text{Annual depreciation charge} = (\text{Historical cost - net residual value}) \times \frac{\text{Annual output}}{\text{Total lifetime output}}$$

$$= (£17{,}000 - £2{,}000) \times \frac{50{,}000}{200{,}000}$$

$$= £15{,}000 \times 0.25$$

$$= £3{,}750 \text{ per year}$$

Revaluation method of depreciation

The methods described so far are not suitable for calculating depreciation for low cost, fixed assets such as hand tools, laboratory equipment or kitchen utensils. It would be time consuming and costly to calculate the annual depreciation charge for every single spanner, screwdriver, socket and hand tool owned by a garage, for example. Under these circumstances, a business might choose the REVALUATION METHOD of calculating depreciation. This method requires the following information:
- a valuation of the fixed assets at the beginning of the year;
- the cost of new fixed assets purchased during the year;
- a valuation of the stock of fixed assets at the end of the year.

To illustrate this method, consider a restaurant that owns a stock of pots, pans and other kitchen utensils. On 1 January 2000 the stock of these items was valued at £2,600. During the year, the restaurant purchased £500 of new utensils and on 31 December 2000 the stock was valued at £2,500. The annual depreciation charge is:

	£
Value of stock on 1.1.00	2,600
Add purchases of stock during the year	500
	3,100
Less value of stock on 31.12.00	2,500
Depreciation charge	600

The advantage of this method is that it simplifies the calculation of depreciation for low cost fixed assets. It is an example of the materiality concept being applied. The main difficulty is that accountants have to place a value on the stock of fixed assets at the end of each year. The valuation of such assets therefore involves a subjective judgment.

The disposal of assets

The net book value of a fixed asset might not be the same as its actual net residual value when sold. This is because the rate of depreciation is estimated, as is the net residual value. Consequently, when a fixed asset is sold, a business might make a 'profit' or a 'loss' on the sale. A 'profit on disposal of fixed assets' is made if an asset is sold for more than its net book value. A 'loss on disposal' is made if it sells for less than its net book value. For example, if a machine with a net book value of £8,000 was sold for £8,700, a profit of £700 would be made. This would be classed as additional income on the profit and loss account. If the machine was sold for £7,500, a loss of £500 would be made. This would be classed as an expense on the profit and loss account.

When calculating the profit or loss on the sale of a fixed asset, a problem arises if the sale is not at the end of the financial year. A decision has to be made whether to take a part of a year's depreciation into account. Different businesses adopt different policies to cope with this problem. One approach is to calculate the value of depreciation to the nearest month. For example, if a fixed asset is sold three months into the year, and the annual depreciation charge is £6,000, the depreciation charge for the three month period is £1,500 (ie $\frac{3}{12} \times £6{,}000$).

An alternative approach is to disregard the exact date on which fixed assets are bought and sold. Depreciation is charged for a full year on any fixed asset owned by a business at the end of the year. But, if an asset is sold before the end of the year, there is no depreciation charge for that year on that asset.

QUESTION 3

Weston Service Station, located in Oxfordshire, is owned by Wilfred Jobson. The garage owns a range of fixed assets including tools and mechanical equipment. A new breakdown truck was purchased by the business in 1998. The truck cost £25,000 and was expected to have a useful life of 5 years and a net residual value of £1,000. However, after two years the breakdown truck was sold for £11,500 because the business was running short of cash. It was decided to lease a truck instead.

(a) Using the sum-of-the-year's digits method, draw up a table to show the annual depreciation charge and the net book value at the end of each year for the breakdown truck.
(b) Calculate the profit/loss on disposal of the breakdown truck.
(c) Using the straight line method, calculate the net book value of the breakdown truck at the end of year two and recalculate the profit/loss on disposal.
(d) Comment on the difference in your answers between (b) and (c).

Revaluation of fixed assets

Although most fixed assets fall in value over time, some such as land and buildings might rise in value. Depending on the accounting policy adopted, businesses sometimes choose to revalue these particular fixed assets. This means that the net book value of the fixed asset is increased in the balance sheet. When a fixed asset is revalued, a reserve is created which increases the value of owner's capital (see unit 38). Businesses might decide to revalue land and buildings because this gives a more accurate, ie 'true and fair', indication of their value. However, other businesses might decide against this policy because any valuation must be based on a subjective estimate of what the assets are worth.

Even though property might be periodically revalued, it is normal accounting practice to make a charge for depreciation on buildings. This is because buildings suffer from wear and tear. A charge for depreciation is also generally made on land that is held on a short lease. This is because the land will soon revert to its owner and is therefore of less value to the leaseholder. However, in the case of freehold land and land held on a long lease, most businesses take the view that depreciation does not occur.

After a fixed asset such as a building has been revalued, depreciation is calculated on the new net book value. To illustrate this, consider a business that bought a warehouse for £50,000. The warehouse was expected to have a useful life of 25 years and to have no residual value. In the 6th year, when the property still had a useful life of 20 years, it was revalued at £90,000. Using the straight line method of depreciation, the annual depreciation charge before the revaluation was £2,000 (ie £50,000 ÷ 25). After the revaluation, the annual depreciation charge was £4,500 (ie £90,000 ÷ 20). The annual depreciation charge and the net book value for the first 10 years are shown in Figure 22.6.

summary questions

1. Explain the link between deprecation and the matching concept.
2. What is meant by a provision for depreciation?
3. State four reasons why assets depreciate.
4. Explain the difference between the straight line method and the reducing balance method of calculating depreciation.
5. Explain why the reducing balance method might be more suitable for an asset such as a lorry.
6. Explain how the annual cost of employing a fixed asset is more equal if the reducing balance method is used.
7. What method would be suitable to depreciate a wasting asset such as an oil well?
8. What types of assets might be depreciated using the revaluation method?
9. Under what circumstances will a loss be made on the disposal of a fixed asset?
10. Under what circumstances might a fixed asset be revalued?

Figure 22.6 *The annual depreciation charge and net book value of the warehouse for the first 10 years of its life*

Year	Historical cost / revaluation	Annual depreciation charge	Accumulated depreciation	Net book value
	£	£	£	£
1	50,000	2,000	2,000	48,000
2	50,000	2,000	4,000	46,000
3	50,000	2,000	6,000	44,000
4	50,000	2,000	8,000	42,000
5	50,000	2,000	10,000	40,000
6	90,000	4,500	14,500	85,500
7	90,000	4,500	19,000	81,000
8	90,000	4,500	23,500	76,500
9	90,000	4,500	28,000	72,000
10	90,000	4,500	32,500	67,500

key terms

Consumed - (in the context of depreciation) the 'using up' of a fixed asset.

Depletion method - a method of calculating the annual depreciation charge which is linked to the rate at which a resource is extracted from a wasting asset, such as a mine.

Machine hour method - a method used to calculate the annual depreciation charge which is linked to the number of hours a machine is operated.

Net residual value - the disposal value or scrap value of an asset at the end of its useful life.

Obsolete - where an asset is no longer used because of changes in technology or economic conditions.

Reducing balance method - a method used to calculate the annual depreciation charge which involves writing off the same percentage rate from the net book value each year.

Revaluation - an increase in the value of a fixed asset in the balance sheet.

Revaluation method - a method used to calculate the annual depreciation charge for low cost fixed assets based on annual valuations.

Straight line method - a method used to calculate the annual depreciation charge which involves writing off exactly the same amount each year.

Sum-of-the-year's digits method (or sum-of-the-digits method) - a method used to calculate the annual depreciation charge which involves writing off the value of an asset according to the sum-of-the-year's digits given the expected life of the asset.

Units of output method - a method used to calculate the annual depreciation charge which is linked to the rate of output for an asset.

UNIT ASSESSMENT   QUESTION 1

West Sussex Removals, based in Chichester, is owned and run by Elizabeth Brown. The business owns three lorries, two of which were bought two years ago and the third which was bought three years ago. They each cost £40,000 and had an expected life of six years when purchased. Three years ago the business bought a van for £20,000. This year, the van was sold because it was under-used. The disposal raised £4,500.

   The business is located on an industrial estate where it has rented premises. The office contains a small amount of office furniture with a current net book value of £1,200. The furniture was bought for £2,200 ten years ago. It had an expected life of twenty years when it was bought and its net residual value is estimated to be £200.

(a) Calculate the current net book value of the three lorries using the reducing balance method of depreciation. Write off the lorries by 40 per cent each year.
(b) Calculate the current net book value of the van. Write off the van by 40 per cent each year.
(c) Calculate the profit/loss on disposal of the van.
(d) Calculate the annual depreciation charge for the office furniture. West Sussex Removals uses the straight line method of depreciation for its furniture.
(e) Suggest reasons why the business uses two different methods of depreciation.

UNIT ASSESSMENT   QUESTION 2

Bert Jackson owns a small dairy farm in Gloucestershire. He purchased the farm for £240,000 in 1995. £100,000 was paid for the land and £140,000 for the farm buildings. In 2000 the farm was revalued. According to a local firm of estate valuers, the land was worth £160,000 and the buildings £220,000. When the farm was purchased, the straight line method was used to depreciate the buildings. A residual value of zero was

assumed and the useful life of the buildings was expected to be 25 years. It was decided that no depreciation charge would be made on the land. Bert also owns a tractor which he bought for £30,000 two years ago. The reducing balance method is used to calculate depreciation on this asset.

(a) Calculate the annual depreciation charge for the farm buildings: (i) between 1995 and 1999; (ii) between 2000 and 2004.
(b) Draw up a table to show the historical cost/revaluation, annual depreciation charge and the net book value of the farm buildings from 1995 to 2004.
(c) Why are fixed assets such as land and property sometimes revalued?
(d) Calculate the current net book value of the tractor. Write off the tractor at a rate of 30 per cent each year.
(e) Suggest two other assets that the farm will depreciate in its accounts.

unit 23 Accounting for depreciation

unit**objectives**

To understand:
- accounting for depreciation;
- accounting for the disposal of a fixed asset;
- how to make end of year adjustments for depreciation.

How is depreciation recorded in the accounts?

In double entry bookkeeping, the purchase of a fixed asset is entered in the ledgers as a credit in the bank account and as a debit in the asset account (see unit 8). However, the depreciation charge on the fixed asset is **not** recorded in the asset account. Instead, it is entered as a credit in a separate **provision for depreciation account**. The corresponding debit entry is in the profit and loss account.

To illustrate how depreciation is recorded in the accounts, consider the example of Brian Cooper who owns a pet shop in Derby. His financial year runs from January 1 to December 31. In January 2000, he purchased a new asset, a van for £8,000. His accountant advised him to write off the cost of the van at 40% per year using the reducing balance method. The annual depreciation charge, accumulated depreciation and net book value of the van are shown in Figure 23.1.

Figure 23.1 *The annual depreciation charge, accumulated depreciation and net book value of the van*

Year	Cost of van	Annual depreciation charge	Accumulated depreciation	Net book value at end of year
	£	£	£	£
2000	8,000	3,200 (40% × 8,000)	3,200	4,800 (8,000 - 3,200)
2001		1,920 (40% × 4,800)	5,120	2,880 (8,000 - 5,120)

Figure 23.1 shows that the depreciation charge was £3,200 in 2000 and £1,920 in 2001. The van account, the provision for depreciation account and extracts from the profit and loss account for Brian Cooper's business are shown in Figure 23.2.

Figure 23.2 *Balanced ledger accounts for Brian Cooper's business*

NOMINAL LEDGER

Dr		Van Account		Cr	
2000		£	2000		£
1.1	Bank	8,000	31.12 Balance c/d		8,000
2001			2001		
1.1	Balance b/d	8,000	31.12 Balance c/d		8,000
2002					
1.1	Balance b/d	8,000			

Dr   Provision for Depreciation (Van) Account   Cr

2000	£	2000	£
31.12 Balance c/d	3,200	31.12 Profit and loss	3,200
2001		2001	
31.12 Balance c/d	5,120	1.1 Balance b/d	3,200
		31.12 Profit and loss	1,920
	5,120		5,120
		2002	
		1.1 Balance b/d	5,120

Extracts from the Profit and Loss Account (for the years ended 31 December)

Dr		Cr	
	£		£
2000 Provision for depreciation	3,200		
2001 Provision for depreciation	1,920		

- The purchase of the van on 1 January 2000 is a debit entry in the van account. This records the historical cost of the van. The corresponding credit entry is in the bank account which is not shown here. The balance on the van account is unaffected by depreciation. It remains unchanged until the asset is disposed of at the end of its useful life to the business.
- The provision for depreciation account is credited with the depreciation charge for each year. The account is credited with £3,200 in 2000 and with £1,920 in 2001. The balance b/d on 1 January 2002 shows the accumulated depreciation up to that date.
- The profit and loss account is debited each year with the provision for depreciation. This depreciation charge is treated as a business expense when it is transferred to the formal profit and loss account in the final accounts (see unit 29).

The example used in Figure 23.2 is simplified as the asset is purchased at the beginning of the business's financial year. The depreciation charge is therefore calculated for a full year. In reality, this might not be the case. If an asset is purchased part way through an accounting period, a number of approaches might be used to account for depreciation. A business might decide:

- to provide for depreciation for the whole year on any asset held at the end of the year, ie the annual depreciation charge is made even if a new asset is bought part way through the year;
- to ignore depreciation for that year on any asset bought part way through a year;
- to calculate the depreciation charge on a monthly basis and to make the provision accordingly. For example, suppose a business buys a machine for £24,000 and decides to use the straight line method of depreciation. The machine has an estimated life of 10 years and no residual value. Therefore the annual depreciation charge is £2,400 and the monthly charge is £200 (ie £2,400 ÷ 12). If the machine is bought on 1 September and the accounting period ends on 31 December, the depreciation charge for the four months is £800 (ie 4 × £200).

QUESTION 1

Mary Grant owns a small textile company that makes swimwear. A new sewing machine was purchased on January 1 2000 to cope with shorter and more varied production runs. The machine cost £4,000 and it was decided to write off the cost of the machine at 30 per cent per year using the reducing balance method.

(a) Calculate the first year's depreciation charge for the new sewing machine.
(b) Show the bookkeeping entries in the sewing machine account and the provision for depreciation account to record the purchase of the machine and the depreciation charge. Assume that the business's financial year runs from January 1 to December 31.
(c) Balance the sewing machine account and the provision for depreciation account.

Recording depreciation in the balance sheet

Fixed assets are shown in the balance sheet at their net book value. The historical cost, accumulated depreciation and the net book value of the van for Brian Cooper's business as at 31 December 2001, are shown in Figure 23.3.

Figure 23.3 *The net book value of the van for Brian Cooper's business as at 31 December 2001*

Brian Cooper
Balance Sheet (extract) as at 31.12.01

	Historical cost	Depreciation to date	Net book value
Fixed asset	£	£	£
Van	8,000	5,120	2,880

- The historical cost is the purchase price of the van. In businesses which own a range of assets such as vehicles, machinery and property, the heading in the balance sheet might be 'Historical cost or valuation'. This is because some of the assets, such as buildings, might have been revalued and are therefore not shown at their historical cost.
- The depreciation charge in the first year (£3,200) is added to the current year's charge (£1,920) to give the accumulated total of £5,120 at 31 December 2001.
- The net book value is calculated by subtracting the depreciation charge from the historical cost.
- For large businesses, the value of all the business's assets would be shown together, or in broad categories, rather than as the separate values of individual assets such as the van.

The information in the balance sheet extract in Figure 23.3 can be presented in a number of ways. An alternative method that is frequently used is shown in Figure 23.4. Note that, in this layout, the net book value is the amount in the right-hand column.

Figure 23.4 *The net book value of the van for Brian Cooper's business as at 31 December 2001 (alternative layout)*

Brian Cooper
Balance Sheet (extract)
as at 31.12.01

Fixed asset	£	£
Van, at cost	8,000	
less provision for depreciation	5,120	2,880

QUESTION 2

Wasim Ahmed has a taxi business in Preston, Lancashire. On 1 February 2000 he paid £9,200 for furniture and fittings for his office. He decided to depreciate these by using the straight line method. He estimated that, at the end of 10 years, their residual value would be zero.

On 1 August 2000, Wasim bought a new taxi costing £15,000. He decided to depreciate the taxi at the rate of 40% per year using the reducing balance method. His financial year ends on 31 December. Any asset purchased in the first six months of the year has a whole year's depreciation written off. Any asset purchased in the second half of the year has a half-year's depreciation charge.

(a) **For the years ended 31 December 2000 and December 2001, prepare (i) a furniture and fittings account; (ii) a provision for depreciation of furniture and fittings account; (iii) a taxi account; (iv) a provision for depreciation of taxi account.**

(b) **Present a balance sheet extract as at 31 December 2001 for furniture and fittings and the taxi.**

Accounting for the disposal of a fixed asset

When a fixed asset is sold by a business, the disposal must be recorded in the ledger accounts. To illustrate the bookkeeping entries, consider the earlier example of Brian Cooper. Suppose he sells his van for £3,000 in 2001. Figure 23.5 shows that a profit of £120 was made on the sale. Note that, in this context, the profit or loss is the difference between the disposal price and the net book value on the date the asset was sold. Because, in this case, the sale price was higher than the net book value, a profit was made. The bookkeeping entries to record the disposal are shown in Figure 23.6.

Figure 23.5 *The profit made on the disposal of Brian Cooper's van on 31 December 2001*

	£
Historical cost of van	8,000
less Accumulated depreciation to date	5,120
equals Net book value on date of sale	2,880
Sale price	3,000
Profit on sale	**120**

Figure 23.6 *Bookkeeping entries to account for the disposal of Brian Cooper's van*

NOMINAL LEDGER

Dr   **Disposal of Van Account**   **Cr**

2001		£	2001		£
31.12	Van	8,000	31.12	Provision for depreciation	5,120
31.12	Profit and loss	120	31.12	Bank	3,000
		8,120			8,120

Dr   **Van Account**   **Cr**

2000		£	2000		£
1.1	Bank	8,000	31.12	Balance c/d	8,000
2001			2001		
1.1	Balance b/d	8,000	31.12	Disposal of van	8,000

Dr   **Provision for Depreciation (Van) Account**   **Cr**

2000		£	2000		£
31.12	Balance c/d	3,200	31.12	Profit and loss	3,200
2001			2001		
31.12	Disposal of van	5,120	1.1	Balance b/d	3,200
			31.12	Profit and loss	1,920
		5,120			5,120

Dr   **Bank Account**   **Cr**

2001		£		£
31.12	Disposal of van	3,000		

Dr   **Profit and Loss Account**   **Cr**
(for the year ended 31 December)

	£		£
		2001 Disposal of van (profit)	120

- A disposal of van (or sale of van) account is opened in order to record the historical cost of the asset, the accumulated depreciation, the sale proceeds and the profit/loss made on the sale.
- The van account is credited and the disposal of van account is debited with the historical cost of the asset.
- The provision for depreciation account is debited and the disposal of van account is credited with the accumulated depreciation.

- The bank account is debited and the disposal of van account is credited with the sale proceeds (assuming that payment is made by cheque).
- The profit and loss account is credited and the disposal of van account is debited as there is a profit on the sale. However, if there was a loss on the sale, the profit and loss account would be debited and the disposal of van account would be credited.
- A profit is recorded as additional income in the profit and loss account.
- A loss would be recorded as an expense in the profit and loss account.

QUESTION 3

Angela Collier runs a swimming pool servicing company in the south east of England. Most of her work comes from contracts with hotels and private sports clubs that own a swimming pool. When she started the business, Angela bought a special machine that sucks debris from the bottom of swimming pools. This machine cost £3,000 when it was purchased. However, it was sold for £600 on 31 December 2000 because Angela decided to lease machinery in the future. Figure 23.7 shows the balances on the machine account and the provision for depreciation account for this machine prior to its disposal. The machine was written off, using the straight line method of depreciation, at £500 per year. Depreciation is calculated until the asset is sold. The financial year end for the business is 31 December.

Figure 23.7 *Machine account and provision for depreciation account for the machine owned by Angela Collier's business*

NOMINAL LEDGER

Dr		Machine Account		Cr	
2000		£	2000		£
1.1	Balance b/d	3,000			

Dr	Provision for Depreciation (Machine) Account		Cr	
2000		£	2000	£
			1.1 Balance b/d	2,000

(a) Calculate the profit or loss on disposal of the machine.
(b) Show the bookkeeping entries in the machine account, the provision for depreciation account and the disposal of machine account to record the disposal.

Accounting for the part-exchange of an asset

Sometimes a business will trade in an old fixed asset to help pay for a replacement. Such a transaction is called a **part-exchange**. To illustrate the bookkeeping entries for this transaction, suppose that in the earlier example Brian Cooper had not sold his van but instead had used it as part-exchange for a new van. If the new van cost £12,000 and the dealer allowed £2,500 for the trade-in, Brian needed to pay £9,500 to complete the purchase. The part-exchange allowance of £2,500 is shown in the accounts as:

- a debit in the van account;
- a credit in the disposal of van account.

The provision for depreciation account is not affected by the transaction. However, in this example, Brian makes a loss on the sale. This is shown in Figure 23.8. The bookkeeping entries to record the transaction are shown in Figure 23.9.

Figure 23.8 *The loss made on the disposal of Brian Cooper's van on 31 December 2001*

	£
Historical cost of van	8,000
less Accumulated depreciation to date	5,120
equals Net book value on date of sale	2,880
Part exchange allowance	2,500
Loss on sale	**380**

Figure 23.9 *Bookkeeping entries to show the part-exchange of a van and the purchase of a new van*

NOMINAL LEDGER

Dr		Van Account	Cr	
2001		£	2001	£
1.1	Balance b/d	8,000	31.12 Disposal of van	8,000
31.12	Disposal of van (part-exchange)	2,500	31.12 Balance c/d	12,000
31.12	Bank	9,500		
		12,000		12,000
2002				
1.1	Balance b/d	12,000		

Dr	Disposal of Van Account	Cr	
2001	£	2001	£
31.12 Van	8,000	31.12 Provision for depreciation	5,120
		31.12 Van	2,500
		31.12 Profit and loss	380
	8,000		8,000

- The van account shows the previous entries from Figure 23.6 which record the historical cost of the old van (£8,000) and the credit entry for its disposal. The new entries which record the part-exchange and the purchase of a new van are the debit entries for disposal of van (the trade-in value of £2,500) and the bank entry for £9,500 which represents a cheque that is paid to the van dealer. The bank account is not shown.
- The £12,000 debit balance b/d in the van account represents the historical cost of the new van.
- The disposal of van account is slightly different from Figure 23.6. The credit entry of 'Van £2,500' replaces 'Bank £3,000'. This shows that a part-exchange allowance of £2,500 was made for the old van rather than it being sold for £3,000. The loss of £380 is shown as a credit on the disposal of van account. This will be a debit on the profit and loss account (not shown here), representing an expense.

Adjusting for depreciation at the end of year

When a trial balance is prepared for a business at the end of a financial year, the usual practice is to show:
- a separate entry for each category of fixed asset at historical cost;
- the annual depreciation charge for each category of fixed asset;
- the accumulated provision for depreciation for each category of fixed asset.

The value of fixed assets is shown as a debit balance and the accumulated provision for depreciation is shown as a credit balance. Each year, the depreciation charge has to be added to the accumulated provision and this adjustment is made in the **extended trial balance** (see unit 29).

To illustrate how an end of year adjustment for depreciation is made, consider the example of Langton & Co. which sells bathrooms from its shop in Nottingham. An extract from the extended trial balance for two years is shown in Figure 23.10. The business owns fixtures and fittings that cost £12,000 when new in 2000. The annual depreciation charge for the fixtures and fittings is £1,000. This, together with the historical cost of these assets and the provision for depreciation, are shown in the extended trial balance for each of the two years up to December 31 2001.

Figure 23.10 *Extracts from the extended trial balance of Langton & Co.*

Langton & Co.
Extended Trial Balance
as at 31.12.00 (extract)

	Ledger balances		Adjustments	
	Dr	Cr	Dr	Cr
	£	£	£	£
Fixtures and fittings - at cost	12,000			
Depreciation charge for the year			1,000	
Provision for depreciation		0		1,000

Extended Trial Balance
as at 31.12.01 (extract)

	Ledger balances		Adjustments	
	Dr	Cr	Dr	Cr
	£	£	£	£
Fixtures and fittings - at cost	12,000			
Depreciation charge for the year			1,000	
Provision for depreciation		1,000		1,000

- The historical cost of the fixtures and fittings is shown as a debit entry.
- The annual depreciation charge is shown as a debit entry in the adjustments column. It is also recorded as an expense in the profit and loss account (not shown here).
- The provision for depreciation is shown as a credit entry. The current total is the sum of the amounts in the ledger balances and the adjustments column. The accumulated depreciation is subtracted from the historical cost of the assets to give the net book value. For example, in 2000 it was £11,000 (ie £12,000 - £1,000) and in 2001 it was £10,000 (ie £12,000 - £2,000). This is recorded in the balance sheet extract shown below in Figure 23.11.

Figure 23.11 *Balance sheet extract to show the net book value*

Langton & Co.
Balance Sheet (extract) as at 31.12.01

	Historical cost	Depreciation to date	Net book value
Fixed asset	£	£	£
Fixtures and fittings	12,000	2,000	10,000

summary questions

1. What does the provision for depreciation account show?
2. What information is needed from the accounts to calculate the net book value of a fixed asset?
3. How is the disposal of a fixed asset recorded in the fixed asset account?
4. To which account is the historical cost of a fixed asset transferred when it is disposed of?
5. Explain why a profit or loss might occur when a fixed asset is disposed of.
6. In which accounts are recorded the profit or loss on the sale of a fixed asset?
7. Which account is (i) debited and (ii) credited when a fixed asset is part-exchanged?
8. What is meant by the term 'accumulated provision for depreciation'?
9. How is the extended trial balance used when making an adjustment for depreciation?
10. What information relating to depreciation is included in a balance sheet?

UNIT ASSESSMENT QUESTION 1

Alice and Jeff Montgomerie own a textile design business in Edinburgh. They bought a new computer which cost £4,000 on 1 January 2000. The depreciation charge for this computer was 40% per year using the reducing balance method. Because of rapid developments in technology, the computer was out of date by the end of 2001. Alice decided to sell the computer and was offered £600, which she accepted. The computer was sold on 31 December 2001. The financial year for the business runs from 1 January to 31 December.

(a) Calculate the accumulated depreciation charge and the net book value of the computer at the end of 2000 and 2001.
(b) Calculate the profit or loss on disposal of the computer.
(c) Show the computer account and the provision for depreciation account for the year ending 31 December 2000.
(d) Show the entries needed to account for the disposal of the computer in the computer account, the provision for depreciation account and the disposal account (do not include the profit and loss account and the bank account).

UNIT ASSESSMENT QUESTION 2

Anna Bremner runs a small manufacturing company which makes safety equipment. On 31 December 2001, the company bought a new computer controlled cutting machine for £45,000. The transaction involved the part-exchange of an old cutting machine for which an allowance of £5,000 was made. The balance of £40,000 was paid to the supplier by cheque. The cutting machine account and the provision for depreciation account are shown in Figure 23.12. These relate to the old machine which had cost £32,000 when new. The annual depreciation charge on the old machine was £8,000 per year and this was calculated using the straight line method. The year end for the business is 31 December.

Figure 23.12 *The cutting machine account and provision for depreciation account for Anna Bremner's business*

NOMINAL LEDGER

Dr	Cutting Machine Account		Cr
2001	£		£
1.1 Balance b/d	32,000		

Dr	Provision for Depreciation (Cutting Machine) Account		Cr
	£	2001	£
		1.1 Balance b/d	16,000

(a) For the year ending 31 December 2001, show the entries in the cutting machine account, the provision for depreciation account and the disposal account to record the part-exchange transaction (ignore the entries in the profit and loss account and the bank account).
(b) Draw up an extract from the extended trial balance to show the historical cost of the old cutting machine and the provision for depreciation at 31 December 2000.

Stock valuation

unit objectives

To understand:
- the nature of stocks;
- the different methods of stock valuation;
- the effect of stock valuation on the accounts;
- the principles of stock control.

What is meant by stock?

Manufacturing and retailing businesses generally hold STOCK (also called stock-in-trade) to help production run smoothly and to keep up with demand from customers. In practice a variety of stocks might be held by a business. They can be categorised in the following ways.

- **Raw materials and components** Stocks of raw materials and components are purchased from suppliers before production can begin. For example, a clothes manufacturer is likely to purchase stocks of fabric, cotton, buttons and zips. Delays in production might be avoided if such items can be supplied quickly from factory stores rather than waiting for a new delivery to arrive.
- **Work-in-progress** In some industries it can take days, weeks or even months to complete the finished product. For example, Morgan Cars, the sports car manufacturer, might spend up to three months making one of its hand-built cars. At any point in time there will be a stock of partly built cars in the factory. These are classed as WORK-IN-PROGRESS.
- **Finished goods** Manufacturers might build up stocks of finished goods so they can cope with unexpected increases in demand. This allows them to meet urgent orders without having to speed up production.
- **Goods for resale** Retailers hold stocks of the goods that they sell. For example, a large supermarket chain will have stocks of goods on its shelves, in its store rooms and in distribution centres around the country.
- **Consumables** These are items that are used by a business, but which are not intended for resale. For example, an office might have stocks of paper, envelopes, stamps and ink cartridges for computers.

In recent years, many businesses have tried to operate in a way that keeps stock holding to an absolute minimum. In some cases, businesses operate with zero stocks. The reasons for this **just-in-time** approach to production, and the principles behind it, are explained at the end of the unit.

The need for stock valuation

In order to produce their **final accounts**, businesses need to determine the end-of-year value of their stock. This is known as the CLOSING STOCK value and is recorded in the balance sheet as one of the business's **current assets**. The closing stock value is also used to calculate the cost of sales in the **profit and loss trading account** (see unit 17). The value of closing stock becomes the value of OPENING STOCK in the accounts at the beginning of the next financial year. Regular stock valuations are needed if accounts are produced more frequently than once a year or if businesses wish to make a security check. STOCKTAKES are carried out in order to confirm that the value of stock in the accounts is the same as the value of the stock that physically exists. If the value of actual stock is less than the value recorded, this suggests that some stock has gone missing. Stocktaking can be a laborious process. Every single item of stock has to be counted and listed on a stock sheet.

Some businesses operate a system of **periodic stocktaking**. This involves the counting of items in stock at the end of an accounting period. An alternative is to use a system of **perpetual stocktaking**. This involves keeping a running total of stock in a ledger or file. The balance of the quantity in stock is updated after each receipt or issue of stock.

How is stock valued?

According to the accounting standard SSAP9 *Stocks and work-in-progress*, stock should be valued at either its cost or its NET REALISABLE VALUE (NRV), whichever is lower. In this context, cost is defined as including any expenses associated with bringing the product to its present location and condition. For example, if a boat manufacturer pays £7,000 in wages and other expenses to convert £15,000 of raw materials and components into a finished boat, the cost of stock would be £22,000 (ie £7,000 + £15,000). The net realisable value is the estimated resale value of stock, less any selling or distribution costs.

If the boat in the above example has a net realisable value of £37,000, this is greater that its cost which is £22,000. So, according to the accounting standard, SSAP9, the boat must be valued at £22,000. By using the lower stock valuation, an accountant is conforming to the concept of prudence.

Usually, the cost of stock is lower than its net realisable value. However, there are circumstances when the net realisable value can fall below cost. This could happen for a number of reasons.
*   A change in fashion. For example, at the end of the summer season, clothes retailers might have to sell stocks at below cost to clear their shelves for the new season's fashions.
*   Stocks might deteriorate whilst being stored. For example, colouring in furniture fabrics might fade after being stored for a period of time.
*   Stocks might become obsolete due to a change in technology or the passage of time. For example, dot matrix computer printers lost their value when low cost ink jet printers were developed. A diary printed with the dates for 2001 would have lost value if it remained unsold in 2002.

Stock valuation for groups of items

The accounting standard SSAP9 states that individual items of stock should be valued separately. However, if this is not practical, groups of similar items should be valued together. For example, it would be time consuming and expensive to value every single bolt kept in stock by an engineering company. In such a case, it is acceptable to place a value on all the bolts together.

In order to illustrate this, consider the example of Outdoor Supplies, a retailer of camping equipment. The stock valuation for the business is based on six groups or categories of stock. These groups and their values are shown in Figure 24.1. At cost, the total stock is valued at £28,100 and at net realisable value (NRV) it is £35,700. This might suggest that the value of £28,100 should be used in the accounts. However, this fails to recognise that the value of footwear at cost (£2,500) is greater than the net realisable value (£1,900). Clearly, if each stock group is valued separately, and then totalled, the valuation is lower than either the total cost or the total net realisable value. The third column in Figure 24.1 shows the valuation that should be used in the accounts.

Figure 24.1 *Stock groups and values for Outdoor Supplies*

Stock group	Cost £	NRV £	Valuation £
Tents	4,500	8,000	4,500
Hardware	6,500	6,800	6,500
Clothing	4,800	6,100	4,800
Footwear	2,500	1,900	1,900
Sleeping bags	2,900	3,000	2,900
Miscellaneous	6,900	9,900	6,900
Total	28,100	35,700	27,500

QUESTION 1

In January 2001, Steve Westwood set up a business selling second hand cars. He rents a garage forecourt in Witney, Oxfordshire and buys his stock of cars at auctions in London. By the end of the trading year, 31 December, Steve had 10 unsold cars. A stock list is shown in Figure 24.2. The cost and the net realisable value of the cars are shown.

(a) **What category of stock do the unsold cars fall into? Explain your answer.**
(b) **What was the value of closing stock on 31 December?**
(c) **What was the value of opening stock on 1 January in the following year?**
(d) **Steve bought the Rover 214 at an auction and paid £2,300 for it, as shown in the stock list. However, the car would not start and could not be driven. Steve paid £100 to a car transport service to bring it to Witney. How might this affect the stock value?**

Figure 24.2 *The stock of cars owned by Steve Westwood's business*

	Cost £	NRV £
Ford Orion (red)	1,200	1,800
Ford Orion (blue)	1,600	2,100
Polo	800	950
Golf Gti	2,100	2,950
Nissan Micra	1,900	2,400
Nissan Almera	600	1,200
Peugeot 106	1,850	2,100
Ford Fiesta	350	590
Rover 214	2,300	2,900
Fiat Brava	1,900	1,500
Total	14,600	18,490

Methods of stock valuation

The valuation of stock is made difficult if the purchase price, ie cost, of items changes over time. Suppose, for example, that a manufacturer pays several different prices for identical components bought during the year. At the end of the year, the business might not know the actual prices paid for the individual items left in stock. Under these circumstances, different methods can be used to value the cost of stocks. Three such methods are:

- FIFO (first in, first out);
- LIFO (last in, first out);
- AVCO (average cost).

Stock valuation – FIFO (first in, first out)

The first in, first out method of valuation assumes that stock is used, or sold, in the order in which it is purchased. So, stocks of goods that are bought first are used first. Any unused stocks at the end of the trading year are therefore those bought most recently.

To illustrate this method of stock valuation, consider the example of Steelcraft, a manufacturer of metal components for containers. Steelcraft buys steel plates from a Spanish supplier. Figure 24.3 shows how a closing stock figure for Steelcraft is calculated using the FIFO method of stock valuation. The table gives the quantity and price of steel plates delivered to Steelcraft each month, ie 'stock received', and the quantity and price used in production each month, ie 'stock issued'. The stock valuation shows the quantity and valuation of stocks held at the end of each month. It is assumed that there were no stocks held at the start of the period.

Figure 24.3 *Stock transactions illustrating how a closing stock figure is calculated using the FIFO method*

| Date | Stock received | | | Stock issued | | | Stock valuation | | | |
	Qty	Price	Value	Qty	Price	Value	Qty	Price	Value	Total
		£	£		£	£		£	£	£
Jan	1,000	5	5,000				1,000	5	5,000	5,000
Feb	2,000	6	12,000				1,000	5	5,000	
							2,000	6	12,000	17,000
March				1,000	5	5,000				
				500	6	3,000	1,500	6	9,000	9,000

In January, Steelcraft took delivery of 1,000 steel plates costing £5 each, which meant that it had £5,000 of steel in stock. In February, a further 2000 steel plates at £6 each were added to stock, making a total value of £17,000. In March, 1,500 plates were issued from stock for production. Since stock is used on the first in, first out basis, the plates taken from stock were the 1,000 plates received in January, at £5 each, and 500 plates from the 2,000 plates received in February, at £6 each. The remaining stock was 1,500 (2,000 - 500) steel plates at £6 each. This gives a closing stock value of £9,000.

The main **advantages** of the FIFO method are that:
- it is realistic because it is based on the assumption that issues from stock are made in the order in which the goods are received;
- it is relatively easy to calculate;
- the stock values are based on prices actually paid for stock;
- the closing stock valuation is based on the most recent prices paid;
- it is acceptable to the Inland Revenue for the purposes of taxation and it conforms to the accounting standard SSAP9 and the Companies Act (see unit 38) relating to the valuation of stocks.

However, there are some **disadvantages** of the FIFO method.
- The prices at which stock is issued to production are likely to be out of date, so the selling price of the finished goods might not accurately reflect the most recent costs.
- When the prices of stock are rising, the FIFO method values the stock at the highest, ie latest, prices. The effect is to reduce the cost of sales and therefore to raise profit (this is explained later in the unit). Such a policy could result in more tax being paid because profits are higher than they might otherwise have been.

Stock valuation – LIFO (last in, first out)

The last in, first out method of stock valuation assumes that the most recent deliveries of stock are used first. So, new stock is always issued before old stock. The value of unused stocks at the end of the trading year is therefore based on the cost of earlier purchases.

To illustrate this method of stock valuation, consider again the example of Steelcraft. Figure 24.4 shows the same stock transactions for steel plates as in Figure 24.3. However, they are adjusted for the LIFO method of stock valuation.

Figure 24.4 *Stock transactions illustrating how a closing stock figure is calculated using the LIFO method*

Date	Stock received			Stock issued			Stock valuation			Total
	Qty	Price	Value	Qty	Price	Value	Qty	Price	Value	
		£	£		£	£		£	£	£
Jan	1,000	5	5,000				1,000	5	5,000	5,000
Feb	2,000	6	12,000				1,000	5	5,000	
							2,000	6	12,000	17,000
March				1,500	6	9,000	1,000	5	5,000	
							500	6	3,000	8,000

In March, when 1,500 steel plates were issued from stock, it was the most recent deliveries that were used. So, all the plates that were used were those that had cost £6. The remaining plates left in stock were 500 (2,000 - 1,500) that had cost £6 each, and 1,000 that had cost £5 each. The total value of stock at the end of March was £8,000 compared with the higher value of £9,000 using the FIFO method.

The main **advantages** of the LIFO method are that:
- the system is based on the prices most recently paid for stock, therefore selling prices will reflect up to date costs;
- it is relatively easy to calculate.

The **disadvantages** include:
- there might be problems in issuing new stock first, particularly if the stock is perishable or is likely to go out of date;
- the closing stock is valued at out of date prices which might be lower than the current prices. For this reason, the method does not conform to the accounting standard SSAP9, nor is it acceptable for tax purposes with the Inland Revenue.

Stock valuation – AVCO (average cost)

This method of stock valuation is sometimes also known as the weighted average cost. It involves recalculating the average cost (AVCO) of stock every time a new delivery arrives. Each unit of stock is valued at the average cost of all units and is calculated using the formula below.

$$(\text{Weighted}) \text{ average cost} = \frac{\text{Existing stock value} + \text{value of latest purchase}}{\text{Number of units in stock}}$$

QUESTION 2

Sorensen Mills is a food processing company. It refines and packs flour for large supermarkets. The business's main raw material is grain that it buys from a Canadian supplier. During April, the following stock transactions were recorded:

3.4	20 tonnes were delivered @ £100 per tonne;
10.4	40 tonnes were delivered @ £110 per tonne;
12.4	40 tonnes were used in production;
18.4	40 tonnes were delivered @ £120 per tonne;
29.4	40 tonnes were used in production.

(a) **Assuming that the opening stock was zero, calculate the value of closing stock at the end of April using the (i) FIFO method; (ii) LIFO method.**

(b) **Which method of valuation is most appropriate for Sorensen Mills? Explain your answer.**

In order to illustrate the AVCO method, consider again the example of Steelcraft, the metal component manufacturer. Figure 24.5 shows the same stock transactions as in Figures 24.3 and 24.4. However, they are adjusted for the AVCO method of stock valuation.

Figure 24.5 *Stock transactions illustrating how a closing stock figure is calculated using the AVCO method*

| Date | Stock received | | | Stock issued | Average cost | Stock valuation | |
	Qty	Price	Value	Qty		Qty	Value
		£	£		£		£
Jan	1,000	5	5,000		5	1,000	5,000
Feb	2,000	6	12,000		5.67	3,000	17,010
March				1,500	5.67	1,500	8,505

When the first delivery of steel plates is received in January, the average cost is the price paid for them, ie £5 each (£5,000/1,000). The value of stock is therefore £5,000. When the next delivery of 2,000 plates costing £6 each is received in February, the average cost is:

$$\text{Average cost} = \frac{£5,000 + £12,000}{3,000} = \frac{£17,000}{3,000} = £5.67$$

This is the cost that is used to calculate stock values until the next delivery. The value of stock in February is therefore £17,010 (£5.67 × 3,000). In March, 1,500 plates are issued, so there are 1,500 remaining in stock. This is valued at £8,505 (£5.67 × 1,500). In this example, the AVCO valuation is approximately midway between the FIFO and LIFO valuations.

The main **advantages** of the AVCO method are that:
- it is logical since all identical units of stock are given an equal value;
- fluctuations in the purchase price of stock are evened out so the impact on costs and profit is reduced;
- it conforms to the accounting standard SSAP9 and is acceptable to the Inland Revenue.

The main **disadvantages** are that:
- the average cost has to be recalculated every time the price of purchased stock changes;
- the average cost might not be the same as any of the prices actually paid for stock;
- if stock prices are rising rapidly, the average cost will be much lower than the replacement price.

QUESTION 3

Mark Peters owns a footwear wholesaling business in Leeds. One of his best selling lines is a pair of hiking boots imported from China. However, the price of these boots is volatile because of fluctuations in exchange rates. During the first six months of the year, the following stock transactions for hiking boots were recorded:

January	200 pairs delivered @ £20 each;
February	150 pairs issued;
March	200 pairs delivered @ £30 each;
April	200 pairs issued;
May	200 pairs delivered @ £24 each;
June	150 pairs issued.

(a) Assuming that opening stock was zero, calculate the value of closing stock of hiking boots using the AVCO method.

(b) Explain the advantages and disadvantages of AVCO to Mark Peters' business.

How does stock valuation affect profits?

The closing stock value is used to determine the **gross profit** of a business. Gross profit is calculated by subtracting the **cost of sales** from **turnover**. The cost of sales is calculated by adding the opening stock to purchases, and then subtracting the closing stock. To illustrate the effect of different stock valuations on gross profit, consider the earlier example of Steelcraft. Assume that Steelcraft's turnover for the first quarter of the year was £40,000, opening stock was zero and purchases of steel were £17,000.

Figure 24.6 shows the effect on Steelcraft's gross profit of using stock valuations based on FIFO, LIFO and AVCO. When the FIFO method is used to calculate the closing stock value, the gross profit is highest, £32,000. The LIFO method results in the lowest gross profit, £31,000, and the AVCO method gives a value in-between.

Figure 24.6 *Gross profit for Steelcraft using three different methods of stock valuation*

	FIFO £	LIFO £	AVCO £
Turnover	40,000	40,000	40,000
Opening stock	0	0	0
Purchases	17,000	17,000	17,000
Less closing stock	9,000	8,000	8,505
Cost of sales	8,000	9,000	8,495
Gross profit	32,000	31,000	31,505

Factors that affect the choice of method when valuing stock

According to SSAP9, UK companies must use either the FIFO or the AVCO method of stock valuation. Whichever method is chosen, it must be applied consistently and should reflect a 'true and fair view' of a business's financial circumstances. However, because there are alternative methods of stock valuation, accountants must use their judgment when selecting an appropriate method. A number of factors influence which method is chosen.

- **Convenience** Some businesses might choose a particular method because it is easier to apply. For example, many businesses avoid using AVCO because of the need to recalculate the average cost of stock whenever the purchase price changes.
- **Taxation** If a business wishes to defer the payment of tax, it is likely to choose the method of valuation that gives the lowest level of profit.
- **Enhancing performance** A business might wish to report high profits to show its performance in a good light. This could happen if senior managers' wages are tied to profit levels or if the business is trying to attract investors or a potential buyer. In this case, it would choose a method of stock valuation that gives the highest value of closing stock.
- **Tradition** A business might use a particular method of stock valuation because it is the custom and practice in a particular industry.
- **Lack of information** A lack of information might restrict a business in its choice of method. For example, if a business does not have detailed records of all stock purchases and issues, the AVCO method is difficult to apply.

It is not acceptable practice for a business to switch between different methods of stock valuation from year to year. The accounting standard SSAP9 states that consistency of approach is important. However, this does not mean that a valuation method can never be changed. But, if a change is made, it should be explained in the notes to the accounts (see unit 38).

It should be noted that methods of stock valuation are not necessarily the same as methods of stock control. To illustrate this, suppose that a business chooses to use the FIFO method of stock valuation. This assumes that the oldest stock is used first, and therefore the closing stock is valued on the basis of the cost of the more recent purchases. However, in practice, this does not mean that stock has to be physically issued on a FIFO basis. For example, if the business has a stock of identical metal components which were bought at different times, the components might all be mixed together in a storage bin. It does not matter which components are used first, and this does not affect the method of stock valuation.

The principles of stock control

When deciding how much stock it should hold, a business must balance the **costs of holding stock** against the benefits. The costs include:
- the cost of warehousing and storage;
- the cost of insuring stock;
- the financial cost of tying up funds in the form of stock rather than as, for example, money in a bank deposit account where it might earn interest;
- the risk of pilferage and obsolescence.

The **benefits of holding stock** include:
- the ability to meet customer demand immediately, and thereby maintain goodwill;
- the ability, for manufacturers, to maintain continuous production without the danger of stock shortages;
- the avoidance of having to reorder at short notice, at prices that might be unfavourable or on time scales that suppliers might be unable to meet;
- the avoidance of having to reorder frequently, and thereby avoiding the administration and other costs associated with making frequent orders.

In order to ensure that stocks are efficiently managed, a number of techniques have been developed. For example, the **stock turnover ratio** is used by some businesses to calculate how many days it takes to sell the average stock holding (see unit 44). Many businesses now use computerised systems so that managers can have up-to-date information on stock levels and speed of turnover (see unit 47).

The ECONOMIC ORDER QUANTITY (EOQ) is a mathematical technique that is used for calculating the optimum, ie best, amount of stock that a business should hold. It assumes that the main costs associated with stock are **holding costs** and **ordering costs**. The cost of holding stock increases as more is held, so managers might wish to decrease the amount. However, by reducing stock levels there will be a rise in the number of orders made, so ordering costs will increase. It is possible to work out the stock level where costs are minimised. This is illustrated in Figure 24.7. It shows that holding costs increase, and ordering costs decrease, as stock levels increase. The point at which total costs are at a minimum is at output OX.

Figure 24.7 *Economic order quantity*

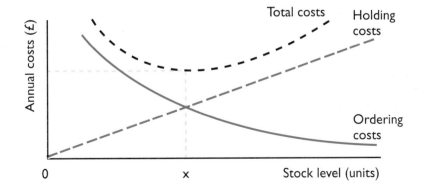

JUST-IN-TIME stock management is a relatively new system of stock control that is used by some manufacturing businesses. The aim is to eliminate stocks by having raw materials and components delivered just-in-time for them to be used in the production process. By adopting this approach, businesses avoid the costs involved in holding stocks. However, the system requires a close planning relationship between the manufacturer and its suppliers. Materials have to be delivered in the correct quantities, at the right quality at the agreed times. Any failure can be very costly in terms of lost production and sales. Just-in-time techniques are also used for finished goods. Production is matched to demand by only supplying goods to order.

UNIT ASSESSMENT   QUESTION 1

Figure 24.8 *Stock groups and closing stock values for Stavely Golf Club shop* ●●●

Stock group	Cost £	NRV £
Golf clubs - irons	4,600	7,600
Golf clubs - drivers & putters	4,100	9,700
Golf bags	1,200	2,800
Clothes	2,900	1,500
Golf shoes	2,100	2,000
Golf accessories	5,900	8,700
Total	20,800	32,300

The equipment shop at Stavely Golf Club records its stock in 6 groups. The end-of-year closing stock valuations are shown in Figure 24.8.

(a) What is the closing stock value for the golf club shop?
(b) Explain why the total cost of stock should not be used in the accounts.
(c) A mistake in the stocktake revealed that the cost of golf accessories is £4,900.
   What effect will this error have on (i) gross profit (ii) the balance sheet?

summary questions

1. Give two examples of work-in-progress.
2. Explain the difference between stocks of finished goods and stocks for resale.
3. State two reasons why a business needs to value stock.
4. Explain the difference between cost and net realisable value.
5. According to the accounting standard SSAP9, how should closing stock be valued?
6. Explain why individual items of stock, or groups of similar items, should be valued separately.
7. Explain the difference between the FIFO and LIFO methods of stock valuation.
8. State one advantage and one disadvantage of each method of stock valuation.
9. What will be the effect on profit if a business switches from the LIFO to the AVCO method of stock valuation?
10. State four factors that might influence the choice of stock valuation method.

UNIT ASSESSMENT QUESTION 2

Luton Taxis is a well established taxi company. Purchases and issues of diesel for a four month period are listed in the table on the right.

June	10,000 litres @ 70p per litre purchased;
June	7,000 litres used;
July	10,000 litres @ 75p per litre purchased;
July	8,000 litres used;
August	15,000 litres @ 80p per litre purchased;
August	15,000 litres used;
September	15,000 litres @ 75p per litre purchased;
September	12,000 litres used.

(a) **Assuming zero opening stock, calculate the value of closing stock in September using (i) the FIFO method (ii) the AVCO method.**
(b) **Which method of stock valuation would you recommend to Luton Taxis if it wishes to minimise payments of tax in the current period? Explain your answer.**
(c) **Explain the disadvantages of using the method chosen in (b).**

key terms

AVCO (average cost) - a method of stock valuation that involves calculating the average cost of total stock every time a new delivery is received.

Closing stock - the value of stock held by a business at the end of an accounting period.

Economic order quantity - a system of ordering raw materials and components so that ordering costs and holding costs are minimised.

FIFO (first in, first out) - a method of stock valuation that involves issuing stock in the order in which it is delivered, so that remaining stock is valued closer to its replacement value.

Just-in-time - a system of stock control in which raw materials and other components are delivered to a manufacturing plant only when they are needed. The system minimises the quantity of stock held by the manufacturer. It also involves producing goods to order, so stocks of finished goods are also minimised

LIFO (last in, first out) - a method of stock valuation that involves issuing the more recent deliveries first, so that closing stock is valued at older purchase prices.

Net realisable value (NRV) - the estimated resale value of stock, less any selling or distribution costs.

Opening stock - the value of stock held by a business at the beginning of an accounting period.

Stock (stock-in-trade) - raw materials, work-in-progress or finished goods that are held by businesses. In North America, stock is called inventory.

Stocktake - physically counting the actual amount of stock that a business owns.

Work-in-progress - the value of partly completed products in a business.

Bank reconciliations

unit objectives

To understand:
- the nature of bank reconciliations;
- the reasons why balances on bank statements might differ from those in the cash book;
- how to prepare a bank reconciliation statement;
- the purposes of bank reconciliation statements.

What is a bank reconciliation statement?

A BANK RECONCILIATION STATEMENT identifies and resolves the differences between a business's cash book and the bank statement issued by a bank. The cash book is used to record details of all bank payments and receipts made by a business (see unit 12). A bank statement is a record of a business's bank transactions from the bank's point of view. It is sent by the bank to a business at regular intervals.

Periodically, the cash book is balanced. The balance b/d on the bank account of the cash book shows how much there is in the bank or how much the business is overdrawn. In theory, the balance b/d on the bank account in the cash book should be the same as the balance on the bank statement. However, in practice the balance on the bank account in a business's cash book might be different from the balance on the bank statement. The process of reconciliation is a means of identifying where the differences occur and of bringing the cash book and bank statement into agreement.

Why might balances be different on a bank statement and in the cash book?

There is a number of reasons why the balance on a bank statement might differ from the balance in the cash book.

Timing differences There is often a time delay in the actual recording of transactions. Cheque payments are generally recorded by a business several days before they are recorded by a bank. For example, a business might send a cheque to a supplier on 12 March and enter the payment in the cash book on the same day. The bank might not record this transaction until, say, 18 March. There are two reasons for this:
- there is a delay between the cheque being sent and the supplier paying the cheque into the bank;
- the bank takes at least three working days to 'clear' the cheque. Clearing is the term used in banking to describe the transfer of funds from one account to another.

Cheques that have been drawn, ie issued, by a business and sent to a payee, but not yet recorded by the bank, are called UNPRESENTED CHEQUES. Since they have not yet been 'cleared' by the bank, they will not appear on the bank statement. Therefore, the balance on the bank statement of the business paying the cheque will be higher than the balance in the cash book.

Time delays also occur when a business receives money and pays it into the bank. When money is paid in, the cashier will complete a paying-in slip showing the value of notes, coins and cheques. This is recorded in the cash book. However, there will be a delay before this transaction appears on the bank statement. This is because it takes time for the bank to process the transaction and to clear any cheques being paid in. The delay is likely to be longer if deposits are made late in the day or at branches other than the one where the account is maintained. Deposits not yet cleared by the bank are called UNCLEARED LODGEMENTS. Their effect is to make the balance on a business's bank statement lower than the balance in its cash book.

A timing difference will also occur if a business receives a cheque from a customer, records it in the cash book and then delays presenting it to the bank. The balance on the bank statement will be lower than the balance in the cash book if there are such uncleared lodgements.

QUESTION 1

Rita Prem runs a beauty salon in Manchester. She keeps up to date records of her business transactions and on the 30 April the balance b/d on the cash book was a debit balance of £1,290. However, two cheques recorded in the cash book as payments were unpresented when Rita received her monthly bank statement. The cheques were for £100 and £160. Rita also knew that a recent cash deposit of £340 was not recorded on the statement.

(a) What will be the balance on the bank statement for Rita's business?
(b) Explain why the two cheques might have been unpresented.

Omissions from the cash book It is possible for a bank statement to contain entries that have not yet been recorded in the cash book. Examples of such payments and receipts might include the following.

- **Standing orders, direct debits and BACS (Bankers' Automated Clearing System)**
  These direct transfers of money can be both payments or receipts. For example, a business might pay an insurance premium by direct debit. It might receive payment from a customer by BACS.
- **Bank charges** These are charges for running a bank account. The charge is levied directly from the account and the amount is notified by an entry on the bank statement.
- **Interest** This is paid by a business to the bank if the account is overdrawn. Some banks pay account holders interest when they have money in the bank.

It is accepted practice for bookkeepers to delay recording such payments and receipts in the cash book until they receive the bank statement.

Errors Differences between bank statements and cash books can occur if errors are made. These could be bookkeeping errors made by a business, such as a failure to record a transaction, or a mistake in addition. Errors by bank staff could include the payment of a cheque into the wrong account or a keyboarding mistake.

Dishonoured cheques A DISHONOURED CHEQUE is a cheque which the drawer's bank refuses to pay. The drawer is the person or organisation which writes and signs the cheque (see unit 4). If this happens, the bank marks the cheque 'refer to drawer' and returns it to the payee, ie to the person or business that received the cheque. There is a number of reasons why a bank might refuse to honour a cheque.

- The drawer does not have enough money in the bank to cover the cheque payment made to the business. In this case, the cheque has 'bounced'.
- The drawer has 'stopped' the cheque. This means that the drawer has contacted the bank and instructed it not to transfer funds.
- An error has been found on the cheque. For example, the drawer might have written an amount in words that is different from the amount in figures on the cheque.
- The cheque has not be signed by the drawer, or the drawer's signature does not match the specimen signature in the bank's records.

If a business receives a dishonoured cheque from a customer, the balance in its cash book will be more than the balance on its bank statement. This is because the receipt of the cheque will be recorded in the cash book, but the business's bank will not have received the money from the customer's bank.

How is a bank reconciliation statement prepared?

A bank reconciliation statement is generally prepared by a business each time that a bank statement is received. This is likely to be at least once per month and might even be on a daily basis in businesses that have large numbers of payments or receipts.

In order to illustrate how a bank reconciliation statement is prepared, consider Victor Hughes, an insurance broker specialising in car insurance. Copies of his business's June bank statement and an extract from the cash book are shown in Figure 25.1. To simplify the explanation, the cash book just

QUESTION 2

Adam Bogdanovic runs a financial consultancy that gives advice on pensions, savings and life assurance. On 31 May, he received the regular monthly bank statement for his business. According to the statement, the business had £2,600 in the current bank account. This was less than Adam expected.

- In another letter from the bank, on the same day that the statement arrived, a dishonoured cheque for £600 was enclosed. The letter explained that the drawer did not have sufficient funds to cover the cheque.
- The statement included quarterly bank charges of £160 which Adam had not accounted for in the cash book.

(a) What is the balance that Adam would have expected on his bank statement?

(b) Explain why bank charges are not likely to be entered in the cash book before the bank statement is received.

contains details of bank transactions. It has been balanced to show that the balance b/d on July 1 is different from the balance on the bank statement. In practice, it is not likely that a business would balance the cash book at this stage. It is more likely that balancing would wait until after any adjustments were made in the reconciliation process.

Figure 25.1 *Bank statement and cash book extract for Victor Hughes*

233 Wright Street
Earlsdon
Coventry
CV2 9PP

NorthWest

Current account
Mr Victor Hughes

Sheet No.35

STATEMENT DATE 30.06.01   Account No. 09875424

Date	Payment details		Payments	Receipts	Balance (£)
1 Jun	Balance b/f from sheet no. 34				✓453.90
6 Jun	Cheque	005567	✓234.80		219.10
8 Jun	Cheque	005568	✓100.00		119.10
10 Jun	Direct Debit	British Gas	45.00		
	Credit	000104		✓345.25	419.35
11 June	Cheque	005570	✓230.00		189.35
21 June	Automated credit C. Jones & Son			200.00	389.35
22 June	Cheque	005571	✓23.65		365.70
23 June	Cheque	005572	✓400.00		34.30 OD
30 June	Credit	000105		✓560.40	
	Cheque	005573	✓166.45		
	Balance c/f to sheet no. 36				359.65

OD = Overdrawn (sometimes Dr is used instead)

	Debit			**CASH BOOK**	Credit		
Date	**Details**		**Bank**	**Date**	**Details**		**Bank**
2001			£	2001			£
1.6	Balance b/d		✓ 453.90	2.6	Advertising 005567		✓ 234.80
10.6	Sales		✓ 345.25	3.6	P. Wilson 005568		✓ 100.00
26.6	Sales		✓ 560.40	6.6	L. Hornchurch 005569		32.00
29.6	Sales		300.00	6.6	Eastern Electric 005570		✓ 230.00
				15.6	Simpsons 005571		✓ 23.65
				19.6	Rent 005572		✓ 400.00
				22.6	Wages (T. Ball) 005573		✓ 166.45
				30.6	Balance c/d		472.65
			1,659.55				1,659.55
1.7	Balance b/d		472.65				

Note that some banks use the heading Debit for payments and Credit for receipts. This is because the transactions are being considered from the bank's point of view. So, for example, when money is paid into a business's bank account it is listed as a **credit** on the statement because it represents an **increase in the bank's liabilities**. The money is owed by the bank to the business. It represents an increase in the business's assets so it is treated as a debit in the business's cash book. When money is paid out of a business's bank account, it is listed as a debit on the statement and is treated as a credit in the cash book.

The following steps are taken when preparing the bank reconciliation statement.
- The opening balance b/d on the cash book, at the start of the period, is compared with the opening balance b/f on the bank statement. In this case, the balances are the same, ie £453.90. To confirm that they are the same, a tick is placed by the side of each amount in Figure 25.1. The term 'balance b/f' is used when a balance is brought forward from a previous page or sheet.
- Transactions that appear in both the cash book and on the bank statement are compared. If they match, a tick is placed by the two entries, once in the cash book and once on the statement. For example, the payment recorded in the cash book on 2 June, for £234.80, is the same amount as the entry on the statement dated 6 June. The entries relate to the same transaction, a payment for advertising, because the cheque numbers are the same. Both these entries are ticked. It is not sufficient to match values alone. The cheque numbers must also be matched. When ticking entries it is helpful to be systematic. One approach is to tick all the receipts in the cash book which match in the bank statement and then tick all the payments from the cash book against those in the bank statement. All the matching entries for Victor Hughes' business are ticked and shown in Figure 25.1.
- When all the matching entries have been ticked, there are some unticked items. These appear in both the cash book and on the bank statement. For Victor Hughes, there are four unticked items, two on the bank statement and two in the cash book.
- The unticked items on the bank statement must be recorded in the cash book to bring it up to date. The two unticked items are for a direct debit of £45.00 and an automated credit for £200.00. The updated cash book is shown in Figure 25.2. The direct debit to British Gas for £45.00 is shown as a payment and the automated credit from C. Jones & Son is shown as a receipt. Note that the items identified on the bank statement are entered at the last date of the

Figure 25.2 *Updated cash book*

Debit			CASH BOOK	Credit		
Date	Details	Bank	Date	Details		Bank
2001		£	2001			£
1.6	Balance b/d	453.90	2.6	Advertising 005567		234.80
10.6	Sales	345.25	3.6	P. Wilson 005568	✓	100.00
26.6	Sales	560.40	6.6	L. Hornchurch 005569	✓	32.00
29.6	Sales	300.00	6.6	Eastern Electric 005570		230.00
30.6	C. Jones & Son (21.6)	200.00	15.6	Simpsons 005571	✓	23.65
			19.6	Rent 005572	✓	400.00
			22.6	Wages (T. Ball) 005573	✓	166.45
			30.6	British Gas (10.6)	✓	45.00
			30.6	Balance c/d		627.65
		1859.55				1,859.55
1.7	Balance b/d	627.65				

Note that the cash book entries include all those from the cash book in Figure 25.1 but this time it is balanced **after** the items 'picked up' from the bank statement are added.

period, 30 June. The date they appear on the bank statement is entered in brackets.

- Once the cash book has been brought up to date and balanced, the bank reconciliation statement can be drawn up. The unticked payment of £32.00 to L. Hornchurch in the cash book is an unpresented cheque. The unticked receipt for £300 is an uncleared lodgement. These unticked items in the cash book are used in the reconciliation statement.
- The reconciliation statement is shown in Figure 25.3. The first entry in the statement is the balance b/d from the updated cash book. For Victor Hughes's business this is £627.65. This is the balance after the adjustments for unticked entries on the bank statement.
- The next entry on the reconciliation statement is the unpresented cheque for £32.00. The cheque number and the value are written in the statement. The value of the cheque is then **added** to the opening balance to give £659.65.
- The next entry is the uncleared lodgement for £300. This is **subtracted** from the subtotal to give a balance of £359.65. The amount is the same as the balance on the bank statement. This completes the reconciliation.

Figure 25.3 *Bank reconciliation statement for Victor Hughes's business*

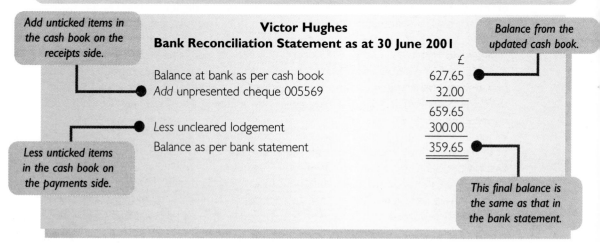

Add unticked items in the cash book on the receipts side.

Balance from the updated cash book.

Victor Hughes
Bank Reconciliation Statement as at 30 June 2001

	£
Balance at bank as per cash book	627.65
Add unpresented cheque 005569	32.00
	659.65
Less uncleared lodgement	300.00
Balance as per bank statement	359.65

Less unticked items in the cash book on the payments side.

This final balance is the same as that in the bank statement.

Using the balance on a bank statement as the opening balance

In Figure 25.3, the bank reconciliation statement starts with the balance from the updated cash book. However, it is also acceptable to start with the bank statement balance and use this as the opening balance. If this method is used, then unpresented cheques must be **subtracted**, and uncleared lodgements must be **added**. To illustrate this alternative approach, the bank reconciliation statement for Victor Hughes is redrawn in Figure 25.4. The opening balance in this statement is taken from the balance on the bank statement, £359.65. The next entry is the uncleared lodgement, £300.00, which is added to the opening balance. The unpresented cheque for £32.00 is then subtracted which gives the balance in the cash book. This is £627.65.

Figure 25.4 *Bank reconciliation statement for Victor Hughes (using the bank statement balance as the opening entry)*

Victor Hughes
Bank Reconciliation Statement as at 30 June 2001

	£
Balance as per bank statement	359.65
Add uncleared lodgement	300.00
	659.65
Less unpresented cheque 005569	32.00
Balance at bank as per cash book	627.65

QUESTION 3

Paulo Mancini runs a restaurant called Mancini's in Cheltenham, Gloucestershire. He prepares monthly bank reconciliation statements to help keep his affairs in order. Figure 25.5 shows a bank statement and an extract from Mancini's cash book.

Figure 25.5 A bank statement and an extract from Mancini's cash book

17 Church Street
Cheltenham
GL14 9TB

NorthWest
Current account
Mancini's Restaurant

Sheet No.66

STATEMENT DATE 31.03.01   Account No. 01366201

Date	Payment details		Payments	Receipts	Balance (£)
1 Mar	Balance b/f from sheet no. 65				540.70
7 March	Cheque	000441	56.10		
	Cheque	000443	200.00		284.60
12 March	Credit	000012		1,299.90	1,584.50
17 March	Direct debit AA Subscription		90.00		1,494.50
22 March	Cheque	000444	345.00		1,149.50
24 March	Bank charges		67.50		1,082.00
25 March	Cheque	000445	580.95		501.05
31 March	Balance c/f to sheet no. 67				501.05

CASH BOOK

	Debit				Credit	
Date	Details	Bank	Date	Details		Bank
2001		£	2001			£
1.3	Balance b/d	540.70	2.3	Squires Supplies 000441		56.10
9.3	Sales	1,299.90	2.3	Robertson's 000442		209.00
			2.3	Telecom Connect 000443		200.00
			16.3	Brown Meats 000444		345.00
			20.3	Wages (C. Raffo) 000445		580.95

(a) Match the entries in the cash book with the entries on the bank statement.
(b) Update and balance Mancini's cash book.
(c) Prepare a bank reconciliation statement for Mancini's.

Bank reconciliation with a bank overdraft

When a business has an overdraft, the adjustments needed for a reconciliation statement are similar to those shown previously. However, because the opening balance is negative, ie the business owes money to the bank rather than the other way around, extra care has to be taken in the calculations.

In order to illustrate how a reconciliation statement is prepared, consider the example of Bampton Steel, a steel wholesaler. A copy of Bampton Steel's bank statement and an extract from the updated cash book are shown in Figure 25.6. The bank statement and cash book both show that the business was overdrawn by £431.10 at the start of the month. But, at the end of the month, the balance on the bank statement was different from the balance b/d in the cash book.

- The first step in preparing the bank reconciliation statement is to identify entries that appear on both the bank statement and cash book. These can then be ticked.
- There are three unticked items. The two in the cash book relate to an unpresented cheque for £158.00 and an uncleared lodgement of £464.90. The one on the bank statement relates to a direct debit payment for £230.00.
- The cash book is updated in Figure 25.7 to include the unticked item on the bank statement. It is balanced and shows a credit balance of £365.15.

Figure 25.6 *A bank statement and extract from the cash book for Bampton Steel*

```
130 Bedford Street          N NorthWest
North Shields
NE29 6LB                    Current account
                            Bampton Steel                    Sheet No.24

STATEMENT DATE 31.05.01              Account No. 07864438

Date      Payment details           Payments      Receipts     Balance (£)

1  May  Balance b/f from sheet no. 23                       ✓431.00 OD
7  May  Cheque   001229            ✓320.10                   751.10 OD
10 May  Direct debit  B'ham BS      230.00                   981.10 OD
12 May  Credit   012665                         ✓654.20      326.90 OD
17 May  Cheque   001231            ✓ 32.45                   359.35 OD
24 May  Cheque   001232            ✓312.70                   672.05 OD
31 May  Balance c/f to sheet no. 25                          672.05 OD

OD = Overdrawn
```

	Debit	CASH BOOK		Credit	
Date	**Details**	**Bank**	**Date**	**Details**	**Bank**
2001		£	2001		£
9.5	Sales	✓ 654.20	1.5	Balance b/d	✓ 431.00
29.5	Sales	464.90	3.5	Cheque 001229	✓ 320.10
31.5	Balance c/d	135.15	5.5	Cheque 001230	158.00
			14.5	Cheque 001231	✓ 32.45
			20.5	Cheque 001232	✓ 312.70
		1,254.25			1,254.25
			1.6	Balance b/d	135.15

Figure 25.7 *Updated cash book*

	Debit	CASH BOOK		Credit	
Date	**Details**	**Bank**	**Date**	**Details**	**Bank**
2001		£	2001		£
9.5	Sales	654.20	1.5	Balance b/d	431.00
29.5	Sales	464.90	3.5	Cheque 001229	320.10
31.5	Balance c/d	365.15	5.5	Cheque 001230	158.00
			14.5	Cheque 001231	32.45
			20.5	Cheque 001232	312.70
			31.5	B'ham BS (10.5)	230.00
		1,484.25			1,484.25
			1.6	Balance b/d	365.15

- The bank reconciliation statement is shown in Figure 25.8. The first entry is the value of the overdraft taken from the updated cash book, £365.15. Since the opening value represents an overdraft, it is placed in brackets to indicate that it is negative. The next step is to **add** the uncleared cheque for £158.00.
- The next step is to **subtract** the uncleared lodgement of £464.90. This gives a figure of (minus) £672.05 which is the same as the balance on the bank statement.

Figure 25.8 *Bank reconciliation statement for Bampton Steel*

Bampton Steel
Bank Reconciliation Statement as at 31 May 2001

	£
Balance at bank as per cash book	(365.15)
Add unpresented cheque	158.00
	(207.15)
Less uncleared lodgement	464.90
Balance as per bank statement	(672.05)

What is the purpose of a bank reconciliation statement?

The preparation of a bank reconciliation statement can serve some useful purposes for a business.

* It helps check the accuracy of the bookkeeping in the cash book. When the entries in the cash book and on the bank statement are matched, items that have not been entered in the cash book, and any errors, will be identified.
* It helps to maintain a check on fraud and embezzlement. Since the bank statement is an independent accounting record, ie not produced by the business, it serves as a means of verifying entries in the cash book. For example, if a business cheque is dishonestly made payable to an employee and not entered in the cash book, it will eventually show up on the bank statement when cashed.
* It can be used to detect errors made by the bank. Although such errors might not be common, they can go undetected for some time if regular reconciliations are not made.
* It helps a business to control its cash flow. By preparing bank reconciliation statements, owners can identify precisely how much money is available.
* Dishonoured cheques will be identified. They will appear on the receipts side in the cash book but will not appear on the bank statement.

key terms

Bank reconciliation statement - a financial statement that brings into agreement the balance in the cash book and the balance on the bank statement.
Dishonoured cheque - a cheque that is paid into a bank but then returned unpaid to the payee (ie recipient) generally because there are insufficient funds in the drawer's (ie payer's) account.
Uncleared lodgements - deposits of cash and cheques that have been recorded in the cash book and paid into the bank, but not yet processed or cleared by the bank.
Unpresented cheques - cheques that have been issued by a drawer but not yet cleared by the bank.

summary questions

1. With reference to bank reconciliations, what is meant by timing differences?
2. State three examples of possible omissions from the cash book.
3. What is the difference between a dishonoured cheque and an unpresented cheque?
4. Give three reasons why a cheque might be dishonoured.
5. What information is required to prepare a bank reconciliation statement?
6. Explain how a bank reconciliation statement is prepared.
7. During the reconciliation process, give two examples of items that might be unticked on the bank statement.
8. During the reconciliation process, give two examples of items that might be unticked in the cash book.
9. How should a bank reconciliation statement be prepared if a business is overdrawn at the bank?
10. State four purposes of a bank reconciliation statement.

UNIT ASSESSMENT QUESTION 1

Data Plus is a market research agency run by Rachel Nichols. At the end of August 2001, Rachel prepared her regular bank reconciliation statement. After matching the entries on the statement with those in the cash book, there were four unticked items remaining in the cash book. Details of these items were as follows:

- unpresented cheque no. 000991 £43.90;
- unpresented cheque no. 000995 £1,528.00;
- unpresented cheque no. 000999 £269.07;
- uncleared lodgement for £670.00.

After updating the cash book, there was a (debit) balance b/d of £1,900.30. The end of month balance on the bank statement was £3,071.27.

(a) Using the balance on the cash book as the opening balance, draw up a bank reconciliation statement for Data Plus.
(b) Redraw the bank reconciliation statement using the balance on the bank statement as the opening balance.
(c) How might drawing up a bank reconciliation statement help Rachel avoid cash flow problems when running Data Plus?

UNIT ASSESSMENT QUESTION 2

Samantha and Dave Russell run a private play group and nursery school called Juniors in Glasgow. Figure 25.9 shows a bank statement for Juniors and an extract from the cash book.

Figure 25.9 *Bank statement and extract from the cash book for Juniors*

16 Woodside Place
Glasgow
G3 7QT

NorthWest
Current account
Juniors Nursery

Sheet No.94

STATEMENT DATE 28.02.01   Account No. 02594427

Date	Payment details		Payments	Receipts	Balance (£)
1 Feb	Balance b/f from sheet no. 93				221.90
4 Feb	Cheque	000431	125.00		96.90
7 Feb	Credit	000220		590.00	686.90
9 Feb	Cheque	000432	23.60		663.30
11 Feb	Cheque	000434	12.50		650.80
12 Feb	Direct Debit	DLR Ins.	45.00		605.80
14 Feb	Credit	000221		670.60	1,276.40
16 Feb	Bank charges		34.50		1,241.90
21 Feb	Credit	000222		561.00	1,802.90
25 Feb	Direct Debit	Stamford BS	450.00		1,352.90
27 Feb	Cheque	000435	1,000.00		352.90
27 Feb	Balance c/f to sheet 95				352.90

	Debit		**CASH BOOK**		Credit	
Date	**Details**	**Bank**	**Date**	**Details**		**Bank**
2001		£	2001			£
1.2	Balance b/d	221.90	1.2	Edinburgh DC 000431		125.00
5.2	Sales	590.00	6.2	T. McDonald 000432		23.60
11.2	Sales	670.60	7.2	B. McDowd 000433		120.00
18.2	Sales	561.00	8.2	Tesco 000434		12.50
26.2	Sales	680.00	25.2	Wages 000435		1,000.00

(a) Update and balance the cash book.
(b) Prepare a bank reconciliation statement for Juniors.
(c) Explain why businesses, such as Juniors, prepare bank reconciliation statements.

Value added tax

What is VAT?

VALUE ADDED TAX (VAT) is an indirect tax which is levied on spending. It is administered and collected by the Customs and Excise which is a UK government department. The standard rate of VAT (in 2002) is 17.5%. This is charged on most goods and services such as petrol, telephone charges and electrical goods. However, there is also a lower rate of 5% which is charged on domestic fuel and on a limited number of other items such as household insulation materials. Some goods and services are **zero rated** which means that the VAT rate is 0%. These include:

- food (except food bought in restaurants);
- books and newspapers;
- medicines;
- children's clothes and footwear;
- domestic housing;
- passenger transport.

Certain goods and services are **exempt** from VAT. From a customer's point of view, there is no difference between buying goods that are zero rated and buying goods that are exempt because, in both cases, no VAT is charged. However, from a business's point of view, there is a difference. This is explained later in the unit. Two types of goods and services are exempt from VAT.

- **Goods and services sold by small businesses** Any business that has a turnover of less than £54,000 (in 2001) does not have to register for VAT. This means that it does not charge VAT or keep VAT records. The turnover below which businesses need to register is called the **VAT threshold**. It generally rises each year in line with other tax thresholds. The purpose of this exemption is to reduce the burden of bookkeeping on small businesses.

- **Exempt supplies** These include services such as insurance, most education and training, health and dental care provided by doctors, most banking services, betting and gaming, postal services and the letting, leasing and sale of most commercial land and buildings.

Businesses that have a turnover above the VAT threshold, and smaller businesses that choose to register, are issued with a VAT registration number. This must be quoted on all their business documents. These businesses are also required to complete a VAT return every quarter. An example of a completed VAT return is given at the end of this unit.

Who pays VAT and how is it collected?

Although it is consumers who ultimately bear the cost of VAT, the tax is actually collected and paid by businesses at each stage in the production process. To illustrate this, consider the example in Figure 26.1 which shows the different stages involved in the production of a wooden table.

- The first stage in the process is that wood is sold by a forester to a timber merchant for £235. The price includes VAT of £35 (17.5% x £200) which is paid by the forester to the Customs and Excise. The sale of the timber by the forester is an **output** and the VAT charged on the sale is known as an OUTPUT TAX (or sales tax). From the timber merchant's point of view, the purchase of the timber is an **input** and the VAT paid on the purchase is known as an INPUT TAX (or purchases tax).

Figure 26.1 *The collection and payment of VAT at different stages of production*

Business	Price		VAT input tax (purchases)	VAT output tax (sales)	VAT paid by each business to Customs & Excise
	excl. VAT	incl. VAT			
	£	£	£	£	£
Forester	200.00	235.00	0	35.00	35.00
Timber merchant	400.00	470.00	35.00	70.00	35.00
Furniture maker	500.00	587.50	70.00	87.50	17.50
Retailer	700.00	822.50	87.50	122.50	35.00
					122.50

Note that, although it is not relevant in this example, when calculating VAT, fractions of a penny are ignored. The amount is always rounded down to the nearest penny.

- The timber merchant then processes the wood and sells it to a furniture maker for £470. This price includes the output tax of £70 VAT (17.5% × £400). However, the timber merchant only pays £35 of this to the Customs and Excise. This is because the timber merchant subtracts the £35 VAT input tax paid to the forester from the £70 output tax collected from the furniture maker.
- The furniture maker produces a table from the wood and sells it to a retailer for £587.50. This includes £87.50 VAT (17.5% × £500). However, the furniture maker only pays £17.50 of this VAT to the Customs and Excise (ie output tax of £87.50 less input tax of £70) because VAT of £70 has already been paid to the timber merchant.
- Finally, the retailer sells the table for £822.50 to a consumer. This includes £122.50 VAT (17.5% × £700). The retailer pays £35.00 of this to the Customs and Excise (output tax of £122.50 less input tax of £87.50). The consumer does not pay any money directly to the Customs and Excise. This is because the £122.50 total VAT has already been collected and paid by the businesses at each stage of production. This is shown by the total in the final column in Figure 26.1 (£35 + £35 + £17.50 + £35 = £122.50).

It is sometimes said that businesses are the unpaid collectors of VAT. This means that businesses are responsible for collecting VAT from customers, calculating how much they owe and paying it to the Customs and Excise. This is shown in the above example. The forester pays £35 to the Customs and Excise, the timber merchant pays £35, and so on. The collection and payment of VAT requires businesses to keep careful records of transactions involving the charging or payment of VAT. They also have to maintain good administrative systems to ensure that VAT payments are made on time.

Zero rated and exempt goods and services

To illustrate the difference between businesses that are either not registered for VAT or that sell exempt supplies, and businesses that sell zero rated goods and services, consider again the example in Figure 26.1. Suppose that the retailer selling the wooden table has a low turnover and is therefore exempt from charging VAT. The price of the table to consumers would be £700.00 because the VAT of £122.50 would not be charged. However, the retailer would have paid £87.50 VAT to the furniture maker in the purchase price of £587.50. The input tax of £87.50 would be borne fully by the retailer because there is no output VAT to set it against.

This contrasts with the position of a retailer who is registered for VAT but who only sells goods that are zero rated, such as childrens' clothes. Any VAT paid on inputs, for example telephone charges, can be reclaimed from the Customs and Excise.

Calculating VAT

When the price of a good **exclusive** of VAT is known, the calculation of VAT is relatively straightforward. For example, in Figure 26.1, wood priced at £200 was sold by the forester. The amount of VAT to be paid can be found by calculating 17.5% of the price. The price of the product including VAT can then be found by:

Price of wood inclusive of VAT = price of wood exclusive of VAT + (price of wood exclusive of VAT × 17.5%)

$$= £200.00 + (£200.00 × 17.5\%)$$

$$= £200.00 + £35.00$$

$$= £235.00$$

It is also possible to calculate the amount of VAT when only the price inclusive of VAT is known. In the previous example, the price of the wood inclusive of VAT is £235. To calculate how much VAT has been paid, the following calculation is necessary:

$$\text{Amount of VAT paid} = \frac{\text{VAT rate}}{100 + \text{VAT rate}} × \text{price inclusive of VAT}$$

$$= \frac{17.5}{117.5} × £235.00$$

$$= £35.00$$

Alternatively, to work out the price of the wood before VAT is added, the following calculation is necessary:

$$\text{Price exclusive of VAT} = \frac{100}{100 + \text{VAT rate}} × \text{price inclusive of VAT}$$

$$= \frac{100}{117.5} × £235.00$$

$$= £200.00$$

QUESTION 1

Angela Cox sells light fittings from her specialist shop in Leamington Spa, Warwickshire. The business is registered for VAT. During the last financial year, her turnover was £125,600 and the cost of sales was £76,800. Both of these figures exclude VAT.

(a) Calculate the following (i) the amount of VAT paid by Angela Cox's business to suppliers; (ii) the amount of VAT charged to customers; (iii) the amount of VAT paid to the Customs and Excise by Angela Cox's business. Assume that the rate of VAT is 17.5%.

(b) One of the light fittings sold by the business is priced at £94.00 inclusive of VAT. How much VAT is being charged?

(c) A supplier sells £763.75 of fittings to Angela Cox inclusive of VAT. Calculate the price exclusive of VAT.

Accounting for VAT – credit sales

The bookkeeping entries needed to record the sale of goods to customers on credit are described in unit 9. In order to simplify the explanation, unit 9 ignores the impact of VAT. To illustrate how VAT is accounted for in practice, consider the example of Perkins & Co, a supplier of pumping equipment. Extracts from the business's sales day book and ledgers are shown in Figure 26.2. Two credit sales are shown. For each sale, the price excluding VAT, the VAT amount, and the total price including VAT are entered in the day book. The double entry postings necessary to record these two credit sales transactions are as follows.

- The customer accounts in the sales ledger are debited with the total price of goods sold inclusive of VAT. For example, the C. Waterman account on page 32 in the sales ledger is debited with £470. This shows that C. Waterman owes Perkins & Co £470 for goods bought. Bolton Pumps owes £164.50.

- The sales account on page 10 in the nominal ledger is credited with the sales total excluding VAT for the accounting period. This is £540. It represents the amount of money that Perkins & Co is owed by customers.

- The VAT account is credited with the total of VAT. This is £94.50. It shows how much VAT is due to be paid to Perkins & Co. By separating sales and VAT totals in the nominal ledger, it is made clear how much money is owed to the business and how much is owed to the Customs and Excise.

Figure 26.2 *Extracts from the sales day book and ledgers of Perkins & Co*

SALES DAY BOOK						(page 23)
Date	Customer	Invoice no.	Folio	Price	VAT	Total
				£	£	£
12.1	C. Waterman	1187	SL32	400.00	70.00	470.00
14.1	Bolton Pumps	1188	SL11	140.00	24.50	164.50
				540.00	94.50	634.50
				NL10	NL34	

SALES LEDGER

	Dr		C. Waterman (page 32)		Cr	
			£			£
12.1	Sales	SDB23	470.00			

	Dr		Bolton Pumps (page 11)		Cr	
			£			£
14.1	Sales	SDB23	164.50			

NOMINAL LEDGER

	Dr		Sales Account (page 10)		Cr	
			£			£
				14.1	Credit sales SDB23	540.00

	Dr		VAT Account (page 34)		Cr	
			£			£
				14.1	SDB23	94.50

QUESTION 2

Premier Packaging manufactures a range of items including polythene bags, disposable cups, serviettes and plates. An extract from the business's sales day book is shown in Figure 26.3.

Figure 26.3 *Extracts from the sales day book and ledgers of Perkins & Co*

SALES DAY BOOK						(page 103)
Date	Customer	Invoice no.	Folio	Price	VAT	Total
				£	£	£
4.4	Swansea Catering	2237	SL32	320.00	56.00	376.00
9.4	Bunters	2238	SL6	560.00	98.00	658.00
13.4	Jones Bros.	2239	SL21	190.00	33.25	223.25
				NL12	NL37	

(a) **The sales day book is added up on 14 April. Calculate the totals.**

(b) **Show the entries in the sales and nominal ledgers to account for the transactions listed in the sales day book.**

(c) **What does the balance on the VAT account represent?**

Accounting for VAT – credit purchases

The bookkeeping entries needed to record the purchase of goods on credit are described in unit 10. As with credit sales, VAT is ignored. To illustrate how VAT is accounted for when credit purchases are made by a business, consider again the example of Perkins & Co. Extracts from the business's purchases day book and ledgers are shown in Figure 26.4. Two credit purchases are shown. For each transaction, the price excluding VAT, the VAT amount and the total including VAT are shown. The entries needed to record these credit purchases are as follows.

- The supplier accounts in the purchases ledger are credited with the amount including VAT that is owed for purchases. For example, the Winsford Steel account is credited with £258.50. This shows that Perkins & Co owes Winsford Steel £258.50 for goods bought on credit. T. Hall is owed £267.90.
- The purchases account on page 23 of the nominal ledger is debited with £448.00. This represents the overall total of purchases exclusive of VAT and is the cost of sales for the accounting period.
- The VAT account is debited with £78.40. This is the input tax that Perkins & Co will **pay** when it makes payment to its suppliers. The amount can be offset against any output tax that is owed to the Customs and Excise. In this example, the VAT account shows that £94.50 is owed as a result of the credit sales made earlier. If the VAT account was to be settled at this point, Perkins & Co would pay the Customs and Excise £16.10 (the difference between output tax of £94.50 and input tax of £78.40). Note that if, for some reason, the input tax was greater than the output tax, Perkins & Co would be owed money by the Customs and Excise rather than the other way around.

Figure 26.4 *Extracts from the purchases day book and ledgers of Perkins & Co*

PURCHASES DAY BOOK (page 87)

Date	Supplier	Invoice no.	Folio	Price £	VAT £	Total £
6.1	Winsford Steel	0128	PL41	220.00	38.50	258.50
11.1	T. Hall	1187	PL12	228.00	39.90	267.90
				448.00	78.40	526.40
				NL23	NL34	

PURCHASES LEDGER

Dr	**Winsford Steel (page 41)**	Cr
£		£
	6.1 Purchases PDB87	258.50

Dr	**T.Hall (page 12)**	Cr
£		£
	11.1 Purchases PDB87	267.90

NOMINAL LEDGER

Dr	**Purchases Account (page 23)**	Cr
£		£
14.1 Credit purchases PDB87 448.00		

Dr	**VAT Account (page 34)**	Cr
£		£
14.1 PDB87 78.40	14.1 SDB23	94.50

QUESTION 3

Oxford Books publishes a variety of children's books. The company is registered for VAT and the books it sells are zero rated. An extract from the business's purchases day book is shown in Figure 26.5. Three credit purchases are listed. The price excluding VAT, the VAT amount and the total price including VAT for each purchase is shown.

Figure 26.5 *Purchases day book extract for Oxford Books*

PURCHASES DAY BOOK						(page 53)
Date	Supplier	Invoice no.	Folio	Price £	VAT £	Total £
2.3	Welford Paper	1298	PL43	320.00	56.00	376.00
9.3	T. Watkins & Co	4496	PL40	160.00	28.00	188.00
14.3	Algo Logistics	11876	PL3	200.00	35.00	235.00
				680.00	119.00	799.00
				NL21	NL41	

(a) **Show the entries in the purchases and nominal ledgers to account for the transactions in the purchases day book.**

(b) **Explain what the balance on the VAT account represents.**

(c) **Explain how being registered for VAT affects Oxford Books.**

Accounting for VAT – returns

The treatment of returns inwards (or sales returns) and returns outwards (or purchases returns) is explained in unit 11. However, in that unit, VAT is ignored.

Returns inwards In order to illustrate the entries needed to account for VAT when goods are returned by customers, consider the example of Weston Mills, a paper supplier. Extracts from the business's sales returns day book and ledgers are shown in Figure 26.6. Two transactions are listed and the columns are totalled. To account for the two returns, which have VAT included, the following entries are necessary.

- The customer accounts in the sales ledger are credited with the total price of the returned goods including VAT. For example, the Thompsons' customer account on page 24 of the sales ledger is credited with £352.50. This is the price of the goods, including VAT, that have been returned to Weston Mills. Wickson Ltd's account is credited with £117.50.
- The returns inwards account in the nominal ledger is debited with £400 which is the total amount of sales returns for the period. This total excludes VAT.
- The VAT account in the nominal ledger is debited with £70. This is the total VAT charged on the returned goods.

Figure 26.6 *Extracts from the returns inwards day book and ledgers of Weston Mills*

RETURNS INWARDS DAY BOOK						(page 68)
Date	Customer	Credit note no.	Folio	Price £	VAT £	Total £
12.5	Thompsons	CN12	SL24	300.00	52.50	352.50
21.5	Wickson Ltd	CN67	SL41	100.00	17.50	117.50
				400.00	70.00	470.00
				NL16	NL38	

Figure 26.6 continued

SALES LEDGER
Dr Thompsons (page 24) Cr

	£			£
		12.5 Returns inwards RIDB68		352.50

Dr Wickson Ltd (page 41) Cr

	£			£
		21.5 Returns inwards RIDB68		117.50

NOMINAL LEDGER
Dr Returns Inwards Account (page 16) Cr

		£		£
31.5 Returns RIDB68		400.00		

Dr VAT Account (page 38) Cr

		£		£
31.5 Returns RIDB68		70.00		

Returns outwards In order to illustrate the entries needed to account for VAT when goods are returned to suppliers, consider again the example of Weston Mills. Extracts from the business's purchases returns day book and ledgers are shown in Figure 26.7. Two transactions are listed and the columns are totalled. To account for the two returns, which have VAT included, the following entries are necessary.

- The supplier accounts in the purchases ledger are debited with the price of the returned goods including VAT. For example, the supplier account for Simpson & Co on page 32 of the purchases ledger is debited with £141. This is the price of the goods, including VAT, that Weston Mills has returned.
- The purchases returns account in the nominal ledger is credited with £300. This is the total amount of returns for the period, excluding VAT.
- The VAT account is credited with the total of VAT relating to the purchases returns. In this case, the account is credited with £52.50.

Figure 26.7 *Extracts from the purchases returns day book and ledgers of Weston Mills*

RETURNS OUTWARDS DAY BOOK (page 74)

Date	Supplier	Credit note no.	Folio	Price £	VAT £	Total £
7.5	Simpson & Co	2349	PL32	120.00	21.00	141.00
26.5	N. Walters	1871	PL41	180.00	31.50	211.50
				300.00	52.50	352.50
				NL32	NL38	

PURCHASES LEDGER
Dr Simpson & Co (page 32) Cr

		£		£
7.5 Returns outwards RODB74		141.00		

Dr N. Walters (page 41) Cr

		£		£
26.5 Returns outwards RODB74		211.50		

NOMINAL LEDGER
Dr Returns Outwards Account (page 32) Cr

	£			£
		31.5 Returns RODB74		300.00

Figure 26.7 continued

Dr	VAT Account (page 38)		Cr
	£		£
		31.5 Returns RODB74	52.50

Accounting for VAT – cash payments and receipts

The way that payments and receipts are recorded in the cash book is described in unit 12. In that unit, payments and receipts involving VAT are ignored. In practice, most cash books have a column to record the VAT element of a transaction. To illustrate the treatment of payments and receipts that involve VAT, consider the example of Bedford Tiles. Extracts from the business's cash book and the VAT account are shown in Figure 26.8. In order to simplify the example, folios are not included. The cash book is totalled and balanced. Note, however, that the VAT columns are not balanced. They are used for memorandum purposes and their totals are transferred to the VAT account in the nominal ledger.

Figure 26.8 Cash book extract and VAT account for Bedford Tiles

		Debit			CASH BOOK		Credit		
Date	Details	VAT	Cash	Bank	Date	Details	VAT	Cash	Bank
			£	£				£	£
1.6	Balance b/d		31.00	569.00	4.6	A. Roberts			345.00
9.6	Sales	35.00	235.00		12.6	Motor repairs	49.00		329.00
15.6	B. McKee			705.00	16.6	L. Lister		63.00	
21.6	D. Lupton			470.00	19.6	Advertising	21.00		141.00
25.6	Sales	31.50	211.50		23.6	C. Benson			528.75
					30.6	Wages		400.00	
					30.6	Balance c/d		14.50	430.25
		66.50	477.50	1,744.00			70.00	477.50	1,774.00
1.7	Balance b/d		14.50	430.25					

NOMINAL LEDGER

	Dr	VAT Account		Cr
		£		£
30.6 Cash book		70.00	30.6 Cash book	66.50

- On the debit side of the cash book, the monthly total of VAT collected from customers when making cash sales, £66.50, is credited to the VAT account. This represents the VAT that is owed to the Customs and Excise. The receipts from B. McKee and D. Lupton do not include any VAT. This is because they are credit transactions which have gone through customer accounts in the sales ledger. The VAT has therefore already been dealt with in the bookkeeping system.
- On the credit side of the cash book, the £70.00 total VAT paid by the business is debited to the VAT account. This represents the amount of input tax that can be deducted from the output tax when calculating the amount of VAT due to the Customs and Excise. The payments to A. Roberts and C. Benson do not include any VAT. This is because these credit transactions have gone through the supplier accounts in the purchases ledger. The VAT has therefore already been accounted for in the bookkeeping system.
- The two payments that do include VAT, motor repairs and advertising, are both expenses. The VAT on such items is usually accounted for in the cash book rather than in the purchases ledger. The wages payment does not include any VAT because wages are not subject to this tax.

QUESTION 4

South Ribble Garden Supplies supplies seeds, fertiliser and other horticultural goods to gardeners, garden centres and builders. An extract from the business's cash book is shown in Figure 26.9.

Figure 26.9 *Cash book extract for South Ribble Garden Supplies*

		Debit			CASH BOOK		Credit		
Date	Details	VAT	Cash	Bank	Date	Details	VAT	Cash	Bank
			£	£			£	£	£
1.9	Balance b/d		96.00	230.00	3.9	Tractor parts	28.00		188.00
6.9	Sales	17.50	117.50		7.9	Robinson Seeds			493.50
11.9	Preston GC			587.50	10.9	L.E.P.	17.50		117.50
21.9	Sales	140.00		940.00	17.9	V. Jones			564.00
25.9	T. Cook			869.50	21.9	Wages			600.00

(a) Balance the cash book.

(b) Show the appropriate postings to the VAT account.

(c) Suggest possible reasons why there is no VAT included for the receipt from Preston GC and the payment to Robinson Seeds.

The VAT account in the nominal ledger

The VAT account in the nominal ledger is used as a means of summarising the total VAT paid by a business, and the total amount charged by a business. The debit side of the account shows the amount of VAT paid. This is an input tax and, as Figure 26.10 shows, it relates to expenditure on purchases, ie raw materials and goods intended for resale, on fixed assets and on expenses. The VAT on returns inwards, ie sales returns, is also entered on the debit side of the account.

On the credit side of the account, where the output tax is recorded, the VAT on all business sales is entered. These sales not only include the goods and services produced by the business, but also the sale of any fixed assets. In addition, the VAT on returns outwards, ie purchases returns, is recorded on this side of the account.

Figure 26.10 *Entries in the VAT account*

Debit (Dr)	VAT Account	Credit (Cr)
VAT on:		**VAT on:**
Purchases		Sales of goods and services
Expenditure on fixed assets		Sale of fixed assets
Expenses		Returns outwards
Returns inwards		

The VAT return

Businesses that are registered for VAT must complete a VAT return on a regular basis, usually every quarter. The VAT return involves completing the form VAT 100 that the Customs and Excise send out (see Figure 26.12). This form is used to state the amount of VAT that a business is paying or claiming back. Businesses that collect more VAT from customers than they pay to suppliers make a payment to the Customs and Excise. Those that pay more to suppliers than they collect from customers claim a VAT refund from the Customs and Excise.

Completing the VAT return involves transferring information from a business's bookkeeping records to the form *VAT 100*. To illustrate how this is done, consider the example of Hunter Foods, an animal feed supplier. Much of the information to be entered on *VAT 100* is contained in the business's VAT account. This is shown in Figure 26.11. It contains entries for the second quarter of 2001.

Figure 26.11 *VAT account for Hunter Foods*

NOMINAL LEDGER

	Dr		VAT Account		Cr	
2001		£	2001			£
30.4	Purchases day book	2,870	30.4	Sales day book		5,950
30.4	Expenses	420	31.5	Sales day book		4,445
30.4	Fixed assets	250	31.5	Fixed assets		875
31.5	Purchases day book	1,785	30.6	Sales day book		3,780
31.5	Expenses	315				
30.6	Purchases day book	1,925				
30.6	Expenses	280				
30.6	Balance c/d	7,205				
		15,050				15,050
20.7	Bank	7,205	1.7	Balance b/d		7,205

Figure 26.12 *Completed form VAT 100 for Hunter Foods*

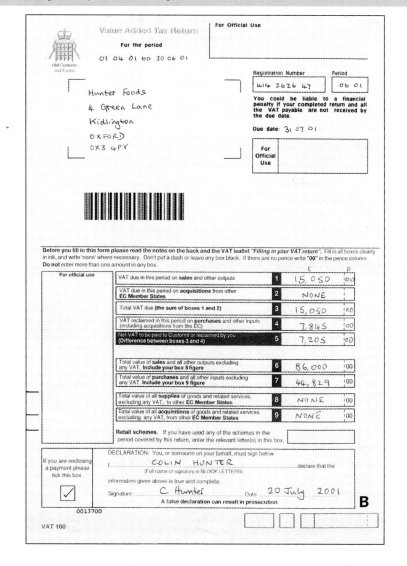

VAT 100 is completed by filling in boxes 1 to 9 as follows.

- **Box 1** The output tax is entered here. This is the value of VAT collected from customers and from any other sales, such as the sale of fixed assets. For this period, Hunter Foods would enter £15,050.00 in this box. This is the total of credits for the quarter as shown in the VAT account in Figure 26.11.
- **Box 2** Businesses enter the amount of VAT due (but not paid) on all goods and services acquired from other EU member states during the quarter. Since Hunter Foods does not trade with any businesses outside the UK, 'none' is written in this box.
- **Box 3** The total VAT due is written in this box. It is calculated by adding together the amounts in boxes 1 and 2. This is called the total output tax and in this example it is £15,050.
- **Box 4** The amount of input tax is entered here. This is the total of all VAT paid during the quarter. It includes any VAT paid on acquisitions of goods and services from other EU member states. For Hunter Foods, the amount is £7,845. This is the total of debit entries in the VAT account, but not including the balance c/d (ie £15,050 - £7,205).
- **Box 5** The amount of money being paid or reclaimed is written in this box. It is the difference between the amounts in boxes 3 and 4. If the value in box 3 is greater than the value in box 4, a cheque for the difference is sent to the Customs and Excise. In this example, Hunter Foods owes £7,205. This amount is equal to the balance c/d on the VAT account.
- **Box 6** The total value of sales made by the business during the quarter is entered here. This figure excludes VAT. The information is taken from the sales account and from the fixed asset accounts if any fixed assets are sold during the period. For Hunter Foods, the amount is £86,000. The value of any sales to other EU member states is also included in the total (from Box 8).
- **Box 7** The total value of purchases and all other inputs are entered in this box. The figure excludes VAT paid, but includes any goods bought from the EU. For Hunter Foods, the total amount is £44,829.
- **Box 8** The value of sales to other EU member states, excluding VAT, is recorded in this box.
- **Box 9** The value of purchases from other EU member states is entered in this box, exclusive of VAT.

At the bottom of *VAT 100*, an authorised signatory for the business signs and dates the form. If a cheque is sent with the form, the box in the bottom left-hand corner is ticked. Note that the payment of £7,205 to the Customs and Excise is also shown in the VAT account by a debit entry on 20 July.

key terms

Input tax (or purchases tax) - VAT that is paid when purchasing goods or services from a VAT registered trader.
Output tax (or sales tax) - VAT that is charged on sales by a VAT registered trader.
Value added tax - an indirect tax levied on spending.

summary questions

1. State two goods or services that are zero rated for VAT.
2. State two goods or services that are exempt from VAT.
3. It is often said that businesses are the unpaid collectors of VAT. Explain what this means.
4. Why does the government allow small businesses to be exempt from VAT?
5. A business sells goods to a customer for £900 (including VAT). How much VAT is paid?
6. Explain the difference between input tax and output tax.
7. Explain how the VAT on credit sales is dealt with in the bookkeeping system.
8. Explain how the VAT on sales returns is dealt with in the bookkeeping system.
9. State the entries that might appear on the debit side of the VAT account.
10. What is the purpose of a VAT return?

UNIT ASSESSMENT QUESTION 1

Henry Cavour manufactures jet skis in a Bournemouth factory. His business supplies dealers throughout the UK. Figure 26.13 shows an extract from the sales day book and the returns inwards day book. Transactions from the first week in August are listed.

Figure 26.13 *Sales day book and returns inwards day book of Henry Cavour's business*

SALES DAY BOOK

Date	Customer	Invoice no.	Folio	Price £	VAT £	Total £
3.8	Brighton Seasport	2219	SL23	6,400	1,120	7,520
6.8	Benson's Skis	2220	SL18	8,800	1,540	10,340
8.8	T. Gordon	2221	SL9	4,600	805	5,405
				19,800	3,465	23,265
				NL25	NL39	

RETURNS INWARDS DAY BOOK (page 68)

Date	Customer	Credit Note no.	Folio	Price £	VAT £	Total £
9.8	Brighton Seasport	331	SL23	800	140	940
12.8	T. Gordon	332	SL9	200	35	235
				1,000	175	1,175
				NL27	NL39	

(a) Show the ledger entries to account for **VAT** resulting from the transactions listed in (i) the sales day book and (ii) the returns inwards day book.
(b) During the first week of August, Henry Cavour's business purchased some new equipment for £3,400 (inclusive of **VAT**).
(i) Calculate how much **VAT** the business would have paid on the equipment.
(ii) Explain how the **VAT** account would be affected by this purchase.
(c) Suggest two services that Henry Cavour's business might buy that would be exempt from **VAT**.

UNIT ASSESSMENT QUESTION 2

Kidz is a childrens' fashions shop in Chelsea, London. The shop does not extend credit to customers and is therefore paid over the counter for all goods sold. The daily receipts and payments are recorded in a cash book. In the first quarter of 2002, the following financial information was extracted from the cash book (all figures are exclusive of VAT). There were no transactions involving other EU member states.

Sales	£123,600
Purchases	£45,500
Wages	£10,000
Other expenses	£16,800

(a) Calculate the **VAT** paid on (i) outputs; (ii) inputs for Kidz.
(b) How much **VAT** was due to the Customs and Excise for the first quarter of 2002?
(c) Kidz was registered for **VAT** in 2000. Prior to that, the business was exempt from **VAT**. Suggest why this was the case.

Control accounts

unit**objectives**

To understand:
- the nature of control accounts;
- the purposes of control accounts;
- how to prepare a sales ledger control account;
- how to prepare a purchases ledger control account;
- how to account for contra entries in control accounts.

What is a control account?

A CONTROL ACCOUNT is an account in the nominal ledger which summarises the transactions in a number of other accounts. It is also sometimes known as a **total account** or a **summary account**. Examples of control accounts include:

- the sales ledger control account, which summarises the individual customer accounts, ie debtor accounts;
- the purchases ledger control account, which summarises the individual supplier accounts, ie creditor accounts;
- the stock control account, which summarises the accounts of different items of stock;
- the wages control account, which summarises individual wages accounts.

For large businesses, with perhaps thousands of customer accounts, the sales ledger might be subdivided into sections. The division could be alphabetical, according to customer names, such as A-E, F-J, K-O and so on, or geographical, by sales region. Each of these subdivisions would then have a control account of its own.

In those businesses that operate control accounts, they form part of the double entry system. The individual accounts which they summarise and 'control' then act as subsidiary or **memorandum** accounts. These subsidiary customer accounts are not part of the double entry system. However, they act as a record or check of what each customer owes. For example, a debit balance on the sales ledger control account shows the total amount owed by customers. It is the amount recorded on the trial balance and it should equal the total of the debit balances on the individual customer accounts.

What is the purpose of control accounts?

Control accounts have a number of uses for businesses.

Localising errors Control accounts allow errors to be confined to relatively small areas in the books and accounts. For example, if a business divides its sales ledger into six sections according to geographical regions, only one section will have to be searched if the balance on the control account is different from the balance on the customer accounts. Without control accounts for each section, the entire sales ledger would have to be searched. This saves time and makes it easier to keep accurate accounts. However, it should be noted that some errors can still occur even when control accounts are used. For example, if a transaction is not recorded at all, the error will not be detected by a control account. The detection and correction of errors using control accounts is explained in the next unit.

Independent checks Control accounts in the nominal ledger act as an independent check on the work of the clerks who maintain the sales and purchases ledgers. Since control accounts in large organisations are usually managed by a more senior member of the accounts department, a fraudulent entry or an error in a customer or supplier account would eventually be detected. This is because the transaction must also be entered in the control account. The control account therefore adds another level of security in the system and deters fraud.

Calculating debtors and creditors totals The total amount owed by debtors, and the total amount owed to creditors, can be determined relatively quickly if control accounts are used. This is because the alternative, ie adding together the balances on all the individual accounts, is far more time consuming and also more likely to lead to errors.

Compiling final accounts Control accounts can be used to compile the profit and loss account and balance sheet, even if a business has **incomplete records** (see unit 31). For example, if details regarding a particular customer's account are lost, the sales ledger control account still contains all the information required.

The sales ledger control account – credit sales and bank receipts

The SALES LEDGER CONTROL ACCOUNT is used to 'control' the sales ledger. This contains the accounts of customers who buy goods on credit. The entries in the sales ledger control account come from the books of prime entry, not from the individual accounts in the sales ledger. This provides a checking facility because, if the information in the books of prime entry is posted directly to the individual accounts and also to the control account, a cross check can be made. The balance on the control account should be the same as the total of all balances on the individual sales accounts. If not, then an error has occurred.

The sales ledger control account is sometimes known as the **debtors control account**. This is because the customers who have bought goods on credit are debtors, ie they owe money to the business that has sold them the goods.

To illustrate the relationship between the individual accounts that make up the control account and the control account itself, consider the example of Hagan Chemicals, a supplier of paint to retailers. Hagan Chemicals uses a control account for each letter of the alphabet in the sales ledger. The accounts for the 'letter A' section in the sales ledger are shown in Figure 27.1. The control account is also shown.

Figure 27.1 *Individual accounts for the 'A' section in the sales ledger, and the sales ledger control account*

SALES LEDGER (A)

Dr Adams Paints Cr

		£			£
1.5	Balance b/d	1,200	30.5	Bank	2,300
31.5	Credit sales	3,000	31.5	Balance c/d	1,900
		4,200			4,200
1.6	Balance b/d	1,900			

Dr T. Andrews Cr

		£			£
31.5	Credit sales	3,400	29.5	Bank	3,200
			31.5	Balance c/d	200
		3,400			3,400
1.6	Balance b/d	200			

Dr D. Armstrong Cr

		£			£
31.5	Balance b/d	2,600	31.5	Bank	2,600

Figure 27.1 continued

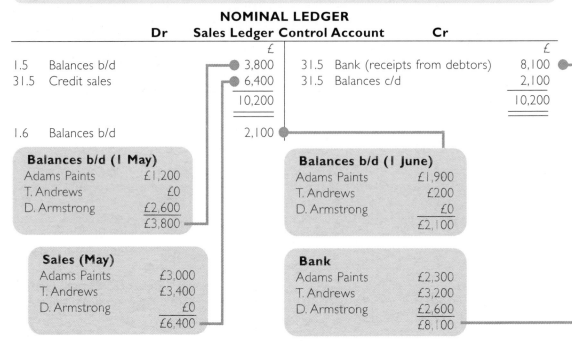

NOMINAL LEDGER
Sales Ledger Control Account

Dr		£		Cr	£
1.5	Balances b/d	3,800	31.5	Bank (receipts from debtors)	8,100
31.5	Credit sales	6,400	31.5	Balances c/d	2,100
		10,200			10,200
1.6	Balances b/d	2,100			

Balances b/d (1 May)
Adams Paints	£1,200
T. Andrews	£0
D. Armstrong	£2,600
	£3,800

Balances b/d (1 June)
Adams Paints	£1,900
T. Andrews	£200
D. Armstrong	£0
	£2,100

Sales (May)
Adams Paints	£3,000
T. Andrews	£3,400
D. Armstrong	£0
	£6,400

Bank
Adams Paints	£2,300
T. Andrews	£3,200
D. Armstrong	£2,600
	£8,100

- The information in the control account is an aggregate of the information in the individual customer accounts. For example, the debit balance b/d of £3,800 on 1 May in the control account is equal to all of the balances b/d on the individual accounts added together (£1,200 + £0 + £2,600).
- Similarly, the total credit sales figure in the control account £6,400 is equal to all of the credit sales amounts in the individual accounts added together (£3,000 + £3,400 + £0).
- The total amount of money received from debtors (ie customers who owe money) as shown in the control account is £8,100. This is the same as the amounts in the individual accounts added together (£2,300 + £3,200 + £2,600).
- The debit balances b/d on the control account is £2,100 on 1 June. This is the same as the balances b/d on the individual accounts added together (£1,900 + £200 + £0). It represents the amount owed to Hagan Chemicals on that date.

The sales ledger control account – sales returns and bad debts

In order to illustrate more complex transactions than credit sales and the receipt of payments, the sales ledger control account for Woodstock Toys is shown in Figure 27.2. The account has been drawn up for the month of March. In this example, the account also shows the sources of information, ie the folios, needed to prepare the control account. In addition to sales and receipts, the account includes other details that are contained in customer accounts. These relate to returns inwards, ie sales returns, and to bad debts.

Figure 27.2 *The sales ledger control account for Woodstock Toys*

NOMINAL LEDGER
Sales Ledger Control Account

Dr		Folio	£		Cr	Folio	£
1.3	Balances b/d		15,720	31.3	Bank	CB	65,900
31.3	Credit sales	SDB	76,890	31.3	Cash	CB	4,500
31.3	Balances c/d		400	31.3	Returns inwards	RIDB	1,180
				31.3	Bad debts	Jnl	1,000
				31.3	Balances c/d		20,430
			93,010				93,010
1.4	Balances b/d		20,430	1.4	Balances b/d		400

Notes: The folios show the books of prime entry that are the sources of information on the account.
SDB: Sales Day Book; CB: Cash Book; RIDB: Returns Inwards Day Book; Jnl: Journal.
The balances b/d on 1 March come from the previous accounting period.

QUESTION 1

A & L Foods manufactures a range of frozen desserts for supermarkets. The company accountant uses control accounts to control the sales ledger. The ledger is divided alphabetically and the individual accounts for the W to Z section are provided in Figure 27.3. The October transactions are shown in the accounts.

Figure 27.3 *Individual customer accounts in the W to Z section of the sales ledger for A & L Foods*

SALES LEDGER (W - Z)

Dr		Wintermart		Cr	
		£			£
1.10	Balance b/d	3,100	31.10 Bank		3,300
31.10	Credit sales	3,000	31.10 Balance c/d		2,800
		6,100			6,100
1.11	Balance b/d	2,800			

Dr		Woburn Stores		Cr	
		£			£
1.10	Balance b/d	4,300	31.10 Bank		11,000
31.10	Credit sales	12,900	31.10 Balance c/d		6,200
		17,200			17,200
1.11	Balance b/d	6,200			

Dr		Young & Son		Cr	
		£			£
1.10	Balance b/d	2,800	31.10 Bank		12,600
31.10	Credit sales	13,400	31.10 Balance c/d		3,600
		16,200			16,200
1.11	Balance b/d	3,600			

Dr		Zimmerman		Cr	
		£			£
1.10	Credit sales	6,700	31.10 Bank		6,700

(a) Prepare the sales ledger control account for the section of the sales ledger shown above.
(b) Explain why the balances on the customer accounts and on the control account are all debit balances when this apparently contradicts the rules of double entry bookkeeping.

- The first entry on the debit side of the sales ledger control account is £15,720 balances b/d. This is the total amount owed to Woodstock Toys by its customers at the beginning of the month. It is equal to the total of debit balances on the customer accounts in the sales ledger.
- The sales figure of £76,890 is the total value of credit sales for the month. This information is obtained from the sales day book.
- The £400 balances c/d on 31 March arises because Woodstock Toys owes some money to its customers. This is unusual but might occur if, for example, a customer returns some goods after they have been paid for, or because a customer has overpaid in error. Note that this amount is brought down as a credit balance on 1 April. It is not subtracted from the debit balance to give a net balance. This is to make clear that one or more customer accounts have a credit balance. The entry is exceptional because it is derived not from a book of prime entry but from the end of month list of balances in the sales ledger.

- The first entry on the credit side of the sales ledger is £65,900. This relates to the total amount of money that customers have paid by cheque to the business for goods bought on credit. This information is taken from the cash book.
- The £4,500 cash receipt is the amount of money paid by credit customers who have settled their accounts in cash during the month. This amount is from the cash book.
- The credit entry of £1,180 relates to goods returned by customers. This information is taken from the returns inwards day book.
- The £1,000 credit is the amount of money written off by Woodstock Toys for bad debts. This information comes from the journal. A **provision for bad debts** is **not** entered in the control account. This is because the bookkeeping entries required for the treatment of bad debts provision do not involve the debtor's personal accounts.
- The credit entry 'Balances c/d' in the control account is for £20,430. This balance, which is brought down on the first day of the following month, represents the amount of money still owing to Woodstock Toys for goods bought on credit. It should be the same as the total debit balances in the customer accounts in the sales ledger.
- Note that the sales ledger control account does not show any discounts allowed. This is because the business does not give discounts. However, if discounts were allowed on sales, the total value of these would be shown as a credit entry in the sales ledger control account. The amount would be taken from the cash book.

The purchases ledger control account

The PURCHASES LEDGER CONTROL ACCOUNT is sometimes known as the **creditors control account**. It is used to control the purchases ledger which contains the accounts of individual suppliers who supply goods on credit. The information needed to prepare the purchases ledger control account comes from the books of prime entry. For example, the total value of purchases during an accounting period comes from the purchases day book. Figure 27.4 shows the purchases control account for Woodstock Toys.

QUESTION 2

Sutherland Ceramics makes vases, bowls, tiles and ornaments. The business supplies a range of retailers, mainly in Scotland. It uses a sales ledger control account as part of its bookkeeping system. The financial information listed below relates to last September.

1 September	Money owed by customers	£5,700
1 September	Money owed to customers	£350
30 September	Sales	£35,680
30 September	Returns inwards	£1,350
30 September	Cheque payments by credit customers	£32,360
30 September	Cash payments by credit customers	£4,300
30 September	Money owed by customers	£3,190
30 September	Money owed to customers	£170

(a) **Produce a sales ledger control account for Sutherland Ceramics. Show the balances b/d on 1 October.**

(b) **Where will the information come from for the entries relating to (i) sales; (ii) returns inwards; (iii) cheque payments?**

(c) **What might be the reason for the £170 credit balance b/d on the control account?**

Figure 27.4 *The purchases ledger control account for Woodstock Toys*

NOMINAL LEDGER
Dr   Purchases Ledger Control Account   Cr

		Folio	£			Folio	£
1.3	Balances b/d		670	1.3	Balances b/d		13,460
31.3	Bank	CB	34,400	31.3	Credit purchases	PDB	36,700
31.3	Returns outwards	RODB	2,300	31.3	Balances c/d		260
31.3	Discounts received	CB	1,200				
31.3	Balances c/d		11,850				
			50,420				50,420
1.4	Balances b/d		260	1.4	Balances b/d		11,850

Notes: The folios show the books of prime entry that are the sources of information on the account.
PDB: Purchases Day Book; CB: Cash Book; RODB: Returns Outwards Day Book.
The balances b/d on 1 March come from the previous accounting period.

- On the debit side of the control account, the balances b/d of £670 shows the amount of money that suppliers owe Woodstock Toys. It is unusual for suppliers to owe money but it might arise if Woodstock Toys has returned goods after paying for them, or because a particular supplier was overpaid by mistake. Total debit balances on supplier accounts are not likely to be very high. This information is brought down from the previous accounting period.
- The £34,400 debit entry represents the total amount of money paid by Woodstock Toys to suppliers during the month. This figure is taken from the cash book.
- The £2,300 debit entry relates to goods returned to suppliers during the month. This is taken from the returns outwards day book.
- Some suppliers give Woodstock Toys cash discounts. During March the business received total discounts of £1,200 from suppliers. This information is taken from the cash book.
- The debit entry balances c/d of £11,850 shows the total amount of money owed by Woodstock Toys to suppliers for goods bought on credit. This balance should be the same as the total of debit balances in the individual supplier accounts. The amount is brought down as a credit balance on 1 April.
- The first entry on the credit side of the purchases ledger control account is the balances b/d for £13,460. This represents the amount that Woodstock Toys owed suppliers at the beginning of March. This information is brought down from the previous accounting period.
- The next entry is the total of goods bought on credit from all suppliers during the month. The figure of £36,700 comes from the purchases day book.
- The final credit entry in the purchases ledger control account is the balances c/d of £260. This represents the small amount owed to Woodstock Toys by suppliers at the end of the month. Note that this amount is brought down as a debit balance on 1 April. It is not subtracted from the credit balance to give a net balance. This is to make clear that one or more supplier accounts have a debit balance. The entry comes from the end of month list of balances in the purchases ledger.

What are contra entries?

CONTRA ENTRIES or **set-off entries** arise if a business sells goods to, and also buys goods from, the same trader. For example, consider the accounts of Nigel Matthews who is a farmer. On 12 March he sells £500 of lambs to Ken Simpson, a butcher, for slaughter. Then, on 28 March, Nigel Matthews buys back some cut meat products from Ken Simpson for £350 to sell in his farm shop. In this case, Ken Simpson will have an account in both the sales ledger and the purchases ledger of Nigel Matthews. This is because he is both a customer and a supplier. The entries needed to record the two transactions are shown in Figure 27.5. These accounts show that:
- Ken Simpson owes Nigel Matthews £500 for lambs bought on 12 March;
- Nigel Matthews owes Ken Simpson £350 for cut meat sold to him on 28 March.

QUESTION 3

Hendon Paper manufactures wallpaper for wholesalers and retailers in the UK. The business operates control accounts for sales and ledgers. The following information is supplied by Hendon Paper from its bookkeeping records. The information relates to last July.

1 July	Money owed to suppliers	£37,450
31 July	Credit purchases	£231,600
31 July	Returns outwards	£12,900
31 July	Total payments	£222,000
31 July	Discounts received	£6,770
31 July	Money owed by suppliers	£560
31 July	Money owed to suppliers	£27,940

(a) Prepare the purchases ledger control account for Hendon Paper. Show the balances b/d on 1 August.

(b) Where will the information come from for the entries relating to (i) returns outwards; (ii) discounts received; (iii) total payments?

(c) What does the debit balance b/d on 1 August represent?

Figure 27.5 *Accounts for Ken Simpson*

SALES LEDGER

Dr	Ken Simpson			Cr	
		£			£
12.3 Credit sales		500			

PURCHASES LEDGER

Dr	Ken Simpson			Cr	
		£			£
			28.3 Purchases		350

The accounts in Figure 27.5 would be settled if Ken Simpson paid a cheque to Nigel Matthews for £500 and Nigel Matthews paid a cheque to Ken Simpson for £350. However, an easier way would be to set-off Ken Simpson's £500 debt against Nigel Matthews's £350 debt. The debt between the traders could then be settled if Ken Simpson sent Nigel Matthews a cheque for the difference of £150. Such a set-off is called a contra entry. Figure 27.6 shows the entries needed to record such a transaction.

Figure 27.6 *Treatment of a contra entry*

SALES LEDGER

Dr	Ken Simpson			Cr	
		£			£
12.3 Credit sales		500	31.3 Contra purchases ledger		350
			31.3 Bank		150
		500			500

PURCHASES LEDGER

Dr	Ken Simpson			Cr	
		£			£
31.3 Contra sales ledger		350	28.3 Purchases		350
		350			350

- The Ken Simpson account in the sales ledger is credited with £350. This is a contra entry and is made to set-off the amount Ken Simpson owes to Nigel Matthews. The difference, £150, is settled by a cheque payment from Ken Simpson to Nigel Matthews.
- The Ken Simpson account in the purchases ledger is debited with £350. This is a contra entry and

is made to cancel out Nigel Matthews's debt with Ken Simpson.

- Contra entries must be recorded in both the sales ledger and the purchases ledger control accounts. In this case, the £350 contra entry appears on the credit side of the sales ledger control account and on the debit side of the purchases ledger control account.

QUESTION 4

Figure 27.7 *The accounts of Elmdon Copper in Kendal Engineering's ledgers*

SALES LEDGER

Dr		Elmdon Copper	Cr	
	£			£
15.4 Credit sales	1,560			

PURCHASES LEDGER

Dr		Elmdon Copper	Cr	
	£			£
		2.4 Purchases		2,600

Kendal Engineering makes metal products for a wide range of customers. One of its suppliers is Elmdon Copper, a stockist of copper sheet, wire and bars. Elmdon Copper also buys from Kendal Engineering. In April, Elmdon Copper placed a £1,560 order with Kendal Engineering for copper components for switchgear. In the same month, Kendal Engineering bought £2,600 of copper sheet from Elmdon Copper. The transactions are shown in the ledgers for Kendal Engineering in Figure 27.7.

(a) Show the necessary contra entries in Elmdon Copper's accounts.
(b) Balance the two accounts (assume that no payment has yet been made).
(c) State whether Elmdon Copper is a debtor or a creditor of Kendal Engineering.

key terms

Contra entry - a bookkeeping entry used in control accounts to set-off balances on accounts in the sales and purchases ledgers when a business buys from, and sells to, the same trader.
Control account - an account that contains totals of entries in a ledger, or section of a ledger, and which can be used to check the arithmetic accuracy of the bookkeeping.
Purchases ledger control account - an account that contains the total of entries in the purchases day book and is used to check the arithmetic accuracy of the entries in the purchases ledger.
Sales ledger control account - an account that contains the total of entries in the sales day book and is used to check the arithmetic accuracy of the entries in the sales ledger.

Celia Dobrowolski runs a discount store in Northampton selling linens, curtains, bedding, soft furnishings and other household products. She has a large number of suppliers and uses control accounts to control the purchases ledger. She introduced control accounts two years ago when she discovered that fraudulent entries had been made in the ledgers. The personal accounts of suppliers from one section of the ledger are shown in Figure 27.8. The accounts show entries for last October.

Figure 27.8 *Personal accounts in a section of Celia Dobrowolski's purchases ledger*

PURCHASES LEDGER (A - C)

Dr	Adams & Son		Cr
	£		£
23.10 Bank	2,000	1.10 Balance b/d	400
29.10 Returns outwards	200	2.10 Purchases	2,150
31.10 Balance c/d	350		
	2,550		2,550
		1.11 Balance b/d	350

Dr	T. Bosworth		Cr
	£		£
26.10 Bank	7,410	1.10 Balance b/d	2,100
31.10 Contra sales ledger	500	11.10 Purchases	8,600
31.10 Balance c/d	2,790		
	10,700		10,700
		1.11 Balance b/d	2,790

Dr	Cartwrights		Cr
	£		£
1.10 Balance b/d	320	4.10 Purchases	12,900
12.10 Returns outwards	700		
31.10 Bank	10,000		
31.10 Balance c/d	1,880		
	12,900		12,900
		1.11 Balance b/d	1,880

Dr	L. Cundall		Cr
	£		£
23.10 Bank	13,600	1.10 Balance b/d	3,100
23.10 Discount received	600	22.10 Purchases	12,000
31.10 Balance c/d	900		
	15,100		15,100
		1.11 Balance b/d	900

(a) Produce a purchases ledger control account for Celia Dobrowolski's business.
(b) Explain how using a control account could help Celia detect fraud.
(c) Explain the contra entry in T. Bosworth's account.

UNIT ASSESSMENT QUESTION 2

Oxplex is a manufacturer of surgical equipment. It supplies the National Health Service with a wide range of surgical equipment that is used in operating theatres. The business uses control accounts for the purchases and the sales ledgers. The control accounts are part of the double entry system. At the end of August, the following information was extracted from the financial records.

Debit balances on the sales ledgers (1.8)	£27,400
Credit balances on the sales ledgers (1.8)	£800
Credit balances on the purchases ledger (1.8)	£14,610
Purchases	£51,090
Sales	£101,000
Dishonoured cheques	£3,900
Money received from credit customers	£102,000
Cheques paid to suppliers	£56,100
Cash paid to suppliers	£1,100
Amounts settled by contra on sales ledger	£2,000
Bad debts written off	£4,600
Returns inwards	£1,400
Returns outwards	£1,200
Discounts allowed	£500
Discounts received	£1,750

(a) Produce a sales ledger control account to determine the amount owed by customers.
(b) Produce a purchases ledger control account to determine the amount owed to suppliers.
(c) If the control accounts are part of the double entry system, what role do the personal accounts play?

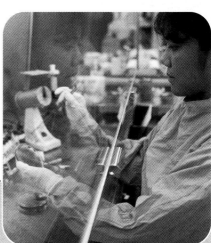

summary questions

1. Explain what a control account aims to control.
2. Give two examples of credit entries on a sales ledger control account.
3. On which side of the sales ledger control account will a dishonoured cheque appear?
4. What will be the sources of information for (i) bad debts written off; (ii) total sales?
5. Give two examples of debit entries on a purchases ledger control account.
6. What will be the sources of information for (i) returns outwards; (ii) discounts received?
7. What will the balance b/d on the purchases ledger control account represent (assuming a credit balance)?
8. Explain why contra entries are used by businesses in control accounts.
9. How will a bookkeeping error be detected when using control accounts?
10. How can fraud be detected when using control accounts?

unit 28

Control accounts and error correction

unitobjectives

To understand:
- how to identify errors using control accounts;
- what might cause errors in control accounts;
- how to correct errors on the sales ledger control account;
- how to correct errors on the purchases ledger control account.

How are errors identified in control accounts?

Bookkeeping errors are more easily detected if control accounts are used by businesses (see unit 27). This is because control accounts help to localise errors and, if regular checks are made on the bookkeeping system, there is less work to do in searching for errors when the trial balance is produced. For example, an error should be identified if the total of balances on the individual accounts in the sales ledger is different from the balance on the sales ledger control account. Since the information used to produce both sets of balancing figures originates from the same source, ie the books of prime entry, the balances should be the same. The procedure for detecting errors in the sales ledger is summarised as follows.

- Make a list of the balances on the individual customer, ie debtor accounts in the sales ledger, and then add up the total balance.
- Balance the sales ledger control account.
- If the two balances are different, an error has been made.
- If the two balances are the same, an error has not been detected. It cannot be said for certain that an error has not been made because some errors do not become apparent when control accounts are used. This point is explained in more detail later in the unit.

Consider Barker & Son, a supplier of cosmetics to retailers which uses control accounts to control the sales and purchases ledgers. A copy of its sales ledger control account for August is shown in Figure 28.1. According to the control account, the balances b/d on 1 September is £13,620. This represents the amount owed to Barker & Son by customers. However, according to the sales ledger (not shown here), the total of debtors is £13,920 which is £300 greater than the control account balance. This means that at least one error has been made in the recording of transactions (assuming that an error has not been made in preparing the control account).

Figure 28.1 *Sales ledger control account for Barker & Son*

SALES LEDGER

Dr		Sales Ledger Control Account		Cr	
		£			£
1.8	Balances b/d	11,670	31.8	Bank	79,600
31.8	Sales	84,500	31.8	Returns inwards	1,600
31.8	Dishonoured cheques	2,100	31.8	Bad debts written off	950
			31.8	Contra purchases ledger	2,500
			31.8	Balances c/d	13,620
		98,270			98,270
1.9	Balances b/d	13,620			

QUESTION 1

Heyford Concrete supplies ready mixed concrete to local construction sites. The company has a large number of regular customers and operates a control account on the sales ledger. This is used every month to check for errors in the bookkeeping. At the end of September, the following information was extracted from the bookkeeping system.

Opening balances	£8,390
Total credit sales	£45,790
Dishonoured cheques	£1,500
Money received from credit customers	£52,500
Returns inwards	£700
Bad debts written off	£470

(a) Produce the sales ledger control account for Heyford Concrete and determine the balances b/d as at 1 October.

(b) According to the customer account balances, the total amount owed to Heyford Concrete at the end of September was £3,010. Explain whether or not an error has been made.

What errors can be detected by control accounts?

There are three main types of error that can be detected by using control accounts.

- A **casting error** is an error of addition. It is also sometimes known as a miscast. An example of this type of error is when the total sales for a period in the sales day book are added incorrectly. If this incorrect figure is then recorded in the sales ledger control account, it will be different from the total derived from the individual customer accounts. When an incorrect total is greater than the correct figure, it is known as an overcast. If the incorrect total is less than the correct figure, it is known as an undercast.

- A **transposition error** is an error in which two digits are transposed. For example, £1,375 might be written as £1,735. Such an error could be made when posting entries, either to the sales ledger control account, or to the individual accounts.

- An error can arise if a transaction is recorded in the control account and not in the memorandum account, or vice versa. For example, a bad debt written off in the sales ledger might not be recorded in the journal and is therefore missing from the control account.

Some bookkeeping errors will not be detected when using control accounts. Such errors are described in unit 16 and include the following.

- **Errors of omission** - a transaction might not be recorded at all in the bookkeeping system. For example, an invoice might not be entered in the sales day book and is therefore also missing from both the customer account and the control account.

- **Errors of commission** - a transaction might be recorded in the wrong account, for example in the P. Harding account rather than the P. Hardman account. Under these circumstances, the balances from the customer accounts will still agree with the control account. This type of error is also known as **misposting**.

- **Errors of original entry** - the wrong amount for a transaction might be entered correctly. For example, £125.00 might be recorded instead of £12.50 in both a customer account and the sales ledger control account. Again, the sales ledger will still agree with the control account.

These types of error which affect both the control account and the customer accounts are not easily identified. They might only come to light if, for example, a customer complains that a statement of account is incorrect.

How are errors corrected on the sales ledger control account?

Once an error has been detected it must be corrected. It is necessary to decide whether the error has affected the individual accounts or the control account, or both. When doing this it is helpful to

remember the following.
* A transaction that is not entered in a book of prime entry will also be omitted from both the individual account and the control account.
* A transaction that is entered incorrectly in the book of prime entry will be repeated in the individual account and the control account.
* A casting error in the book of prime entry will affect the control account but not the individual account.
* If a transaction is misposted from the prime record to the individual account, the control account is not affected.

In order to illustrate the correction of errors that are identified when using control accounts, consider the example of Jones Hardware, a supplier of tools and equipment to mechanics and garages. At the end of December, the sales ledger control account was balanced and the amount carried down was £24,700. The total debtors for the period according to the list of debtors in the sales ledger was £21,300. Since the balances did not agree, an investigation was carried out and four errors were detected.
* **Error 1** A bad debt of £500 was written off in the sales ledger but not entered in the journal and therefore not recorded in the control account.
* **Error 2** A debit balance of £2,700 from a customer account was not included in the total of debtors list.
* **Error 3** Discounts allowed to the value of £200 were recorded in the individual accounts but not the control account.
* **Error 4** An invoice for the sale of £2,600 of goods to V. Patel was completely omitted from the records.

The following steps were taken to correct the errors and determine the correct balance on the control account and to adjust the amount on the debtors list.

Step 1 Each error was examined to decide whether it affected the individual accounts or the control account, or both. In this example, the errors are analysed as follows.
* **Error 1** The individual account is correct and only the control account is affected. The £500 bad debt that has been written off must be credited to the control account. This in effect reduces the balance on the control account.
* **Error 2** The omitted debit balance of £2,700 must be added to the debtors list in the sales ledger. The control account will be unaffected.
* **Error 3** The individual accounts will not be affected. The control account must be credited with the omitted £200 discounts allowed.
* **Error 4** The omitted invoice must be debited, which means that the total of debtors in the sales ledger must be raised by £2,600. The sales figure in the control account must also be debited with £2,600.

Step 2 The balance on the sales ledger control account needs to be adjusted to compensate for the errors. This is done by redrawing the control account, starting with the balances b/d from the original account. This is £24,700 as stated earlier. Errors 1, 3 and 4 affect the control account and the entries needed to correct them are explained in Step 1. The entries are shown below in the control account. When the entries are in place, the account can be balanced again and the new balance on the account is £26,600.

SALES LEDGER

Dr		Sales Ledger Control Account		Cr
	£			£
31.12 Balances b/d	24,700	31.12 Bad debt written off		500
31.12 Credit sales	2,600	31.12 Discounts allowed		200
		31.12 Balances c/d		26,600
	27,300			27,300
1.1 Balances b/d	26,600			

Step 3 The total debtors amount from the sales ledger needs to be adjusted. This can involve adding some amounts, because they have been missed off, and subtracting others. Whether amounts

are added or subtracted depends on the nature of the error. In this case, two additions are necessary. They are explained in **Step 1**. The adjustment to the total of debtors is shown below.

Calculation of revised debtors balance

	£
Balance as per sales ledger	21,300
Add	
Omitted debtor balance	2,700
Further debit - V. Patel	2,600
Balance as per control account	26,600

After the control account has been amended to compensate for the errors, and the total of debtors has been adjusted, the two balances are the same. The balances b/d on the amended control account for Jones Hardware is £26,600. The total of debtors after adjustment is also £26,600. The **reconciliation** is now complete.

QUESTION 2

Leung Sing Contractors provides factory cleaning and maintenance services in the West Midlands. The business uses a control account to control the sales ledger. At the end of last April, the balance on the sales ledger control account was £11,800. However, the total of debtors from the sales ledger accounts was £14,000. After an investigation by the company accountant, three errors were discovered.

- **Error 1** One of the debtor balances on the debtors list, N. Thompson, was read as £2,100 when the correct amount was £1,200.
- **Error 2** A sale for £3,400 to A. Watkins was not entered at all in the records.
- **Error 3** A sale for £1,300 to B. Peters was correctly entered in the customer account but omitted from the sales day book.

(a) Produce an amended sales ledger control account for Leung Sing Contractors.
(b) Revise the total for the debtors list for Leung Sing Contractors.

How are errors corrected on the purchases ledger control account?

The procedure for correcting errors on the purchases ledger when using control accounts is similar to that used when correcting errors on the sales ledger. In order to illustrate the procedure, consider the example of Arco, a manufacturer of fire and burglar alarms. Arco uses a purchases ledger control account and, at the end of June, the value of creditors was £15,530. However, the credit balance on the purchases control account was £16,700. Since the balances were different, an investigation was carried out and the following four errors were detected.

- **Error 1** The total in the purchases day book for June was overcast by £1,000.
- **Error 2** A returns outwards for £650 was not entered in the books at all. The supplier's name was B. Denton.
- **Error 3** A discount received for £170 was entered in the individual account but not in the cash book.
- **Error 4** An amount of £450 was entered in the purchases day book when the correct amount was £850. This was on a purchase from K. Ricketts.

The following steps were taken to determine the correct balance on the purchases ledger control account and to adjust the total amount of creditors in the purchases ledger.

Step 1 Each error was examined in turn. It is necessary to decide whether the error affects the individual accounts or the purchases ledger control account, or both. In this example, the errors are analysed as follows.

- **Error 1** The individual account is correct and only the control account is affected. The control account must be debited with £1,000. This is because the total amount of purchases has been overstated in the control account.
- **Error 2** The omitted returns outwards amount of £650 affects both the individual supplier's account and the control account. The B. Denton account must be debited which means that the total of creditors in the purchases ledger must be reduced by £650. The returns outwards amount

in the control account must be increased by £650. Therefore the control account must be debited with £650.

- **Error 3** The individual accounts will not be affected. The control account must be debited with £170.
- **Error 4** This error will affect both the individual account and the control account. The K. Ricketts account must be debited with £400 to account for the difference between the actual amount of the transaction and the amount already entered. This increases the amount owed to this supplier by £400. The total amount of purchases must also be increased in the control account, therefore the control account must be credited with £400.

Step 2 The balance on the purchases ledger control account needs to be adjusted to compensate for the errors. This is done by redrawing the control account starting with the balances b/d from the original account. This is £16,700 as stated earlier. In this example, all of the errors affect the control account. The entries needed to correct them are explained in **Step 1** and the entries are shown below in the control account. When the entries are in place, the account can be balanced again. The new balances b/d on the account is £15,280.

PURCHASES LEDGER

Dr	Purchases Ledger Control Account		Cr	
		£		£
30.6	Adjustment of purchases (overcasting error)	1,000	30.6 Balances b/d	16,700
			30.6 Adjustment of purchases	400
30.6	Adjustment of returns outwards	650		
30.6	Adjustment of discount received	170		
30.6	Balances c/d	15,280		
		17,100		17,100
			1.7 Balances b/d	15,280

Step 3 The total amount of creditors needs to be adjusted. This involves adding some amounts, because they have been missed off, and subtracting others. Whether amounts are added or subtracted depends on the nature of the error. In this example, there is one addition and one deduction. They are explained in Step 1 and relate to errors 2 and 4. The adjustments to the creditors balance are shown below.

Calculation of revised creditors balance

	£
Balance as per purchases ledger	15,530
Add	
Further credit - K. Ricketts	400
	15,930
Deduct	
To record goods returned to B. Denton	650
Balance as per control account	15,280

After the control account has been amended to compensate for the errors, and the total of creditors has been adjusted for the errors, the two balances are the same. The balance b/d on the amended purchases ledger control account for Arco is £15,280 and the value of creditors after adjustment is also £15,280. The reconciliation is now complete.

Recording corrections in the journal

It is standard practice to record the correction of errors in the journal. The entry in the journal also serves as a record of prime entry for the correction. The use of the journal for error correction is explained in unit 14.

QUESTION 3

Waltham Meats supplies meat to butchers, hotels, public houses, restaurants and caterers in the London area. Three years ago, a system of control accounts was introduced into the bookkeeping to help reduce the number of errors made by staff. Although errors continued to be made, the time spent searching for them was significantly reduced. At the end of last February, the balances b/d on the purchases ledger control account was £23,760. The total of creditors in the purchases ledger accounts was £24,670. Since the two figures were different, an investigation was carried out and the following three errors were detected.

- **Error 1** A purchase from T. Williams for £2,100 was completely omitted from the records.
- **Error 2** The discounts received column in the cash book was overcast by £1,000.
- **Error 3** A purchase in the purchases day book for £980 was posted to the F. Keane account as £890.

(a) Analyse the errors and decide how they should be corrected.
(b) Produce the amended purchases ledger control account for Waltham Meats.
(c) Produce the revised creditors total for Waltham Meats.

UNIT ASSESSMENT QUESTION 1

Kim Williams runs CanAd, an advertising agency in Devizes, Wiltshire. The business was set up five years ago and now has several hundred regular clients on its books. CanAd uses a sales ledger control account to speed up the bookkeeping process. At the end of last March, the sales ledger control account was drawn up (see Figure 28.2). However, the balance on the control account did not match the total of debtors at the end of the month which was £13,020. After checking the books, four errors were discovered.

Figure 28.2 *Sales ledger control account for CanAd*

SALES LEDGER

Dr		Sales Ledger Control Account		Cr	
		£			£
1.3	Balances b/d	17,420	1.3	Balances b/d	800
31.3	Credit sales	78,010	31.3	Bank	74,600
31.3	Dishonoured cheques	1,100	31.3	Bad debts written off	2,000
			31.3	Contra purchases ledger	1,600
			31.3	Discounts allowed	2,310
			31.3	Balances c/d	15,220
		96,530			96,530

- **Error 1** The cash book was undercast by £2,000.
- **Error 2** A sales invoice issued to Johnson & Co for £1,670 was omitted from the books.
- **Error 3** A discount allowed entered in the cash book for £100 was not posted to the F. Crow customer account.
- **Error 4** A bad debt for £300 was written off in the sales ledger but not entered in the journal.

(a) Bring down the balance before adjustments in the control account and adjust the account with correcting entries.
(b) Revise the total amount of debtors for CanAd.

UNIT ASSESSMENT QUESTION 2

A. Hajaig manufactures clothing in his Peterborough factory. In an effort to remain competitive, A. Hajaig continually switches between suppliers to get the best prices when buying materials. This has resulted in extra work for the purchases ledger clerk and in order to keep a control of the purchases ledger, a control account is used. At the end of last July, the balance on the purchases ledger control account was £32,190. However, the total amount of creditors according to the purchases ledger was £32,040. The ledger clerk was instructed to carry out a check on the bookkeeping and, as a result, the following five errors were found in the system.

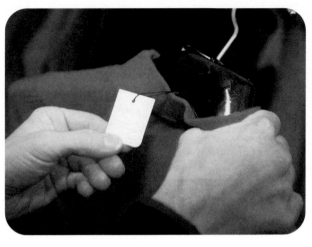

- **Error 1** The purchases day book had been undercast by £1,000.
- **Error 2** A contra entry for £650 with the sales ledger had been recorded twice in the control account.
- **Error 3** Credit balances of £1,800 had been omitted from the list of creditor balances from the purchases ledger.
- **Error 4** A. Hajaig had recorded returns outwards for £2,000 but the supplier then refused to accept the goods. The goods were sent back to A. Hajaig. This had gone unrecorded.
- **Error 5** A return to T. Orchard for £3,600 was made but not recorded at all in the ledger.

(a) Analyse the five errors and decide how they should be corrected.
(b) Produce an adjusted purchases ledger control account for A. Hajaig.
(c) Calculate and show the revised creditors balance for A. Hajaig.

summary questions

1. How are control accounts used to identify errors in the bookkeeping system?
2. What corrections are necessary if a returns inward has been completely omitted from the returns inwards day book?
3. What corrections are necessary if a customer payment is correctly entered in the cash book but not entered in the customer's account?
4. What corrections are necessary if the sales day book is undercast?
5. What corrections are necessary if the purchases day book is overcast?
6. What corrections are necessary if a discount allowed is not entered in the customer account?
7. State two types of error that would result in the need to add amounts to the list of creditors balances.
8. State two types of error that would result in the need to subtract amounts from the list of debtors balances.

unit 29

The extended trial balance

unit objectives

To understand:
- the nature and purpose of the extended trial balance;
- how to use the extended trial balance to prepare final accounts.

What is the extended trial balance?

Unit 16 explains how the trial balance is used to produce the final accounts. However, the examples in that unit do not incorporate end of year adjustments such as the provision for bad and doubtful debts, depreciation, errors, and accruals and prepayments. The only adjustment taken into account in unit 16 is the change in stock values between the beginning and the end of the trading year. It is necessary to take into account all the other end of year adjustments to ensure that the final accounts provide a 'true and fair' view of a business's activities.

The EXTENDED TRIAL BALANCE is used to incorporate end of year adjustments into the final accounts. The layout of an extended trial balance is shown in Figure 29.1;
- the first column of figures shows the ledger balances from the trial balance;
- the second column is used to record end of year adjustments;
- the third column is used to record the entries for the profit and loss account, incorporating the trading account;
- the final column is used to record the entries for the balance sheet.

Figure 29.1 *The layout of an extended trial balance*

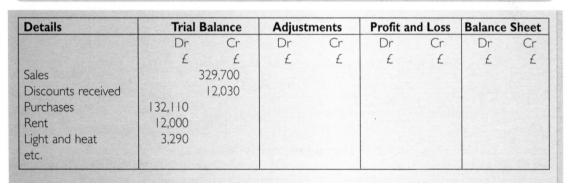

Details	Trial Balance		Adjustments		Profit and Loss		Balance Sheet	
	Dr	Cr	Dr	Cr	Dr	Cr	Dr	Cr
	£	£	£	£	£	£	£	£
Sales		329,700						
Discounts received		12,030						
Purchases	132,110							
Rent	12,000							
Light and heat	3,290							
etc.								

The extended trial balance is used as a 'posting sheet' to prepare the final accounts. Entries listed in the trial balance and adjustments columns are posted to the profit and loss account and the balance sheet columns in the extended trial balance. These entries are then posted to the appropriate positions in the profit and loss account and balance sheet. In each of the columns of the extended trial balance, the total of debits must equal the total of credits. This acts as a checking facility, as is explained later in the unit.

How is the extended trial balance prepared?

In order to illustrate how the extended trial balance is used to incorporate the end of year adjustments, consider the example of Mary O'Brien, a retailer of computers and computer accessories. A copy of the trial balance for her business is shown in Figure 29.2. The total cost of fixtures and fittings is £4,000. This is the cost when these assets were first purchased and is shown as

a debit. The accumulated depreciation on these fixtures and fittings to date (ie before the current year) is £1,200. It is treated as a liability and is shown as a credit. This is standard practice and coincides with the treatment of depreciation described in unit 23. The following information is also supplied with regard to end of year adjustments:
- closing stock is £25,120;
- depreciation on fixtures and fittings for the current year is £400;
- an electricity bill for £210 is still outstanding - this is therefore treated as an accrual.

Figure 29.2 Trial balance for Mary O'Brien's business as at 31.12.01

Mary O'Brien
Trial Balance as at 31.12.01

	Debit £	Credit £
Sales		141,110
Opening stock	23,100	
Purchases	74,090	
Wages	6,700	
Rent and rates	5,800	
Electricity	560	
Telephone	420	
Sundry expenses	2,420	
Fixtures and fittings	4,000	
Provision for depreciation - fixtures & fittings		1,200
Cash at bank	4,200	
Cash in hand	2,010	
Trade creditors		4,380
Capital		13,000
Drawings	36,390	
	159,690	159,690

When constructing the extended trial balance, the following stages are followed.
- Transfer the trial balance information to the extended trial balance.
- Record the end of year adjustments in the adjustments column.
- Extend the entries to the profit and loss column.
- Extend the entries to the balance sheet column.

Transferring the trial balance information The information in the trial balance is first transferred to the extended trial balance document. All written details and amounts should be transferred. This is shown in Figure 29.3. It is useful to check again the total of debits and credits. They should be the same as in the original trial balance, ie £159,690. The items from the trial balance are listed so that those relating to the profit and loss account are at the top and those that relate to the balance sheet are at the bottom. This makes it easier to construct the final accounts.

Recording the end of year adjustments The end of year adjustments are then recorded in the adjustments column. In this case there are three adjustments. Each adjustment has both a debit entry and a credit entry. The treatment required for each adjustment is explained below.
- **Closing stock** The closing stock value, £25,120, is recorded twice in the adjustments column. In this example, the entry is made underneath the entries from the original trial balance. It is standard procedure to write:
    'Closing stock - Profit and loss' (this is a credit entry);
    'Closing stock - Balance sheet' (this is a debit entry).

In a computerised bookkeeping system where it is relatively easy to insert lines, entries for adjustments are usually made in their 'correct' position in the trial balance. So, for example, in this case 'Closing stock - Profit and loss' would be entered immediately under 'Purchases', ie where it appears in a profit and loss account.

- **Depreciation** The £400 depreciation for the current year is recorded twice in the adjustments column. One entry is made at the bottom of the extended trial balance. This is a debit entry and is described as 'Depreciation expense'. The £400 matching credit entry is made against 'Provision for depreciation - fixtures and fittings'.
- **Accrual** Again there are two entries in the adjustments column to record the £210 electricity accrual. One entry is made at the bottom of the extended trial balance. It is a credit entry and is described as 'Accrual'. The £210 debit entry is made against 'Electricity'. If there had been no previous payments for Electricity, a new entry 'Electricity - expense' would be written above 'Accrual' and the debit entry would be made against this.

Prepayments are treated in a similar way to accruals except that the entries are reversed. If there had been a prepayment of electricity, there would be a credit entry against 'Electricity' and, at the bottom of the extended trial balance, there would be a debit entry made against 'Prepayments'.

At this stage it is useful to add up the debit and credit entries in the adjustments column to check that they are equal. In this case they are both £25,730. The totals are entered at the bottom of the adjustments column in Figure 29.3.

Figure 29.3 *Extended trial balance for Mary O'Brien's business as at 31.12.01*

Details	Trial Balance Dr £	Trial Balance Cr £	Adjustments Dr £	Adjustments Cr £	Profit and Loss Dr £	Profit and Loss Cr £	Balance Sheet Dr £	Balance Sheet Cr £
Sales		141,110				141,110		
Opening stock	23,100				23,100			
Purchases	74,090				74,090			
Wages	6,700				6,700			
Rent and rates	5,800				5,800			
Electricity	560		210		770			
Telephone	420				420			
Sundry expenses	2,420				2,420			
Fixtures and fittings	4,000						4,000	
Provision for depreciation- fixtures and fittings		1,200		400				1,600
Cash at bank	4,200						4,200	
Cash in hand	2,010						2,010	
Trade creditors		4,380						4,380
Capital		13,000						13,000
Drawings	36,390						36,390	
Closing stock - P & L				25,120		25,120		
Closing stock - Bal. sheet			25,120				25,120	
Depreciation expense			400		400			
Accrual				210				210
Net profit					52,530			52,530
	159,690	159,690	25,730	25,730	166,230	166,230	71,720	71,720

Extending the entries to the profit and loss column The next stage in constructing the extended trial balance is to extend the relevant entries in the trial balance and adjustments columns to the profit and loss column. Relevant entries are those which are **revenue** or **expense** items. Debit entries in the trial balance and adjustments columns are entered as debit entries in the profit and loss account. Credit entries in the trial balance and adjustment columns are entered as credit entries in the profit and loss account. For example, in Figure 29.3, the credit entry for sales in the trial balance of £141,110, is recorded as a credit entry in the profit and loss column. The debit entry for opening stock in the trial balance, £23,100, is recorded as a debit entry in the profit and loss column.

The three adjustments described previously are also posted across to the profit and loss column.

QUESTION 1

The Worcester Wool Company is a wholesale business which buys wool from sheep farmers in Wales, Hereford and Worcestershire. The wool is washed and processed before being sold to manufacturers. The trial balance for the business as at 31.7.01 is shown in Figure 29.4.

(a) Transfer the information in the trial balance to the extended trial balance.

(b) Make the appropriate entries in the adjustments column of the extended trial balance.

Figure 29.4 *Trial balance for the Worcester Wool Company as at 31.7.01*

The Worcester Wool Company
Trial Balance as at 31.7.01

	Debit £	Credit £
Sales		219,300
Opening stock	12,390	
Purchases	143,980	
Wages	43,750	
Rent and rates	15,600	
Motor expenses	5,340	
Electricity	2,420	
Telephone	750	
Bank charges	560	
Sundry expenses	4,320	
Machinery	24,000	
Provision for depreciation – machinery		15,000
Motor vehicles	41,500	
Provision for depreciation – motor vehicles		20,000
Debtors	3,270	
Cash at bank	6,260	
Trade creditors		2,300
Capital		74,320
Drawings	26,780	
	330,920	330,920

Additional information
- Closing stock is valued at £14,320.
- Depreciation on machinery for the current year is £3,000.
- Depreciation on motor vehicles for the current year is £4,000.
- Rates have been prepaid by £350.
- A telephone bill for £310 is outstanding.

The first is the debit entry relating to the accrual for electricity. This £210 accrual is added to the £560 debit entry in the trial balance and the total, £770, is debited to the profit and loss column. If there had been a prepayment rather than an accrual, the amount would be subtracted from the trial balance total before being entered in the profit and loss column. The credit entry for closing stock, £25,120, is extended to the profit and loss column on the credit side. Finally, the £400 debit entry for the depreciation expense is extended to the profit and loss column on the debit side.

The debit and credit entries in the profit and loss column are then totalled. If the debit total is less than the credit total, **the difference is net profit**. This is entered at the bottom of the extended trial balance and the total is inserted as a debit. Debits are now the same as credits. If debits are greater than credits, the difference represents a loss and should be recorded as a credit. In this example, the difference of £52,530 represents a net profit. The two totals of debits and credits are now £166,230.

Extending entries to the balance sheet column The remaining entries in the trial balance, ie those relating to **assets**, **liabilities**, **capital** and **drawings**, are extended to the balance sheet column. Debit entries in the trial balance are extended to the debit side of the balance sheet column. For example, the debit entry showing cash at bank in the trial balance for £4,200 is extended to the debit side of the balance sheet column. Similarly, the credit balances in the trial balance are extended to the credit side of the balance sheet column. For example, the credit entry in the trial balance for trade creditors, £4,380, is extended to the credit side of the balance sheet column.

The three adjustments in the adjustments column also have to be extended to the balance sheet column. The £400 credit balance representing the provision for depreciation for fixtures and fittings is added to the £1,200 total provision shown as a credit in the trial balance. The total of £1,600 is entered on the credit side of the balance sheet column. The £25,120 debit balance representing closing stock in the adjustments column is extended to the debit side of the balance sheet column. The £210 credit entry representing accruals in the adjustments column is extended to the credit side of the balance sheet column Finally, the net profit (debit) in the profit and loss becomes a credit in the balance sheet column.

The debits and credits in the balance sheet are then added to check the totals. If they are the same, then errors have been avoided. In this case the total debits and total credits are both £71,720. The extended trial balance is now complete.

QUESTION 2

Plymouth Furniture Supplies sells office furniture such as desks, chairs, filing cabinets and cupboards to businesses in the South West. A copy of the business's trial balance as at 31.3.01 is shown in Figure 29.5.

(a) **Transfer the information in the trial balance to the extended trial balance.**
(b) **Make the appropriate entries in the adjustments column.**
(c) **Extend the appropriate entries to the profit and loss account column.**
(d) **Extend the appropriate entries to the balance sheet column.**

Figure 29.5 *Trial balance for Plymouth Furniture Supplies as at 31.3.01*

Plymouth Furniture Supplies
Trial Balance as at 31.3.01

	Debit £	Credit £
Sales		211,110
Opening stock	31,900	
Purchases	121,190	
Carriage	1,100	
Wages	31,000	
Rent and rates	23,150	
Light and heat	2,440	
Motor expenses	2,230	
Insurance	1,220	
Advertising	2,210	
Motor vehicles	15,000	
Provision for depreciation - motor vehicles		6,000
Fixtures & fittings	3,500	
Provision for depreciation - fixtures & fittings		1,050
Debtors	4,100	
Cash in hand	760	
VAT		2,440
Trade creditors		7,010
Bank overdraft		1,900
Capital		45,040
Drawings	34,750	
	274,550	274,550

Additional information
- Closing stock is £35,330.
- Depreciation on motor vehicles for the year is £3,000.
- Depreciation on fixtures and fittings for the year is £350.
- Accountancy fees of £2,000 are outstanding.

How is the extended trial balance used to prepare the final accounts?

Once the extended trial balance is completed, the final accounts for Mary O'Brien's business can be prepared (see Figure 29.7). All the figures required to prepare the accounts are contained in the extended trial balance (see Figure 29.7). No further adjustments are necessary. Certain aspects of the process are worth noting.

- When constructing the profit and loss account, an entry must be made for depreciation in the list of expenses. There is no entry in the original trial balance (see Figure 29.2) for depreciation. It is one of the end of year adjustments.
- When constructing the balance sheet, both the cost of fixtures and fittings and the total provision for depreciation are shown under the fixed assets heading. In this case, the cost of fixtures and fittings is £4,000 and the provision for depreciation is £1,600. This means that the book value for fixtures and fittings is now £2,400 (£4,000 - £1,600).
- The £210 credit entry for accruals in the balance sheet column of the extended trial balance is entered as a current liability in the balance sheet.

QUESTION 3

Marco Bellini owns a fishing tackle shop in Wolverhampton. Marco bought the business in 1996 and, since then, his enthusiasm for the sport and his good customer relations have resulted in steady profit growth. The trial balance for Marco Bellini's business is shown in Figure 29.6.

(a) Transfer the information in the trial balance to the extended trial balance.

(b) Make the appropriate entries in the adjustments column.

(c) Extend the appropriate entries to the profit and loss account column.

(d) Extend the appropriate entries to the balance sheet column.

(e) Prepare the trading and profit and loss account for Marco Bellini.

(f) Prepare the balance sheet for Marco Bellini.

Additional information
- Closing stock is £15,300.
- Depreciation on the van for the year is £500.
- Depreciation on fixtures and fittings for the year is £300.
- An amount of £240 is outstanding for lighting and heating.
- Rent amounting to £400 has been prepaid.

Figure 29.6 *Trial balance for Marco Bellini's business as at 31.12.01*

Marco Bellini
Trial Balance as at 31.12.01

	Debit £	Credit £
Sales		81,310
Opening stock	13,250	
Purchases	46,730	
Motor expenses	1,380	
Rent and rates	8,590	
Light and heat	1,560	
Telephone	520	
Bank interest	180	
Van	4,300	
Provision for depreciation - van		2,500
Fixtures and fittings	3,000	
Provision for depreciation - fixtures & fittings		1,500
Trade debtors	320	
Cash at bank	780	
Cash in hand	310	
Trade creditors		2,310
Capital		5,000
Drawings	11,700	
	92,620	92,620

Figure 29.7 *Final accounts for Mary O'Brien's business*

Mary O'Brien
Trading and Profit and Loss Account
for the year ended 31.12.01

	£	£
Sales		141,110
Opening stock	23,100	
Purchases	74,090	
	97,190	
Less closing stock	25,120	
Cost of sales		72,070
Gross profit		69,040
Less expenses		
Wages	6,700	
Telephone	420	
Rent and rates	5,800	
Electricity	770	
Depreciation	400	
Sundry expenses	2,420	
		16,510
Net profit		52,530

Mary O'Brien
Balance Sheet as at 31.12.01

	£	£	£
Fixed assets			
Fixtures and fittings at cost		4,000	
Less depreciation		1,600	
			2,400
Current assets			
Stock		25,120	
Cash at bank		4,200	
Cash in hand		2,010	
		31,330	
Current liabilities			
Trade creditors	4,380		
Add accruals	210		
		4,590	
Net current assets			26,740
Net assets			29,140
Financed by			
Capital			
Opening capital			13,000
Add net profit			52,530
			65,530
Less drawings			36,390
Capital employed			29,140

The extended trial balance and the final accounts – a further example

As a further illustration of how the extended trial balance is used to produce final accounts, consider the example of Bedford Construction. This business specialises in building garages and extensions. The trial balance for the business as at 30.6.01 is shown in Figure 29.8. Some additional information regarding end of year adjustments is also provided.

Figure 29.8 *Trial balance for Bedford Construction as at 30.6.01*

Bedford Construction
Trial Balance as at 30.6.01

	Debit £	Credit £
Sales		132,560
Opening stock	3,110	
Purchases	67,300	
Motor expenses	3,120	
Rent and rates	4,390	
Casual wages	9,500	
Insurance	2,300	
Telephone	420	
Sundry expenses	3,110	
Lorry	12,500	
Provision for depreciation – lorry		6,000
Tools and equipment	14,000	
Provision for depreciation – tools and equipment		8,400
Trade debtors	3,260	
Cash at bank	3,220	
Trade creditors		5,330
Bank loan		3,000
Capital		15,340
Drawings	44,400	
	170,630	170,630

Additional information
- Closing stock is £3,670.
- Depreciation on the lorry for the year is £2,000.
- Depreciation on the tools and equipment is £1,400.
- Accountancy fees of £2,300 are owed by the business.
- A provision for doubtful debts of £1,000 is to be made.
- Rent for £320 has been prepaid.
- The owner of the business took £500 of the business's timber for his own use.

The following steps are taken to construct the extended trial balance.

Transferring the trial balance information The information in the trial balance is transferred to the extended trial balance. The debit and credit totals must be checked to make sure they are the same. This is shown in Figure 29.9.

Recording the end of year adjustments The seven end of year adjustments are then recorded in the adjustments column. Each adjustment has both a debit entry and a credit entry in the adjustments column. The treatment required for each adjustment is explained below.
- **Closing stock** The value of stock, £3,670, is entered twice in the adjustments column. The entry is made underneath the entries from the original trial balance. It is standard procedure to write:
    'Closing stock – Profit and loss' (this is a credit entry).
    'Closing stock – Balance sheet' (this is a debit entry).

Details	Trial Balance Dr £	Trial Balance Cr £	Adjustments Dr £	Adjustments Cr £	Profit and Loss Dr £	Profit and Loss Cr £	Balance Sheet Dr £	Balance Sheet Cr £
Sales		132,560				132,560		
Opening stock	3,110				3,110			
Purchases	67,300			500	66,800			
Motor expenses	3,120				3,120			
Rent and rates	4,390			320	4,070			
Casual labour	9,500				9,500			
Interest	2,300				2,300			
Telephone	420				420			
Sundry expenses	3,110				3,110			
Lorry	12,500						12,500	
Provision for depreciation-lorry		6,000		2,000				8,000
Tools and equipment	14,000						14,000	
Provision for depreciation-tools and equipment		8,400		1,400				9,800
Trade debtors	3,260						3,260	
Cash at bank	3,220						3,220	
Trade creditors		5,330						5,330
Bank loan		3,000						3,000
Capital		15,340						15,340
Drawings	44,400		500				44,900	
Closing stock - P & L				3,670		3,670		
Closing stock - Bal. sheet			3,670				3,670	
Depreciation: lorry			2,000		2,000			
Depreciation: tools + equip.			1,400		1,400			
Accountancy expense			2,300		2,300			
Accrual				2,300				2,300
Provision for doubtful debt				1,000				1,000
Provision for doubtful debt - adjustment			1,000		1,000			
Prepayment			320				320	
Net profit					37,100			37,100
	170,630	170,630	11,190	11,190	136,230	136,230	81,870	81,870

- **Depreciation** There are two adjustments for depreciation, one for the lorry and one for tools and equipment. The debit entries are listed at the bottom of the extended trial balance, £2,000 for the lorry and £1,400 for tools and equipment. These depreciation expenses are added together when constructing the profit and loss account. The credit entries are made against the 'Provision for depreciation' entries in the trial balance.
- **Accountancy fees** The debit entry for this provision is made at the bottom of the extended trial balance. The £2,300 is listed as an 'Accountancy expense'. The credit entry is also listed at the bottom of the extended trial balance as an 'Accrual' since the money is still owed by the business.
- **Doubtful debt provision** The debit entry for this provision is listed at the bottom of the extended trial balance. The £1,000 is listed as a 'Provision for doubtful debt - adjustment'. The credit entry is also listed at the bottom of the extended trial balance as 'Provision for doubtful debt'. In the balance sheet it is subtracted from the debtors total.
- **Prepayment** The £320 debit entry for the prepayment of rent is made at the bottom of the extended trial balance. It is listed as 'Prepayment'. The credit entry for the prepayment is made against the rent and rates entry in the trial balance.
- **Stock drawings** The effect of the business owner using £500 worth of timber stock for his own use is to increase drawings and to reduce purchases. The £500 is debited against drawings and is credited against purchases.

The debit and credit entries in the adjustments column are then added to check that they are equal. In this case they are both £11,190. The totals are entered at the bottom of the adjustments column.

Extending the entries to the profit and loss column The third stage in preparing an extended trial balance is to extend the relevant entries in the trial balance and adjustments columns to the profit and loss column. Relevant entries are those which are revenue or expense items. Debit entries in the trial balance and adjustments columns are recorded as debit entries in the profit and loss account. Credit entries in the trial balance and adjustment columns are recorded as credit entries in the profit and loss account. For example, the credit entry for sales in the trial balance of £132,560, is recorded as a credit entry in the profit and loss column. The debit entry for motor expenses in the trial balance, £3,120, is recorded as a debit entry in the profit and loss column.

All of the end of year adjustments are posted across to the profit and loss column. The first in the list is the credit entry relating to the £500 of timber used by the owner. This has the effect of reducing purchases to £66,800 (ie £67,300 - £500). The prepayment for rent of £320 is subtracted from the debit balance of £4,390 for rent and rates in the trial balance. The result is that £4,070 is debited to the profit and loss column. The credit entry for closing stock for £3,670 is extended to the profit and loss column on the credit side.

The two debit entries for the depreciation charge, £2,000 and £1,400, are extended to the profit and loss column on the debit side. The £2,300 accountancy expense is extended to the debit side of the profit and loss column, as is the £1,000 provision for doubtful debt.

The difference between the debit and credit totals in the profit and loss column is £37,100. This represents net profit and is entered in the extended trial balance on the debit side of the profit and loss column. The two totals are now £136,230.

Extending the entries to the balance sheet column The remaining entries in the trial balance are extended to the balance sheet column. Debit entries in the trial balance are extended to the debit side of the balance sheet column. For example, the debit entry relating to the lorry in the trial balance for £12,500 is extended to the debit side of the balance sheet column. Similarly, the credit balances in the trial balance are extended to the credit side of the balance sheet column. For example, the credit entry in the trial balance for the bank loan, £3,000, is extended to the credit side of the balance sheet column.

The end of year adjustments are also extended to the balance sheet column. The two credit balances representing the provision for depreciation for the lorry and the tools and equipment are added to the total provisions shown as credit balances in the trial balance. Therefore a total of £8,000 (£6,000 + £2,000) is entered on the credit side of the balance sheet column for the lorry and £9,800 (£8,400 + £1,400) for the tools and equipment.

The £3,670 debit balance representing closing stock in the adjustments column is extended to the debit side of the balance sheet column. The £2,300 credit entry representing accruals in the adjustments column is extended to the credit side of the balance sheet column. The £1,000 provision for doubtful debts is posted to the credit side of the balance sheet column and the £320 prepayment to the debit side. The adjusted total for drawings, ie the original amount of £44,400 plus the £500 timber taken by the owner is posted to the debit side of the balance sheet column. The total is now £44,900.

The debits and credits in the balance sheet are added to obtain the totals. If they are equal, then errors have been avoided. In this case, the total debits and total credits are both £81,870. The extended trial balance is now complete.

Preparing the final accounts for Bedford Construction

When the extended trial balance is complete, the final accounts can be prepared (see Figure 29.10 and Figure 29.11).

- When constructing the profit and loss account, an entry is made for depreciation in the list of expenses. Note that there was no entry in the original trial balance for depreciation, it was one of the end of year adjustments. In this case there are two adjustments for depreciation and they are added together. The total depreciation expense is £3,400 (£2,000 + £1,400).
- An entry is made for the doubtful debts provision in the profit and loss account. Again, there was

no entry in the original trial balance for this because it is an end of year adjustment. It is £1,000.

- When constructing the balance sheet, the cost of fixed assets, the total provision for depreciation and the book value are all shown. For example, in this case, the original cost of the lorry is recorded as £12,500 and the provision for depreciation is £8,000. This means that the current net book value is £4,500 (£12,500 - £8,000).
- The £2,300 credit entry for accrued accountancy fees in the balance sheet column of the extended trial balance is entered as a current liability in the balance sheet.
- The £320 prepayment is shown as a current asset in the balance sheet.

Figure 29.10 *The trading and profit and loss account for Bedford Construction*

Bedford Construction
Trading and Profit and Loss Account
for the year ended 31.12.01

	£	£
Sales		132,560
Opening stock	3,110	
Purchases	66,800	
	69,910	
Less closing stock	3,670	
Cost of sales		66,240
Gross profit		66,320
Less expenses		
Casual labour	9,500	
Motor expenses	3,120	
Telephone	420	
Rent and rates	4,070	
Interest	2,300	
Depreciation	3,400	
Accountancy fees	2,300	
Provision for doubtful debts	1,000	
Sundry expenses	3,110	
		29,220
Net profit		37,100

Balance sheet extracts Note that, sometimes, students might be asked to prepare a balance sheet extract rather than a full balance sheet as in Figure 29.11. For example, if a balance sheet extract for the lorry is requested, as at 31.12.01, it would be:

	£	£
Fixed assets		
Lorry at cost	12,500	
Less depreciation	8,000	4,500

Figure 29.11 *The balance sheet for Bedford Construction*

Bedford Construction
Balance Sheet as at 31.12.01

	£	£	£
Fixed assets			
Lorry at cost		12,500	
Less depreciation		8,000	4,500
Tools and equipment		14,000	
Less depreciation		9,800	4,200
			8,700
Current assets			
Stock		3,670	
Debtors	3,260		
Less provision for doubtful debt	1,000		
		2,260	
Prepayments		320	
Cash at bank		3,220	
		9,470	
Current liabilities			
Trade creditors	5,330		
Accruals	2,300		
		7,630	
Net current assets			1,840
			10,540
Less long-term liabilities			
Bank loan			3,000
Net assets			7,540
Financed by			
Capital			
Opening capital			15,340
Add net profit			37,100
			52,440
Less drawings			44,900
Capital employed			7,540

summary questions

1. What are the four headings of figures that appear in the extended trial balance?
2. What is the adjustments column used for in the extended trial balance?
3. Explain how an accrued telephone charge for £120 is treated in the adjustments column.
4. Explain how a provision for a doubtful debt of £6,790 is treated in the adjustments column.
5. Explain how depreciation is treated in the adjustments column.
6. Where does the information in the profit and loss column in the extended trial balance come from?
7. If an owner takes stock from the business for personal use, the total of purchases is affected. Explain how this is dealt with in the adjustments column.
8. How are drawings dealt with in the extended trial balance?
9. How are sales dealt with in the extended trial balance?
10. How is net profit dealt with in the extended trial balance?

key terms

Extended trial balance - a document that is used to incorporate the end of year adjustments into the final accounts. It contains the trial balance, details of adjustments, entries for the profit and loss account and entries for the balance sheet.

UNIT ASSESSMENT QUESTION 1

Figure 29.12 *Trial balance for Damien McGill's business as at 31.1.01*

Damien McGill
Trial Balance as at 31.1.01

	Debit £	Credit £
Sales		98,450
Opening stock	14,360	
Purchases	34,210	
Rent	6,000	
Casual labour	6,100	
Motor expenses	1,440	
Telephone	340	
Sundry expenses	2,130	
Vehicle	15,000	
Provision for depreciation - vehicle		6,000
Fixtures & fittings	13,500	
Provision for depreciation - fixtures & fittings		8,100
Trade debtors	3,210	
Cash at bank	2,340	
Trade creditors		2,110
Capital		12,340
Drawings	28,370	
	127,000	127,000

Additional information
- Closing stock is £12,220.
- Depreciation on the vehicle for the year is £2,000.
- Depreciation on fixtures and fittings for the year is £1,350.
- Wages of £200 are owed to a casual labourer.
- Accountancy fees of £1,300 are also owed.

Damien McGill manufactures and mends cricket bats and other equipment in his Hampshire workshop. He supplies a large number of specialist retailers and also makes bats to order for top class cricketers. The trial balance for his business is shown in Figure 29.12.

(a) Prepare the extended trial balance for Damien McGill's business.
(b) Prepare the final accounts for Damien McGill's business.

UNIT ASSESSMENT QUESTION 2

Jean Watkinson owns a fish and chip shop in Burnley, Lancashire. The business faces fierce competition from new fast food outlets. A copy of the trial balance for the business for the year ended 31.12.01 is shown in Figure 29.13.

(a) **Prepare an extended trial balance for Jean Watkinson's business.**
(b) **Prepare the final accounts for the business.**
(c) **Do you think the business is successful? Explain your answer.**

Figure 29.13 *Trial balance for Jean Watkinson's business as at 31.12.01*

Jean Watkinson
Trial Balance as at 31.12.01

	Debit £	Credit £
Sales		32,680
Opening stock	640	
Purchases	21,010	
Rent	5,000	
Casual labour	2,200	
Insurance	560	
Interest	760	
Telephone	230	
Sundry expenses	3,220	
Equipment	9,500	
Provision for depreciation - equipment		4,750
Cash in hand	440	
Trade creditors		1,260
Bank overdraft		1,210
Capital		9,700
Drawings	6,040	
	49,600	49,600

Additional information
- Closing stock is £1,060.
- Depreciation on the equipment is £950.
- An amount of £200 for rent has been prepaid.
- A telephone bill for £70 is owed.
- The owner took £350 of goods for her own use.

Suspense accounts and error correction

What is a suspense account?

A SUSPENSE ACCOUNT is a temporary account. It is used when there is a difference between the total credits and total debits on the trial balance. This difference indicates that a bookkeeping error has been made. If the source of the error cannot be found after an initial search, the difference between the credits and debits is posted to a suspense account in the nominal ledger. The balance on the suspense account is then listed in the trial balance and the final accounts can be prepared. The final accounts will not be complete until the cause of the difference on the trial balance is identified and the suspense account is 'cleared'. In this context, clearing the suspense account means that the correcting entries have been made and the account is then balanced and closed.

To illustrate how a suspense account is used, consider the example of Bookends, a specialist bookshop. A copy of the trial balance for Bookends as at 31 May 2001 is shown in Figure 30.1. The total of debits is £100,870 and the total of credits is £99,090. It does not balance because there is a difference of £1,780 between the two totals. The difference between the debit and credit totals is placed in a suspense account and listed at the bottom of the trial balance. It is a credit balance of £1,780 (ie £100,870 - £99,090). Including it ensures that the trial balance actually balances. The suspense account can have a debit or a credit balance depending on what errors have caused the difference in the trial balance.

Figure 30.1 *Trial balance for Bookends*

Bookends
Trial Balance as at 31.5.01

	Debit	Credit
	£	£
Sales		79,430
Opening stock	6,420	
Purchases	43,280	
Returns outwards		1,330
Rent and rates	12,700	
Heat and light	980	
Sundry expenses	1,540	
Fixtures & fittings	4,500	
Provision for depreciation - fixtures and fittings		2,500
Cash at bank	2,640	
Cash in hand	340	
Trade creditors		3,210
Capital		12,620
Drawings	28,470	
Suspense		1,780
	100,870	99,090

The suspense account is entered here as a credit.

The suspense account is kept in the nominal ledger of Bookends. This is shown in Figure 30.2. The entry in the suspense account is the same amount, and on the same side of the account, as that shown in the trial balance. In this case the suspense account has a credit balance of £1,780. The suspense account will be cleared when the errors causing the difference are found and corrected.

If the errors cannot be found before the final accounts are prepared, the balance on the suspense account is shown in the balance sheet. A debit balance on the suspense account is shown as an asset in the balance sheet. A credit balance is shown as a liability.

Figure 30.2 *The suspense account for Bookends*

NOMINAL LEDGER

Dr		Suspense Account	Cr	
	£	2001		£
		31.5 Difference per trial balance		1,780

QUESTION 1

Gill Knight owns a dog training school in Bradford called Canine Concerns. Her business specialises in training dogs and overcoming bad behaviour such as disobedience, nuisance barking and aggression. A copy of the trial balance for Canine Concerns as at 31 March 2001 is shown in Figure 30.3. There is an error in the bookkeeping which has caused a difference between the total debits and total credits on the trial balance.

(a) **Calculate the difference between debits and credits and open a suspense account in the trial balance so that it does balance.**
(b) **Show the suspense account in the nominal ledger.**
(c) **If the final accounts are produced without clearing the suspense account, where will the suspense account balance appear in the final accounts?**

Figure 30.3 *Trial balance for Canine Concerns as at 31.3.01*

Canine Concerns
Trial Balance as at 31.3.01

	Debit £	Credit £
Fees		59,060
Interest received		230
Motor expenses	2,450	
Insurance	670	
Advertising	1,560	
Telephone	730	
Sundry expenses	3,520	
Motor vehicle	12,500	
Provision for depreciation – motor vehicle		4,000
Cash at bank	6,500	
Trade creditors		740
Capital		6,000
Drawings	43,050	

Reasons for opening a suspense account

A suspense account will be opened for two main reasons. First, if a bookkeeper is unsure where to post an item, a suspense account might be opened until the correct destination is found. For instance, suppose a payment for goods is received but it is not clear who has sent the money. A suspense account will be opened and credited with the amount. Then, when it is discovered who has paid the money, the books can be corrected and the customer's account can be credited.

The second and more common reason for opening a suspense account is when there is a difference on the trial balance that cannot quickly be traced and corrected. The types of error that result in a difference between total debits and total credits are explained in unit 28. They are summarised on the next page.

- Transposition. This is where two digits in a number are accidentally reversed. For example, an amount for £5,670 might be posted as £6,570. There is a difference of £900.
- One sided omission. This is where a transaction is entered correctly on one side of an account but not included at all in another account.
- A transaction is entered twice on the same side of an account.
- One amount is recorded on the debit side of an account and a different amount is recorded on the credit side of another account.
- An account balance is entered on the wrong side of the trial balance.
- An account is omitted when constructing the trial balance.
- A casting (ie addition) error has occurred in an account.
- A casting error has occurred in the trial balance.

Some errors made in the bookkeeping system do not affect the trial balance. These types of error, such as errors of original entry, errors of omission, errors of principle and errors of commission, are explained in unit 16. Since the trial balance will still balance when these types of error are made, a suspense account is not needed to correct them.

Error correction

Once a suspense account has been opened it is good practice to clear the account as soon as possible. To do this the bookkeeping errors that have caused the difference on the trial balance must be identified and corrected. The process summarised in Figure 30.4 can be used to correct errors.

Figure 30.4 *A procedure for correcting errors to clear the suspense account*

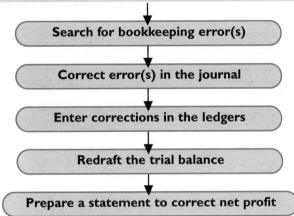

In order to illustrate the correction process, consider again the example of Bookends. Figure 30.1 showed that the credit balance on the suspense account was £1,780.

Searching for errors The first step is to search the bookkeeping system to find the errors. After a check was carried out on 7.6.01, the following two errors were discovered in Bookends' ledgers:
- the sales account was undercast, ie added up incorrectly, by £1,000;
- a rates rebate for £780 from the local council had not been entered in the rent and rates account, but it had been recorded in the cash book.

Correct errors in the journal When an error is identified it must be recorded in the journal. The journal entry serves as a primary record for the correction. It states which accounts are debited and credited, and by how much. In this case the casting error is corrected by debiting the suspense account with £1,000 and crediting the sales account with £1,000. The second error is corrected by debiting the suspense account with £780 and crediting the rent and rates account with £780. These two corrections are shown in the journal for Bookends in Figure 30.5. Note that debit entries are recorded first in the journal. Folio entries are ignored.

Figure 30.5 *The journal entries required to correct the two errors*

JOURNAL				
Date	Details	Folio	Debit	Credit
			£	£
2001 7.6	Suspense Sales *Correction of casting error*		1,000	1,000
7.6	Suspense Rent and rates *Correction of error, completion of double entry*		780	780

Entering corrections in the ledgers The bookkeeping system needs to be amended by including the corrections shown in the journal. In this case, the suspense account, sales account and rent and rates account in the nominal ledger all need to be updated. These accounts are illustrated in Figure 30.6.

Figure 30.6 *Suspense account, sales account and the rent and rates account for Bookends after corrections have been made*

NOMINAL LEDGER

Dr	Suspense Account		Cr	
2001		£	2001	£
7.6 Sales		1,000	31.5 Difference per trial balance	1,780
7.6 Rent and rates		780		
		1,780		1,780

Dr	Sales Account		Cr	
2001		£	2001	£
			31.5 Balance b/d	79,430
7.6 Balance c/d		80,430	7.6 Suspense	1,000
		80,430		80,430
			7.6 Balance b/d	80,430

Dr	Rent and Rates Account		Cr	
2001		£	2001	£
31.5 Balance b/d		12,700	7.6 Suspense	780
			7.6 Balance c/d	11,920
		12,700		12,700
7.6 Balance b/d		11,920		

The accounts show the balances brought down on 31 May 2001 and the corrections entered in the journal. The suspense account is now cleared. The two debit entries for £1,000 and £780 match the credit entry of £1,780. This means that there will be no suspense account in the trial balance when it is redrafted on 7 June 2001. The sales account shows the correction for the undercasting error. The account is credited with £1,000 and the new balance b/d is £80,430. This new balance will appear in the trial balance when it is redrafted. Finally, the rent and rates account shows the correction for the omission error. The account is credited with £780 and the new balance b/d is £11,920. This new balance will also appear in the redrafted trial balance.

Redraft the trial balance The amended trial balance for Bookends is shown in Figure 30.7. There are three changes to the trial balance shown in Figure 30.1.
- The suspense account is cleared and therefore removed from the trial balance.
- The total of sales is increased from £79,430 to £80,430 to allow for the error.
- The total of rent and rates is reduced from £12,700 to £11,920 to allow for the error.

As a result of these changes, the trial balance now balances without a suspense account. The new balancing totals are £100,090.

Figure 30.7 *Redrafted trial balance for Bookends as at 7.6.01*

Bookends
Trial Balance as at 7.6.01

	Debit	Credit
	£	£
Sales		80,430
Opening stock	6,420	
Purchases	43,280	
Returns outwards		1,330
Rent and rates	11,920	
Heat and light	980	
Sundry expenses	1,540	
Fixtures & fittings	4,500	
Provision for depreciation - fixtures and fittings		2,500
Cash at bank	2,640	
Cash in hand	340	
Trade creditors		3,210
Capital		12,620
Drawings	28,470	
	100,090	100,090

What effect do errors have on the final accounts?

The errors which cause a difference between the total debits and total credits on the trial balance can affect the final accounts. For example, if the total of sales is undercast by £100, gross and net profit are both understated by £100. Some errors only affect the balance sheet. For example, if the drawings account is undercast by £100, the total of drawings in the balance sheet is understated by £100.

Once errors are detected and corrected in the ledgers, it is common practice to prepare a statement showing the effect on net profit. This is the final stage in the procedure shown in Figure 30.4. Such a statement is prepared if the final accounts are drawn up before the errors have been found. The statement shows the net profit before adjustment, any additions to net profit arising from error correction and any deductions from net profit arising from error correction.

To illustrate how errors are dealt with in the trading and profit and loss account, consider again the errors in the trial balance of Bookends in Figure 30.1. The statement of corrected net profit for Bookends is shown in Figure 30.9. The first entry in the statement is the net profit before adjustments are taken into account. In this case, assume that the net profit made by Bookends before the errors were detected was £23,840. Both of the errors in this example require additions to the net profit. The undercasting error on the sales account adds £1,000 to net profit and the unrecorded rates rebate adds £780 to net profit. There are no deductions from net profit in this example. The adjusted net profit for Bookends is £25,620.

QUESTION 2

Garden World is a large garden centre in Sussex. The trial balance for the business was drawn up on 31 October 2001. It is shown in Figure 30.8 and, because it did not balance, a suspense account was opened. On 4 November 2001, the bookkeeper located the following two errors.

- The purchases account was undercast by £100.
- The owner had used a business cheque to buy his mother's birthday present for £680. This was recorded in the bank account but not in the drawings account.

(a) Show the journal entries for the errors detected by the bookkeeper (ignore folio entries).

(b) Redraft the trial balance for Garden World as at 4.11.01.

Figure 30.8 *Trial balance for Garden World as at 31.10.01*

Garden World
Trial Balance as at 31.10.01

	Debit £	Credit £
Sales		151,520
Opening stock	12,410	
Purchases	84,320	
Wages	32,180	
Motor expenses	2,060	
Rates and insurance	3,280	
Heat and light	1,450	
Sundry expenses	650	
Van	13,400	
Provision for depreciation - van		6,000
Fixtures and fittings	3,500	
Provision for depreciation - fixtures and fittings		1,400
Cash at bank	2,270	
Cash in hand	670	
Trade creditors		3,740
Capital		13,180
Drawings	18,870	
Suspense	780	
	175,840	175,840

Figure 30.9 *Statement of corrected net profit for Bookends*

	£
Net profit (before adjustment)	23,840
Add	
Sales undercast	1,000
Rates rebate not recorded	780
Adjusted net profit	25,620

In the Bookends example, because sales were understated and expenses, ie rent and rates, were overstated, the effect of the errors was to lower net profit. If the figure for net profit is incorrect, it also makes the balance sheet incorrect because this incorporates the net profit figure. Different errors have an impact on different parts of the final accounts. The impact is summarised in Figure 30.10.

Figure 30.10 *The impact of errors on the final account*

Error	Final accounts affected
Sales figure incorrect	Trading account, profit and loss account and balance sheet
Purchases figure incorrect	Trading account, profit and loss account and balance sheet
Expenses incorrect	Profit and loss account and balance sheet
Non-operating income incorrect	Profit and loss account and balance sheet
Assets figure incorrect	Balance sheet
Liabilities figure incorrect	Balance sheet
Capital figure incorrect	Balance sheet
Drawings figure incorrect	Balance sheet

QUESTION 3

Rajesh Kumar runs a business in Manchester that supplies, reconditions and repairs snooker and pool tables. When the trial balance was prepared on 31 December 2001 the total of debits did not equal the total of credits. A suspense account was opened so that the final accounts could be produced. The net profit made by the business was stated as £45,310. Two weeks later, on 14 January 2002, the bookkeeper discovered the following errors.

- The total of purchases was overcast by £1,000.
- The balance for motor expenses was read as £2,540 instead of £2,450 when being transferred to the trial balance.

(a) Show the journal entries required to correct the errors (ignore folio entries).
(b) Show the statement of corrected net profit for Rajesh's business on 14.1.01.

Error correction – a further example

The bookkeeping errors relating to Bookends described earlier in this unit are relatively straightforward. Different issues are raised if the two following situations arise.

- Some errors discovered by bookkeepers do not require the drawing up of a suspense account because they do not affect the trial balance. Examples include errors of commission and errors of omission. However, such errors should be corrected in the journal, entered in the ledgers and included in the statement of corrected net profit.
- Unlike in the Bookends example, where both the errors (£1,000 and £780) are recorded on the debit side of the suspense account, a combination of errors might occur on both the credit side and the debit side.

In order to illustrate the effect of these two issues, consider the example of Ralph Butler, a clothes retailer in Kidderminster. On 30 November 2001, the trial balance for his business was prepared but there was a difference between total debits and total credits. A suspense account was opened with a debit balance of £8,870. The final accounts were prepared and the net profit was £51,090. On 7 December 2001, the bookkeeper identified the six errors described below.

- **Error 1** The sales day book was totalled at £176,321 and should have been £167,321.
- **Error 2** A payment in the cash book for £230 for motor expenses was not posted to the motor expenses account in the nominal ledger.
- **Error 3** The purchase of a display cabinet for £780 was debited to the sundry expenses account rather than the fixtures and fittings account.
- **Error 4** The debit side of the wages account was overcast by £1,000.
- **Error 5** Cash drawings amounting to £250 were completely omitted from the bookkeeping system.
- **Error 6** A £320 payment by cheque to a creditor, Dale Fashions, was mistakenly posted to the credit side of the supplier account instead of the debit side.

The first step in correcting the errors is to enter them in the journal.

- **Error 1** This is a transposition error which has resulted in the sales being overstated by £9,000. To correct this error the sales account is debited with £9,000 and the suspense account is credited with £9,000.
- **Error 2** This has arisen because only one entry has been made for a transaction. A £230 payment for motor expenses has been entered in the cash book but not in the motor expenses account. To correct this error the motor expenses account is debited with £230 and the suspense account is credited with £230.
- **Error 3** This does not affect the suspense account because it has no impact on the trial balance. The purchase of a display cabinet for £780 was posted to the sundry expenses account by mistake. This is an error of principle. To correct this error the fixtures and fittings account is debited with £780 and the sundry expenses account is credited with £780.
- **Error 4** This is a casting error which results in the total of wages being overstated by £1,000. To correct this error the suspense account is debited with £1,000 and the wages account is credited with £1,000.
- **Error 5** This is an error of omission that does not affect the suspense account. To correct the error the drawings account is debited with £250 and the cash book is credited with £250.

Figure 30.11 *Journal entries for Ralph Butler's business to correct errors*

	JOURNAL			
Date	**Details**	**Folio**	**Debit**	**Credit**
			£	£
7.12	Sales		9,000	
	Suspense			9,000
	Correction of transposition error			
7.12	Motor expenses		230	
	Suspense			230
	Correction of error, completion of double entry			
7.12	Fixtures and fittings		780	
	Sundry expenses			780
	Correction of error of principle			
7.12	Suspense		1,000	
	Wages			1,000
	Correction of casting error			
7.12	Drawings		250	
	Cash book			250
	Correction of omission error			
7.12	Dale Fashions		640	
	Suspense			640
	Correction of misposting error			

- **Error 6** This is a posting error. The payment was posted to the wrong side of the supplier account. To correct the error, the suspense account must be credited with £640, ie double the amount of the transaction value. This is because an entry of £320 is required to cancel out the misposting and £320 is required to complete the double entry. The corresponding journal entry is to debit the Dale Fashions account with £640.

These corrections are shown in the journal for Ralph Butler's business in Figure 30.11. The folios are omitted.

Figure 30.12 shows the entries in the suspense account after the errors are corrected. The suspense account is cleared and balanced. Not all errors are recorded in the suspense account. In this case, the third error is an error of principle and the fifth error is an error of omission which have no impact on the trial balance. Note that a combination of errors, both on the debit and credit side of the bookkeeping system, contributed to the difference on the trial balance. The difference in this case, £8,870, was the result of one debit error of £1,000 and three credit errors of £9,000, £230 and £640.

Figure 30.12 *The suspense account for Ralph Butler's business*

NOMINAL LEDGER

Dr		Suspense Account	Cr	
2001		£	2001	£
30.11 Difference per trial balance	8,870		7.12 Sales	9,000
7.12 Wages	1,000		7.12 Motor expenses	230
			7.12 Dale Fashions	640
	9,870			9,870

Once the errors are corrected, the net profit for the year can be adjusted. The statement of corrected net profit is shown in Figure 30.13. As a result of the corrections, the net profit for Ralph Butler's business is now lower at £43,640. The statement includes the correction for the third error even though it does not affect the suspense account. The £780 should not have been classed as expenses because it was spent on an asset, fixtures and fittings. This should be entered in the balance sheet. The overstated expenses of £780 are added to net profit. The same applies to the overstated wages of £1,000 which are also added to net profit. The overstated sales and motor expenses are subtracted from net profit to give the amended total.

The error involving the drawings account relates to the balance sheet and does not affect net profit. It is therefore not included in the statement. The sixth error also does not affect the profit and loss account. This is because it relates to the personal account of a supplier, and therefore it affects the creditors figure which appears in the balance sheet.

Figure 30.13 *Statement of corrected net profit for Ralph Butler's business*

	£	£
Net profit (before adjustment)		51,090
Add		
Wages overstated (error 4)		1,000
Sundry expenses overstated (error 3)		780
		52,870
Less		
Sales overstated (error 1)	9,000	
Motor expenses (error 2)	230	
		9,230
Adjusted net profit		43,640

QUESTION 4

Collins Labels makes and supplies labels for commercial and industrial customers. The business is located in Leeds and produces self adhesive labels in paper, vinyl, metal and polycarbonate. At the end of the financial year, 31.5.01, there was a difference between total debits and total credits on the trial balance and a suspense account was opened. The suspense account had a debit balance of £2,730. The final accounts were prepared and a net profit of £54,330 was reported. The following four errors were detected by the bookkeeper on 3.6.01.

Error 1 A cheque received from a debtor, P. Hendry, for £290, was posted to the debit side of his account by mistake.

Error 2 The purchases day book was undercast by £3,000.

Error 3 A credit sale to A. Larkin for £340 was completely omitted from the bookkeeping system.

Error 4 A payment to British Telecom for £310 was entered correctly in the cash book but was omitted from the telephone account.

(a) Show the journal entries required to correct the above errors (ignore folio entries).

(b) Show the balanced suspense account after making the appropriate entries for the corrections.

(c) What would be the effect on the net profit of the first error?

(d) Prepare a statement of corrected net profit for Collins Labels.

What happens if the suspense account cannot be cleared?

It is important for accountants to clear the suspense account so that the final accounts are accurate. However, in practice, if the balance left on a suspense account is insignificant or 'immaterial', it might be written off against profit. Accountants need to use their judgment when deciding when to write off the suspense account. A business with a turnover of £500 million is not likely to spend very much time searching for an error of £500. The time spent searching for the difference would not be worth it. This decision would be justified according to the concept of **materiality**. However, a £500 difference in the trial balance for a business with a turnover of, say, £45,000 is significant. Therefore, more effort might be made to find the errors. Accountants will also realise that a small difference can conceal two or more errors involving larger values. For example, a debit balance of £110 might result from a single error of this amount, or it could result from two errors of, say, £41,950 on the debit side and £41,840 on the credit side (£41,950 - £41,840 = £110). This has to be taken into account when deciding whether or not to write off a difference on the suspense account.

How can errors be minimised?

Businesses that undertake very large numbers of transactions during the year are likely to find mistakes in their bookkeeping. Since searching for errors takes time and can cause delays in the accounting process, it is important to minimise the number of errors that occur. Certain measures can be taken to help reduce the number of errors.

- The use of computers in accounting helps to reduce errors. Computers tend to be more reliable than humans when processing large amounts of information. Also, many software programmes are able to alert users to errors as they arise. The advantages of computerised accounts are explained in unit 47.

- The bookkeeping system can be divided between a number of people. If different staff are responsible for the upkeep of different ledgers, for example, specialisation occurs. This allows each individual member of staff to become more proficient in their area and therefore minimises errors.

- Control accounts can be used to increase the number of checks that are made in the bookkeeping process. This is explained in unit 27.

- The regular dispatch of statements to customers helps to reduce errors. This is because customers check the statements against their own records and raise queries if there are discrepancies.

- Checking statements from suppliers ensures that records coincide with those of suppliers. If there are differences, errors can be detected and corrected.

- Preparing a trial balance on a regular basis, for example monthly, can reduce errors. However, it should be remembered that not all errors can be detected by this practice.
- Preparing regular bank reconciliation statements can help detect particular types of error. For example, errors in the cash book might be highlighted .
- Checking the amount of cash in the petty cash box against the petty cash book. This helps detect errors in the recording of cash transactions.

Figure 30.14 *Trial balance for Errol Drakes' business as at 31.3.01*

UNIT ASSESSMENT QUESTION 1

Errol Drakes runs a delicatessen and catering business in North London. A wide range of fresh food is prepared and supplied on the premises. At the end of the year, 31 March 2001, a trial balance was prepared for the business. However, there was a difference on the trial balance which was posted to a suspense account. Following a search through the books, the accountant detected four errors.

- **Error 1** A credit note for £210, received from a supplier, had been entered in the returns outwards day book but not in the creditor's account.
- **Error 2** The (correct) bank balance of £2,550 had been incorrectly entered on the trial balance as an overdraft, ie as a credit instead of a debit.
- **Error 3** The payment of an electricity bill for £320 had been entered in the cash book but not in the heat and light account.
- **Error 4** The purchases day book had been overcast by £300.

Errol Drakes
Trial Balance as at 31.3.01

	Debit £	Credit £
Sales		172,020
Interest received		540
Opening stock	6,320	
Purchases	91,960	
Wages	49,450	
Motor expenses	2,100	
Insurance	210	
Advertising	650	
Telephone	430	
Heat and light	860	
Sundry expenses	2,560	
Motor vehicle	21,000	
Provision for depreciation - motor vehicle		8,000
Cash at bank		2,550
Trade creditors		4,300
Capital		23,290
Drawings	29,830	
	205,370	210,700

(a) **Determine the balance on the suspense account.**
(b) **Show the journal entries necessary to correct the errors.**
(c) **Show the balanced suspense account with all the entries.**
(d) **Redraw the trial balance for 1.4.01.**
(e) **What would be the effect on the net profit for Errol Drakes' business of the first error?**

key terms

Suspense account - a temporary account used to post the difference in the trial balance caused by errors in the bookkeeping system.

UNIT ASSESSMENT QUESTION 2

Rupert Johnson owns a menswear shop called RJ's. At the end of the financial year, 31.7.01, the trial balance did not agree and a suspense account was opened. The suspense account had a debit balance of £230. The final accounts were prepared and a net profit of £24,020 was reported. The following six errors were detected by the bookkeeper on 7.8.01.

Error 1 The sales day book was overcast by £400.

Error 2 A payment of £145 for a telephone bill was mistakenly posted to sundry expenses instead of to the telephone account.

Error 3 A rates payment for £650 was posted to the rates account as £560.

Error 4 A credit purchase by A. Wilson for £430 was completely omitted from the accounts.

Error 5 The owner withdrew £200 cash from the business for personal use. This was recorded in the cash book but not elsewhere.

Error 6 A cash sale for £460 was entered in the cash book but not in the sales account.

(a) **Show the journal entries required to correct the errors.**
(b) **Show the balanced suspense account after making the appropriate entries for the corrections.**
(c) **Prepare a statement of corrected net profit for Rupert Johnson's business.**

summary questions

1. Why is the suspense account a temporary account?
2. What happens to the balance on the suspense account if the final accounts are prepared before the suspense account is cleared?
3. In addition to a difference on the trial balance, why else might a bookkeeper open a suspense account?
4. State five types of error that will cause a difference on the trial balance.
5. State four types of error that will not affect the trial balance.
6. State the journal entries required if the sales account is undercast by £1,000.
7. State the journal entries required if a £430 payment to a supplier is posted to the wrong side of the supplier's personal account.
8. If the purchases day book is undercast by £600, what will be the effect on net profit?
9. Explain what might happen if the suspense account cannot be cleared.
10. Suggest four ways in which errors in the bookkeeping system might be minimised.

Incomplete records–statement of affairs

unitobjectives

To understand:
- the nature of incomplete records;
- how to calculate profit using the accounting equation;
- how to prepare a statement of affairs;
- how to use a statement of affairs to calculate profit.

What are incomplete records?

A business is said to have INCOMPLETE RECORDS if it does not have a full set of books and ledger accounts. Some businesses have incomplete records because books or ledgers have been accidentally lost or destroyed. A more common explanation is that a business owner has decided not to use the double entry system of bookkeeping. There is a number of possible reasons for this.

- The owners of small businesses, such as market stall holders, taxi operators and guest house proprietors, might decide that their business income is not large enough to justify such a system.
- Cash-based businesses, ie those that do not buy or sell goods on credit, might decide not to use all of the books associated with the double entry system.
- Some business owners might feel that they do not have sufficient time or resources to carry out double entry bookkeeping.

Despite the difficulties involved in bookkeeping, business owners are required by the Inland Revenue to provide a record of their earnings for tax assessment. Consequently many businesses rely on accountants to produce a set of accounts from incomplete records.

Accountants encourage business owners to keep at least some basic records. Accounts can be prepared more quickly if accountants have the relevant information. From the business owner's point of view, there is good reason to supply accountants with accurate and complete details of transactions. This is because fees charged by accountants are often determined by the amount of time spent preparing a client's accounts.

Businesses that do not use the double entry system of bookkeeping might use a SINGLE ENTRY SYSTEM. This involves recording all payments, receipts and other transactions in one cash book. However, there will be no matching entries in other books. Although this method does give a full record of transactions, it fails to distinguish between, for example, drawings, expenses, purchases or capital spending.

QUESTION 1

Shelly Rafferty is a market trader. She sells football programmes which she buys in bulk from collectors, auctions, football clubs and other dealers. She travels around the West Midlands setting up her stall at car boot sales and at small markets in towns and villages. She estimates that, last year, she made £6,800 profit, but she is not really certain. Shelly decided to make an appointment with an accountant so that her profit could be calculated for tax assessment. She was apprehensive as the date for the appointment drew nearer because she had not kept detailed records regarding sales from her stall. However, she had paid most of her takings into the bank each week after she had taken some cash for herself. Shelly had a good idea how much she had spent on the purchase of programmes because she had kept receipts, and she had also kept receipts for expenses when travelling. But she had not kept a written record of her other expenses.

(a) Using Shelly's business as an example, explain what is meant by incomplete records.

(b) State three pieces of financial information that Shelly might not be able to give to her accountant.

(c) Explain why it will be in Shelly's interests to keep proper records in the future.

Calculating profit using the accounting equation

If a business owner has kept neither a cash book nor a record of transactions it might not be possible to produce a set of final accounts. However, it might still be possible to calculate the profit made by the business. Profit can be determined if the amounts of opening capital and closing capital are known. The difference between the two amounts represents profit or loss for the year. Capital can be calculated if the total of assets and liabilities are known. The accounting equation, explained in unit 5, can be used to calculate capital:

Capital = assets - liabilities

To illustrate this, suppose that on 1 January a business's assets are valued at £23,100 and its liabilities are valued at £12,430. At the end of the financial year, 31 December, the assets are valued at £39,420 and its liabilities are valued at £11,390. To calculate the profit made by the business, it is necessary to calculate the opening and closing capital, ie at 1 January and 31 December.

At 1 January
Opening capital = assets - liabilities
Opening capital = £23,100 - £12,430
Opening capital = £10,670

At 31 December
Closing capital = £39,420 - £11,390
Closing capital = £28,030

Profit is calculated by subtracting the opening capital from the closing capital. Since capital has increased by £17,360 (£28,030 - £10,670), the business has made a profit of £17,360. This example assumes that there are no drawings and that capital has not been introduced during the year. However, if capital is introduced and drawings are taken, profit can be calculated using the equation:

Profit = closing capital - opening capital - capital introduced + drawings

QUESTION 2

Edward Tregaron is a part time taxi driver in St Ives, Cornwall. He does not keep proper accounting records and it is impossible for his accountant to produce a set of meaningful final accounts. However, Edward is able to supply the following information for his accountant to calculate the annual profit of the taxi business.

1 February 2001   Assets = £28,540; Liabilities = £2,100
31 January 2002   Assets = £33,700; Liabilities = £3,490

During the year Edward withdrew £14,500 for his own personal use. No fresh capital was introduced.

(a) Calculate the opening capital and closing capital for Edward Tregaron's taxi business.
(b) Calculate the profit made by Edward Tregaron's business.
(c) After his annual profit had been calculated, Edward remembered that he had paid £350 for repairs to his taxi from his own money. What effect would this have on profit?

Statement of affairs

A STATEMENT OF AFFAIRS is sometimes used to determine a business's capital if the total of assets and liabilities are known. It is a statement which lists all the assets and liabilities of a business at a given date. It is similar to a balance sheet in appearance and is set out in a formal way.

In order to illustrate how profit can be calculated using a statement of affairs, consider the example of Rita Howarth who runs a mobile grocery shop in Lincolnshire. Rita does not consistently record transactions and she does not maintain a cash book. However, some financial details regarding her assets and liabilities are available and are shown on the next page.

	As at 30 June, 2002	As at 1 July, 2001
	£	£
Motor van	10,000	12,000
Equipment	2,350	1,800
Stock	3,860	3,430
Debtors	510	330
Cash at bank	2,180	1,290
Cash in hand	420	450
Trade creditors	1,430	1,210
Bank loan	3,000	3,500

During the year, Rita withdrew £12,000 from the business for her personal use. No new capital was introduced. To determine the profit made by Rita's business, the following steps are taken.
- Prepare a statement of affairs as at 1 July, 2001 to calculate the opening capital.
- Prepare a statement of affairs as at 30 June, 2002 to calculate the closing capital.
- Calculate profit using the formula:

Profit = closing capital - opening capital - capital introduced + drawings

The two statements of affairs as at 1 July, 2001 and 30 June, 2002 for Rita's business are shown in Figure 31.1. The fixed assets are listed and totalled. The current assets are listed, totalled and then added to fixed assets. The liabilities are also listed and totalled. Liabilities are then subtracted from the assets to determine the opening capital as at 1 July and the closing capital as at 30 June.

Figure 31.1 *Statements of affairs for Rita Howarth's business*

Rita Howarth
Statement of Affairs

	As at 30.6.02		As at 1.7.01	
	£	£	£	£
Fixed assets				
Motor van		10,000		12,000
Equipment		2,350		1,800
		12,350		13,800
Current assets				
Stock	3,860		3,430	
Debtors	510		330	
Cash at bank	2,180		1,290	
Cash in hand	420		450	
		6,970		5,500
		19,320		19,300
Less current liabilities				
Trade creditors		1,430		1,210
		17,890		18,090
Less long term liabilities				
Bank loan		3,000		3,500
Net assets		14,890		14,590
Financed by				
Capital		14,890		14,590

The statements of affairs in Figure 31.1 show that Rita's business had an opening capital of £14,590 and a closing capital of £14,890. The profit for Rita Howarth's business is calculated below.

Profit = closing capital - opening capital - capital introduced + drawings
= £14,890 - £14,590 - 0 + £12,000
= £12,300

QUESTION 3

Gary Manning owns a business which manufactures wrought iron gates, railings, security grills and garden furniture. Gary is always very busy and, as a result, he has never devoted sufficient time to keep proper records of his financial transactions. At the end of the financial year, 31 August, 2001, he supplied his accountant with the following information regarding his assets and liabilities.

	As at 31.8.01 £	As at 1.9.00 £
Motor vehicle	6,500	8,000
Tools and equipment	8,100	5,400
Stock	5,890	4,430
Debtors	2,600	2,270
Prepayments	1,000	800
Cash at bank	3,920	2,290
Trade creditors	4,380	3,430

During the year, Gary withdrew £21,500 from the business for personal use. He also introduced £2,000 of capital during the year to help fund the purchase of some new welding equipment.

(a) Produce a statement of affairs for Gary's business as at 1 September, 2000 to determine the opening capital.
(b) Produce a statement of affairs for Gary's business as at 31 August, 2001 to determine the closing capital.
(c) Calculate the profit made by Gary's business during the year.

Limitations of statements of affairs

The usefulness of statements of affairs depends on the accuracy of the information used in their preparation. For example, if a business owner forgets that £50 is owed by a customer, current assets will be understated. This means that when closing capital is being calculated it will also be understated by £50. As a result, the profit for the business will be understated by £50.

The calculation of profit using the opening and closing capital amounts is less reliable than using detailed double entry records of transactions. Lapses of memory and mistakes often occur. Also, it is not possible to produce a full trading and profit and loss account using just the statements of affairs. Only by using a proper bookkeeping system is it possible to produce a complete set of final accounts.

UNIT ASSESSMENT   QUESTION 1

Elizabeth Baker operates a secretarial agency in Brighton. She has an office at home which she has converted from a spare bedroom. Elizabeth does not keep proper records of her transactions but can supply the information below.

	As at 31.10.02	As at 1.11.01
	£	£
Motor car	4,500	5,000
Computer	1,600	2,000
Books and other equipment	1,250	1,500
Prepayments	400	350
Cash at bank	2,430	670
Cash in hand	120	150
Bank loan	3,000	5,000

During the year, Elizabeth withdrew £5,500 from the business for her own private use. No fresh capital was introduced.

(a) Prepare a statement of affairs as at 1.11.01 for Elizabeth Baker.
(b) Prepare a statement of affairs as at 31.10.02 for Elizabeth Baker.
(c) Calculate the profit made by Elizabeth's business during the year.
(d) After her accountant calculated the profit, Elizabeth remembered that she had withdrawn an extra £500 from the business at Christmas. She also remembered that £320 was owed to a local garage for repairs to her car.
(i) Redraft the statement of affairs as at 31.10.02; (ii) Recalculate the profit made by Elizabeth's business.
(e) With reference to the information in (d), outline the limitations of using this method to calculate business profit.

summary questions

1. Suggest three reasons why business owners might not use the double entry system to record transactions.
2. State four pieces of information that business owners with incomplete records might not be able to provide accountants.
3. Give two reasons why business owners need to know how much profit they have made.
4. How can the accounting equation be used to calculate profit?
5. Explain the purpose of a statement of affairs.
6. What are the disadvantages of purely using a statement of affairs to calculate a business's profit?
7. The opening capital for a business is £43,200, closing capital is £52,900, drawings are £25,100 and no new capital is introduced during the year. Calculate the profit made by the business.
8. The opening capital for a business is £21,300, closing capital is £8,900, drawings are £11,100 and no new capital is introduced during the year. Calculate the profit made by the business.

Gordon Poole owns a plumbing business in Swansea. He specialises in fitting new bathroom suites but he also deals with emergency work repairing leaking and burst pipes. He is often very busy and he sometimes fails to keep a written record of his transactions. However, Gordon is able to supply the financial information below.

	As at 31.12.01	As at 1.1.01
	£	£
Van	6,500	8,000
Tools and equipment	3,300	1,500
Stocks	710	430
Trade creditors	1,340	1,290
Other creditors	600	450
Cash at bank	-	1,010
Cash in hand	610	350
Bank overdraft	340	-

- During the year Gordon withdrew £15,500 from the business for his own private use.
- On 24 November, 2001, Gordon received a £200 deposit for a job that he was to start in the following January. The amount is included in 'cash at bank' but no other record has been made. It should be recorded in the statement of affairs as 'income prepaid' in the current liabilities.
- Gordon introduced £1,000 into the business in January to buy some new tools.

(a) **Prepare a statement of affairs as at 1.1.01 for Gordon Poole.**
(b) **Prepare a statement of affairs as at 31.12.01 for Gordon Poole.**
(c) **Calculate the profit made by Gordon's business during the year.**
(d) **After the profit was calculated, Gordon remembered that he owed a supplier £300. What effect would this have on profit?**

key terms

Incomplete records - accounting records from which some details are missing. The term implies that the double entry system of bookkeeping is not used.

Single entry system - a bookkeeping system which involves making one entry for each business transaction, usually in a cash book.

Statement of affairs - a list of a business's assets and liabilities at a given date.

unit**objectives**

To understand:
- how to use a cash book summary to find missing information;
- how to use control accounts to find missing information;
- how to use accounting ratios to calculate the cost of sales and total sales;
- how to prepare final accounts from incomplete records;
- how to calculate the value of missing stock and missing cash.

How can final accounts be produced from incomplete records?

If a business can only provide incomplete records, it might still be possible to produce final accounts if sufficient information is available. When accountants are faced with incomplete records their first task is to find the missing figures. One of the problems is that different businesses provide accountants with different sets of information. No two 'jobs' are the same. However, a number of techniques can be used to find the missing figures. These techniques include the following.
- Producing a cash book summary to determine the cash and bank balances. This might involve reconstructing the cash book.
- Using control (or total) accounts to find the total sales and purchases for the year.
- Using accounting ratios (see unit 44) to determine the total sales or purchases.
- Compiling a statement of affairs.

How is a cash book summary prepared?

If a business keeps a cash book, it should be possible to prepare a **cash book summary**. This can be used to find missing figures, such as the closing bank balance or the total of drawings. A cash book summary will generally show:
- the opening and closing cash and bank balances;
- the amount of all receipts and payments regardless of whether they relate to capital or revenue items;
- a record of all amounts received and paid during the year irrespective of the time periods to which they relate.

An example of a cash book summary is shown in Figure 32.1. It is prepared for a business run by Alf Ormerod, a mechanic who owns a garage in Leicester. Alf maintains a cash book but he has not drawn up a cash book summary. However, there is no missing information and the summary is based on records extracted from the cash book. The summary shows the opening and closing balances on the cash and bank accounts, the total of cash sales (£3,490) and credit sales (£43,020), the total of purchases (£23,790), the total of expenses (£6,320) and the total drawings (£15,890).

Figure 32.1 *Cash book summary for Alf Ormerod's business*

Date	Debit Details	Cash	Bank	Date	Credit Details	Cash	Bank
		CASH BOOK					
2001		£	£	2001		£	£
1.1	Balances b/d	250	610		Payments to creditors	1,890	21,900
	Cash sales	3,490			Expenses	760	5,560
	Receipts from debtors		43,020		Drawings	850	15,040
				31.12	Balances c/d	240	1,130
		3,740	43,630			3,740	43,630
2002							
1.1	Balances b/d	240	1,130				

If a cash book has not been kept, it might still be possible to reconstruct one from bank statements, paying-in slips and cheque counterfoils. However, there is a chance that some of the information required to produce the cash book summary will not be available. A figure that is sometimes missing is cash drawings. This is because some business owners do not always record the amount of cash they take from the business for personal use.

To illustrate how a cash book summary can be prepared even if the amount of drawings is not known, consider the example of Allen Harper, a supplier and installer of suspended ceilings. Allen does not keep a cash book. However, he can provide the opening balance on the cash account and he has kept all bank statements, cheque counterfoils and paying-in slips. He also knows the total of cash sales and purchases for the year. He does not know the exact amount of cash drawings, nor does he know the closing bank balance. Allen's accountant is able to analyse the bank documents and use the information provided by Allen to produce the information shown in in Figure 32.2. The details relate to Allen's trading year which runs from 1 April to 31 March.

Figure 32.2 *Information available to produce a cash book summary for Allen Harper*

Information needed to produce a cash book summary		Source of information
	£	
Cash at 1 April	480	Allen Harper
Bank at 1 April	2,310	Analysis of bank documents
Cash sales	8,320	Allen Harper
Cheques received from debtors	19,690	Analysis of bank documents
Cheques paid to creditors	12,190	Analysis of bank documents
Cash paid to creditors	1,540	Allen Harper
Cash paid for expenses	870	Allen Harper
Cheques paid for expenses	2,430	Analysis of bank documents
Bank drawings	6,460	Analysis of bank documents
Cash drawings	**missing**	
Cash at 31 March	520	Allen Harper
Bank at 31 March	**missing**	

The information in Figure 32.2 can be used to prepare a cash book summary, even though Allen does not maintain a cash book and some information is missing. The cash book summary is shown in Figure 32.3. The opening balances for the cash and bank account are entered on the debit side of the summary. The cash sales and receipts from debtors are also entered on the debit side. On the credit side of the summary, the cash and bank payments to creditors, the cash and cheques paid for expenses and drawings from the bank are all entered. However, there are two missing figures on the credit side. Both the amount of cash drawings and the closing bank balance are unknown.

In order to find the missing amounts, both sides of the cash book summary are totalled. Because the two sides must balance, the missing amounts are the balancing figures in the cash account and the bank account respectively. Therefore cash drawings must be £5,870 and the bank account balance c/d must be £920. The completed cash book summary is shown below and the two balancing figures are shown in bold.

Figure 32.3 *Cash book summary for Allen Harper*

	Debit			CASH BOOK		Credit		
Date	Details	Cash	Bank	Date	Details	Cash	Bank
		£	£			£	£
1.4	Balances b/d	480	2,310		Payments to creditors	1,540	12,190
	Cash sales	8,320			Expenses	870	2,430
	Receipts from debtors		19,690		Drawings	**5,870**	6,460
				31.3	Balances c/d	520	**920**
		8,800	22,000			8,800	22,000

Figure 32.4 *Financial information supplied by Victoria O'Keefe*

	£
Cash at I January	210
Bank at I January	920
Cash sales	3,410
Cheques received from debtors	20,000
Cheques paid to creditors	8,190
Cash paid to creditors	1,110
Cheques paid for expenses	2,830
Bank drawings	530
Cash drawings	**missing**
Cash at 31 December	520
Bank at 31 December	**missing**

Victoria O'Keefe runs a small restaurant in Southend. She does not keep a cash book, but Victoria can supply a full set of bank records and a certain amount of information regarding transactions. She receives both cash and cheques for sales. She uses both cheques and cash to make payments. Victoria does not know exactly how much she has taken from the business for personal use and she is not aware of the closing bank balance. A summary of the information supplied by Victoria O'Keefe is shown in Figure 32.4. Her financial year runs from I January to 31 December.

(a) Prepare a cash book summary for Victoria O'Keefe's business.
(b) Calculate the (i) cash drawings; (ii) the closing bank balance.
(c) Explain how an accountant might determine how much was paid by cheque to creditors, and for expenses.

Calculating purchases and sales

In order to produce a set of accounts for a business, the totals of cash and credit sales and purchases must be known. Business owners can often provide totals for cash sales and cash purchases if they keep till rolls and receipts. In order to find the total of credit sales and credit purchases, control accounts can be used.

To illustrate how the total of credit sales can be calculated, consider the example of Maureen Perkins, a frozen food wholesaler. At the beginning of the last financial year, she knew that her customers owed her business £1,870. She also knew from her cash book that customers had paid £23,210 for goods bought on credit during the year. Finally, after checking customer accounts, she knew that £2,390 was owed to the business at the end of the year. This information can be used to construct a **sales ledger control account** or debtors control account and therefore determine the total of credit sales for the year. The account is shown in Figure 32.5. Given that the total on the credit side of the account is £25,600, the sales figure on the debit side must be £23,730 in order for the account to balance.

Figure 32.5 *Calculating credit sales for Maureen Perkins' business*

Dr		Sales Ledger Control Account		Cr
		£		£
1.1	Balances b/d	1,870	Receipts from debtors	23,210
	Sales	**23,730**	31.12 Balances c/d	2,390
		25,600		25,600

It is possible to calculate the total of credit sales without constructing a sales ledger control account. Using the same example as above, the credit sales can be determined by using the following equation.

Credit sales for the year = Debtors at end of year + receipts from debtors - debtors at beginning of year

Credit sales for the year = £2,390 + £23,210 - £1,870

$$= £23,730$$

The total of credit purchases can be determined in a similar way to credit sales. Suppose, for example, that Maureen Perkins knew her business owed £910 to suppliers at the beginning of the year and £1,430 at the end of the year, and that she had paid £13,520 to suppliers for credit purchases during the year. Using this information, a **purchases ledger control account** or creditors control account can be constructed. The account is shown in Figure 32.6. Given that the total on the debit side is £14,950, the total of purchases must be £14,040 for the account to balance.

Figure 32.6 *Calculating credit purchases for Maureen Perkins' business*

	Dr	Purchases Ledger Control Account		Cr	
		£			£
	Payments to creditors	13,520	1.1 Balances b/d		910
31.12	Balances c/d	1,430	**Purchases**		**14,040**
		14,950			14,950

It is also possible to calculate total purchases for Maureen Perkins' business without constructing a purchases ledger control account. The method is shown below.

Credit purchases for the year   = Creditors at end of year + total paid to creditors - creditors at beginning of year

Credit purchases for the year   = £1,430 + £13,520 - £910

$$= £14,040$$

QUESTION 2

Matthew Grant runs a small engineering company that makes components for tractor manufacturers. At the beginning of the last financial year, on 1 January, he knew that customers owed his business £12,880. He also knew from his cash book that customers had paid £213,210 for goods bought on credit during the year. Finally, after checking customer accounts, he knew that £11,390 was owed to the business at the end of the year.

(a) Calculate the total of sales by preparing a sales ledger control account.

(b) After a further check of his figures, Matthew Grant realised that he had omitted a debtor from the debtors list at the year end. The amount owed by this debtor was £890. What effect would this have on the total of sales for the year?

Accounting ratios

It is sometimes possible to use **accounting ratios** (see unit 44) when producing accounts from incomplete records. Two ratios that are particularly helpful when calculating sales and purchases are the following.

- GROSS (PROFIT) MARGIN. This can be expressed as the ratio of gross profit to selling price. It is usually expressed in percentage terms, ie gross profit as a percentage of the selling price. Sometimes it is simply known as the gross margin.
- MARK-UP. This is the amount by which the cost of a good has been increased to arrive at the selling price. It can be expressed either as the ratio of gross profit to purchase cost or as gross profit as a percentage of cost of sales.

For example, suppose a business buys an item of stock for £80 and sells it for £100, so making a gross profit of £20. The relationship between cost of sales, gross profit and selling price is given by:

$$\text{Selling price} = \text{cost of sales} + \text{gross profit}$$
$$£100 = £80 + £20$$

The gross (profit) margin is given by:

$$\text{Gross profit margin} = \frac{\text{Gross profit}}{\text{Selling price}} \times 100$$

$$= \frac{£20}{£100} \times 100 = 20\% \; (\text{or } \tfrac{1}{5})$$

The mark-up is given by:

$$\text{Mark-up} = \frac{\text{Gross profit}}{\text{Cost of sales}} \times 100$$

$$= \frac{£20}{£80} \times 100 = 25\% \; (\text{or } \tfrac{1}{4})$$

To illustrate how accountants use ratios to calculate the totals of sales or purchases when records are incomplete, consider the following example. Jamil Khan is a retailer who can supply the following information relating to the past trading year:
- mark-up = 25%;
- purchases = £54,000;
- opening stock = £4,890;
- closing stock = £5,210.

Sales The total sales for the year can be found by working out the cost of sales and then adding on the gross profit. In this example, set out in the table below, cost of sales are £53,680.

	£
Opening stock	4,890
Plus purchases	54,000
	58,890
Less closing stock	5,210
Cost of sales	53,680

Then, using the equation for mark-up from above and rearranging it, gross profit is calculated.

$$\text{Mark-up} = \frac{\text{Gross profit}}{\text{Cost of sales}} \times 100$$

So:

$$\text{Gross profit} = \frac{\text{Mark-up} \times \text{Cost of sales}}{100}$$

$$= \frac{25 \times £53,680}{100}$$

$$= £13,420$$

Total sales can now be calculated by adding the gross profit to the cost of sales.

$$\text{Total sales} = £13,420 + £53,680 = £67,100$$

Purchases To illustrate how the total purchases can be found when records are incomplete, consider again the example of Jamil Khan. The following financial information comes from a previous trading year:
- opening stock = £2,600;
- gross margin = 30%;
- closing stock = £2,800;
- sales = £80,000;

In order to determine total purchases, a trading account for Jamil Khan must be prepared (see Figure 32.7).

Figure 32.7 *Statement of corrected net profit for Bookends*

Jamil Khan
Trading Account

	£	£
Sales		80,000
Opening stock	2,600	
Purchases	**56,200**	
	58,800	
Closing stock	**2,800**	
Cost of sales		**56,000**
Gross profit (30% × £80,000)		24,000

The sales total, opening stock and closing stock are all given, so they can be entered in the account. Some figures have to be calculated. The gross profit is calculated by taking 30% of the sales revenue (£24,000 = 30% of £80,000). The cost of sales is then found by subtracting the gross profit from sales (£56,000 = £80,000 - £24,000). It is now possible to work out purchases using the equation below.

$$\text{Cost of sales} = \text{opening stock} + \text{purchases} - \text{closing stock}$$

So:

$$\text{Purchases} = \text{cost of sales} - \text{opening stock} + \text{closing stock}$$
$$= £56,000 - £2,600 + 2,800$$
$$= £56,200$$

QUESTION 3

Kim Williams runs a toy shop in Richmond, North Yorkshire. She operates with a gross profit margin of 40%. At the end of the financial year, 31 December, she provided her accountant with the following information.
- sales = £120,000;
- opening stock = £15,340;
- closing stock = £17,450.

(a) Prepare a trading account for Kim Williams' business.
(b) Calculate the mark-up used by Kim Williams.

Preparing final accounts from incomplete records

When preparing final accounts from incomplete records it is useful to adopt a consistent approach. This involves a series of steps:
- identifying the missing information;
- using the techniques already described to calculate the missing figures;
- preparing a trading and profit and loss account;
- preparing a balance sheet.

To illustrate this approach, consider the example of Angela Rice. She owns a shop which sells greetings cards, wrapping materials and small gifts. Angela does not use a double entry system to record transactions, but she can provide the information listed below.

- All of her sales are for cash. According to records from till rolls, the total of sales for the year ending 31 December 2001 was £49,420. She banked £21,500 and used the rest for the payment of expenses and for drawings.
- During the year, £20,050 was paid by cheque to suppliers for purchases of cards, gifts and

wrapping materials.
- General expenses of £1,400 were paid in cash and £1,600 by cheque.
- Wages of £4,000 were paid to part-time staff in cash.
- Fixtures and fittings at the beginning of the year had a book value of £1,200. Each year £200 is written off for depreciation.
- Additional information relating to assets and liabilities is shown in the table below.

	31.12.01	1.1.01
	£	£
Stock	1,620	1,410
Bank balance	n/a	1,340
Cash balance	360	240
Trade creditors	1,300	980
Outstanding loan (from parents)	2,000	2,000

Identifying the missing information The first task when attempting to produce final accounts from incomplete records is to identify what information is missing. In this example, the missing information includes:
- opening capital;
- closing bank balance;
- drawings;
- purchases.

 If it is not clear what information is missing, one technique is to draw up the trading and profit and loss account and balance sheet and insert the figures that are clearly available. The missing figures can be identified by the gaps that appear in the accounts.

Calculating the missing figures The figures that are missing can be calculated by using the techniques outlined in this unit and in unit 31.

 The **opening capital** can be found by producing a statement of affairs for Angela's business on 1 January, ie the first day of her trading year. It involves listing the assets of the business and then subtracting the liabilities. This is shown in Figure 32.8. According to the statement, the total of capital at the beginning of the financial year was £1,210.

Figure 32.8 *Statement of affairs for Angela Rice's business*   ● ● ●

Angela Rice
Statement of Affairs
as at 1.1.01

	£	£
Fixed assets		
Fixtures and fittings		1,200
Current assets		
Stock	1,410	
Cash at bank	1,340	
Cash in hand	240	
		2,990
		4,190
Less current liabilities		
Trade creditors		980
		3,210
Less long term liabilities		
Loan from parents		2,000
Net assets		1,210
Financed by		
Capital		1,210

The total of **drawings** and the **closing bank balance** can be found by preparing a cash book summary. This is done by listing the total receipts and total payments for the year, and balancing the accounts (see Figure 32.9).

- The opening cash and bank balances are b/d on 1 January.
- The debit side has two other entries. These represent the total cash sales for the year, £49,420, and the proportion of this paid into the bank, £21,500. The money paid into the bank is shown as a contra entry (see unit 12) because it is an internal transfer within the cash book from the cash account to the bank account.
- On the credit side there are cash payments of £4,000 for wages and £1,400 for expenses. The contra entry for the £21,500 cash paid into the bank is also shown.
- The credit side also shows cheque payments of £20,050 paid to creditors and £1,600 for expenses.
- Because the cash book summary must balance, the figures for drawings and bank balance c/d can be calculated. They are both shown in bold. Drawings are £22,400 and the closing bank balance is £1,190.

Figure 32.9 *Cash book summary for Angela Rice's business*

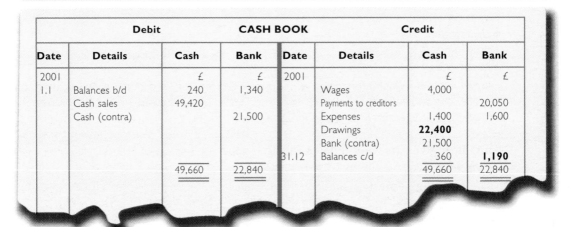

Debit				CASH BOOK		Credit		
Date	Details	Cash	Bank	Date	Details	Cash	Bank
2001		£	£	2001		£	£
1.1	Balances b/d	240	1,340		Wages	4,000	
	Cash sales	49,420			Payments to creditors		20,050
	Cash (contra)		21,500		Expenses	1,400	1,600
					Drawings	**22,400**	
					Bank (contra)	21,500	
				31.12	Balances c/d	360	**1,190**
		49,660	22,840			49,660	22,840

The total **purchases** can be found by preparing a purchases ledger control account (see Figure 32.10). The total of creditors at the beginning and at the end of the year is known. The amount paid to suppliers is also known. This means that the balancing figure on the account will represent the total of purchases for the year. It is £20,370 and is shown in bold.

Figure 32.10 *Purchases ledger control account for Angela Rice's business*

Dr		Purchases Ledger Control Account		Cr
2001		£	2001	£
	Payments to suppliers	20,050	1.1 Balances b/d	980
31.12	Balances c/d	1,300	**Purchases**	**20,370**
		21,350		21,350

Preparing a trading and profit and loss account There is now enough information to prepare the trading and profit and loss account. This is shown in Figure 32.11. The total sales, £49,420, is the first entry in the account. This figure was provided by Angela Rice along with the opening and closing stock values. The opening stock is added to purchases, calculated above, and then closing stock is subtracted to give the cost of sales, £20,160. This is subtracted from sales to give a gross profit of £29,260 (£49,420 - £20,160). Finally, the expenses are listed and subtracted from gross profit to determine net profit. Notice that depreciation has been included and that general expenses include both cash and cheque payments (£1,400 + £1,600). The net profit made by Angela Rice's business is £22,060. This is used in the balance sheet to calculate capital employed.

Figure 32.11 *Trading and profit and loss account for Angela Rice's business*

Angela Rice
Trading and Profit and Loss Account
for the year ended 31.12.01

	£	£
Sales		49,420
Opening stock	1,410	
Purchases	20,370	
	21,780	
Less closing stock	1,620	
Cost of sales		20,160
Gross profit		29,260
Less expenses		
Wages	4,000	
General expenses	3,000	
Depreciation	200	
		7,200
Net profit		22,060

Preparing a balance sheet The final step in drawing up final accounts is to prepare the balance sheet for Angela Rice's business (see Figure 32.12). The only fixed asset on the balance sheet is fixtures and fittings. £200 depreciation is subtracted from the book value at the beginning of the year. This gives a value on 31 December of £1,000 (£1,200 - £200). The figure for the bank balance (£1,190) is the closing balance that comes from the cash book summary. When the liabilities are subtracted from assets, the value of net assets can be determined. It is £870.

Figure 32.12 *Balance sheet for Angela Rice's business*

Angela Rice
Balance Sheet as at 31.12.01

	£	£
Fixed assets		
Fixtures and fittings at cost	1,200	
Less depreciation	200	1,000
Current assets		
Stock	1,620	
Cash at bank	1,190	
Cash in hand	360	
	3,170	
Current liabilities		
Trade creditors	1,300	
Net current assets		1,870
		2,870
Less long term liabilities		
Loan from parents		2,000
Net assets		870
Financed by		
Capital		
Opening capital		1,210
Add net profit		22,060
		23,270
Less drawings		22,400
Capital employed		870

The opening capital in the balance sheet (£1,210) is the figure obtained from the statement of affairs. The net profit for the year (£22,060) from the trading and profit and loss account is added to opening capital to give a total of £23,270. To determine the closing capital, ie capital employed, drawings of £22,400 are subtracted. The total of drawings is obtained from the cash book summary. Closing capital is £870. This is the same as net assets, and therefore indicates that the balance sheet is correct.

QUESTION 4

Clive Cox owns a fruit and vegetable wholesale business in Chester. He supplies retailers, hotels and public houses in the area. Clive buys his produce from a market in Liverpool and pays by cheque. He does not use the double entry system when recording transactions but can provide the following financial information relating to the year ending 31 December 2001.

1. According to bank statements and cheque counterfoils, the total of purchases for the year was £34,070.
2. At the beginning of the year, customers owed the business £2,300. At the end of the year this had risen to £3,290. The total of cash sales was £12,310 during the year and £54,700 was received in cheques from customers.
3. General expenses of £3,290 were paid in cash and £3,200 by cheque.
4. A total of £1,300 was paid in direct debits for mortgage interest.
5. Wages of £14,000 were paid by cheque to two part-time staff. However, a total of £240 was owing to one member of staff.
6. Premises at the beginning of the year had a book value of £56,000. Each year £4,000 is written off for depreciation.
7. Additional information relating to assets and liabilities is shown in the table below.

	31.12.01	1.1.01
	£	£
Stock	2,110	2,360
Bank balance	n/a	2,440
Cash balance	2,430	1,660
Mortgage	20,000	20,000

(a) Prepare a statement of affairs as at 1.1.01 to determine the opening capital.
(b) Produce a cash book summary to determine the closing bank balance and the total of cash drawings.
(c) Produce a sales ledger control account to determine the total of credit sales for the year. Add this figure to cash sales to give the overall total sales.
(d) Prepare a trading and profit and loss account for Clive Cox's business.
(e) Prepare a balance sheet for Clive Cox's business.

A further example of preparing final accounts

When preparing final accounts from incomplete records, the missing information might not be the same as in the examples so far. To illustrate a different type of problem, consider the example of George McGregor, a timber merchant operating from a timber yard in Dundee. George set up his business on 1 January 2001. He opened a business bank account and deposited £12,000 of his savings to use as start-up capital. He also took out a bank loan for £7,000. The following information is provided regarding his first year of trading.

1. George decided not to offer trade credit in his first year, but all his purchases were on credit. He operated with a 50% mark-up to determine the selling price of his timber.
2. All takings were banked except for his drawings plus wages of £2,400 which were paid for casual labour and £870 for general expenses.
3. The value of stock on 31 December 2001 was £4,240.
4. A annual depreciation allowance of £500 was made on the van.
5. On 31 December, George held £860 in cash and owed £2,600 to timber suppliers.
6. The total of bank receipts and payments are given in the table below.

	£
Receipts	
Takings banked	82,400
Payments	
Van	5,000
Purchases	65,400
Interest	900
Rent	6,000
General expenses	3,620

Identifying the missing information In this example, the information needed to prepare the final accounts are the figures for:

• purchases;
• sales;
• drawings;
• closing bank balance.

Calculating the missing figures Note that a statement of affairs is not needed in this example. This is because the opening capital is known. It is the £12,000 put into the business by the owner on 1 January.

To calculate the total **purchases**, a purchases ledger control account can be used (see Figure 32.13). The opening balance is zero because it was the first year of the business. The amount paid for purchases during the year was £65,400 and the amount owed at the end of the year to creditors was £2,600. The balancing figure in the account, £68,000, represents purchases for the year.

Figure 32.13 *Purchases ledger control account for George McGregor's business*

Dr	**Purchases Ledger Control Account**		**Cr**
2001	£	**2001**	£
Payments to suppliers	65,400	1.1 Balances b/d	0
31.12 Balances c/d	2,600	**Purchases**	**68,000**
	68,000		68,000

The total **sales** is calculated below. The closing stock is first subtracted from purchases to work out the cost of sales. Then, applying the 50% mark-up gives the gross profit which is added to the cost of sales to give the total sales figure.

		£
Opening stock		0
Purchases		68,000
		68,000
Less closing stock		4,240
Cost of sales		63,760

$$\text{Gross profit} = \frac{\text{Mark-up} \times \text{Cost of sales}}{100}$$

$$= \frac{50 \times £63,760}{100}$$

$$= £31,880$$

$$\text{Total sales} = \text{Gross profit} + \text{Cost of sales}$$

$$= £31,880 + £63,760$$

$$= £95,640$$

To determine the total **drawings** and the **closing bank balance**, a cash book summary can be prepared (see Figure 32.14). The opening balances are zero since the business was in its first year. After payments and receipts are recorded, drawings must be £9,110 and the balance on the bank account must be £20,480 in order for the cash book to balance. These figures are both shown in bold.

Figure 32.14 *Cash book summary for George McGregor's business*

	Debit				CASH BOOK		Credit	
Date	Details	Cash	Bank	Date	Details	Cash	Bank
2001		£	£	2001		£	£
1.1	Balances b/d	0	0		Payments to creditors		65,400
	Capital		12,000		General expenses	870	3,620
	Bank loan		7,000		Rent		6,000
	Sales	95,640			Casual labour	2,400	
	Cash (contra)		82,400		Bank (contra)	82,400	
					Van		5,000
					Interest		900
					Drawings	**9,110**	
				31.12	Balances c/d	860	**20,480**
		95,640	101,400			95,640	101,400

Preparing a trading and profit and loss account Now that the missing information has been determined, the trading and profit and loss account can be prepared to find the net profit. This is shown in Figure 32.15. The trading account includes the sales and purchases figures calculated above. The gross profit is £31,880. The net profit is calculated by subtracting all the expenses shown in the cash book summary plus the depreciation allowance. The net profit made by George McGregor's business in his first year of trading as a timber merchant was £17,590.

Figure 32.15 *Trading and profit and loss account for George McGregor's business*

George McGregor
Trading and Profit and Loss Account
for the year ended 31.12.01

	£	£
Sales		95,640
Opening stock	0	
Purchases	68,000	
	68,000	
Less closing stock	4,240	
Cost of sales		63,760
Gross profit		31,880
Less expenses		
Rent	6,000	
General expenses	4,490	
Interest	900	
Casual labour wages	2,400	
Depreciation	500	
		14,290
Net profit		17,590

Preparing a balance sheet The balance sheet for George McGregor's business is shown in Figure 32.16. The opening capital is the amount that George invested in the business when it was set up at the beginning of the year.

Figure 32.16 *Balance sheet for George McGregor*

George McGregor
Balance Sheet as at 31.12.01

	£	£
Fixed assets		
Fixtures and fittings at cost	5,000	
Less depreciation	500	4,500
Current assets		
Stock	4,240	
Cash at bank	20,480	
Cash in hand	860	
	25,580	
Current liabilities		
Trade creditors	2,600	
Net current assets		22,980
		27,480
Less long term liabilities		
Bank loan		7,000
Net assets		20,480
Financed by		
Capital		
Opening capital		12,000
Add net profit		17,590
		29,590
Less drawings		9,110
Capital employed		20,480

Accounting for missing stock

Businesses sometimes lose stock because of theft or due to events such as fire and flood. If a quantity of stock is lost, its value must be determined in order to prepare the final accounts. The missing stock value will also be needed to make an insurance claim. If proper and up-to-date stock records are kept, the value of missing stock can be determined relatively easily by conducting a **stocktake**. This involves comparing the actual amount of stock present with the records of what stock should be present. However, some businesses do not keep up-to-date records. Therefore the value of missing stock must be determined by using the accounting techniques already outlined.

In order to illustrate how the value of missing stock might be determined, consider the example of Leonard Potts, a watchmaker. During a burglary at his workshop, the entire stock of watches was stolen. His stock was last valued at the end of the previous financial year, 31 December 2000, when it was worth £4,100. The theft occurred on 12 April 2001. Leonard had kept some financial records and knew that the current year's sales up until the burglary were £24,000. During that time he had also made purchases of £11,900. Leonard operates with a gross profit margin of 60%.

To work out the value of missing stock, the gross profit and cost of sales first need to be calculated.

- The **gross profit** can be found using the gross profit margin. It is given by the equation:

    Gross profit = sales × gross profit margin
    Gross profit = £24,000 × 60% = £14,400

- The **cost of sales** is the difference between gross profit and sales. It is given by:

    Cost of sales = sales - gross profit
    Cost of sales = £24,000 - £14,400
    = £9,600

- In this example, the **missing stock** is the same as the closing stock because it was all stolen. It is equivalent to the difference between the cost of sales and the total of purchases and opening stock added together. It is given by:

    Closing stock = (purchases + opening stock) - cost of sales
    Closing stock = (£11,900 + £4,100) - £9,600
    = £16,000 - £9,600
    = **£6,400**

The trading account for the period ending 12 April 2001 is shown in Figure 32.17. It shows the relationship between the gross profit, cost of sales and closing stock calculated above.

Figure 32.17 *Trading account for Leonard Potts' business*

Leonard Potts
Trading Account
for the period ended 12.4.01

	£	£
Sales		24,000
Opening stock	4,100	
Purchases	11,900	
	16,000	
Less *closing stock*	**6,400**	
Cost of sales		9,600
Gross profit		14,400

When drawing up the trading and profit and loss account, the missing stock must be taken into consideration. In the trading account, when calculating the cost of sales, the closing stock must include any missing stock in order to calculate the gross profit accurately. **In the profit and loss account, missing stock is written off as an expense when working out the net profit.** However, missing stock is not included in the balance sheet because it cannot be considered an asset.

Accounting for missing cash

If a business loses some of its cash, the amount can usually be determined if there is an accurate record of all cash transactions. In order to illustrate how to calculate an amount of missing cash, consider the example of Ruth Watts, a newsagent. She suspects that cash has been stolen from her business, but is not sure of the amount or by whom. She can provide the following information regarding cash transactions.

	£
Cash balance at 1 January	1,060
Cash balance at 31 December	740
Cash sales	98,430
Cash purchases	12,450
Cash banked	48,190
Drawings	12,000
Wages	11,610
Other cash payments	8,430

A summary of the cash account for Ruth Watts' business is shown in Figure 32.18. The opening and closing balances are entered and all the payments and receipts made in cash are listed. As the summary shows, the amount of missing cash, shown in bold, is £6,070. This is the balancing figure in the account. When the final accounts are prepared, the missing cash will be written off in the profit and loss account as an expense.

Figure 32.18 *A summary of the cash account for Ruth Watts' business*

Debit			CASH BOOK	Credit	
Date	**Details**	**Cash**	**Date**	**Details**	**Cash**
2001		£	2001		£
1.1	Balance b/d	1,060		Purchases	12,450
	Sales	98,430		Bank	48,190
				Drawings	12,000
				Wages	11,610
				Other payments	8,430
				Missing cash	**6,070**
			31.12	Balance c/d	740
		99,490			99,490

summary questions

1. What is a cash book summary?
2. Give two examples of missing figures that could be found by using a cash book summary.
3. At the beginning of the year, customers owed a business £3,890. By the end of the year this had risen to £4,220. If £43,290 was paid by customers during the year, what was the total of sales?
4. At the beginning of the year, a business owed suppliers £340. By the end of the year this had risen to £1,790. If £21,450 was paid to suppliers during the year, what was the total of purchases?
5. A business buys a product for £12 and sells it for £15. What is the mark-up?
6. A business makes a gross profit of £24,000 on sales of £68,000. What is the gross profit margin?
7. What is the relationship between gross profit margin and mark-up?
8. How can the opening capital be determined for a business that does not keep complete records?
9. How can the value of missing stock be determined by a business?
10. How can the total of missing cash be determined by a business?

key terms

Gross profit margin - the ratio of gross profit to selling price; in percentage terms it is gross profit as a percentage of sales turnover.

Mark-up - the ratio of gross profit to purchase cost; in percentage terms it is gross profit as a percentage of total purchases.

UNIT ASSESSMENT   QUESTION 1

Helen Wallace runs a public house called the College Arms in west London. The pub is leased from a local brewery and was taken over by Helen in 1999. Although Helen built up trade and made the business profitable, she experienced staffing problems. At the end of the trading year, 31 July 2001, she provided her accountant with the information that is listed below. During the preparation of the final accounts, the accountant told Helen that some cash was missing.

1. All sales are for cash. During the year ending 31 July 2001, takings amounted to £126,000 of which £93,070 were banked.
2. The total of payments to creditors by cheque was £63,000.
3. Helen withdrew £10,400 cash for personal use.
4. Wages paid in cash were £17,200.
5. The leasing charge made by the brewery for premises was £15,000. It was paid by standing order through the bank.
6. A vehicle that is owned by the business is depreciated using the straight line method. The annual charge is £1,000.
7. General expenses were a total of £5,830, of which £1,720 was paid in cash and the rest by cheque.
8. The total paid for heat and light for the year by cheque was £3,220. However, £310 was still owing at the end of the year.
9. Details of assets and liabilities are given below.

	31.7.01	1.8.00
	£	£
Vehicle (historical cost)	7,000	7,000
Stock	6,220	5,160
Bank	n/a	1,220
Cash	1,020	810
Trade creditors	3,140	2,460

(a) Prepare a statement of affairs as at 1.8.00 to determine the opening capital for Helen's business.

(b) Prepare a cash book summary and determine the amount of missing cash and the closing bank balance.

(c) Calculate the total purchases for the year.

(d) Prepare a trading and profit and loss account for Helen's business and identify the missing cash.

(e) Prepare a balance sheet for Helen's business.

UNIT ASSESSMENT   QUESTION 2

Sara Jarvis set up in business on 1 March 2001 with £10,000 of her own capital and a £5,000 bank loan. She leased a retail unit in a new shopping centre in Ipswich and sold casual wear aimed at the young adults market. Sara's strategy was to generate business by undercutting competitors in the area. She reckoned that if she operated with a 30% gross profit margin this would be significantly lower than her rivals. The shop was successful but it was clear to Sara that some stock was being stolen. At the end of the first year of trading she provided the following financial information to her accountant.

1. Total sales for the year were £93,000. Of this £71,670 was banked. There were no credit customers.
2. At the end of the year, the business owed trade creditors £12,310.
3. Rent paid by cheque was £13,000 of which £1,000 related to the next trading year.
4. Sara had not kept a record of cash drawings.
5. Sundry expenses of £2,100 had been paid with cash.
6. Fixtures and fittings are depreciated using the straight line method with an annual charge of £1,000.
7. The business had £2,780 in cash at the end of the year.
8. The value of Sara's stock at the end of the year was £10,500. This does not include the missing stock.
9. A summary of the bank account for the year ending 28 February 2002 is given below.

Debit			CASH BOOK	Credit		
Date	**Details**	**Bank**	**Date**	**Details**		**Bank**
2001		£	2001			£
1.3	Balance b/d	0		Purchases		65,620
	Capital	10,000		Rent		13,000
	Loan	5,000		Fixtures and fittings		9,000
	Sales banked	71,670		Heat and light		1,800
2002				Interest		780
28.2	Balance c/d	4,650		Sundry expenses		1,120
		91,320				91,320

For Sara's first year of business:
(a) Calculate the total purchases.
(b) Calculate the value of missing stock.
(c) Calculate the total drawings by preparing a cash account summary.
(d) Prepare a trading and profit and loss account.
(e) Prepare a balance sheet.

unit 33

Types of business organisation

What is a business organisation?

Business organisations sell goods and services to consumers and to other businesses. Most aim to make a profit. There are, however, some organisations such as clubs and societies that are non-profit making. This unit considers the legal structure of these different organisations and compares their advantages and disadvantages. The way organisations present their accounts is explained in units 36, 38 and 39, and their sources of finance are considered in units 34 and 35.

Most business activity in the UK is undertaken in the PRIVATE SECTOR. The private sector includes all businesses that are owned by individuals or groups of individuals. The types of business in the private sector can vary considerably. Some are small retailers with a single owner. Others are large multinational companies with billions of pounds of assets such as Vodafone, HSBC and BP Amoco. The legal structure of businesses in the private sector will vary according to the form of ownership.

- **Unincorporated businesses** These businesses tend to be small, owned by an individual (a sole trader) or a number of partners (a partnership). There is no legal distinction made between the owners of these businesses and the business itself.
- **Incorporated businesses** Incorporated businesses or corporations have a separate legal identity from their owners. These businesses are known as limited companies in the UK and they tend to be larger than sole traders or partnerships. The difference between private limited companies and public limited companies is explained later in the unit.

Figure 33.1 shows the main types of business organisation in the private sector, their legal status and their ownership. Non-profit making organisations such as charities, clubs and societies are not shown. PUBLIC SECTOR organisations are also excluded. These organisations, such as the BBC and NHS, are owned by the government.

Figure 33.1 *Business organisations in the private sector*

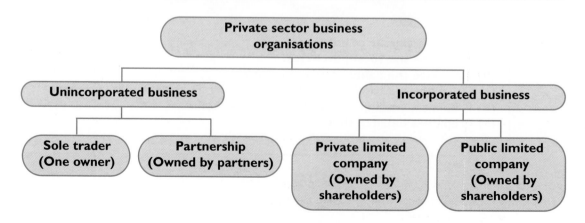

Sole traders

The simplest and most common form of business organisation is owned by a SOLE TRADER or SOLE PROPRIETOR. This is where the business is owned by one person. The owner runs the business but might employ other people to help. Sole traders are found in many different industries. Examples include farmers, fishermen, small scale manufacturers, builders, retailers, financial advisers, restaurant owners, hairdressers, gardeners, interior designers and taxi drivers.

Setting up as a sole trader is straightforward. There are no legal formalities needed. However, sole traders do have some legal responsibilities once they become established. In addition, some types of business need to obtain special permission before trading.

- Once sales revenue reaches a certain level, sole traders must register for VAT (see unit 26).
- Sole traders must pay income tax and National Insurance Contributions.
- Some types of business activity need a licence, such as the sale of alcohol or the operation of a public transport service.
- Sometimes planning permission is needed in certain locations. For example, if a business owner wishes to change the use of premises from a clothes retailer to a fast food outlet, permission from the local authority is needed before trading can begin.
- Sole traders must comply with health and safety legislation, and employment legislation if they employ staff.

There are certain **advantages** to being a sole trader.

- The lack of legal restrictions. A sole trader does not face a lengthy setting up period or incur expensive administration costs.
- Any profit made after tax belongs to the owner.
- The owner is in complete control and is free to make decisions without any interference. Independence is one of the key attractions of running a business.
- A sole trader has flexibility to choose hours of work and the timing of holidays.

However, there are also **disadvantages**.

- A sole trader has UNLIMITED LIABILITY. This means that the owner is personally liable for any business debts. As a result, a sole trader might be forced to sell personal possessions or use personal savings to cover debts incurred by the business.
- Sole traders might have difficulty in raising finance. They are often seen as risky investments by banks and other money providers.
- Although independence is often an advantage, it can also be a disadvantage because decision making and the burden of responsibility are not shared.
- In cases where the sole trader has no employees, if the owner is ill the business might have to close down temporarily. This leads to a loss of revenue and a possible loss of customers.
- Because sole traders are unincorporated businesses, the owner can be sued by customers in the event of a dispute.
- Sole trader businesses cease to exist if the owner withdraws or dies.

Partnerships

A PARTNERSHIP exists when the ownership of a business is shared between at least two people. In most cases, the maximum number of partners is 20, although exceptions occur in certain cases such as accountants and solicitors. Partnerships exist in all types of business but are particularly common amongst professionals such as doctors, accountants, solicitors, estate agents and auctioneers. After sole traders, partnerships form the largest proportion of business organisations in the UK.

There are no legal formalities to complete when forming a partnership. However, partners often draw up a DEED OF PARTNERSHIP. This is a legal document which states partners' rights in the event of a dispute. It covers issues such as:

- how much capital each partner will contribute;
- the rate of interest, if any, to be paid on capital;
- how profits (and losses) will be shared;
- the procedure for ending the partnership;
- partners' salaries;
- how much control each partner has;

QUESTION 1

In June 2001, Beryl Robinson opened a shop in a Birmingham suburb selling camping and hiking equipment. She invested £20,000 of her own money to buy stock, fixtures and fittings and other equipment. Beryl was surprised at how easy it was to start trading. There were no solicitor's fees, planning permission to seek nor any other restrictions. She was confident that her venture would be successful because there was no other similar retailer in the area.

In the first months of trading, Beryl enjoyed the independence associated with running her own business and she looked forward to spending the profits. She worked very hard, often 12 hours a day, 7 days a week. However, despite advertising in the local newspaper, it became clear that sales were too low to continue. So, after 14 months the business was forced to close. At the time of closure, the business's only assets (at cost) were:

Stock	£26,260
Fixtures and fittings	£2,900

(a) Use the accounting equation (Assets - Liabilities = Capital) to calculate the amount of money Beryl's business owed in total.
(b) When the business closed and the stock and fixtures and fittings were disposed of, they only raised £8,000. How would this affect Beryl?
(c) With reference to Beryl's business, outline the advantages and disadvantages of being a sole trader.

- rules for recruiting new partners.

If no deed of partnership is drawn up, the arrangement between partners is subject to the **Partnership Act (1890)**. This states that:
- profits and losses will be shared equally;
- there is no interest to be allowed on capital;
- interest should not be charged on drawings;
- salaries are not allowed;
- a partner who contributes more money than the original capital is entitled to receive 5% interest on the additional amount.

There is a number of **advantages** to forming a partnership.
- There are no legal formalities that must be completed when setting up.
- Partners can specialise. For example, a firm of solicitors with four partners might find that each partner can specialise in one aspect of law such as conveyancing, divorce, criminal law and contract law.
- More finance can be raised since there are more contributors.
- The workload and the burden of responsibility can be shared. For example, partners can share ideas when making decisions.
- Partnerships might find it easier to raise money than sole traders because they tend to be larger businesses.

However, there are also **disadvantages**.
- With the exceptions that are explained below, partners have unlimited liability. Under the provisions of the Partnership Act, business debts are shared equally between partners.
- The more partners there are, the more that profits have to be shared out.
- Partners might disagree. For example, their views might differ regarding the future direction of the business.
- The amount of capital that can be raised from owners is limited by the number of partners.
- Any decision made by one partner is legally binding on all other partners. For example, if one partner signs a contract to lease an office for 5 years, all partners must honour this.
- Partnerships must be wound up when one of the partners dies. This allows the partner's family to retrieve the money invested in the business. It is normal for the remaining partners to form a new partnership afterwards.
- Since partnerships are unincorporated, partners can be sued by customers.

Exceptions to the principle of unlimited liability for partners occur in a relatively small number of cases.

- The **Limited Partnership Act (1907)** allows a business to become a LIMITED PARTNERSHIP if some partners provide capital but take no part in management. These 'sleeping' partners have LIMITED LIABILITY which means that they can only lose the amount of money they invest in the business. In other words, they cannot be made to use personal funds to meet business debts. However, there must always be a least one partner with unlimited liability.
- The **Limited Liability Partnership Act (2000)** allows all the partners in a partnership to have limited liability. However, in order to gain this advantage, the Act requires that a Limited Liability Partnership (LLP) must comply with a number of regulations. For example, it must file its annual accounts with the Registrar of Companies.

QUESTION 2

Chris Smith and Tom Hayden formed a partnership in January 2001. They leased an office in Manchester and advertised their services as financial advisors. Chris was a qualified accountant and Tom was a former Inland Revenue tax inspector. They both contributed £5,000 capital which they used to buy computers and office furniture. A secretary was recruited and the business developed quite rapidly. In the first year of trading, the partnership made £22,600 profit. Most of the income was generated from commission on the sale of pensions. They also charged small companies for tax advice and pension scheme management.

In the second year, Chris and Tom decided to expand the partnership. They recruited a new partner, Kirsten Lavelle, who would be responsible for providing clients with investment advice. She contributed £5,000 of capital. However, the development of the business required some expensive software and Tom contributed a further £3,000 of capital. The partners agreed that it would not be necessary to draw up a Deed of Partnership.

(a) **What is the annual interest on capital that the partners are entitled to in the absence of a Deed of Partnership?**

(b) **In what ways does the case study illustrate the advantages of a partnership?**

(c) **What problems might arise from the decision by the partners not to draw up a Deed of partnership?**

Limited companies

The main feature of a LIMITED COMPANY is that it has a separate legal identity from that of its owners. This means that the company can own assets, form contracts, employ people, sue and be sued in its own right. The owners of a company all have limited liability. Therefore, if the company collapses, they cannot be forced to use personal funds to pay off business debts. They only lose the amount that they originally invested in the company.

The **capital** of a limited company is raised by selling **shares**. The **shareholders** are the joint owners of the company. They are entitled to a share of the profit and some control over the company. The amount of control, and the precise share of profit, is proportionate to the size of the shareholding. Control is exercised through a vote when appointing **directors** to run the company. The board of directors, headed by a **chairperson**, is accountable to shareholders and should run the company in line with shareholder expectations. If the shareholders are unhappy with the performance of the company, directors can be removed from the board when shareholders cast their votes at the **Annual General Meeting (AGM)**.

Forming a limited company involves following a set legal procedure. The first step is to draw up two documents - the **Memorandum of Association** and the **Articles of Association**. The Memorandum sets out the constitution and gives details about the company. The **Companies Act 1985** states that the following details must be included in the Memorandum.

- The name of the company.

- The name and address of the company's registered office.
- The objectives of the company, and the scope of its activities.
- The liability of its members, ie shareholders.
- The amount of capital to be raised and the number of shares to be issued.
- A limited company must have a minimum of two members, but there is no upper limit.

The Articles of Association deal with the internal running of the company. It includes details such as:

- the rights of shareholders;
- the procedures for appointing directors and the scope of their powers;
- the length of time directors can serve before re-election;
- the timing and frequency of company meetings;
- the arrangements for auditing the company's accounts.

The Memorandum and Articles of Association, together with the names of directors, must be sent to the Registrar of Companies. Then, assuming that the documents are in order, the Registrar will award a **Certificate of Incorporation** which allows the company to start trading. Other regulations that a limited company must comply with include an obligation to send a copy of its accounts each year to the Registrar, and to inform shareholders in writing of the date and venue of the AGM.

There are two types of limited company - private limited companies and public limited companies. These are explained in the next two sections.

Private limited companies

PRIVATE LIMITED COMPANIES are not allowed to offer their shares for sale to the public. Their names end in Ltd or Limited. Many private limited companies are family businesses where the family members are the shareholders. Most are relatively small although there are exceptions. Clarks, the shoe manufacturer and retailer is one of the largest private limited companies in the UK with an annual turnover of over £800 million. The directors of private limited companies are often major shareholders and are involved in the running of the business.

There is a number of **advantages** to forming a private limited company.
- Shareholders have limited liability. As a result, more people might be willing to risk their money than in a partnership which does not have limited liability.
- Again, compared with a partnership, it is relatively easy to raise capital in a private limited company because there is no limit to the number of shareholders.
- Control of the company cannot easily be lost to outsiders. This is because shares can only be sold to new members with the agreement of the other shareholders.
- The business can continue even if one of the owners dies because shares can be transferred to other people.

However, there are also **disadvantages.**
- Because there are generally more owners in a private limited company than in a partnership, profits have to be shared out between more people.
- The legal procedures to set up the business take time and cost money.
- Because shares cannot be offered for sale to members of the general public, this might restrict the amount of capital that can be raised.
- Financial information filed with the Registrar of Companies is open to public scrutiny. Competitors might use this to their advantage.
- In practice, it might be difficult for a shareholder to sell shares.

Public limited companies

There are over 1 million limited companies in the UK but only about 1% of them are PUBLIC LIMITED COMPANIES. They tend to be larger than private limited companies, so they contribute far more to national output and employ far more people. Examples include household names such as Cadbury Schweppes plc and Tesco plc. Public limited companies are allowed to sell shares to the public on the **stock market** (see unit 34). The names of these companies end in plc.

QUESTION 3

Simon Parker set up in business in 1997 after leaving his job as a systems analyst for a large supermarket chain. He decided to invest £12,000 of his own money in a business providing software systems. His products were fairly advanced and, since his overheads were low, he was able to market them at a competitive price. He also offered a back-up service which was free of charge for six months after the installation of his software.

By March 2000, Simon's business had grown so much that he could no longer keep up with demand. After consulting his accountant, Simon decided to form a private limited company and invited his two sisters, Julie and Helen, to become shareholders. They each bought 24% of the shares and contributed a total of £10,000 to the business. Simon was the only other shareholder. With the extra money raised from the share issue, and some retained profit, Simon moved his location from Bristol to Reading. Much of the money was used to buy computer equipment so that more staff could be recruited.

Simon was wary about operating as a private limited company because of the formal legal procedure needed to set up. He was also reluctant to disclose private financial information about his company and did not want to be distracted by what he called the 'paper work' when setting up. However, since he was about to sign a 10 year lease on an office in Reading for £50,000, he felt that he needed some financial protection. On 1st July 2000, his company StockSystems Ltd was awarded a Certificate of Incorporation.

(a) Explain why you think Simon decided to form a private limited company.
(b) Why do you think Simon only sold 48% of the shares to his sisters?
(c) Explain what Simon meant by the 'paper work' when forming a limited company.
(d) In December 2000, one of Simon's sisters, Helen, decided to emigrate and wanted to sell all of her shares. Explain why this could create a problem.

In addition to the Memorandum and Articles of Association, a third document is required by the Registrar of Companies when a public limited company is formed. This is called a **statutory declaration** and it states that the requirements of all the relevant Company Acts have been met. When a public limited company has been issued with a Certificate of Incorporation, it then generally publishes a **prospectus**. This is a document which advertises the company to potential investors and invites them to buy shares in a FLOTATION. This process is also known as 'going public'.

'Going public' is expensive for a number of reasons.
- The company needs to hire lawyers to ensure that the prospectus complies with company law.
- A large number of 'glossy' prospectuses have to be sent to potential investors.
- The company is likely to pay a financial institution to process share applications.
- The share issue has to be **underwritten**. This means that the company must insure against the possibility that some shares remain unsold. A fee is paid to the underwriter, who will agree to buy any unsold shares.
- The company might incur promotion and advertising costs to generate interest in the flotation.

A public limited company cannot begin trading until it has completed these tasks and has received at least 25% payment for the value of its shares. It will then receive a Trading Certificate so it can begin operating, and the shares will be quoted on the stock market.

There is a number of **advantages** to forming a public limited company.
- There is no limit to the number of owners so very large amounts of money can be raised from the sale of shares to the public.
- Because of their size, plcs sometimes are able to raise extra finance more cheaply than smaller companies.
- As with private limited companies, all shareholders enjoy limited liability.
- Again, as with private limited companies, if one owner, ie a shareholder dies, the company can carry on trading.

However, there are also **disadvantages**.
- Flotation costs can be very high, often running into millions of pounds.
- The share capital must be a minimum of £50,000.
- Outsiders can take over ownership of plcs if they are able to buy more than 50% of the shares.

- Plcs have to publish much more detailed financial information than private limited companies. Competitors might be able to use some of this information to their advantage.
- Plcs must comply with a range of company legislation which is designed to protect shareholders.

QUESTION 4

Egg is an internet bank. In June 2000, 20% of the shares in the company were floated on the stock market in a wave of publicity. The shares were on offer for £1.60 but, by the end of the first day of trading, they had risen to £1.77. The share issue was oversubscribed which meant that demand for the available shares was greater than the supply. The flotation raised around £86 million for Prudential who had set up Egg eighteen months previously. The flotation also raised £150 million for Egg to use for marketing and acquisitions.

When Egg was originally launched by Prudential, it was a telephone bank based on the model of First Direct. However, technical problems, coupled with huge demand generated by generous interest rates on deposits, forced the company to focus on customers with access to computers. Despite restricting access, Egg recruited over 1 million customers. The company hoped to make a profit by selling these customers other products such as mortgages, insurance and pensions.

Several weeks after the flotation, Egg unveiled losses for the first six months of the year. The bank had lost £80.7 million which sent the share price falling to a low of £1.28 on 26 July 2000. Egg also reported a slowdown in customer growth and a net withdrawal of deposits, due to severe competition from other new online banks.

Source: adapted from the *Financial Times* 12.6.00, 13.6.00 and 27.7.00.

(a) With reference to Egg, suggest two advantages of operating as a public limited company.

(b) Suggest any actual or potential disadvantages of floating Egg from Prudential's point of view.

Other types of business organisation

Retail co-operatives The first retail co-operative in the UK was established in 1844 by a group of workers in Rochdale, Lancashire. They bought food from wholesalers and opened a shop for their members. The profits were shared in proportion to the amount members spent in the shop. The principles of the co-operative were:

- voluntary and open membership;
- democratic ownership, with one member one vote;
- the surplus, or profit, to be distributed according to spending;
- educational facilities to be provided for members and workers.

Today, retail co-operatives are mainly organised on a regional basis. The principles outlined above are still important, with profits being shared according to how much each customer spends in the stores. The co-op is best known for its grocery outlets. However, intense competition from supermarkets has eroded its market share in the last 20 years. The co-operative movement also operates its own bank and an insurance society, together with travel agents, chemists, funeral parlours and opticians.

Mutual organisations These organisations, which include a number of building societies and friendly societies, are owned by their customers, or members, rather than by shareholders. They generally have a policy of reinvesting all their profits to improve customer services and products. However, in recent years, many building societies have 'demutualised' and now operate as plcs. One of the main reasons for this change is to gain access to capital from shareholders.

Clubs and societies Non-profit making organisations such as sports and social clubs exist because their members are drawn together by a common interest. The assets of clubs and societies are the property of the members and most income comes from members' subscriptions. Clubs and societies do not have a profit and loss account because they do not aim to make a profit. However, they are likely to produce an income and expenditure account so that all payments and receipts are accounted for.

Charities Charities exist to support 'worthy' causes. For example, Mencap raises money on behalf of the mentally handicapped and the National Trust promotes the preservation of the national heritage. Charities mainly rely on donations for their revenue but might also organise fund raising events. Some charities run business ventures to raise money. For example, Oxfam runs a chain of charity shops which sells second-hand goods and 'fair trade' items. The Charities Act (1993) introduced regulations to govern the accounting practices of charities.

key terms

Deed of partnership - a legally binding document which states the formal rights of partners.

Flotation - the process of a company 'going public', ie selling shares to the public.

Limited company - a business organisation which has a separate legal identity from that of the owners.

Limited liability - a business owner is only liable for the amount of money invested in the business.

Limited partnership - a partnership in which one or more partners has limited liability. These partners contribute capital and enjoy a share of profit, but do not participate in the running of the business. At least one partner in the business must have unlimited liability.

Partnership - a business organisation which is usually owned by between 2 and 20 people (except in certain professions such as solicitors and accounting where there is no upper limit).

Private limited company - a business organisation that is owned by shareholders who cannot sell their shares without the consent of the other shareholders.

Private sector - businesses that are owned by individuals or groups of individuals.

Public limited company - a business organisation in which shares can be bought by members of the public.

Public sector - organisations that are owned by the government.

Sole trader - an individual who is the sole owner of a business.

Unlimited liability - the owner of a business is personally liable for all business debts.

summary questions

1. What is meant by an unincorporated business?
2. State four advantages of being a sole trader.
3. Explain why independence can be a disadvantage for a sole trader.
4. How much interest on capital is allowed on partner's capital if there is no deed of partnership?
5. State four disadvantages of partnerships.
6. What is meant by a 'sleeping partner'?
7. What is the difference between the Memorandum of Association and the Articles of Association?
8. What is the purpose of a Certificate of Incorporation?
9. What is the main difference between private and public limited companies?
10. How do clubs and societies differ from most business organisations?

UNIT ASSESSMENT QUESTION 1

Kerry Marriot set up in business in 1998 selling antiques in an Oxfordshire village. The success of the business exceeded her expectations and, in the first year of trading, the business made £29,600 profit. In the second year, this rose to £36,700. Kerry reckoned that her success was due to:

- specialising in expensive European furniture;
- having a large number of useful contacts, many of which were through family and friends;
- the ability to extract the highest possible price from customers;
- the development of a loyal customer base;
- the quality of the personal service she provided;
- her expert buying skills based on having a good 'eye' for a bargain.

Kerry was enthusiastic and extremely ambitious, with a long term aim of building a chain of antiques shops. However, she felt that she could not do this alone. Most of the buying was done at weekends and in the evenings. She spent most weekdays in the shop serving customers. She relied on her mother at weekends to be in charge of the shop but noticed that the prices her mother negotiated with customers were not as high as she could obtain. Her mother was willing to help out but she did not want a long term commitment.

Kerry felt that the way forward was to form a partnership. She knew two people who might be interested. They both owned antiques shops in the Oxfordshire area and seemed honest and reliable. However, they would have to share the same ambitions and business views as herself. Kerry also believed that it would be important to draw up some form of partnership agreement since there would be a lot of money at stake.

(a) Why do you think Kerry needed to change her business from a sole trader to a partnership?
(b) Why do you think Kerry felt the need to draw up a partnership agreement?
(c) What information might be included in the partnership agreement?
(d) What might be the drawbacks to Kerry of forming a partnership in this case?

UNIT ASSESSMENT QUESTION 2

One of the most successful business start-ups in recent years has been the development of Carphone Warehouse, the mobile phone retailer. The business was started in 1989 by Charles Dunstone in a Marylebone flat with £6,000 of savings. It is now a pan-European retailer of mobile phones and accessories, with 800 outlets and an annual revenue of over £700 million. On July 14th 2000, the company was floated on the stock market. Before that date, Carphone Warehouse was a private limited company. The investment bank handling the issue was Credit Suisse First Boston. The shares were priced at £2.00 each which valued the company at around £1.6 billion. Carphone raised £185 million from the flotation and Charles Dunstone, the chairman, and David Ross, the chief operating officer, made £56.3 million and £39.4 million respectively.
Source: adapted from the *Financial Times* 27.6.00, 15.7.00 and 18.7.00.

(a) Outline the benefits of going public to: (i) the founder; (ii) Carphone Warehouse.
(b) With reference to Carphone Warehouse, what are the actual and potential disadvantages of going public?

unit 34

Business finance–share capital

unitobjectives

To understand:
- the sources of business finance;
- the nature and types of shares;
- share capital;
- the bookkeeping records needed for share issues;
- stock markets.

Sources of finance

New businesses need funds to buy equipment, raw materials and premises. Once established and successful, businesses then often require additional finance to expand.

Figure 34.1 is a summary of the sources of finance that are available to businesses. These sources can be divided into **internal sources**, ie arising from inside the business, and **external sources**, ie arising from outside the business. The external sources of finance are often classified into long term sources, such as share capital, and short term sources such as bank overdrafts. This unit looks at share capital in detail. Unit 35 looks at the other sources of finance.

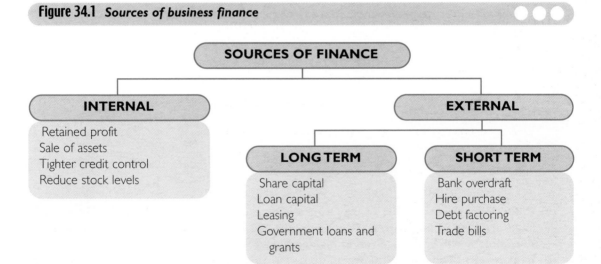

Figure 34.1 *Sources of business finance*

SOURCES OF FINANCE

INTERNAL
- Retained profit
- Sale of assets
- Tighter credit control
- Reduce stock levels

EXTERNAL

LONG TERM
- Share capital
- Loan capital
- Leasing
- Government loans and grants

SHORT TERM
- Bank overdraft
- Hire purchase
- Debt factoring
- Trade bills

Types of shares

Limited companies can raise capital by selling shares. Share capital is sometimes referred to as **permanent capital**. This is because it is rarely **redeemed**, ie it is not repaid by the company. It is only when shares are first sold, ie when they are **issued**, that a company raises capital from their sale. When shares are subsequently sold 'secondhand', money is simply transferred between the buyer and the seller. No money is paid to the company.

In return for owning shares, shareholders are paid a **dividend**. This is a share of the company's profit. In the UK, it is usual for companies to pay a dividend every six months. The largest portion is generally paid at the end of the financial year and is known as a final dividend. A smaller portion, paid half way through the year, is known as an interim dividend.

Ordinary shares These are the most common type of shares. The ordinary share capital of a company is sometimes known as its **equity**. Ordinary shares are said to be the riskiest form of shareholding because the dividend on the shares is discretionary and variable. This means that the directors of a company might decide not to pay a dividend if the company makes a loss, or if they decide to reinvest the profit in the business. However, if a company is successful, there is no upper limit to the dividend payment that ordinary shareholders might receive.

Many shareholders in public limited companies buy shares to make a CAPITAL GAIN, ie they hope to sell the shares at a higher price than they paid for them. Often, for short-term investors, the prospect of a capital gain is more important than the size of dividends. It is possible, however, that a share price might fall for a variety of reasons, such as a decline in profits or fears of a recession in the wider economy. In this case, a capital loss is made.

Ordinary shareholders are usually entitled to vote at a company's Annual General Meeting (AGM). They exercise control by electing, or re-electing, the board of directors who oversee the management of the company.

Preference shares Preference shareholders are subject to less risk than ordinary shareholders. This is because their dividend is paid before ordinary shareholders receive their share of profits. The dividend on preference shares is generally fixed. For example, the owners of 4% £1 preference shares will receive 4p (ie 4% x £1) for every share they own, assuming that a dividend is paid. Because dividends are fixed, the price of preference shares tends to be less volatile than ordinary shares.

Preference shareholders usually carry preferential rights if a company is **liquidated**, ie if it ceases to trade and its assets are sold. This means that capital is repaid to them before ordinary shareholders, providing there is any money left. In most cases, preference shareholders do not have any voting rights at a company's Annual General Meeting.

There are several different types of preference share.
- **Cumulative preference shares** - these entitle shareholders to receive any dividends not paid in previous years. For example, if a dividend is not declared for one year, cumulative preference shareholders are entitled to the arrears in the next year that a dividend is paid.
- **Participating preference shares** - these entitle the holder to extra dividends in addition to the fixed rate. The extra payments are only paid after ordinary shareholders have received their dividend.
- **Redeemable preference shares** - the issuing company has the right to redeem these shares. This means that shareholders receive back the money for their shares at a future date.

QUESTION 1

Crenshaw Holdings plc owns a chain of newsagents in the UK. The company made profits of £12.6 million in 2001 and declared dividends to both preference and ordinary shareholders. Ordinary shareholders received 5.3p per share.

(a) Colin Wright owns 10,000 £1 preference shares in Crenshaw Holdings. These shares pay a fixed dividend of 4%. Jenny Bartlett owns 10,000 ordinary shares. Calculate how much each shareholder will have received in dividends in 2001.
(b) Explain why dividend payments made by companies such as Crenshaw Holdings are discretionary.
(c) What are the advantages and disadvantages of Colin's preference shareholding compared with Jenny's ordinary shareholding?

How are shares issued?

There is a number of ways in which shares in a public limited company are **issued**, ie sold by a company for the first time. This is sometimes called an **initial public offering (IPO)**.
- **Public issue** This method is generally used for large issues of shares. The issue is announced in a **prospectus**, which sets out details of the offer. Potential investors fill in an application form and send cheques with their applications. An ISSUING HOUSE, which is a financial institution such as a bank, might be asked by the company issuing the shares to give advice and administer the issue.
- **Offer for sale** This method involves selling shares to an issuing house, which then issues them to the public. Prospectuses might not be widely circulated but are likely to be distributed to potential investors on a specialised mailing list.

- **Sale by tender** This method is designed to maximise the amount of share capital to be raised. Prospective investors are invited to bid for blocks of shares stating the price that they are prepared to pay. Shares are then sold to the highest bidders. Those investors that make low tenders might not obtain any shares at all.
- **Placing** This method involves issuing shares directly to selected groups of individuals or financial institutions. It is a relatively inexpensive way of issuing shares because it avoids the expense of large public issues.
- **Rights issue** A RIGHTS ISSUE is where existing shareholders are given the right to buy new shares at a discounted price. Shareholders are generally allowed to buy the new shares in proportion to their existing holding. For example, in 2001, British Telecom announced a 3 for 10 rights issue at £3 per share. This means that a shareholder owning 1,000 shares in BT was allowed to buy 300 of the new shares at £3. BT planned to raise £5.9 billion to help reduce its debt. The rights issue in this case was heavily discounted because the price of BT shares at the time of the rights issue was over £5. Rights issues are a relatively inexpensive and easy method of issuing shares for companies.
- **Bonus issue** A BONUS ISSUE, also called a scrip issue, involves giving new shares to existing shareholders. It might happen, for example, if a company has built up reserves in its balance sheet. Suppose that the company has accumulated £100m of profits in a reserve, but only wishes to retain £60m. The remaining £40m can be transferred to shareholders in the form of a bonus issue. No new capital is raised, but the shareholders now own more shares.

QUESTION 2

Fitness UK runs a chain of health clubs. In March 2001, the company reported a 65% increase in profits to £2.2 million, with turnover rising by 74% to £11.8 million. In order to fund an expansion abroad, Fitness UK raised £10.2 million through a 1-for-9 rights issue at 267p in October 2000. When the rights issue was announced, the shares fell in price by 6p to 291p. However, by 4 June 2001, Fitness UK shares were trading at 317.5p.

(a) **With reference to Fitness UK, explain what is meant by a rights issue.**
(b) **In October 2000, a shareholder who owned 4,500 shares in Fitness UK decided to exercise her rights in the share issue. Calculate (i) how much it will have cost the shareholder to buy the shares to which she was entitled; (ii) the capital gain if she sold her *new* shares on 4.6.01 (ignore dealing costs).**
(c) **Explain two advantages of a rights issue to Fitness UK.**

Share capital

Share capital is that part of the finance of a company that is received from its owners (ie its shareholders) in exchange for shares. There is a number of different terms associated with share capital.

- **Authorised share capital** This is the maximum amount of share capital that a limited company can issue. The Memorandum of Association will state the total of AUTHORISED SHARE CAPITAL. However, company law does allow a company to raise its authorised share capital if shareholders agree. Authorised share capital includes both ordinary and preference shares. The total of authorised share capital is not shown on the balance sheet.
- **Issued share capital** Companies are not obliged to issue all of their authorised share capital. That part of authorised share capital that is actually issued to shareholders is called ISSUED SHARE CAPITAL or subscribed share capital.
- **Called-up capital** When shares are issued, a company might not require shareholders to pay the amount owed for their purchase in full. It might 'call up' the amount of money that the

business needs for its immediate purposes and allow shareholders to pay the difference at a later date. Consequently, the total of 'called-up' capital is often less than the total of issued capital. Called-up share capital is the total shown on the balance sheet.

- **Uncalled capital** This is the amount of money that shareholders still owe the company once they have paid their called-up capital. For example, if a company issues 50,000,000 £1 ordinary shares and 'calls up' 25p per share, the total of called up capital is £12,500,000 (50,000,000 × 25p). Therefore the uncalled capital, the amount still owed by shareholders, is £37,500,000 (50,000,000 × 75p).
- **Paid up capital** This is the total amount of money that shareholders have paid to a company for their fully paid shares.
- **Calls in advance** This is money that some shareholders have paid for shares in advance of calls being made by the company.
- **Calls in arrears** This is money owed by some shareholders who have not yet paid for shares after calls have been made by the company.
- **Forfeited shares** If shareholders do not pay money owed for shares after calls have been made, they risk losing them. Shares lost by shareholders for non-payment are called forfeited shares. The circumstances under which shares are forfeited will be outlined in the Articles of Association.

When a company states its authorised share capital in the Memorandum of Association it also often states how this is divided into shares. For example, an authorised share capital of £2,000,000 might be divided into 2 million ordinary shares of £1 each. This face value of a share is known as its NOMINAL or PAR VALUE. The nominal value is likely to be a figure such as £1, 50p or even 5p. The 'secondhand' or **market** value of shares often bears little relationship to their nominal value. The market price is determined by supply and demand, ie the interaction between buyers and sellers.

It is quite common for companies to issue shares at a price that is higher than the nominal value. This is particularly true for established companies when they issue new shares. For instance, if the nominal value of a share is £1 and the market price is £3, new shares will generally be issued at a price nearer the market price. If the nominal value of a share is £1 and new shares are issued for £2.80, the £1.80 difference is known as a **premium**. The £1.80 is credited to a **share premium account**. This is explained later in the unit.

QUESTION 3

NetVen plc invests money in internet-based companies. It provides sums of between £100,000 and £5,000,000 for businesses that show potential. The company was established in 1997 and has survived despite the collapse of many internet companies in recent years. The founders of the company decided in 2001 to raise some more capital to help expansion into European markets. The advert below is an extract from the prospectus published by NetVen in June 2001.

Figure 34.2 *An extract from a share prospectus*

NetVen plc
(Incorporated in England and Wales on 4 October 1997 under the Companies Act 1985)
Offer for subscription
of
40,000,000 Ordinary shares of 5p each at an issue price of £1.50 per share with 50p payable on application.

According to the terms of the share issue, applicants had to submit their application forms with a cheque for the initial payment by 31 July 2001. The remainder of the money fell due on 31 July 2002.

(a) What was the nominal value of the shares?
(b) How much money in total is being raised by NetVen?
(c) What is the amount of the share premium (per share)?

The bookkeeping entries needed for share issues

The issue of shares by a company involves a number of transactions that require bookkeeping entries in the nominal ledger (see Figure 34.3). To illustrate the process, suppose a company decides to sell shares by prospectus. Investors are invited to buy shares at an issue price of £2.50, with £1.00 payable on application. The issuing process is as follows.

- Prospective investors submit their application forms and cheques (£1.00 per share). In contract law, this represents an **offer** to purchase the shares.
- **Acceptance** of the offer by the company is indicated by a letter of ALLOTMENT sent to the investors. When an offer has been accepted, a legally binding contract has been entered into both by the purchaser and seller of the shares.
- If the issue is **oversubscribed**, ie if there are more applications than shares available, unsuccessful applicants are repaid their money.
- The allocation of shares might be decided in a number of ways. A random draw could be used, or all applications could be scaled down by a fixed percentage. Some companies choose to favour investors who apply for large numbers of shares whereas others favour those investors who only apply for a few.
- On allotment, a further amount of money is requested from the successful applicants who are now shareholders. In this example, the company might request £1.50 per share, ie the balance between the issue price and the amount paid by the investor on application.
- Alternatively, the company might only request part of the balance outstanding. Then, at some time in the future, the company might make further **calls** until the shares are fully paid.

Figure 34.3 shows that when money is first received from applicants, it is credited to the application and allotment account. This is a temporary account and will be closed when the share issue is completed. Only when allotment has taken place and the applicants have been accepted as shareholders is the share capital account credited. A similar process occurs when a company requests call money. As the money is received, it is credited to the call account. Then, when the process is complete and it is clear which shareholders have made the payment, the money is credited to the share capital account. If, at any stage, there is a share premium, the money is credited to the share premium account rather than the share capital account.

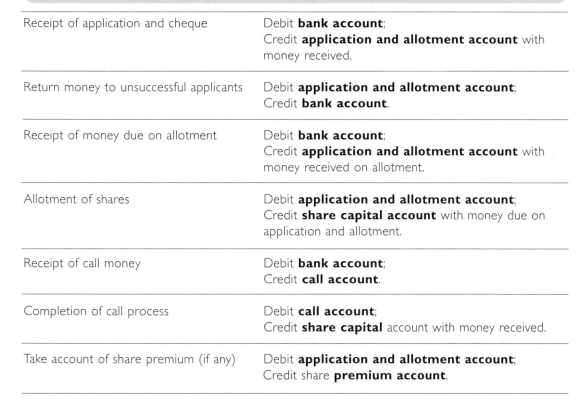

Figure 34.3 *The bookkeeping entries relating to the issue of shares*

Receipt of application and cheque	Debit **bank account**; Credit **application and allotment account** with money received.
Return money to unsuccessful applicants	Debit **application and allotment account**; Credit **bank account**.
Receipt of money due on allotment	Debit **bank account**; Credit **application and allotment account** with money received on allotment.
Allotment of shares	Debit **application and allotment account**; Credit **share capital account** with money due on application and allotment.
Receipt of call money	Debit **bank account**; Credit **call account**.
Completion of call process	Debit **call account**; Credit **share capital** account with money received.
Take account of share premium (if any)	Debit **application and allotment account**; Credit share **premium account**.

To illustrate the bookkeeping entries associated with the issue of shares, consider the example of Hoskins plc, a manufacturer of water pumps. On 1 May 2001, the company arranged a public issue of 60 million ordinary shares with a nominal value of £1 and an issue price of £1.80. The following terms applied to the issue:

- On application: 80p per share (this represents the share premium);
- On allotment: 50p per share;
- First and final call: 50p per share.

The share issue was oversubscribed, with 72,650,000 applications for shares. This meant that some applicants were unsuccessful. The directors of Hoskins decided to allocate the 60 million shares by a random draw. The ledger entries required to record the transactions associated with Hoskins' share issue are shown in Figure 34.4.

- The cheques received from all applicants are deposited in the bank. Therefore the bank account is debited with £58,120,000 (80p × 72,650,000). The credit entry for this transaction is in the application and allotment account.
- When the shares are allotted, the unsuccessful investors applying for 12,650,000 shares have their money refunded. Therefore the bank account is credited with £10,120,000 (12,650,000 × 80p). The debit entry for the refund is in the application and allotment account.
- The balance received on allotment is then deposited in the bank. The total amount due on allotment according to the terms of the issue is 50p × 60 million. Therefore the bank account is debited with £30m (60 million × 50p). The credit entry for this transaction is in the application and allotment account.
- Once shares have been allotted, the ordinary share capital account is credited with the money paid (excluding the premium). The amount is £30m (60 million × 50p). The debit entry for this transaction is in the application and allotment account.
- Since Hoskins issued the shares at 80p above the nominal value, a share premium account must be opened. The share premium account is credited with £48m (60 million × 80p). The debit side of this transaction is in the application and allotment account.
- When the call is made for the money owing on the shares, a call account is opened. The money received from the call is debited to the bank account. This is £30m (60 million × 50p). The call account is credited with the same amount.
- Once the call is complete, the call account is closed by debiting the call account with £30m and crediting the ordinary share capital account with £30m.

The accounts in Figure 34.4 are balanced. Note that the balance b/d on the bank account is equal to the total amount of money raised from the share issue, ie £108m (60 million × £1.80). This excludes all administration and other issuing costs.

Figure 34.4 *Ledger accounts recording the issue of share for Hoskins plc (dates are ignored)*

NOMINAL LEDGER

Dr	Bank Account		Cr
	£		£
Application and allotment	58,120,000	Application and allotment	10,120,000
Application and allotment	30,000,000	Balance c/d	108,000,000
Call	30,000,000		
	118,120,000		118,120,000
Balance b/d	108,000,000		

Dr	Application and Allotment Account		Cr
	£		£
Bank *(refunds to investors)*	10,120,000	Bank *(application money)*	58,120,000
Ordinary share capital	30,000,000	Bank *(balance on allotment)*	30,000,000
Share premium	48,000,000		
	88,120,000		88,120,000

Figure 34.4 continued

Dr	Ordinary Share Capital Account		Cr
	£		£
Balance c/d	60,000,000	Application and allotment	30,000,000
		Call	30,000,000
	60,000,000		60,000,000
		Balance b/d	60,000,000

Dr	Call Account		Cr
	£		£
Ordinary share capital	30,000,000	Bank	30,000,000

Dr	Share Premium Account		Cr
	£		£
Balance c/d	48,000,000	Application and allotment	48,000,000
		Balance b/d	48,000,000

Share issues and the balance sheet

When the share issue for Hoskins plc is completed, the new capital will be recorded on the company's balance sheet. The increase in the bank account of £108m will be shown as an increase in current assets. In the 'Financed by' section of the balance sheet, £60m will be added to the ordinary share capital and a share premium reserve of £48m will be created. The reason for this is that the Companies Act states that UK companies must show how much money is raised as a share premium. By dividing the new capital into ordinary share capital and a share premium reserve, this is made clear. The creation of reserves in the balance sheet is explained in more detail in unit 38.

QUESTION 4

Delworth plc produces fasteners and other small metal products for the engineering industry. On 1 July 2001, the company issued 20,000,000 ordinary shares with a nominal value of £1 and an issue price of £1.50. The following terms applied:

- On application: 50p per share (share premium);
- On allotment: 50p per share;
- First and final call: 50p per share.

The share issue was oversubscribed, there were applications for 22,250,000 shares. The directors of Delworth decided to allot the shares on the basis of a random draw. The money paid by unsuccessful applicants was returned when the shares were allotted.

(a) Draw up the ledger accounts to show the bookkeeping entries associated with the share issue for Delworth plc.

(b) How much money was raised by the share issue?

(c) How would the increase in capital be recorded on the company's balance sheet?

Accounting entries for a rights issue

If a company decides to raise finance by a rights issue, it generally offers shares to existing shareholders at a price between the nominal value and the current market value. For example, suppose the market value of a company's shares is £5.00 and the nominal value is £1.00. The company might choose to offer its shareholders the chance to buy 1 million shares at a price of £4.00 each. This would be attractive to shareholders because they would be obtaining shares at £1.00 less than their current market value. From the company's point of view, it would be raising £4m of new capital, assuming that the offer was fully subscribed. Because the offer price is more than the nominal value, the difference would be credited to the share premium account.

The accounting entries to record the transaction are similar to those for a new share issue (see Figure 34.4):

- debit bank account £4m;
- credit share capital account £1m;
- credit share premium account £3m.

On the balance sheet, current assets would increase by £4m. In the 'Financed by' section, ordinary share capital would increase by £1m and the share premium reserve would increase by £3m. To illustrate this, consider the simplified balance sheet of RTP plc in Figure 34.5. On the left hand side is the balance sheet before the rights issue and, on the right hand side, is the balance sheet after the rights issue.

Figure 34.5 *Balance sheet changes*

	RTP plc Balance Sheet (before rights issue)		RTP plc Balance Sheet (after rights issue)	
	£	£	£	£
Fixed assets		25,000,000		25,000,000
Current assets	5,000,000		9,000,000	
Current liabilities	4,000,000		4,000,000	
Net current assets		1,000,000		5,000,000
Net assets		26,000,000		30,000,000
Financed by				
Ordinary share capital		15,000,000		16,000,000
Share premium reserve		6,000,000		9,000,000
Profit and loss account reserve		5,000,000		5,000,000
Capital employed		26,000,000		30,000,000

- Before the rights issue, the company had issued 15 million shares with a nominal value of £1 each. Net assets and capital employed were both £26m.
- Also before the rights issue, the company had a share premium reserve of £6m. In addition there was a profit and loss account reserve of £5m. This represented accumulated profits that had been retained by the company.
- As a means of raising new capital, the company made a rights issue of 1 million shares at £4 per share.
- The rights issue increased current assets by £4m, from £5m to £9m. This is the amount of money that shareholders paid RTP plc for the new shares.
- The ordinary share capital increased by £1m, from £15m to £16m.
- The share premium reserve increased by £3m, from £6m to £9m.
- The overall effect was to raise net assets and capital employed by £4m.
- Note that fixed assets, current liabilities and the profit and loss account reserve were all unaffected by the rights issue.

Accounting entries for a bonus issue

If a company decides to make a bonus issue it is, in effect, transferring capital from a reserve to its ordinary shareholders. Suppose, for example, that RTP plc decided that it had retained more profits than it needed in its profit and loss account reserve. The company could choose to transfer some of this in the form of a bonus issue to its ordinary shareholders. The accounting entries would be:

- debit the profit and loss account reserve;
- credit the ordinary share capital account.

To illustrate how this would affect the balance sheet, consider the (right hand) balance sheet of RTP plc in Figure 34.5. If it was decided to make a bonus issue of 2 million shares, the changes to the balance sheet would be as shown in Figure 34.6.

Figure 34.6 *Balance sheet after bonus issue*

	RTP plc Balance Sheet (before bonus issue)		RTP plc Balance Sheet (after bonus issue)	
	£	£	£	£
Fixed assets		25,000,000		25,000,000
Current assets	9,000,000		9,000,000	
Current liabilities	4,000,000		4,000,000	
Net current assets		5,000,000		5,000,000
Net assets		30,000,000		30,000,000
Financed by				
Ordinary share capital		16,000,000		18,000,000
Share premium reserve		9,000,000		9,000,000
Profit and loss account reserve		5,000,000		3,000,000
Capital employed		30,000,000		30,000,000

- The bonus issue of 2 million £1 shares has the effect of increasing ordinary share capital from £16m to £18m.
- The bonus issue was financed from the profit and loss account reserve so this fell by £2m, from £5m to £3m.
- The overall totals of net assets and capital employed remain unchanged at £30m.

Stock markets

Shareholders who buy a new issue of shares from a public limited company generally cannot sell the shares back to the company (unless the shares are redeemable). However, shareholders can sell their shares on a STOCK MARKET. The main market for shares in the UK is the **London Stock Exchange**. At one time, shares were bought and sold by **stockbrokers** on the floor of the Stock Exchange. Today, dealing is carried out electronically using computers, telephones and the internet. Dealers operate from different locations, generally in the City of London.

The main function of the Stock Exchange is to provide a market where buyers and sellers are brought together. Shareholders are more willing to invest in companies if they know that there is a market for the shares if they decide to sell.

Approximately 4,000 plcs are listed on the London Stock Exchange. In order for these shares to be quoted, the London Stock Exchange insists that companies must comply with regulations that are designed to protect the interests of shareholders. The high costs of compliance and of obtaining a listing mean that it is only worthwhile for large plcs to go through the process. A less regulated and less expensive means of raising capital is provided by the **Alternative Investment Market (AIM)**. This was established in 1995 and gives small and growing companies the opportunity to raise capital and to trade their shares more widely, without the cost of a full Stock Exchange listing.

key terms

Allotment - the distribution of previously unissued shares in a public limited company.

Authorised share capital - the maximum amount of share capital that a business can issue as stated in the Memorandum of Association.

Bonus issue (or scrip issue) - involves giving new shares to existing shareholders. No new capital is raised.

Capital gain - the money made by selling a share (or any asset) for more than it cost to buy.

Issued share capital - the amount of share capital actually issued to shareholders.

Issuing house - a financial institution, such as a bank, that advises businesses and deals with the administration of applications when new shares are issued.

Nominal or par value - the face value of a share, as opposed to the market price at which the share trades on the stock market.

Ordinary share - a share in a company that carries the right to a variable dividend. Ordinary shareholders generally have the right to vote at a company's Annual General Meeting.

Preference share - a share in a company that carries the right to a fixed percentage dividend. Preference shareholders generally do not have the right to vote at a company's Annual General Meeting, but if the company ceases trading, preference shares are paid out before ordinary shares.

Rights issue - existing shareholders are given the right to buy new shares at a discounted price.

Stock exchange or stock market - a market where shares are traded.

UNIT ASSESSMENT   QUESTION 1

Tenon Group plc was founded in February 2000 and was floated on the Alternative Investment Market a month later. The flotation raised £50 million which was used by the company for acquisitions. Tenon bought a number of small regional accountancy firms. The company is developing services such as tax advice, corporate finance, consultancy, business services and corporate recovery as well as e-commerce and internet consultancy. Ian Buckley, the chief executive, said that the group would expand into areas such as investment advice where it had an advantage over small firms that often struggled with increasingly complex regulation. The company aims to generate a £100 million turnover within three years. Current turnover is around £30 million.

In March 2001, Tenon Group announced expansion plans that involved raising £40 million through a placing and an offer for sale. The issue was of 31.3 million new shares at 130p each. On 7 June 2001, the shares were trading at 149p.

Tenon is owned mainly by institutional investors rather than by private individual shareholders. For example, Henderson Investors has 14.85% of the shares and Gartmore Investment owns 10.4%. The directors of Tenon own less than 2% of the shares.

Source: adapted from the *Financial Times*, 21.3.00, 2.1.01 and 31.3.01.

(a) Explain the terms (i) placing; (ii) offer for sale.

(b) Suggest two possible reasons why Tenon Group floated on AIM rather than the London Stock Exchange.

(c) Explain why institutions such as Henderson Investors and Gartmore Investment might buy shares in companies like Tenon Group.

UNIT ASSESSMENT QUESTION 2

Horace Group was incorporated in February 1996 as a private limited company. The main objective of Horace Group, as set out in its Memorandum of Association, is to manufacture packaging materials. On 1 February 2000, Peter Marsh the founder, floated the company on the London Stock Exchange and issued 80,000,000 ordinary shares. The shares had a nominal value of £1 and this was also their issue price. The following terms applied:

- On application: 25p per share;
- On allotment: 25p per share;
- First and final call: 50p per share.

The share issue was oversubscribed, there were applications for 82,250,000 shares. The directors of Horace Group decided to reject applications for 2,250,000. The money paid by unsuccessful applicants was returned when the shares were allotted.

(a) Draw up the ledger accounts to show the bookkeeping entries associated with the share issue for Horace Group.

(b) Horace group paid a dividend of 15.6p per share in 2000. If 30% of net profit was paid out in dividends, what was the total net profit?

(c) In 2001, Horace Group issued a further 20,000,000 ordinary shares in a 1-for-4 rights issue. The shares were issued at £2.20 against a market price of £2.68. Suggest why the shares were issued at a discount, ie at less than the market price.

(d) Assuming that it was fully subscribed, describe how the rights issue would affect the balance sheet of Horace Group.

(e) Explain the difference between a rights issue and a bonus issue. Compare how they would affect the balance sheet.

summary questions

1. State two entitlements of shareholders.
2. What is the main difference between ordinary shares and preference shares?
3. Explain how shares might be issued by prospectus.
4. What is the difference between a rights issue and a bonus issue?
5. Who can own shares in plcs?
6. Why might a company decide to use an Issuing House?
7. What is meant by (i) called-up capital (ii) calls in advance?
8. Explain why the application and allotment account is a temporary account.
9. Under what circumstances is a share premium account opened?
10. Why might a company prefer to be listed on AIM rather than the London Stock Exchange?

Business finance–loan capital and other sources

unit**objectives**

To understand:
- external sources of long term finance;
- external sources of short term finance;
- internal sources of finance;
- capital structure.

External sources of long term finance

External sources of finance are funds raised from outside the business. At some stage in their existence, most businesses will need to raise finance from external sources. This is because they might not be able to generate sufficient funds from internal sources, such as retained profits, to finance their activities.

Funds that are raised from external sources can be divided into short term and long term finance. In general, accountants classify any money that is borrowed or obtained for more than one year as long term finance. Money that is borrowed or obtained for less than one year is called short term finance. Examples of long term finance include **share capital** and **loan capital**. Share capital involves the issuing of shares, as described in unit 34. LOAN CAPITAL is money that has been borrowed for a lengthy period of time. It includes debentures, bank loans and mortgages.

Debentures A DEBENTURE is a certificate which indicates that a loan has been made to a company. The certificate usually states the terms of the loan, for example its length, and the interest rate payable. Debentures are the most common form of loan capital borrowed by UK limited companies. This source of finance is not available to sole traders and partnerships. Debentures have a number of features.

- They are often secured on the assets of a company. This means that if the company fails to pay the interest on the debenture, or fails to repay the debenture on its maturity, the lender can take ownership of the assets. Some debentures are secured on specified assets, these are called **fixed charge** debentures. If the assets are not specified, the debentures are called **floating charge** debentures. If they are issued without security, they are said to be **naked** debentures.
- Most debentures are **redeemable**. This means that the loan will be repaid on a specified future date. However, some debentures are irredeemable, which means that the loan will never be repaid by the company whilst it continues to trade.
- The interest paid on debentures is fixed. It does not depend on the amount of profit made by the company. This is one of the key differences between shares and debentures. The dividend paid to shareholders is discretionary and often depends on the size of profit.
- One of the attractions to companies of debentures is that interest is charged against profit in the profit and loss account. This means that the cost of debenture funding is paid before tax. So, unlike share capital, where the dividend is paid after tax, a business should pay less tax because less profit will be made.
- Debenture holders are not members, ie owners, of the company. So they do not have any voting rights. However, if the company is wound up, debenture holders are repaid before shareholders.
- Some debentures are **convertible**. This means that, at some future date, these debenture holders will have an option to convert the loan into shares at a predetermined price. Debenture holders are likely to exercise this option if the market price of the shares rises above the predetermined price.

Mortgages A MORTGAGE is a long term loan which is generally used to purchase land or property. The loan is secured on the land or property. So, if the borrower cannot repay what is owed, the lender can repossess the assets that have been used as security. Mortgages can be repaid over very long periods of time, typically 25 years. Banks and building societies are the main providers of mortgages.

An advantage of a mortgage is that the interest rate charged is relatively low. For example, for most of 2001, the mortgage rate offered by many lenders was around 7%. This compared with around 15% to 20% for unsecured loans. Mortgages are a cheap source of finance because lenders are not exposed to very much risk.

Unsecured loans Banks and other financial institutions are sometimes prepared to make UNSECURED LOANS to businesses. The money is lent without any security which means that lenders are exposed to more risk. If the business is not able to maintain its repayments, the bank might not be able to recover all of the money lent. Consequently, the interest rates charged on unsecured loans is higher than those charged on mortgages.

Venture capital A number of specialist organisations provide funds for businesses which have difficulty in raising finance from conventional sources such as banks. In recent years there has been a significant growth in the number of these VENTURE CAPITALISTS. They provide funds mainly, but not exclusively, for small and medium sized businesses. The best known venture capitalist in the UK is 3i. Venture capitalists use their own funds but also attract money from financial institutions and **business angels**. These are individuals or institutions who invest in businesses which they believe have potential. They often take a stake, ie a shareholding, in the company and sometimes become involved in decision making.

QUESTION 1

Tom Hunter, a Scottish entrepreneur, is creating a £200 million venture capital fund called West Coast Capital. The fund will make investments in retailing, property, leisure and 'high risk' technology companies. It will be Scotland's biggest venture capital fund compared with the recent £80 million raised by Scottish Equity Partners and the £100m raised by by Penta Capital. Only the operations of 3i in Scotland are bigger. The £200m for the fund will come entirely from Mr Hunter. He earned £260 million when he sold Sports Division, the sports shoe company which he founded, to JJB in 1998. He has since re-invested £20 million in several UK companies as a business angel. He now says that he wants to formalise his investment strategy.
Source: adapted from the *Financial Times*, 5.2.01.

(a) Describe the role that venture capitalists such as West Coast Capital, Scottish Equity Partners and Penta Capital, play in the provision of capital for businesses.
(b) Suggest why a business might seek finance from a Venture Capital fund.
(c) Why might business angels and venture capitalists prefer to take a shareholding stake in a business when they make an investment?

Government and EU sources of finance A wide range of grants and loans are available to businesses from central and local government agencies, and from the European Union. The main qualification for this funding is that businesses must secure or create employment. The EU provides support in the form of 'structural funds'. These are allocated to regions categorised as Objective 1 or Objective 2. Objective 1 status means that a region's average income is less than 75% of the EU average. Objective 2 status means that a region is seriously affected by industrial or agricultural decline. In the UK, Merseyside, South Yorkshire, Cornwall, West Wales and the Welsh Valleys have Objective 1 status. Funds are allocated in a bidding process and are granted for training, Research and Development, and for providing premises for small and medium size local enterprises (SMEs).

A network of government funded agencies called Business Link in England, with similar agencies in Wales, Scotland and Northern Ireland, provide advice to businesses that are seeking information on grants and loans. The main advantage of this funding is that the money is either in the form of a grant or a low interest loan.

An example of the scale of finance available to businesses occurred in the late 1990s when the Welsh Development Agency offered LG (a Korean company) a £200 million package to locate in South Wales. At the other extreme, in 2001, European Union and regional development grants were used to help regenerate parts of inner Liverpool. Cash grants of a few thousand pounds were available for craft and media workshops that located in the area.

Leasing A LEASE is a contract in which a business acquires the use of an asset in return for regular payments (see unit 6). Leasing is a form of finance that is increasingly used by businesses to acquire expensive plant, machinery and equipment. In this type of finance, the ownership never passes to the business that is using the asset. With a **finance lease**, the arrangement is often for 3 years or longer and, at the end of the period, the business might be given the option of then buying the asset. In accounting, the payments are treated as capital expenditure. With an **operating lease**, the arrangement is generally for a shorter period of time and the payments are treated as revenue expenditure.

The advantages of leasing include:
- cash flow is improved because payments are spread out over a longer period than if the asset is bought outright;
- maintenance and repair costs are not the responsibility of the user;
- leasing companies usually offer the most up to date equipment;
- leasing is useful if equipment is only required for a relatively short period of time;
- a leasing agreement is generally easier for a new company to obtain than other forms of loan finance. This is because the assets remain the property of the leasing company.

Leasing does, however, have some disadvantages.
- If assets are leased for a long period of time, the cost can be very high, sometimes higher than purchasing the assets outright.
- Loans cannot be secured against assets that are leased.

QUESTION 2

Welland Farm, a 1,200 hectare arable farm in Suffolk, is owned by Harry Stocker. He grows barley and wheat and employs 4 staff. In July 2001, his combine harvester was destroyed when it overheated and caught fire. This incident could not have occurred at a worse time. Harry was in the middle of the busy harvest period. Replacing the machine was a very urgent priority.

Harry would have preferred to purchase a new combine harvester outright. However, his business did not have sufficient cash to buy a new machine. One option would have been to fund the purchase with a bank loan and wait for the proceeds of an insurance claim. However, arranging a loan would not have been easy and the insurance company could take weeks, or even months, to pay out. Harry therefore decided to arrange an operating lease for a new combine harvester that could be delivered the next day.

(a) (i) Explain why leasing was a suitable option for Harry. (ii) State two other possible advantages of leasing farm equipment.
(b) Explain how the leasing charge would be treated by an accountant.

External sources of short term finance

Bank overdraft An OVERDRAFT is a loan in which a business is allowed to withdraw more money than it has in its bank account, usually up to a specified limit. This is one of the main sources of short term finance for businesses. The main attraction of an overdraft is its flexibility. Once an overdraft facility has been agreed with a bank, a business can draw different amounts of funds whenever it wishes. The amount which businesses draw depends on their needs at any particular point in time. Businesses only pay interest on the amount that they are overdrawn.

Hire purchase (HP) This form of finance is sometimes used by small businesses to purchase plant, machinery and equipment. A HIRE PURCHASE agreement generally requires a down payment by the borrower, who then agrees to pay the remainder in instalments over a period of time. FINANCE HOUSES specialise in the provision of funds for such agreements.

To illustrate the working of a hire purchase agreement, consider the purchase of a van by a business, Pizza Deliveries.
- Pizza Deliveries makes a down payment of money, ie a deposit, to the vehicle dealer and takes

delivery of the van.
- The finance house pays the vehicle dealer the amount outstanding and arranges to collect instalments (including interest) from Pizza Deliveries.
- The van does not legally belong to Pizza Deliveries until the last instalment is made to the finance house.
- If Pizza Deliveries falls behind with the repayments, the finance house can repossess the van.

Finance houses are often prepared to enter into HP agreements with businesses and individuals that are considered a 'high risk' by banks. Consequently the interest rates on HP are generally much higher than those charged by banks.

Trade credit It is common practice for businesses to buy raw materials and components on credit. They take delivery of the goods and arrange to pay at a later date, typically after 30 days. This arrangement allows businesses time to buy, and then sell, goods before payment is due. In effect, trade credit is a short term loan from a supplier to a purchaser. If a business is short of funds, it might request a longer period of trade credit. However, delays in the payment of bills can result in poor business relations with suppliers and might eventually lead to a refusal to supply.

Debt factoring Debt factoring involves a financial institution, a debt factor, advancing money to a business against the security of unpaid sales invoices. The invoices provide evidence of sales and show the amount of money owed to the business. Typically, a debt factor might advance a business 80% of the value of outstanding invoices. The balance of 20% might then be paid when customers settle their bills. The debt factor makes a charge for this service, usually a percentage of the business's sales turnover. Many commercial banks offer debt factoring services.

The advantages of using a factor are that cash flow is improved and business personnel do not have to devote time to debt collection. The disadvantages are that the factor charges a fee and also that some other businesses might believe that the need to use a factor indicates a financial problem has arisen.

Trade bills (or **bills of exchange**) This method of raising finance has fallen in importance but is still sometimes used as a source of finance, particularly in overseas transactions. A bill of exchange is a document in which a purchaser of goods promises to pay for the goods at a specified date, usually 90 days later. The holder of the bill might choose to sell the bill at a discount, ie at less than face value, before the maturity date to a specialist financial institution. The new holder then receives payment at the end of the period from the debtor.

QUESTION 3

Berwick Rugs Ltd is a family run business that produces woollen mats, rugs and small carpets. Since incorporation in 1987, the company has enjoyed a stable financial position. The main source of short term funding used by the business is a bank overdraft. The company has a £9,000 overdraft limit and is charged 14% p.a. The overdraft is often used by Berwick Rugs to pay suppliers of wool.

On June 1st 2001, the company took out a 12 month bank loan. Berwick Rugs needed the money to purchase a new machine costing £5,000. The loan was to be repaid in 12 monthly instalments plus interest charged at 12% p.a.

(a) Outline the differences between a bank overdraft and a bank loan.
(b) Suggest why Berwick Rugs chose to finance its new machine with a bank loan rather than the overdraft or a hire purchase agreement.
(c) Outline the advantages and disadvantages to Berwick Rugs of using a debt factor rather than a bank loan to raise short term finance.

Internal sources of finance

Internal sources of finance come from within a business. These sources have the advantages that they give a business flexibility to make its own decisions about the timing and amount of finance. They also tend to be cheaper than external sources.

Retained profit A large proportion of all funding in UK companies comes from retained profit. The advantage of this source of finance is that there is no interest to pay and no potential loss of control that arises if new shares are issued. However, there is an opportunity cost involved. If profits are reinvested rather than distributed to shareholders as dividends, shareholders might become dissatisfied. As a consequence, they might decide to sell shares and so cause their price to fall. This creates the danger of a takeover in a public limited company. It also makes it more difficult in the future to issue new shares.

Sale of assets Businesses sometimes sell assets to raise finance. For example, in April 2001, BT sold Yell, its yellow pages operation, for £2.14 billion. The money was required by BT to reduce its debts.

A growing trend is for businesses to sell assets and then lease them back. For example, many nursing homes have sold their properties to specialist leaseback companies in recent years. A **sale and leaseback** arrangement provides an immediate cash injection, yet allows the business to continue using the assets. However, the rental payments must be made throughout the term of the lease and there is a possibility that the lease might not be renewed. In addition, the value of the property might rise in future and this capital gain would be lost to the business that sells the property.

Tighter credit control A business can release funds for other purposes by improving its system of credit control and reducing the amount owed by trade debtors. However, the benefits gained from earlier payment must be weighed against the possible loss of customer goodwill and lost sales.

Reduce stock levels Reducing the stock level releases funds for other uses. However, if stocks fall so much that the business sells out of particular items, customer goodwill could be lost and sales might fall.

What factors influence business financing?

A number of factors is important when business owners and managers choose between different sources of finance.

Use of funds When a company undertakes large scale capital expenditure, it is usually funded by a long term source of finance. For example, the building of a new factory might be financed by a share issue or a mortgage. Revenue expenditure tends to be funded by short term sources. For example, the purchase of raw materials by a manufacturer might be funded by trade credit or a bank overdraft.

Cost The cost of different sources of funds is a major influence on the type of finance that a business chooses. Businesses will clearly prefer sources which are less expensive, both in terms of interest charges and administrative costs. For example, share issues can carry very high administration costs. Even relatively small issues of shares can cost several hundred thousand pounds in fees. Probably the least expensive long term source of finance is a mortgage, whereas a low cost short term source is trade credit or a bank overdraft. Hire purchase and debt factoring tend to be more expensive. The lowest cost source of all is retained profit. However, although the use of profit for funding does not carry a direct financial cost, there is an impact on shareholders to consider.

Status and size Sole traders and partnerships, which tend to be small, have a relatively narrow range of choice because they cannot issue shares or debentures. Limited companies, particularly plcs, can generally obtain finance from many different sources. In addition, due to their size and security, they can often demand lower interest rates from lenders.

Financial situation If a business is making losses or has high debts, lenders might be reluctant to offer finance. The cost of borrowing is also likely to rise. This is because banks and other institutions charge more if there is greater risk. Financial institutions are more willing to lend to secure businesses which have **collateral**, ie assets which provide security for loans.

Gearing GEARING can be defined as the relationship between long term, fixed interest loan capital and share capital. A company is said to be high geared if it has a large proportion of loan capital to share capital. A low geared company has a relatively small amount of loan capital. For example, two companies might have total capital of £100 million. If the first has loan capital of £75 million and share capital of £25 million, it is relatively **high geared**. If the second has loan capital of £10 million and share capital of £90 million, it is relatively **low geared**.

The gearing of a company can influence its funding. If a business is already high geared, it might be reluctant to raise even more money by borrowing. It might choose to issue more shares instead, rather than increasing the interest to be paid on loans. However, issuing shares carries the risk of losing control of the company. Figure 35.1 summarises the advantages and disadvantages of being high geared and low geared.

Figure 35.1 *Advantages and disadvantages of being high geared and low geared*

	ADVANTAGES	DISADVANTAGES
LOW GEARED	The burden of loan repayments and interest payments is reduced. Volatile interest rates are less of a threat.	Dividend payments have to be made indefinitely. Ownership of the company is diluted. Dividends are paid after tax.
HIGH GEARED	The interest on loans can be set against tax. Ownership is not diluted. Once loans are repaid, the company's debt is reduced.	Interest payments must be met. Interest rates can change, so creating uncertainty. Loans must be repaid and might become a burden, so increasing the risk of insolvency.

Capital structure

Businesses raise funds from many different sources. The relative importance of each source is shown by its CAPITAL STRUCTURE. For example the capital structure of a limited company will show how money has been raised from shares, loans and short term sources. The capital structure for Leeds Sporting plc, the company which owns Leeds United Football Club, is shown in Figure 35.2. The pie chart shows that more than a third of the company's funding comes from short term sources. It also shows that more than half of long term funding is provided by the shareholders.

Figure 35.2 *The capital structure of Leeds Sporting plc*

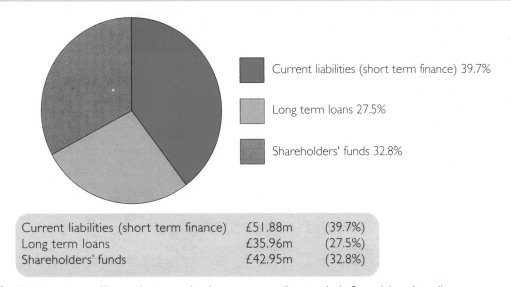

Current liabilities (short term finance) 39.7%

Long term loans 27.5%

Shareholders' funds 32.8%

Current liabilities (short term finance)	£51.88m	(39.7%)
Long term loans	£35.96m	(27.5%)
Shareholders' funds	£42.95m	(32.8%)

Capital structure will vary between businesses according to their financial and trading circumstances. For example, the capital structure of JCB, the earth moving equipment manufacturer, shows that very little money is raised from long term loans. This is because, over the years, the owners of JCB have continually reinvested large proportions of profit to fund expansion. Consequently, most of JCB's long term funding is provided by shareholders. In contrast, the capital structure of BT at the beginning of 2001 was quite different. The company had accumulated £30 billion of debt and its capital structure consisted of a very large proportion of long term loan capital. Indeed, during 2001, the size of the debt was seen as a serious problem and a number of measures were taken to reduce it. As a result of these changes, such as selling assets and a rights issue, BT's capital structure changed significantly.

There is no 'typical' or 'ideal' capital structure for a business. However, there are certain features that might be considered good financial practice.

- It is generally argued that fixed assets should be funded by long term sources of finance, such as shares or mortgages. Therefore, a business with a very large proportion of fixed assets should have a capital structure that consists mainly of long term capital. If a business tries to fund the purchase of fixed assets with short term sources, it might face liquidity problems. In other words, it might have insufficient cash or liquid assets to pay its bills.
- The amount of short term funding should be linked to the size of current assets. It is often stated that the value of current assets should be between 1.5 and 2 times the size of current liabilities. Therefore, if a business has £50m of current assets, it should ideally have around £35m of short term funds in its capital structure.

QUESTION 4

MFI Furniture Group plc manufactures and sells a wide range of furniture products. The company owns brands such as Hygena, Schreiber and MFI itself. In recent years the company has encountered problems such as falling sales and industrial unrest at some of its factories. However, in 2000 it reported an increase in profits from £3.6 million to £10.4 million.

Kewill Systems plc is a leading company in the internet sector. It has a customer base of 47,000 businesses. One of the company's services is to provide links, via the internet, between small suppliers and their main trading partners to enable the exchange of orders, invoices and other trading information. In 2000, sales rose by 25% to £75.2 million. However, profits fell slightly from £10.8 million to £9.6 million. The capital structures for both companies are shown in Figure 35.3.

Source: adapted from the *Annual Reports and Accounts* of MFI and Kewill Systems.

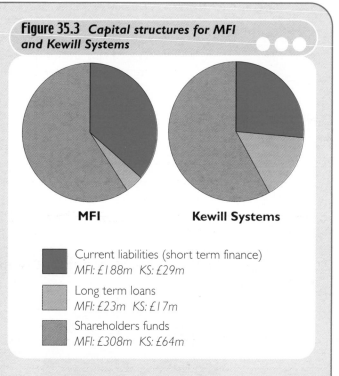

Figure 35.3 *Capital structures for MFI and Kewill Systems*

MFI   **Kewill Systems**

Current liabilities (short term finance)
MFI: £188m KS: £29m

Long term loans
MFI: £23m KS: £17m

Shareholders funds
MFI: £308m KS: £64m

(a) **Compare the capital structures of the two companies.**
(b) **Which of the two companies was the most highly geared?**
(c) **In 2000, the value of MFI's fixed assets was £325m and current assets was £194m. Comment on this in relation to MFI's capital structure.**

summary questions

1. What is the difference between short term and long term loan capital?
2. State four features of debentures.
3. Why is the interest rate on a mortgage relatively low?
4. What is meant by venture capital?
5. How is leasing different from hire purchase?
6. Why is a bank overdraft said to be flexible?
7. State three sources of internal finance.
8. How will the capital structure differ between a sole trader and a plc?
9. State the advantages and disadvantages of being highly geared.
10. Explain three factors that would be considered by a business when choosing between different sources of finance.

key terms

Capital structure - the balance between different sources of capital finance in a business.

Debenture - a certificate indicating that a loan has been made to a company. The certificate generally states the terms of the loan.

Finance House - a financial institution which specialises in hire purchase finance.

Gearing - the relationship between funds raised from long term, fixed interest loans and funds raised from issuing shares. Note that some definitions of gearing suggest that it is the ratio between loan capital plus preference shares and ordinary capital, ie between funds with a fixed interest charge and funds with a variable charge.

Hire Purchase - an agreement in which a purchaser usually makes a down payment and then pays the remainder, plus interest, in instalments over a period of time. The purchaser does not own the item being purchased until the final instalment is made. Payments are made to a finance house which pays the supplier the amount due at the beginning of the agreement.

Lease - a contract in which a business acquires the use of an asset in return for regular payments.

Loan capital - money borrowed for a lengthy period of time.

Mortgage - a long term loan, often up to 25 years, secured by assets such as property or land.

Overdraft - a loan in which a business's bank account is allowed to be overdrawn, usually up to a specified limit.

Unsecured bank loan - money lent by a bank without any security.

Venture capitalist - a provider of funds for small and medium-sized businesses that might be considered too risky by other investors. Individual venture capitalists are sometimes called **business angels**.

UNIT ASSESSMENT QUESTION 1

Daimler to sell stake in air-leasing company

DaimlerChrysler has put its airline leasing business up for sale as the loss-making German-US vehicle maker seeks to concentrate on its core operations.

Daimler is seeking a buyer for its 45% stake in Debis Air-Finance, one of the world's five largest airline leasing businesses. The company has a portfolio of more than 220 jets and turbo-props which the company values at around $5bn.

At DaimlerChrysler's Annual General Meeting in March 2001, a loss of $900m was reported for the fourth quarter of 2000. Despite reassurances from directors who claimed that the company's problems were being tackled, the 11,000 small shareholders present at the AGM were unimpressed. They had come to vent their anger about the declining share price.

Source: adapted from the *Financial Times*, 20.6.01.

(a) **Suggest why airlines might prefer to lease aircraft rather than buy them outright.**

(b) **Explain why DaimlerChrysler needed to raise funds.**

(c) **Outline the reasons why DaimlerChrysler chose to sell assets rather than issue new shares or seek loan finance.**

UNIT ASSESSMENT QUESTION 2

Pinkerton Ltd was set up by Angela and Graham Pinkerton in 1994. The company manufactures high quality clothing for 'up-market' retailers. Although the company is profitable, it is burdened with a large debt in the form of a mortgage and bank loan. Despite the debt, dividends of £2 million were paid to shareholders in January 2001. 75% of the company is owned by Angela and Graham. The remainder of the shares are held by family and friends.

In March 2001, Angela and Graham decided that they would try and launch their own label of men's clothes, Fashion Plus. However, the design, new equipment and marketing costs would be £6m. Raising the money would not be easy. One suggestion made by Angela was to involve a business angel or a venture capitalist in the funding. Graham was not keen on this idea. Some financial information for Pinkerton Ltd is shown in Figure 35.4.

Figure 35.4 *Financial information for Pinkerton Ltd*

Current liabilities (short term finance)	£15.2m
Long term loans	£15.0m
Shareholders funds	£12.8m
Fixed assets:	£24.2m
Current assets:	
Stock	£8.8m
Debtors	£8.4m
Cash	£1.6m

(a) Outline in a memo to the company the possible alternative sources of finance to raise the £6m.

(b) Suggest why Graham might not be keen to involve a business angel or a venture capitalist.

(c) How might the gearing of the company affect its choice of funding?

Partnership accounts

unit**objectives**

To understand:
- the differences between sole trader and partnership accounts;
- how to prepare the appropriation account for partnerships;
- how to treat interest on drawings and loans by partners;
- the difference between capital and current accounts;
- how to produce the final accounts for a partnership.

Sole trader and partnership accounts

The preparation of the trading and profit and loss account and the balance sheet for sole traders is described in units 17 and 18. The same accounts are produced for partnerships. However, since a partnership has more than one owner, certain sections of the accounts are different.

- **Profit and loss appropriation account** In the case of partnerships, the profit and loss account includes an appropriation account to show how net profit is divided between the partners. The appropriation account is shown below the trading and profit and loss account and does not usually have a separate heading.

- **Balance sheet** In the balance sheet of a sole trader, the 'financed by' section shows how much capital has been introduced by the owner of the business. This is the balance on the owner's CAPITAL ACCOUNT. For a partnership, there is a capital account for each partner and the balance on these accounts is included in the balance sheet. The partnership balance sheet usually also includes a CURRENT ACCOUNT for each partner. This records transactions such as partners' drawings, salaries, interest on capital and profit distribution.

The profit and loss appropriation account

The profit and loss appropriation account of a partnership shows:
- how the net profit, or loss, is allocated between partners;
- the salaries to which the partners are entitled, assuming that salaries are paid;
- the interest on capital allowed to each partner, assuming that interest is paid on capital.

The **drawings**, ie withdrawals of cash or other assets made by partners, do **not** appear in the appropriation account. They are recorded in the balance sheet.

To illustrate the appropriation account of a partnership, consider the example of Gill Thompson and Pauline Clarke who run a catering business called Thompson and Clarke. According to the Deed of Partnership, which they drew up when the partnership was formed, any profits or losses are shared equally. However, since Gill works more hours than Pauline, Gill is entitled to an annual salary of £25,000 and Pauline's salary is £15,000. Gill provided £10,000 capital and Pauline provided £14,000 when the business started. According to the partnership agreement, 5% interest is allowed on this capital.

In 2001, the business made a net profit of £72,000. To prepare the appropriation account (see Figure 36.1), the following steps are taken.
- The net profit, £72,000, is brought down from the profit and loss account.
- The interest on capital for each partner is subtracted from the net profit. The interest paid to Gill is £500 (5% × £10,000). The interest paid to Pauline is £700 (5% × £14,000). After interest has been subtracted, the amount of profit c/d is £70,800.
- The salaries paid to each partner are subtracted from the balance. The salaries are £25,000 and £15,000 respectively for Gill and Pauline. The amount of net profit after salaries have been deducted is £30,800.
- The remaining profit is divided between the partners. In this case, according to the partnership agreement, the profit is shared equally. Therefore, both partners receive £15,400.

Figure 36.1 *Profit and loss appropriation account for Thompson and Clarke*

Thompson and Clarke
Profit and Loss Appropriation Account for the year ended 31.7.01

	£	£
Net profit b/d		72,000
Less interest on capital:		
Thompson	500	
Clarke	700	
		1,200
		70,800
Less salaries:		
Thompson	25,000	
Clarke	15,000	
		40,000
		30,800
Share of remaining profit:		
Thompson (50%)	15,400	
Clarke (50%)	15,400	
		30,800

- Note that if the business had made a £72,000 loss instead of a profit, it could be recorded in the account as (£72,000). Some businesses use the convention of showing negative numbers in brackets.

If a Deed of Partnership did not exist between Thompson and Clarke, the arrangements between the partners would be subject to the Partnership Act. This would affect the appropriation of profit because the following provisions apply:
- salaries are not paid to partners;
- no interest is paid on capital, or charged on drawings;
- profits or losses are shared equally;
- interest can be paid on partners' loans to the business at a rate of 5% per year.

Under such circumstances, the appropriation account would be as shown in Figure 36.2.

Figure 36.2 *Profit and loss appropriation account for Thompson and Clarke (under the terms of the Partnership Act)*

Thompson and Clarke
Profit and Loss Appropriation Account for the year ended 31.7.01

	£	£
Net profit b/d		72,000
Share of profit:		
Thompson (50%)	36,000	
Clarke (50%)	36,000	
		72,000

Interest on drawings

Some partnership agreements specify that partners must pay interest on the drawings they make. The partners are, in effect, being charged for withdrawing money. The purpose of this is to reduce or postpone the cash flow out of the business. If interest is charged on drawings, the interest contributes to business profits which all the partners share.

Interest on drawings is usually charged at an agreed rate on the amount that is withdrawn. It is calculated from the date of the withdrawal to the end of the financial year. Details of drawings made

QUESTION 1

Tom Wilson and Salim Patel are solicitors trading as partners. Their office is in Tooting, South London, and when the partnership was formed they drew up a Deed of Partnership. The terms of the agreement were as follows.

- Profits / losses are shared equally.
- Tom provided £15,000 capital.
- Salim provided £5,000 capital.
- Interest of 5% is paid on partners' capital.
- Tom is paid an annual salary of £30,000.
- Salim is paid an annual salary of £40,000.

In 2000, the business made a net profit of £83,000. The year end for the business is 31 December.

(a) Draw up the profit and loss appropriation account for Wilson and Patel for the year ended 31 December 2000.

(b) In 2001, net profit fell to £58,000. Assuming that the terms in the partnership agreement were unchanged, draw up the profit and loss appropriation account for 2001.

by George Botham and Ian McKee, who jointly own a building business, are shown in Figure 36.3. The interest is charged at 5% and the amount charged to the partners is calculated and shown. For example, the £500 withdrawn by George Botham on 1 January is charged at 5% interest for the full year. The financial year of the business ends on 31 December.

Figure 36.3 *Drawings and interest charged*

George Botham				Ian McKee			
Date	Drawings	Interest		Date	Drawings	Interest	
	£	£			£	£	
1.1.01	500	25.00	(12/12 x 5% x 500)	1.2.01	700	32.08	(11/12 x 5% x 700)
1.3.01	800	33.33	(10/12 x 5% x 800)	1.5.01	700	23.33	(8/12 x 5% x 700)
1.5.01	600	20.00	(8/12 x 5% x 600)	1.9.01	700	11.66	(4/12 x 5% x 700)
1.7.01	1,000	25.00	(6/12 x 5% x 1,000)				
1.9.01	600	10.00	(4/12 x 5% x 600)				
1.11.01	1,000	8.33	(2/12 x 5% x 1,000)				
Total	**4,500**	**121.66**		**Total**	**2,100**	**67.07**	

George Botham was charged more interest because he withdrew more cash than Ian McKee. Drawings made earlier in the financial year were charged more interest than those made later. The interest charged to the two partners is added to net profit in the profit and loss appropriation account. This is illustrated by the extract from the partners' profit and loss appropriation account in Figure 36.4. It assumes that the partnership made a net profit of £40,000 for the year. Figures are rounded to the nearest pound.

Figure 36.4 *Profit and loss appropriation account for Botham and McKee (extract)*

Botham and McKee
Profit and Loss Appropriation Account for the year ended 31.12.01

	£	£
Net profit b/d		40,000
Add interest on drawings:		
Botham	122	
McKee	67	
		189
		40,189

Loans made by partners

If a partner provides the business with a loan, it is classified in the balance sheet as a liability and not as capital. This is because the money has to be repaid to the partner at some time in the future, unlike capital which might never be repaid. The interest payable on a partners' loan to the business is treated as an expense. Like other expenses it is subtracted from the gross profit to give net profit. This is different from the way that interest paid on partners' capital is treated. As outlined earlier in the unit, the interest on partners' capital is recorded in the appropriation account at the end of the profit and loss account, ie after net profit is calculated.

The terms and conditions for partners' loans are usually outlined in the Deed of Partnership. In the absence of such a partnership agreement, a provision is made in the Partnership Act. This states that interest on partners' loans should be charged at 5%.

QUESTION 2

Abbot, Cox and Cairns is a marketing agency in Devon. The partnership specialises in market research for customers in the tourism and leisure industry. The Deed of Partnership sets out the following terms.

- The amount of capital contributed by Sarah Abbot, Christine Cox and Matthew Cairns is £10,000, £10,000 and £20,000 respectively.
- Interest is paid on capital at 6%.
- Interest is charged on drawings at 10%, from the date of withdrawal.
- Interest is paid on loans at 6%.
- Salaries paid to Sarah Abbot, Christine Cox and Matthew Cairns are £25,000, £25,000 and £5,000 respectively.
- Profits or losses are shared as follows: Sarah Abbott 40%, Christine Cox 40% and Matthew Cairns 20%.

The net profit made by the business for the year ending 31 December 2000 was £78,000. Drawings made by the partners during the year are shown in Figure 36.5.

(a) Calculate the interest charged on the partners' drawings during the year in question.

(b) Prepare a profit and loss appropriation account for the partnership for the year ended 31 December 2000.

(c) In May, 2001, Matthew Cairns lent the business £5,000. Explain how interest on this loan will have been treated.

Figure 36.5 *Drawings made the partners*

Date	Sarah Abbot	Christine Cox	Matthew Cairns
	£	£	£
1.1.00	3,000	2,000	
1.3.00	3,300	2,000	2,500
1.5.00	3,000	2,000	
1.7.00	4,000	2,000	
1.9.00	4,000	2,000	2,500
1.11.00	4,000	2,000	
Total	21,300	12,000	5,000

Capital accounts and current accounts

Two different approaches are used when recording transactions between partners and the business they own. One approach is for partners to have two accounts, a FIXED CAPITAL ACCOUNT and a current account. The alternative, less common approach, is to combine the accounts in a single FLUCTUATING CAPITAL ACCOUNT. In both cases, the balances on the accounts and a summary of the transactions are included in the balance sheet. This is dealt with in the next section.

Fixed capital account and current account The fixed capital account shows the amount of capital that each partner has contributed to the business. This account only changes if partners contribute more capital or withdraw capital. To illustrate the fixed capital accounts of a partnership, consider again the example of Thompson and Clarke.

Gill Thompson contributed £10,000 and Pauline Clarke contributed £14,000 when the partnership was formed. Since then there have been no further introductions or withdrawals of capital. Therefore the fixed capital accounts for both partners have remained unchanged. They are shown in

Figure 36.6. Because they indicate the contribution of capital to the business, both accounts show a credit balance.

Dr		Gill Thompson - Fixed Capital Account		Cr	
	£	2000			£
		1.8	Balance b/d		10,000

Dr		Pauline Clarke - Fixed Capital Account		Cr	
	£	2000			£
		1.8	Balance b/d		14,000

The fixed capital accounts can also be shown in columnar form. This makes it easier to compare each partner's contribution. They are shown in Figure 36.7 for Gill Thompson and Pauline Clarke.

Dr			Partners' Fixed Capital Accounts		Cr	
	Thompson	Clarke			Thompson	Clarke
	£	£	2000		£	£
			1.8	Balances b/d	10,000	14,000

The current account shows all the transactions between partners and the business, apart from the contribution and withdrawal of capital. These transactions are recorded as debits or credits, as shown in Figure 36.8.

Dr	Partner's Current Account	Cr
Drawings	Salary	
Interest on drawings	Interest on capital contributed	
Share of loss	Interest on loan made to partnership	
	Share of profit	

The entries in the profit and loss appropriation account for Thompson and Clarke, in Figure 36.1, are shown as entries in the current accounts in Figure 36.9. The current accounts of Gill Thompson and Pauline Clarke are:
* credited with interest on capital of £500 and £700 respectively;
* credited with salaries of £25,000 and £15,000 respectively;
* credited with a 50% share of the profit, ie £15,400 each.

At the start of the year, 1 August 2000, the credit balances b/d on the current accounts for Gill Thompson and Pauline Clarke were £1,200 and £1,400 respectively. During the year, Gill withdrew a total of £31,500 from the business and Pauline withdrew £21,400. These amounts are shown as debit entries. As agreed in the Deed of Partnership, interest is not charged on drawings. At the end of the year, the balance b/d on the current account of Gill Thompson was £10,600 and was £11,100 for Pauline Clarke. These balances, since they are credit balances, represent the amount of money owed by the business to the partners. It is money that the partners could withdraw.

Figure 36.9 *Current accounts for Gill Thompson and Pauline Clarke*

Dr	Gill Thompson - Current Account		Cr	
2001		£	2000	£
31.7 Cash - drawings		31,500	1.8 Balance b/d	1,200
31.7 Balance c/d		10,600	2001	
			31.7 Interest on capital	500
			31.7 Salary	25,000
			31.7 Profit	15,400
		42,100		42,100
			1.8 Balance b/d	10,600

Dr	Pauline Clarke - Current Account		Cr	
2001		£	2000	£
31.7 Cash - drawings		21,400	1.8 Balance b/d	1,400
31.7 Balance c/d		11,100	2001	
			31.7 Interest on capital	700
			31.7 Salary	15,000
			31.7 Profit	15,400
		32,500		32,500
			1.8 Balance b/d	11,100

As with the fixed capital accounts, the partners' current accounts can be presented in columnar form. This makes it easier to compare the partners' transactions. The current accounts shown above, in Figure 36.9, are presented in columnar form in Figure 36.10.

Figure 36.10 *Current accounts presented in columnar form*

Dr	Partners' Current Accounts			Cr		
		Thompson	Clarke		Thompson	Clarke
2001		£	£	2000	£	£
31.7 Cash - drawings		31,500	21,400	1.8 Balances b/d	1,200	1,400
31.7 Balances c/d		10,600	11,100	2001		
				31.7 Interest on capital	500	700
				31.7 Salaries	25,000	15,000
				31.7 Profit	15,400	15,400
		42,100	32,500		42,100	32,500
				1.8 Balances b/d	10,600	11,100

Note that a debit balance on a current account would indicate that a partner has withdrawn more money than she is entitled to receive in profit, interest and salary. It is by keeping the capital and current accounts separate that this is made clear. If the capital and current accounts are combined, it is less easy to see whether a partner has taken more profit than she is entitled to, and has therefore withdrawn some of her original capital contribution.

Fluctuating capital account If it is decided to show all the partners' transactions with the business in just one account, the account is called a FLUCTUATING CAPITAL ACCOUNT. This account combines all the transactions that appear in both the current account and the fixed capital account. Consequently the balance on the account is likely to change, or fluctuate, at the end of each year.

The transactions described previously for Thompson and Clarke are recorded in the fluctuating capital account shown in Figure 36.11. For Gill Thompson, the balance b/d on the account at the start of the year equals the capital introduced by Gill, £10,000, and the balance b/d on her current account, £1,200. Therefore the balance b/d is £11,200 (£10,000 + £1,200). For Pauline Clarke the balance b/d is £15,400 (£14,000 + £1,400). At the end of the year, the balance c/d on the Gill Thompson account is £20,600. For Pauline Clarke it is £25,100. These are the total amounts of money that the business, in effect, owes the partners. They represent the share of profit, salary and interest, plus the contribution of capital, that relates to each partner.

Figure 36.11 *Fluctuating capital account*

Dr	Gill Thompson - Fluctuating Capital Account		Cr	
2001		£	2000	£
31.7 Cash - drawings		31,500	1.8 Balance b/d	11,200
31.7 Balance c/d		20,600	2001	
			31.7 Interest on capital	500
			31.7 Salary	25,000
			31.7 Profit	15,400
		52,100		52,100
			1.8 Balance b/d	20,600

Dr	Pauline Clarke - Current Account		Cr	
2001		£	2000	£
31.7 Cash - drawings		21,400	1.8 Balance b/d	15,400
31.7 Balance c/d		25,100	2001	
			31.7 Interest on capital	700
			31.7 Salary	15,000
			31.7 Profit	15,400
		46,500		46,500
			1.8 Balance b/d	25,100

QUESTION 3

Tillett and Hopkins is an employment agency in Brighton. Sheila Tillett and Jason Hopkins drew up a Deed of Partnership when they started the business and each contributed £7,000 capital to cover the set up costs. Some details of the partnership agreement are as follows.

- No interest is paid on capital.
- No interest is paid on drawings.
- An annual salary of £26,000 is paid to Sheila Tillett and £14,000 to Jason Hopkins who only works part-time.
- Remaining profits/losses are shared equally.

The following additional information is taken from Tillett and Hopkin's books for the year ended 31 December 2001.

	£
Net profit	71,400
Current account balance (1 January 2001)	
Tillett	2,300
Hopkins	3,800
Drawings	
Tillett	30,500
Hopkins	16,000

(a) Draw up a fixed capital account and a current account for the partners for the year ended 31 December 2001. Use a columnar format.

(b) Balance the accounts and explain the changes on the end of year balances in the current accounts.

The balance sheet

The balance sheet for a partnership is similar to that of a sole trader. The assets and liabilities are recorded in the same way. However, there is a difference in the 'financed by' section of the balance sheet. This arises because there is more than one owner in a partnership and the balance sheet must reflect this.

In the 'financed by' section of a sole trader's balance sheet, net profit is added to opening capital, and drawings are then deducted. This gives the closing balance on the owner's capital account. The balance sheet for a partnership must show the capital and current accounts of all partners. It is also usual to show a summary of the transactions that have taken place during the year on each account. The balance sheet for Thompson and Clarke, the partnership described previously in this unit, is shown in Figure 36.12.

Figure 36.12 *Balance sheet for Thompson and Clarke*

Thompson and Clarke
Balance Sheet as at 31.7.01

		£	£
Fixed assets			
Equipment			15,500
Vehicle			19,500
			35,000
Current assets			
Stocks		4,300	
Debtors		6,400	
Bank		5,500	
		16,200	
Less current liabilities			
Trade creditors		2,500	
Net current assets			13,700
			48,700
Less long term liabilities			
Bank loan			3,000
Net assets			45,700

Financed by			
Capital accounts			
Thompson		10,000	
Clarke		14,000	
			24,000

Current accounts	Thompson	Clarke	
	£	£	
Opening balance	1,200	1,400	
Add			
Salary	25,000	15,000	
Interest on capital	500	700	
Share of profit	15,400	15,400	
	42,100	32,500	
Less			
Drawings	31,500	21,400	
Closing balance	10,600	11,100	
			21,700
Capital employed			45,700

- In Figure 36.12, the sections of the balance sheet relating to fixed assets, current assets, current liabilities and long term liabilities are no different from a sole trader's balance sheet. However, the section relating to the capital of the business contains much more detail. It is customary to show the fixed capital account first. The balance sheet shows that Gill Thompson contributed capital of £10,000 and Pauline Clarke £14,000. The amounts are added together in the balance sheet to show the total, ie £24,000.

- The current accounts are shown underneath the capital accounts in the balance sheet. The opening balance for each partner is shown and interest on capital, salaries and share of profit are added. This gives a total of £42,100 for Gill Thompson and £32,500 for Pauline Clarke. Drawings are subtracted to give the closing balance on each current account. For Gill this is £10,600 and for Pauline it is £11,100. These are added to show the total amount, ie £21,700.

- The balances on the current accounts are added to the balances on the capital accounts. This shows the total amount that is, in effect, owed by the business to the partners. It is £45,700 (£21,700 + £24,000) and is the same as the total of net assets for the partnership.

QUESTION 4

Joy Lee and Gerry Wong trade together as partners. They run an import agency shipping a wide range of products from Hong Kong and China into the UK. In the year ended 30 June 2001, the business made a net profit of £63,600. When the partnership was formed, both partners contributed £12,000 capital.

The opening balances on the partners' current accounts on 1 July 2000, were £4,100 and £200 for Joy Lee and Gerry Wong respectively. The profits are not shared equally. Joy takes 60% and Gerry takes 40%. This is in recognition that Joy originally started the business. Both partners take a salary of £25,000. During the year, Joy withdrew £25,000 from the business and Gerry withdrew £28,600.

(a) Draw up the 'financed by' section of the balance sheet for Lee and Wong as at 30 June 2001.

(b) What was the value of net assets for the business at the end of year?

Preparing the final accounts of a partnership from a trial balance

The procedure for compiling final accounts for a partnership is similar to that for preparing sole trader accounts. As already explained, the only differences are in the profit and loss appropriation account and in the section of the balance sheet that relates to capital. To illustrate how the final accounts of a partnership can be prepared from a trial balance, consider the example of George Truman and Ian Robbins who own a business called Trade Wines. The trial balance for Trade Wines as at 31 March 2001, is shown in Figure 36.13.

328

Figure 36.13 *Trial balance for Trade Wines*

Trade Wines
Trial Balance as at 31.3.01

	Dr	Cr
	£	£
Sales		407,100
Purchases	145,900	
Stock at 1.4.00	67,500	
Rent	12,000	
Employees' wages	67,200	
Motor expenses	21,400	
Other overheads	34,300	
Van	12,500	
Provision for depreciation - van		6,000
Equipment	6,000	
Provision for depreciation - equip.		4,000
Trade debtors	34,000	
Bank	23,200	
Trade creditors		45,300
Capital: Truman		10,000
Capital: Robbins		10,000
Current account: Truman		3,500
Current account: Robbins		4,100
Drawings: Truman	36,000	
Drawings: Robbins	30,000	
	490,000	490,000

The following additional information is also provided as at 31.3.01.
- Stocks of wine were valued at £73,500.
- Depreciation for the current year on the van was £2,000 and on the equipment was £500.
- George Truman earns an annual salary of £40,000 and Ian Robbins earns an annual salary of £20,000.
- No interest is paid on capital or charged on drawings.
- Profits are shared equally between the partners.

The **trading and profit and loss account**, including the appropriation account, for Trade Wines is shown in Figure 36.14.
- The gross profit is £267,200. It is calculated by deducting the cost of sales from the sales revenue.
- The net profit is £129,800. It is calculated by subtracting expenses, including the current year's depreciation, from the gross profit.
- The appropriation account shows the deduction of partners' salaries from net profit and the distribution of the remaining profit. According to the information given, George Truman is paid a larger salary than Ian Robbins. After the salaries are deducted from net profit, the remaining profit of £69,800 is divided equally between the two partners.

Figure 36.14 *The trading and profit and loss account for Trade Wines*

Trade Wines
Trading and Profit and Loss Account for the year ended 31.3.01

	£	£
Sales		407,100
Opening stock	67,500	
Add purchases	145,900	
	213,400	
Less closing stock	73,500	
Cost of sales		139,900
Gross profit		267,200
Less expenses		
Rent	12,000	
Employees wages	67,200	
Motor expenses	21,400	
Other overheads	34,300	
Depreciation	2,500	
		137,400
Net profit		129,800
Salaries:		
Truman	40,000	
Robbins	20,000	
		60,000
		69,800
Share of remaining profit:		
Truman	34,900	
Robbins	34,900	
		69,800

The **balance sheet** for Trade Wines is shown in Figure 36.15.

- The fixed and current assets of Trade Wines are entered in the balance sheet in the same way as for a sole trader. The value of fixed assets takes into account the adjustment for depreciation, ie the accumulated provision shown in the trial balance plus the current year's depreciation.
- The value of net current assets for Trade Wines is £85,400. This is calculated by subtracting the current liabilities from the total current assets. There are no long term liabilities so the total of net assets is calculated by adding fixed assets to net current assets. Net assets are £91,400 for the business.
- The 'financed by' section of the balance sheet shows the partners' capital accounts and current accounts. The capital accounts are fixed and show that the partners both contributed £10,000 capital. The current accounts show the opening balances, the deduction of salaries, the share of profit and the deduction of drawings. The closing balances on the current accounts of George Truman and Ian Robbins are £42,400 and £29,000 respectively. The total capital of the business is calculated by adding together the balances on the partners' capital and current accounts. It is £91,400 and is equal to net assets.

Figure 36.15 *Balance sheet for Trade Wines*

Truman and Robbins
Balance Sheet as at 31.3.01

		£	£
Fixed assets			
Van		12,500	
Less depreciation		8,000	4,500
Equipment		6,000	
Less depreciation		4,500	1,500
			6,000
Current assets			
Stocks		73,500	
Debtors		34,000	
Bank		23,200	
		130,700	
Less current liabilities			
Trade creditors		45,300	
Net current assets			85,400
Net assets			91,400

Financed by
Capital accounts

		£	£
Truman		10,000	
Robbins		10,000	
			20,000

Current accounts	Truman	Robbins	
	£	£	
Opening balance	3,500	4,100	
Add			
Salary	40,000	20,000	
Share of profit	34,900	34,900	
	78,400	59,000	
Less			
Drawings	36,000	30,000	
	42,400	29,000	
			71,400
Capital employed			91,400

key terms

Capital account - see fixed capital account.
Current account - (in the context of balance sheets) an account that records a partner's transactions with the business, excluding capital transactions.
Fixed capital account - an account that records the introduction and withdrawal of capital in the business by a partner.
Fluctuating capital account - an account that records all a partner's transactions with the business, including capital transactions.

summary questions

1. State three differences between sole trader accounts and partnership accounts.
2. Describe the information that may be found in the profit and loss appropriation account of a partnership.
3. Explain why interest is sometimes charged on partners' drawings.
4. Explain how the interest charged on drawings is calculated for a partner.
5. Explain the difference between a partner's capital account and current account.
6. How is the interest on a partner's loan treated in the final accounts?
7. What is a disadvantage of using a fluctuating capital account for a partner?
8. Give three examples of credits that might appear in a partner's current account.
9. Explain how profit is allocated between partners if there is no Deed of Partnership.
10. How is the closing balance on a partner's current account calculated in the balance sheet?

UNIT ASSESSMENT   QUESTION 1

Laura Willis and Simon Daly are partners in a business that supplies hotels with cleaning and maintenance services. They did not draw up a Deed of Partnership when the business was set up. Laura put in £20,000 of capital and Simon provided £25,000. In the year ended 31 December 2001, the business made a net loss of £24,600. During this year Laura withdrew £14,000 from the business and Simon took £11,500. The credit balances on their current accounts at the start of the year had been £12,300 for Laura and £14,300 for Simon.

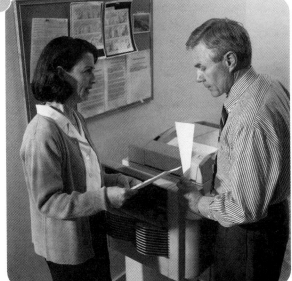

(a) **Draw up a profit and loss appropriation account for the business.**
(b) **Show the (i) fixed capital accounts; (ii) current accounts of the two partners. Use the columnar method of presentation.**
(c) **If the partners had a Deed of Partnership which specified a salary of £20,000 for Laura and £10,000 for Simon, how would this affect the profit and loss appropriation account?**

UNIT ASSESSMENT QUESTION 2

Helen Davies and Mary Bishop own a large veterinary practice in South Wales. They operate as a partnership and employ four administrative staff and 3 other vets. When the partnership was formed, Helen contributed £20,000 capital and Mary contributed £10,000. A Deed of Partnership specifies the following details.
- Interest of 5% is paid on capital.
- No interest is charged on drawings.
- Helen is paid a salary of £33,000 and Mary is paid £30,000.
- Helen, who is the senior partner, receives 75% of the remaining profit and Mary receives 25%.

The trial balance for the partnership is shown in Figure 36.16.

Figure 36.16 Trial balance for Davies and Bishop as at 31.1.01

Davies and Bishop
Trial Balance as at 31.1.01

	Dr £	Cr £
Fees		406,600
Purchases	76,200	
Employees wages and salaries	112,600	
Leasing charge	24,000	
Motor expenses	53,500	
Office expenses	12,400	
Insurance	3,200	
Other overheads	3,900	
Equipment at cost	45,000	
Provision for depreciation - equipment		20,000
Vehicles at cost	32,000	
Provision for depreciation - vehicles		14,000
Stocks (at 1.2.00)	5,300	
Debtors	42,700	
Bank	9,500	
Trade creditors		3,400
Capital: Davies		20,000
Capital: Bishop		10,000
Current account: Davies	400	
Current account: Bishop		3,900
Drawings: Davies	31,800	
Drawings: Bishop	25,400	
	477,900	477,900

The following additional information is also provided.
- Stocks were valued at £6,300 at 31.1.01.
- Depreciation on the equipment and vehicles for the current year is £5,000 and £3,500 respectively.
- £500 is owing on an insurance premium.

(a) Prepare a trading, profit and loss and appropriation account for the partnership
(b) Prepare a balance sheet for the partnership.
(c) Suggest a possible reason why one partner takes a higher share of the profit than the other.

unit 37

Changes in partnerships

unit objectives

To understand:
- the changes that occur in partnerships;
- how goodwill and other assets are treated in partnerships;
- the impact of changes on partnership accounts.

Why do partnerships change?

Partnerships can change for a variety of reasons. These include:
- a new partner being admitted to the partnership;
- the partners deciding to change the profit and loss sharing ratio;
- the partnership being DISSOLVED. A partnership might end, for example, if there is a disagreement between partners or if a partner retires or dies.

Such changes in partnerships affect the accounts. For example, a change in the number of partners will affect the capital structure as shown on the balance sheet. Whenever a change occurs, it is accepted practice to produce a set of accounts for the period up to the date of the change and another for the period after. This unit looks at how accountants deal with changes in the ownership of partnerships and how changes in the value of certain assets affect the partners' financial positions.

Goodwill in partnerships

Goodwill is defined as the difference in value between the net assets of a business, if sold separately, and what the whole business could be sold for (see unit 21). It is an intangible (ie non-physical) asset. Businesses are likely to generate goodwill if they are successful. This success might be the result of building good relations with customers and developing a reputation for quality and service.

The value of goodwill is usually entered in the accounts only if one business is purchased by another and the goodwill is included in the purchase price. However, an exception occurs in the case of partnerships when a partner decides to leave. Under these circumstances, the partner is entitled to a share in the value of the goodwill and therefore its value must be calculated.

The precise value of goodwill is never known until a business is sold. It is determined through negotiation between the buyer and seller. Inevitably the seller of a business will place a higher value on goodwill than the buyer. However, there are several ways of estimating the value of goodwill if a valuation is required at a time other than the sale of the business.

- One approach is to look at the current year's net profit, the highest net profit made in the past few years, or the average net profit over a number of years, and then multiply this by a given number 'X'. The size of 'X' depends on what is expected to happen to profits in the near future. It will be influenced by the nature of the industry, the expected changes in the economy and the particular factors that might influence the performance of the business. If profit is expected to be stable, 'X' might be 1 - 3. If profit is expected to grow, a factor of 4 or 5 might be used. For example, if a business makes an annual profit of £26,000, and profit is expected to grow, the value of goodwill might be £104,000 (4 × £26,000). Here 'X' is 4.

- Another approach involves using **super profits** as a basis for valuation. Super profit is the value of net profit made by a business less the cost to the owner of being involved. This cost includes the salary that the owner could have earned from full time employment elsewhere and also the interest the owner could have earned on any capital invested in the business. Once the amount of super profit has been determined, it is multiplied by a factor 'X' to calculate the value of goodwill. This method is often used for partnerships and sole traders because, in these businesses, net profits are not always an accurate reflection of 'true' profits. Owners often do not charge the full cost of the labour and capital they have invested.

An alternative to using profits in the valuation of goodwill is to focus on sales levels or fee income. For example, businesses that sell professional services, such as accountants, often base goodwill on their gross annual fees. Again the figure for gross fees will be multiplied by a factor 'X'.

A range of other, more sophisticated, methods can also be used to calculate goodwill. For example, discounted cash flow (see unit 57) or the return on capital employed in an industry (see unit 44) might be used.

Goodwill is usually divided among partners in the same ratio as profit unless otherwise agreed. The treatment of goodwill when the structure of a partnership changes is explained later in this unit.

QUESTION

After 25 successful years trading as building contractors in Woking, Tony Skinner and Dennis Giles decided to sell their business. Over the years they had built up a reputation for reliability and quality. Most of their work involved maintenance contracts with local schools and hospitals. Figure 37.1 shows the balance sheet for the partnership as at 31 December 2001. The net profit made by the business over five years is shown in Figure 37.2.

Figure 37.2 *Net profit made by Skinner and Giles over a 5 year period*

Year	Net profit
2001	£42,000
2000	£38,000
1999	£41,000
1998	£37,000
1997	£33,000

(a) Calculate the value of goodwill for the business using average profit over the five years as the basis. Assume X = 4.

(b) Using your answer in (a) and the balance sheet in Figure 37.1, suggest the selling price that Tony Skinner and Dennis Giles might ask for their business.

(c) What factors might influence the value of 'X' in this case?

Figure 37.1 *Balance sheet for Skinner and Giles*

Skinner and Giles
Balance Sheet as at 31.12.01

	£	£
Fixed assets		
Van	15,000	
Less depreciation	10,000	5,000
Tools and equipment	19,000	
Less depreciation	15,000	4,000
		9,000
Current assets		
Stocks	2,700	
Debtors	5,600	
Bank	5,200	
	13,500	
Less current liabilities		
Trade creditors	3,700	
Net current assets		9,800
Net assets		18,800
Financed by		
Capital accounts		
Skinner	8,000	
Giles	5,000	
		13,000

Current accounts	Skinner	Giles
	£	£
Opening balance	600	4,800
Add		
Salary	15,000	15,000
Share of profit	21,000	21,000
	36,600	40,800
Less		
Drawings	34,500	37,100
	2,100	3,700

		5,800
Capital employed		18,800

Revaluation and partnerships

A change in a partnership, such as a partner leaving, will require a REVALUATION of asset values. This is because the partner will want to withdraw any profit that has resulted from the increase in asset values.

Revaluations are necessary when the book values of assets in the balance sheet are not the same as their **net realisable value**, ie their market value. This arises for the following reasons.

- Assets such as land and buildings are likely to appreciate in value over time. This is particularly true for property values in times of inflation.
- Assets such as vehicles, machinery and computers might fall in value faster than expected due to excessive wear and tear or obsolescence.

To illustrate how accountants deal with revaluations of assets, consider the example of Darren Hanson and Matthew Williams, who trade as butchers. A simplified balance sheet for their business, before a revaluation of their assets on 1 January 2002, is shown in Figure 37.3.

Figure 37.3 *Balance sheet of Hanson and Williams (before revaluation of assets)*

Hanson and Williams
Balance Sheet as at 31.12.01

	£	£
Fixed assets		
Premises	85,000	
Less depreciation	5,000	80,000
Van	15,000	
Less depreciation	1,000	14,000
		94,000
Current assets	18,000	
Less current liabilities	11,000	
Net current assets		7,000
Net assets		101,000
Financed by		
Capital accounts		
Hanson	20,000	
Williams	15,000	
		35,000

Current accounts	Hanson	Williams	
	£	£	
	44,000	22,000	
			66,000
Capital employed			101,000

The revaluation of the partnership's assets showed that the value of premises had risen by £40,000 and the value of the van had fallen by £3,000. The nominal ledger entries for these revaluations are in Figure 37.4. It shows the revaluation account, the assets accounts (for the premises and the van) and the partners' capital accounts.

- The entry on the credit side of the revaluation account shows that the premises were revalued upwards by £40,000. The matching debit entry in the premises account shows the increase in the asset value.
- The first entry on the debit side of the revaluation account shows that the van was revalued downwards by £3,000. The matching credit entry in the van account shows the fall in the asset value.
- The balance on the revaluation account represents a profit or loss depending on whether the overall value of assets increased or decreased. In this case, the value of assets increased, ie credits exceeded debits by £37,000 (£40,000 - £3,000), so a profit was made. The profit is credited to the owners' capital accounts and is divided equally between Darren Hanson and Matthew

Williams, £18,500 each. Note that the profit is credited to the partners' capital accounts rather than their current accounts because the profit has not yet been realised. In other words, the profit has not actually been made until the property is sold. If the profit was credited to the partners' current accounts it might be withdrawn and then place a financial strain on the business. Since the profit has not been realised, there might not be enough money in the business for partners to draw on.

Figure 37.4 *Revaluation account, asset accounts and capital account*

Dr		Revaluation Account	Cr	
	£			£
Van	3,000	Premises		40,000
Capital accounts:				
Hanson (1/2)	18,500			
Williams (1/2)	18,500			
	40,000			40,000

Dr		Premises Account	Cr	
	£			£
Balance b/d	80,000	Balance c/d		120,000
Revaluation	40,000			
	120,000			120,000
Balance b/d	120,000			

Dr		Van Account	Cr	
	£			£
Balance b/d	14,000	Revaluation		3,000
		Balance c/d		11,000
	14,000			14,000
Balance b/d	11,000			

Dr	Partners' Capital Accounts			Cr		
	Hanson	Williams			Hanson	Williams
	£	£			£	£
Balances c/d	38,500	33,500	Balances b/d		20,000	15,000
			Revaluation		18,500	18,500
	38,500	33,500			38,500	33,500
			Balances b/d		38,500	33,500

Admission of a new partner

The structure of a partnership will change when a new partner is admitted. This is relatively common and might occur, for example, if a partnership is growing and needs more capital or if someone with different expertise is required. Alternatively it might simply be to replace a partner who has left. Since a new partner will not have made any contribution to the accumulation of goodwill, a payment might be required upon entry. A payment might also be required as a contribution towards the ownership of the partnership's other assets. These must therefore be revalued when the new partner joins.

Adjustments for goodwill To illustrate the bookkeeping entries required to deal with the admission of a new partner and the payment for goodwill, consider the following example. Carol Pugh and James Lister trade as partners in a publishing business and recently admitted a new partner, Helen Grant. Profits were formerly shared equally between Carol and James. When Helen joined, the new arrangement was for Carol and James to take 40% each and Helen 20%. At the time it was agreed that goodwill built up in the business was worth £20,000. It was also agreed that

Helen would pay £18,000 cash into the business's bank account. Carol and James had both contributed £15,000 capital when the business was set up.

One approach for recording these transactions is to open a goodwill account with the agreed valuation. Then, after Helen Grant is admitted, this account is closed by transferring the goodwill to all three partners' capital accounts according to the agreed profit sharing ratios. This is shown in Figure 37.5.

> **Figure 37.5** *Goodwill and capital accounts for Carol Pugh, James Lister and Helen Grant*

Dr	Goodwill Account		Cr	
	£			£
Value divided:		Value divided:		
Pugh (50%)	10,000	Pugh (40%)		8,000
Lister (50%)	10,000	Lister (40%)		8,000
		Grant (20%)		4,000
	20,000			20,000

Dr	Partners' Capital Accounts				Cr		
	Pugh	Lister	Grant		Pugh	Lister	Grant
	£	£	£		£	£	£
Goodwill written off	8,000	8,000	4,000	Balances b/d	15,000	15,000	
Balances c/d	17,000	17,000	14,000	Goodwill created	10,000	10,000	
				Bank			18,000
	25,000	25,000	18,000		25,000	25,000	18,000
				Balances b/d	17,000	17,000	14,000

- The goodwill account is opened and is debited with £20,000. Since Carol Pugh and James Lister originally shared profits equally, the total goodwill is divided between the two partners in the goodwill account, £10,000 each.
- The balances b/d on the capital account reflect the amount of capital each of the two original partners contributed when the business was set up, ie £15,000 each. The capital accounts of the two original partners are also credited with the amount of goodwill they are each entitled to. Carol Pugh's and James Lister's capital accounts are both credited with £10,000.
- The £18,000 paid into the business by Helen Grant is shown by a credit entry in her capital account. A corresponding debit entry is made in the partnership bank account (not shown here).
- The goodwill is now 'written off' in accordance with the agreed profit sharing ratios following the admission of Helen. This is done by debiting Carol Pugh's capital account with £8,000 (40% × £20,000), James Lister's with £8,000 (40% × £20,000) and Helen Grant's with £4,000 (20% × £20,000). The goodwill account is credited with these amounts and the account is closed. Goodwill is written off in this way in order to conform with the accounting standard SSAP22 *Accounting for goodwill*. This recognises that it is difficult to separate goodwill from the value of the business as a whole and is largely a subjective valuation agreed between the partners. Therefore it should not be included on the balance sheet in these circumstances.
- The effect of these adjustments for goodwill is shown by the opening and closing balances in the capital accounts. The balances for Carol Pugh and James Lister have increased by £2,000 each, from £15,000 to £17,000. This is because Helen Grant has, in effect, paid them £4,000 (£2,000 each) for a 20% share of the goodwill they have built up in the business. The £18,000 capital introduced by Helen Grant has fallen by £4,000 to £14,000. This reduction reflects the amount she has paid for goodwill.

Another way of arranging the adjustment for goodwill is for the new partner to make a private cash payment to the original partners. Once the value of goodwill has been agreed, money is paid by the new partner which does not pass through the books of the business. In the example above, if no goodwill account was opened, Helen Grant would pay £2,000 each to Carol Pugh and James Lister. Helen would also pay £14,000 into the business's bank account as her share of capital.

John Fox and Gillian Ball own a restaurant in London and trade as partners sharing profits equally. They set up the business in 1996 and have enjoyed a great deal of success. They have now decided to open another restaurant and have invited Ricardo Benni, the head chef, to join the partnership. Ricardo will pay £50,000 capital into the business bank account when he joins. The credit balances on John Fox's and Gillian Ball's capital accounts are £25,000 each. The value of goodwill in the business has been agreed between the three partners as £60,000. In future, profits will be shared equally between the three partners.

(a) Show the entries needed in the goodwill account and partners' capital accounts when Ricardo Benni is admitted.
(b) What is the value of each partner's capital in the business after the admission of Ricardo Benni?
(c) Explain why there is no balance on the goodwill account.

Adjustments for revaluation To illustrate the adjustments necessary for revaluation when a new partner is admitted to a partnership, consider the example of Michael Proctor and Damien Slater. They operate as estate agents and in April 2001 they admitted Marcia Jennings as a new partner. Profits had been shared equally between Michael and Damien and, when Marcia joined, the partners agreed to take a third each. It was also agreed that two assets should be revalued. The premises had increased in value by £30,000 due to a rise in property prices. However, it was decided that the value of vehicles was £4,000 less than their book value.

The closing balance sheet for Proctor and Slater is shown in Figure 37.6. It shows the position prior to the revaluation of assets and the admission of the new partner.

Figure 37.6 *Closing balance sheet for Proctor and Slater*

Proctor and Slater
Balance Sheet as at 31.3.01

	£	£
Fixed assets		
Premises (net book value)		75,000
Vehicles (net book value)		18,000
		93,000
Current assets		
Debtors	23,600	
Bank	11,300	
	34,900	
Less current liabilities		
Trade creditors	4,300	
Net current assets		30,600
Net assets		123,600
Financed by		
Capital accounts		
Proctor	50,000	
Giles	50,000	
		100,000

Current accounts	Proctor	Slater
	£	£
Opening balance	2,300	4,200
Add		
Share of profit	41,000	41,000
	43,300	45,200
Less		
Drawings	30,000	34,900
	13,300	10,300

		23,600
Capital employed		123,600

Marcia Jennings was admitted to the partnership on 1 April 2001 and on that date she paid £50,000 into the firm's bank account as capital. The book entries needed for the revaluation and on the admission of the new partner are shown in Figure 37.7.

- A revaluation account is opened with a £30,000 credit and £4,000 debit. The credit entry shows that the premises have increased in value by £30,000. The debit entry for this transaction will appear in the premises account (not shown here). The debit entry in the revaluation account shows that vehicles have fallen in value by £4,000. The credit entry for this transaction will appear in the vehicles account (also not shown here).
- The balance of £26,000 on the revaluation account represents a profit. This profit is credited to the capital accounts of Michael Proctor and Damien Slater. The profit is shared equally so the original partners' capital accounts are both credited with £13,000 with the balance rising from £50,000 to £63,000 each.

Figure 37.7 *Revaluation account and partners' capital accounts for Proctor and Slater*

Dr		**Revaluation Account**	**Cr**	
	£			£
Vehicles	4,000	Premises		30,000
Capital:				
Proctor (50%)	13,000			
Slater (50%)	13,000			
	30,000			30,000

Dr			**Partners' Capital Accounts**	**Cr**		
			(before Marcia Jennings joined)			
	Proctor	**Slater**			**Proctor**	**Slater**
	£	£			£	£
Balances c/d	63,000	63,000	Balances b/d		50,000	50,000
			Revaluation		13,000	13,000
	63,000	63,000			63,000	63,000
			Balances b/d		63,000	63,000

Figure 37.9 shows an opening balance sheet for the partnership on the date that Marcia Jennings joined. It records the effect of the revaluation, the payment by Marcia, and the capital accounts of the three partners. When Marcia Jennings joined the partnership on 1 April 2001, she deposited £50,000 into the business bank account. The fixed assets are recorded at their new valuation so that premises now have a net book value of £105,000 and vehicles have a net book value of £14,000. The balance at the bank has risen by £50,000 to £61,300 to reflect Marcia's payment on admission. The balances on the capital accounts of Michael Proctor and Damien Slater have risen by £13,000 to reflect the profit on revaluation, and Marcia Jenning's capital account is now included.

QUESTION 3

Darlene Peters and Heather Moss run a private nursery school in Southampton. In 2001 they decided to admit a new partner to share the responsibility of running the business. They also needed an injection of capital to cover the cost of complying with new health and safety legislation. Jean Cherry was admitted to the partnership on 1 May 2001 paying £25,000 into the business bank account. The school premises originally cost £78,000 but were valued at £190,000 in April 2001. However, the value of the computer system had fallen and was estimated to be worth only £200. Before admitting their new partner, Darlene and Heather decided to make an extra provision for bad debts of £1,500. The original partners shared profits equally and it was agreed that the new ratio would be 2:2:1 respectively for Darlene, Heather and Jean. The partnership balance sheet prior to the revaluation and admission of Jean is shown in Figure 37.8.

Figure 37.8 *Balance sheet for Peters and Moss*

Peters and Moss
Balance Sheet as at 30.4.01

	£	£
Fixed assets		
Premises (net book value)		78,000
Fixtures and fittings (net book value)		18,000
Equipment (net book value)		6,500
Computer (net book value)		2,300
		104,800
Current assets		
Debtors and prepayments	7,200	
Bank	4,200	
	11,400	
Less current liabilities		
Trade creditors	5,300	
Net current assets		6,100
		110,900
Less long term liabilities		
Mortgage		60,000
Net assets		50,900
Financed by		
Capital accounts		
Peters	25,000	
Moss	25,000	
		50,000

Current accounts	Peters	Moss	
	£	£	
Opening balance	1,500	2,100	
Add			
Share of profit	26,200	26,200	
	27,700	28,300	
Less			
Drawings	27,600	27,500	
	100	800	
			900
Capital employed			50,900

(a) **Prepare a revaluation account for Darlene Peters and Heather Moss.**
(b) **Redraw the balance sheet for the new partnership as at 1 May 2001.**

Figure 37.9 *Balance sheet for Proctor, Slater and Jennings*

Proctor, Slater and Jennings
Balance Sheet as at 1.4.01

	£	£
Fixed assets		
Premises (net book value)		105,000
Vehicles (net book value)		14,000
		119,000
Current assets		
Debtors	23,600	
Bank	61,300	
	84,900	
Less current liabilities		
Trade creditors	4,300	
Net current assets		80,600
Net assets		199,600
Financed by		
Capital accounts		
Proctor	63,000	
Giles	63,000	
Jennings	50,000	
		176,000

Current accounts	Proctor £	Slater £	Jennings £
Opening balance	2,300	4,200	-
Add			
Share of profit	41,000	41,000	-
	43,300	45,200	-
Less			
Drawings	30,000	34,900	-
	13,300	10,300	-

	£
	23,600
Capital employed	199,600

Retirement of a partner

When a partner leaves a business it is necessary to calculate exactly how much money that partner is entitled to. This requires a valuation of all assets, including goodwill, and all liabilities. To illustrate the bookkeeping entries on the retirement of a partner, consider the example of Thomas Wilson, Dilip Solanki and George Betts who run a shipping agency. George decided to retire from the partnership on 1 January 2002. The partners agreed that goodwill in the business was worth £30,000 and also that premises were worth £105,000 and fixtures and fittings were worth £14,500. Profits in the partnership were shared equally and, when George left, a payment of £10,000 was made to him. The remainder of the money owed to George was left in the business as a loan to be repaid at a future date. The balance sheet for Wilson, Solanki and Betts as at 31 December 2001 is shown in Figure 37.10.

Figure 37.10 *Balance sheet for Wilson, Solanki and Betts*

Wilson, Solanki and Betts
Balance Sheet as at 31.12.01

	£	£
Fixed assets		
Premises		60,000
Fixtures and fittings		17,500
		77,500
Current assets		
Debtors	3,600	
Bank	24,100	
	27,700	
Less current liabilities		
Trade creditors	5,600	
Net current assets		22,100
Net assets		99,600
Financed by		
Capital accounts		
Wilson	30,000	
Solanki	30,000	
Betts	30,000	
		90,000
Current accounts		
Wilson	2,600	
Solanki	3,300	
Betts	3,700	
		9,600
Capital employed		99,600

To calculate how much is owed to George Betts on his retirement from the partnership, the following steps are taken. The accounts are shown in Figure 37.11.

- A goodwill account is opened and goodwill of £30,000 is recorded as a debit. It is shared equally between the partners (£10,000 each) and credited to their capital accounts. The goodwill account is then closed by crediting the goodwill to the remaining partners, Thomas Wilson and Dilip Solanki (£15,000 each) and debiting the amounts to their capital accounts.
- A revaluation account is opened to determine the share of any profit on revaluation. The account is credited with £45,000. This represents the increase in value of the premises from £60,000 to £105,000. The account is debited with £3,000. This reflects the fall in value of fixtures and fittings from £17,500 to £14,500. The balance on the account, which is a debit balance of £42,000, represents profit on revaluation. This is shared equally between the partners (£14,000 each) and is credited to their capital accounts.
- The opening balances b/d in the partners' capital account is £30,000 each. The capital accounts must now be balanced. However, since George Betts is leaving, his account must be closed. The balance of £54,000 is transferred as a credit to a loan account. The balances on the capital accounts of Thomas Wilson and Dilip Solanki are now £39,000.
- The loan account for George Betts shows the £10,000 payment to him as a debit entry. The credit entry for the transaction is in the business bank account (not shown here). The balance on George Betts' current account, £3,700, is also transferred to the loan account. The balance on the loan account, £47,700, is recorded in the balance sheet and eventually George will be repaid what is owed to him. This is a relatively common practice since paying off a partner at once might place a financial strain on the business.

Figure 37.11 *Partnership accounts on retirement*

Dr	Goodwill Account		Cr	
	£			£
Value divided:		Value divided:		
Wilson (1/3)	10,000	Wilson (1/2)		15,000
Solanki (1/3)	10,000	Solanki (1/2)		15,000
Betts (1/3)	10,000			
	30,000			30,000

Dr	Partners' Capital Accounts			Cr		
	Wilson	Solanki	Betts	Wilson	Solanki	Betts
	£	£	£	£	£	£
Goodwill written off	15,000	15,000		Balances b/d	30,000	30,000	30,000
Loan account - Betts			54,000	Goodwill	10,000	10,000	10,000
Balances c/d	39,000	39,000		Revaluation	14,000	14,000	14,000
	54,000	54,000	54,000		54,000	54,000	54,000
				Balances b/d	39,000	39,000	

Dr	Revaluation Account		Cr	
	£			£
Fixtures and fittings	3,000	Premises		45,000
Capital accounts:				
Wilson	14,000			
Solanki	14,000			
Betts	14,000			
	45,000			45,000

Dr	Loan Account - Betts		Cr	
	£			£
Bank	10,000	Capital a/c - transfer		54,000
Balance c/d	47,700	Current a/c - transfer		3,700
	57,700			57,700
		Balance b/d		47,700

The opening balance sheet for the new partnership of Wilson and Solanki as at 1 January 2002 is shown in Figure 37.12. The premises and fixtures and fittings have been revalued (premises to £105,000 and fixtures and fittings to £14,500). The bank account has fallen to £14,100 from £24,100 because £10,000 was used to pay George Betts. In addition, a new liability has been created representing the amount owed to George (£47,700). The new balances in the capital accounts are entered for Thomas Wilson and Dilip Solanki (£39,000), and George Betts' capital and current accounts are deleted because the balances have been transferred to a loan account.

One of the effects of the adjustments is that Thomas Wilson and Dilip Solanki have bought George Betts' share of the goodwill in the business. If the business is sold in the future, the two partners would then benefit from the sale of this goodwill.

Figure 37.12 *Opening balance sheet for Wilson and Solanki*

Wilson and Solanki
Balance Sheet as at 1.1.02

	£	£
Fixed assets		
Premises		105,000
Fixtures and fittings		14,500
		119,500
Current assets		
Debtors	3,600	
Bank	14,100	
	17,700	
Less current liabilities		
Trade creditors	5,600	
Net current assets		12,100
		131,600
Less long term liabilities		
Loan - Betts		47,700
Net assets		83,900
Financed by		
Capital accounts		
Wilson	39,000	
Solanki	39,000	
		78,000
Current accounts		
Wilson	2,600	
Solanki	3,300	
		5,900
Capital employed		83,900

Death of a partner

If a partner dies, the accounting procedure is similar to that for a retiring partner. However, because a loan account cannot be opened for the deceased partner, the amount owing is placed into an executor's (or administrator's) loan account before a final settlement is made.

Change in profit sharing ratio

Sometimes partners agree to change their profit sharing ratios. Such action might be necessary because there has been a change in the amount of:
- time a partner works;
- capital a partner contributes;
- responsibility a partner has in the business.

When a change in the profit sharing ratio takes place, adjustments are necessary to account for the goodwill that has built up in the period before the change. The purpose of this is to share out the goodwill according to the old ratio before the new ratio is introduced. To illustrate the bookkeeping entries required, consider the example of David Poon and Christine Francis who trade as insurance brokers. When they formed their partnership, they agreed to share profits equally. However, after three years they decided to change the ratio to 3:2 in favour of David Poon to reflect the extra workload he had undertaken. The partners agreed at the time of the change that the value of goodwill in the business was £50,000. The opening balances on the capital accounts of David Poon and Christine Francis were £20,000 and £25,000 respectively. The bookkeeping entries are shown in Figure 37.13.

- A goodwill account is opened and £50,000 of goodwill is recorded as a debit. This is shared equally between the two partners according to the old profit sharing ratio. The partners' capital accounts are credited with £25,000 each.
- The goodwill account is closed by crediting the account with £50,000. This is divided between David Poon and Christine Francis in the new profit sharing ratio of 3:2. Therefore David's capital account is debited with £30,000 and Christine's with £20,000.

Figure 37.13 *Goodwill account and partners' capital accounts for Poon and Francis* ○○○

Dr	Goodwill Account		Cr	
		£		£
Value divided:			Value divided:	
Poon (1/2)		25,000	Poon (3/5)	30,000
Francis (1/2)		25,000	Francis (2/5)	20,000
		50,000		50,000

Dr	Partners' Capital Accounts		Cr		
	Poon	Francis		Poon	Francis
	£	£		£	£
Goodwill written off	30,000	20,000	Balances b/d	20,000	25,000
Balances c/d	15,000	30,000	Goodwill created	25,000	25,000
	45,000	50,000		45,000	50,000
			Balances b/d	15,000	30,000

The balances on the capital accounts are adjusted to reflect the change in the profit sharing ratio. It might seem odd that David Poon's balance has fallen by £5,000 from £20,000 to £15,000, and that Christine Francis' balance has increased by £5,000 from £25,000 to £30,000, when the profit sharing ratio has changed in favour of David. However, what has happened is that Christine has been compensated for her loss of goodwill. In effect David has paid Christine £5,000 to increase his share of profits and goodwill in the future from $\frac{1}{2}$ to $\frac{3}{5}$.

QUESTION 4

Kate Done, Angus Bryce and Alastair Wallace are partners in a business that provides financial services in Newcastle. When the partnership started they decided to share profits equally but, on 1 January 2001, they agreed to change the profit sharing ratio. It was felt by all partners that the success of the business was increasingly the result of Alastair's efforts in introducing new clients. It was agreed that future profits would be divided in a ratio of 1:1:2 in favour of Alastair. It was also decided that goodwill in the business was worth £90,000 at the time of the change. The balances on the partners' capital accounts prior to the change are shown in Figure 37.14.

Figure 37.14 *Capital accounts for Done, Bryce and Wallace* ○○○

Dr	Partners' Capital Accounts				Cr		
	Done	Bryce	Wallace		Done	Bryce	Wallace
	£	£	£		£	£	£
				Balances b/d	10,000	15,000	15,000

(a) Show the entries needed in the goodwill account and the partners' capital accounts to adjust for the changes in the profit sharing ratio.

(b) Explain why the balance on Wallace's capital account has fallen in relation to the other two partners.

(c) Explain why there is no balance on the goodwill account.

Dissolution of a partnership

When a partnership ceases trading, its affairs are dissolved. This means that all of its accounts have to be closed. The causes of dissolution might be:

- the death, retirement or ill health of a partner;
- an inadequate level of profits;
- the business becoming a limited company;
- a disagreement between partners about the future direction of the business.

When a partnership is dissolved, the assets of the business are sold and the proceeds are distributed according to the Partnership Act (1890). This states that money should be paid in the following order:

1 - to business creditors (not including partners);
2 - to partners that have lent money to the business;
3 - to partners in respect of their current accounts;
4 - to partners in respect of their capital accounts.

Any profit or loss on dissolution is divided according to the agreed profit sharing ratios. If a loss is made, the money paid to partners in respect of their capital accounts will be reduced. If the loss is so great that it is not covered by the partners' capital, current or loan accounts, then partners have to pay money into the business's bank account. This is because partners have unlimited liability for the business's debts.

When disposing of a business's assets, the partners might decide to take personal ownership of some of those assets that formerly belonged to the business. For example, they might keep the cars that they have used. If this happens, the value of any assets taken are debited to the partner's capital account.

The dissolution of a partnership requires a **realisation account** to be opened. This account records the book values of the assets to be disposed of on the debit side and the proceeds from disposal on the credit side. The balance on the account represents the profit or loss on disposal. If the value of debits is greater than the value of credits, a loss is made. If credits exceed debits, a profit is made. Any profit or loss is transferred to the partners' capital accounts.

To illustrate the bookkeeping entries involved when dissolving a partnership, consider the example of Steve Price and Kumar Patel who ran an airport taxi service together in Bristol. The partners agreed to dissolve the partnership because Steve decided to move to Birmingham. The balance sheet for Price and Patel as at 31 May 2001 is shown in Figure 37.15.

The realisation account, bank account and partners' capital accounts relating to the dissolution of the partnership are shown in Figure 37.16.

- All asset accounts, except for the cash and bank accounts, are closed by transferring the balances to the realisation account. The asset accounts are credited and the realisation account is debited. In this case, for example, the minibus account and the motor car account are credited with £18,000 and £6,000 respectively (not shown here). The realisation account is debited with £18,000 and £6,000.
- Provisions accounts, such as depreciation and bad debts, are closed by transferring the balances to the realisation account. The realisation account is credited and the provisions accounts is debited with the value of the balances. There are no such entries in this example.
- The proceeds from the disposal of assets are listed on the credit side of the realisation account. In this case, the Minibus is sold for £21,000 and the amount obtained from debtors is £500. The debit entries for these transactions are shown in the bank account.
- Steve Price took ownership of the motor car at an agreed value of £7,000. Therefore his capital account is debited with £7,000 and the realisation account is credited with £7,000.
- The creditors were paid off with money from the bank. In this case, trade creditors were owed £1,200 so the bank account is credited with £1,200 and the trade creditors account is debited (not shown here). There was also a £6,000 bank loan that had to be repaid. The loan account is debited with £6,000 (not shown here) and the bank account is credited with £6,000. These transactions do not affect the realisation account.
- The dissolution of a partnership often incurs some administration costs or 'realisation expenses'. For example, advertising costs might be incurred when disposing of assets. In this case, realisation expenses for Steve Price and Kumar Patel were £500. This payment is debited to the realisation

Figure 37.15 *Balance sheet for Price and Patel as at 31.5.01*

Price and Patel
Balance Sheet as at 31.5.01

	£	£
Fixed assets		
Minibus		18,000
Motor car		6,000
		24,000
Current assets		
Debtors and prepayments	600	
Bank	2,200	
Cash	300	
	3,100	
Less current liabilities		
Trade creditors	1,200	
Net current assets		1,900
		25,900
Less long term liabilities		
Bank loan		6,000
Net assets		19,900
Financed by		
Capital accounts		
Price	7,000	
Patel	7,000	
		14,000
Current accounts		
Price	2,900	
Patel	3,000	
		5,900
Capital employed		19,900

account and is credited to the bank account.

- The balance on the realisation account is transferred to the partners' capital accounts once all disposals have been made. In this case, a profit of £3,400 was made on the realisation account which is divided equally between the two partners. Therefore the partners' capital accounts are credited with £1,700 each.

- Any loans made by the partners to the business have to be repaid. The bookkeeping entries required for this transaction are to debit the partners' loan accounts and credit the bank account. In this case, neither partner had lent the business any money.

- In order to close the partners' current accounts, the balances are transferred to their capital accounts. In this case, the capital accounts of Steve Price and Kumar Patel are credited with their current balances of £2,900 and £3,000 respectively. If one or both the partners had a negative balance on his current account, the amount would be debited to the capital account.

- The remaining cash in hand or at the bank is used to repay the credit balances on the partners' capital accounts. Steve Price is paid £4,600 and Kumar Patel is paid £11,700. Note that Kumar takes £11,400 from the bank and £300 in cash to clear his capital account.

- If either partner had a debit balance on his capital account, this would mean that money is owed to the business. Therefore cash must be introduced by that partner. However, this is not the case in this example. The final balances on the partners' capital accounts must be equal to the combined balances on the cash and bank accounts. If they are not, an error has been made in the bookkeeping when dissolving the business.

Figure 37.16 *Realisation account, bank account and partners' capital accounts for Price and Patel*

Dr	Realisation Account		Cr	
	£			£
Minibus	18,000	Minibus		21,000
Motor car	6,000	Debtors		500
Debtors and prepayments	600	Motor car (taken by Price)		7,000
Bank - realisation expenses	500			
Profit on realisation				
Price (1/2)	1,700			
Patel (1/2)	1,700			
	28,500			28,500

Dr	Bank Account		Cr	
	£			£
Balance b/d	2,200	Trade creditors		1,200
Realisation: assets sold		Bank loan		6,000
Minibus	21,000	Realisation expenses		500
Debtors and prepayments	500	Capital accounts		
		Price		4,600
		Patel		11,400
	23,700			23,700

Dr	Partners' Capital Accounts			Cr		
	Price	Patel			Price	Patel
	£	£			£	£
Realisation (motor car)	7,000		Balances b/d		7,000	7,000
Bank to close	4,600	11,400	Profit on realisation		1,700	1,700
Cash to close		300	Current accounts		2,900	3,000
	11,600	11,700			11,600	11,700

The Garner v Murray (1904) rule

As stated before, when a partnership is dissolved and a partner has a debit balance on his or her capital account, the partner must pay money into the business bank account. If that partner does not have sufficient financial resources to settle the account, the remaining partners must bear the loss. However, the loss should **not** be shared according to the profit/loss sharing ratios, but according to the **balances on their capital accounts**. This ruling, which relates to England, Wales and Northern Ireland, was established in 1904 in a court case *Garner v Murray*. The court stated that, subject to any agreement to the contrary, any deficiency on a partner's capital account resulting from the dissolution of that partnership, should be shared by the other partners not in their profit and loss sharing ratio but in the ratio of 'last agreed capitals'. This refers to the credit balances on their capital accounts in the balance sheet at the end of the last trading year. It does not mean the balances after assets have been realised.

To illustrate the Garner v Murray ruling, consider the example of Ann Gibbs, Trisha Crawley and Ben Smith who agreed to dissolve their partnership at the end of 2001. The credit balances on their capital accounts shown in the balance sheet as at 31 December 2001 were £20,000, £10,000 and £10,000 respectively. After the assets were realised, the capital account balances were £5,000, £3,000 and minus £6,000 respectively. Ben Smith was unable to pay off his £6,000 deficit. Consequently, according to the Garner v Murray ruling, the deficit was paid by the remaining two partners according to the ratio of the balance on their capital accounts at the end of the trading year. The amount paid by each partner is calculated as follows.

$$\text{Ann Gibbs} \quad = \quad \frac{£20,000}{£20,000 + £10,000} \quad \times \quad £6,000 \quad = \quad £4,000$$

$$\text{Trisha Crawley} = \quad \frac{£10,000}{£20,000 \ + \ £10,000} \quad \times \quad £6,000 \quad = \quad £2,000$$

Since Ann Gibbs' capital balance was bigger than Trisha Crawley's, Ann was obliged by the ruling to pay off a greater proportion of Ben Smith's deficit. Note, however, that this would not have been the case if the partners had made a different arrangement in their original Deed of Partnership.

key terms

Dissolution - the ending of a business entity. In this context it occurs when a partnership is dissolved.

Revaluation - the increase, or sometimes decrease, in the value of assets to reflect the change from their historical value to their current market value.

summary questions

1. State three reasons why partnerships might change.
2. Explain two ways in which goodwill might be valued.
3. Why is a revaluation of assets necessary when a partnership structure changes?
4. Suggest two examples of entries that might appear on the credit side of the revaluation account.
5. Why should a new partner make a payment for goodwill when joining a partnership?
6. If a profit is made on revaluation, on which side of the revaluation account will it appear?
7. A loan account is sometimes opened in the name of a retired partner. Explain why this might be necessary.
8. What is a realisation account used for?
9. If a profit is made on realisation, which side of the account will it appear on?
10. Outline the Garner v Murray ruling.

UNIT ASSESSMENT QUESTION 1

George Hart and Henry Brown traded as partners for 25 years and shared profits or losses equally. They ran an advertising agency but decided to end the partnership in 2001 because they both wished to retire. The balance sheet for the business is shown in Figure 37.17. Note that Henry Brown had a negative balance on his current account. The following information is also available.

- The premises were sold for £84,000.
- Fixtures and fittings were sold for £1,000.
- George Hart took possession of the computer at an agreed value of £1,000.
- Realisation and dissolution expenses were £1,200.
- Debtors realised £2,900.
- Trade creditors and the mortgage loan were repaid at the values shown in the balance sheet.

Figure 37.17 *Balance sheet for Hart and Brown*

Hart and Brown
Balance Sheet as at 31.7.01

	£	£
Fixed assets		
Premises		64,000
Fixtures and fittings		4,300
Computer		1,500
		69,800
Current assets		
Debtors and prepayments	3,200	
Bank	5,200	
	8,400	
Less current liabilities		
Trade creditors	4,000	
Net current assets		4,400
		74,200
Less long term liabilities		
Mortgage		30,000
Net assets		44,200
Financed by		
Capital accounts		
Hart	20,000	
Brown	20,000	
		40,000
Current accounts		
Hart	5,800	
Brown	(1,600)	
		4,200
Capital employed		44,200

(a) Prepare a realisation account for George Hart and Henry Brown
(b) How much profit was made on realisation?
(c) Show the entries required in (i) the bank account; (ii) the partners' capital accounts when the partnership is dissolved.

Aysha Hussain, Karen Munton and Elizabeth Rose were partners in a mini-market selling groceries, confectionery, alcohol and fresh produce in Slough. Although the business was very successful, Karen decided to retire from the partnership due to ill health. It was agreed that she would leave at the end of the financial year, 31 December 2001. The value of goodwill in the business was estimated to be £90,000. The partners shared all profits equally and, when Karen left, it was agreed to pay the money owed to her at a later date and to open a loan account in her name. The partners also agreed that:

- the premises were worth £120,000;
- fixtures and fittings were worth £4,800.

The balance sheet for the partnership is shown in Figure 37.18.

Figure 37.18 Balance sheet for Hussain, Munton and Rose

Hussain, Munton and Rose
Balance Sheet as at 31.12.01

	£	£
Fixed assets		
Premises		83,000
Van		7,000
Fixtures and fittings		5,200
		95,200
Current assets		
Stock	18,400	
Debtors	5,300	
Bank	27,400	
	51,100	
Less current liabilities		
Trade creditors	16,600	
Net current assets		34,500
Net assets		129,700
Financed by		
Capital accounts		
Hussain	40,000	
Munton	40,000	
Rose	40,000	
		120,000
Current accounts		
Hussain	3,100	
Munton	1,900	
Rose	4,700	
		9,700
Capital employed		129,700

(a) **Prepare the following accounts for the partnership at the time of Karen Munton's retirement: (i) goodwill; (ii) revaluation; (iii) partners' capital; (iv) Karen Munton loan and (v) premises.**

(b) **Prepare a balance sheet for the new partnership, Hussain and Rose, as at 1.1.02.**

Limited company accounts

unitobjectives

To understand:
- company accounts;
- the requirements of the Companies Acts;
- published accounts.

Limited company accounts

Limited companies are businesses in which the liability of owners, ie shareholders, is limited to the amount (if any) unpaid on their shares. This is unlike sole traders and partnerships, where the owners have unlimited liability for their business's debts.

The accounts of limited companies differ slightly from those of sole traders and partnerships. One reason is because they have different capital structures. For example, limited companies raise capital by the sale of shares and certain details relating to this share capital are shown in the balance sheet. Another difference is in the terminology used. For instance, the term TURNOVER is used instead of 'sales'. Also, the term 'creditors: amounts falling due within one year' is used instead of 'current liabilities'.

Limited companies in the UK are obliged to publish accounts in order to conform to the Companies Acts. These Acts of Parliament require companies to disclose certain information about their financial affairs and to present the information in a particular format. The requirements of the Companies Acts and the format for **published accounts** are discussed later in this unit. Limited companies also produce accounts for **internal use**. These accounts provide directors and managers with financial information to help them monitor performance and make decisions.

The profit and loss account

The profit and loss account of companies, like that of partnerships, is divided into three sections:
- the trading account which shows the gross profit;
- the profit and loss account which shows the net profit;
- the appropriation account which shows how the net profit is shared out to shareholders, how much is retained in reserves and how much is paid in tax.

Figure 38.1 shows a profit and loss account for Bracken Ltd. This is a private limited company that produces domestic gas fires and other appliances. The account has been prepared for internal use and therefore does not necessarily conform to any legal standard format. The style of presentation for internal accounts varies from company to company, depending on which information is required.

- **Turnover** (or sales) This is the amount of revenue generated from the sale of goods and services. For Bracken Ltd this was £2,469,000 in 2001.
- **Cost of sales** Unlike in the accounts of sole traders and partnerships, it is not usual to show the adjustments made for opening and closing stock when preparing the trading account for limited companies. The main reason for this is to avoid including too much detail. Examples of cost of sales for Bracken Ltd are direct costs such as components, materials used in production, and the wages of employees directly involved in production.
- **Gross profit** As with other types of business, the purpose of preparing a trading account is to calculate gross profit. For Bracken Ltd gross profit was £1,488,000. It is found by subtracting cost of sales from turnover (£2,469,000 - £981,000).
- **Selling and distribution expenses** The expenses, or overheads, in the profit and loss account of limited companies are generally classified as either selling and distribution expenses or administration expenses. For Bracken Ltd, examples of selling and distribution expenses include the salaries of salespeople, motor expenses and warehouse costs. Some businesses might choose

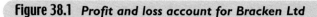

Figure 38.1 *Profit and loss account for Bracken Ltd*

Bracken Ltd
Profit and Loss account
for the year ended 31.12.01

	£000s	£000s
Turnover		2,469
Cost of sales		981
Gross profit		1,488
Less expenses		
Selling and distribution	114	
Administration	451	565
		923
Interest paid		21
Profit before taxation		902
Taxation		220
Profit after taxation		682
Dividends paid and proposed		
Interim dividends paid:		
Preference shares	50	
Ordinary shares	120	
Final dividends proposed:		
Preference shares	50	
Ordinary shares	150	
		370
Retained profit for the year		312
Retained profit b/f		4,391
Retained profit c/f		4,703

to list specific selling and distribution expenses. In this case, Bracken Ltd has chosen to list the total (£114,000).

- **Administration expenses** All other expenses are listed under administration expenses. For Bracken Ltd, these include the salaries of office staff, directors' remuneration, auditor's fees, insurance and depreciation. Again, some businesses might list further details of these costs but Bracken Ltd has listed the total (£451,000). All expenses are added together and subtracted from gross profit. This gives a sub-total of £923,000.
- **Interest or financial charges** The interest paid by Bracken Ltd is shown as a separate entry in the profit and loss account. This helps to show how much debt the company has. For example, large interest payments (in relation to profit) will indicate that the company has a significant amount of debt. Businesses usually show the total interest paid and not the details. Interest paid might include that paid to banks or debenture holders. Bracken Ltd paid a total of £21,000 interest which is subtracted from £923,000 to give profit before taxation of £902,000. If Bracken Ltd had received any interest, for example from money in a bank deposit account, the amount would also be shown here as 'interest received'. Some companies simply record 'net interest' which is the interest paid less the interest received.
- **Profit before taxation** This is the amount of money left over for distribution. It represents the starting point for the profit and loss appropriation account which shows shareholders and other stakeholders what has happened to profit.
- **Taxation** Limited companies pay corporation tax on their profits. Accountants estimate how much corporation tax is due and the amount is deducted from the profit before tax. The same amount is shown as a current liability in the balance sheet. For Bracken Ltd, corporation tax is estimated to be £220,000. Corporation tax rates are determined by the government and might change. Note that this aspect of the accounts is different from sole traders and partnerships, where taxation is not recorded in the final accounts.

- **Profit after taxation** Bracken Ltd made a profit of £682,000 after tax. This money is available to the business and can be distributed according to the wishes of the directors subject to the support of shareholders.
- **Dividends paid and proposed** If the business has made sufficient profit, the directors will generally distribute some of it to shareholders. If dividends are paid, it is common to pay an INTERIM DIVIDEND. This is a payment that is made to shareholders before the end of the trading year. A FINAL DIVIDEND is then paid early in the following financial year. The bookkeeping entries required to record dividends are to debit the appropriation account and credit the dividend account. Then, when dividends are actually paid, the dividend account is debited. Proposed dividends appear in the balance sheet as a current liability. Bracken Ltd paid an interim dividend to both preference and ordinary shareholders, £50,000 and £120,000 respectively. Bracken's directors also proposed a final dividend of £50,000 and £150,000 to preference and ordinary shareholders respectively.
- **Retained profit** Any profit that is not distributed is called RETAINED PROFIT and is transferred to reserves in the balance sheet. In the case of Bracken Ltd, £312,000 was retained. The bookkeeping entries to record this are to debit the appropriation account and credit the reserve account. In effect, the retained profit is added to the balance of retained profits that have accumulated since the company began trading. This is shown at the bottom of the appropriation account. The balance of retained profit was £4,391,000, therefore the total retained profit carried forward was £4,703,000 (£312,000 + £4,391,000). Profit is retained by companies as a precaution in case trading becomes difficult or to help fund future investment.

Balance sheet

Figure 38.3 shows the balance sheet for Bracken Ltd, the company used in the earlier example. Note that the section dealing with capital and reserves of a limited company is different from the balance sheet of sole traders and partnerships.

QUESTION 1

Weston Toys Ltd is owned by the Weston family and manufactures soft toys. The information shown in Figure 38.2 relates to the trading year ended 30 November 2001. The company does not pay interim dividends but the directors proposed a final dividend of £1,000,000 to shareholders.

Figure 38.2 *Financial information for Weston Toys Ltd, year ended 30.11.01*

Turnover	£12,432,000	Depreciation	£176,000
Cost of sales	£5,332,000	Other administration expenses	£732,000
Salaries of sales staff	£210,000	Interest paid	£153,000
Distribution	£312,000	Taxation	£800,000
Other selling expenses	£448,000	Directors' remuneration	£560,000
Office expenses	£1,237,000	Retained profit brought forward	£6,920,000

(a) **Prepare the trading, profit and loss and appropriation accounts for Weston Toys Ltd.**
(b) **What is the amount of retained profit carried forward?**
(c) **Suggest why the directors of Weston Toys Ltd might have retained some of the profit.**

Figure 38.3 *Balance sheet for Bracken Ltd as at 31.12.01*

Bracken Ltd
Balance Sheet as at 31.12.01

	£000	£000	£000
Fixed assets			
Tangible assets			12,500
Investments			2,600
			15,100
Current assets			
Stock		3,100	
Debtors		1,280	
Cash		2,758	
		7,138	
Creditors: amounts falling due within one year			
Creditors	2,180		
Taxation (220 + 45)	265		
Dividends proposed	200	2,645	
Net current assets			4,493
			19,593
Creditors: amounts falling due after more than one year			
Mortgage			1,500
Net assets			18,093
Capital and reserves			
Authorised share capital			
10,000,000 ordinary shares of £1 each		10,000	
2,000,000 5% preference shares of £1 each		2,000	
		12,000	
Issued and fully paid up			
5,000,000 ordinary shares of £1 each			5,000
2,000,000 preference shares of £1 each			2,000
Share premium account			2,500
Revaluation reserve			2,890
Capital redemption reserve			1,000
Profit and loss account			4,703
Shareholders' funds			18,093

- **Tangible assets** The value of fixed assets are generally listed under three headings - tangible assets, intangible assets and investments. Tangible assets are the physical assets of the business. Examples for Bracken Ltd include its premises, plant and machinery, tools and equipment, and vehicles. The net book value of tangible assets for Bracken Ltd is £12,500,000. It is usual to give just a total for tangible assets in the balance sheet in order to avoid too much detail. If Bracken Ltd had any intangible assets such as purchased goodwill or brand names, their value would also be given.

- **Investments** These are shareholdings in other companies, for example subsidiaries. They are classed as investments if the business intends to hold them for more than one year. Bracken Ltd has £2,600,000 of investments.

- **Current assets** The current assets held by limited companies are similar to those held by sole traders and partnerships, such as stock, debtors and cash. Bracken Ltd has a range of current assets which total £7,138,00. If the company owned financial assets, such as shares, which it intended to sell within one year, these assets would be listed as investments under current assets.

- **Creditors: amounts falling due within one year** This term is used to describe the current liabilities of limited companies. Examples include trade creditors, accruals and bank overdrafts which might all appear on the balance sheets of sole traders and partnerships. However, there are likely to be some additional entries in the accounts. These are explained below.

- **Taxation** The amount of taxation owed to the Inland Revenue includes any outstanding amounts from the previous year, plus the provision for the current year. Bracken Ltd made a provision for taxation of £220,000 in the profit and loss account shown in Figure 38.1. The total amount owed, according to the balance sheet, is £265,000. This means that Bracken had £45,000 outstanding from the previous year.
- **Dividends proposed** The dividends proposed by the directors were not paid during the period before the final accounts were published. Consequently they appear on the balance sheet as a liability. According to the profit and loss account for Bracken Ltd, the proposed dividend was £200,000 (£50,000 for preference shareholders plus £150,000 for ordinary shareholders). This amount is shown in the balance sheet as a liability until it is actually paid.
- **Net current assets** This is calculated by subtracting the value of creditors: amounts falling due within one year from current assets. The total of net current assets for Bracken Ltd is £4,493,000. This is an important item of information for managers and directors. It shows the total of liquid resources or WORKING CAPITAL available to the business (see unit 44).
- **Creditors: amounts falling due after more than one year** This term is used to describe the long term liabilities of limited companies. Examples of items in this category include mortgages, debentures and long term bank loans. Bracken Ltd has a mortgage for £1,500,000. This is subtracted from net current assets and fixed assets to give net assets.
- **Net assets** This value is the difference between the total assets of a company and its total liabilities. For Bracken Ltd, net assets are £18,093,000.
- **Capital and reserves** The lower section of the balance sheet shows the share capital of the company and its RESERVES. Profit that has been retained by the business, and any unrealised profit that the business might have, is classified as reserves.
- **Authorised share capital** This is the maximum amount of capital that could be raised by the company, as set out in its Memorandum of Association. The amount cannot be exceeded, although it is possible to increase it. Bracken Ltd has £12,000,000 authorised share capital. It is made up of 10,000,000 £1 ordinary shares and 2,000,000 £1 preference shares. The value is double underlined to show that it does not feature in any other balance sheet calculations.
- **Issued and fully paid up share capital** This represents the amount of money that shareholders have actually paid the company for shares that have been issued. Bracken Ltd has issued 5,000,000 £1 ordinary shares and 2,000,000 £1 preference shares.
- **Share premium account** This results from the issue of shares above their nominal value. It is classified as a **capital reserve** which means that it cannot be distributed to shareholders as dividends. However, it can be used to issue fully paid shares to existing shareholders as a bonus. Bracken Ltd has £2,500,000 in its share premium account.
- **Revaluation reserve** Revaluation arises when the value of fixed assets appreciate. Although it represents profit made by the business, the profit has not been realised, therefore it is non-distributable. It is therefore classified as a capital reserve and it cannot be used to pay dividends. However, if any asset that has been revalued is sold, the balance of the revaluation becomes realised and is available for distribution. Bracken Ltd has £2,890,000 in its revaluation account.
- **Capital redemption reserve** This is a capital reserve which is created when a company buys back some of the shares it has issued. There is a number of reasons why a company might wish to buy its own shares. In the case of a private limited company, the company might buy some of its own shares if a shareholder wishes to sell them and no other buyer can be found. In the case of a plc, the company might have surplus cash which it wishes to return to shareholders by buying back their shares. Sometimes shares are issued by a plc as 'redeemable'. This means that they were issued on the understanding that the company would buy them back at a future date. The process of buying them back is known as **redemption**. Whenever a company buys back its own shares, the amount of money it is going to spend is transferred to a capital redemption reserve. Bracken Ltd has £1,000,000 in its capital redemption reserve.
- **Profit and loss account** Any undistributed profit is added to the total accumulated retained profit of the business. Bracken Ltd has a total of £4,703,000 retained profit. This is made up of the current year's retained profit of £312,000 and the total amount of accumulated retained profit of £4,391,000. This is classified as a **revenue reserve** and can be distributed to shareholders as dividends in the future. It might be used, for example, to maintain dividend payments to

QUESTION 2

Heyford plc makes specialist equipment for the rail industry. The small public limited company owns a factory in Buckinghamshire and employs 16 staff. In the financial year ended 30 June 2001, the company made a record profit after taxation of £4,329,000. As a result, the directors raised dividends to £2,100,000. The following information relates to the shareholders' funds.

- Authorised share capital: 25,000,000 50p ordinary shares.
- Issued share capital: 10,000,000 50p ordinary shares.
- Revaluation: £12,400,000.
- Retained profit brought forward: £18,400,000.
- Share premium: £6,000,000.

(a) **Prepare an extract from the balance sheet of Heyford plc showing the capital and reserves section.**

(b) **What is the value of net assets for Heyford plc?**

(c) **A significant proportion of Heyford's shareholders' funds are tied up in the revaluation and share premium accounts. Explain why this cannot be distributed as dividends to shareholders.**

shareholders in a year when a company's profit is small or negative.

- **Shareholders' funds** This is the total amount of money that is, in effect, owed by the company to its shareholders. It is equal to the value of net assets. For Bracken Ltd, the total of shareholders' funds is £18,093,000. Note that it is called **capital employed** by some companies.

Requirements of the Companies Acts

In the UK, the first Companies Act was passed by Parliament in 1862. Since then, a number of other acts aimed at regulating companies and protecting shareholders have come into force. The Companies Act 1985 (as amended by the Companies Act 1989) consolidated much of this legislation. The Act requires directors, who have **stewardship** (ie responsibility for looking after the affairs) of limited companies, to publish accounts which show a 'true and fair view' of the company's financial position. Company accounts must be sent to all shareholders and debenture holders and to the **Registrar of Companies** at Companies House where they are available for inspection by the public.

The main provisions of the Companies Act, in relation to the publication of accounts, are that a company must:

- keep **statutory books of account** that show and explain the company's transactions, plus records of the assets and liabilities of the company and stock held at the end of the year. These records must be kept for a minimum of 3 years for a private limited company and for 6 years in the case of a plc;
- ensure that accounts are drawn up in accordance with commonly accepted accounting practices, consistently and without ambiguity;
- ensure that all information relevant to the proper understanding of the accounts is disclosed, whilst maintaining a balance between completeness of disclosure and summarisation for clarity;
- produce **statutory accounts**. Large companies must publish a directors' report, an auditor's report, notes to the accounts, a statement of total recognised gains and losses, a profit and loss account and a balance sheet. Small and medium sized companies are allowed to file abbreviated accounts which summarise their position.

Directors' report This must include:
- a description of the principal activities of the company;
- a fair review of the current and future prospects of the business;

- information on the sale, purchase or valuation of assets;
- recommended dividends;
- employee statistics, including information relating to health and safety and, in the case of larger companies, relating to the employment of people with disabilities;
- the names of the directors and their interests, eg shareholding, in the company;
- details of political or charitable donations.

Auditors' report This states whether, in the auditors' opinion, the accounts give a 'true and fair' view of the company's affairs. Auditors are independent accountants who are registered to carry out this work. The auditors are also required to certify that the accounts are drawn up in accordance with the requirements of the Companies Act.

Notes to the accounts These must include:
- disclosure of the accounting policies used, for example relating to depreciation, together with any changes to these policies;
- an explanation for any deviation from accounting standards;
- the sources of turnover from different geographical markets (if applicable);
- details of fixed assets, investments, share capital, debentures and reserves;
- directors' emoluments, ie earnings including pensions and other benefits;
- earnings per share.

Statement of total recognised gains and losses This is a summary of all the profits and losses made by a business during the year. It is deemed necessary because not all gains and losses are shown on the profit and loss account. For example, an upward revaluation of a fixed asset, such as a building, is not classed as revenue from trading operations, so it will not be included on the profit and loss account. However, it will add to the revaluation reserve in the balance sheet.

A published profit and loss account

A number of different formats for published accounts is allowed by the Companies Act. The most commonly used format for the profit and loss account, with entries arranged vertically, is shown in Figure 38.4. Although the Act outlines how accounts should be presented, in practice there is a great deal of variation between companies.

Figure 38.4 *Profit and loss account*

A	Turnover
B	Cost of sales
C	Gross profit or loss
D	Distribution costs
E	Administrative expenses
F	Other operating income
G	Income from shares in group companies
H	Income from shares in related companies
I	Income from other fixed asset investments
J	Other interest receivable and similar income
K	Amounts written off investments
L	Interest payable and similar charges
M	Tax on profit or loss on ordinary activities
N	Profit or loss on ordinary activities after taxation
O	Extraordinary income
P	Extraordinary charges
Q	Extraordinary profit or loss
R	Tax on extraordinary profit or loss
S	Other taxes not shown in the above items
T	Profit or loss for the financial year

- **Turnover** This refers to any money generated by the sale of goods or services from the company's **ordinary activities**. Trade discounts, VAT and any other sales-based tax should be excluded from this figure. A company must disclose in the notes to the accounts an analysis of turnover if it is generated from substantially different business activities or geographical areas.

- **Expenditure** When calculating the cost of sales, distribution costs and administrative expenses, the following items must be included:

  1 provision for depreciation;
  2 directors' and employees' emoluments, ie wages, salaries and other earnings;
  3 amounts paid for the hire of plant and machinery;
  4 auditor's fees;
  5 amounts paid for **exceptional** items. These are transactions falling within the ordinary activities of the company but are of an exceptional magnitude. An example might be the cost of relocating and retraining staff if a company decides to close one of its branches.

The exact sums paid in each case must be shown in the notes to the accounts if not disclosed in the profit and loss account.

- **Other operating income** Sometimes businesses receive income that is not linked to their ordinary operating activities. An example might be if a retailer owns a building and obtains rent from an upstairs property that is not used by the business. Such income is shown as non-operating income. It would also include any profit made on the disposal of assets.

- **Other investment income** The Companies Act requires companies to list any income or losses from subsidiaries, associated companies and trade investments separately. Details should be published in the notes to the accounts.

- **Other interest receivable and similar income** This refers to interest received from deposits held by companies at banks and similar institutions. It also includes income from holding bonds and other securities which are issued by the government. The purpose of listing these sources of income separately is to prevent companies from 'boosting' income from ordinary activities with non-operating income. This could be misleading.

- **Amounts written off investments** If there is a fall in the value of their financial investments, companies should disclose the amount written off in the profit and loss account.

- **Interest payable and similar charges** Many companies borrow money to help fund their activities. Any interest paid on bank loans, overdrafts and debentures is shown separately.

- **Profit or loss on ordinary activities before and after taxation** This is the net figure resulting from the additions to, and deductions from, gross profit of the separate items described above. The figure is given before and after the deduction of corporation tax.

- **Extraordinary items** These are costs, or income, that do not derive from the ordinary activities of the company. Under Financial Reporting Standard 3 *Reporting financial performance*, extraordinary items are only permitted in very unusual circumstances. An example might be if a hotel chain discovered that a building it had acquired contained a valuable work of art. The sale of the art would be classed as extraordinary income.

- **Profit or loss for the year** This represents the amount available to the business and its owners. It is often referred to as **net profit**.

An example of a published profit and loss account is shown in Figure 38.5. The account is for Majestic Wine PLC. Majestic operates the largest wine warehouse chain in Britain, specialising in the direct sale of wine to the public.

- It is customary to show figures for the current year and also for the previous year. This allows the reader to make immediate comparisons.

- Figures for each year are presented in a single column. Negative numbers are shown in brackets.

- The term **operating profit** is used here to describe gross profit plus rental income, less costs. The term is increasingly used in published accounts and is generally defined as the profit made by a company as a result of its ordinary trading activities.

- Profit on ordinary activities is also known as net profit. It is shown before and after taxation. The amount after taxation is available to shareholders as dividends or it is kept by the company as retained profits.

- Further details relating to some entries are to be found in the notes to the accounts. For example, note 3 shows how net interest receivable has been calculated. Although not shown here, the note states that it has been calculated as follows:

interest received - interest paid = £126,000 - £60,000 = £66,000.

- The company experienced an increase in turnover from £81,183,000 to £86,764,000. However, profit after taxation fell slightly from £3,105,000 to £3,088,000.
- The directors of Majestic decided to pay approximately one third of the profit after taxation in dividends. £2,117,000 was retained by the company.
- It is customary to show the **earnings per share** for the company. This is a measure of profitability and is explained in unit 44.

Figure 38.5 *Profit and loss account for Majestic Wine PLC.*

Profit and Loss Account
for the year ended 2 April 2001

	Note	Year to 02.04.01 £000	Year to 27.03.00 £000
Turnover		**86,764**	81,183
Cost of sales		**(69,929)**	(65,979)
Gross profit		**16,835**	15,204
Distribution costs		**(8,285)**	(7,160)
Administrative costs		**(4,449)**	(3,957)
Rental income		**342**	321
Operating profit	1	**4,443**	4,408
Net interest (paid)/received	3	**66**	97
Profit on ordinary activities before taxation		**4,509**	4,505
Taxation	4	**(1,421)**	(1,400)
Profit on ordinary activities after taxation		**3,088**	3,105
Dividend			
Interim - paid		**(310)**	(285)
Final - proposed		**(661)**	(614)
Retained profit for the year	14	**2,117**	2,206
Earnings per share	5	**21.42p**	22.15p

Source: adapted from *Majestic Wine PLC Annual Report and Accounts*, year ended 2 April 2001.

QUESTION 3

Dana Petroleum plc is a leading British independent oil and gas exploration company. The company owns assets in Europe, Africa and the Far East. An extract from Dana's profit and loss account is shown in Figure 38.6.

Figure 38.6 *Profit and loss account for Dana Petroleum*

**Profit and Loss Account
for the year ended 31 December 2000**

	2000 £000	1999 £000
Turnover	**29,865**	20,746
Cost of sales	**(19,359)**	(14,212)
Gross profit	**?**	6,534
Administrative expenses	**(2,399)**	(1,956)
Other operating income-	**-**	2,013
Operating profit	**8,107**	6,591
Share of loss of associated company	**(7)**	(30)
Loss on disposal of subsidiary undertaking	**-**	(204)
Operating profit on ordinary activities before interest and taxation	**8,100**	6,357
Interest receivable	**1,063**	1,127
Interest payable and similar charges	**(1,729)**	(1,044)
Profit on ordinary activities before taxation	**?**	6,440
Taxation	**(1,813)**	(1,187)
Profit on ordinary activities after taxation	**5,621**	5,253
Profit per share	**0.52p**	0.51p

Source: adapted from *Dana Petroleum PLC Annual Report and Accounts*, year ended 31 December 2000.

(a) Calculate the missing values for (i) gross profit and (ii) profit on ordinary activities before taxation for 2000.
(b) Give three possible examples of administrative expenses for Dana Petroleum.
(c) Comment briefly on the financial performance of Dana Petroleum over the two years shown.

A published balance sheet

The Companies Act provide two formats for the presentation of balance sheets, one vertical and the other horizontal. Most companies in the UK use the vertical format which is outlined in Figure 38.7. One reason for using the vertical format is that it makes it easier to show the working capital, ie current assets less current liabilities. However, as with the profit and loss account, there is a great deal of variation in the details that companies include.

Figure 38.7 *Balance sheet*

A   Called-up share capital not paid
B   Fixed assets
    I   Intangible assets
    II   Tangible assets
    III   Investments
C   Current assets
    I   Stocks
    II   Debtors
    III   Investments
    IV   Cash at bank and in hand
D   Prepayments and accrued income
E   Creditors: amounts falling due within one year
F   Net current assets (or liabilities) / working capital
G   Total assets less current liabilities
H   Creditors: amounts falling due after more than one year
I   Provisions for liabilities and charges
J   Accruals and deferred income
K   Capital and reserves
    I   Called-up share capital
    II   Share premium account
    III   Revaluation reserve
    IV   Other reserves
    V   Profit and loss account

- **Called-up share capital not paid** This represents money owing from shareholders who have not paid for shares issued and 'called' (see unit 34). The amount is also sometimes recorded as a current asset under 'debtors'.
- **Fixed assets** It is usual to show only the totals under this heading. Details are given in the notes to the accounts. These details include the net book value of the assets at the beginning and end of the year, the provision for depreciation, and any acquisitions and disposals made during the year.
- **Intangible assets** Examples include patents, licences, trade marks, brand names and goodwill. It is now accepted practice that only intangible assets that have been purchased can be included on the balance sheet.
- **Tangible assets** These include land and buildings, plant and machinery, fixtures and fittings, tools and equipment and assets in the course of construction.
- **Investments** These include shares in other companies and loans that have been made to other companies or to the government in the form of government securities. If these assets are intended to be held for more than a year, they are generally classed as fixed assets. Otherwise, they are classed as current assets.
- **Current assets** Stocks include raw materials, work-in-progress, finished goods for resale and payments on account. Debtors include trade debtors and amounts owed by group or related companies. Cash held at the bank and in hand is also listed here.
- **Prepayments and accrued income** This is shown as a separate item on the balance sheet.
- **Creditors: amounts falling due within one year** These are the current liabilities of the business. They can include debenture loans, bank loans and overdrafts, payments received on account, trade creditors, bills of exchange payable, amounts owed to group or related companies, and taxation and social security owed.
- **Net current assets** This equals current assets less creditors: amounts falling due within one year. It is also known as working capital.
- **Total assets less current liabilities** This is calculated by adding fixed assets to net current assets.
- **Creditors: amounts falling due after more than one year** These are long term liabilities, such as a mortgage or debenture loans which have more than one year to maturity.
- **Provisions for liabilities and charges** This category relates to the concept of prudence

which states that companies should provide for any foreseeable losses. Examples might include possible pension obligations and deferred taxation.

- **Accruals and deferred income** These anticipated expenses and income are shown as a separate item on the balance sheet.
- **Capital and reserves** The total under this category is equal to net assets. It includes the called-up share capital, the balance on the share premium account, the revaluation reserve and the balance on the profit and loss account which is made up of the current year's retained profit plus retained profit from previous years.

An example of a published balance sheet is shown in Figure 38.8. It is for Majestic Wine PLC, the company described earlier.

Figure 38.8 *Balance sheet for Majestic Wine PLC*

Balance Sheet
as at 2 April 2001

	2001 £(000)	2000 £(000)
Fixed assets		
Tangible assets	15,479	13,091
Current assets		
Stocks	15,699	13,848
Debtors	3,109	2,815
Cash at bank and in hand	2,420	3,318
	21,228	19,981
Creditors: amounts falling due within one year	(19,191)	(17,998)
Net current assets	2,037	1,983
Total assets less current liabilities	17,516	15,074
Creditors: amounts falling due after more than one year	-	-
Provisions for liabilities and charges	(338)	(287)
Net assets	17,178	14,787
Capital and reserves		
Called-up share capital	4,398	4,282
Shares to be issued	10	12
Share premium account	3,537	3,172
Revaluation reserve	22	22
Profit and loss account	9,211	7,299
Equity shareholders' funds	17,178	14,787

Source: adapted from *Majestic Wine PLC Annual Report and Accounts*, year ended 2 April 2001.

- A single column is used to present the figures for each of the two years.
- The balance sheet shows that the value of net assets increased from £14,787,000 to £17,178,000.
- The amount of long term debt is relatively small. Majestic made a provision of just £338,000.
- The amount of money owed in the short term is considerably higher. According to the notes to the accounts, which are not shown here, most of the £19,191,000 due within one year was owed to trade creditors. In the case of Majestic, this was money owed to its suppliers of wine and other stock.

summary questions

1. What is the difference between published accounts and accounts prepared for internal use?
2. What is meant by dividends proposed?
3. State two reasons why profit is retained.
4. Why is interest shown as a separate item on the profit and loss account of a limited company?
5. Explain the difference between tangible and intangible assets.
6. Give 3 examples of creditors: amounts falling due within one year.
7. Give 3 examples of creditors: amounts falling due after more than one year.
8. Where will 'dividends proposed' appear in the balance sheet?
9. Explain the difference between a capital reserve and a revenue reserve.
10. State 3 requirements of the Companies Act when preparing published accounts.

UNIT ASSESSMENT QUESTION 1

Robson's Locks Ltd manufactures a wide range of locking mechanisms. Figure 38.9 shows the trial balance for Robson's Locks Ltd.

Figure 38.9 *Trial balance for Robson's Locks Ltd*

Robson's Locks Ltd
Trial Balance as at 31.12.01

	£	£
Share capital, authorised and issued:		
500,000 ordinary shares £1 each		500,000
Debentures at 6%		50,000
Stock at 31.12.01	43,000	
Creditors		21,500
Debtors	27,400	
Cash at bank	16,300	
Gross profit (year ended 31.12.01)		672,100
Office wages and salaries	166,300	
Directors' salaries	102,300	
Motor expenses	43,100	
Advertising and marketing	21,900	
Bad debt written off	2,400	
General expenses	32,400	
Half yearly debenture interest paid	1,500	
Factory at cost	1,300,000	
Motor vehicles at cost	41,800	
Depreciation on motor vehicles		20,000
Plant and equipment at cost	65,000	
Depreciation on plant and equipment		36,000
Profit and loss account		563,800
	1,863,400	1,863,400

Additional information

(i) Depreciation for the year ended 31.12.01 was as follows:
  Motor vehicles   £4,000
  Plant and equipment   £6,000
(ii) Six month's debenture interest had accrued by 31.12.01.
(iii) The directors proposed a full and final dividend of 12p per share.
(iv) A £50,000 provision for taxation was made for the current year.

(a) Prepare a profit and loss account for Robson's Locks Ltd for internal use.

(b) Prepare a balance sheet for Robson's Locks Ltd for internal use. (Show the assets at cost and the depreciation to date).

key terms

Final dividend - the dividend paid to shareholders after the end of the financial year.

Interim dividend - a preliminary dividend payment to shareholders during the financial year.

Reserves - part of the capital of a company arising, for example, from retained profits, the revaluation of assets, or the issue of shares at more than their nominal value. Reserves are classified into **capital reserves** (or statutory reserves) which are not available for distribution, and **revenue reserves** (or non-statutory reserves) which are available for distribution.

Retained profit - profit held in reserve by a company, as opposed to being distributed to shareholders.

Turnover - the amount of revenue generated from the sale of goods or services.

Working capital - the value of creditors: amounts falling due within one year subtracted from current assets. It is a measure of the total of liquid assets available to a business, ie the amount of cash and assets that can be readily turned into cash.

UNIT ASSESSMENT   QUESTION 2

Somerfield plc, the supermarket chain, grew in the late 1990s as a result of various acquisitions and mergers, the biggest of which was the merger with Kwik Save. However, in 2000, its turnover fell from £6.3 billion to £5.8 billion and profit before tax fell from £226.4 million to £15.9 million. One of the main reasons for the huge fall in profits was an exceptional charge of approximately £100 million to pay for restructuring the organisation. Some financial information for Somerfield is shown in Figure 38.10.

Figure 38.10 *Financial information for Somerfield, year ended 29.4.00*

Tangible assets	£960.3m
Investments	£4.4m
Stock	£372.6m
Debtors	£145.4m
Short term investments	£3.9m
Cash at bank and in hand	£238.3m
Creditors:	
amounts falling due within one year	£655.5m
Creditors:	
amounts falling due after more than one year	£328.8m
Provisions for liabilities and charges	£24.8m
Called-up share capital	£49.4m
Share premium account	£32.8m
Revaluation reserve	£82.4m
Other reserves	£335.3m
Profit and loss account	£215.9m

Source: adapted from *Somerfield Annual Report and Accounts* 1999/2000.

(a) Prepare a balance sheet for Somerfield plc. Present it in the format used for published accounts.

(b) Give 3 possible examples of tangible assets for Somerfield.

(c) With reference to Somerfield, explain what is meant by an exceptional item.

(d) Explain the difference between investments and short term investments as shown on the Somerfield balance sheet.

The accounts of non-profit making organisations

unit**objectives**

To understand:
- non-profit making organisations;
- receipts and payments accounts;
- income and expenditure accounts.

What are non-profit making organisations?

Unlike businesses, whose main aim is to make a profit, NON-PROFIT MAKING ORGANISATIONS exist to provide services to their members or to promote a 'good cause'. Examples include **clubs and societies** such as sports clubs, social clubs, amateur dramatics societies and charities. These organisations might receive income in the form of:
- membership fees or annual subscriptions;
- donations;
- funds raised from raffles, fetes and car boot sales;
- revenue from the sale of food and drinks to members.

The money raised is used to meet running expenses, such as rent, light and heat, equipment and travel expenses.

Non-profit making organisations are usually run by a committee. A TREASURER, who is likely to be an elected member of the committee, is responsible for keeping financial records, maintaining the organisation's bank account and reporting to the members at a general meeting. Records for small clubs and societies are generally kept using a system of single entry as opposed to double entry bookkeeping. Most treasurers use a cash book to record all payments and receipts made during the year.

The type of annual accounts produced by non-profit making organisations depends to a large extent on their size. Smaller clubs and societies generally produce a simple receipts and payments account. Larger organisations often produce a more complex income and expenditure account, and a balance sheet.

The receipts and payments account

The RECEIPTS AND PAYMENTS ACCOUNT is a summary of the cash book. It shows where money has come from, where it has been spent, and how much money is left at the end of the year. An example of a receipts and payments account is shown in Figure 39.1. It is for the Woodstock Chess Club. This meets every week in a school classroom which the club rents for £20 per session. The club has 31 members and its purpose is to provide them with an opportunity to play chess on a regular basis, discuss and develop chess strategies, listen to visiting speakers and participate in chess tournaments. The club raises most of its funds from subscriptions.

The debit side of the receipts and payments account shows details of club receipts. The credit side shows a summary of payments made by the club. According to the account, the club had £340 left over from the previous year's activities. It received £620 subscriptions from members, £300 from donations and it made a profit of £360 on a Christmas raffle. During the year, the chess club's main item of expenditure was the £840 paid to the school for renting the classroom. Other payments included a total of £210 to visiting speakers for their expenses, £130 entrance fees for tournaments and competitions, and £240 for new chess sets. At the end of the year, the club had £200 left over. This amount is brought down to start the new financial year.

Figure 39.1 *Receipts and payment account for the Woodstock Chess Club*

Woodstock Chess Club
Receipts and Payments Account for the year ended 31.12.01

Receipts	£	Payments	£
Balance b/d	340	Rent	840
Subscriptions received	620	Visiting speaker's expenses	210
Donations	300	Competition and tournament fees	130
Net proceeds from Xmas raffle	360	New chess sets	240
		Balance c/d	200
	1,620		1,620
Balance b/d	200		

Small clubs, such as the Woodstock Chess Club, often use this relatively simple method of reporting. The club's transactions are straightforward and the members do not need any further detail. However, there are disadvantages of reporting the finances in this way.

- The receipts and payments account does not record transactions such as accruals and prepayments, nor does it show depreciation of assets. For example, some of the subscriptions from members of the Woodstock Chess Club were paid in advance, and some were outstanding at the end of the year. The receipts and payments account does not show this.
- There is no distinction made between revenue and capital expenditure. For example, the chess sets bought by the Woodstock Chess Club will last for many years and therefore could be classified as capital items.
- There is not enough information to produce a balance sheet. For example, the Woodstock Chess Club owns assets such as chess clocks that it bought in previous years. The club also owes money to the local chess league. Such details are not revealed when using a receipts and payments account.

QUESTION 1

The Wheatsheaf Rambling Club meets every month in the Wheatsheaf public house, Maidenhead, rent free. The club organises walks and visits to rural locations on most Sundays. There are 98 members who pay £10 annual subscription. On the more popular walks, a coach is hired and members pay a flat £5 per trip. The coach trips are subsidised to encourage participation. During the year ended 31 December 2001, a total of £780 was collected from members to help pay for coach hire. In addition, two jumble sales raised £430 and £490 respectively after all expenses were paid. The club also received £200 sponsorship from the Wheatsheaf. This was given on the understanding that the club would include the name and location of the pub on its T-shirts, and would also continue to use the pub for their meetings. The net proceeds from the sale of 50 T-shirts during the year was £110. During the year ended 31 December 2001, the club also made payments totalling £2,930. An analysis of these payments is as follows:

- coach hire   £1,660;
- advertising   £340;
- maps   £280;
- first aid kits   £240;
- stationery   £190;
- miscellaneous expenses £220.

(a) Prepare a receipts and payments account for the Wheatsheaf Rambling Club for the year ended 31 December, 2001. (The balance brought down from the previous year was £260.)

(b) How much money was left over at the end of the year?

(c) Explain why this and other clubs produce a receipts and payments account.

The income and expenditure account

The problems associated with receipts and payments accounts can be overcome by drawing up an INCOME AND EXPENDITURE ACCOUNT. This is similar to a profit and loss account and can be used to show transactions such as depreciation. It also provides sufficient information to help produce a balance sheet. The income and expenditure account lists the receipts and expenditure for the year, takes prepayments, accruals and other adjustments into account, and subtracts expenditure from income. If income is greater than expenditure there is a **surplus**. If income is less than expenditure, there is a **deficit**.

To illustrate how an income and expenditure account is prepared, consider the Darton Cricket Club. The club has over 60 members and runs first and second eleven teams. It also organises regular fixtures for an under 15 team. The club rents a pavilion and cricket ground from a landowner. In addition to members' subscriptions, the club gains additional income from sponsorship by a local sportswear manufacturer.

In order to draw up the income and expenditure account, a receipts and payments account is first prepared (see Figure 39.2). Additional information is also supplied.

Figure 39.2 *Receipts and payments account for the Darton Cricket Club*

Darton Cricket Club
Receipts and Payments Account for the year ended 31.10.01

Receipts	£	Payments	£
Balance b/d	380	Rent	1,000
Subscriptions received	1,100	Heat and light	200
Net proceeds – monthly draw	2,100	Cricket equipment	1,100
Net proceeds – presentation dinner	1,340	Groundsman's wages	420
Sponsorship	500	Team travelling expenses	740
		Furniture	600
		Miscellaneous expenses	220
		Balance c/d	1,140
	5,420		5,420
Balance b/d	1,140		

Additional information
(i)   £60 is owed by members for subscriptions.
(ii) £40 is owed for heat and light.
(iii) £50 insurance has been prepaid (included in miscellaneous expenses).
(iv) Depreciation of £400 for cricket equipment and £200 for furniture is estimated for the year. This includes depreciation on new equipment purchased during the year.

Either a vertical or horizontal format can be used when preparing an income and expenditure account. In this case, the account for the Darton Cricket Club is presented in a vertical format. It is shown in Figure 39.3.

- The £380 balance b/d in the receipts and payments account is not included. It does not represent income for the current year.
- Sources of income are listed for the current year and adjustments are made for any income owed to the club. In this case, the club is owed £60 in subscriptions and this is added to the amount received during the year, £1,100. This makes a total of £1,160.
- Other income includes net proceeds from the weekly draw, £2,100. Any expenses, such as prizes, are deducted because the figure in the account is a net figure. Similarly, the net proceeds from the annual presentation dinner is listed after expenses, £1,340. The sponsorship income, £500, is also listed. The total income received by the Darton Cricket Club during the year was £5,100.
- The revenue expenditure incurred by the club includes rent of £1,000, groundsman's wages of £420 and travelling expenses of £740. Capital expenditure on cricket equipment of £1,100 and furniture of £600 is not included.
- Adjustments are made for accruals and prepayments. In this case, the club owed £40 for heat and light. This must be added to the amount paid for heat and light during the year of £200. This makes a total of £240. The club had also made a £50 prepayment for insurance which is included

Figure 39.3 *Income and expenditure account for the Darton Cricket Club*

Darton Cricket Club
Income and Expenditure Account for the year ended 31.10.01

	£	£
Income		
Subscriptions (1,100 + 60)		1,160
Net proceeds from weekly draw		2,100
Net proceeds from annual presentation dinner		1,340
Sponsorship		500
		5,100
Expenditure		
Rent	1,000	
Heat and light (200 + 40)	240	
Groundsman's wages	420	
Travelling expenses	740	
Miscellaneous expenses (220 - 50)	170	
Depreciation	600	
		3,170
Surplus of income over expenditure		1,930

in miscellaneous expenses of £220. This must be subtracted so the figure for miscellaneous expenses is £170 (£220 - £50).
- Depreciation is included in the list of expenses. A total of £600 is charged.
- The total amount of revenue expenditure for the club during the year was £3,170. This is subtracted from income to give £1,930 (£5,100 - £3,170). This is shown as the surplus of income over expenditure in the account. It is added to the club's **accumulated fund**.

QUESTION 2

The Werndene Tennis Club owns a small pavilion and six grass courts. It has over 200 members who pay subscriptions. The club also raises money from social events. A receipts and payments account for the Werndene Tennis Club is shown in Figure 39.4.

Figure 39.4 *The Werndene Tennis Club receipts and payments account*

The Werndene Tennis Club
Receipts and Payments Account for the year ended 31.3.01

Receipts	£	Payments	£
Balance b/d	720	Affiliation to county tennis assoc.	400
Subscriptions received	2,100	Heat and light	270
Net proceeds - summer ball	3,130	Tennis equipment	2,400
Net proceeds - presentation dinner	2,100	Groundsman's wages	680
Net proceeds - summer fete	450	Lawn mower	1,500
		General expenses	380
		Balance c/d	2,870
	8,500		8,500
Balance b/d	2,870		

Additional information:
(i) £140 is owed by members for subscriptions.
(ii) £230 has been paid in advance for subscriptions for the next year.
(iii) The club owes the groundsman £50 wages.
(iv) Depreciation charges of £1,000 for the pavilion, £500 for tennis equipment and £300 for the lawn mower should be made.

(a) Prepare the income and expenditure account for the Werndene Tennis Club, year ended 31 March 2001.

(b) Suggest two advantages of using this type of account when reporting the financial position of a club.

The balance sheet

Non-profit making organisations with a significant amount of fixed assets generally prepare a balance sheet. This shows the organisation's assets and liabilities and states its net worth. The balance sheet for a non-profit making organisation is similar to that for a business. However, there are likely to be differences in the amount of detail shown. Also, the capital section is replaced by an ACCUMULATED FUND. This represents the difference in value between the assets and the liabilities of the organisation, ie its net assets. Each year, the surplus or deficit on the income and expenditure account is added to the accumulated fund.

A balance sheet for a non-profit making organisation is shown in Figure 39.5. It is for the Darton Cricket Club whose income and expenditure account is shown earlier. The following information from the start of the club's financial year, on 1 November 2000, was also available:

- cash at bank and in hand £1,140;
- cricket equipment (net book value) £3,000;
- furniture (net book value) £1,400;
- interest free loan from a member £2,000;
- accumulated fund (1.11.00) £2,780.

Figure 39.5 *Balance sheet for the Darton Cricket Club as at 31.10.01*

Darton Cricket Club
Balance Sheet as at 31.10.01

	£	£
Fixed assets		
Cricket equipment (3,000 + 1,100)	4,100	
Less depreciation	400	3,700
Furniture (1,400 + 600)	2,000	
Less depreciation	200	1,800
		5,500
Current assets		
Debtors (subscriptions owing)	60	
Prepayments	50	
Cash at bank and in hand	1,140	
	1,250	
Current liabilities		
Accrual	40	
Working capital		1,210
		6,710
Long term liabilities		
Loan (member)		(2,000)
Net assets		4,710
Financed by		
Accumulated fund		2,780
Surplus of income over expenditure for the year		1,930
		4,710

- There are two fixed assets listed on the balance sheet. The net book value of cricket equipment is £3,700. This is calculated by adding the value of new equipment bought (shown in the receipts and payments account in Figure 39.2) to the balance as at 1 November 2000 and subtracting depreciation (£3,000 + £1,100 - £400). The net book value of furniture, £1,800, is calculated in the same way (£1,400 + £600 - £200).
- Three current assets are listed. The £60 debtors arises because some members had not yet paid their subscriptions. In the future, this might be written off if, for example, the members leave the club. The £50 prepayment arises from insurance that had been paid in advance. The £1,140 cash at bank and in hand represents the bank balance of the cricket club and the amount of cash held by the treasurer.

- Only one current liability is listed. This is a £40 accrual and results from the amount owing for heat and light.
- Working capital is calculated by subtracting current liabilities from current assets (£1,250 - £40 = £1,210).
- Sometimes a non-profit making organisation might have long term liabilities. In this case, the Darton Cricket Club owes £2,000 to a member. It is an interest free loan from a member who supported the club financially in the past.
- The value of net assets of the club, £4,710, is calculated by adding fixed assets to working capital and subtracting the long term liabilities (£5,500 + £1,210 - £2,000).
- The lower section of the balance sheet shows the accumulated fund of the club. Each year this rises or falls depending on whether the club has a surplus or a deficit on the income and expenditure account. The accumulated fund for the Darton Cricket Club was £2,780 at the beginning of the year. During the year there was a surplus on the income expenditure account of £1,930. This is added to the accumulated fund to calculate the end of year balance. In this case it is £4,710 (£2,780 + £1,930). It is equal to the net assets of the club.

QUESTION 3

The Hampton Rowing Club has more than 70 members. The club owns a number of boats and rents a boathouse by the side of the River Avon. Membership fees are high and two big social functions each year are well supported. An income and expenditure account for the year ended 31 May 2001 is shown in Figure 39.6. During the year, the club bought new rowing equipment for £1,200. Some additional information is also available:

- cash at bank and in hand £4,560;
- insurance prepayment £400;
- boats and equipment (net book value as at 1.6.00) £21,500;
- accrual (electricity) £130;
- subscriptions owing £300;
- interest free loan from a member £5,000;
- accumulated fund (1.6.00) £18,800.

Figure 39.6 *Income and expenditure account for the Hampton Rowing Club.*

Hampton Rowing Club
Income and Expenditure Account for the year ended 31.5.01

	£	£
Income		
Subscriptions		7,100
Net proceeds from summer ball		4,100
Net proceeds from Xmas dance		2,040
Interest		230
		13,470
Expenditure		
Rent	3,000	
Electricity	290	
Competition entry fees	850	
Insurance	1,950	
Travelling expenses	2,480	
Sundry expenses	870	
Depreciation	3,500	
		12,940
Surplus of income over expenditure		530

(a) Prepare a balance sheet for the Hampton Rowing Club.
(b) Explain why this balance sheet might be helpful to the members of the club.

Fund-raising events and trading activities

It is common for non-profit organisations to supplement subscription income with money from other sources. For example, clubs and societies organise fund-raising events such as raffles, monthly draws, fetes, and social events like summer balls and Christmas dances. In the examples so far in this unit, the net proceeds of such events are shown in the receipts and payments account or in the income and expenditure account. This is acceptable accounting practice. However, it is sometimes useful if the treasurer can provide a separate statement for each fund-raising event to show how the net proceeds are calculated. Figure 39.7 shows such a statement for the Christmas raffle organised by the Woodstock Chess Club. The net proceeds in the receipts and payments account shown in Figure 39.1 are £360. It is calculated by subtracting total expenses of £180 from ticket revenue of £540.

Figure 39.7 *Calculating net proceeds from the Christmas raffle for the Woodstock Chess Club*

	£	£
Sale of raffle tickets		540
Less		
Prizes	110	
Printing	40	
Guest expenses	30	
		180
Net proceeds		360

Another source of income for clubs and societies is profit from trading activities which are run on a regular or permanent basis. For example, some sports and social clubs run a bar for their members. Under these circumstances, a bar trading account is likely to be prepared at the end of the year. Such an account is shown for the Thetwell Football Club in Figure 39.8. The bar sales for the year amounted to £12,890. The cost of sales, £6,380, is calculated by subtracting the closing stock from the total of opening stock plus purchases. It is then subtracted from sales to determine gross profit, £6,510. The Thetwell Football Club made a net profit on the bar of £3,010. This is calculated by subtracting other expenses, in this case wages, from gross profit. The net profit would be shown as a source of income in the income and expenditure account. The closing stock would be shown on the balance sheet as a current asset. If any money was owed to drinks or other suppliers, this would be shown as a current liability on the balance sheet.

Figure 39.8 *Bar trading account for the Thetwell Football Club*

Thetwell Football Club
Bar Trading Account for the year ended 31.7.01

	£	£
Sales		12,890
Less cost of sales		
Opening stock	1,300	
Purchases	6,330	
	7,630	
Closing stock	1,250	6,380
Gross profit		6,510
Less wages to bar staff		3,500
Net profit on bar		3,010

Life membership

Some non-profit making organisations have a system of life membership. This allows a new member to pay a substantial 'one-off' membership fee and nothing thereafter. Such payments are dealt with in accordance with the matching concept. This means that the money should not all be treated as income in the income and expenditure account in the year that it is received. Instead, when a life membership fee is received, it should be credited to a life membership (or subscriptions) account and then credited to the income and expenditure account in equal annual instalments. At the end of the financial year, it is added to the accumulated fund in the balance sheet.

The amount to be transferred to the income and expenditure account each year would be a decision of the treasurer or committee. They could base their decision on what they consider to be an average length of time for life membership. This might depend on the nature of the club. For example, some golf clubs might have life members whose membership lasts for over 50 years. Therefore, life subscriptions would continue to be transferred for that amount of time. Alternatively, it might be decided to transfer the subscriptions over a 10 or 20 year period.

To illustrate how life membership and other subscriptions are treated, consider the example of the Lostock Tennis Club. This club was founded in 1998. Subscriptions for the first four year period are shown in Figure 39.9. Life membership subscriptions are initially credited to a life membership account and then credited to the income and expenditure account in 10 equal instalments.

Figure 39.9 *Membership subscriptions received by the Lostock Tennis Club*

	1998	1999	2000	2001
	£	£	£	£
Annual subscriptions received	4,300	4,100	4,400	5,500
Of which, subscriptions in advance	-	250	400	300
Life subscriptions received	600	600	1,200	1,800

The amount of subscriptions credited to the income and expenditure account in 2000 is shown in Figure 39.10. Because the life membership subscriptions are credited to the income and expenditure account in 10 equal instalments, one-tenth of the amount received is transferred each year for ten years. So, in this example, the amount credited in 2000 is one-tenth of the life subscriptions received up to and including that year (ie one-tenth of £2,400). Note also that the annual subscriptions for 2000 are adjusted to take into account the subscriptions paid in advance, both for 2000 and 2001.

Figure 39.10 *Subscriptions for 2000*

	£	£
Annual subscriptions		
Received in 2000	4,400	
Less received in advance for 2001	400	
	4,000	
Add received in advance for 2000	250	
		4,250
Life subscriptions		
One-tenth of 1998 life subscriptions	60	
One-tenth of 1999 life subscriptions	60	
One-tenth of 2000 life subscriptions	120	
		240
Total subscriptions for 2000		4,490

Donations

Non-profit making organisation deal with donations in different ways. The simplest way is to treat a donation as income in the year that it is received. An alternative method, often used for large sums, is to **capitalise** donations and add them to the accumulated fund on the balance sheet. However, if a donor gives money for a specific purpose, such as the building of a new clubhouse, the donation could be credited to a special fund on the balance sheet, separate from the accumulated fund.

key terms

Accumulated fund - the difference between the value of assets and liabilities of a non-profit making organisation.

Income and expenditure account - an account, similar to a profit and loss account, that summarises the annual income and revenue expenditure of a non-profit making organisation. It takes into account the **accrual** concept.

Non-profit making organisation - a club, society or charity which exists to provide services to its members or to promote a 'good cause'.

Receipts and payments account - an account that summarises all payments and receipts made by an organisation.

Treasurer - someone who is elected by members of an organisation to keep financial records and report the financial affairs.

summary questions

1. How do non-profit making organisations differ from businesses?
2. State three possible sources of income for a non-profit making organisation.
3. What does a receipts and payments account show?
4. State two disadvantages of a receipts and payments account.
5. What sort of expenditure is shown in an income and expenditure account?
6. Where will the surplus or deficit on the income and expenditure account also be recorded?
7. Under what circumstances might the books of a non-profit making organisation include an account which shows a profit or loss?
8. State three examples of current assets that a non-profit making organisation might have on its balance sheet.
9. Explain how accountants treat life membership subscriptions.
10. Explain how accountants might treat donations to clubs and societies.

The Glenroyd Rugby Club runs a number of teams and competes in a Scottish regional league. The club owns its clubhouse, pitches and a training area. It has over 250 members, many of whom are non-playing social members. The club has a bar which contributes significantly to club funds. It is run by a full-time steward. Figure 39.11 shows a receipts and payments account for the year ended 31 December 2001. The following information was also available on that date:

- members owed £125 in subscriptions;
- £150 was owed for electricity;
- £450 was owed to suppliers of beer and spirits to the bar;
- bar stocks were £2,360 on 1.1.01 and £3,100 on 31.12.01;
- depreciation of £4,200 was estimated. This breaks down as £3,000 for the clubhouse, £600 for furniture and £600 for fixtures and fittings;
- rugby kit is replaced each year and is therefore treated as a revenue expense rather than a capital expense.

Figure 39.11 *Receipts and payments account for Glenroyd Rugby Club* ●●●

Glenroyd Rugby Club
Receipts and Payments Account for the year ended 31.12.01

Receipts	£	Payments	£
Balance b/d	3,960	Travelling expenses	1,500
Subscriptions received	6,250	Purchases for bar	11,780
Bar takings	32,100	Salary - bar steward	14,000
Donations	850	Committee expenses	560
Proceeds from presentation event	1,190	Stationery	120
Sponsorship	500	Heat and light	650
		New furniture	1,500
		Rugby kit	5,200
		Groundstaff wages	3,600
		Water rates	720
		Sundry expenses	1,670
		Balance c/d	3,550
	44,850		44,850
Balance b/d	3,550		

(a) Prepare a bar trading account to determine the profit made by the bar during the year.

(b) Prepare an income and expenditure account for the year ended 31 December 2001.

(c) The value of the accumulated fund for Glenroyd Rugby Club was £28,560 on 1 January 2001. What was the value on 31 December 2001?

The Knighton History Society meets every two weeks in a functions room at the Black Sheep public house. The members hold debates, show films and invite guest speakers to their meetings. The society owns a mini-bus and regularly visits places of historic interest. Members pay £5 to help cover expenses for each trip they make. The society also has a small history library with books that are available to members to borrow free of charge. Figure 39.12 shows the receipts and payments account for the society and a summary of its assets and liabilities at the beginning of the financial year. The following information was also available at the year end:

- £100 motor insurance was prepaid;
- £230 was owed to a book supplier;
- £80 was owed to a history film company;
- a £900 charge was made for depreciation (£600 for the minibus, £200 on books, £50 on the projector and £50 on a camera).

Figure 39.12 *Receipts and payments account and a summary of assets and liabilities for the Knighton History Society*

Knighton History Society
Receipts and Payments Account for year ended 31.12.01

Receipts	£	Payments	£
Balance b/d	650	Expenses to guest speakers	430
Subscriptions	670	Motor expenses	760
Fares from visits	1,200	Rent for functions room	260
Net proceeds from Xmas raffle	810	Books purchased	730
		Fees for film hire	240
		Society camera	400
		Sundry expenses	130
		Balance c/d	380
	3,330		3,330
Balance b/d	380		

	£
Assets as at 1.1.01	
Minibus	4,300
Books	1,200
Film projector	350
Prepayment - motor insurance	50
Cash at bank and in hand	650
Liabilities	
Accrual - film	60
Book supplier	130

(a) Calculate the value of net assets as at 1 January 2001 to determine the value of the accumulated fund for the Knighton History Society.

(b) Prepare an income and expenditure account for the year ended 31 December 2001.

(c) Prepare a balance sheet as at 31 December 2001.

unit objectives

To understand:
- the costs incurred by manufacturers;
- how to prepare a manufacturing account;
- the manufacturing, trading and profit and loss account;
- transfer prices and factory profit.

The costs incurred by manufacturers

Manufacturers are businesses that process raw materials and components into **intermediate goods** or **final goods**. Intermediate goods are those, such as circuit boards, wheels and components, that are bought by other businesses. Final goods are those, such as cars, computers and furniture, that are bought by consumers. The processes used by manufacturers might include cutting, shaping, welding, pressing, painting and assembly. Resources such as labour and machinery are used in these processes.

Manufacturing accounts are slightly different from those described in earlier units. This is because, in order to calculate the cost of goods sold, manufacturers must take into account not only the cost of raw materials but also the other **production costs**. These are also known as factory costs or manufacturing costs and they include labour and fuel costs. All these costs are recorded in a MANUFACTURING ACCOUNT. Because it includes production costs, this account is unlike the trading account of retailers who simply buy in goods and then resell them to the public without altering their condition.

Figure 40.1 illustrates the costs that are incurred by a manufacturer. Production costs are divided into DIRECT COSTS and INDIRECT COSTS (see unit 48). Like other businesses, manufacturers incur administrative expenses, such as office wages, and selling and distribution expenses, such as advertising and carriage. These are also indirect costs.

Figure 40.1 *Costs incurred by manufacturers*

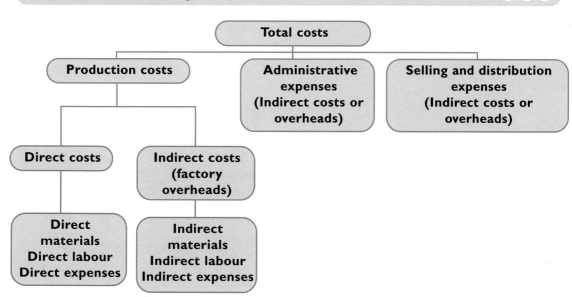

- Direct costs are those that can be attributed in full to a particular product, process or department. They are broken down into **direct materials**, **direct labour** and **direct expenses**. To illustrate the difference between these, consider the example of a manufacturer producing computer keyboards. The raw materials and components, such as circuit boards, plastic and wire, are direct materials. The wages paid to the workers assembling the keyboards are direct labour costs. An example of a direct expense would be a licence fee that is paid to a patent holder for every item produced. This might occur, for instance, if the manufacturer is copying a product with the permission of an inventor who has taken out a patent. A similar fee, or royalty, might be charged if the manufacturer was using a trade name or logo with the copyright holder's permission. The total of direct materials, direct labour and direct expenses is known as the PRIME COST.

- Indirect costs are also known as OVERHEADS. They are costs that cannot be attributed directly and in full to a particular product, process or department. **Factory overheads** are classified as production costs. They include indirect materials, indirect labour and indirect expenses. Cleaning fluids and lubricants are examples of indirect materials. Indirect labour costs include the wages of workers who are not directly involved in making the product, such as supervisors, maintenance workers and store workers. Indirect expenses include factory rates, rent, depreciation on machinery and insurance.

Note that factory overheads are not the same as administrative or selling and distribution overheads. These expenses, such as auditors' fees, office expenses and freight charges, are not production costs and are not included in the manufacturing account.

QUESTION 1

Figure 40.2 *Production worker in pottery factory*

(a) **Look at the photograph. Suggest one example of (i) direct materials (ii) direct labour (iii) direct expenses.**
(b) **With reference to the photograph, explain the difference between direct and indirect production costs.**

Manufacturing accounts

The basic structure of a manufacturing account is shown in Figure 40.3. There are two main sections in the account. The first section contains the direct materials, direct labour and other direct costs. These are added together to give the prime cost. The second section contains the factory overheads, ie indirect materials, indirect labour and other indirect expenses. These overheads are added to prime cost to give the production cost.

Figure 40.3 *Structure of a manufacturing account*

```
    Direct materials
  + Direct labour
  + Direct expenses
  = Prime cost
  + Indirect materials
  + Indirect labour
  + Indirect expenses
  = Production cost
```

In order to illustrate the preparation of a manufacturing account, consider the example of Welshpool Stoves Ltd, a manufacturer of cookers and stoves. Figure 40.4 shows the manufacturing account for this company.

Figure 40.4 *Manufacturing account for Welshpool Stoves Ltd*

Welshpool Stoves Ltd
Manufacturing Account for the year ended 31.12.01

	£000	£000
Direct materials		
Stock at 1.1.01	191	
Purchases	2,189	
	2,380	
Less stock at 31.12.01	221	2,159
Direct labour		3,336
Direct expenses		2,870
Prime cost		8,365
Add production overheads		
Indirect materials	411	
Indirect labour	1,305	
Indirect expenses	122	1,838
		10,203
Add work-in-progress at 1.1.01		1,420
		11,623
Less work-in-progress at 31.12.01		1,711
Production cost		9,912

- The first entry in the account is the direct materials cost incurred by Welshpool. These costs are adjusted for stock and amount to £2,159,000. The stock adjustments are shown in the first column. The opening stock is added to purchases of direct materials and the closing stock is subtracted to give the cost of materials used during the year.
- Direct labour costs of £3,336,000 and direct expenses of £2,870,000 are added to the direct materials cost to give the prime cost. The prime cost for Welshpool Stoves Ltd is £8,365,000.
- The production overheads of indirect materials, indirect labour and indirect expenses are listed and totalled. This is £1,838,000 (£411,000 + £1,305,000 + £122,000). The total is added to the prime cost to give a total production cost of £10,203,000.
- The total production cost of £10,203,000 includes goods that have not yet been finished and are in a partly completed state. These goods are called **work-in-progress**. Any work-in-progress from the last period, which is now complete and available for sale, must be added to the production cost. However, any work-in-progress from the current period must be subtracted from

QUESTION 2

Cartwright Holdings Ltd manufactures metal products including mountings and casings for speed cameras. The information listed below relates to production costs, stocks and work-in-progress for the year ended 31 March 2001.

Direct materials	£12,001,000	Indirect materials	£7,443,000
Direct labour	£15,332,000	Indirect labour	£4,009,000
Direct expenses	£4,880,000	Indirect expenses	£2,773,000
Stocks of materials at 1.4.00	£1,769,000	Stocks of materials at 31.3.01	£1,988,000
Work-in-progress at 1.4.00	£2,122,000	Work-in-progress at 31.3.01	£2,431,000

(a) **Prepare a manufacturing account for Cartwright Holdings Ltd.**
(b) **Explain why the total production cost must be adjusted for work-in-progress.**

the total production cost. The purpose of these adjustments is to ensure that the production cost accurately represents the cost of goods available for sale. For Welshpool Stoves Ltd, the work-in-progress on 1 January 2001 is £1,420,000. This is added to the total production cost of £10,203,000 to give £11,623,000. The value of work-in-progress at 31 December 2001, £1,711,000, is subtracted to give the final figure in the account. The production cost for Welshpool Stoves Ltd for the year ended 31 December 2001 is £9,912,000.

The manufacturing, trading and profit and loss account

The manufacturing account forms the first part of the overall manufacturing, trading and profit and loss account of a company. Figure 40.5 shows the manufacturing, trading and profit and loss account for Welshpool Stoves Ltd.

Figure 40.5 *Manufacturing, trading and profit and loss account*

Welshpool Stoves Ltd
Manufacturing, Trading and Profit and Loss Account
for the year ended 31.12.01

	£000	£000
Direct materials		
Stock at 1.1.01	191	
Purchases	2,189	
	2,380	
Less stock at 31.12.01	221	2,159
Direct labour		3,336
Direct expenses		2,870
Prime cost		8,365
Add production overheads		
Indirect materials	411	
Indirect labour	1,305	
Indirect expenses	122	1,838
		10,203
Add work-in-progress at 1.1.01		1,420
		11,623
Less work-in-progress at 31.12.01		1,711
Production cost		9,912
Sales		38,706
Less cost of sales		
Stocks of finished goods (1.1.00)	987	
Production cost	9,912	
	10,899	
Less stocks of finished goods (31.12.01)	1,110	9,789
Gross profit		28,917
Less expenses		
Selling and distribution expenses	2,344	
Administration expenses	4,510	6,854
		22,063
Interest paid		3,210
Net profit		18,853

Production cost transferred to trading account

• The account begins with the manufacturing account shown in Figure 40.4. The total production cost is £9,912,000.
• The next section is the trading account which is used to calculate gross profit. Sales for the year

are £38,706,000. To calculate the cost of sales, the production cost of £9,912,000 is transferred from the manufacturing account and adjusted for stocks of finished goods. For Welshpool Stoves Ltd the adjusted total is £9,789,000. This is subtracted from sales to give gross profit which is £28,917,000.

- The final section is the profit and loss account, which is used to calculate net profit. Selling and distribution expenses of £2,344,000 and administrative expenses of £4,510,000 are subtracted from gross profit to give £22,063,000. Finally, interest paid of £3,210,000 is subtracted to give net profit. The net profit made by Welshpool Stoves Ltd for the year ended 31 December 2001 is £18,853,000. Note that, in this example, the profit and loss appropriation account is not shown.

When drawing up the accounts for a manufacturing company, it is sometimes necessary to divide certain overheads between the manufacturing account and the profit and loss account. For example, a business that rents a factory which includes some office space might divide the total rent paid between factory overheads and administrative overheads. This could be done, for example, in proportion to the floor space of the factory and the floor space of the office. The rent apportioned to the factory will appear in the manufacturing account as an indirect expense. The rent apportioned to the office will appear in the profit and loss account as an administrative expense. The apportionment of costs is explained in detail in unit 50.

When preparing the balance sheet of a manufacturing company, the value of all stocks should be listed as current assets. This includes stocks of raw materials, work-in-progress and stocks of finished goods. The valuation of stocks is explained in unit 24. Figure 40.6 shows a balance sheet extract for Welshpool Stoves. The figures come from the manufacturing, trading and profit and loss account in Figure 40.5.

Figure 40.6 *Balance sheet extract for Welshpool Stoves Ltd*

Welshpool Stoves Ltd
Balance Sheet (extract)
as at 31.12.01

	£000
Current assets	
Direct materials	221
Work-in-progress	1,711
Finished goods	10,089
	12,021

QUESTION 3

Celtic Plastics Ltd manufactures a range of plastic products for the construction industry. The business is family owned and employs 31 people. The information listed below is for the year ended 31 July 2001. During that financial year, Celtic Plastics had a turnover of £9,156,000.

Direct materials	£2,331,000	Indirect materials	£1,222,000
Direct labour	£1,911,000	Indirect labour	£987,000
Direct expenses	£199,000	Indirect expenses	£1,852,000
Stocks of materials (1.8.00)	£169,000	Stocks of materials (31.7.01)	£188,000
Work-in-progress (1.8.00)	£340,000	Work-in-progress (31.7.01)	£401,000
Stocks of finished goods (1.8.00)	£421,000	Stocks of finished goods (31.7.01)	£459,000
Selling and distribution expenses	£768,000		
Administrative expenses	£889,000		
Interest paid	£100,000		

(a) Prepare a manufacturing, trading and profit and loss account for Celtic Plastics Ltd.

(b) Prepare a balance sheet extract to show the total value of stocks at the end of the financial year.

Transfer prices and factory profit

A number of companies in recent years have ceased manufacturing to focus on other, more profitable, areas of business. For example, Greenhalls, the pub and restaurant chain, stopped brewing to concentrate on selling food and drink. After the change it bought in drinks, such as beer, from other companies. In order for such companies to assess whether manufacturing is worthwhile, they must estimate how much profit they make in different parts of their operations. One way of doing this is to set a TRANSFER PRICE for completed goods being moved from the factory to the warehouse. This transfer price is equal to the production cost of a manufactured good plus an additional amount, say 20 per cent, for FACTORY PROFIT. The reason for charging this notional profit is to apportion some of the company's overall profits to the manufacturing part of its

Figure 40.7 *Manufacturing, trading and profit and loss account, including a 50% factory profit*

Welshpool Stoves Ltd
Manufacturing, Trading and Profit and Loss Account
for the year ended 31.12.01

	£000	£000
Direct materials		
Stock at 1.1.01	191	
Purchases	2,189	
	2,380	
Less stock at 31.12.01	221	2,159
Direct labour		3,336
Direct expenses		2,870
Prime cost		8,365
Add production overheads		
Indirect materials	411	
Indirect labour	1,305	
Indirect expenses	122	1,838
		10,203
Add work-in-progress at 1.1.01		1,420
		11,623
Less work-in-progress at 31.12.01		1,711
Production cost		9,912
Factory profit at 50%		4,956
Production cost incl. factory profit (transfer price)		14,868
Sales		38,706
Less cost of sales		
Stocks of finished goods (1.1.00)	987	
Production cost including factory profit	14,868	
	15,855	
Less stocks of finished goods (31.12.01)	1,110	14,745
Gross profit		23,961
Less expenses		
Selling and distribution expenses	2,344	
Administration expenses	4,510	6,854
		17,107
Interest paid		3,210
Trading profit		13,897
Factory profit		4,956
Net profit		18,853

operations. If the profit from trading is significantly higher than the profit from manufacturing, a business might decide to cease manufacturing in the way that Greenhalls did.

To illustrate how a transfer price is shown in the accounts, consider the Welshpool Stoves example used previously. Figure 40.7 shows the manufacturing, trading and profit and loss account for Welshpool Stoves Ltd after a 50% notional factory profit has been added to the production cost.

- The 50% profit is shown at the end of the manufacturing account. It is calculated by multiplying the production cost by 50%. The factory profit for Welshpool Stoves is £4,956,000 (50% × £9,912,000). This is transferred to the trading account as in Figure 40.5.
- As a result of charging a transfer price for the goods made in the factory, the gross profit made by Welshpool Stoves falls by £4,956,000 to £23,961,000.
- The profit and loss account now shows both the profit resulting from trading, ie selling, and the profit made from manufacturing. The trading profit is found by subtracting the various non-manufacturing expenses from gross profit. This gives a total of £13,897,000. When the factory profit is added back to this, net profit is £18,853,000, the same as in Figure 40.5.
- The advantage of dividing net profit between manufacturing and trading is that it helps in decision making. In this example, the profit from trading, £13,897,00, is significantly higher than the profit from manufacturing, £4,956,000. This might suggest that Welshpool Stoves should review its business strategy since trading appears to be so much more profitable than manufacturing. It might be worthwhile for the company to consider buying stoves from elsewhere rather than manufacturing them.

QUESTION 4

Anslow Furnishings Ltd manufactures a range of specialist furniture. In recent years the board of directors has wondered whether the company should close down the manufacturing side of its business and focus on wholesaling. In the last financial year the company enjoyed a turnover of £540,100. The information below relates to the year ended 31 January 2001.

Turnover	£540,100
Prime cost	£184,200
Production overheads	£65,800
Opening stocks (finished goods)	£41,000
Closing stocks (finished goods)	£43,200
Selling costs	£78,000
Administration costs	£56,000

(a) Prepare a manufacturing, trading and profit and loss account for Anslow Furnishings Ltd. Include a charge for factory profit of 40% of production cost.

(b) What factors might the board of directors take into account when deciding if the company should close down the manufacturing side of the business?

Provision for unrealised profit

Although transfer pricing has the advantage of making clear the profit from different parts of a company's operations, it does have a disadvantage. This arises because, in the accounts, the value of stocks of finished goods includes not only their production cost but also an element of factory profit. This does not conform to generally accepted principles of accounting. In particular, it conflicts with Statement of Standard Accounting Practice 9 (*Stocks and work-in-progress*). According to SSAP 9, stocks should be valued at either cost or net realisable value, whichever is lower. Because the stocks in question have not been sold, any profit is unrealised and therefore should not be included in their valuation.

To overcome this problem, it is necessary to reduce the value of the stock by the amount of factory profit added. This reduced value then appears in the balance sheet. To illustrate the bookkeeping entries necessary, consider the manufacturing account for Welshpool Stoves Ltd in Figure 40.7. The opening stock of finished goods is £987,000 and the closing stock is £1,110,000. Both of these figures include factory profit which is unrealised, and which must therefore be subtracted. Since 50% was added on in the first place, the amount to be subtracted is given by:

For opening stock: $£987,000 \times \dfrac{50}{150} = £329,000$

For closing stock: $£1,110,000 \times \dfrac{50}{150} = £370,000$

A provision for unrealised profit account is used to adjust the stock figures. The account for Welshpool Stoves Ltd is shown in Figure 40.8. The account is debited with the unrealised profit in the closing stock (£370,000) and credited with the unrealised profit in the opening stock (£329,000). The balance of £41,000 is deducted from factory profit in the profit and loss account.

Figure 40.8 *Provision for unrealised profit account for Welshpool Stoves Ltd*

Dr	Provision for Unrealised Profit Account		Cr
2001	£	2001	£
31.12 Balance c/d	370,000	1.1 Balance b/d	329,000
(closing stock adjustment)		(opening stock adjustment)	
		31.12 Profit and loss account	41,000
	370,000		370,000
		2002	
		1.1 Balance b/d	370,000

The deduction of unrealised profit from factory profit is shown in Figure 40.9. Since factory profit has been reduced by £41,000, the net profit for the year has also been reduced by the same amount. Note that if closing stock had been less than opening stock there would have been a debit balance on the provision for unrealised profit account. This would then have to be added to factory profit and net profit for the year would be higher.

Figure 40.9 *An extract from the profit and loss account for Welshpool Stoves Ltd*

	£000	£000
Trading profit		13,897
Factory profit	4,956	
Less increase in provision for unrealised profit	41	4,915
Net profit		18,812

summary questions

1. Explain the difference between direct materials and indirect materials.
2. How is prime cost calculated?
3. Give two examples of indirect labour costs.
4. What is the purpose of a manufacturing account?
5. What is meant by work-in-progress?
6. To which account is the total production cost transferred?
7. Why might a manufacturer use a transfer price?
8. Why is factory profit said to be notional?
9. What is a provision for unrealised profit account used for?
10. What happens if there is a credit balance on the provision for unrealised profit account?

UNIT ASSESSMENT QUESTION 1

Quentin Carmichael Ltd is a manufacturer of aircraft components. The company has faced intense competition in recent years but has been able to survive as a result of increased efficiency. For example, flexible working practices have been introduced to cut down the amount of overtime. The information below relates to costs incurred in two financial years. The financial year end for Quentin Carmichael Ltd is 31 December.

	2000	2001
	£	£
Factory wages	451,000	377,800
Supervisors' salaries	67,000	61,000
Maintenance staff wages	54,000	48,000
Purchases of raw materials	120,000	124,000
Purchases of components	340,200	342,100
Royalties and other direct expenses	146,200	144,500
Indirect materials	45,600	43,800
Factory rent	100,000	100,000
General factory overheads	78,500	81,200

	31.12.99	31.12.00	31.12.01
Stocks of raw materials and components	£24,000	£25,600	£27,800
Stocks of work-in-progress	£38,000	£41,000	£45,000

(a) Prepare manufacturing accounts for Quentin Carmichael Ltd for 2000 and 2001.

(b) Comment on the changes in costs over the two years.

UNIT ASSESSMENT QUESTION 2

Boswell, Burns & Co. is a boot and shoe manufacturer. The company has a policy of charging a transfer price when goods are moved from the factory to the warehouse. A 25% factory profit is added to total production cost. In the last financial year, the business raised its turnover by 15% to £2,520,000. Production costs and other financial information for the year ended 31 December 2001 were:

Direct materials	£351,000	Indirect materials	£28,000
Direct labour	£511,000	Indirect labour	£98,000
Direct expenses	£110,000	Indirect expenses	£52,000
Stocks of materials (1.1.01)	£30,000	Stocks of materials (31.12.01)	£32,000
Work-in-progress (1.1.01)	£54,000	Work-in-progress (31.12.01)	£60,000
Stocks of finished goods (1.1.01)	£70,000	Stocks of finished goods (31.12.01)	£80,000
Selling and distribution expenses	£290,000		
Administrative expenses	£341,000		

(a) Prepare a manufacturing, trading and profit and loss account for Boswell, Burns & Co. for the year ended 31 December 2001.

(b) Comment on the contribution made by manufacturing to the business.

key terms

Direct costs - costs that can be directly attributed to a particular product, process or department.

Factory profit - the amount added to the production cost of a manufactured good to give its transfer price.

Indirect costs - costs that cannot be directly attributed to a particular product, process or department.

Manufacturing account - a financial statement that sets out the costs incurred in production.

Overheads - costs that cannot be attributed directly to a particular product.

Prime cost - the total of direct materials, direct labour and direct expenses.

Transfer price - the notional price of a manufactured good when it is transferred between parts of the same company. It is calculated by adding factory profit to the production cost.

Departmental accounts

unit**objectives**

To understand:
- the nature and purpose of departmental accounts;
- the preparation of departmental accounts;
- how departmental accounts are used.

What are departmental accounts?

Some businesses measure the performance of different departments within their organisation. This can be helpful to managers in calculating the amount of profit each department contributes to the total. The information allows them to make decisions on whether a particular department should be closed or expanded, for example. Also, in some cases, staff in each department might receive bonuses that are related to their department's profit. In order to make such decisions, it is necessary to prepare DEPARTMENTAL ACCOUNTS. These generally consist of a trading and profit and loss account for each individual department in the organisation. The balance sheets for departments are not usually drawn up. This is because it is difficult to divide the assets and liabilities of a whole business between different departments.

Figure 41.1 shows the annual profit/loss made by five departments in Marshall's, a large department store. The total profit was £204,100. However, the children's wear department made a loss of £12,000. Without this loss, the profit made by Marshall's would have been £216,100. Given this information, managers might decide to make changes in the children's wear department or even close it down. Figure 41.1 also shows that women's wear made the highest profit. Managers might wish to investigate why the performance of this department was so much better than the others. They could then help other departments to improve their profitability.

Figure 41.1 *Departmental profit/loss at Marshall's*

	Profit/(loss)
	£
Men's wear	67,000
Women's wear	92,000
Children's wear	(12,000)
Soft furnishings	22,500
Electrical goods	34,600
Total profit	204,100

Departmental trading accounts

To produce departmental accounts it is necessary to record all the transactions that individual departments undertake. Analysed day books are often used to record the sales and purchases made by each department. This information is then posted to separate departmental accounts. Figure 41.3 shows the departmental trading accounts for Fenton's, a large DIY store and garden centre, for the year ended 31 December 2001. The store operates four departments and the various trading account entries are shown for each department. It is usual to present departmental accounts in a columnar format. This makes comparisons between the different departments easier. The totals for the business are shown in the final column.

QUESTION 1

S.T. Sports is a large discount store that specialises in sports goods and outdoor clothing and equipment. It is divided into three departments, each of which has its own manager. These managers are paid a profit-related bonus equivalent to 5% of their department's net profit.

Figure 41.2 *Profit made by each department at S.T. Sports in the last financial year.*

	Profit £
Outdoor clothing and equipment	17,000
Sports wear and equipment	38,000
Fashion wear	86,000
Total profit	141,000

(a) Suggest two advantages to S.T. Sports of calculating departmental profit in its store.
(b) State one possible disadvantage of rewarding managers according to departmental profit.

Figure 41.3 *Departmental trading accounts for Fenton's*

	Garden Centre £	Kitchens & Bathrooms £	Painting & Decorating £	Tools & Accessories £	Total £
Sales	341,900	355,300	411,600	755,900	1,864,700
Opening stock	32,200	42,100	43,900	53,900	172,100
Purchases	135,800	166,500	209,700	399,700	911,700
	168,000	208,600	253,600	453,600	1,083,800
Closing stock	33,200	41,300	46,400	56,400	177,300
Cost of sales	134,800	167,300	207,200	397,200	906,500
Gross profit	207,100	188,000	204,400	358,700	958,200
Gross profit margins	60.57%	52.91%	49.66%	47.45%	51.39%

- Fenton's made a total gross profit of £958,200.
- The Tools and Accessories department had the highest turnover and the highest gross profit.
- The Garden Centre had the lowest turnover and profit of all departments.
- One way of comparing the performance of each department using these accounts is to calculate the gross profit margins. This measures the gross profit in relation to the sales revenue. For example, the gross profit margin for the Garden Centre was:

$$\text{Gross profit margin} = \frac{\text{Gross profit}}{\text{Sales}} \times 100 = \frac{£207,100}{£341,900} \times 100 = 60.57\%$$

- The gross profit margins of the other departments were 52.91% (Kitchens and Bathrooms), 49.66% (Painting and Decorating) and 47.45% (Tools and Accessories).
- The profit margins show that, although the Garden Centre had the lowest gross profit and lowest turnover, it had the highest gross profit margin. Also, the department with the highest gross profit and turnover, Tools and Accessories, had the lowest gross profit margin. The use of gross profit margins as a means of analysing performance is described in more detail in unit 44.

QUESTION 2

Cedars is a large furniture store on the outskirts of Reading. It has three departments which sell different types of furniture. Information for each department is presented below.

Department	Sales	Stock 1.9.00	Stock 31.8.01	Purchases
	£	£	£	£
Bedroom	236,800	24,100	23,800	132,900
Dining room	155,400	21,900	22,700	111,100
Suites	733,900	53,900	54,000	363,500

(a) Prepare departmental trading accounts for Cedars.
(b) What was the total gross profit made by Cedars?
(c) (i) Calculate the gross profit margins for each department and (ii) comment briefly on the relative performance of each department.

Departmental profit and loss accounts

One of the problems when producing profit and loss accounts for departments is deciding how to **apportion** indirect costs or overheads. These are costs such as insurance, interest payments, rent and administrative expenses. One simple way is to split the costs equally between each department. Another method is to apportion overheads in relation to the departments' direct costs. This means that departments with high direct costs 'soak-up' more of the overheads. However, neither of these methods is considered satisfactory because they are arbitrary and do not reflect actual costs.

In order to apportion indirect costs more accurately, specific information about the way a business and each department operates is required. For example, in some businesses it might be appropriate to apportion costs according to the floor space occupied by each department. For other businesses, it might be best to apportion costs in proportion to the value of net sales for each department. The way in which indirect costs are apportioned is explained in more detail in unit 50.

To illustrate how departmental profit and loss accounts are prepared, consider again the example of Fenton's. During the year ended 31 December 2001, the company's total indirect costs were £440,000. An analysis of these costs is given in Figure 41.4.

Figure 41.4 *An analysis of indirect costs for Fenton's*

Managers' salaries	£100,000	(all departmental managers are paid exactly the same)
Rent	£200,000	
Heat and light	£60,000	
Other administration expenses	£80,000	
Total	£440,000	

Fenton's has a policy of apportioning rent, heat and light according to the floor space that each department uses. The Garden Centre takes up $\frac{1}{4}$ of the floor space, Kitchens and Bathrooms also $\frac{1}{4}$, Painting and Decorating $\frac{1}{8}$ and Tools and Accessories $\frac{3}{8}$. Other administrative expenses are apportioned equally between each department. Using this information, the profit and loss accounts can be prepared for each department. These are shown in Figure 41.5.

Figure 41.5 *Departmental profit and loss accounts for Fenton's*

	Garden Centre	Kitchens & Bathrooms	Painting & Decorating	Tools & Accessories	Total
	£	£	£	£	£
Gross profit	207,100	188,000	204,400	358,700	958,200
Manager's salaries	25,000	25,000	25,000	25,000	100,000
Rent	50,000	50,000	25,000	75,000	200,000
Heat and light	15,000	15,000	7,500	22,500	60,000
Other admin. exp.	20,000	20,000	20,000	20,000	80,000
	110,000	110,000	77,500	142,500	440,000
Net profit	97,100	78,000	126,900	216,200	518,200
Net profit margins	28.40%	21.95%	30.83%	28.60%	27.79%

- Total net profit for Fenton's was £518,200.
- The Tools and Accessories department made the highest net profit, £216,200, ie nearly half of the total net profit made by the business.
- The Kitchens and Bathrooms departments made the lowest net profit of £78,000.
- To help compare the performance of each department, the net profit margins for each department can be calculated. These measure the net profit in relation to the sales revenue (from Figure 41.3). For example, the net profit margin of the Garden Centre was:

$$\text{Net profit margin} = \frac{\text{Net profit}}{\text{Sales}} \times 100 = \frac{£97,100}{£341,900} \times 100 = 28.40\%$$

- The net profit margins of the other departments were 21.95% (Kitchens and Bathrooms), 30.83% (Painting and Decorating) and 28.60% (Tools and Accessories).
- The Kitchens and Bathrooms department had the lowest net profit margin. The other three departments had fairly similar net profit margins. The use of net profit margins is explored in more detail in unit 44.

Closing departments

The main reason for producing departmental accounts is to monitor the performance of individual sections of a business. When a poorly performing department is identified, managers might consider whether it should be closed down. However, before closure, the following factors might be taken into account.

- Have overheads been apportioned fairly? The accurate apportionment of overheads between departments can be difficult. If overheads have been apportioned unfairly, this might result in an otherwise profitable department appearing to make a loss.
- Has a gross profit been made? Although a department might be making a net loss, its gross profit might be making a contribution to the overheads of a business. Sometimes, when a section of a business is closed down, there is very little reduction in overheads. Consequently, a department which makes a gross profit and also pays some of the overheads might be worth keeping open.
- What will be the impact on the rest of the business? A loss making department might attract customers who then buy goods or services from the more profitable departments. Closing a loss making department could reduce the choice offered by a business and, as a result, customers might go elsewhere.
- What costs will be incurred in closing down sections of the business? For example, staff in the department might be entitled to redundancy payments.
- Will spare resources be created? When a department is closed, consideration has to be given to any unused resources. For example, in a department store, there might be empty floor space if a department closes. Possibly this could be rented out to other retailers. Alternatively, a business might expand one of the profitable departments into the vacant area.

Branch accounts

• • • • • • • • • • •

Some businesses, such as supermarket chains, operate with a head office and a number of branches. The manager in each branch might be responsible for purchasing, staff recruitment, financial management, marketing and customer relations. However, other businesses are more centralised, with greater control exercised by the head office. Whichever system of organisation is adopted, it is usual to draw up separate accounts for each branch. These accounts are similar to departmental accounts allowing senior managers to monitor performance.

QUESTION 3

The Great Barr Discount Centre is a retail store in Birmingham. It sells goods in three departments.

● **Food hall** This department takes up the most space occupying half of the entire floor space. It sells canned and packaged food, wines, spirits and beers. The department employs 12 staff and the manager is paid £24,000 p.a.

● **Electrical goods** This department occupies a quarter of the floor space. It sells electrical products such as televisions, video recorders, personal stereos, car sound systems and personal computers. The department employs 8 staff and the manager is paid £29,000 p.a.

● **Sports and leisure wear** This department is relatively new. It sells casual clothes and footwear, sports wear and toddlers clothes. The department employs 4 staff and occupies a quarter of the floor space in the store. The manager, who is paid £27,000 p.a. believes that higher gross margins in the department will lead to its expansion within the store.

Figure 41.6 shows financial information for the Great Barr Discount Centre. The company is keen to raise the profitability of all departments and closely monitors the performance of each. When preparing departmental accounts, heat, light and depreciation are apportioned according to the floor space occupied by each department. Advertising costs are apportioned equally between departments.

Figure 41.6 *Financial information for the Great Barr Discount Centre, year ended 31 January 2002*

	Food	Electrical goods	Sports and leisure wear
Sales	£664,000	£543,000	£211,000
Gross profit	£221,400	£150,900	£99,000

	Overheads
Managers' salaries	£80,000
Heat and light	£40,000
Depreciation	£20,000
Advertising	£45,000
Total	185,000

(a) Prepare departmental profit and loss accounts for the Great Barr Discount Centre.

(b) Comment on the view of the sports and leisure wear manager that high gross margins will result in the expansion of the department.

key terms

Departmental accounts - separate accounts for each section of a business.

UNIT ASSESSMENT QUESTION 1

Nicholson's is a large fashion store in Edinburgh. It has four departments: shoes and accessories, lingerie, evening wear and casual wear. In recent years, sales have declined due to competition. As a consequence, the owner of the store is considering the closure of the casual wear department. Departmental accounts are kept to help monitor performance. When apportioning overheads, wages are apportioned according to the number of staff in each department. Rent and rates and heat and light are apportioned according to floor space. Other expenses are shared equally between the four departments. Figure 41.7 shows some information for the store. It relates to the past financial year which ended on 31 March.

Figure 41.7 *Financial information for Nicholson's*

	Shoes and accessories	Lingerie	Evening wear	Casual wear
	£	£	£	£
Sales	127,400	106,500	231,000	163,900
Purchases	46,300	43,200	117,000	102,000
Opening stock	12,500	14,300	27,500	16,400
Closing stock	13,900	15,300	26,400	19,800
Number of staff	3	2	3	4
Floor space	20%	20%	20%	40%

Overheads	£
Wages	240,000
Rent and rates	50,000
Heat and light	20,000
Other expenses	12,000
Total	322,000

(a) Prepare a trading and profit and loss account for each department.
(b) Do you think there are grounds for closing the casual wear department?
(c) What factors should be taken into account before the department is closed?

UNIT ASSESSMENT QUESTION 2

Alexander Jones owns a small chain of grocers shops in the Midlands. He keeps accounts to monitor the performance of each branch and pays a bonus to branch managers equivalent to 10% of net profit. One of the branches has an office where Alexander works. The expenses for this office, including Alexander's own salary, are £45,000 p.a. In the accounts, this is apportioned equally between the branches. Figure 41.8 shows additional financial information for each branch. It relates to the past financial year which ended on 30 September.

Figure 41.8 *Financial information for Alexander Jones's business*

	Dudley	Gornal	Sedgley	Oldbury	Walsall
	£	£	£	£	£
Sales	65,000	69,000	86,700	43,100	121,900
Purchases	32,100	36,400	43,800	17,500	64,000
Opening stock	1,200	1,500	1,300	1,100	2,700
Closing stock	1,300	1,600	1,200	1,300	3,000
Branch overheads	6,400	7,500	8,500	5,300	21,000
Branch manager's salary	15,000	15,000	15,000	15,000	15,000

(a) **Prepare a trading and profit and loss account for each branch.**

(b) **Calculate the salary bonus for each manager.**

(c) **Calculate the net profit margin for each branch and comment briefly on the results.**

(d) **What are the advantages and disadvantages of rewarding the branch managers according to the size of their net profit?**

summary questions

1. What types of business are likely to prepare departmental accounts?
2. State two reasons why a business might produce departmental accounts.
3. How is the gross profit margin calculated?
4. State two ways in which overheads might be apportioned in an arbitrary way.
5. How might rent and rates be fairly apportioned between departments?
6. What does the net profit margin measure?
7. Why is it difficult to produce a balance sheet for departments?
8. State four factors that might be considered before closing a department.
9. What are branch accounts?

unit 42

Cash flow statements

unit objectives

To understand:
- the nature and purpose of cash flow statements;
- how to prepare a cash flow statement for a sole trader;
- how to prepare a cash flow statement for a limited company.

What is cash and cash flow?

It is important for businesses to keep a record of the money they receive and the payments they make. This is shown in a CASH FLOW STATEMENT. In the context of cash flow statements, cash consists of:

- notes and coins;
- deposits in banks, or similar financial institutions, that are repayable to the business on demand;
- CASH EQUIVALENTS, which are short-term investments that can be converted into cash within three months.

Cash is the most **liquid asset** that a business owns. This means it can be used to make payments immediately. Cash equivalents are the next most liquid asset after notes, coins and bank deposits. Other assets, such as stocks of goods, are less liquid because they generally take longer to convert into cash.

Cash is important because, without it, a business cannot survive. For example, if a manufacturer does not have enough cash to pay wages, factory workers are unlikely to continue working. Similarly, without cash to pay for raw materials, suppliers will eventually refuse to make deliveries. Again the result is that production is likely to cease.

Since cash is so important, owners and managers must monitor the movement of cash into and out of a business. This movement is known as **cash flow**. Cash balances rise or fall according to the type and volume of transactions that are undertaken. For example, the cash flow of a business will improve if, on a particular day, £57,200 is received from customers and £45,300 is paid to suppliers. The result is a positive net cash flow of £11,900 (£57,200 - £45,300). A negative cash flow occurs if payments are greater than receipts.

The nature and purpose of cash flow statements

A cash flow statement is a summary of a business's actual cash inflows and cash outflows over a given period of time. This is different from cash flow forecasts or cash budgets which are both concerned with future cash flows (see unit 54).

All medium and large-sized UK companies must publish a cash flow statement in their annual accounts. This regulation was issued in 1991 (and revised in 1996) by the **Accounting Standards Board** in its Financial Reporting Standard *Cash flow statements* (FRS1). In practice, most companies publish cash flow statements for the past two financial years. This is to show how the cash position of the company has changed.

The reasoning behind FRS1 was the belief that the profit and loss account and balance sheet do not disclose enough information about a business's financial circumstances. In particular, they fail to highlight how much cash is available for a business to pay its outgoings.

A common misconception is that if a business is profitable it must have sufficient cash for its needs. However, this is not always the case because profit and cash are not the same. For example, suppose that a business has a bank balance of £5,000 at the start of the year and makes a profit of £75,000. It is very unlikely that the bank balance at the end of the year will be £80,000 (£5,000 + £75,000). There is a number of reasons for this.

- The profit and loss account matches revenues recognised in a particular trading period with the costs incurred in earning that revenue. This is known as 'accruals based' accounting. It does not record revenues actually received and costs actually incurred. For example, at the end of a trading year, a business might be owed £4,000 for goods sold on credit. Even though payment has not been made, the sale and resulting profit are 'realised' and will still appear in the current year's account. However, the business will only receive the cash when the customer eventually pays for the goods.

- Capital expenditure is not recorded as an expense in the profit and loss account. Instead it is recorded in the fixed asset section of the balance sheet. So, for example, a £100,000 payment for a new machine will not appear in the profit and loss account and therefore will not reduce profit. However, it will reduce the business's bank balance by £100,000. Similarly, the proceeds from the sale of a fixed asset will boost the amount of cash that a business has, but it will have no effect on the profit and loss account.

- If a business receives a loan and deposits the money in its bank account, this will be recorded on the balance sheet but will not be shown on the profit and loss account. However, it will affect the amount of cash that the business has at its disposal. Similarly, when a loan is repaid, the bank balance will fall, but there will be no effect on the profit made by the business.

- Drawings by owners do not appear on the profit and loss account because they are not classed as business expenses. Therefore they do not affect profit but they do reduce the amount of cash available. Owners who draw too much money can threaten a business's survival by draining its cash resources.

- The profit and loss account includes transactions such as depreciation which do not affect the amount of cash held. The depreciation is listed as an expense in the profit and loss account and therefore reduces the amount of profit reported. However, no cash leaves the business.

A cash flow statement helps makes the distinction between cash and profit clear. For instance, it can show if a business has made a healthy profit, but has little cash in the bank. Alternatively, it can show if a business has made a loss but still has sufficient cash for its needs.

QUESTION 1

The following list of business transactions were undertaken by Basingstoke Building Supplies plc during the past financial year. In each case, state the immediate effect (increase, decrease, no change) on both profit and cash.

1 Bought a new delivery van for cash.
2 Repaid a short-term bank loan.
3 Issued new shares for cash.
4 Received cash from a trade debtor.
5 Made a large sale of bricks on credit.
6 Increased provision for depreciation on its buildings.
7 Sold a surplus fork lift truck for cash.
8 Arranged a long term bank loan.

Cash flow statement format

Companies are required by FRS1 *Cash flow statements* to present cash flow statements using a standard format. This is shown in Figure 42.1. Each of the entries listed represents a cash inflow or outflow resulting from the various activities of the business. Figure 42.2 shows how Enodis plc, a manufacturing company, has used this format to present a cash flow statement.

Net cash flow from operating activities
plus or minus
Returns on investments and servicing of finance
plus or minus
Taxation
plus or minus
Capital expenditure and financial investment
plus or minus
Acquisitions and disposals
plus or minus
Equity dividends paid
plus or minus
Management of liquid resources
plus or minus
Financing
equals
Increase or decrease in cash over the period

Figure 42.2 *Cash flow statement for Enodis plc*

	52 weeks to 20 September 2000
	£m
Net cash inflow from operating activities	160.5
Return on investments and servicing of finance	
Net interest paid	(37.5)
Taxation	
Overseas and UK tax paid	(10.2)
Capital expenditure and financial investment	
Payments to acquire tangible fixed assets	(32.1)
Receipts from sale of tangible fixed assets	8.2
Proceeds from / (payments to acquire) financial investments	0.6
	(23.3)
Acquisitions and disposals	
Purchase of subsidiary undertakings and minority interests	(47.8)
Investment in joint venture	(0.4)
	(48.2)
Equity dividends paid	(28.6)
Cash inflow / (outflow) before use of liquid resources and financing	12.7
Management of liquid resources	
Cash transferred from term deposits	1.0
Financing	
Issue of shares	0.6
(Repayment of) / increase in long-term loans	(32.9)
Net increase / (decrease) in other loans	18.5
	(13.8)
(Decrease) / increase in cash in the period	(0.1)

Source: adapted from *Enodis Annual Report and Accounts 2000*.

The cash flow statement for Enodis contains the following features.
- **Net cash flow from operating activities** This figure shows the amount of cash that has been generated from trading activities. The way that it is calculated is explained in the next section of this unit. For Enodis, the net cash inflow from operating activities during the financial year was £160.5m.

- **Returns on investments and servicing of finance** This section shows the net interest paid on loans and received on deposits. It also includes any dividend income from shares owned by the business, and dividend payments to preference shareholders. It does not include dividend payments to ordinary shareholders. This is dealt with later. During the year, Enodis paid interest of £38.5m and received interest of £1m, giving a net payment of £37.5m. Note that cash outflows are shown in brackets.
- **Taxation** This mainly relates to payments of corporation tax by limited companies. It also includes any corporation tax rebates that might be received from the Inland Revenue. Enodis paid a total of £10.2m tax which also included tax payments to foreign governments.
- **Capital expenditure and financial investment** Expenditure on fixed assets and investments is included in this section. Receipts from the sale of fixed assets are also shown. During the year, Enodis spent £32.1m on tangible fixed assets and received £8.2m from the sale of tangible assets. The company also received £0.6m from the sale of financial investments. This resulted in a net cash outflow of £23.3m.
- **Acquisitions and disposals** This section shows cash flows resulting from the purchase or sale of businesses. These might include subsidiaries, associated companies or joint ventures. Enodis spent £47.8m on new businesses during the year. It also invested £0.4m in a joint venture. This caused a total cash outflow of £48.2m. There were no disposals of businesses during the year.
- **Equity dividends paid** This section shows the cash outflow resulting from the payment of dividends to ordinary shareholders. Enodis paid a total of £28.6m in dividends during the financial year. In the case of partnerships and sole traders, any drawings made by the owners would be entered here.
- **Cash inflow/outflow before the management of liquid resources and financing** This figure is calculated by adding all the cash inflows and subtracting all the cash outflows listed in the statement so far. For Enodis, the cash inflow before liquid resources and financing was £12.7m (£160.5m - £37.5m - £10.2m - £23.3m - £48.2m - £28.6m).
- **Management of liquid resources** This involves the transfer of money between bank accounts. For instance, a business could decide to transfer money from its current bank account, where the cash is instantly available, to a 'term' account where the money is deposited for a fixed period and interest is paid. The management of liquid resources also includes the purchase and sale of short term securities. For example, a business might decide to use some of its cash to buy treasury bills which are, in effect, 90 day loans to the government. In the case of Enodis, there was a cash inflow of £1m resulting from the transfer of money from term deposits.
- **Financing** This section of the statement shows the cash flows arising from share issues, borrowing money or repaying loans. The cash flow statement for Enodis states that £0.6m was raised by selling shares and a further £18.5m was borrowed. However, £32.9m of long-term loans were repaid. The net cash flow resulting from Enodis's financing activities was an outflow of £13.8m.
- **Increase/decrease in cash** The overall change in cash is shown at the bottom of the cash flow statement. In this case it states that Enodis experienced a relatively small net cash outflow of £0.1m.

Calculating net cash flow from operating activities

Two approaches can be used when calculating the net cash flow from operating activities of a business. The most widely used is called the INDIRECT METHOD. This method starts with the figure for operating profit and then adjusts it for non-cash transactions. An alternative approach is the **direct method**. It involves an analysis of a business's cash records, identifying all the payments and receipts relating to operating activities. Relatively few businesses use this method because it can be laborious and time-consuming.

The indirect method of calculating net cash flow from operating activities is summarised in Figure 42.3. It starts with the operating profit which is taken from the profit and loss account.

Figure 42.3 *The indirect method of calculating net cash flow from operating activities*

Operating profit
plus
Depreciation and amortisation
plus or minus
Profit (minus) or loss (plus) on disposal of fixed assets
plus or minus
Increase (minus) or decrease (plus) in stock
plus or minus
Increase (minus) or decrease (plus) in debtors
plus or minus
Increase (plus) or decrease (minus) in creditors
equals
Net cash flow from operating activities

To illustrate how the net cash flow from operating activities is calculated by the indirect method, consider again the example of Enodis. Using figures from the company's profit and loss account and balance sheet, Figure 42.4 shows the calculation of net cash flow from operating activities.

Figure 42.4 *The net cash flow from operating activities for Enodis*

	£m
Operating profit	118.3
Depreciation	23.8
Amortisation of goodwill	21.1
Profit on sale of fixed assets	(0.3)
Increase in stock	(4.8)
Decrease in debtors	6.0
Decrease in creditors	(3.6)
Net cash flow from operating activities	**160.5**

Source: adapted from *Enodis Annual Report and Accounts 2000*.

- **Operating profit** This is the net profit before taxation and interest. In the case of Enodis, operating profit was £118.3m.
- **Depreciation and amortisation** Non-cash transactions such as depreciation and amortisation are classed as expenses in the profit and loss account, but do not result in any outflow of cash from the business. Therefore they are added back to profit in the calculation. In the case of Enodis, depreciation of £23.8m and £21.1m amortisation of goodwill are added back.
- **Sale of fixed assets** Any profit or loss on the disposal of a fixed asset must be taken into account. A gain on disposal is subtracted and a loss is added. Such gains and losses arise when a fixed asset is sold at a price different from its net book value. In the case of Enodis, fixed assets were sold for £0.3m more than their net book value.
- **Stock** An increase in the value of stock arises if fewer goods are sold than are replaced. This results in a net cash outflow. In the case of Enodis, there was an increase in stock of £4.8m. This amount is deducted in the calculation.
- **Debtors** If debtors decrease this means that the amount of money being paid by debtors is more than the amount of new debtors created. This results in a net cash inflow and therefore the decrease must be added in the calculation. The value of debtors for Enodis decreased by £6.0m so this amount must be added. If the value of debtors had increased, the amount would be subtracted.
- **Creditors** If creditors decrease this means that more cash is paid to creditors than new creditors are created. This results in a net cash outflow and therefore the decrease must be deducted in the calculation. The value of creditors for Enodis decreased by £3.6m and is therefore deducted. If the value of creditors had increased, the amount would be added.

QUESTION 2

Hedges Ltd produces leather goods such as handbags, suitcases, briefcases and other leather accessories. In 2001 the company made an operating profit of £11,500,000. Extracts from the balance sheet for Hedges Ltd are shown in Figure 42.5. During the year there were no acquisitions or disposals of fixed assets so the difference in the balance sheet totals for fixed assets is the result of depreciation.

Figure 42.5 *Extracts from the balance sheet of Hedges Ltd*

	2001 £000	2000 £000
Fixed assets	13,400	15,000
Stocks	2,300	2,600
Debtors	4,300	3,200
Creditors	3,200	3,800

(a) Calculate the net cash flow from operating activities for Hedges Ltd for the year 2001.
(b) Explain why depreciation should be added to operating profit in the above calculation.

The net cash flow from operating activities is found by adding or subtracting the figures in the column of adjustments. For Enodis, the total gives the value for net cash flow from operating activities as £160.5m. Limited companies must show this reconciliation in their published accounts as a note. It is called a **reconciliation of operating profit to net cash inflow from operating activities**.

Preparing a cash flow statement for a sole trader

The format described in Figure 42.1 is used to produce cash flow statements for all types of business organisation. However, there are likely to be fewer entries in the cash flow statement of a sole trader than in that for a limited company. Consider the example of Brian Anderson, a sole trader who owns a paint wholesaling business. A copy of the balance sheet for the business is shown in Figure 42.6. The fixed assets are shown at their net book value.

Figure 42.6 *Balance sheet for Brian Anderson's business*

Brian Anderson
Balance Sheet as at

	31.12.01 £	31.12.00 £
Fixed assets		
Vehicle	8,000	10,500
Fixtures and fittings	12,000	14,000
Computer	3,000	-
	23,000	24,500
Current assets		
Stock	15,600	16,400
Debtors	14,900	10,100
Bank	1,000	6,200
	31,500	32,700
Current liabilities		
Trade creditors	7,300	8,600
Working capital	24,200	24,100
Net assets	47,200	48,600
Financed by		
Opening capital	48,600	51,000
Add net profit	43,700	39,200
	92,300	90,200
Less drawings	48,100	41,600
	44,200	48,600
Add capital introduced	3,000	-
Closing capital	47,200	48,600

Additional information:
(i) During the year, there were no disposals of fixed assets.
(ii) Net interest of £140 was paid during the year.
(iii) Brian introduced £3,000 of capital during the year.
(iv) A computer costing £4,000 was purchased during the year.

The first step in preparing the cash flow statement is to calculate the net cash flow from operating activities. The calculation is shown in Figure 42.7.

- The first figure is the operating profit of £43,840. In the case of a sole trader (and also a partnership) it is equal to the net profit shown in the balance sheet plus the net interest paid.

  Operating profit = Net profit + Net interest paid
  = £43,700 + £140

- Depreciation is calculated by subtracting the difference between the net book values of the fixed assets in the two years. The depreciation for the vehicle was £2,500 (£10,500 - £8,000) and for the fixtures and fittings it was £2,000 (£14,000 - £12,000). The calculation of depreciation for 2001 also needs to take into account the purchase of a new fixed asset, the computer, during the year. The computer was purchased for £4,000 and, according to the balance sheet, the net book value was £3,000 at the end of 2001. So, depreciation on the computer must have been £1,000 (£4,000 - £3,000). Total depreciation for the year was therefore £5,500 (£2,500 + £2,000 + £1,000).

- The adjustments for stock, debtors and creditors are calculated by comparing the amounts in the balance sheets for the two years. So, for stock, there was a decrease of £800 (£15,600 - £16,400). Debtors rose by £4,800 (£14,900 - £10,100) and creditors fell by £1,300 (£7,300 - £8,600).

Figure 42.7 *Calculating the net cash inflow from operating activities for Brian Anderson's business*

	£
Operating profit	43,840
Depreciation	5,500
Decrease in stock	800
Increase in debtors	(4,800)
Decrease in creditors	(1,300)
Net cash flow from operating activities	44,040

After the various adjustments for depreciation and changes in current assets, the net cash inflow from operating activities is shown as £44,040. This is transferred to the cash flow statement for Brian Anderson's business shown in Figure 42.8.

- For a sole trader, the return on investments and financing generally involves only interest payments. In the case of Brian Anderson's business, net interest of £140 was paid during the year.
- The entry for taxation is left blank. This is because sole traders do not pay corporation tax.
- During the year, Brian Anderson purchased a new computer for £4,000. This is a cash outflow and is entered under the heading of capital expenditure and financial investment.
- The next item in the cash flow statement is acquisitions and disposals. Sole traders generally do not own subsidiaries and associated companies and there is no entry in this case.
- Since sole traders do not issue shares, there are no equity dividends in the cash flow statement. However, drawings must be included in this section. Drawings represent cash outflows to the owner of the business. This is the equivalent to dividend payments to shareholders. During the year, Brian Anderson withdrew £48,100 from the business. This is shown as an outflow of cash.
- When all the entries listed so far are added, the figure for cash outflow before the use of liquid resources and financing is obtained. According to Figure 42.8, Brian Anderson's business experienced a cash outflow of £8,200 before the use of liquid resources and financing.
- The financing section shows whether a business has raised any money during the year, either from the **owner** or in **loans**. According to the balance sheet, Brian Anderson introduced £3,000 capital during the year and this is shown as a cash inflow. His business did not receive any loans. If any had been received, they would have been shown on the balance sheet as long-term liabilities.
- The final entry in the cash flow statement shows what has happened to the cash position of the business over the trading period. According to the statement, there was a net outflow of cash of £5,200 in Brian Anderson's business. This reconciles with the change in the bank balance shown in the balance sheet in Figure 42.6. A reconciliation statement is shown below.

Cash at bank (31.12.00)	£6,200
Decrease in cash (as in cash flow statement)	(£5,200)
Cash at bank (31.12.01)	£1,000

Figure 42.8 *Cash flow statement for Brian Anderson's business*

Brian Anderson
Cash Flow Statement for the year ended 31.12.01

	£
Net cash flow from operating activities	44,040
Returns on investments and servicing of finance	
Net interest paid	(140)
Taxation	-
Capital expenditure and financial investment	
Payment for computer	(4,000)
Acquisitions and disposals	-
Equity dividends	
Drawings	(48,100)
Cash outflow before use of liquid resources and financing	(8,200)
Financing	
Introduction of capital by owner	3,000
Decrease in cash in the period	(5,200)

QUESTION 3

Jason Simmons owns a successful car showroom in Cardiff. One of the reasons why the business is successful is that Jason stocks a wide range of makes and models. However, holding large stocks is expensive and for much of the time the business is overdrawn at the bank. Following a request from the bank, Jason produces regular cash flow statements to help monitor the position.

(a) Calculate the operating profit that Jason's business made during 2001.

(b) Calculate the net cash flow from operating activities for the business. There were no purchases or disposals of fixed assets during the year.

(c) Produce a cash flow statement for Jason Simmons's business for 2001.

(d) Produce a statement that reconciles the change in cash in hand and at the bank with the net cash flow.

(e) (i) State what happened to the cash position of the business. (ii) Suggest two possible reasons for the position.

Figure 42.9 *Balance sheet for Jason Simmons's business*

Jason Simmons Balance Sheet as at

	31.12.01	31.12.00
	£	£
Fixed assets		
Motor car	8,000	10,000
Fixtures and fittings	4,500	5,000
	12,500	15,000
Current assets		
Stock	184,300	176,400
Debtors	2,300	3,400
Cash	500	1,200
	187,100	181,000
Current liabilities		
Trade creditors	3,400	4,200
Bank	23,400	18,700
	26,800	22,900
Working capital	160,300	158,100
Long-term liabilities		
Bank loan	55,000	50,000
Net assets	117,800	123,100
Financed by		
Opening capital	123,100	110,500
Add net profit	51,100	56,200
	174,200	166,700
Less drawings	56,400	43,600
Closing capital	117,800	123,100

Additional information:
(i) Net interest of £9,300 was paid during the year.

Preparing a cash flow statement for a limited company

To illustrate the preparation of a cash flow statement for a limited company, consider the example of Cummings Ltd, a second hand car trader. The balance sheet for the business as at 31 December 2001 is shown in Figure 42.10.

Figure 42.10 *Balance sheet for Cummings Ltd*

Cummings Ltd
Balance Sheet as at

	31.12.01 £	31.12.00 £
Fixed assets		
Premises	95,000	100,000
Office equipment	12,000	14,000
	107,000	114,000
Investments	12,000	8,000
	119,000	122,000
Current assets		
Stocks	123,900	111,000
Debtors	4,300	5,200
Bank and cash	4,300	2,100
	132,500	118,300
Creditors: amounts due in less than one year		
Trade creditors	6,400	7,400
Taxation	12,800	15,000
Dividends proposed	10,000	10,000
	29,200	32,400
Net current assets	103,300	85,900
Creditors: amounts due in more than one year		
Mortgage	60,000	60,000
Bank loan	5,000	
	65,000	60,000
Net assets	157,300	147,900
Capital and reserves		
Called up share capital	50,000	50,000
Revaluation	25,000	25,000
Profit and loss account	82,300	72,900
	157,300	147,900

Additional information:
(i) Net interest of £7,800 was paid during the year.
(ii) The tax and dividends recorded in the profit and loss account for the year were the same as the amounts owed at the end of the year.

Operating profit can be derived from the company's balance sheet by the following method.
- First calculate the difference in the profit and loss account between the two years. This gives the amount of retained profit.
- Then add net interest paid, tax owed and dividends proposed for that year to retained profit to give the operating profit.

The calculation is shown on the next page.

Operating profit = Change in profit and loss account + Taxation owed + Dividends proposed + Net interest paid

= (£82,300 - £72,900) + £12,800 + £10,000 + £7,800

= £9,400 + £12,800 + £10,000 + £7,800

= £40,000

The operating profit of £40,000 is used to calculate the net cash inflow from operating activities, shown in Figure 42.11. The other entries in the reconciliation statement are obtained by taking the differences between the two years' figures which are listed in the balance sheet. For example, the increase in stock of £12,900 is found by subtracting £111,000 from £123,900. The decrease in creditors of £1,000 excludes taxation and dividends because these do not form part of operating activities.

Figure 42.11 *Reconciliation of operating profit to net cash inflow from operating activities for Cummings Ltd*

	£
Operating profit	40,000
Depreciation	7,000
Increase in stock	(12,900)
Decrease in debtors	900
Decrease in creditors	(1,000)
Net cash flow from operating activities	34,000

The net cash flow from operating activities of £34,000 is the first entry in the cash flow statement shown in Figure 42.12.

- During the year, net interest of £7,800 was paid so this is shown as an outflow.
- Taxation of £15,000 is paid. It is the amount listed in the balance sheet as owed at 31 December 2000.
- During the year, £4,000 of financial investments were purchased by the business and these are shown under the heading of capital expenditure and financial investment.
- There were no acquisitions or disposals of businesses during the year.
- Equity dividends of £10,000 were paid. It is the amount listed in the balance sheet as owed at 31 December 2000.
- The resultant cash outflow before the use of liquid resources and financing was £2,800.
- During the year, according to the balance sheet, Cummings Ltd took out a £5,000 bank loan. This is shown in the financing section of the cash flow statement.
- The statement shows that Cummings Ltd had a £2,200 increase of cash. This is confirmed by looking at the change in the cash and bank balance in the balance sheet. It shows an increase of £2,200 from £2,100 in 2000 to £4,300 in 2001.

Figure 42.12 *Cash flow statement for Cummings Ltd for the year ended 31.12.01*

Cummings Ltd
Cash Flow Statement for the year ended 31.12.01

	£
Net cash flow from operating activities	34,000
Returns on investments and servicing of finance	
Net interest paid	(7,800)
Taxation	
Tax paid	(15,000)
Capital expenditure and financial investment	
Purchase of investments	(4,000)
Acquisitions and disposals	-
Equity dividends paid	(10,000)
Cash outflow before use of liquid resources and financing	(2,800)
Financing	
New bank loan	5,000
Increase in cash in the period	2,200

key terms

Cash - notes, coins and bank deposits repayable on demand. In the context of cash flow statements, *cash equivalents* are also counted as cash. These are short-term investments that can be converted into known amounts of cash without notice and were within three months maturity when acquired.

Cash flow statement - this shows the inflows and outflows of cash in a business over a particular trading period.

Indirect method (of calculating net cash flow from operating activities) - this method starts with the figure for operating profit and then adjusts it for non-cash transactions.

UNIT ASSESSMENT   QUESTION 1

Cheryl Rickets owns a fabric and soft furnishings store in Southampton. During 2001, Cheryl took out a bank loan to purchase a new van that was urgently required. Figure 42.13 shows a cash flow statement for Cheryl's business and a reconciliation statement showing how the net cash inflow from operating activities was calculated.

Figure 42.13 *Reconciliation of operating profit to net cash inflow from operating activities and cash flow statement for Cheryl Rickets's business*

	£
Operating profit	24,300
Depreciation	4,300
Decrease in stock	10,700
Decrease in debtors	2,100
Increase in creditors	2,400
Net cash flow from operating activities	43,800

Cheryl Rickets
Cash Flow Statement for the year ended 31.10.01

	£
Net cash flow from operating activities	43,800
Returns on investments and servicing of finance	
Net interest paid	(1,200)
Taxation	-
Capital expenditure and financial investment	
Payment for new van	(6,000)
Acquisitions and disposals	-
Equity dividends	
Drawings	(27,800)
Cash inflow before use of liquid resources and financing	8,800
Financing	
Bank loan	6,000
Increase in cash in the period	14,800

(a) **Using examples from Cheryl's business, explain the difference between net cash inflow from operating activities of £43,800 and the increase in cash of £14,800.**

(b) **Suggest possible reasons for the improvement in the cash position of Cheryl's business.**

UNIT ASSESSMENT QUESTION 2

Scottish Fabrics Ltd manufactures and markets a range of tartan woollen products. In order to increase efficiency, the directors decided to invest in new computerised machinery. This was an expensive process and in order to fund the investment a £200,000 rights issue was undertaken. However, during the installation of the new machines, there were a number of teething problems and production was held up for longer than expected. The balance sheet for Scottish Fabrics is shown in Figure 42.14.

Figure 42.14 Balance sheet for Scottish Fabrics Ltd as at 31.8.01

Scottish Fabrics Ltd
Balance Sheet as at

	31.8.01 £	31.8.00 £
Fixed assets		
Factory	490,000	500,000
Plant and machinery	650,000	270,000
	1,140,000	770,000
Investments	20,000	30,000
	1,160,000	800,000
Current assets		
Stocks	34,300	41,900
Debtors	45,200	43,200
Bank and cash	-	12,700
	79,500	97,800
Creditors: amounts due in less than one year		
Trade creditors	16,300	14,300
Bank overdraft	8,600	-
Taxation	11,000	25,000
Dividends proposed	10,000	12,000
	45,900	51,300
Net current assets	33,600	46,500
Creditors: amounts due in more than one year		
Mortgage	80,000	50,000
Bank loan	100,000	-
	180,000	50,000
Net assets	1,013,600	796,500
Capital and reserves		
Called up share capital	900,000	700,000
Revaluation	25,000	25,000
Profit and loss account	88,600	71,500
	1,013,600	796,500

Additional information:

(i) Net interest of £16,300 was paid during the year.

(ii) Depreciation of £10,000 was charged on the factory.

(iii) Depreciation of £70,000 was charged on plant and equipment.

(iv) New plant and equipment worth £550,000 was purchased.

(v) Old plant and equipment were sold at book value for £100,000.

(vi) The tax and dividends recorded in the profit and loss account were the same as the amounts owed at the end of the year.

(a) Calculate the operating profit made by Scottish Fabrics Ltd in 2001.

(b) Produce a reconciliation of operating profit to net cash inflow from operating activities for Scottish Fabrics Ltd.

(c) Prepare a cash flow statement for Scottish Fabrics Ltd.

(d) Explain why the company's cash position worsened.

summary questions

1. What is liquidity?
2. What is the difference between a cash equivalent and cash?
3. What is meant by the term cash flow?
4. Which types of business must publish a cash flow statement according to FRS1?
5. State three reasons why cash and profit are different.
6. What is the difference between net profit and operating profit?
7. Describe the standard format for a cash flow statement.
8. What is meant by operating activities?
9. State three examples of cash inflows from operating activities.
10. State three examples of cash outflows that would appear on a cash flow statement.

Analysing accounts

Who uses accounts?

A wide variety of individuals and organisations use information that is contained in business accounts. Those users who have an interest in a particular business are called **stakeholders**. They include owners, managers and employees. Other users of business information include the media, financial analysts and competitors.

Company legislation and regulatory bodies have introduced certain requirements to make it easier to analyse accounts. The Companies Act (see unit 38) sets out which businesses must publish their accounts, what content must be included and how the accounts are to be presented. This makes comparison easier. The Accounting Standards Board and its predecessor, the Accounting Standards Committee (see unit 45), have issued Accounting Standards which specify how profit and asset values are to be calculated. Again this is intended to make it easier to compare the performance of companies and to prevent manipulation of the accounts.

The needs of different users of accounts are outlined below.

- **Owners** These include sole traders, partners and shareholders of limited companies. They are likely to be interested in the amount of profit the business has made because this can influence whether they will be paid a dividend.
- **Managers and directors** The role of managers and directors is to plan, organise and control a business. Information in the accounts indicates how well they are achieving their objectives.
- **Employees and trade unions** People who work for a business are interested in how much profit is being made. This will, to some extent, affect how much the business can afford to pay in wages and salaries. Employee representatives, such as Trade Unions, are likely to take the performance of a business into account when bargaining for wage increases. The financial position of a business in the future will also be of interest to such groups because it can influence job prospects.
- **Government agencies** A number of government agencies have the right to inspect business accounts. In some cases, such as the **Inland Revenue** and **Customs and Excise**, it is to check that the correct amount of tax is being paid. It is a legal obligation for companies to file their accounts with the **Registrar of Companies** annually. The information is then available to members of the public.
- **Bankers and creditors** Before providing finance, bankers will assess whether a business is creditworthy. They are likely to scrutinise several years' accounts when judging whether a business has the ability to repay a loan, for example. Similarly, suppliers are not likely to grant a new customer large amounts of trade credit until they are reasonably confident that they will be paid. The balance sheet is particularly helpful when assessing creditworthiness. For example, the balance sheet shows whether a business already has loans to repay.
- **Potential investors** Venture capitalists, fund managers and other investors will study the accounts when deciding whether to invest in a business. They will be interested in the profitability of the business and the rate of return on their investment. They are also likely to be interested in the value of assets, which could be used as security if loan capital is being provided.
- **Customers** In some cases, customers will wish to assess the financial position of a business and its ability to maintain continuity of supplies. Customer pressure groups such as the Consumers' Association might be interested in the level of profits in order to assess, for example, whether

consumers are being overcharged.

- **Competitors** It is useful for businesses to compare their sales turnover, market share, costs of production, profitability and return on assets with those of their rivals. This information can be used by both owners and managers as an indicator of how well a business is performing.
- **Investment analysts** Financial institutions such as pension funds and insurance companies employ specialist investment analysts. Their role is to advise fund managers on the risks and rewards of investing in particular industries and businesses. The analysts require detailed knowledge and understanding of business accounts in order to provide their advice.
- **Media** Newspapers, magazines, radio, television and web sites all use information from business accounts. For example, most newspapers have financial sections in which they comment on the performance of particular businesses. Often they also give advice to stock market investors about possible shares to buy and sell.
- **Community** Local communities are dependent on businesses to provide employment and services. Residents and councils therefore have an interest in the financial affairs and prospects of locally based businesses. Environmental groups are concerned by pollution and other side-effects of business activity. Organisations such as Friends of the Earth and Greenpeace therefore monitor all aspects of those businesses which they consider are harming the environment. Financial and other information from the annual reports of targeted companies is used in publicity campaigns.

QUESTION 1

Carol Blake is a sole trader who runs a shop in Kings Lynn selling blinds, canopies and awnings. She sells to a wide range of customers including shops, offices, schools and the general public. Her business has expanded in recent years supplying blinds to people who have new conservatories. During the financial year ended 31 March 2001, Carol had set a target to increase net profit by 25%. Figure 43.1 shows a summary of the trading and profit and loss account for Carol's business.

(a) How might the account in Figure 43.1 be of use to the Inland Revenue?

(b) (i) Did Carol reach her target?
(ii) How else might the account in Figure 43.1 be of use to Carol?

(c) Under what circumstances might bankers wish to see the account in Figure 43.1?

Figure 43.1 *Summary of the trading and profit and loss account for Carol Blake's business*

Carol Blake Trading and Profit and Loss Account	Year ended 31.3.01	Year ended 31.3.00
	£	£
Sales	176,500	145,800
Cost of sales	91,000	78,500
Gross profit	85,500	67,300
Less expenses	55,400	41,200
Net profit	30,100	26,100

Methods of analysis

There are several methods by which accounts can be analysed. They are outlined below.

Comparisons over time When business accounts are published, the results for two years are usually shown. This allows the reader to make an immediate comparison between two different time periods, ie the current financial year and the previous one. However, comparing just two years does not reveal longer term trends. Public limited companies often publish key accounting information in their annual reports (see unit 38) for a five year, or even a ten year, period. Comparisons over this length of time are much more meaningful. Trends are easier to detect and abnormal years are revealed.

When accounts are examined, a mathematical technique known as **ratio analysis** is sometimes used. This method is described in detail in unit 44.

Inter-business comparisons Comparing the financial information of one business with that of another is something that might be done by managers, owners or potential investors. Such comparisons help to show the strengths and weaknesses of businesses within the same industry. However, when making these comparisons, it is important to compare 'like with like'. This means that the businesses whose accounts are being compared must have similar characteristics. For example, they must be in the same industry, have a similar turnover and have access to similar resources.

Inter-business comparisons over time It is sometimes useful to combine the two approaches described above in order to make comparisons over time. For example, a potential investor who is considering investing in the retail sector might compare the accounts of Tesco, Safeway, Sainsbury and Asda over a 5 year period before committing any funds. Such comparisons are widely used and provide a meaningful way of analysing the performance of a whole industry over a period of time.

Comparison with a budget It is common practice within businesses to compare actual results with those that were predicted or planned. For example, managers often prepare **budgets** (see unit 54) which represent spending or sales plans for a future time period. Comparing the actual results of spending and sales patterns with plans can be helpful to managers. Any variations can be identified, investigated and acted upon.

Analysing the trading and profit and loss account

In order to illustrate how a trading and profit and loss account can be analysed, consider the account in Figure 43.3. It is prepared for Norris Ltd, a ship repair company.

QUESTION 2

Cynthia McDonald is the managing director of Quest plc, a construction company. When reviewing the performance of the company, she makes an inter-business comparison over time with two local rivals, Carter's Construction plc and Millstone plc. Figure 43.2 shows the sales and profit for the 3 companies over a 5 year period.
- Quest plc is a relatively new entrant to the market, set up in 1994. It builds houses, factories, warehouses and some large buildings. Around 65% of its contracts are for houses.
- Carter's Construction plc is an established local firm which builds houses, factories, warehouses and other large buildings such as school extensions. About 50% of Carter's contracts are for houses.
- Millstone plc is a much larger construction company. Not only does it build houses and other commercial buildings, it often wins government contracts for roads and bridges.

Figure 43.2 *Sales and profit figures for three construction companies*

		1997 £m	1998 £m	1999 £m	2000 £m	2001 £m
Quest plc	Sales	27.4	29.8	32.3	35.3	37.9
	Profit	4.1	4.7	4.2	4.9	5.2
Carter's Construction plc	Sales	24.5	25.6	25.8	23.8	22.1
	Profit	3.8	3.8	3.7	3.1	1.8
Millstone plc	Sales	67.2	69.5	89.1	71.4	72.6
	Profit	4.9	5.2	8.6	5.8	5.4

(a) Comment on the performance of Quest plc compared with its two rivals over the time period.
(b) To what extent is Cynthia comparing 'like with like' in her analysis?
(c) What is the main advantage of making comparisons over a long time period?

Figure 43.3 *Trading and profit and loss account for Norris Ltd*

Norris Ltd
Trading and Profit and Loss Account

	Year ended 31.12.01	Year ended 31.12.00
	£000	£000
Turnover	2,300	2,240
Cost of sales	1,200	1,300
Gross profit	1,100	940
Selling and distribution	340	360
Administration	150	170
Operating profit	610	410
Net interest received	40	45
Net profit before taxation	650	455
Taxation	160	120
Net profit after taxation	490	335
Dividends	100	100
Retained profit	390	235

- **Turnover** This is often used as an indicator of the size and growth of a business. It depends upon the volume of sales and the price charged to customers. In this case, Norris Ltd experienced a relatively small 2.7% rise in turnover to £2,300,000 over the two years. Turnover can also be used to calculate market share if the size of the overall market is known.
- **Gross profit** The rise in gross profit of Norris Ltd was caused by an increase in turnover and a decrease in the cost of sales. This latter might have resulted from the purchase of cheaper materials or an improvement in the efficiency of how the materials were used. For a company to reduce its cost of sales while at the same time increasing its turnover generally indicates a good management performance.
- **Expenses** Overheads include expenses associated with selling, distribution and administration. They fell by a total of £40,000 over the two years. This suggests that the company was operating more efficiently.
- **Operating profit** The operating profit of £610,000 in 2001 came from Norris Ltd's ordinary trading activities. Non-operating income which in this example consists of the net interest received, is then added to give net profit before taxation. If non-operating income had formed a large proportion of net profit, this might raise concerns that the business was 'bolstering' its profit and therefore exaggerating its performance. However, in the case of Norris Ltd, this does not appear to be happening.
- **Net interest received** When analysing the profit and loss account, some users, such as bankers and creditors, are likely to be interested in how much money is owed by the business. An indication of this is given by the net interest paid or received during the year. In the case of Norris Ltd, the accounts show that it received relatively large net payments of interest in both years. This suggests that the company had substantial amounts of money either deposited in bank accounts or possibly in the form of short-term securities.
- **Net profit after taxation** Most users of accounts are likely to be interested in the net profit after taxation. It is often described as 'the bottom line'. This is because it is the final figure in the profit and loss account before appropriation, ie before dividends and retained profit. In the case of Norris Ltd, the net profit after tax in 2001 was £490,000. This was significantly higher than the previous year, representing just over a 46% increase. The owners are likely to have been pleased with this result.
- **Net profit and turnover** A good indicator of business performance is to compare net profit with turnover. In the case of Norris Ltd, net profit rose by a much bigger percentage than turnover. This suggests that the company was being successful in reducing its costs.
- **Retained profit** The account shows that profit of £390,000 was retained in 2001 and £100,000

was paid to shareholders in the form of dividends. Potential investors and shareholders who are interested in short-term returns might prefer that more is paid in dividends. On the other hand, employees and shareholders who are more concerned about the long-term future of the business might prefer more profit to be reinvested.

Analysing the balance sheet

In order to illustrate how a balance sheet is analysed, consider again the example of Norris Ltd. The balance sheet for the company is shown in Figure 43.5.

QUESTION 3

Popplewell Ltd supplies paper to magazine and newspaper publishers. During the early 1990s the company made between £100,000 - £150,000 net profit each year. However, since then, its profits declined. As a result, the directors decided to increase the amount spent on promoting the company's products. Figure 43.4 shows the trading and profit and loss account for Popplewell Ltd.

Figure 43.4 *Trading and profit and loss account for Popplewell Ltd*

Popplewell Ltd
Trading and Profit and Loss Account

	Year ended 31.5.01	Year ended 31.5.00
	£	£
Turnover	810,000	640,000
Cost of sales	320,000	310,000
Gross profit	490,000	330,000
Selling and distribution	240,000	140,000
Administration	65,000	74,000
Operating profit	185,000	116,000
Net interest paid	165,000	90,000
Net profit before taxation	20,000	26,000
Taxation	5,000	6,000
Net profit after taxation	15,000	20,000

(a) **Suggest possible reasons why turnover might have increased over the two years.**
(b) **Account for the difference between gross profit and net profit before taxation in each year.**
(c) **Comment on the size of Popplewell's debt over the two years.**

Figure 43.5 *Balance sheet for Norris Ltd*

Norris Ltd
Balance Sheet

	As at 31.12.01	As at 31.12.00
	£	£
Fixed assets		
Premises	100,000	110,000
Tools and equipment	180,000	128,900
Vehicles	46,000	52,000
	326,000	290,900
Current assets		
Stocks	15,000	16,500
Debtors	76,000	61,300
Bank	560,000	190,800
	651,000	268,600
Creditors: amounts falling due within one year		
Trade creditors	10,600	23,100
Taxation	160,000	120,000
Dividends proposed	100,000	100,000
	270,600	243,100
Net current assets	380,400	25,500
Net assets	706,400	316,400
Shareholders funds		
Share capital	100,000	100,000
Revaluation reserve	20,000	20,000
Profit and loss account	586,400	196,400
Capital employed	706,400	316,400

- **Assets** The ASSET STRUCTURE of a business refers to its range of assets. In 2001, Norris Ltd had current assets that were significantly higher in value than its fixed assets, mainly because of its large bank balance. A company in Norris's position is often described as being **cash rich**. It could be argued that the company should invest more money in machinery and productive capacity or return cash to its shareholders. On the other hand, the company might be considered prudent in maintaining its cash reserves so that it can cope with unforeseen circumstances. Norris Ltd's balance sheet also reveals that the value of its tools and equipment rose by £51,100 (£180,000 - £128,900) over the two years. This could suggest that the company was committed to investment and expansion. Also revealed by the balance sheet was an increase in debtors from £61,300 to £76,000. Although this is small in relation to turnover, the amount of money owed to the company is clearly a significant figure to be noted when analysing final accounts.
- **Net current assets** This is the value of current assets less current liabilities. It is also known as **working capital**. It represents the amount of liquid resources that a business has available to pay for its everyday needs. If a business does not have sufficient working capital, it might face difficulty in paying suppliers or employees, or in repaying loans. The balance sheet shows that this was not a problem for Norris Ltd. The company increased its working capital from £25,500 to £380,400, mainly because it retained £390,000 from its net profit (see Figure 43.3). Working capital and liquidity are discussed in detail in unit 44.
- **Net assets** The value of net assets serves as a rough guide to the 'worth' of a business. In 2001, the net assets of Norris Ltd were £706,400. This was over double the previous year's figure, which could indicate a rise in the company's value. However, net assets are not always a reliable guide. This is because intangible assets such as goodwill are not generally shown on the balance sheet. Also, the net book value of fixed assets might not be the same as the disposal value of

these assets. The limitations of accounts are discussed in more detail in unit 45.

- **Capital structure** This refers to the proportions of share capital, reserves and long term borrowing of a company. Norris Ltd does not have any long-term debts. Most of the company's finance has come from the reinvestment of profit. The profit and loss account entry in the shareholders funds section of the balance sheet shows that £586,400 was retained by the business since it began trading. The amount of share capital, £100,000, was unchanged over the two years. There is a revaluation reserve of £20,000. It is the result of a rise in the value of fixed assets. This, and other reserves, are described in more detail in unit 38.

- **Loan capital and share capital** Loan capital refers to fixed interest borrowing. Share capital, or **equity**, is the amount of money raised from ordinary shareholders. The relationship between loan capital and share capital is known as GEARING or LEVERAGE. A company is said to be high geared if it has a relatively large amount of loan capital in relation to its share capital. This is not the case for Norris Ltd. As the balance sheet shows, the company had no long term loans outstanding in either year. Gearing is discussed in more detail in unit 44.

QUESTION 4

Stealth UK is a small public limited company which makes specialist boards for windsurfing. During 2000 and 2001, the board of directors decided to invest in new machinery in order to improve efficiency. This was expected to have an impact on profits in two or three years' time. Figure 43.6 shows the balance sheet for Stealth UK.

(a) Suggest how the investment undertaken by Stealth UK was funded.

(b) What happened to the value of the company over the two years?

(c) Comment on the size of working capital for Stealth UK.

(d) What happened to the gearing of the company over the two years?

Figure 43.6 *Balance sheet for Stealth UK*

Stealth UK
Balance Sheet

	As at 31.12.01	As at 31.12.00
	£m	£m
Fixed assets		
Premises	5,400	5,000
Plant and equipment	12,800	8,200
	18,200	13,200
Current assets		
Stocks	2,400	2,600
Debtors	3,900	4,100
Bank	1,100	6,300
	7,400	13,000
Creditors: amounts falling due within one year		
Trade creditors	4,100	3,500
Taxation	400	1,400
Dividends proposed	-	2,000
	4,500	6,900
Net current assets	2,900	6,100
Creditors: amounts falling due after one year		
Debentures	3,000	3,000
Net assets	18,100	16,300
Shareholders funds		
Share capital	8,000	8,000
Revaluation reserve	1,200	800
Profit and loss account	8,900	7,500
Capital employed	18,100	16,300

UNIT ASSESSMENT **QUESTION 1**

In early 2002, Julie and Barry Price decided to buy a small shop. They contacted a commercial estate agent and were given some information regarding two shops for sale. Both shops sold newspapers, magazines, confectionery and some groceries. Julie and Barry had £40,000 cash and were confident that they could raise more from a bank if necessary. Details regarding the two shops for sale are given below.

● Leonard Matthews was selling his business because he had accumulated enough money on which to retire. The asking price was £95,000. This included the premises, with living accommodation above the shop. It had been a profitable business for 15 years since being acquired by the current owner.

● Denise Wignall was selling her shop because of increasing health problems. The shop was run down with sales revenue falling by 50% in the previous 3 years. It was priced at £25,000 for a quick sale. The premises were rented and the current landlord was happy to continue the lease with the new owners on the same terms.

The profit and loss accounts for the businesses are shown in Figure 43.7.

Figure 43.7 *Profit and loss accounts for Leonard Matthews and Denise Wignall*

Leonard Matthews Profit and Loss Account for the year ended 31.12.01			Denise Wignall Profit and Loss Account for the year ended 31.12.01		
	£	£		£	£
Sales		153,400	**Sales**		92,300
Cost of sales		110,700	Cost of sales		67,500
Gross profit		42,700	**Gross profit**		24,800
Less expenses			*Less expenses*		
Wages for casual labour	3,200		Wages for part-time staff	9,000	
Heat and light	1,100		Rent and rates	6,500	
Bad debts	4,100		Heat and light	800	
Advertising	600		Other overheads	4,200	
Other overheads	2,300		Depreciation	600	
Depreciation	1,000				21,100
		12,300	**Net profit**		3,700
Net profit		30,400			

(a) **Outline the advantages and disadvantages of buying each of the two businesses.**

(b) **What evidence is there to indicate whether the businesses have outstanding debts?**

(c) **Suggest what other information Julie and Barry might wish to analyse before deciding to buy one of the businesses.**

key terms

Asset structure - the range of assets owned by a business.
Gearing or leverage - the proportion of fixed interest, loan capital to share capital or equity.

summary questions

1. Why might business owners wish to analyse accounts?
2. How might business accounts be used by managers and directors?
3. Which agencies have a legal right to financial information produced by companies?
4. Why might the media be interested in business accounts?
5. Why might business managers make an inter-firm comparison?
6. How can the profit and loss account be used to assess whether a business has grown?
7. How can the profit and loss account be used to assess how well a business has controlled its overheads?
8. How might a banker use the balance sheet of a business?
9. What is meant by the term capital structure?
10. How can a balance sheet be used to assess the liquidity of a business?

UNIT ASSESSMENT QUESTION 2

Vision Ltd owns a large television and video recorder shop in Coventry. The company also has a servicing and repairs department. The Thompson family, who own the business, decided to expand and open a new store in Rugby where they would lease premises in the shopping centre. However, they needed to borrow £50,000 to finance this development. Their bank manager requested a copy of the current year's accounts and a full business plan before making a decision on whether to advance a loan. Figure 43.8 shows the profit and loss account and balance sheet for Vision Ltd.

Figure 43.8 *Profit and loss account and balance sheet for Vision Ltd*

Vision Ltd
Profit and Loss Account

	Year ended 31.7.01	Year ended 31.7.00
	£000	£000
Turnover	1,500	1,300
Cost of sales	860	790
Gross profit	640	510
Selling and distribution	410	390
Administration	130	140
Operating profit/(loss)	100	(20)
Net interest paid	10	10
Profit/(loss) before taxation	90	(30)
Taxation	30	-
Profit/(loss) after taxation	60	(30)
Dividends	40	40
Retained profit/(loss)	20	(70)

Figure 43.8 continued

Vision Ltd
Balance Sheet

	As at 31.7.01 £	As at 31.7.00 £
Fixed assets		
Premises	100,000	105,000
Fixtures and fittings	33,000	26,000
	133,000	131,000
Current assets		
Stocks	85,000	.64,000
Debtors	14,300	6,500
Bank	21,000	4,500
	120,300	75,000
Creditors: amounts falling due within one year		
Trade creditors	28,600	31,300
Taxation	30,000	
Dividends proposed	40,000	40,000
	98,600	71,300
Net current assets	21,700	3,700
Creditors: amounts falling due after one year		
Mortgage	75,000	75,000
Net assets	79,700	59,700
Shareholders funds		
Share capital	40,000	40,000
Profit and loss account	39,700	19,700
Capital employed	79,700	59,700

(a) **What evidence is there in the profit and loss account and balance sheet to suggest that the performance of the business has improved over the two years?**

(b) **On what grounds might the bank manager (i) grant a loan (ii) refuse a loan?**

unit 44

Ratio analysis

unit**objectives**

To understand:
- the ratios used in financial analysis;
- the relationship between profitability and efficiency;
- the limitations of ratio analysis.

What is ratio analysis?

RATIO ANALYSIS involves the use of mathematics to analyse business performance. In particular, it examines the relationship between variables such as turnover, profit and capital employed. In conducting ratio analysis, comparisons are often made between different time periods and between different businesses within the same industry.

Ratios can be expressed in various ways. The most common method is to show the number of times one variable can be divided into another. For example, if a business's current assets are valued at £10,000 and its current liabilities are £5,000, the ratio of current assets to current liabilities is 2:1. Another method of expressing a ratio is to use percentages. For example, if a business has debts of £20,000 and total capital of £50,000, the ratio of debt to capital can be expressed as 40%, ie (£20,000 ÷ £50,000) × 100.

There is a number of different ratios and they can be grouped together in the following ways.

- **Performance (or profitability) ratios** Performance ratios help assess whether a business has met its objectives. The most widely used performance ratios relate profitability to other indicators such as capital employed and turnover. Owners, managers, directors and potential investors are likely to be interested in this information.
- **Activity ratios** These are used to assess how efficiently a business has used its resources. For instance, the performance of the credit control department can be assessed by measuring how quickly debts are collected. Activity ratios are likely to be used internally within a business, by managers for example.
- **Liquidity (or solvency) ratios** Liquidity ratios assess the ability of a business to pay its bills. They focus on short-term assets and liabilities. Bankers and suppliers are likely to be interested in liquidity ratios to help decide whether the business is creditworthy. Managers might also use them to ensure that the business has enough liquid resources to operate effectively.
- **Gearing ratios** Gearing ratios are used to assess the burden of long-term debt that a business has accumulated. They show the relationship between loans, on which interest is paid, and shareholders' funds, on which dividends are paid. Existing and new creditors will be concerned about a company's gearing. For example, creditors might be wary of lending money to a high geared company, where loan capital is high relative to share capital. On the other hand, shareholders might prefer to raise additional capital from loans rather than issuing more shares. This is because profits will be diluted and some control will be lost if there are more shares in circulation.
- **Shareholders' (or investors') ratios** The owners of limited companies and potential investors will be interested in ratios that measure the rate of return on their investment. Such ratios focus on the earnings and dividends from shares in relation to the share prices.

Performance ratios

To illustrate how ratio analysis can be used to assess the performance of a business, consider Phelps plc, a wholesaler of children's clothing. A profit and loss account and balance sheet for Phelps plc is shown in Figure 44.1. The accounts relate to the year ended 31 March 2002.

Figure 44.1 *Profit and loss account and balance sheet for Phelps plc*

Phelps plc Profit and Loss Account

	Year ended 31.3.02	Year ended 31.3.01
	£000	£000
Turnover	23,900	20,100
Cost of sales	11,300	10,600
Gross profit	12,600	9,500
Selling and distribution costs	2,800	2,700
Administration costs	3,200	3,400
Operating profit	6,600	3,400
Net interest paid	500	500
Profit on ordinary activities before tax	6,100	2,900
Taxation	1,500	700
Profit on ordinary activities after tax and interest	4,600	2,200
Preference dividend	500	500
Ordinary dividend	1,000	500
Retained profit	3,100	1,200

Phelps plc Balance Sheet

	As at 31.3.02	As at 31.3.01
	£000	£000
Fixed assets		
Tangible assets	46,000	40,000
Investments	4,500	4,500
	50,500	44,500
Current assets		
Stocks	2,100	2,800
Debtors	4,300	1,400
Bank	3,200	2,900
	9,600	7,100
Creditors: amounts falling due within one year		
Trade creditors	1,200	900
Other liabilities	4,300	2,800
	5,500	3,700
Net current assets	4,100	3,400
Total assets less current liabilities	54,600	47,900
Creditors: amounts falling due after one year		
Mortgage	8,000	8,000
Net assets	46,600	39,900
Capital and reserves		
Ordinary share capital	10,000	10,000
Preference share capital	5,000	5,000
Share premium	15,000	11,000
Revaluation reserve	4,300	4,700
Profit and loss account	12,300	9,200
Shareholders funds	46,600	39,900

Additional information:	2002	2001
(i) Number of ordinary shares issued	50m	50m
(ii) Share price as at 31 March	130p	41p

Return on capital employed One of the most important ratios that is used to measure the performance of a business is the RETURN ON CAPITAL EMPLOYED (ROCE). This is sometimes also referred to as the **primary ratio**. It compares the profit, ie return, made by a business with the amount of money invested, ie its capital. There is a number of ways in which the ratio is calculated. This is because there are different definitions of capital employed. Four definitions of capital employed are given below and are calculated for Phelps for the year ended 31 March 2002:

Long term capital = total share capital + reserves + loan capital
= £30m + £16.6m + £8m
= £54.6m

Total share capital is made up of ordinary share capital (£10m) plus preference share capital (£5m) plus the share premium (£15m).
Reserves are made up of, in this example, the revaluation reserve (£4.3m) plus the profit and loss account (£12.3m).
The loan capital is, in this example, the mortgage (£8m).

Total capital = total share capital + reserves + loan capital + current liabilities
= £30m + £16.6m + £8m + £5.5m
= £60.1m

Current liabilities are the trade creditors (£1.2m) plus the other liabilities (£4.3m).

Shareholders' capital = total share capital + reserves
= £30m + £16.6m
= £46.6m

Shareholders' equity = ordinary share capital + reserves
= (£10m +£15m) + £16.6m
= £41.6m

The particular definition of capital employed that will be used by an analyst depends on what is being measured. For example, if an analyst wishes to know the return on all the money invested in the business, the definition for total capital will be used. Alternatively, if the analyst is measuring the return on the amount of money contributed by ordinary shareholders, the definition for shareholders' equity will be used.

When calculating ROCE, it is standard practice to define profit as net profit before tax and interest. This is sometimes described as **earnings before interest and tax** or **EBIT**. For Phelps, this is equivalent to the operating profit, £6.6m, that is shown in its profit and loss account. Tax is ignored because it is determined by the government and is therefore outside the control of the company. Interest is excluded because it does not relate to the business's ordinary trading activities.

The **return on long-term capital employed** for Phelps is calculated using the formula below. Note that figures are rounded to two decimal places unless otherwise stated.

$$\text{ROCE} = \frac{\text{Profit before tax and interest}}{\text{Long-term capital employed}} \times 100$$

For 2002 $\text{ROCE} = \dfrac{£6,600,000}{£54,600,000} \times 100 = 12.09\%$

For 2001 $\text{ROCE} = \dfrac{£3,400,000}{£47,900,000} \times 100 = 7.10\%$

When a ratio has been calculated, it requires interpretation. In this case, there was clearly an improvement in the ROCE, with a rise from 7.1% in 2001 to 12.09% in 2002. However, this ROCE also needs to be compared with the ROCE made by businesses in the same industry in order to judge whether the company's performance was satisfactory. In addition, an investor might compare the ROCE with the potential return if the capital was invested elsewhere. For example, if the £54.6m was placed in a bank account in 2002, it might have earned a 5% return. Consequently, the 12.09% ROCE in 2002 appears satisfactory. However, an investor in the company will also wish to be rewarded for the risk involved. The £54.6m investment in Phelps is at risk if the business collapses. Therefore, for the investment to be worthwhile, the ROCE must be substantially above the return that could be earned in a 'safe' investment.

Return on net assets This ratio compares the profit of a business with **shareholders' capital** rather than with long-term capital as in the previous example. It uses the third definition of capital given above. However, it is conventional to use the term net assets rather than shareholders' capital. The balance sheet in Figure 44.1 shows that shareholders' capital is £46.6m. This is exactly the same as the value of net assets. The RETURN ON NET ASSETS is calculated using the formula:

$$\text{Return on net assets} = \frac{\text{Profit before tax and interest}}{\text{Net assets}} \times 100$$

For 2002 $\quad \text{Return on net assets} = \dfrac{£6,600,000}{£46,600,000} \times 100 = 14.16\%$

For 2001 $\quad \text{Return on net assets} = \dfrac{£3,400,000}{£39,900,000} \times 100 = 8.52\%$

Over the two years, the return on net assets improved significantly from 8.52% to 14.16%. However, as with the ROCE, whether these returns are satisfactory depends on factors such as the returns earned by competitors and the rate of interest. The return on net assets will always be higher than ROCE. This is because the denominator is lower, ie shareholders' capital must, by definition, be lower than total capital.

Return on equity The RETURN ON EQUITY looks specifically at the return on the money contributed by, and belonging to, ordinary shareholders. It uses the fourth definition of capital employed given before, ie shareholders' equity, made up of ordinary share capital plus reserves. It is calculated using the formula:

$$\text{Return on equity} = \frac{\text{Profit accruing to ordinary shareholders*}}{\text{Ordinary share capital} + \text{reserves}} \times 100$$

*This is equivalent to net profit after tax less payments on fixed interest bearing capital (ie preference share dividend).

For Phelps, the net profit after tax in 2002 was £4.6m. The preference shareholders' dividend was £0.5m, therefore the profit accruing to ordinary shareholders was £4.1m (£4.6m - £0.5m). The value of ordinary share capital and reserves, or **shareholders' equity**, was £41.6m. So:

For 2002 $\quad \text{Return on equity} = \dfrac{£4,100,000}{£41,600,000} \times 100 = 9.86\%$

For 2001 $\quad \text{Return on equity} = \dfrac{£1,700,000}{£34,900,000} \times 100 = 4.87\%$

Phelps' return on equity improved significantly from 4.87% to 9.86%. As with all ratio analysis, judgment on whether this was satisfactory depends to a large extent on comparisons with similar companies in the same industry.

Gross profit margin The GROSS PROFIT MARGIN is also known as the **mark-up**. It is the percentage amount by which the cost of a good is increased to give the selling price. Figures for this calculation come from the profit and loss account for Phelps in Figure 44.1. The gross profit margin is calculated by using the formula:

$$\text{Gross profit margin} = \frac{\text{Gross profit}}{\text{Turnover}} \times 100$$

For 2002 $\quad$ Gross profit margin $= \dfrac{£12,600,000}{£23,900,000} \times 100 = 52.72\%$

For 2001 $\quad$ Gross profit margin $= \dfrac{£9,500,000}{£20,100,000} \times 100 = 47.26\%$

Higher gross profit margins are clearly preferable to lower ones. The gross profit margin for Phelps improved over the two years from 47.26% to 52.72%. The improvement might have resulted from charging a higher price, or from a fall in the cost of goods bought in for resale. To determine whether the gross margin earned by Phelps is satisfactory, it has to be compared with other similar businesses. Gross profit margins can vary considerably between different industries. As a rule, the quicker the turnover of stock, the lower the gross profit margin. For example, a supermarket with a fast stock turnover is likely to have a lower gross profit margin than a car retailer with a much slower stock turnover.

Net profit margin The NET PROFIT MARGIN helps to measure how well a business controls its overheads. If the difference between the gross profit margin and the net profit margin is small, this suggests that overheads are low. This is because net profit equals gross profit less overheads. When calculating the net profit margin, it is conventional to define net profit as the profit before tax and interest. For Phelps in 2002, it was £6.6m, and the turnover was £23.9m. The net profit margin is calculated by using the formula:

$$\text{Net profit margin} = \frac{\text{Net profit before tax and interest}}{\text{Turnover}} \times 100$$

For 2002 $\quad$ Net profit margin $= \dfrac{£6,600,000}{£23,900,000} \times 100 = 27.62\%$

For 2001 $\quad$ Net profit margin $= \dfrac{£3,400,000}{£20,100,000} \times 100 = 16.92\%$

QUESTION 1

Hawkins Ltd sells jewellery. In the 1990s, competition from larger competitors caused a fall in turnover for the company. In response to this, Jenny Hawkins, the managing director, implemented some changes to improve financial performance. Prices were reduced and staffing cuts were made to reduce labour costs. Figure 44.2 shows turnover, gross profit and net profit before taxation for 2001 and 2000.

Figure 44.2 *Turnover, gross profit and net profit for Hawkins Ltd*

	2001	2000
Turnover	£148,000	£119,000
Gross profit	£30,200	£28,000
Net profit before taxation and interest	£10,500	£7,000

(a) **Calculate the (i) gross profit margins (ii) net profit margins for Hawkins Ltd for the two years.**
(b) **To what extent did the changes made by Jenny account for the changes in the ratios over the two years?**
(c) **In 2001, the long-term capital employed by Hawkins Ltd was £240,000. (i) Calculate the return on long-term capital employed. (ii) How might Hawkins Ltd judge whether this was satisfactory?**

Phelps experienced a significant increase in its net profit margin over the two years, from 16.92% to 27.62%. This suggests that the company was able to restrict overhead spending, as a proportion of turnover, more effectively in 2002 than in 2001. In 2002, the gross profit margin was almost twice the size of the net profit margin. In 2001, however, the gross profit margin was almost three times the size of the net profit margin. This perhaps confirms that overheads were controlled more effectively in 2002.

Activity ratios

Activity ratios or 'asset usage ratios' are used to measure how efficiently a business employs its resources.

Asset turnover The ASSET TURNOVER ratio measures the productivity of assets. It looks at how much turnover is generated by the assets employed in the business. The ratio is often expressed as the number of times by which the net assets can be divided into the turnover. The following example considers how efficiently the net assets of Phelps are used. Other asset turnover ratios measure the efficiency of total assets, fixed assets or current assets.

According to Figure 44.1, the turnover for Phelps in 2002 was £23.9m and the value of net assets was £46.6m. Asset turnover is calculated by the formula:

$$\text{Asset turnover} = \frac{\text{Turnover}}{\text{Net assets}}$$

For 2002 $\text{Asset turnover} = \dfrac{£23,900,000}{£46,600,000} = 0.51 \text{ times}$

For 2001 $\text{Asset turnover} = \dfrac{£20,100,000}{£39,900,000} = 0.50 \text{ times}$

The ratio shows that, in 2002, for every £1 invested in net assets by Phelps, 51p of turnover was generated. There was little difference in the ratio between the two years. The asset turnover ratio varies considerably between different industries. In retailing, where turnover is high and the value of fixed assets is relatively low, the asset turnover can be 3 or more. By contrast, in manufacturing, where there is often more investment in fixed assets, the ratio is generally lower. For example, it can be 1 or less. These figures might suggest that the asset turnover of Phelps was low. However, a comparison with other companies in the same line of business would be necessary to determine this.

Some analysts prefer to use a slightly different ratio when considering how effective the capital employed by a business has been in generating sales turnover. It is called the **sales to capital employed ratio**. Instead of using net assets as an indication of capital employed, long-term loans are also included. So, for Phelps, the capital employed in 2002 was £54.6m, ie £46.6m plus £8m (creditors: amounts falling due after one year).

$$\text{Sales to capital employed} = \frac{\text{Sales}}{\text{Shareholders' funds + long term loans}}$$

For 2002 $\text{Sales to capital employed} = \dfrac{£23,900,000}{£54,600,000} = 0.48 \text{ times}$

For 2001 $\text{Sales to capital employed} = \dfrac{£20,100,000}{£47,900,000} = 0.42 \text{ times}$

These figures indicate that there was a marginal improvement in the sales to capital employed ratio between 2001 and 2002.

Stock turnover (or inventory turnover) The STOCK TURNOVER ratio measures how quickly a business uses or sells its stock. It is generally considered desirable to sell, or 'shift', stock as quickly as possible. One method of measuring stock turnover is to calculate how many days it takes to sell the average stock holding. This uses the formula:

$$\text{Stock turnover} = \frac{\text{Average stock}}{\text{Cost of sales}} \times 365$$

An alternative method of measuring stock turnover is to calculate by how many times the cost of sales can be divided by the average stock. This uses the formula:

$$\text{Stock turnover} = \frac{\text{Cost of sales}}{\text{Average stock}}$$

The average stock for a business is calculated by adding the opening stock for the year to the closing stock, and dividing the total by 2. According to its balance sheet, the average stock for Phelps in 2002 was £2.45m ([£2.8m + £2.1m] ÷ 2). The cost of sales for 2002 as recorded in the profit and loss account was £11.3m.

$$\text{For 2002} \quad \text{Stock turnover} = \frac{£2,450,000}{£11,300,000} \times 365 = 79 \text{ days (to the nearest day)}$$

$$\text{Or} \quad \text{Stock turnover} = \frac{£11,300,000}{£2,450,000} = 4.61 \text{ times}$$

Stock turnover for 2001 cannot be calculated in the same way because the opening stock figure for 2001 is not given in the balance sheet. Under these circumstances, the closing stock might be used instead of average stock. However, the two ratios would not then be strictly comparable. To determine whether the stock turnover of 79 days was satisfactory, it would be necessary to make a comparison with other wholesalers of children's clothes.

Stock turnover differs considerably between different industries. Retail supermarkets, such as Tesco and Sainsbury, have a relatively quick stock turnover of around 14 to 28 days. This means that they sell the value of their average stock every two to four weeks. Manufacturers generally have a much slower stock turnover than this because of the time spent in processing raw materials. However, in recent years, many manufacturers have adopted **just-in-time production** techniques (see unit 24). This involves ordering stocks only when they are required in the production process and, therefore, stock levels tend to be lower. As a result, the stock turnover is faster.

Businesses which supply services, such as banks, travel agents and dry cleaners, do not hold stock. Therefore the stock turnover ratio is not used by service industry analysts.

Debt collection period This ratio measures the efficiency of a business's credit control system. The DEBT COLLECTION PERIOD is the average number of days it takes to collect debts from customers. It can be calculated using the formula below. Some businesses prefer to use 'credit sales' rather than turnover in the calculation so that cash sales are excluded. However, in this example, the figure for credit sales is not shown in Phelps' accounts.

$$\text{Debt collection period} = \frac{\text{Debtors}}{\text{Turnover}} \times 365$$

According to Phelps' accounts, the amount owed by debtors in 2002 was £4.3m and turnover was £23.9m.

$$\text{For 2002} \quad \text{Debt collection period} = \frac{£4,300,000}{£23,900,000} \times 365 = 66 \text{ days (to the nearest day)}$$

$$\text{For 2001} \quad \text{Debt collection period} = \frac{£1,400,000}{£20,100,000} \times 365 = 25 \text{ days (to the nearest day)}$$

Businesses that sell goods on credit typically give customers a period of 30, 60 or 90 days in which to pay. If credit customers are slow to pay their debts, cash flow problems can arise. It is therefore important to monitor the debt collection period. Over the two years, Phelps' performance deteriorated, with the debt collection period increasing from 25 to 66 days. One reason for the deterioration might have been because the company had 'eased' its credit policy to encourage sales. In other words, some customers were given a longer credit period. Another reason might have been that several large customers got into financial difficulties and were slow to settle their debts.

Creditors payment period This ratio measures how quickly a business pays its debts to its suppliers and other short term creditors. The CREDITORS PAYMENT PERIOD is the average number of days it takes to pay debts. It can be calculated using the formula below. As with the debtors collection period, some businesses prefer to use 'credit purchases' rather than cost of sales so that cash purchases are excluded.

$$\text{Creditors payment period} = \frac{\text{Creditors}}{\text{Cost of sales}} \times 365$$

According to Phelps' accounts, the amount owed to short-term creditors in 2002 was £5.5m and the cost of sales was £11.3m.

For 2002 $\quad$ Creditors payment period $= \dfrac{£5,500,000}{£11,300,000} \times 365 = 178$ days (to the nearest day)

For 2001 $\quad$ Creditors payment period $= \dfrac{£3,700,000}{£10,600,000} \times 365 = 127$ days (to the nearest day)

For Phelps, the creditors payment period increased from 127 days in 2001 to 178 days in 2002. Both these payment periods were significantly longer than the debt collection period. It is possible that Phelps' suppliers might be unhappy with the increase in time taken to pay bills.

Liquidity ratios

A business must ensure that it has enough liquid assets to pay any immediate bills that arise. Liquid assets include cash and assets that can be quickly switched into cash, such as stocks, debtors and short-term investments. Two widely used ratios that are used to monitor liquid assets are the current

---

QUESTION 2

DLC Ltd is a small engineering company. In order to improve cash flow, the management decided to put pressure on customers to settle their debts more quickly. Unfortunately this resulted in a fall in turnover because some customers decided to buy their supplies from other manufacturers. Figure 44.3 shows some extracts from DLC's accounts.

(a) (i) Calculate the debt collection period for 1999, 2000 and 2001 (to the nearest day).
(ii) Did the company's pressure on customers result in quicker payment?
(b) (i) Calculate the stock turnover for 2001 and 2000 (to the nearest day).
(ii) How might DLC's attempt to speed up customer payments account for the change in stock turnover?

Figure 44.3 *Extracts from DLC Ltd accounts 1999 - 2001*

	2001	2000	1999
	£	£	£
Turnover	780,000	810,000	970,000
Cost of sales	320,000	330,000	340,000
Gross profit	460,000	480,000	630,000
Current assets			
Stocks	85,000	55,000	35,000
Debtors	150,000	180,000	250,000
Cash	45,000	30,000	5,000

ratio and the acid test ratio.

Current ratio The CURRENT RATIO focuses on current assets and current liabilities. It is also known as the **working capital ratio** and is calculated using the formula:

$$\text{Current ratio} = \frac{\text{Current assets}}{\text{Current liabilities}}$$

It is also sometimes expressed as:

Current assets : Current liabilities

According to the balance sheet of Phelps, current assets were £9.6m in 2002 and current liabilities were £5.5m.

For 2002 $\quad$ Current ratio $= \dfrac{£9,600,000}{£5,500,000} = 1.75$ or $\quad 1.75 : 1$

For 2001 $\quad$ Current ratio $= \dfrac{£7,100,000}{£3,700,000} = 1.92$ or $\quad 1.92 : 1$

There is no simple rule about what constitutes a 'correct' current ratio. However, a low ratio, eg under 1 : 1, might raise concern that a business has insufficient working capital to meet its needs. This can arise if a business expands too rapidly, a situation known as **overtrading**. On the other hand, if a business has a current ratio in excess of 2 : 1, it might indicate poor management of working capital. This could arise, for example, if too much money was held in the form of cash that does not earn any return.

The current ratio for Phelps hardly changed over the two years, falling slightly from 1.92 : 1 to 1.75 : 1. As with other ratios, judgment on whether this is satisfactory depends to a large extent on comparisons within the industry. Some businesses, such as supermarkets, have relatively low current ratios because they only hold fast-selling stocks of finished goods and they generate mostly cash sales. Manufacturing businesses tend to have relatively high current ratios. This is because they must hold stocks of raw materials and work-in-progress that are being processed.

Acid test ratio The ACID TEST RATIO is a more rigorous test of liquidity than the current ratio. It is also known as the **quick ratio** or **liquid ratio**. It is often regarded as a better test of a business's liquidity because it excludes stocks from the total of liquid assets.
This is because a business cannot be sure that all its stock will be sold. For Phelps, the information required to calculate the acid test ratio is contained in the balance sheet in Figure 44.1. It is calculated using the formula:

$$\text{Acid test ratio} = \frac{\text{Current assets - stocks}}{\text{Current liabilities}}$$

It is also sometimes expressed as:

Current assets - stocks : Current liabilities

For 2002 $\quad$ Acid test ratio $= \dfrac{£9,600,000 - £2,100,000}{£5,500,000} = 1.36$ or $1.36 : 1$

For 2001 $\quad$ Acid test ratio $= \dfrac{£7,100,000 - £2,800,000}{£3,700,000} = 1.16$ or $1.16 : 1$

If a business has an acid test ratio of less than 1 (ie 1 : 1) it means that its liquid current assets do not cover its current liabilities. This could indicate a potential liquidity problem. However, as with the current ratio, there is considerable variation between the typical acid test ratios of businesses in different industries. For example, supermarket chains with a strong positive cash flow can have an

QUESTION 3

Brockhurst plc is a manufacturer of sofas, armchairs and three piece suites. In 1999, the company decided to stop holding stocks of finished goods. Instead, it would only produce goods to order. It was hoped that this would improve the liquidity of the business. Figure 44.4 shows extracts from the balance sheet of Brockhurst plc.

Figure 44.4 *Extracts from Brockhurst's balance sheet, 1998 to 2001*

	2001 £000	2000 £000	1999 £000	1998 £000
Current assets				
Stocks	300	1,100	4,500	4,400
Debtors	4,100	4,200	3,800	3,700
Bank	2,200	1,400	1,200	1,100
Current liabilities	4,900	4,800	4,900	4,600

(a) Calculate (i) the current ratio and (ii) the acid test ratio for Brockhurst for each year between 1998 and 2001.
(b) What effect did the change in policy have on the company's liquidity?

acid test ratio of only 0.5 (ie 0.5 : 1). For Phelps, the acid test ratio above 1 suggests that it has adequate liquid resources to meet its immediate payments.

Gearing ratios

Gearing ratios are a means of analysing the **capital structure** of a company (see unit 35). They compare the amount of capital raised from ordinary shareholders with that raised in loans and, in some cases, from preference shareholders. This is important because the interest on loans and dividends for preference shareholders are fixed commitments whereas the dividends for ordinary shareholders are not.

Gearing ratio There are several different versions of the GEARING RATIO. Two are described here. Both are used to analyse the burden of fixed interest payments on a company. One widely used version relates the total of long-term loans and other fixed interest capital to the total of shareholders' funds plus long-term loans. According to the balance sheet of Phelps in Figure 44.1, long term loans in 2002 were £8m. This was the mortgage entered under the heading 'Creditors: amounts falling due after one year'. Added to this is the fixed interest capital, ie the preference share capital of £5m. As long as the company is trading profitably, Phelps must pay fixed interest dividends to its preference shareholders. Although not relevant in this example, if Phelps had raised loans in the form of debentures, they would also be included here. The total of long-term loans and fixed interest capital in 2002 was £13m (£8m + £5m). The total of shareholders' funds plus long-term loans was £54.6m (£46.6m + £8m). This version of the gearing ratio is calculated by the formula:

$$\text{Gearing ratio} = \frac{\text{Fixed cost capital}}{\text{Long term capital}}$$

$$= \frac{\text{Long term loans + Preference share capital}}{\text{Shareholders' funds (incl. pref. share capital) + Long term loans}} \times 100$$

For 2002   Gearing ratio $= \dfrac{£8,000,000 + £5,000,000}{£54,600,000} \times 100 = 23.80\%$

For 2001   Gearing ratio $= \dfrac{£8,000,000 + £5,000,000}{£47,900,000} \times 100 = 27.14\%$

When this definition of gearing is used, it is sometimes said that a ratio above 50% means that a company is high geared. Below 50% it is low geared. However, this type of analysis has been criticised on the grounds that 50% is an arbitrary figure and takes no account of the particular industry average. For example, if the average gearing for an industry is 70%, it could be argued that a company within that industry with a gearing ratio of 60% is relatively low geared.

A second version of the gearing ratio relates debt to equity. In this context, debt is defined as long term loans. For Phelps, it is the mortgage of £8m. Equity is defined as ordinary share capital plus reserves. According to Phelps' balance sheet, in 2002, equity was £41.6m (ie ordinary share capital £10m + share premium £15m + other reserves £4.3m + profit and loss account £12.3m). This version of the gearing ratio is calculated by the formula:

$$\text{Gearing ratio} = \frac{\text{Debt}}{\text{Equity}} \times 100$$

For 2002 $\text{Gearing ratio} = \dfrac{£8,000,000}{£41,600,000} \times 100 = 19.23\%$

For 2001 $\text{Gearing ratio} = \dfrac{£8,000,000}{£34,900,000} \times 100 = 22.92\%$

When this definition of gearing is used, a ratio that is greater than 100% means that debt is greater than equity. In most industries, this would be considered to be high gearing and could pose an unacceptably high risk to potential lenders. This is because, if there was a downturn in profits, the company might not be able to meet its interest payments. However, this is not the case for Phelps. Both versions of the gearing ratio suggest that the company is not unduly burdened by debt. The significance of gearing is discussed in more detail in unit 35.

Interest cover The gearing ratio is an assessment of a company's debt burden derived from its balance sheet. INTEREST COVER, however, is derived from the profit and loss account. It assesses the burden of interest payments by comparing interest paid with net profit before interest and tax. It is calculated by using the formula:

$$\text{Interest cover} = \frac{\text{Profit before interest and tax}}{\text{Interest}}$$

The profit before tax and interest (ie operating profit) for Phelps in 2002 was £6.6m as shown in its profit and loss account. The amount of interest paid during the year was £0.5m.

For 2002 $\text{Interest cover} = \dfrac{£6,600,000}{£500,000} = 13.2 \text{ times}$

For 2001 $\text{Interest cover} = \dfrac{£3,400,000}{£500,000} = 6.8 \text{ times}$

If interest cover is 1, this means that all of a company's profit would be used to pay interest. This is obviously not sustainable in the long term. In the case of Phelps, interest cover rose from 6.8 to 13.2, indicating an improved ability to meet its interest payments.

Shareholders' ratios

Shareholders' ratios provide information which can help investors to make decisions about buying or selling shares. They are often used to analyse the performance of public limited companies. However, they can also be helpful to the owners of private limited companies.

Earnings per share The EARNINGS PER SHARE (EPS) is a measure of how much profit each ordinary share earns after tax and dividend payments to preference shareholders. It does not, however, show how much money is actually paid to ordinary shareholders because some profit might be retained as a reserve. The EPS is generally shown at the bottom of the profit and loss account in the published accounts of plcs. For Phelps, which has issued both ordinary shares and preference shares, the EPS is:

$$\text{Earnings per share} = \frac{\text{Profit available to ordinary shareholders*}}{\text{Number of ordinary shares}}$$

*This is equivalent to net profit after tax less payment on fixed interest bearing capital (ie preference share dividend).

For Phelps in 2002, the net profit (after tax) was £4.6m as shown in the profit and loss account. £0.5m was paid to preference shareholders so the profit available to ordinary shareholders was £4.1m (£4.6m - £0.5m). According to the additional information given in Figure 44.1, the number of ordinary shares issued in 2002 was 50m.

$$\text{For 2002} \quad \text{Earnings per share} = \frac{£4,100,000}{50,000,000} = £0.082 = 8.2p$$

$$\text{For 2001} \quad \text{Earnings per share} = \frac{£1,700,000}{50,000,000} = £0.034 = 3.4p$$

Over the two years, the EPS for Phelps improved significantly, more than doubling from 3.4p to 8.2p. However, on its own, this does not necessarily indicate a satisfactory performance. Only when the EPS is compared with the company's share price and with the EPS of comparable companies is it possible to make a judgment.

Price earnings ratio The PRICE EARNINGS (P/E) RATIO is one of the main indicators used by investors in deciding whether to buy or sell particular shares. The P/E ratio relates the current share price to the earnings per share. It is calculated using the formula below. The ratio is often expressed as the number of times by which the share price can be divided by the earnings per share.

$$\text{Price earnings ratio} = \frac{\text{Share price (stock market price)}}{\text{Earnings per share}}$$

In the case of plcs which are listed on the Stock Market, their share price is published daily in the Financial Times and other newspapers. The share price for Phelps on 31 March 2002, is shown as additional information in Figure 44.1. It was 130p. The earnings per share was 8.2p as calculated above.

$$\text{For 2002} \quad \text{Price earnings ratio} = \frac{130p}{8.2p} = 15.85 \text{ times}$$

$$\text{For 2001} \quad \text{Price earnings ratio} = \frac{41p}{3.4p} = 12.06 \text{ times}$$

The P/E ratio of 15.85 means that the market price of a share is 15.85 times higher than its current level of earnings. Assuming that nothing changes, it would take 15.85 years for these shares to earn their current market value. The P/E ratio of Phelps rose over the two years from 12.06 to 15.85, indicating that investors had increased confidence in the future profitability of the company. As a result, demand for the shares rose, causing the price to jump from 41p to 130p. Rising investor confidence was justified since the earnings per share for Phelps had increased significantly from 3.4p to 8.2p.

Price earnings ratios provide a useful guide to market confidence and can be helpful in comparing different companies. However, a general rise or fall in share prices will clearly affect P/E ratios, so care must be taken when interpreting changes.

Dividend per share The DIVIDEND PER SHARE shows how much money ordinary shareholders receive per share.

$$\text{Dividend per share} = \frac{\text{Dividend paid to ordinary shareholders}}{\text{Number of ordinary shares}}$$

According to the profit and loss account in Figure 44.1, the dividend paid to Phelps' ordinary shareholders in 2002 was £1m. The number of ordinary shares is shown as additional information and was 50m.

For 2002   Dividend per share $= \dfrac{£1,000,000}{50,000,000} = £0.02 = $ 2p per share

For 2001   Dividend per share $= \dfrac{£500,000}{50,000,000} = £0.01 = $ 1p per share

The dividend per share paid to Phelps' shareholders doubled from 1p per share to 2p over the two years. To determine whether this would be satisfactory to investors, the dividend per share must be compared with the share price. This involves calculating the dividend yield.

Dividend yield The DIVIDEND YIELD is the dividend per ordinary share expressed as a percentage of the current share price.

$$\text{Dividend yield} = \frac{\text{Dividend per ordinary share}}{\text{Ordinary share market price}} \times 100$$

For Phelps, the share price on 31 March 2002 was 130p. The dividend per share was 2p.

For 2002   Dividend yield $= \dfrac{2p}{130p} \times 100 = 1.54\%$

For 2001   Dividend yield $= \dfrac{1p}{41p} \times 100 = 2.44\%$

Over the two years, the dividend yield fell significantly for Phelps, despite the doubling of the dividend per share. The reason for this is that the share price more than trebled and this accounts for the fall. Whether a dividend yield of 1.54% is adequate depends on what might be earned in other companies and in other forms of investment. However, when making this judgment, it must be remembered that dividends are not the only reward for owning shares. Investors might make a capital gain if the shares are sold for a higher price than when they were bought.

Dividend cover The DIVIDEND COVER measures how many times a company's dividends to ordinary shareholders could be paid from net profit.

$$\text{Dividend cover} = \frac{\text{Profit available to ordinary shareholders*}}{\text{Dividends (ordinary shares)}}$$

* This is equivalent to net profit after tax less payment on fixed interest bearing capital (ie preference share dividend).

For Phelps, the profit available to ordinary shareholders in 2002 was £4.1m. The dividend paid to ordinary shareholders was £1m.

For 2002   Dividend cover $= \dfrac{£4,100,000}{£1,000,000} = 4.1$ times

For 2001   Dividend cover $= \dfrac{£1,700,000}{£500,000} = 3.4$ times

For Phelps, the dividend cover improved slightly over the two years. A cover of 4.1 means that the dividends could have been paid 4.1 times over in 2002. If the dividend cover is high, shareholders might argue that bigger dividends should be paid. If it is low, it could mean that profits are low or that the company is not retaining enough profit for new investment.

It is possible for a business to pay dividends even when there is not sufficient profit in the current year to cover the payment. A company might do this to help retain the loyalty of shareholders. The money to cover the payment would have to come from reserves.

QUESTION 4

DataCall plc specialises in setting up and operating call centres. At the end of 2001, an investor in the company who owned 1,500,000 ordinary shares was contemplating selling the

Figure 44.5 *Financial information for DataCall*

	2001	2000
Earnings per share	42p	39p
End of year share price	490p	520p
Dividends	£10.5m	£12m
Number of shares issued	105m	100m

stake completely. Figure 44.5 shows some financial information for the company for the financial years 2000 and 2001. All the figures relate to ordinary shares.

(a) Calculate the (i) price earnings ratio; (ii) dividend per share; and (iii) dividend yield for DataCall for 2001 and 2000.
(b) On the basis of your answer in (a) explain whether you would advise the investor to sell the shares or not.
(c) What other information might be helpful to the investor before making a final decision on selling the stake?

The relationship between profitability and efficiency

Earlier in this unit, the return on capital employed (ROCE) is described as the primary ratio. This is because it is generally regarded as the key indicator of business performance. It is dependent on two subsidiary or 'secondary' factors, the net profit margin and asset turnover. The relationship between these ratios is given by the following equation.

Return on capital employed* $=$ Net profit margin $\times$ Asset turnover

$$\frac{\text{Profit before tax and interest}}{\text{Net assets}} = \frac{\text{Profit before tax and interest}}{\text{Turnover}} \times \frac{\text{Turnover}}{\text{Net assets}}$$

* In this context, ROCE is defined as the return on net assets, ie on shareholders' capital.

Using the 2002 figures for Phelps plc that are given in Figure 44.1:
- profit before tax and interest was £6.6m;
- net assets were £46.6m;
- turnover was £23.9m.

Substituting these figure in the equation above:

Return on capital employed $=$ Net profit margin $\times$ Asset turnover

$$\frac{£6,600,000}{£46,600,000} = \frac{£6,600,000}{£23,900,000} \times \frac{£23,900,000}{£46,600,000}$$

$$14.16 = 27.62 \times 0.51$$

By breaking down the ROCE ratio in this way, it is clear that the return on capital is determined both by the profitability of sales and the efficiency in the use of capital.

Limitations of ratio analysis

Although ratios offer a useful method of analysing business performance, they do have several limitations. The following factors all affect their usefulness.

The basis for comparison It is important when analysing the differences between businesses to compare 'like with like'. This means that valid comparisons can only be made between businesses within the same industry. Even then, differences in the size of the businesses, in their accounting policies and in their financial year-ends can make comparisons difficult.

The quality of final accounts Ratios are usually based on published financial statements and therefore depend upon the quality of these statements. One factor that can affect the quality of accounting information is the change in monetary values caused by inflation. Rising prices distort comparisons between different time periods. For example, in times of high inflation, asset values and turnover might rise rapidly in monetary terms. However, when the figures are corrected for inflation, there might be no increase in real terms. The limitations of published accounts are described in more detail in unit 45.

Limitations of the balance sheet Because the balance sheet is a 'snapshot' of a business at the financial year-end, it might not be representative of the business's performance throughout the year. If, for example, a business experiences its peak trading activity in summer, and has its year-end at a time when trade is slow, in the New Year, balance sheet figures for stock and debtors will be unrepresentative.

Narrowness of view Ratios only provide a restricted view of how a business is performing. For example, they do not show absolute differences in scale. Suppose two companies have a ROCE of 20% and 25% respectively. Although it might appear that the second company is performing better, if its net profit is £50,000 and the net profit of the first company is £250,000, a different judgment might be made.

Numerical values Ratios are expressed in numerical terms. They do not indicate reasons or provide explanations for what is happening in businesses. Further investigation is generally necessary for a full understanding.

Summary of accounting ratios

Return on capital employed $= \dfrac{\text{Profit before tax and interest}}{\text{Long-term capital employed}} \times 100$

Return on net assets $= \dfrac{\text{Profit before tax and interest}}{\text{Net assets}} \times 100$

Return on equity $= \dfrac{\text{Profit available to ordinary shareholders*}}{\text{Ordinary share capital + reserves}} \times 100$

* This is equivalent to net profit after tax less payment on fixed interest bearing capital (ie preference share dividend).

Gross profit margin $= \dfrac{\text{Gross profit}}{\text{Turnover}} \times 100$

Net profit margin $= \dfrac{\text{Net profit before tax and interest}}{\text{Turnover}} \times 100$

Asset turnover $= \dfrac{\text{Turnover}}{\text{Net assets}}$

Sales to capital employed $= \dfrac{\text{Sales}}{\text{Shareholders' funds + long-term loans}}$

Stock turnover $= \dfrac{\text{Average stock}}{\text{Cost of sales}} \times 365$ **or** $\dfrac{\text{Cost of sales}}{\text{Average stock}}$

Debt collection period $= \dfrac{\text{Debtors}}{\text{Turnover}} \times 365$ **or** $\dfrac{\text{Debtors}}{\text{Credit sales}} \times 365$

Creditors payment period $= \dfrac{\text{Creditors}}{\text{Cost of sales}} \times 365$ **or** $\dfrac{\text{Creditors} \times 365}{\text{Credit purchases}}$

Current ratio (or working capital ratio) $= \dfrac{\text{Current assets}}{\text{Current liabilities}}$

Acid test ratio (or quick ratio or liquid ratio) $= \dfrac{\text{Current assets - stocks}}{\text{Current liabilities}}$

Gearing ratio (1) $= \dfrac{\text{Long-term loans + Preference share capital}}{\text{Shareholders' funds (incl. pref. share capital) + Long-term loans}} \times 100$

Gearing ratio (2) $= \dfrac{\text{Loans}}{\text{Equity}} \times 100$

Interest cover $= \dfrac{\text{Profit before interest and tax}}{\text{Interest}}$

Earnings per share $= \dfrac{\text{Profit available to ordinary shareholders*}}{\text{Number of ordinary shares}}$

* This is equivalent to net profit after tax less payment on fixed interest bearing capital (ie preference share dividend).

Price earnings ratio $= \dfrac{\text{Share price}}{\text{Earnings per share}}$

Dividend per share $= \dfrac{\text{Dividend (ordinary shares)}}{\text{Number of ordinary shares}}$

Dividend yield $= \dfrac{\text{Dividend per ordinary share}}{\text{Ordinary share price}} \times 100$

Dividend cover $= \dfrac{\text{Profit available to ordinary shareholders*}}{\text{Dividends (ordinary shares)}}$

* This is equivalent to net profit after tax less payment on fixed interest bearing capital (ie preference share dividend).

key terms

Acid test ratio - a liquidity ratio that relates current assets less stocks to current liabilities.

Asset turnover ratio - a measure of asset productivity that relates current, fixed, total or net assets, or capital employed, to turnover.

Creditors payment period - the average number of days it takes to pay debts.

Current ratio - a liquidity ratio that relates current assets to current liabilities.

Debt collection period - the average number of days it takes to collect debts from customers.

Dividend cover - the number of times the dividend can be paid from the current year's earnings.

Dividend per share - the amount of money that shareholders receive for each share owned.

Dividend yield - the amount of money received by shareholders expressed as a percentage of the market share price.

Earnings per share - the amount of money that each share earns.

EBIT - earnings (or profit) before interest and tax.

Gearing ratio - the relationship between the funds provided to a company by its owners, ie ordinary shareholders, and other long-term funds with a fixed interest charge.

Gross profit margin (or mark-up) - the gross profit as a percentage of turnover.

Interest cover - the relationship between interest payments and net profit.

Net profit margin - the net profit as a percentage of turnover.

Price earnings ratio - the current market price of a share divided by the earnings per share.

Ratio analysis - a mathematical technique that examines the relationship between variables such as turnover, profit and capital employed.

Return on capital employed (ROCE) - the profit of a business expressed as a percentage of the amount of money invested in that business.

Return on equity - the profit of a business expressed as a percentage of the amount of money provided by ordinary shareholders (plus reserves).

Return on net assets - the profit of a business expressed as a percentage of net assets.

Stock turnover - measures how quickly a business uses or sells its stock.

summary questions

1. Explain the difference between shareholders' equity, total capital and long-term capital.
2. What is the difference between performance ratios and activity ratios?
3. If the return on capital employed for a business is 3.4% and the current rate of interest is 5%, how might you interpret the company's performance?
4. How might a rise in the net profit margin be interpreted by a business?
5. What does the current ratio measure?
6. What is the difference between the current ratio and the acid test ratio?
7. If the price earnings ratio for a business is 12, what does this imply?
8. What is the difference between the gearing ratio and interest cover?
9. Which ratio measures the amount of money that shareholders actually receive per share?
10. What will happen to the dividend yield if the share price falls but dividends remain unchanged?

UNIT ASSESSMENT QUESTION 1

Arken plc manufactures components for the telecommunications industry. In 2001, the company was hit hard by a fall in demand from some of its big customers. As a result, the company's profit before interest and tax fell from £5.6m in 2000 to £1.2m in 2001. The amount of interest paid by the company rose from £500,000 in 2000, to £800,000 in 2001. The company also experienced some bad debts and asked its bank for a £5m, 10 year loan.

Figure 44.6 Balance sheet for Arken plc

Arken plc
Balance Sheet

	As at 31.7.01 £000	As at 31.7.00 £000
Fixed assets		
Tangible assets	54,000	51,000
Investments	5,400	5,400
	59,400	56,400
Current assets		
Stocks	6,400	6,900
Debtors	9,700	4,300
Bank	-	1,200
	16,100	12,400
Creditors: amounts falling due before one year		
Trade creditors	5,300	4,200
Bank overdraft	5,400	
Other liabilities	4,500	3,200
	15,200	7,400
Net current assets	900	5,000
Total assets less current liabilities	60,300	61,400
Creditors: amounts falling due after one year		
Debentures	20,000	20,000
Net assets	40,300	41,400
Capital and reserves		
Ordinary share capital	10,000	10,000
Share premium	5,000	5,000
Other reserves	2,300	4,600
Profit and loss account	23,000	21,800
Shareholders funds	40,300	41,400

(a) Calculate the (i) current ratio; (ii) acid test ratio; (iii) gearing (debt to equity) ratio; and (iv) interest cover for Arken plc in 2000 and 2001.
(b) Based on your answers in (a), explain whether you think a bank would lend the company £5m.
(c) (i) Calculate the debt collection period for 2000 and 2001. Turnover was £36.8m and £45.6m in these years respectively. (ii) How do your answers in (i) reconcile with the company's problem of rising bad debts?

Shelly Hadlee is a fund manager for a large pension company. Her job is to invest client's money in companies that offer a safe but steady rate of return. In 2000, the possibility of recession in the economy prompted Shelly into purchasing more 'defensive stocks', ie shares in companies that might not be too severely affected by a recession. However, she also wished to invest in companies that showed potential for future growth. Two companies that Shelly considered were:

- A K Foods plc: a food processing company based in Manchester. It is a long established business and has no long-term debts. The company employs 140 staff and it supplies supermarkets with canned meats, vegetables and soups.
- CanCo plc: a food processing company based in Milton Keynes. It is a relatively new company that has enjoyed increasing success. When it was set up, it invested heavily in up to date plant and equipment. The company employs 109 staff and it supplies supermarkets, wholesalers and some department stores with a wide range of canned and bottled foodstuffs.

Figure 44.7 *Financial ratios for A K Foods and CanCo*

A K Foods	1996	1997	1998	1999	2000
Return on capital employed	12.40%	11.90%	12.10%	12.40%	11.90%
Dividend yield	1.80%	1.70%	1.80%	2.00%	1.80%
Price earnings ratio	13.1	16.2	17.6	16.7	16.9

CanCo	1996	1997	1998	1999	2000
Return on capital employed	4.10%	6.20%	9.40%	12.30%	13.70%
Dividend yield	0.10%	0.90%	1.20%	1.40%	1.80%
Price earnings ratio	11.1	16.4	17.4	18.1	21.2

(a) Given the information provided, in which company would you have advised Shelly to invest? Give reasons for your answer.

During 2001, the analysts who work for Shelly provided her with updated information regarding the two companies. This is shown in Figure 44.8.

Figure 44.8 *Updated information for A K Foods and CanCo*

	Capital employed	Net profit before tax & interest	Earnings per share	Dividends per share	Share price
A K Foods	£98m	£11.96m	45p	14p	751p
CanCo	£87m	£12.65m	36p	19p	828p

(b) Using the updated information in Figure 44.8, calculate the (i) ROCE; (ii) Dividend yield; and (iii) price earnings ratio for 2001.

(c) Would your recommendation in (a) change as a result of the calculations made in (b)? Explain your answer.

(d) Explain how five years of figures for the two companies would be helpful in making a decision in this case.

unit 45 Limitations of published accounts

unitobjectives

To understand:
- the limitations of published accounts;
- the factors that can cause accounts to be misleading;
- the regulations that protect shareholders.

Limitations

Published accounts provide information that can be used to assess the performance of a business. By comparing figures and calculating ratios, accounts can be used to analyse a company's profitability, efficiency and solvency. However, it is important to recognise that a study of published accounts is not likely to provide a comprehensive assessment of a company's performance. For example, accounts do not provide information on non-financial factors such as the quality of the workforce and the location of the business.

A large number of factors can limit the usefulness of accounts. Some factors are outside the control of businesses, such as inflation. Others are within the control of businesses, such as changes in the accounting policies used. In some circumstances, businesses might wish to deliberately mislead shareholders and investors by using practices known as 'window dressing'. These, and the other factors that limit the usefulness of published accounts, are described below.

Lack of detail

Published accounts only provide a summary of a business's financial circumstances. So, for example, they do not contain details on the relative performance of different parts of a business. A further limitation of published accounts is that they generally only contain the figures for two years. Although this allows comparison between the two years, it does not provide information on longer term trends.

Historical information

Information in published accounts is based on historical data. The profit and loss account and cash flow statement contain figures from the past financial year. The balance sheet is based on a 'snapshot' valuation of assets and liabilities on the last day of the financial year. The information in these financial statements is therefore outdated by the time it is published. Therefore it might not be a reliable guide to the current and future performance of the business. To illustrate the point, suppose that an important customer became insolvent on the last day of a business's financial year. This would have a major impact on future turnover. However, it would have no impact on that year's accounts.

Non-monetary factors and intangible assets

The information contained in accounts focuses on factors that can be measured in monetary terms. However, a company's performance and circumstances are also influenced by non-monetary factors that the accounts do not show. Consequently, the analysis of accounts cannot provide a full assessment of a business's prospects. Examples of non-financial factors that might be important are as follows.

- **Workforce and management** The quality of the people working for a business can have a major influence on its performance. If the workforce is well trained, highly motivated, flexible and loyal, the performance of the business is likely to be enhanced.

- **Location** A business can benefit from, or be adversely affected by, its location. For example, a hotel that is located next to a new motorway is likely to be more successful than a hotel that is bypassed by a new road.
- **Intangible assets** Following the issue of Financial Reporting Standard *Goodwill and intangible assets* (FRS10), it is standard accounting practice to exclude the value of most intangible assets from the balance sheet (unless they have been purchased). However, assets such as goodwill, brand names, patents and trademarks can be extremely valuable for a business. The balance sheet will tend to undervalue a business when intangible assets are not included. For example, the brand names owned by companies such as Coca-Cola and Cadbury Schweppes are estimated to be worth many millions of pounds, but they are not shown on the balance sheet. This is because it is difficult to put an objective valuation on them until they are sold.

Subjectivity

Although regulatory authorities have attempted to reduce the scope for subjective judgments in published accounts, there are still instances where they occur. In these cases, accounts have to be interpreted with care. For example, businesses can choose whether to value fixed assets such as buildings at their historical cost or at a current market valuation. Similarly, a business has flexibility in deciding when to write off bad debts. Both these issues have an impact on the balance sheet.

Differences in accounting policy

Businesses have considerable leeway in deciding how to draw up their accounts. For example, some businesses choose to depreciate their fixed assets by the straight line method, while others choose the reducing balance method. The Financial Reporting Standard *Tangible fixed assets* (FRS15) does not specify the depreciation policy that a business has to use. Instead, companies must select a method that 'reflects as fairly as possible the pattern in which the asset's economic benefits are consumed'. Because different methods are used, comparing the accounts of companies can be misleading. Comparisons over time can also be misleading if a company changes its method of depreciation.

Window dressing

Despite the existence of accounting standards, it is possible for accountants to disguise the true financial position of a business. Information can be presented so that the position appears better or worse than it really is. This is called WINDOW DRESSING. There is a number of reasons why businesses might wish to 'window dress' their accounts.

- **To fend off a takeover bid** By making a company look stronger than it really is, shareholders might be encouraged to retain their shares, thereby discouraging a potential predator from making an unwanted bid. A strong and well performing company will be more expensive to buy than a failing company whose share price has collapsed.
- **To attract investment** By exaggerating the financial strength of a business, it might be possible to persuade potential lenders to provide funding.
- **To increase the market price of shares** This might happen if the managers of a company have received share options. A share option gives someone the right to buy a share at a particular price. A profit can then be made if the share price rises above the option price.
- **To lower the market price of shares** In exceptional circumstances a company might deliberately wish to show itself in a poor light. This could encourage shareholders to sell shares causing their price to fall. Directors of the company could then buy the shares at the lower price, knowing that the market share price is based on a false impression.
- **To reduce taxation** A company might try to disguise the amount of profits it makes in order to reduce the amount of corporation tax paid.

Even though the law requires that accounts should give a 'true and fair view', the practice of window dressing is not illegal. Therefore it is important for shareholders and analysts to understand how accounts can be manipulated. Some examples of how it is done are given on the next page.

Earnings management In some industries it is possible for a business to choose when to 'recognise' business income. For example, a TV production company can choose to recognise the income for a new programme when the programme contract is signed, or when the programme is delivered, or when the invoice is issued. By choosing to recognise income in the next financial year, the current year's profit will be reduced. This therefore reduces the tax liability for the year.

Depreciation Companies can choose the method of depreciation to be used in their accounts. This means that it is possible for assets to be depreciated at a slower or a faster rate. Switching from one method of calculating depreciation to another can affect both the balance sheet and the profit and loss account. For example, if a company buys a new lorry for £54,000 (with a 5 year estimated life and a residual value of £4,000), the depreciation charge in the first year would be £10,000 using the straight line method. It would be £20,000 using the reducing balance method if it was decided to use a depreciation rate of 40%. The higher the depreciation charge, the lower will be both the company's profit and the value of its assets in the balance sheet.

Another way in which companies can use depreciation to window dress their accounts is by changing their policy relating to research and development. The Statement of Standard Accounting Practice *Accounting for research and development* (SSAP13) allows companies to choose how they treat development expenditure. They can either write it off immediately as an expense or they can 'capitalise' it and treat it as an intangible asset. In the latter case, the asset is then depreciated or 'amortised' over a period of time. If the expenditure is written off as it occurs, it immediately reduces profits. If the expenditure is capitalised, the effect is to reduce profits in the future, but not in the current year.

Creditors and debtors Changes in the total of debtors and creditors can affect the apparent financial strength of a business. By making a special effort to collect debts just before the end of a financial year, a company can reduce the total of debtors on its balance sheet. Similarly, if a business pays some of its bills early, just before the end of the financial year, the total of creditors will appear lower.

Stock valuation According to the Statement of Standard Accounting Practice *Stocks and work in progress* (SSAP9), UK companies can choose the FIFO (first in, first out) method or the AVCO (average cost) method of stock valuation. By changing its method of stock valuation, a business can affect both the profit and loss account and the balance sheet. For example, suppose a company uses the FIFO method and the value of its closing stock is £108,000. By using the AVCO method, suppose the value is reduced to £93,000. A switch from FIFO to AVCO in this case means that the cost of sales will rise by £15,000 (£108,000 - £93,000). Therefore, profit will fall by £15,000. In the balance sheet, the value of current assets will be £15,000 lower.

QUESTION 1

Tesco, the supermarket chain, was criticised in 2001 for flattering its profits by changing its accounting policies. ABN Amro, the stockbroker, published a research note suggesting that Tesco's earnings would have been 10% lower if the company had kept its accounting policies unchanged since 1997. 'Following the publication of the 2001 report and accounts, it seems to us that the issue of depreciation is far more serious than we first thought' the note said. The depreciation charge shown in the profit and loss account had hardly changed even though Tesco had invested heavily in fixtures and fittings in recent years. A financial analyst from Merrill Lynch suggested that earnings growth might have been

flattered by 3% in 1999 - 2000 and by 2% last year. Tesco denied that it had made any changes beyond those disclosed in the accounts.

Source: adapted from the *Sunday Times* 10.6.01.

(a) According to the allegation in the report, Tesco 'flattered' its profits? What might have been its motive?

(b) Explain how a business can 'window dress' its accounts using depreciation.

Asset manipulation A business can improve its liquidity by selling some of its fixed assets and then leasing them back. This provides an immediate injection of cash which can then be used to pay creditors. The effect is to raise the liquid ratio. However, in the longer term, the effect will be to reduce profits because a leasing charge has now to be paid. An additional effect is that if assets are sold for more than their net book value, a profit will be made and this will be shown in the profit and loss account.

External factors

Businesses operate in a dynamic environment and are subject to external factors that are beyond their control. These factors can have a significant effect on turnover and profitability but are not shown in published accounts.

- **The economic cycle** Periods of economic prosperity in which consumer spending and business confidence are high are often followed by a recession in which demand and investment falls and business failures increase. All businesses within the economy are affected to some extent by such changes.
- **Government legislation** Changes in the law can affect the performance of businesses. For example, a minimum wage was introduced in 1999. This raised labour costs for some businesses.
- **Exchange rate** Changes in the exchange rate can affect the profitability of many businesses. Directly affected are those businesses that import or export goods and services. Indirectly affected are those businesses that produce goods with foreign components and also those businesses that compete with foreign suppliers. For example, if the pound rises in value, UK businesses find it more difficult to sell their goods abroad and the cost of imported goods falls. On the other hand, if the pound loses value, exporters find it easier to sell goods abroad and the cost of imports rises.
- **Interest rates** When interest rates change, the cost of borrowing also changes. The impact can vary between companies. For example, a rise in interest rates will increase the costs more for a high geared business with large bank loans than for a low geared business with few debts.
- **Inflation** This is a general and persistent rise in prices. It can distort the information provided in accounts. This is particularly true when making comparisons over time. One of the problems of using accounts when inflation is high is that turnover and profit might be overstated. For example, if a business made a profit of £2m in year 1, and £2.1m in year 2, this represents an increase of 5%. However, if inflation during the year was 10%, the profit would have fallen in **real terms**. Another problem relates to asset values. According to SSAP9, businesses should value their stock at the 'lower of historical cost or net realisable value'. But, at times of high inflation, the historical cost might be much less than the replacement cost. This means that stock values will be understated in the balance sheet.

Comparing 'like for like'

When analysing published accounts, it is usual to make comparisons between companies. For these comparisons to be valid, it is important to compare 'like for like'. This means that the businesses should have the following characteristics.

- They should be operating in the same industry. For example, comparing the performance of a car manufacturer with that of a supermarket would not be appropriate. One company is a manufacturer which mainly sells goods on credit and the other is a retailer which mainly sells goods for cash. Consequently the values for the debt collection period and the acid test ratio are likely to be quite different. But this does not necessarily mean that one company is performing any better than the other.
- The businesses should be roughly the same size. For example, comparing the performance of a small independent pizza restaurant with that of Pizza Hut is not comparing 'like for like', even though they are both restaurants. Pizza Hut is a national chain with a turnover of millions of pounds. The turnover of the independent might only be a fraction of this. Even though the independent will make lower profits than Pizza Hut, it does not necessarily mean that the business is performing less effectively.
- The businesses should have similar capital structures. For example, two manufacturers might produce very different financial results if one is funded mainly by share capital and the other is funded from loans. The business funded from borrowed money will have to pay interest which

reduces profit, earnings per share and the price earnings ratio.

When making comparisons, it is important to compare the performances of businesses within the same time period. External events such as a rise in interest rates or a collapse of consumer confidence can have a major impact on accounts. If one company published its accounts for the period before these events, and one published after, any comparison would be invalid. However, companies often have different financial year-ends, so obtaining information for exactly the same time period can be difficult.

Shareholder protection

An important aim of the Companies Act and the Accounting Standards Board is to make it easier to analyse published accounts and to compare companies. By reducing the scope for inconsistency, fraud and misrepresentation, shareholders and investors can have more certainty and confidence in their analysis of company performance. They can be reasonably sure that calculations of profit and asset values have been made in accordance with the relevant standards.

The Companies Act 1985 This Act (as amended by The Companies Act 1989) sets out rules for the presentation and content of published accounts. It also states that it is the directors' responsibility to ensure that accounts give a 'true and fair view' of the state of affairs of a company (see unit 38).

The Accounting Standards Board (ASB) The ASB issues regulations that are known as Financial Reporting Standards (FRSs). Regulations issued by the predecessor of the ASB, the Accounting Standards Committee (ASC), are known as Statements of Standard Accounting Practice (SSAPs). The aim of the regulations is to standardise accounting policies and to ensure that accounts are drawn up and presented in a consistent, logical and 'transparent' fashion. The accounting standards that are particularly relevant in this context are summarised below.

* **FRS1 *Cash flow statements*** - medium and large-sized UK companies must publish a cash flow statement with their annual accounts.
* **FRS3 *Reporting financial performance*** - companies must provide an analysis of their turnover, cost of sales, operating expenses and profit.
* **FRS10 *Goodwill and intangible assets*** - companies should not include goodwill and other intangible assets on their balance sheets unless these intangible assets have been purchased.
* **FRS15 *Tangible fixed assets*** - companies can choose which method of depreciation they use but the method must be 'fair and appropriate'. The standard also states that a depreciation charge should be made on a 'systematic basis over an asset's useful economic life'. The method of depreciation must be stated in the notes to the accounts and any change in depreciation policy must be made clear. This standard replaces **SSAP12 *Accounting for depreciation***.
* **FRS18 *Accounting policies*** - companies should regularly review their accounting policies to ensure that they remain the most appropriate to the business's particular circumstances. Specific disclosure about the policies used, and any changes to the policies, must be made. The policies should be judged against the objectives of relevance, reliability, comparability and understandability. This standard replaces **SSAP2 *Disclosure of accounting policies***.
* **SSAP9 *Stocks and work in progress*** - companies must value stock at the lower of cost and net realisable value. The FIFO or AVCO methods of stock valuation are both acceptable.
* **SSAP13 *Research and development*** - companies must write-off research expenditure as an expense when it occurs. Development costs can be either written-off as they occur or capitalised.

Since the first SSAP was issued, in 1971, it has been necessary to keep the standards under constant review. When it is felt that changes are necessary, the ASB first issues a Financial Reporting Exposure Draft (FRED) as a consultation paper for discussion. Then, if it is decided to go ahead with a change, a new FRS is issued. Sometimes the ASB needs to act quickly, for example to close a loophole that some companies might be exploiting. When this happens, the Urgent Issues Task Force (UITF) has the power to issue new guidelines.

The International Accounting Standards Board (IASB) Although shareholders and investors can be relatively confident that UK companies are conforming to UK accounting standards, difficulty arises with foreign and multinational companies. Different countries have different standards, some of which are not the same as UK standards. There is the additional problem that the regulatory authorities in some countries are not as vigilant as in others. In an attempt to create a global system of regulations, the International Accounting Standards Board (IASB) has been established. It has the difficult and controversial task of harmonising standards between countries that sometimes have very different accounting traditions.

key terms

Window dressing - a way of presenting published accounts so that the financial position of a business appears to be better than it really is.

summary questions

1. State four limitations of published accounts.
2. State two non-monetary factors that might affect a business's performance.
3. Explain how subjective judgments can affect the balance sheet.
4. How might a change in accounting policy affect the accounts?
5. Why might a company window dress its accounts?
6. Explain what is meant by earnings management.
7. What is the effect of excluding intangible assets from the balance sheet?
8. How does inflation affect the usefulness of accounts?
9. What factors must be taken into account to ensure that a like for like comparison is made between companies?
10. How do the government and regulatory authorities attempt to protect the interests of shareholders?

UNIT ASSESSMENT   QUESTION 1

Route 1 and Direct Delivery both offer a 24 hour, door-to-door delivery service.
- Route 1 is a relatively new company but has grown quickly. It is located in Hillingdon, near London, and 80% of its work is based in the South East. The company owns 10 vans and rents premises on a trading estate close to many of its regular customers. Recently the company set up a motorcycle courier service to transport documents and small parcels within the London area. It purchased four motorcycles for this venture.
- Direct Delivery was established in 1985 and operates from a base in Wolverhampton, just 1 mile from the M6 motorway. This central location is ideal because its customers are dispersed across Britain. The company leases 12 vans and rents its premises from the local council.

Figure 45.1 *Financial information for Route 1 and Direct Delivery, year ended 31.3.01*

	Route 1	**Direct Delivery**
	£	£
Turnover	231,000	240,000
Net profit	56,000	40,300
Tangible assets	86,000	6,500
Share capital	50,000	5,000
Loan capital	60,000	0

(a) What factors limit the usefulness of comparisons between Route 1 and Direct Delivery?

(b) Explain why it is important to use the same trading period when making comparisons.

(c) Suggest possible reasons why the two companies had different levels of profitability.

UNIT ASSESSMENT QUESTION 2

Condor Medics plc is a biotechnology research company. It has a number of joint ventures with big pharmaceutical companies and it generates revenue from undertaking research on their behalf. In 2001, the company had a number of setbacks. A clinical trial for one of its products was suspended due to unforeseen side effects. In addition, one of the senior research staff left to join a rival company. The setbacks had a destabilising effect. Within 6 months, the share price fell from 136p to 31p. The company was also running short of cash and urgently required an injection of new capital. After a board meeting, the directors agreed to the following measures.

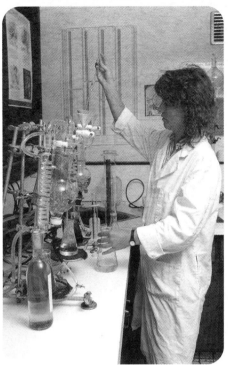

- Tangible assets worth £2,500,000 would be sold for cash and then leased back. The cash would be used immediately to reduce trade creditors.
- All development expenditure for the current and future years would be capitalised instead of being written off as at present.
- Earnings from new research contracts with pharmaceutical companies would be recognised as soon as the research contract was signed instead of later when the invoice was issued.

(a) Explain the possible motives for Condor Medics' measures.
(b) Explain which of the measures would affect the current year's profits.
(c) How would the sale of tangible assets and leaseback arrangement affect the balance sheet?
(d) What protection do shareholders have when directors decide to 'window dress' the accounts?

unit 46

Social accounting

unitobjectives

To understand:
- the nature and purpose of social accounting;
- why some businesses produce social accounts;
- how social accounting is carried out.

What is social accounting?

SOCIAL ACCOUNTING is a means of reporting how a business affects society as a whole. It involves measuring and assessing the impact of a business not just on its shareholders but on its **stakeholders** in the wider community. These stakeholders include employees, customers, suppliers and the local population.

Current UK legislation does not provide a framework for producing social accounts. It is left to individual businesses to decide whether or not to report on social issues. Some companies include only the minimum amount of information as required by company law (see unit 38). Others produce detailed social accounts that describe the impact of the company on all of their stakeholders. The majority of companies fall somewhere in-between these extremes.

Why do companies produce social accounts?

There is a wide variety of motives that lie behind the social accounting policies of different companies.

Social responsibility In some cases, the owners and directors of companies take the view that they have a SOCIAL RESPONSIBILITY. This means that they take into account the interests of society in general rather than purely the interests of their shareholders. Therefore business decisions are not solely made on the basis of increasing profits. Other factors, such as the impact on employees and on the local community, are taken into account. The Co-operative Bank is an example of a company that adopts this policy. Its Partnership Report 2000 states that the Bank aims to conduct its business in 'a socially responsible manner'.

Some businesses take the view that their social responsibility involves a commitment to **sustainable development**. Although this term can be defined in many different ways, it broadly means that economic activity should take place in a way that does not harm future generations. John Laing plc, the property development company, is an example of a business that states its aim is to 'promote the principles of sustainable development'. To achieve this, one of its policies is to 'minimise waste through re-use, reduction and recycling'.

Image Businesses are increasingly concerned with their image. Being seen as a good 'corporate citizen' and developing a reputation of caring for its stakeholders can improve a company's image with the public. This can lead to higher sales and profits. However, a company with a poor image in the eyes of the public might face difficulties. An example of this occurred in the 1990s when Shell decided to dispose of the disused Brent Spar oil platform by sinking it in the North Atlantic. Environmental protesters objected to the pollution that this would cause and organised a consumer boycott of Shell products. Eventually, the company bowed to pressure and agreed to have the platform dismantled on land.

Workforce The loyalty and motivation of the workforce can be improved if companies make efforts to identify, improve and report on employees' needs. For example, Pilkington, the multinational glass producer, has a policy of promoting employee safety. In its 2001 Annual Review the company announced that it had improved its health and safety record. The 'lost time accident rate' (the number of accidents per 200,000 hours worked by employees) had fallen from 6.8 in 1997 to 1.91 in 2001. Including statistics in its annual report on the reduction in injuries, demonstrates the company's commitment to employee welfare.

Consumers Some companies try to increase sales and improve competitiveness by appealing to potential consumers' sense of social responsibility. For instance, the growth of **ethical consumerism** has led to companies launching new products and services. The Body Shop is an example of a company that buys Third World products at 'fair' prices rather than the lowest possible market price. The company includes details of its suppliers and trading policies in its annual report.

In the financial services sector, a number of institutions now offer 'ethical' investments. These are shareholdings in companies that are not engaged in producing, for example, armaments, nuclear power and tobacco. In order to satisfy investors that they are 'ethical', a growing number of companies set out their policies relating to ethical issues in their annual reports.

Legal requirements Although UK company law does not require companies to produce social accounts, it does require disclosure of certain issues that might be regarded as social. They include:
- any political or charitable gifts that exceed £200 per year;
- in the case of larger companies, information relating to the employment of people with disabilities.

How are social accounts produced?

When a company decides to produce social accounts, there are several stages that it must go through. They are shown in Figure 46.2.

QUESTION 1

John Laing plc, the property development company, reported in its Annual Review 2000 that it had achieved a substantial reduction in carbon dioxide emissions from its fleet of cars. Carbon dioxide is a 'greenhouse gas' and is widely blamed for global warming. The long-term impact of global warming is expected to be a general rise in sea levels and an increase in severe weather events. Figure 46.1 shows an extract from Laing's Annual Review.

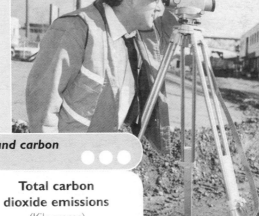

Figure 46.1 *Car fleet fuel consumption and carbon dioxide emissions*

Year	Total fuel consumption	Total carbon dioxide emissions
	(litres)	(Kilograms)
1999	9,534,712	22,404,846
2000	7,607,095	13,581,071

Source: adapted from John Laing plc *Annual Review and Summary Financial Statements 2000*.

(a) **Which stakeholders are likely to benefit from Laing's policy on car fuel consumption? In each case, briefly outline how they will benefit.**
(b) **Outline other possible motives for Laing's policy on sustainable development.**

Figure 46.2 *Stages of social accounting*

Identify stakeholders The first stage in social accounting is for a company to identify those groups and individuals who are affected by its activities. For example, the Co-operative Bank lists seven groups of stakeholders in its annual report.

- **Shareholders** These are the owners of the company.
- **Customers** These are the people who buy goods and services from the company.
- **Staff and their families** These are the paid employees of the company and their families.
- **Suppliers** These are the individuals and businesses that supply goods and services to the company.
- **Other organisations** The Co-operative Bank has a special responsibility to related organisations, such as co-operative supermarkets. In other businesses, there are often inter-dependent relationships between companies, for example between parent companies and their subsidiaries.
- **Local communities** Business activity has a wide ranging impact on the local community. The economic impact can include the employment of local people and the demand for local goods and services. The social impact includes charitable donations and sponsorship of sporting or artistic events. The environmental impact includes the visual impact that the business makes and possible pollution from its activities.
- **National and international society** To some extent, the impact on national and international society is similar to the local impact, though on a bigger scale. So for instance, the emissions of pollutants from burning fossil fuels can cause acid rain across national boundaries. Ethical issues such as the human rights and working conditions of employees in the Third World also become important in this context.

Different companies identify different stakeholders as being important. Some include 'the environment' in their list of stakeholders. The Co-operative Bank, for example, accepts that the environment is affected by its activities, but takes the view that it is the environmental impact on people that is the key issue.

It is sometimes argued that the local and national government are stakeholders in business because of the taxes they receive. For example, corporation tax on company profits and business rates paid to local councils are important sources of government revenue. An alternative view is that it is the local and national community that is the ultimate beneficiary from government spending, and the government is simply an intermediary.

Some stakeholders have more than one interest in a business. For example, employees are often members of the local community and might also be shareholders. This can lead to conflicts of interest. For example, suppose a cement company wishes to open a new plant. Some people might welcome the new plant if they are shareholders or if they are seeking employment. However, if they fear that the plant will pollute the local environment, they might object.

Select indicators This is the second stage in social accounting. In order to assess objectively the effect that a business has on its stakeholders, some means must be found of measuring the impact. For shareholders, this is relatively easy because traditional measures of company performance can be used. For example, the level of dividends per share gives a good indication of how well a company is meeting the needs of its shareholders. For other stakeholders, the issue is more complex because it is not always clear what their needs are. The Co-operative Bank's solution to this difficulty is to ask its stakeholders' opinions. Where this is not practical, as in the case of 'national and international society', the Bank asks for the opinion of experts and interested pressure groups.

For indicators to be of use, they must be measurable. So, for example, rather than a vague statement such as 'employee safety' as an indicator, it is more useful to have something specific, such as 'number of industrial injuries per 1,000 employees'. By quantifying the data, it makes it easier to judge performance.

Measure and report performance Once indicators have been selected, the next stage in social accounting is for the business to gather relevant information. This can be a costly and time consuming process and the more indicators that are chosen, the more expensive it becomes. Gathering information from within a company is generally easier than gathering information from outside. It is for this reason that more companies report on industrial injuries than on customer satisfaction, for example.

The Co-operative Bank goes much further than most UK businesses in its social accounting policies. Not only does it select indicators against which its performance can be measured, it also sets targets for each indicator. So for example, in its 2000 Annual Report, the Bank set 66 targets which it hoped to achieve. These targets ranged from 'achieving a 70% plus satisfaction rating from its staff regarding their salaries', to the aim of 'increasing paper recycling by 5%'. A selection of the indicators used by the Co-operative Bank is given in Figure 46.3.

Figure 46.3 *Selected indicators used in the social accounts of the Co-operative Bank*

Stakeholder	Indicator
Shareholders	Net profit before taxation.
	Return on equity.
Customers	Customer satisfaction (as measured by opinion surveys).
	Number of branches.
Staff	Staff satisfaction with salary package (as measured by opinion surveys).
	Job security (as measured by opinion surveys).
Suppliers	Supplier satisfaction (as measured by opinion surveys).
	Prompt payment of bills.
Co-operative movement	Installation of cash machines in co-operative supermarkets.

In order to meet the needs of its staff, the local community and national and international society, the Bank uses ethical and ecological indicators.

Ethical	Screen suppliers for compliance with ethical codes of conduct.
	Equal employment opportunities for staff.
	Health and safety measures for staff.
	Support charities.
Ecological	Emissions to air, water and land.
	Usage of public transport by employees.
	Energy efficiency.
	Recycling of paper and other materials.

Figure 46.3 shows how the impact of the Co-operative Bank on its stakeholders is measured. So, for instance, the impact on staff is measured by opinion surveys that ask them how they feel about their wages and job security. The company also assesses its performance as an employer by monitoring equal opportunities and the health and safety of its staff.

The impact on suppliers is measured by opinion surveys that ask the suppliers whether they are satisfied with the treatment they receive from the Bank. The time taken to pay suppliers is also monitored. In order to meet its wider, ethical aims, the Bank checks with suppliers that they are conforming to agreed ethical codes of conduct. So, for instance, furniture suppliers might be asked to give an assurance that only timber from sustainably managed forests is used.

Social audit Some companies arrange for a SOCIAL AUDIT of their accounts. For example, the Co-operative Bank assesses how many of its social targets from the previous year it has achieved and this data is then checked or audited by an independent social accounting consultancy. The process is similar to the audit that takes place with traditional accounts. It acts as a safeguard against misleading information and serves to protect the interests of stakeholders.

summary questions

1. State three reasons why a business might wish to demonstrate social responsibility.
2. State two legal requirements for disclosures in published accounts relating to social responsibility.
3. What is meant by an 'ethical investment'?
4. How might a business demonstrate a commitment to sustainable development?
5. How might a business demonstrate social responsibility to its employees?
6. Which stakeholders have a mainly financial interest in a business?
7. Why might stakeholders have conflicting interests?
8. How might a business gather information for its social accounts?
9. What criteria might be used when a company chooses which indicators to use?
10. Explain the difference between social accounting and a social audit.

UNIT ASSESSMENT QUESTION 1

Tate & Lyle is a multinational company that produces sugar and other foodstuffs. In its 2001 Annual Report, Tate & Lyle includes a Social Responsibility Review in which the company states 'our key objective is to create long-term value for our shareholders. However, in addition to commercial results, there are other criteria by which the company's performance should be judged. The Social Responsibility Review will concentrate on three important areas: our people, the effects of our operations on the environment and the communities where we operate'.

Figure 46.4 *Extracts from Tate & Lyle's Social Responsibility Review*

People
For calendar year 2000, the company's safety record improved significantly. Compared with 1999, the company improved the safety index by 35%. (The safety index combines the injury statistics for a plant, creating a single number that can be compared across the company.)

Environment
The company has committed itself to reduce energy consumption, per unit manufactured, by 3% per annum.

Community
In the 12 months to March 2001, total worldwide charitable donations amounted to £1.06m. The target for these allocations remains 50% for Education and Youth, 25% for Civic and Environment, 15% for Health and Welfare and 10% for Culture and Arts.

(a) **Which groups of stakeholders will be directly affected by the policies that Tate & Lyle outlines in the extracts from its Social Responsibility Review? Explain how each group will be affected.**
(b) **Explain how other groups of stakeholders might be affected by Tate & Lyle's operations.**

UNIT ASSESSMENT   QUESTION 2

The House of Fraser is a company that owns department stores throughout Great Britain. Its stores operate under different names but includes Dickins & Jones in London, Kendals in Manchester and Howells in Cardiff. In the House of Fraser Annual Report and Accounts 1999/2000, the company announced the opening of new stores in Reading and in the Bluewater shopping mall in Kent, the £14m redevelopment of its Guildford store and the £12m redevelopment of its Oxford Street store.

The Report and Accounts also included a five year summary of financial results. An extract is shown below.

Key performance measures	1999/2000	1995/1996
Gross profit margin before exceptionals	33.7%	31.1%
Earnings per share before exceptionals	5.7p	5.0p
Dividends per share	5.5p	5.5p
Gearing	4%	36.4%

spring
summer
autumn
winter

House of Fraser annual report
and accounts 1999/00

BRITAIN'S
LEADING
RETAILER OF
DESIGNER
BRANDS

HOUSE OF FRASER

(a) **Which group of stakeholders will be most interested in the key performance measures outlined above? Explain your answer.**

(b) **Suppose that the House of Fraser decided to open a new department store in a city where it did not already operate. List the groups of people and organisations that would be affected and explain how they would be affected.**

(c) **Choose three groups of stakeholders (other than shareholders) and outline how the House of Fraser might produce social accounts for each group.**

key terms

Social accounting - gathering information and reporting how a business affects society as a whole. It involves measuring the impact of a business not just on its shareholders but on its stakeholders in the wider community.

Social audit - a review and verification of social accounts by an independent body.

Social responsibility - a commitment to society in general rather than purely to the shareholders.

Information technology and accounting

unit**objectives**

To understand:
- management information systems;
- IT applications in accounting;
- the advantages and disadvantages of using computers in accounting.

Management Information Systems

MANAGEMENT INFORMATION SYSTEMS (MIS) convert data from internal or external sources into information that is useful for managers. Many businesses have a computerised MIS. Others, however, use a manual, paper-based system. Figure 47.1 shows how a MIS operates.

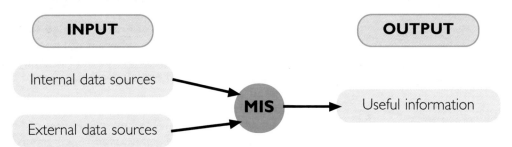

Figure 47.1 *Management Information System*

- **Internal sources** These sources of data are generated from within a business. For example, a manufacturer might collect weekly timesheets from its employees. The data on the timesheets could include the number of hours worked and the jobs or tasks that have been completed. Another internal data source is a sales invoice. This contains the name and address of a customer and the quantity and value of sales.
- **External sources** These sources of data come from outside the business. For example, invoices from suppliers contain details of purchases. Bank statements contain data that relates to the business's cash flow.
- **Output** The information that is provided by a MIS is used by managers to make decisions and improve the running of the business. For example, a business might have hundreds of customers, some of which need to be 'chased' for payment. A MIS can be used to identify customers who have outstanding debts, for example more than 90 days. The credit control manager can be provided with the names and telephone numbers of these debtors and so can direct the department's efforts into recovering these debts. Other examples of useful information generated by a MIS include monthly sales totals, weekly production totals and end-of-year stock totals.

The data collected by a MIS has to be processed for it to be useful. The bigger and more complex the business organisation, the greater the need for a MIS. Each day in a large business, masses of raw data must be recorded, sorted, classified, summarised and stored.

Data is usually stored in files. Quite often, the data contained on one source document has to be put into more than one file. For example, the data contained on a sales invoice might be recorded in the sales ledger, the debtors list, the sales day book, the VAT account and the stock register. A computerised MIS has the advantage that these tasks will be performed automatically once the initial data is input.

What makes an effective Management Information System?

The essential requirements of an effective MIS include the following.

- **Speed** It is important that information is processed quickly so that managers can respond to events.
- **Up-to-date** Managers need information that is up-to-date. For example, if a customer wishes to place a large order, it would be useful for the sales manager to have an instant print-out of stock levels.
- **Accuracy** For information to be useful, it must be accurate. Inaccurate information might lead to managers making decisions that can harm the business. For example, suppose a production manager is informed that stocks of raw materials are higher than is actually the case. If the business then accepts an order that it cannot fulfil, the reputation of the business will be damaged.
- **Clarity** Information must be communicated in a format that is clear, appropriate, easy to understand and concise. This allows managers to focus on the key issues and reduces the danger of mistakes or misinterpretation.
- **Relevance** An effective MIS provides information that is relevant to the user. For example, the credit control manager needs information that relates to debtors. The production manager needs different information, for example relating to stocks of components and sales forecasts.
- **Reliable** For a MIS to be useful it must not 'crash' or break-down. If the system is unreliable, it can damage a business. Suppose, for example, that cash flow information became unavailable at a time when the business was negotiating a bank loan. The consequence might be a delay to the loan and a shortage of cash.
- **Security** Some information contained in a MIS is sensitive and is restricted to particular managers on a 'need-to-know' basis. For example, it is usual to restrict access to wage details to avoid embarrassment or disputes. Only senior managers and directors are likely to be allowed access to the most sensitive information, such as current levels of profitability.

General applications of IT to accounting

Some IT applications that are in general use are also useful in accounting.

Word processing Documents such as letters, reports and memos are often produced by accounting personnel. Using a computer for wordprocessing has a number of advantages:

- presentation can be of a high quality;
- text documents can be drafted and 'polished' efficiently, for example by cutting and pasting and by using a spell-checker;
- standard formats can be used which save time and build up a corporate image;
- graphs and tables can easily be incorporated into text from spreadsheets or databases.

Databases A database is an electronic filing system. It stores information in a format that can be sorted, searched and manipulated. In accounting, databases are used in applications such as stock control where, for example, the quantity and value of different components can be quickly updated.

Spreadsheets This application is used in accounting to produce tables, graphs and charts. Information is input into rows and columns of 'cells'. It can then be used to perform arithmetic operations. For example, a column of weekly sales figures can be totalled to give an annual total, or calculated as a percentage of the previous year's figures. This information can then be used to produce a graph. Spreadsheets are particularly useful in 'what-if' calculations. For example, a cash flow 'model' can be set up on a spreadsheet to show the effect of various possibilities. For instance, the impact on a business's cash flow of, say, a 10% fall in sales receipts or a 5% rise in expenses can be illustrated very quickly.

Specialist accounting applications

A wide range of specialist accounting programmes has been developed. Many of these are integrated so that the different functions are linked. For instance, if a business enters details from a purchase invoice into the system, both the individual supplier account in the purchases ledger and the purchases account in the nominal ledger will be automatically updated. Then, when payment is made, the supplier account, the purchases account and the bank account will all be updated.

In financial accounting, the most widely used accounting applications include:
- invoicing;
- sales ledger, with customer accounts;
- purchases ledger, with supplier accounts;
- nominal ledger, with sales, purchases, expenses and bank accounts;
- stock records;
- payroll records;
- trading and profit and loss account;
- balance sheet.

In management and cost accounting, the most widely used accounting applications include:
- budgeting/forecasting;
- costing;
- estimating special orders;
- capital investment appraisal;
- credit control.

To illustrate how an integrated computer system might operate, consider the following example. Suppose a manufacturing company receives a sales order from a customer. The stages in processing the order are shown in Figure 47.2.

Figure 47.2 *Stages in processing an order using an integrated computer system*

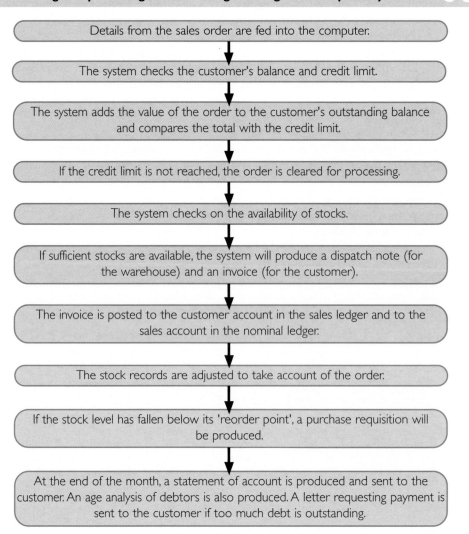

Details from the sales order are fed into the computer.

↓

The system checks the customer's balance and credit limit.

↓

The system adds the value of the order to the customer's outstanding balance and compares the total with the credit limit.

↓

If the credit limit is not reached, the order is cleared for processing.

↓

The system checks on the availability of stocks.

↓

If sufficient stocks are available, the system will produce a dispatch note (for the warehouse) and an invoice (for the customer).

↓

The invoice is posted to the customer account in the sales ledger and to the sales account in the nominal ledger.

↓

The stock records are adjusted to take account of the order.

↓

If the stock level has fallen below its 'reorder point', a purchase requisition will be produced.

↓

At the end of the month, a statement of account is produced and sent to the customer. An age analysis of debtors is also produced. A letter requesting payment is sent to the customer if too much debt is outstanding.

Advantages of computerised systems

Computerised accounting systems have many advantages.

- **Speed** Transactions can be processed much more quickly in computerised systems than in manual systems.
- **Capacity** Some businesses conduct millions of transactions each year. If records of these transactions were stored in manual systems, a huge amount of resources would be required. In addition, access to information that is stored in a computer is very easy. From the millions of transactions that might be recorded, an operator can instantly call up details of one single transaction.
- **Efficiency** Because large volumes of data can be processed quickly, computer systems require a smaller workforce than manual systems. Therefore the cost of collecting and recording transactions can be reduced.
- **Data handling** By using computers, information can be input and accessed from different locations around the country or even the world. For example, a supermarket chain might have several hundred branches in the UK, each with twenty or more checkouts. The sales information from all of these sources is transferred to one central processing unit where it is sorted and stored in the appropriate accounts. Information from every store can be retrieved and monitored from head office.
- **User friendly** The design of accounting programmes means that staff do not need a detailed knowledge of bookkeeping and accounts to be able to input and retrieve data. Consequently, training costs could be lower and a business might be able to employ non-specialist staff in the accounts department to keep labour costs down.
- **Accuracy** Computerised systems are more accurate than manual systems when processing data. Partly this is because computers do not become distracted or tired when performing large numbers of routine operations.
- **Security** By using a system of passwords, it is possible to restrict access to computerised systems. This prevents the unauthorised use of sensitive information.

Disadvantages of computerised systems

The widespread use of computerised accounting systems suggest that the benefits outweigh the drawbacks. Nevertheless, there are certain disadvantages.

- **Cost** The cost of purchasing and then upgrading computer hardware and software can be expensive. Staff training costs can also be high. It is sometimes necessary for a business to employ specialist IT staff to monitor and maintain the system. This adds to the cost.
- **Technical problems** There is a wide range of computer systems on sale and it is not always easy for a business to choose the most appropriate package. If an incorrect choice is made, the mistake can be costly. Problems often arise when a new computer system is installed. It might not run smoothly because of 'bugs' in the system. Other difficulties arise if a 'virus' is downloaded from the internet or via an email, or if inexperienced staff cause the system to crash. When this occurs, it can cause severe problems and delays to staff, customers and suppliers.
- **Industrial relations** The use of computerised systems might lead to industrial relation problems. If staff regard new technology as a threat to their jobs or status, they might not co-operate with management when systems are installed. This can result in delays and friction between managers and employees.
- **Security** Although security can be increased by the use of passwords, employees or outsiders might still be able to 'hack' into the system. This unauthorised access might be used by a disgruntled employee to sabotage the business, or by a competitor who hopes to gain an advantage.
- **Operator error** Computer systems are only effective if data is correctly input. If inaccurate data is entered, the reports that are generated will also be inaccurate, misleading and of little use. This problem is sometimes described as 'GIGO', ie garbage in, garbage out.

key terms

Management Information System (MIS) - a system that converts data from internal or external sources into information that is useful for managers.

summary questions

1. What makes an effective Management Information System?
2. State two internal sources of data for a MIS.
3. State two external sources of data for a MIS.
4. In what ways are manual bookkeeping systems different from computerised systems?
5. Why is a detailed knowledge of computing unnecessary when operating a computerised bookkeeping system?
6. Computerised bookkeeping systems are usually integrated. What does this mean?
7. State two costs of implementing a computerised bookkeeping system.
8. State two advantages of spreadsheets to accountants?
9. Explain how computerised accounting systems might reduce business costs.
10. Why might staff resist the introduction of a computerised accounting system?

UNIT ASSESSMENT QUESTION 1

Phoenix Chemicals is a large multinational company with operations in seven different countries. The company produces a range of chemicals used in the production of synthetic materials. It has thousands of customers all over the world and employs 63,000 staff. Its bookkeeping and accounting system is completely computerised and has recently been upgraded at a cost of £4.5 million. As a result of the upgrade, it was necessary to retrain all 2,200 staff employed in the accounts departments around the world. Part of the training involved a virus awareness programme.

(a) In what ways does Phoenix Chemicals highlight the drawbacks of computerised accounting systems?
(b) What security systems might Phoenix Chemicals need in its computerised accounting system?
(c) Phoenix Chemicals produces final accounts every month. The accounts show a breakdown of performance in each of the seven countries. To what extent will the computerised accounting system aid this reporting pattern?

UNIT ASSESSMENT QUESTION 2

Mary Lam runs Mailwear Ltd, a mail order business selling women's fashion wear. In recent years, the business has expanded and the number of staff employed has grown from 9 to 40. Every week, the business gains around 20 new customers. Once customers have made a purchase of over £50, they are offered credit facilities. They can buy up to £300 of goods on 90 days credit.

At the moment Mary, operates a manual bookkeeping system and pays a part-time bookkeeper to record all transactions. Her accounts are produced by a local accountant who charges £2,500 per year. She also pays a local business £100 a week for administering the company payroll. Her accountant has recommended that she invests £5,000 in a computerised bookkeeping and accounting system. The accountant suggests that this will reduce long term costs, improve financial control and improve access to financial information.

(a) Write a report, using an appropriate format, explaining the advantages and disadvantages to Mailwear of investing in a computerised bookkeeping system.

Costs and revenue

unit**objectives**

To understand:
- the nature of cost accounting;
- the different definitions of cost;
- how revenue is calculated.

Cost accounting

Cost accountants collect and report on information relating to the production costs and sales revenue of a business. This information is mainly intended for internal use within the business. Managers use the information to plan and control production. For example, information on costs and revenue might be used to:

- set the selling price of a new product or service;
- assess the profitability of a department;
- calculate the value of stocks held in a warehouse;
- compare actual production costs with planned production costs.

Businesses develop systems of cost accounting to meet their own needs. There are no legal requirements that specify how information is to be gathered or used, unlike financial accounting, which is primarily concerned with reporting the results and financial position of a business. Strict guidelines are laid down in the way that **financial accountants** prepare and present final accounts. This is because the information is intended for people who are not concerned with the day-to-day running of the business, such as shareholders or the Inland Revenue.

Costs of production

COSTS are the expenses that a business incurs when producing and supplying products and services to customers. Examples of costs for a florist might include wages paid to part-time staff, purchases of flowers for resale, rent for shop premises, business rates paid to the local council and electricity for heating and lighting.

Costs, such as those described, can be classified in a variety of ways depending to how the information is going to be used. One approach, which is taken by economists, is to consider costs as OPPORTUNITY COSTS. For example, a business might wish to buy a van, a computer system and a new range of stock, but only has enough money to buy one of these. The business might decide that its order of preference is:

1. computer system;
2. new range of stock;
3. van.

According to this order of preference, the business would buy the computer system. The opportunity cost is the benefit lost from not purchasing the next best alternative, which in this case is the new range of stock.

Although opportunity costs are important in decision making, accountants are more generally concerned with the monetary cost of resources used by a business. It is these costs which are classified and described in this unit.

For cost accounting purposes, business organisations can be divided into **cost centres**. A cost centre acts as a 'collecting point' for costs before they are analysed further. For instance, a business might have departmental cost centres which include all the costs of a particular department, such as sales or production. Other examples of cost centres might be all the costs associated with a machine or group of machines, or a project such as the installation of a new computer system. The product or service being produced is called a **cost unit**. For example, the cost unit in a restaurant could be a meal served. In a steel mill it could be a tonne of steel produced and in a hospital it could be an operation performed.

Direct and indirect costs

In cost accounting, a distinction is often made between the DIRECT COSTS and INDIRECT COSTS of production.

Direct costs These are business costs that can be attributed in full to a product, service or cost centre. Direct costs can be subdivided into:

- **direct materials costs** such as components or raw materials;
- **direct labour costs** such as wages paid to workers who make a product or provide a service;
- **direct expenses** which are costs incurred in producing a specific good or service, apart from direct materials and direct labour. They might include the costs of hiring machinery, maintenance costs or the cost of specific technical designs or drawings.

The total cost of direct materials, direct labour and direct expenses is known as the PRIME COST.

Indirect costs or OVERHEADS These are costs that cannot be attributed directly and in full to a particular product, service or cost centre. Indirect costs can be subdivided into:

- **production overheads** such as the rent, rates and insurance on a factory, the depreciation, fuel and maintenance of production machinery, the wages of non-productive workers in the production department, such as supervisors, and the cost of any materials that cannot be traced in the finished product, such as lubricating oil for a machine;
- **administration overheads** such as the salaries of office staff, the office rent, rates and other running costs, telephone and bank charges, and depreciation on office equipment. Sometimes included in this category are **financial overheads** such as the interest paid on a bank loan;
- **selling overheads** such as advertising and promotion costs, salaries and commission of sales staff;
- **distribution overheads** such as transport costs, handling and packaging charges and the running costs of delivery vehicles.

The total of all direct and indirect costs is known as TOTAL COST. The term **analysis of total cost** is sometimes used to describe the process of classifying a business's costs of production into the categories listed above.

QUESTION 1

From the following information relating to a manufacturing company, calculate the annual:
(a) prime cost;
(b) total indirect cost;
(c) total cost.

	£
Raw materials	
Purchases of stock during the year	53,000
Wages and salaries	
Production staff	110,000
Administration staff	56,000
Production overheads	16,000
Administration expenses other than wages	42,000
Selling and distribution overheads	34,000

Fixed and variable costs

Cost accountants are sometimes asked to provide information on how costs will vary at different levels of output. **Cost behaviour** is the term used to describe these changes in costs. When analysing cost behaviour, it is necessary to calculate the FIXED COSTS and VARIABLE COSTS of production.

Fixed costs These are costs that stay the same when a business changes the level of output. Examples include rent, business rates, interest payments and depreciation. The basic pay and salaries paid to many full-time employees are also fixed. These costs remain unchanged whether a business produces nothing or is working at full capacity. For example, business rates must be paid to the local council even if the factory is closed for a holiday period.

Figure 48.1 is a graphical illustration of the fixed costs for a small manufacturer. The line on the graph is horizontal. It shows that fixed costs are £40,000 at all levels of output between 0 and 80,000 units.

Figure 48.1 *Fixed costs*

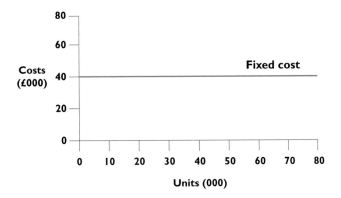

One common misconception regarding fixed costs is that they do not change at all. Fixed costs **can** vary due to changes in circumstances other than changes in output. For example, the interest payment on an overdraft will rise if the rate of interest in the economy is increased. Similarly, the rent paid for business premises might rise at a time of a rent review.

Fixed costs might also increase if a business approaches full capacity. For example, if all the machines in a manufacturing company are fully utilised, the company must buy a new machine to increase output. This has the effect of raising fixed costs because, for example, the depreciation charge increases and new employees are required. Such an increase in fixed costs is called a STEP COST, or stepped cost. Another example might occur if a business needs to increase its office space. The increase in rent paid for the new accommodation is a step cost. Figure 48.2 illustrates several 'steps' in the fixed costs of a manufacturer.

Figure 48.2 *Stepped fixed costs*

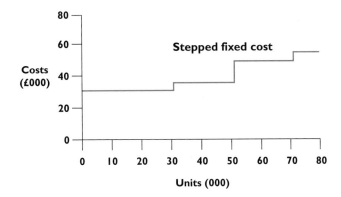

QUESTION 2

Eric Harding Ltd is a medium sized clothes manufacturer in Manchester. The business has the capacity to produce up to 100,000 garments per month. Production workers are paid a basic wage and then receive a 'piece rate' of £1 per garment produced. The table below shows the costs which the company incurred in one month.

Basic pay and salaries	£40,000
Piecework pay	£60,000
Factory rent	£10,000
Bank interest	£3,000
Materials	£45,000
Other fixed overheads	£2,000
Other non-fixed costs	£60,000

(a) **Using the information provided, show the firm's monthly fixed costs on a graph.**
(b) **What would the company's monthly fixed costs be at (i) an output of 90,000;**
    (ii) an output of zero?
(c) **What might happen to fixed costs if it was decided to raise output beyond 100,000 units per month? Explain your answer.**

Variable costs These are costs that vary directly with changes in the level of output. For example, a haulage company will pay more in fuel costs the greater the number of loads it carries. A manufacturer will need more raw materials, components and packaging the more it produces. Bonus payments to employees, commission and overtime are also generally classed as variable costs. If a business does not produce any output, its variable costs are zero. Figure 48.3 shows the variable costs for a business over a range of output from zero to 80,000 units. The straight line indicates that the variable cost per unit of output is constant over this range of output.

Figure 48.3 *Variable costs*

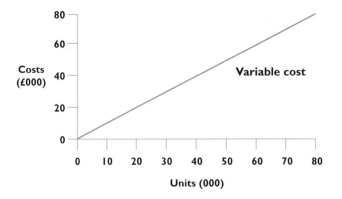

Semi-variable costs Some business costs do not fit neatly into the categories of either fixed or variable because they combine elements of both. Such costs are said to be SEMI-VARIABLE. An example is the cost of operating a delivery van. Operating costs such as the road fund licence, insurance and annual MOT are fixed. They do not vary according to how many miles the van is driven. However, other operating costs, such as fuel, oil and maintenance, will rise if the van is used more frequently. They are therefore variable costs. Another example is the cost of telephones for a business. This cost usually consists of a fixed 'standing charge', plus an extra charge which varies according to the number of calls made.

Total costs and unit costs When fixed and variable costs are added together, they show the TOTAL COSTS of a business. This is shown in Figure 48.4. It illustrates the costs of a component manufacturer, Collins Engineering. Fixed costs are £40,000 at every level of output and variable costs are £1 per unit of output. When output is zero, fixed costs are £40,000 and variable costs are zero. Therefore total costs are £40,000. When output is 80,000 units, total costs are £120,000. This is made up of £40,000 of fixed costs and £80,000 of variable costs. The information in Figure 48.4 is presented as a graph in Figure 48.5.

Figure 48.4 *Costs for Collins Engineering*

Output (units)	Fixed cost £	Variable cost £	Total cost £
0	40,000	0	40,000
10,000	40,000	10,000	50,000
20,000	40,000	20,000	60,000
30,000	40,000	30,000	70,000
40,000	40,000	40,000	80,000
50,000	40,000	50,000	90,000
60,000	40,000	60,000	100,000
70,000	40,000	70,000	110,000
80,000	40,000	80,000	120,000

Figure 48.5 *Graph of Collins Engineering costs*

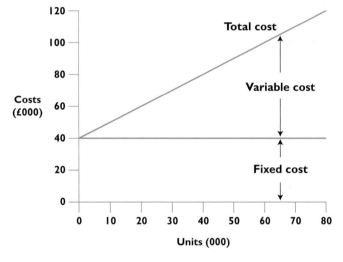

Using the information in Figure 48.4, it is possible to calculate the UNIT COST, or average cost, of each item produced. This is equal to the total cost of production divided by the number of units produced. So, for example, for Collins Engineering, the unit cost when 50,000 units are produced is:

$$\text{Unit cost} = \frac{\text{Total cost}}{\text{Output}} = \frac{£90,000}{50,000} = £1.80$$

QUESTION 3

Hargreaves & Son make a variety of display cabinets for jewellers. The cabinets are hand made in a workshop in Crewe. The variable cost for one of their best selling cabinets is £100 per cabinet. Figure 48.6. shows additional cost information for this business, however, the cost table is incomplete.

(a) Give two examples of variable costs that Hargreaves & Son is likely to incur.
(b) Complete the cost table in Figure 48.6.
(c) What is the unit cost if 20 cabinets are produced?
(d) If fixed costs were to increase by £400, what effect would this have on total costs over the range of output shown in the table?
(e) With reference to Hargreaves & Son, suggest an example of a semi-variable cost. Explain why it is a semi-variable cost.

Figure 48.6 *Cost information for Hargreaves & Son*

Output (units)	Fixed cost £	Variable cost £	Total cost £
0	5,000		
5			
10			
15			
20			
25			
30			
35			
40			

The relationship between fixed, variable, direct and indirect costs

It is sometimes mistakenly believed that fixed costs are the same as indirect costs and that variable costs are the same as direct costs. This is not the case. Although there is a tendency for fixed costs to be indirect costs, there are many exceptions. Likewise, although many variable costs are direct costs, some are not. For example, the telephone costs of a sales department are variable indirect costs. These costs vary with the volume of sales but they are indirect because their cost cannot be traced to particular units of output. Another example relates to labour costs. In many businesses, wages are an important element of direct costs, yet often they are fixed, at least in the short term.

The relationship between the different costs is illustrated in Figure 48.7. It shows that total costs are made up of either fixed costs plus variable costs or direct costs plus indirect costs. Which classification is used depends on the purpose of the analysis. The classification into fixed or variable relates to cost behaviour, ie how costs change in relation to output. The classification into direct and indirect relates to how costs can be traced directly or otherwise to particular units of production.

Figure 48.7 *The relationship between costs*

	Direct costs	Indirect costs (overheads)
Fixed costs		
Variable costs	TOTAL COSTS	

Marginal cost

Marginal cost is the cost of increasing output by a single unit. The calculation of marginal cost is the basis of a system of pricing known as marginal cost pricing (see unit 51). In effect, the marginal cost of a unit of a product or service is the variable cost of producing that unit. Fixed costs are excluded because, by definition, they do not change when output rises. Marginal cost can be calculated by using the following equation.

$$\text{Marginal cost} = \frac{\text{change in total cost}}{\text{change in output}}$$

For example, if the total cost for Collins Engineering of producing 60,000 components is £100,000 and the total cost of producing 60,001 components is £100,001, then the marginal cost of producing the last unit is:

$$\text{Marginal cost} = \frac{£100,001 - £100,000}{60,001 - 60,000} = \frac{£1}{1} = £1$$

QUESTION 4

Lindsey Turner supplies local retailers, offices and factories with lunch time snacks. One of her popular lines is a beef sandwich. She makes 240 of these every week. The costs of producing beef sandwiches are listed below:

Fixed costs per week	£20
Bread	20p per sandwich
Beef	30p per sandwich
Other variable costs	20p per sandwich

(a) Calculate the total cost of making a week's supply of beef sandwiches.
(b) What is the marginal cost of a beef sandwich?

Controllable and uncontrollable costs

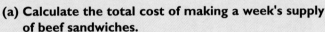

One of the main roles of cost accountants is to provide information to managers. Some costs will be identified as CONTROLLABLE, ie they can be influenced by a particular level of management. It is clearly important to supply this cost information to the relevant manager who is able to influence or control events. At some levels of management, certain costs are UNCONTROLLABLE and it is therefore not sensible to expect these managers to exert control over them. However, at a more senior management level, these costs might become controllable.

To illustrate the classification of costs into controllable and uncontrollable, consider the example of a retail chain of chemists. The basic pay rates of the chemist shops' staff are set nationally and are therefore out of the control of the individual shop managers. However, each shop's total pay bill is also affected by factors that are under the control of the shop managers. These factors include the number of staff employed, overtime payments, rates of sickness and absenteeism, and the proportion of the staff on different grades. Each shop manager is therefore in a position to influence part of the overall wage cost. So, it is good management practice for the managers to be provided with a breakdown of the wage costs that highlights the proportion that is controllable at the shop level.

Total revenue

The amount of money that a business receives from selling its products or supplying its services is its TOTAL REVENUE. Total revenue is calculated by multiplying the number of units sold by the price of each unit:

Total revenue = quantity sold x price

In the case of Collins Engineering described earlier, if 60,000 components were produced and sold to customers for £2 each, the total revenue would be:

Total revenue = 60,000 x £2.00 = £120,000

Figure 48.8 shows the total revenue for Collins Engineering over a range of output from zero to 60,000 units. Clearly, as the business sells more output, total revenue rises.

Figure 48.8 *Total revenue for Collins Engineering when price is £2 per component*

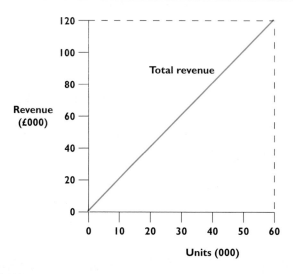

key terms

Controllable costs - costs identified as being controllable by a particular level of management.
Costs - the expenses incurred by a business when making or supplying goods and services.
Direct costs - costs that can be associated with the making of a particular product or linked to a particular process, department or cost centre.
Fixed costs - costs that do not change in the short term when the level of output is changed.
Indirect costs - costs that cannot be attributed to particular products, processes or cost centres.
Opportunity cost - the benefit lost of the next best option foregone when making a choice between different alternatives.
Overhead - another term for an indirect cost.
Prime cost - the total of all direct costs.
Semi-variable costs (or mixed costs) - costs that have both a fixed and a variable element.
Stepped fixed costs - an increase in fixed costs when a business, for example, buys a new machine or rents new premises. It often occurs when a business reaches full capacity.
Total costs - the total costs of production.
Total revenue - the amount of money a business receives from selling its output found by multiplying price by quantity.
Unit cost (or average cost) - the average cost of producing one unit of output.
Variable costs - costs that vary in proportion to the level of output.

summary questions

1. How is opportunity cost different from the costs which accountants generally use?
2. State three ways in which costs can be classified.
3. Using a hospital as an example, state two direct and two indirect costs.
4. What is the difference between prime cost and total cost?
5. Explain why business rates are a fixed cost.
6. Explain what will happen to variable costs if output is cut by 40%.
7. Give two examples of semi-variable costs.
8. Explain why fixed costs do not form part of marginal cost.
9. Why might a manager be more interested in controllable costs than uncontrollable costs.
10. If a firm sells 4 million units for a total revenue of £20 million, what price is being charged?

UNIT ASSESSMENT   QUESTION 1

Lorraine Day is a taxi driver in Gillingham. In an average week she travels 1,000 miles transporting customers. Lorraine leases a car for £150 a week and estimates that her variable costs are 50p per mile. Details of fixed costs are given in Figure 48 9. (Assume a 52 week year.)

Figure 48.9 *Fixed costs for Lorraine Day's taxi business*

Car (leasing charges)	£150 per week
Insurance	£400 per year
Licences (road fund and taxi)	£1,700 per year
Other fixed costs	£14,000 per year

(a) **Give two possible examples of variable costs for Lorraine's business.**
(b) **Calculate the annual (i) fixed costs; (ii) variable costs; (iii) total costs for Lorraine's business.**
(c) **What is the marginal cost for Lorraine of carrying a passenger one mile?**
(d) **Calculate the annual total revenue if Lorraine charges customers £1.05 per mile.**
(e) **If Lorraine took a four week holiday in the winter, what effect would this have on total costs?**

UNIT ASSESSMENT QUESTION 2

Giles Engineering is a small engineering company that produces components for much larger engineers. The company leases a punching machine for £500 per week and a metal folding machine for £600 per week. In March 2001, the business received an order from a regular customer. This was for 1,000 components, reference X12, and 1,000 components, reference C33. The X12 is produced using the punching machine and it takes three weeks to make 1,000. The C33 is produced using the folding machine and it also takes 3 weeks to make 1,000. Details of other production costs for these components are given in Figure 48.10.

Figure 48.10 Production costs for Giles Engineering

Direct costs per unit (excluding leasing charge)	X12 £	C33 £
Labour	1.20	1.50
Materials	2.30	2.00
Other direct costs	1.00	1.50

Overheads	Weekly £
Rent	500.00
Rates	50.00
Other indirect costs	150.00

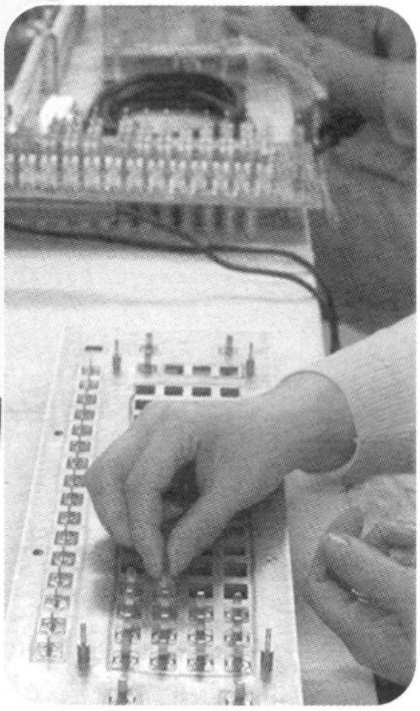

(a) With reference to Giles Engineering, explain the difference between direct and indirect costs.
(b) Calculate the total direct cost of making 1,000 X12s and 1,000 C33s.
(c) Calculate the total cost of meeting the order. Assume that nothing else is produced during the three week period of production.
(d) Explain why the leasing charges for the machines can be classified as both direct costs and fixed costs.

unit 49 Break-even analysis

unit objectives

To understand:
- the nature of break-even;
- how to calculate the break-even point;
- how to interpret and construct break-even charts;
- the advantages and limitations of break-even analysis.

What is meant by break-even?

The level of sales or output where total costs and total revenue are exactly the same is called the BREAK-EVEN POINT. For example, if a business produces 500 units at a total cost of £3,000, and sells them for £6 each, total revenue will also be £3,000 (£6 × 500). At this level of sales, the business is making neither a profit nor a loss, it is breaking even.

Break-even analysis is also known as **cost-volume-profit (CVP)** analysis. It has a number of applications and is used by some businesses to:
- calculate the level of sales and price needed to cover total costs;
- see how changes in sales affect profit.

How is the break-even point calculated?

There are two methods of calculating a business's break-even point. Both methods require the following information:
- the fixed cost of production (FC);
- the variable cost of production per unit (VC);
- the selling price per unit (SP).

In order to illustrate how the break-even point can be calculated using both methods, consider the example of Carl Wright, a market trader who makes and then sells teddy bears for £19 each. The variable cost of producing each bear is £14. This is also the **marginal cost** of producing one extra bear. It is made up of:
- **direct materials**, ie the cost of raw materials that are used in producing the bears;
- **direct labour**, ie the labour costs involved in making the bears;
- **other direct costs**, ie those costs other than materials and labour that vary directly with output. For example, in this case, Carl pays a royalty of 50p per bear to a charity whose logo he uses on the bears;
- **variable production overheads**, ie the indirect expenses such as electricity that vary with the number of bears produced.

Carl has to pay **fixed costs** of £200 a week for his sales pitch at an indoor market.

Using contribution CONTRIBUTION is the difference between the revenue earned from selling one unit of production (ie the selling price) and the variable cost of production per unit. It represents a contribution to the fixed costs of production. If contribution is greater than fixed cost, any excess contributes to profit.

In the case of Carl Wright's teddy bears, the contribution made by each bear is:

Contribution per unit = selling price (SP) - variable cost (VC)
= £19 - £14
= £5

Contribution is sometimes expressed as a percentage of the selling price, known as the **contribution margin**. In Carl Wright's business, the contribution margin is 26.3% (ie [£5÷£19] × 100).

Contribution can be used with the 'profit model' to calculate the break-even point. This shows how profit is derived from costs and revenue. To illustrate the model, consider the example of Carl Wright and suppose that he produces and sells 60 teddy bears in one week. At that level of sales, Figure 49.1 shows that the contribution per unit is £5 and the total contribution is £300 (60 units × £5). When the fixed cost of £200 is subtracted, there is a profit of £100 (total contribution of £300 - fixed cost of £200).

Figure 49.1 *The profit model*

	£
Selling price (SP)	19
Less variable cost (VC)	14
Equals contribution per unit	5
Multiplied by number of units	60
Equals total contribution	300
Less fixed cost	200
Equals profit	100

At what level of sales will Carl Wright's business break-even? It is the number of sales which result in profit being zero. This is 40, as shown in Figure 49.2. The selling price, variable cost and total cost are the same as in Figure 49.1.

Figure 49.2 *The profit model at break-even*

	Break-even (where profit =0)
	£
Selling price (SP)	19
Less variable cost (VC)	14
Equals contribution per unit	5
Multiplied by number of units	**40**
Equals total contribution	200
Less fixed cost	200
Equals profit	0

Figure 49.2 shows that the total contribution must equal the fixed cost when profit is zero. Therefore the break-even level of sales = 40 (200 ÷ 5). This can be expressed as a formula:

$$\text{Break-even point} = \frac{\text{Fixed costs (FC)}}{\text{Contribution per unit}}$$

So, in the case of Carl Wright's business:

$$\text{Break-even point} = \frac{£200}{£5}$$

$$= \quad 40 \text{ teddy bears}$$

Using total revenue and total cost equations Another way of calculating the break-even point is to use the equations for total revenue and total cost. In this example, the total cost and total revenue for Carl Wright's business are:

Total cost (TC) = Fixed cost (FC) + (Variable cost per unit (VC) × quantity sold (Q))
= £200 + £14Q

Total revenue (TR) = Price (P) × quantity sold (Q)
= £19Q

At the break-even point, the total revenue is equal to total cost (ie TR = TC). The break-even quantity (Q) is calculated as follows.

$$
\begin{aligned}
\text{Total revenue} &= \text{Total cost} \\
£19Q &= £200 + £14Q \\
£19Q - £14Q &= £200 \\
£5Q &= £200 \\
Q &= \frac{£200}{5} \\
Q &= 40 \text{ teddy bears}
\end{aligned}
$$

This answer confirms that the break-even point is the same as that calculated using the contribution and profit model method.

QUESTION 1

Norfolk Press specialises in publishing cookery books. A new book is being planned with a likely selling price of £24 per copy. The costs associated with the new publication are listed below.

Fixed costs (office overheads and editorial expenses)	£90,000
Variable costs per book:	
Direct materials:	£5.50
Direct labour:	£0.50
Other direct costs - royalties:	£1.50
Variable overheads - postage, packing and distribution:	£1.50

(a) **Calculate the contribution that each book makes.**
(b) **Calculate the number of books that Norfolk Press needs to sell in order to break-even (use the contribution and profit model method).**
(c) **Calculate the total contribution if Norfolk Press sells exactly its break-even figure.**
(d) **If Norfolk Press needed to reprint the book, the variable costs would remain the same. However, the fixed costs would fall to £60,000. If the selling price stayed the same, how many of the reprint must be sold to break-even? (Use the total revenue and total cost equation method.)**

Break-even charts

A BREAK-EVEN CHART is a graph on which sales revenue and costs of production are plotted. The point at which a business breaks even is where the total revenue line intersects the total cost line. Figure 49.3 shows the break-even chart for Carl Wright's business using the figures given previously. Sales and output are shown on the horizontal axis and revenue and costs are shown on the vertical axis.

- Total revenue is shown over a range of sales from zero to 70 teddy bears. For example, when Carl sells no bears, total revenue is zero. If 60 bears are sold, total revenue is £1,140 (ie price of £19 x sales of 60).
- Fixed costs of £200 are shown as a horizontal line. This illustrates the point that fixed costs are always £200, no matter how much output is sold.
- Total cost equals fixed costs plus variable costs. For example, if Carl sells 60 bears, total costs are £1,040 (ie fixed costs of £200 + variable cost of £840 [£14 x 60]).
- Variable costs are indicated by the vertical distance between the line of fixed cost and the line of total cost. For example, when sales are 60, the variable costs are £840 (£14 x 60).
- The break-even point for Carl Wright's business is where the line of total cost intersects the line of total revenue. This is when 40 bears have been sold. At this point total cost and total revenue are both £760.
- If sales exceed the break-even point, a profit is made. This is because total revenue is greater than total cost. For example, if 60 bears are sold, profit is £100, ie total revenue of £1,140 (60 x £19)

less total cost £1,040 (£200 + [60 x £14]).

- If sales fall below the break-even point of 40, the business makes a loss. This is because total costs are greater than total revenue. For example, if 30 bears are sold, the loss is £50, ie total revenue £570 (30 x £19) less total cost £620 (£200 + [30 x £14]).

Figure 49.3 *Break-even chart for Carl Wright's business*

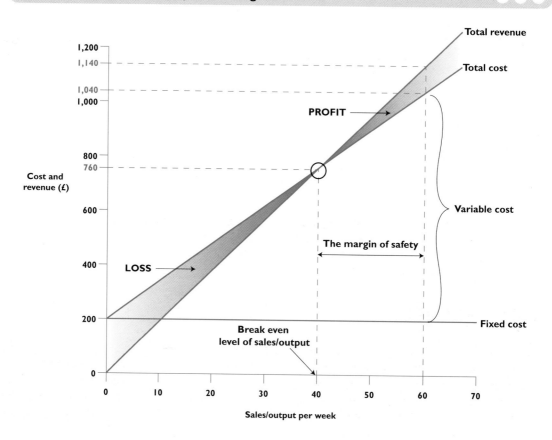

The margin of safety Figure 49.3 shows the MARGIN OF SAFETY if 60 bears are sold per week. This is the amount by which sales can fall before a loss is made. Stated another way, it is the range of sales over which a profit is made. It is the distance between the break-even level point of 40 and the weekly sales figure of 60. So, in this case the margin of safety is 20 bears.

Sometimes the margin of safety is expressed as a percentage of the current sales level. Using the previous figures, if weekly sales are 60 bears and the margin of safety is 20 bears, the margin of safety expressed as a percentage is:

$$\text{Margin of safety} \quad = \quad \frac{20}{60} \times 100 \quad = \quad 33.3\%$$

Profit-volume charts

The shaded areas in Figure 49.3 show the profit or loss that is made at different levels (or volumes) of sales. This information can be extracted from the break-even chart and presented on its own in a PROFIT-VOLUME CHART, as in Figure 49.4. The chart uses similar axes as the break-even chart except that the vertical axis has a negative section. The line of profit (and loss) is plotted against sales volume and the break-even point is where the line cuts the horizontal axis. Although the profit-volume chart does not contain any different information from the break-even chart, it does present it in a simpler fashion. It is therefore easier to see at a glance how much profit, or loss, is made at any given level of sales.

Figure 49.4 *Profit-volume chart for Carl Wright's business*

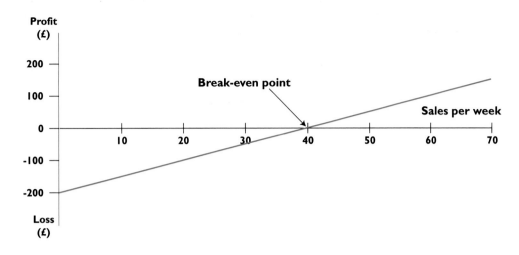

- The information required to plot the profit line is derived from Figure 49.3.
- When weekly sales are zero, a loss of £200 is made.
- Break-even occurs when weekly sales are 40 teddy bears.
- When sales are 60, profit is £100.

QUESTION 2

In January 2000, Ian Taylor began a small business supplying 5-a-side football sets. The sets consist of a football and two goals with nets. Ian advertises them in football magazines and sells them by mail order. The components are bought direct from manufacturers for a total of £25 per set. Fixed costs are £20,000 per year, with advertising making up more than half these costs. Ian sells the sets for £75 each and, in the first year, he sold 300. In the next year, Ian doubled sales to 600 sets. The break-even chart for Ian Taylor's business is shown in Figure 49.5.

(a) (i) How many sets must be sold to break-even? (ii) What was the size of the loss when 300 sets were sold? (iii) How much profit is made if 600 sets are sold? (iv) What is the variable cost of producing 600 sets? (v) What is the total contribution if 600 sets are sold?

(b) (i) What is the margin of safety if sales remain at 600 sets? (ii) What is the margin of safety expressed as a percentage of this sales level?

Figure 49.5 *Break-even chart for Ian Taylor's business*

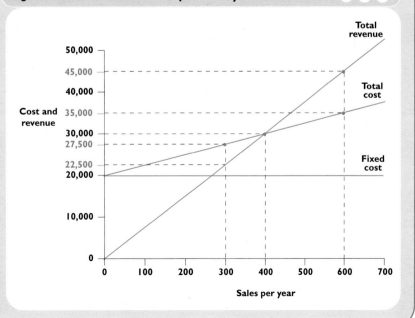

Constructing break-even charts

The break-even chart in Figure 49.3 is constructed by plotting the total cost and total revenue lines. Because both lines are straight, ie they are **linear functions**, it is only necessary to plot two points for each and then draw a straight line through the points. However, to avoid possible error when constructing a break-even chart, it is advisable to plot three points on each line. It is also advisable to use the break-even point as one of the points then to plot total cost and total revenue when sales are zero, and again at a sales level somewhere above break-even.

To illustrate how the points on a break-even chart can be plotted, consider again the information from Carl Wright's business. Remember that the break-even point was calculated as $Q = 40$ and TC and $TR = £760$. The total cost and total revenue were given by the following equations.

Total cost (TC) = Fixed costs (FC) + (Variable cost per unit (VC) × quantity sold (Q))
= £200 + £14Q

Total revenue (TR) = Price (P) × quantity sold (Q)
= £19Q

So, if sales are zero (ie $Q = 0$),

Total cost (TC) = £200 + £14Q
= £200

Total revenue (TR) = £19Q
= £0

If sales are 60 (ie $Q = 60$),

Total cost (TC) = £200 + £14Q
= £200 + (£14 × 60)
= £1,040

Total revenue (TR) = £19Q
= £19 × £60
= £1,140

If total cost and total revenue are plotted at the three sales levels (ie 0, 40 and 60), the result is a graph identical to the one shown in Figure 49.3. The costs and revenue figures that are used in the graph can also be presented in the form of a table (see Figure 49.6). The break-even point is the level of sales where total cost equals total revenue. The table confirms that, in this case, the break-even level of sales is 40 units.

Figure 49.6 *Costs and revenue at three different levels of sales*

Sales	Fixed cost	Variable cost (VC per unit = £14)	Total cost	Total revenue (price = £19)
(units)	£	£	£	£
0	200	0	200	0
40	200	560 (14 × 40)	760	760 (19 × 40)
60	200	840 (14 × 60)	1,040	1,140 (19 × 60)

QUESTION 3

Readymeals supplies cabin meals to a large airline. Demand for meals can fluctuate depending on how many passengers the airline is carrying in a particular week. The fixed costs incurred by Readymeals are £600 per week. The variable costs, mainly food and labour, are £2.00 per meal. The airline pays Readymeals £3.00 per meal.

(a) Show the equations for total cost (TC) and total revenue (TR).

(b) Calculate the number of meals that Readymeals needs to sell in order to break-even.

(c) Construct a break-even chart for Readymeals.

(d) Show the margin of safety if the current output is 1,000 meals per week.

(e) Construct a profit-volume chart for Readymeals.

(f) Reading from your chart, how much profit is made when 1,000 meals are sold?

Advantages of break-even analysis

Break-even analysis has a number of advantages.

Visual impact The break-even chart provides a visual means of analysing a business's financial position at different levels of output. Business decision makers can see at a glance the amount of profit or loss that will be made at different sales levels.

Risk assessment The margin of safety shown on a break-even chart provides businesses with an assessment of risk. It shows by how much sales can fall before a loss is made. It therefore gives an indication of the business's ability to withstand unfavourable trading conditions.

'What-if' considerations Break-even analysis can also be used to consider what would happen to profitability if, for instance, price or costs changed. Suppose, for example, that a business was considering raising its prices. By drawing a new total revenue line on the break-even chart, the amount of profit at each level of sales could easily be seen. Similarly, if, for example, it was known that fixed costs were going to rise, the effect on total cost and profits could be shown by plotting a new graph.

Limitations of break-even analysis

Break-even analysis has a number of limitations. In particular, it is sometimes criticised because certain of its assumptions are unrealistic.

Uncertain data The precise figures for total cost and total revenue are not likely to be known over the full range of sales. This is particularly true in the longer term. For example, changes in technology, raw material costs or market conditions might affect the total costs and total revenue.

Fixed and variable costs Break-even analysis assumes that costs can be divided into fixed and variable costs. This is not always the case. For example, fuel costs are generally 'semi-variable'. They have a fixed standing charge and a variable charge that depends on how much gas or electricity is used. Another difficulty is that some fixed costs are **stepped** or 'semi-fixed'. For example, if a manufacturer raises production, larger premises might have to be obtained, and this will raise rent costs. Different types of stepped cost such as rent, administration costs or interest payments on machinery might have their steps at different output levels. These factors make it difficult to construct an accurate break-even chart.

Non-linear relationships In most break-even analysis, it is assumed that the lines of total revenue and total cost are straight. In practice this is unlikely. Total cost is not likely to rise at a constant rate when output expands. For example, businesses might exploit 'economies of scale', such as bulk buying of raw materials. These result in costs rising less quickly than output. Similarly, total revenue might not rise at a constant rate if, for example, discounts are offered for large orders. Because the relationship between sales, costs and revenue is not linear, any analysis based on straight line graphs might be inaccurate.

Multi-product businesses Because most businesses do not produce and sell just one good, fixed costs have to be shared between different goods (see unit 50). This creates a problem for break-even analysis because the way that fixed costs are shared will affect the break-even point. To illustrate this, consider the example of Carl Wright, the market trader described earlier. Suppose he decided to start selling a new range of soft toys in addition to teddy bears. Depending on the proportion of his fixed costs that he decided the new toys should bear, the break-even point for bears could be higher or lower. An arbitrary decision about the allocation of fixed costs is likely to lead to inaccurate break-even analysis.

Unsold production Break-even analysis assumes that all the goods produced are then sold. Although businesses always hope to sell everything they produce, sometimes this is not the case. Stock might become outdated, unfashionable or damaged, and therefore impossible to sell. If this happens, the costs of production will not relate to the number of goods sold, but to the number of goods produced. Under these circumstances, break-even analysis becomes inaccurate.

summary questions

1. What does the contribution contribute towards?
2. If fixed costs are £10,000 and contribution per unit is £50, what output is needed to break-even?
3. How is the break-even point calculated using the equations for total cost and revenue?
4. What is plotted on the horizontal axis when constructing a break-even chart?
5. How are fixed costs shown on a break-even chart?
6. Why might a business wish to know its margin of safety?
7. What is shown on a profit-volume chart?
8. At what point on a profit-volume chart does break-even occur?
9. Explain three advantages of break-even analysis.
10. Explain five limitations of break-even analysis.

UNIT ASSESSMENT QUESTION 1

Price, Porter & Co manufactures packs of writing equipment and instruments for schools. The annual fixed costs of producing the packs are £40,000 and the variable costs are £3 per pack. The packs are sold for £5 each.

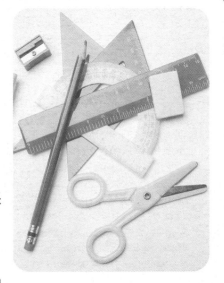

(a) **Calculate the number of packs that the company needs to sell in order to break-even (use the contribution and profit model method).**
(b) **Construct a break-even chart for Price, Porter & Co and show the number of packs that must be sold to break-even. (Construct your graph with axes between £0 and £200,000, and between 0 and 40,000 sales.)**
(c) **If Price, Porter & Co produces and sells 35,000 packs in one year, show the margin of safety on the break-even chart.**
(d) **How much profit will be made if sales are 35,000 per year?**
(e) **Suppose that fixed costs rise by 50%. Draw the new line for total cost on your break-even chart and state the new break-even level of sales.**

UNIT ASSESSMENT | QUESTION 2

The Wine Shop sells cases of wine by mail order. The owner of the business produced the break-even chart shown in Figure 49.7.

Figure 49.7 *Break-even chart for the Wine Shop*

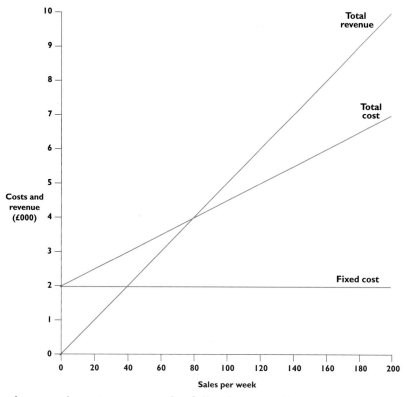

Use the break-even chart to answer the following questions.

(a) State the (i) weekly break-even level of sales and (ii) the total sales revenue and total costs at this point.

(b) State the expected profit or loss that would be made by the Wine Shop if weekly sales were (i) 40 cases and (ii) 120 cases.

(c) If actual sales were 160 cases per week, state the (i) selling price per case, (ii) the fixed cost per case, (iii) the variable cost per case, (iv) the profit per case and (v) the margin of safety.

(d) Calculate (i) the contribution per case and (ii) the total contribution if sales were 160 cases per week.

(e) Taking the role of the Wine Shop owner, write a memo to a new Wine Shop manager outlining the advantages and disadvantages of using break-even analysis.

key terms

Break-even chart - a graph on which sales revenue and costs of production are plotted. The point at which a business breaks even is shown where the line of total revenue intersects the line of total costs.

Break-even point - the level of sales where total costs and total revenue are the same, and therefore no profit or loss is made.

Contribution - the difference between the revenue earned from selling a unit of production and the variable cost of production per unit.

Margin of safety - the range of sales between the break-even point and the current level of sales, over which a profit is made.

unit 50
Absorption costing

unit**objectives**

To understand:
- the nature of costing;
- cost centres and cost units;
- the nature of absorption costing;
- the allocation and apportionment of overheads;
- overhead absorption.

What is costing?

COSTING involves calculating the cost of specific business activities. For example, a cost accountant in an engineering company might calculate the cost of making a number of components for a customer. To do this, it is necessary to gather information on the **direct costs**, such as the cost of materials used, and the **indirect costs** or **overheads**, such as administration costs. It is important to gather accurate information so that the cost of meeting the order is calculated as precisely as possible. If the cost of meeting the order is underestimated, the business could set a price that is too low. Under these circumstances, the business might not cover its costs and would therefore make a loss on the order. On the other hand, if a price is set that is too high, the business might lose the order to a competitor.

In addition to pricing decisions, cost accountants might provide information that helps a business:
- calculate the cost of a new investment project;
- determine the cost of relocating premises;
- calculate the cost of making staff redundant;
- compare the cost of carrying out a particular function, for example distribution, within the business or buying the service in from an outside provider.

A number of different costing methods can be used when calculating costs. ABSORPTION COSTING is described in this unit. Marginal costing and job and batch costing are explained in units 51 and 52. The particular method chosen depends on the nature of the activity being costed and the type of information that decision-makers require.

Cost centres and cost units

In order to carry out absorption costing, the production costs and overheads of running a business must be collected and recorded. A COST CENTRE is a particular area or point of a business for which costs are collected. Depending on the type of business, a cost centre might be:
- a geographical location, such as a factory, a sales region or a shop;
- a functional department, such as production or distribution;
- an item of equipment or machinery, such as a vehicle or photocopier;
- a person, such as a sales representative or maintenance worker.

In the case of manufacturing businesses, there are two main types of cost centre.
- **Production cost centres**, for example production departments such as machining or assembly.
- **Service cost centres**, for example service departments such as administration or distribution. Sometimes these are sub-divided into smaller cost centres such as 'stores' or 'canteen', or into items of expense that are shared between departments, such as 'heat and light' or 'rent and rates'.

When costs have been collected and recorded in cost centres, the process of absorption costing involves calculating the cost of each unit of production or COST UNIT. This might be a single finished product, such as a chair, a batch of finished products, such as a thousand loaves of bread, or a sub-assembly, such as an aircraft wing.

What is absorption costing?

Absorption costing is also known as **full** or **total** costing. The key principle of absorption costing is that all overheads are 'absorbed' in cost units. In other words, all overheads are included when calculating the cost of producing particular items. The main difficulty in absorption costing is deciding how to divide the cost of overheads between these cost units.

There are four main stages in the absorption costing process.

- The first stage is the ALLOCATION of those overhead costs that are directly incurred by particular cost centres.
- The second stage is to APPORTION, ie divide, all shared overheads between the production and service cost centres.
- The third stage is to apportion (or 'reapportion') all service cost centre overheads to the production cost centres.
- The final stage is to ABSORB the allocated and apportioned overheads into the costs of production of cost units.

Cost allocation

When cost accountants calculate the total cost of operating a cost centre, they must include both the **direct** and **indirect costs** of production. Direct costs are, by definition, associated with particular products or cost units and can therefore be charged to the relevant cost centre. For example, the wages paid to assembly line workers can be allocated directly to the production department.

Indirect costs or overheads that are wholly associated with a particular cost centre can also be charged 'directly' to that cost centre. The process is known as **cost allocation**. For example, the wages of an assembly line supervisor or the depreciation on an assembly line machine can both be allocated directly to the production department.

Examples of cost allocation also occur in service cost centres. For instance, the paper used in a photocopying machine might be charged directly to the administration department. The rent payable for a sales office might be charge directly to the sales department.

Apportionment of overheads to cost centres

In many cases, it is not possible to allocate overheads directly to cost centres because the costs are shared between several. For example, the cost of heating, insurance and maintenance might all be shared between a number of production and service departments. Under these circumstances, **cost apportionment** is used to divide the costs between the various cost centres.

A number of methods or **bases** can be used to apportion overheads. Some of the most commonly used are outlined in Figure 50.1. There are no set guidelines when it comes to selecting bases for apportionment. However, the basis should be **equitable**. This means that a fair share of the overheads should be apportioned to the relevant cost centre.

It is important for overheads to be apportioned fairly because businesses will want to determine as accurately as possible the true cost of operating each cost centre. If overheads are not apportioned fairly, the business might charge an inappropriate price to its customers. Another reason is to avoid unfair discrimination between cost centres. Managers responsible for cost centres might be demotivated if their centres are charged an unrealistic share of overheads. It would suggest that their centres are more expensive to operate than they really are.

To illustrate how overheads might be apportioned, consider the example of Dentons Ltd, a clothing manufacturer. Three overheads incurred by Dentons are £10,000 for heating, £40,000 in wages for two supervisors and £20,000 for insuring equipment. The business is divided into four cost centres, details of which are provided in Figure 50.2. The cutting and assembly departments are both production cost centres and the canteen and maintenance departments are both service cost centres.

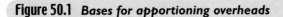

Figure 50.1 *Bases for apportioning overheads*

Overhead	Possible basis of apportionment
Rent and rates	Floor area of cost centres
Heating and lighting	Floor area, or volume of space, occupied by cost centres
Personnel costs such as health and welfare	Number of staff employed by each cost centre
Buildings insurance	Floor area, or book value of buildings, in each cost centre
Machinery and equipment insurance	Book value of machinery / equipment in each cost centre.
Depreciation (plant, machinery and tools)	Book value of assets in each cost centre
Maintenance	Book value of assets in each cost centre
Supervisory costs	No. of staff, or hours worked by supervisor, in each cost centre
Staff canteen	No. of staff employed in each cost centre
Administration	No. of staff employed or direct labour costs in each cost centre

Figure 50.2 *The four cost centres in Dentons Ltd*

	Cutting	Assembly	Canteen	Maintenance	Total
Floor area	25m^2	200m^2	100m^2	75m^2	400m^2
Staff employed	15	30	2	3	50
Book value of equipment	£50,000	£135,000	£10,000	£5,000	£200,000

Heating The heating cost of £10,000 can be apportioned according to the proportion of total floor space that each cost centre occupies. The amount to be apportioned to each cost centre is calculated using the formula:

$$\text{Cost to be apportioned} = \frac{\text{floor space occupied by cost centre}}{\text{total floor space}} \times \text{total heating cost}$$

So:

$$\text{Cutting} = \frac{25m^2}{400m^2} \times £10,000 = £625$$

$$\text{Assembly} = \frac{200m^2}{400m^2} \times £10,000 = £5,000$$

$$\text{Canteen} = \frac{100m^2}{400m^2} \times £10,000 = £2,500$$

$$\text{Maintenance} = \frac{75m^2}{400m^2} \times £10,000 = £1,875$$

Supervision The supervisory costs of £40,000 can be apportioned according to the proportion of total staff employed in each cost centre. The amount to be apportioned to each centre is calculated using the formula:

$$\text{Cost to be apportioned} = \frac{\text{number of staff employed by cost centre}}{\text{total number of staff}} \times \text{total supervision cost}$$

So:

$$\text{Cutting} = \frac{15}{50} \times £40,000 = £12,000$$

$$\text{Assembly} = \frac{30}{50} \times £40,000 = £24,000$$

$$\text{Canteen} = \frac{2}{50} \times £40,000 = £1,600$$

$$\text{Maintenance} = \frac{3}{50} \times £40,000 = £2,400$$

Insurance The insurance cost of £20,000 can be apportioned according to the proportion of the total book value of equipment used in each cost centre. The amount to be apportioned to each centre is calculated using the formula:

$$\text{Cost to be apportioned} = \frac{\text{book value of equipment in cost centre}}{\text{total book value}} \times \text{total insurance cost}$$

So:

$$\text{Cutting} = \frac{50,000}{200,000} \times £20,000 = £5,000$$

$$\text{Assembly} = \frac{135,000}{200,000} \times £20,000 = £13,500$$

$$\text{Canteen} = \frac{10,000}{200,000} \times £20,000 = £1,000$$

$$\text{Maintenance} = \frac{5,000}{200,000} \times £20,000 = £500$$

The share of overheads apportioned to each centre is summarised in Figure 50.3. Sometimes more than one basis of apportionment could be used in a particular cost centre. For example, heating costs could be apportioned according to floor area or to the volume of space occupied by each cost centre. It is, to some extent, a **subjective judgment** which basis is chosen. However, the decision should be consistent and appropriate, and it should always be made clear which basis is chosen.

Figure 50.3 Share of overheads apportioned to cost centres

	Basis of apportionment	Cutting £	Assembly £	Canteen £	Maintenance £	Total £
Heating	Floor area	625	5,000	2,500	1,875	10,000
Supervisory	No. of employees	12,000	24,000	1,600	2,400	40,000
Insurance	Book value	5,000	13,500	1,000	500	20,000
Total		17,625	42,500	5,100	4,775	70,000

QUESTION 1

Castle's is a small department store in Lancaster. It has five departments and each department is operated as a cost centre to help monitor the costs of running the business. A newly appointed cost accountant has suggested that the current method of apportioning overheads is inappropriate and should be reviewed. Figure 50.4 shows some details relating to the various cost centres. An analysis of overheads is also given. During the last financial year, Castle's incurred £500,000 overheads.

Figure 50.4 Information for each cost centre operated by Castle's

	Food Hall	Women's wear	Men's wear	Electrical	Toys	Total
Staff employed	12	8	4	6	10	40
Floor space	800m²	400m²	200m²	400m²	200m²	2,000m²

Overheads		
Rent and rates	£200,000
Electricity	£100,000
Administration	£200,000
Total	£500,000

(a) **Suggest equitable bases of apportionment for the three overheads. Explain your reasoning.**

(b) **Use the bases for apportionment chosen in (a) to calculate the share of overheads that would be charged to each cost centre if the overheads were apportioned accordingly.**

Apportionment of service cost centre overheads

In order to calculate the full cost of producing each cost unit, it is necessary to apportion the service cost centre overheads to the production cost centres. This process is sometimes called REAPPORTIONMENT or **secondary apportionment**. So, for example, the costs involved in operating service departments, such as stores, planning, canteen and maintenance, must be shared between the production departments. The reason for this is that it is only the production cost centres that are directly associated with the manufacture of the cost units.

A number of different apportionment bases can be used when apportioning service cost centre overheads. They are summarised in Figure 50.5.

Figure 50.5 Bases for apportioning service centre cost overheads

Service cost centre	Possible basis of apportionment
Canteen	Number of staff or meals served in each cost centre
Maintenance	Hours of maintenance work carried out for each cost centre
Planning	Number of hours worked in each cost centre
Stores	Number of times that materials are requisitioned by each cost centre

To illustrate how service cost centre overheads are apportioned to production cost centres, consider again the example of Dentons Ltd. Figure 50.6 shows how the company's overheads are allocated and apportioned to four cost centres. The first line shows that some costs are allocated directly to the cost centres. These costs include, for example, overheads such as depreciation on equipment that is used in each cost centre. They also include some direct costs such as direct labour. The second line shows the apportioned costs from Figure 50.3.

Figure 50.6 Share of overheads allocated and apportioned to cost centres

	Cutting (production) £	Assembly (production) £	Canteen (service) £	Maintenance (service) £	Total £
Allocated costs	8,500	10,500	4,400	6,600	30,000
Apportioned costs	17,625	42,500	5,100	4,775	70,000
Total	26,125	53,000	9,500	11,375	100,000

The costs associated with the two service cost centres are reapportioned in the following ways:
- canteen: according to the number meals served to staff employed in each cost centre;
- maintenance: according to the number of hours that maintenance staff work in each cost centre.

Figure 50.7 shows that 30% (ie 3,750 meals ÷ 12,500 meals) of the costs associated with the canteen are apportioned to the cutting department and 60% (ie 7,500 meals ÷ 12,500 meals) are apportioned to the assembly department. Note also that 10% (1,250 meals ÷ 12,500 meals) of the canteen costs are apportioned to the other service department, maintenance. This is because the maintenance workers also make use of the canteen. The costs associated with the maintenance department are split equally between the cutting and assembly departments. This is because, in this example, they both use half the total number of maintenance hours.

Figure 50.7 Service cost centre apportionment

	Cutting	Assembly	Canteen	Maintenance	Total
Canteen: No. of meals	3,750	7,500	-	1,250	12,500
(as a % of total)	30%	60%	-	10%	100%
Maintenance: No. of hours	3,000	3,000	-	-	6,000
(as a % of total)	50%	50%	-	-	100%

Figure 50.8 shows how the total overhead costs are charged to the two production departments.
- The first step is to reapportion the overheads associated with the canteen. Using the information from Figure 50.7, 30% of the costs are charged to the cutting department, ie £2,850 (30% × £9,500), 60% are charged to the assembly department, ie £5,700 (60% × £9500) and 10% are charged to the maintenance department ie, £950 (10% × £9,500).
- The next stage is to reapportion the maintenance overheads to the production departments. In this example these include some of the apportioned canteen overheads. The maintenance costs are split equally with £6,162.50 (50% × [£11,375+£950]) being charged to each production department.

Figure 50.8 Total overheads apportioned

	Cutting £	Assembly £	Canteen £	Maintenance £	Total £
Total overheads (from Figure 50.6)	26,125	53,000	9,500	11,375	100,000
Canteen overheads apportioned	2,850	5,700	(9,500)	950	
Sub-total	28,975	58,700	-	12,325	100,000
Maintenance o/heads apportioned	6,162.50	6,162.50		(12,325)	
Total o/heads apportioned	35,137.50	64,862.50	-	-	100,000

QUESTION 2

Nichol's Plastics Ltd is based in Slough. The company produces a wide variety of plastic products such as downpipes, gutters and storage bins. In order to ensure that all overheads are absorbed into production, the company operates 5 cost centres. There are 3 production departments (planning, moulding and finishing) and 2 service departments (stores and maintenance). The stores department provides services to the maintenance department in addition to the production departments. The maintenance department only provides services to the production departments. The overheads charged to the cost centres and some additional information is shown in Figure 50.9.

Figure 50.9 *Overheads charged to cost centres*

	Planning	Moulding	Finishing	Stores	Maintenance	Total
Overheads	£200,000	£500,000	£100,000	£50,000	£150,000	£1,000,000
No. of requisitions from stores dept.	1,000	6,000	4,000	-	1,000	12,000
Book value of assets	£40,000	£100,000	£60,000	-	-	£200,000

(a) Apportion the stores overheads to the other cost centres.
(b) Apportion the maintenance overheads to the production cost centres.
(c) Explain why it is necessary for Nichol's Plastics to apportion the overheads incurred by service departments.

Overhead absorption

When all overheads have been charged to production cost centres, they can then be **absorbed** into cost units. This ensures that all costs are taken into account when calculating the cost of producing the goods that are to be sold. The rate at which overheads are charged to cost units is called the OVERHEAD ABSORPTION RATE (OAR) or recovery rate. Several different methods of calculation are used. Three are explained below.

Note that the overheads are not absorbed on the basis of actual overheads incurred but on the basis of estimated or **budgeted** figures. This is because actual overheads will not be known precisely until the end of the financial year.

Machine hour overhead absorption rate This method is most suitable when production is capital intensive, ie where there is a high investment in fixed assets, such as machinery, relative to labour. Under these circumstances, most of the overheads are related to the cost of using the machinery. They include, for example depreciation, power, insurance, maintenance and repairs. It is appropriate to recover these overheads according to the amount of time that machinery is used on each cost unit. The machine hour OAR is given by:

$$\frac{\text{Total cost centre overheads}}{\text{Number of machine hours}} = \text{rate per machine hour}$$

Suppose, for example, that in a machining department, the total annual overheads are estimated to be £250,000. The budgeted annual total of machine hours in this cost centre is 10,000. Therefore, the machine hour OAR is:

$$\frac{£250,000}{10,000} = £25 \text{ per machine hour}$$

Consequently, if a particular cost unit takes 6 hours to produce in the machining department, £150 (6 x £25) overheads will be charged to the production of that single unit.

Direct labour hour overhead absorption rate This method is most suitable when production is labour intensive, ie when direct labour costs are high relative to capital costs. Under these circumstances, it is appropriate to recover overheads according to the number of hours it takes employees to produce each cost unit. The direct labour hour OAR is given by:

$$\frac{\text{Total cost centre overheads}}{\text{Total direct labour hours}} = \text{rate per direct labour hour}$$

Suppose, for example, that in a packaging department the total annual overheads are estimated to be £60,000. The budgeted annual total of direct labour hours in the department is 20,000. Therefore, the direct labour hour OAR is:

$$\frac{£60,000}{20,000} = £3 \text{ per direct labour hour}$$

Consequently, if it takes half an hour to pack a cost unit, then £1.50 (0.5 × £3) overheads will be charged to each unit.

Cost unit overhead absorption rate This method is appropriate when cost units are identical. For example, it would be suitable in a brewery where the only output is a single type of bottled beer. However, the method is unsuitable if a cost centre produces a wide range of different products that each take a different length of time to produce. The cost unit OAR is given by:

$$\frac{\text{Total cost centre overheads}}{\text{Total cost units}} = \text{rate per unit}$$

Suppose, for example, that a small brewery which produces just one type of bottled beer incurs an estimated £10,000 annual overheads. The budgeted annual total number of bottles produced is 40,000. Therefore, the cost unit OAR is:

$$\frac{£10,000}{40,000} = £0.25 \text{ per unit}$$

The overhead to be charged to each bottle produced is £0.25.

QUESTION 3

Frampton Holdings manufactures boilers for heating systems. The company operates three production cost centres and incurs the overheads shown in Figure 50.10. The budgeted number of machine and labour hours, and the OAR method used by each department is also shown.

Figure 50.10 *Overheads charged to three production departments*

Production department	Overheads £	Budgeted number of machine hours	Budgeted number of labour hours	Overhead absorption rate method
Cutting	60,000	16,000	2,000	Machine hours
Welding	180,000	3,000	20,000	Direct labour hours
Finishing	40,000	2,000	8,000	Direct labour hours

(a) **Calculate the overhead absorption rates in each production department.**
(b) **Suppose that Frampton Holdings receives an order for 100 boilers. The amount of time it takes to make a single boiler is 3 hours in the cutting department, 6 hours in the welding department, and 2 hours in the finishing department. Calculate the overhead charge for the order.**
(c) **Suggest why Frampton Holdings might use the machine hours OAR in the cutting department.**

Calculating unit costs using absorption costing

In order to illustrate how unit costs are calculated using the absorption costing process, consider the example of Wright Ltd, a manufacturer of sailing boat kits. The company manufactures some parts of the boats and buys in a variety of other components that are used to make up the rest of the kits. The business is divided into four cost centres.

- Body shop - produces the fibre glass parts that are needed to construct the boat shell.
- Sub-assembly - assembles the bought-in components.
- Packing and dispatch - packs and dispatches the kits to customers.
- Quality control - oversees quality control in the three production cost centres. This is a service cost centre.

A machine hours OAR is used in the body shop to charge overheads and a direct labour hours OAR is used in the other two production departments. Details of overheads and additional information are shown in Figure 50.11.

Figure 50.11 *Overheads and additional information for Wright Ltd*

	Body shop	Sub-assembly	Packing & dispatch	Quality control	Total
Floor space	8,000m²	4,000m²	2,000m²	2,000m²	16,000m²
Book value of assets	£600,000	£200,000	£200,000	-	£1,000,000
Number of employees	10	40	20	10	80
Quality control hours	2,000	8,000	4,000	-	14,000

Overheads	£
Rent	1,600,000
Heat and light	400,000
Depreciation	200,000
Administration	800,000
Total	3,000,000

Annual budgeted machine hours in the body shop:	50,000
Annual budgeted direct labour hours in the sub-assembly dept:	40,000
Annual budgeted direct labour hours in the packing and dispatch dept:	20,000

Cost of direct materials per boat:	£500
Cost of direct labour per boat:	£2,500

Time taken to produce one boat kit in each department:
Body shop:	10 hours
Sub-assembly:	15 hours
Packing and dispatch:	8 hours

In order to calculate the cost to Wright Ltd of producing one boat, the following steps are taken.

Step one
- The first step is to apportion the £3m overheads to the 4 cost centres. This is shown in Figure 50.12.
- The rent of £1,600,000 is apportioned according to the floor space used by each centre. For example, £800,000 (£1,600,000 × 8,000 ÷ 16,000) is charged to the body shop.
- Heat and light costs of £400,000 are also apportioned according to floor space. For example, £200,000 (£400,000 × 8,000 ÷ 16,000) is charged to the body shop.

- Depreciation of £200,000 is apportioned according to the book value of assets employed by each centre. For example, £120,000 (£200,000 × 600,000 ÷ 1,000,000) is charged to the body shop. Note that depreciation is not charged to the quality control cost centre. This is because the department does not use any machinery or equipment.
- The administration costs of £800,000 are apportioned according to the number of staff employed in each cost centre. For example, £100,000 (£800,000 × 10 ÷ 80) is charged to the body shop.

Figure 50.12 *The apportioned overheads for Wright Ltd*

	Body shop	Sub-assembly	Packing & dispatch	Quality control	Total
	£	£	£	£	£
Rent	800,000	400,000	200,000	200,000	1,600,000
Heat and light	200,000	100,000	50,000	50,000	400,000
Depreciation	120,000	40,000	40,000	0	200,000
Administration	100,000	400,000	200,000	100,000	800,000
Total	1,220,000	940,000	490,000	350,000	3,000,000

Step two
- The next step is to apportion (or reapportion) the overheads of the service department to the production departments. This is done according to the number of hours that the quality control department is estimated to spend working for them. So, for example, £50,000 (£350,000 × 2,000 ÷ 14,000) is apportioned to the body shop. The amended analysis of overheads is shown in Figure 50.13.

Figure 50.13 *Service cost centre overheads apportioned to production cost centres*

	Body shop	Sub-assembly	Packing & dispatch	Quality control	Total
	£	£	£	£	£
Total overheads	1,220,000	940,000	490,000	350,000	3,000,000
Quality control reapportioned	50,000	200,000	100,000	(350,000)	
Total	1,270,000	1,140,000	590,000	-	3,000,000

Step three
- When all the overheads have been apportioned to production cost centres, the next step is to calculate the overhead absorption rates.
- The body shop uses the machine hours OAR and the annual budgeted number of machine hours is 50,000. Therefore the OAR of this department is:

$$\frac{£1,270,000}{50,000} = £25.40 \text{ per machine hour}$$

- The sub-assembly department uses the direct labour OAR and the annual budgeted number of direct labour hours is 40,000. Therefore the OAR of this department is:

$$\frac{£1,140,000}{40,000} = £28.50 \text{ per direct labour hour}$$

- The packing and dispatch department also uses the direct labour OAR and the annual budgeted number of direct labour hours is 20,000. Therefore the OAR of this department is:

$$\frac{£590,000}{20,000} = £29.50 \text{ per direct labour hour}$$

Step four
- The fourth step is to calculate the overheads that are to be charged to each cost unit, ie boat. In order to do this, it is necessary to multiply the relevant OAR by the length of time it takes to process a single cost unit in each department. This is given in Figure 50.14

Figure 50.14 *Overheads charged to each cost unit*

OAR	Number of hours				Cost per unit
	£				£
Body shop	25.40	×	10	=	254.00
Sub-assembly	28.50	×	15	=	427.50
Packing & dispatch	29.50	×	8	=	236.00
Total					917.50

Step five
- The final step is to calculate the total cost of each boat or cost unit by adding the total overheads charged per cost unit to the direct labour cost and the direct materials cost. These figures were given in Figure 50.11. The total cost is £3,917.50 as shown below.

	£
Direct material per cost unit	500.00
Direct labour per cost unit	2,500.00
Overheads per cost unit	917.50
Total	3,917.50

Under and over absorption

The overhead absorption rate (OAR) is based on budget estimates of overhead costs and the expected level of activity in the business. These estimates will be inaccurate if either the actual overhead costs or activity level are higher or lower than budgeted estimates. If this happens, the OAR will also be inaccurate.

To illustrate how the OAR might be incorrect, consider the following example. Suppose a business estimates that overheads in a particular department will be £100,000. The budgeted number of machine hours is 20,000. Therefore, the machine hour OAR is £5 (£100,000 ÷ 20,000). However, during the year, actual overheads are only £80,000. If the department runs at full capacity, and all the hours are used, a total of £100,000 will be recovered. When this happens, overheads are said to be **over absorbed**.

Although a business might consider that over absorption is acceptable because more costs have been recovered than actually incurred, a disadvantage can arise. If the business has set the price it charges to customers on the basis of covering its costs of production, it will have set too high a price. In a competitive market, this might cause it to lose sales and therefore revenue.

Overheads will be over absorbed when:
- the actual level of overheads is lower than the predicted level (as in the case above);
- the activity level is higher than predicted, possibly because there have been fewer breakdowns than expected.

Overheads are said to be **under absorbed** if insufficient overheads are included in the cost of production. This might occur if:
- the actual level of overheads is higher than the predicted level;
- the activity level is lower than predicted.

To illustrate how under absorption might occur, consider the previous example where the machine hour OAR is £5. This is derived from budgeted overheads of £100,000 and an estimate of 20,000 machine hours. Suppose that the actual overheads are £100,000 but the number of machine hours is only 16,000 due to mechanical breakdowns. Under these circumstances, only £80,000 (£5 × 16,000) overheads will be recovered, leaving a shortfall of £20,000.

If overheads are under absorbed, the business might set a price that is too low to recover all its overheads. Under these circumstances, the price charged to customers will not cover costs and therefore profit will be reduced.

If overheads are over absorbed, the required **bookkeeping entries** are:
- debit overheads account;
- credit profit and loss account.

If overheads are under absorbed, the bookkeeping entries are:
- credit overheads account;
- debit profit and loss account.

Advantages and disadvantages of absorption costing

Advantages Absorption costing is a widely used method of costing because it ensures that costs are fully recovered. This means that businesses will cover their costs as long as the actual costs and level of activity are similar to the budgeted figures.

A second advantage of absorption costing is that it conforms to the accounting standard SSAP9 *Stocks and work-in-progress*. SSAP9 states that absorption costing should be used when valuing stocks in the final accounts. This is because absorption costing includes a share of fixed costs. It therefore recognises these fixed costs in the same period as revenues, and so conforms to the 'matching' principle.

Disadvantages The main disadvantage of absorption costing is that it is based on budgeted figures which might be inaccurate. This is because the figures are generally based on historical data that might not reflect future costs or activity levels. As a result, businesses might under or over absorb their overheads, and therefore set prices that are too low or too high.

A second disadvantage is that it can be complex, time consuming and expensive to gather detailed information from different cost centres. This is particularly the case in small to medium size companies that do not employ specialist cost accountants.

key terms

Absorb - the process of charging overheads to cost units.
Absorption costing (or **full** or **total costing**) - a method of costing that involves charging all overheads to cost units.
Absorption rate (or **recovery rate**) - the rate at which overheads are charged to cost units.
Allocation (or **cost allocation**) - the process of charging indirect costs or overheads that are wholly associated with a particular cost centre to that cost centre.
Apportion (or **cost apportion**) - the process by which shared overheads are divided between cost centres.
Costing - calculating the cost of specific business activities.
Cost centre - a point or area within a business where costs are incurred and recorded.
Cost unit - an item or batch of items that are produced and whose cost of production is calculated.
Reapportionment - charging the overheads incurred by service cost centres to production cost centres.

summary questions

1. Give four examples of specific costing activities.
2. What is the purpose of a cost centre?
3. What is the difference between a cost centre and a cost unit?
4. Explain the difference between cost allocation and cost apportionment.
5. State 3 ways in which overheads could be apportioned.
6. What is meant by secondary apportionment?
7. State 3 ways of calculating the overhead absorption rates.
8. What is meant by over absorption?
9. Why might overheads be under absorbed?
10. State two disadvantages of absorption costing.

UNIT ASSESSMENT QUESTION 1

Berwick Printers Ltd is divided into five departments which are each treated as separate cost centres - Artwork, Typesetting, Graphics, Printing and Distribution. The total overheads of the company amount to £1,000,000. The main direct cost is employees' wages. Some additional information is shown in Figure 50.15.

Figure 50.15 *Information regarding cost centres at Berwick Printers Ltd*

	Artwork	Typesetting	Graphics	Printing	Distribution	Total
	£	£	£	£	£	£
Book value of assets	300,000	600,000	200,000	150,000	250,000	1,500,000
Direct labour	280,000	224,000	322,000	350,000	224,000	1,400,000
Other direct costs	15,000	17,000	8,000	6,000	4,000	50,000
Floor area	1,000m²	1,000m²	1,000m²	2,000m²	3,000m²	8,000m²

Overheads:

Heat and light	£80,000
Administration	£520,000
Cleaning and maintenance	£100,000
Depreciation	£300,000
Total	£1,000,000

(a) Using appropriate bases for apportioning overheads, calculate the cost of operating each cost centre. State which bases for apportionment you have used.

(b) Explain why direct costs must be included when calculating the cost of operating each department.

UNIT ASSESSMENT QUESTION 2

Lockwoods Ltd is an engineering company that uses a system known as 'cell production' in its factory. There are three cells and each is responsible for its own design, purchasing, production, maintenance and distribution. The three cells are classed as production cost centres and the factory canteen is treated as a service cost centre. Figure 50.16 shows information about each cost centre. Overheads have already been apportioned. Lockwoods operates a system of absorption costing. It uses direct labour hours in Cells 1 and 2, and machine hours in Cell 3 to calculate the OARs. The budgeted cost of direct labour is £10 per hour in all three production cells.

Figure 50.16 *Information on Lockwoods' cost centres*

	Cell 1	Cell 2	Cell 3	Canteen	Total
Apportioned overheads	£600,000	£300,000	£250,000	£50,000	£1,200,000
No. of employees (direct labour)	250	100	50	na	400
Budgeted direct labour hours	200,000	200,000	30,000		430,000
Budgeted machine hours	30,000	40,000	100,000		170,000

(a) **Using a suitable basis, apportion the canteen overheads to the production cost centres. State which basis you have used.**

(b) **Calculate the OARs for each cell. Use direct labour hours for Cells 1 and 2, and machine hours for Cell 3.**

(c) **Suppose that a customer places an order with Cell 1 for 1,000 units of a particular component. A single component takes 10 hours to make and uses £25 of materials. Calculate the total cost of the order.**

(d) **Another customer wishes to buy 2,000 components from Cell 3. Each component will take 5 hours to make and will use £45 of material. Calculate the cost of producing the 2,000 components.**

Marginal costing

Marginal costing

MARGINAL COST is defined as the cost of raising output by one more unit. For example, if a business can produce 10 units for £250 and 11 units for £260, the marginal cost of producing the eleventh unit is £10 (£260 - £250). Marginal cost is the same as the variable cost of production. It only includes those costs that vary with the level of output. Examples of these costs include:
- direct materials, for example the raw materials and components that are used in producing an extra unit;
- direct labour, for example the wages of employees who are paid according to the number of items they produce;
- variable indirect costs or overheads, for example the cost of electricity that powers the machines in a production department.

All other costs, such as rent, insurance and administration, are classed as fixed costs. In the long run, these costs might change but, in the short run, they do not vary with the level of production.

MARGINAL COSTING is a costing and decision making technique that is used by business managers. It is an alternative method of costing to absorption costing (see unit 50). It is also sometimes known as **variable costing** or **direct costing**. Unlike absorption costing, which ensures that all costs are charged to a cost unit, marginal costing charges only the variable cost of production. Fixed costs are ignored.

Marginal cost and contribution

In businesses that use marginal costing, managers will often consider the size of the **contribution** when making production decisions. This is the difference between the revenue received from selling a particular output and the variable costs incurred when producing that output (see unit 49). For a single unit of production, the contribution equals the selling price less the variable cost.

To illustrate how contribution is calculated, suppose a market gardener charges a customer £10 for a bunch of flowers. The marginal cost to the market gardener might be £4. This is the variable cost of producing the flowers. Therefore the contribution is £6 (ie £10 - £4). This amount pays towards meeting the market gardener's fixed costs and, once these are paid, towards profit.

Generally, if the revenue received from an order is greater than the variable cost, the order is likely to be worth accepting. This is true provided the business has spare capacity. However, if the business does not have spare capacity, any attempt to increase output will involve incurring extra fixed costs, for example buying new premises. Under these circumstances, it might not be worth accepting the order.

To show how marginal costing is used in deciding whether to accept a particular order, consider the following example. Suppose a glove manufacturer receives an order for 1,000 pairs of leather gloves at a selling price of £6.70 per pair. The manufacturer has a policy of accepting orders if the total contribution exceeds £500. The costs incurred in meeting this order are listed on the next page.

Materials (per pair)	£1.00
Direct labour (per pair)	£3.00
Other variable costs (per pair)	£2.00
Total variable costs (per pair)	£6.00

The contribution made by the order is calculated as follows.

$$\text{Contribution per unit} = \text{selling price} - \text{variable cost}$$
$$= £6.70 - £6.00$$
$$= £0.70$$

So:

$$\text{Total contribution} = \text{contribution per unit} \times \text{number of units}$$
$$= £0.70 \times 1,000$$
$$= £700$$

In this case, since the contribution made by the order (£700) is greater than £500, the order would be accepted. This assumes that the glove manufacturer has sufficient capacity to complete the order. Note that the decision is based on the marginal cost of the order, not on the fixed or total costs.

Marginal costing has a number of applications. For example, it might be used in the following circumstances:

- evaluating special order decisions;
- deciding whether to make or buy-in a particular product or component;
- deciding which products to produce;
- deciding what to produce when resources are scarce;
- deciding what price to charge.

These issues are explained in the following sections of the unit.

QUESTION 1

J. Mansur & Son manufactures tents and marquees. The company is located in Nottingham and employs 24 staff. The total fixed costs for the year are £150,000. Recently there has been an enquiry from the Ministry of Defence regarding the supply of tents for the army. The company has been asked to quote a price for the supply of 100 tents made from high-grade canvas. The variable cost of manufacturing one of these tents is shown below:

Canvas	£80
Other materials	£20
Direct labour	£25
Other variable costs	£10

(a) What is the marginal cost of making one of the tents?
(b) What would be the total contribution if the company could sell the tents for £160 each?
(c) What would be the impact on fixed costs of accepting the order?

Special order decisions

Marginal costing can be used when making decisions about whether to accept a SPECIAL ORDER. This is generally defined as an order for goods at below the usual list price. In some circumstances it might be worthwhile for a manufacturer to accept such an order. An important factor in the decision will be the contribution that the order makes. To illustrate this, consider the example of Middleton Aviation, a manufacturer of microlight aircraft. Some financial details are given below.

- Fixed costs are £500,000 per year and variable costs are £18,000 per aircraft.
- The usual selling price of the aircraft is £23,000.
- The company plans to produce and sell 120 aircraft during the year.

Should Middleton Aviation accept an order from a customer who wishes to buy 10 aircraft but is only prepared to pay £19,000 per aircraft? Before making the decision, the company would calculate the contribution and profit made with and without the special order. This is shown in Figure 51.1.

Figure 51.1 *The contribution and profit made by Middleton Aviation*

	Without the special order	**Special order**
	£	£
Selling price (SP)	23,000	19,000
Less variable cost (VC)	18,000	18,000
Equals contribution per unit	5,000	1,000
Multiplied by number of units	120	10
Equals total contribution	600,000	10,000
Less fixed cost	500,000	0
Equals profit	100,000	10,000

Figure 51.1 shows that, without the special order, Middleton Aviation's profit would be £100,000. This is calculated by working out the contribution per unit (£5,000) and the total contribution if 120 units are produced (ie £5,000 × 120 = £600,000) and then subtracting the fixed cost (£500,000). The contribution per unit from the special order would be £1,000 and the total contribution of the special order would be £10,000. As long as fixed costs were covered by the sale of aircraft at the usual price, the special order would raise profit by £10,000, from £100,000 to £110,000. Under these circumstances, Middleton Aviation might accept the order.

It is unlikely that the company would accept an order that made a negative contribution. The revenue earned from such an order would not even cover the variable costs. Therefore each item sold would reduce overall profit.

Although Middleton Aviation would increase its profit if it accepted the special order, a number of other factors would have to be taken into consideration before a decision was made.

- **Capacity** The company must ensure that it has enough resources to complete the order. For example, would workers be prepared to work overtime if necessary? Is there enough space in the factory to produce more aircraft? Would the order replace other, more profitable orders? If the company was already operating at full capacity, by how much would the special order raise fixed costs? Would the expansion in capacity require extra workers to be employed or new machines to be purchased? For the special order to be profitable, the contribution must be sufficient to cover any rise in fixed costs.
- **Current utilisation** A special order that only makes a small positive contribution might be accepted if a business is experiencing difficulty in finding work. It is important to keep staff occupied and other resources, such as tools and machinery, employed. Therefore it is often better for a business to keep permanent staff employed working on orders with small contributions than doing nothing at all.
- **Future orders** The company might be prepared to accept a lower contribution in the hope that the customer will make bigger, more profitable orders in the future.
- **Retaining customer loyalty** The company might accept an order that makes only a small contribution as a means of retaining a regular customer's loyalty.
- **Customer response** If existing customers discovered that identical aircraft were being sold at a lower price than they paid, it could cause resentment. This might damage the image of the company and could lead to a loss of sales in the future. If Middleton Aviation was forced to lower its price to £19,000 for all customers, ie to the special order price, the company would make an overall loss of £370,000. This is shown in Figure 51.2.

Figure 51.2 *Losses if Middleton Aviation was forced to lower its price*

	£
Selling price (SP)	19,000
Less variable cost (VC)	18,000
Equals contribution per unit	1,000
Multiplied by number of units	130
Equals total contribution	130,000
Less fixed cost	500,000
Equals profit/(loss)	(370,000)

QUESTION 2

Barton Toys is a supplier of train sets to large toy distributors and retailers in the UK. The company's main product is a train set designed for the 7- 9 age group. Barton Toys plans to produce 11,000 sets during the year selling them for £85 each. The variable cost of producing each train set is £55 and fixed costs are £120,000 per year. In January, just after a very busy Christmas period, the company received an order from a new customer for 500 train sets. However, the new customer was only prepared to pay £65 each for the sets.

(a) Calculate the profit made by Barton Toys when producing 11,000 train sets at the usual selling price.

(b) Calculate the contribution made by the new order.

(c) On financial grounds would you advise Barton Toys to accept the order?

(d) What other factors might Barton Toys take into account?

Make or buy decisions

Marginal costing can help a business decide whether to make a component itself or to buy it in from an outside supplier. For example, Cranshaw Ltd manufactures bicycles in Leamington Spa. In recent years, the number of parts that the company makes 'in-house' has been reduced because it has become more profitable to buy-in parts. Butler's, a local engineering company, has offered to supply handlebars at a price of £7.50 each. The current costs associated with handle bar production are shown in Figure 51.3. Annual output of handlebars is 100,000.

Figure 51.3 *Cranshaw Ltd's fixed and variable costs (relating to handlebars)*

Materials (per unit)	£1.90
Direct labour (per unit)	£3.00
Variable overheads (per unit)	£2.50
Fixed costs per year (total)	£80,000

In this example, since the marginal cost of making each handlebar is £7.40 (£1.90 + £3.00 + £2.50) and the price offered by Butler's is £7.50, it is not worth buying them in. Note that the **fixed costs of £80,000 are irrelevant** because they are paid whether handlebars are manufactured by Cranshaw Ltd or bought-in. Figure 51.4 shows cost statements for the production of 100,000 handlebars illustrating 'in-house' costs and buying-in costs. The statements show clearly that the total cost of in-house production is £10,000 lower than buying-in the handle bars from Butler's.

The decision for Cranshaw Ltd appears straightforward because the buying-in price is higher than the 'in-house' cost. However, there might be other factors to take into account. For example, if the handlebars were bought-in, resources currently used in handlebar production would be released. If, as a result, factory space became empty, it could be rented out. Then, if the rent exceeded £10,000, buying-in the handle bars would become a profitable option. The same applies to other resources such as labour and machinery. If these were released from producing handlebars and, instead, were used more profitably, the company would benefit.

> **Figure 51.4** *Statements comparing the cost of handlebars produced in-house and bought-in*

Production 'in-house'	£	Buying-in	£
Variable cost	7.40	Purchase price per unit	7.50
Multiplied by number of units	100,000	*Multiplied by* number of units	100,000
Equals total variable cost	740,000	*Equals* total purchase price	750,000
Plus fixed cost	80,000	*Plus* fixed cost	80,000
Equals total cost	820,000	*Equals* total cost	830,000

If a business does decide to buy-in products or components, the following additional factors might also be taken into account.

- Before contracting-out to an external supplier, a business must be confident that the supplier can meet delivery times and quantities. A new supplier might be able to supply components at a cheaper price but, if the supplier is unreliable, this could lead to lost production and sales.
- The quality of the sub-contractor's work must also be considered. If the new supplier cannot maintain quality standards, it might not be worth using cheaper components.
- Once internal production facilities have been closed down, a business becomes vulnerable to future price increases by its suppliers. However, a long term contract might overcome such a difficulty.

QUESTION 3

Sanjay's Balti House is a restaurant in Blackburn. It currently buys-in one of its starter dishes, vegetable samosas, from a local supplier for 17p each. Each month, 3,000 samosas (10 batches) are purchased. However, a recent order for samosas failed to arrive at Sanjay's due to delivery problems. To meet demand, Sanjay asked one of his chefs to make a week's supply of samosas in-house. When regular customers were served with the chef's version of the samosas, there were some very positive comments. As a result, Sanjay decided to see whether it would be worthwhile making the samosas on a permanent basis. Some cost information is given below.

Ingredients (per batch of 300)	£25
Direct labour (per batch of 300)	£20
Other variable costs (per batch of 300)	£10
Restaurant overheads per year	£65,000

(a) Calculate the marginal cost of making 3,000 samosas in-house.

(b) On purely financial grounds, should Sanjay buy-in samosas or make them in-house?

(c) Suggest two non-financial reasons why it might be preferable for Sanjay to make the samosas in-house.

Ranking products

Sometimes a business might produce a range of different products. Marginal costing can be used to rank the products according to the size of their contribution. To illustrate this, consider the example of Brian Peters, a sole trader. He currently manufactures dog kennels, rabbit hutches and cat boxes for local pet shops. In the last year, Brian made and sold 1,000 of each product. The business has fixed costs of £4,000 per annum.

Brian is considering specialising in producing just one product. In order to decide whether this would be more profitable, he must first calculate which product generates the highest contribution. Figure 51.5 is a statement that shows the costs of production and the contribution of each product. The dog kennels generate the highest contribution, £13, and the cat boxes the lowest, just £5.

Figure 51.5 *Financial information for Brian Peters' business*

	Dog kennels		Rabbit hutches		Cat boxes	
	£	£	£	£	£	£
Selling price		35		28		16
Raw materials - wood	7		3		1	
Other raw materials	4		4		1	
Labour	8		8		8	
Other variable costs	3		1		1	
Total variable cost		22		16		11
Contribution		13		12		5

If Brian specialises in manufacturing the product that makes the highest contribution, he can increase his profit. This is shown in Figure 51.6. When Brian makes and sells 1,000 of each product, he makes a net profit of £26,000. However, if he makes and sells 3,000 dog kennels, his profit will rise to £35,000.

Figure 51.6 *Statements showing the net profit made by Brian Peter's business with and without specialisation*

	Without specialisation					With specialisation	
	Kennels	Hutches	Boxes	Total			Kennels
	£	£	£	£			£
Sales revenue	35,000	28,000	16,000	79,000		Sales revenue	105,000
Less variable costs	22,000	16,000	11,000	49,000		*Less* VC	66,000
Contribution	13,000	12,000	5,000	30,000		Contribution	39,000
Less fixed costs				4,000		*Less* FC	4,000
Profit				26,000		Profit	35,000

Although Brian can increase his profit by specialising, this involves three assumptions that might not always hold true.
● The calculation assumes that the amount of time it takes to produce 3,000 kennels is the same as the time it takes to produce 1,000 of each product. If, in fact, it takes longer, then the extra labour costs would have to be considered.
● The calculation also assumes that Brian's customers are willing to buy the extra kennels instead of hutches and boxes. This might not be the case.
● Customers will be prepared to buy from a supplier who can only supply one item.

Production decisions when resources are scarce

Sometimes businesses are faced with a situation in which some of the resources used in production are scarce. In these circumstances, marginal costing can be used to decide what option to take.

In manufacturing, scarce resources are sometimes called **limiting factors** or **constraints** to production. Examples of limiting factors are:
● a shortage of skilled labour;
● a shortage of raw materials;
● a limited number of machine hours available;
● a shortage of factory space.

To illustrate how marginal costing can be used to calculate the most profitable option when there are limiting factors, consider the following example. Blakes is an engineering company that produces three components for the computer industry. Some information relating to each product manufactured by Blakes is shown in Figure 51.7. Within the company, direct labour costs are charged at £8 per hour and machine hours at £10 per hour. Currently, Blakes is experiencing a problem recruiting qualified staff and this limits the number of labour hours to 600,000 per year.

●●● ○

Figure 51.7 *Information relating to Blakes' products*

Component	A	B	C
Selling price (per unit)	£39.00	£51.00	£39.00
Annual demand (units)	50,000	200,000	100,000
Cost of materials (per unit)	£6.80	£4.90	£7.10
Direct labour hours (per unit)	2	4	2
Machine hours (per unit)	1.5	1.25	1.5

Figure 51.8 shows the calculations that are required when making production decisions. The first step is to calculate the contribution made by a single unit of each component. This is found by subtracting the variable cost from the revenue.

- The variable cost is made up of the material cost, the direct labour cost and the machine hours cost for each unit. The direct labour cost is found by multiplying the hourly rate by the amount of time it takes to produce one unit. So, for component A, this is £16 (2 x £8). The machine hours cost is found by multiplying the hourly rate by the number of machine hours it takes to produce one unit. For component A, this is £15.00 (1.5 x £10). The variable cost of producing one unit of component A is therefore £37.80 (£6.80 + £16.00 + £15.00)
- The contribution for component A is £1.20 (£39.00 - £37.80). The contributions made by the other two components are also shown.

Once the contribution has been calculated for each component, the next step is to calculate the contribution per hour of the limiting factor.

- In this example, direct labour is the limiting factor. The contribution per labour hour for component A is £0.60. This is calculated by dividing the contribution by the number of direct labour hours it takes to produce each unit (£1.20 ÷ 2). For component B, it is £0.40 (£1.60 ÷ 4) and for component C it is £0.45 (£0.90 ÷ 2).
- The contributions are ranked according to their contribution. So, for example, component A is ranked 1st because it has the highest contribution.

Figure 51.8 *Contribution statement for Blakes*

Component	A	B	C
	£	£	£
Selling price (per unit)	39.00	51.00	39.00
Cost of materials (per unit)	6.80	4.90	7.10
Labour cost (per unit)	16.00	32.00	16.00
Machine hours cost (per unit)	15.00	12.50	15.00
Total variable cost (per unit)	37.80	49.40	38.10
Contribution (per unit)	1.20	1.60	0.90
Number of labour hours (per unit)	2	4	2
Contribution (per labour hour)	£0.60	£0.40	£0.45
Ranked order	1st	3rd	2nd
Annual demand (units)	50,000	200,000	100,000
Hours available 600,000			
Hours needed to meet full demand	100,000	800,000	200,000
Hours allocated	100,000	300,000	200,000
Production according to ranking (units)	50,000	75,000	100,000
Contribution (per unit)	£1.20	£1.60	£0.90
Contribution from each component	£60,000	£120,000	£90,000
Total contribution £270,000			

When the contribution per labour hour has been calculated, it is possible to work out the most profitable option. To meet the demand for all three components 1,100,000 hours of labour are required in total. This is made up of:

- 100,000 (2 × 50,000) hours for component A;
- 800,000 (4 × 200,000) hours for component B;
- 200,000 (2 × 100,000) hours for component C.

However, Blakes is faced with a shortage of labour and only 600,000 hours are available. Given this constraint, the best option is to allocate the hours to the products that give the highest contribution per labour hour.

- Therefore, 100,000 hours should be used to meet fully the demand for component A, the product with the highest contribution per labour hour, 200,000 hours should then be used to meet the demand for component C, the product with the second highest contribution. The remaining 300,000 hours should be used to produce component B, which has the lowest contribution per labour hour. However, as a result of the labour shortage, demand for component B would not be fully satisfied. There would be a shortfall of 500,000 hours, which is equivalent to 125,000 units (62.5% × 200,000). As a result, only 75,000 (200,000 - 125,000) units would be produced.
- The total contribution from each component is calculated by multiplying the actual production by the contribution per unit.
- The overall contribution from components A, B and C is shown as £270,000 (£60,000 + £120,000 + £90,000). Blakes' profit can be calculated by subtracting fixed costs from this amount.

Pricing decisions

Marginal costing can be used to help make pricing decisions. For example, a business might consider charging a lower price than usual in order to gain a foothold in a new market or to compete with a rival. However, when reducing the price of a product, businesses are unlikely to set a price that will result in a loss.

QUESTION 4

Forshaw & Co is a manufacturing company based in Cumbria. It makes three designs of walking boots called the Arctic, the Moorlander and the Trekker. The business is profitable with a strong demand for its products. However, recently the company has experienced some breakdowns with its machinery. As a result of the breakdowns, Forshaw & Co expects that it will only have 55,000 machine hours available in the next month whilst repairs are carried out. Direct labour is currently charged at £7 per hour and machine hours cost £5 per hour. Some additional information relating to the production of each product is shown in Figure 51.9.

Figure 51.9 *Information relating to Forshaws & Co's products*

Product	Arctic	Moorlander	Trekker
Price	£60	£40	£30
Demand (monthly, in pairs)	5,000	10,000	20,000
Material cost (per pair)	£8	£7	£4
Direct labour hours (per pair)	3	2	1.5
Machine hours (per pair)	4	3	2.5

(a) **Calculate the unit contribution made by each product.**
(b) **Calculate the contribution per machine hour made by each product.**
(c) **Calculate the number of pairs of each product that should be made given the restriction on the number of machine hours available.**
(d) **Calculate the profit made by Forshaw & Co in the month that machine hours are restricted. Monthly fixed costs are £36,000.**

To illustrate how marginal costing can be used in pricing decisions, consider Jennings Ltd, a manufacturer of dust extractors. The usual selling price for one of its products is £40. However, the company wishes to break into an overseas market and is considering a price reduction. The costs of production are as follows:
- materials per unit: £12.00;
- direct labour per unit: £7.50;
- variable overheads per unit: £4.50;
- shipping costs per unit: £2.00;
- total fixed costs: £45,600.

Provided that Jennings can cover the marginal cost of production in the overseas market, the company will be no worse off than before. The marginal cost per unit is £26 (£12 + £7.50 + £4.50 + £2). Therefore the lowest price Jennings can charge without cutting its profit is £26. As long as the price is above this amount, the contribution will be positive. The £45,600 fixed costs are not taken into account because they will be incurred whether these extra units are sold in the new market or not.

If the pricing strategy is successful and the products are accepted in the new market, it might be possible for Jennings to raise the price in the future so that there is a bigger contribution towards fixed costs and profit.

Sensitivity analysis

Businesses sometimes use a technique known as SENSITIVITY ANALYSIS to evaluate the effects of changes in sales volume, selling price and costs on the break-even point and profits. In order to carry out this analysis, the variable and fixed costs of production must be known.

To illustrate this, consider the example of a business that has fixed costs of £5,000 per year, variable costs of £12 and a selling price of £20 per unit. Figure 51.10 shows that the contribution per unit is £8 and the profit is £3,000 if annual sales are 1,000 units. It also shows that the break-even level of sales is 625 units. This is calculated by dividing the fixed cost by the contribution per unit (£5,000 ÷ £8).

Figure 51.10 *Contribution and profit when annual sales are 1,000 units and at break-even*

	Current position £	Break-even £
Selling price	20	20
Less variable cost	12	12
Equals contribution per unit	8	8
Multiplied by number of units	1,000	**625**
Equals total contribution	8,000	5,000
Less fixed cost	5,000	5,000
Equals profit	3,000	0

Given this information, it is possible, using sensitivity analysis, to consider how certain changes might affect a business. Assume that current sales are 1,000 per year.

A fall in sales How much would sales have to fall for the business to break-even? Figure 51.10 shows that if sales fell to 625 units, the business would break-even. This is a fall of 375 units from the current level of sales. If sales fell below 625 units, a **loss** would be made. Expressed in percentage terms:

$$\text{Fall in sales to break-even point} = \frac{1,000 - 625}{1,000} \times 100 = 37.5\%$$

A fall in price How much would price have to fall for the business to break-even? This is shown in Figure 51.11.

Figure 51.11 *Selling price at break-even*

	Current position £	Break-even £
Selling price	20	**17**
Less variable cost	12	12
Equals contribution per unit	8	5
Multiplied by number of units	1,000	1,000
Equals total contribution	8,000	5,000
Less fixed cost	5,000	5,000
Equals profit	3,000	0

At break-even, profit is zero. Given that fixed costs are £5,000 and current sales are 1,000 per year, the contribution per unit must be £5 at break-even. If the variable cost is £12, the selling price at break-even must therefore be £17. This is a fall of £3 from the current price. If the selling price falls lower that £17, a **loss** is made. Expressed in percentage terms:

$$\text{Fall in price to break-even point} = \frac{20 - 17}{20} \times 100 = 15\%$$

A rise in variable costs How much would variable costs have to rise for the business to break-even? This is shown in Figure 51.12.

Figure 51.12 *Variable cost at break-even*

	Current position £	Break-even £
Selling price	20	20
Less variable cost	12	**15**
Equals contribution per unit	8	5
Multiplied by number of units	1,000	1,000
Equals total contribution	8,000	5,000
Less fixed cost	5,000	5,000
Equals profit	3,000	0

At break-even, the contribution per unit is £5. Given that the selling price is £20, this means that the variable cost at break-even must be £15. This is a rise of £3 from the current figure. If variable costs rise above £15, the business will make a **loss**. Expressed in percentage terms:

$$\text{Rise in variable costs to break-even point} = \frac{15 - 12}{12} \times 100 = 25\%$$

A rise in fixed costs How much would fixed costs have to rise for the business to break-even? This is shown in Figure 51.13.

Figure 51.13 *Fixed cost at break-even*

	Current position £	Break-even £
Selling price	20	20
Less variable cost	12	12
Equals contribution per unit	8	8
Multiplied by number of units	1,000	1,000
Equals total contribution	8,000	8,000
Less fixed cost	5,000	**8,000**
Equals profit	3,000	0

At break-even, the total contribution is £8,000. Therefore, fixed costs at break-even must also be £8,000. This is a rise of £3,000 from the current figure. If fixed costs rise above £8,000, the business will make a **loss**. Expressed in percentage terms:

$$\text{Rise in fixed costs to break-even point} = \frac{8{,}000 - 5{,}000}{5{,}000} \times 100 = 60\%$$

Stock valuation

A major difference between marginal costing and absorption costing lies in the way that stocks are valued. In marginal costing, closing stocks are valued at their marginal (or variable) production cost. However, in absorption costing, closing stocks are valued at their full production cost, ie their fixed and variable cost.

To illustrate how this difference affects the calculation of profits, consider the following example. Rhoslyn Ltd manufactures slate plaques. The company sells all of its production to a large wholesaler for £5 per unit. Some additional information relating to Rhoslyn Ltd is given in Figure 51.14.

Figure 51.14 *Rhoslyn Ltd sales and production for a three year period*

	1999	2000	2001
Units sold (000s)	75	60	80
Units produced (000s)	75	75	75
Opening stock (000s)	-	-	15
Closing stock (000s)	-	15	10

Variable cost of production (per unit)	£3
Fixed costs (manufacturing overheads)	£75,000
Fixed costs (sales, distribution and administration)	£40,000

When marginal costing is used, the opening and closing stock is valued at its marginal cost. This is the same as the variable cost of production, £3 per unit. Figure 51.15 shows the calculation of the contribution and the profit using this valuation.

Figure 51.15 *Profit statement for Rhoslyn Ltd using marginal costing*

	1999		2000		2001	
	£(000s)	£(000s)	£(000s)	£(000s)	£(000s)	£(000s)
Sales (£5 × number of units sold)		375		300		400
Opening stock (£3 × number of items)	-		-		45	
Add variable production cost (£3 × 75,000)	225		225		225	
Less closing stock (£3 × number of items)	-		45		30	
Cost of sales		225		180		240
Contribution (sales - cost of sales)		150		120		160
Less manufacturing fixed costs		75		75		75
Gross profit		75		45		85
Less other fixed costs		40		40		40
Net profit		35		5		45

The profit statement in Figure 51.15 shows, for each year, the amount of profit made by the company. When stocks are taken into account, the contribution is calculated by working out the cost of sales and then subtracting this from the sales revenue. Gross profit equals the contribution less the manufacturing fixed costs. Net profit equals the gross profit less the other fixed costs.

When absorption costing is used to calculate net profit, the opening and closing stock is valued at £4 per unit. This is the full production cost. It is equal to the variable cost £3, plus the absorption rate for the fixed manufacturing overhead which is £1 per unit (ie fixed costs of £75,000 divided by the output of 75,000). Figure 51.16 shows the calculation of net profit using this valuation. Note that, in this case, the production cost that is used to calculate the cost of sales is the full production cost, ie the variable cost plus the fixed manufacturing cost.

Figure 51.16 *Profit statement for Rhoslyn Ltd using absorption costing*

	1999		2000		2001	
	£(000s)	£(000s)	£(000s)	£(000s)	£(000s)	£(000s)
Sales (£5 × number of units sold)		375		300		400
Opening stock (£4 × number of units)	-		-		60	
Add production cost (VC + manuf. FC)	300		300		300	
Less closing stock (£4 × number of units)	-		60		40	
Cost of sales		300		240		320
Gross profit		75		60		80
Less other fixed costs		40		40		40
Net profit		35		20		40

Figures 51.15 and 51.16 show the differences between marginal costing and absorption costing. In 1999, although different methods are used in the calculation, the net profit is the same for both (£35,000). This is because sales are equal to production and therefore there is no closing stock. However, in 2000, net profit using absorption costing is £20,000, whereas the net profit using marginal costing is £5,000. This is because the closing stock is given a higher valuation using absorption costing (£4 per unit) than the valuation using marginal costing (£3 per unit). It is always the case that profit will be higher using absorption costing if stocks increase, ie when production is greater than sales. In this example, Figure 51.15 shows that the opening stock in 2000 was zero and the closing stock was 15,000 units.

However, if production is lower than sales and therefore stocks decrease, profit is lower using absorption costing. This is shown in 2001 with an opening stock of 15,000 units and a closing stock of 10,000 units. Sales were therefore 5,000 more than production, so the closing stock valuation fell from £60,000 to £40,000. The net profit using marginal costing is £45,000 whereas it is only £40,000 using absorption costing.

Advantages and disadvantages of marginal costing

Advantages Marginal costing is relatively simple to operate. Unlike absorption costing, the difficulty of sharing fixed costs between different products and units of production is avoided. There is the extra advantage that under and over absorption of overheads does not occur.

Marginal costing can also be very useful in decision making. For example, it helps when ranking products or deciding whether to make a particular product or to buy it in from outside. Absorption costing is not suitable for such decision making because the inclusion of overheads makes it impossible to work out the extra costs incurred or saved.

Disadvantages When valuing the closing stocks of a business in the final accounts, the accounting standard SSAP 9 *Stocks and work-in-progress* states that the absorption costing method should be used and not the marginal costing method. As a result, marginal costing is not used in the published accounts of UK companies.

It might not always be possible to identify the marginal costs associated with production. For example, the extent to which production overheads, such as the cost of electricity, vary according to changes in output might not be easy to determine.

It is particularly difficult to calculate marginal cost if a business is running at full capacity. Under these circumstances, any rise in output would incur a higher level of fixed costs, such as the purchase of a new piece of machinery. If this is the case, the marginal cost will be much higher than the marginal cost of a unit when there is spare capacity.

For production to be profitable, all production costs must be recovered. A business that only uses marginal costing might find that it does not recover its fixed costs and will therefore make a loss. This is illustrated in those industries where marginal cost is almost zero. For example, the cost to a train or bus operator of carrying one more passenger is close to zero. Most of the train or bus operator's costs are fixed and the variable cost of transporting one more passenger is limited to the cost of issuing a ticket. In these circumstances, if the mass of customers only pay fares that cover the low marginal costs, a business will make losses because it is not covering its high fixed costs. However, marginal costing does explain the benefit of filling empty seats at discount fares, as long as fixed costs are already covered. The revenue earned from these extra passengers adds much more to revenue than it does to costs.

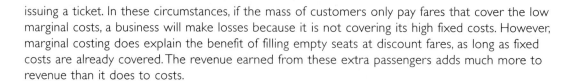

key terms

Marginal cost - the cost of raising output by one extra unit.
Marginal costing - a costing method based on the variable costs of production, which disregards fixed costs.
Sensitivity analysis - the analysis of changes in sales volume, selling price and costs on the break-even point and profits.
Special order - an order for goods at below the usual list price.

UNIT ASSESSMENT QUESTION 1

Richards & Son constructs UPVC conservatories. The company offers three designs called the Oval, the Majestic and the Fen. During the winter, business is usually very quiet. Until recently Richards & Son has offered the full range of products during the quiet period. However, the company is now considering whether it would be more cost effective to withdraw the least profitable design. Some financial information regarding the construction of the conservatories is given below.

	Oval	Majestic	Fen
	£	£	£
Price	8,000	6,000	12,000
Materials	2,500	2,000	3,000
Direct labour	3,000	2,500	5,000
Variable overheads	1,000	1,000	1,500

(a) Calculate the contribution per unit of each design.
(b) Which design should be withdrawn by Richards & Son during the winter?

In order to make more use of its resources during the winter, Richards & Son is considering whether to manufacture greenhouses that could be erected by customers. The greenhouse kits could be made in the winter and then sold during the spring. However, the greenhouse market is very competitive. In order to penetrate the market, the company believes that the kits would have to be sold cheaply to begin with. The estimated costs of producing a single greenhouse kit are shown below.

Materials	£300
Direct labour	£200
Variable overheads	£100

(c) What is the lowest price that Richards & Co could charge for a greenhouse kit without reducing its overall profits?
(d) Could the company charge this price indefinitely? What factors would it need to take into consideration?

UNIT ASSESSMENT QUESTION 2

Boxit Ltd makes pallets for breweries and soft drink producers. The company sells each pallet for £3. Some additional information regarding production, sales and costs is given below.

	2000	2001
Units sold (000s)	100	130
Units produced (000s)	120	120
Opening stock (000s)	-	20
Closing stock (000s)	20	10
Variable cost of production (per unit)		£2
Fixed costs (manufacturing overheads)		£60,000
Fixed costs (sales, distribution and administration)		£30,000

(a) **Prepare a profit statement using marginal costing for Boxit Ltd for the two years.**

(b) **Prepare a profit statement using absorption costing for Boxit Ltd for the two years.**

(c) **Under which method of costing does Boxit Ltd make the most net profit?**

summary questions

1. Explain why marginal costs are variable costs.
2. State three examples of costs that will rise when one more unit of output is produced.
3. If a boat maker sells a boat for £12,000 and incurs £8,700 in variable costs, what is the contribution?
4. What is meant by a special order decision?
5. State three non-financial factors that a business might consider before making a special order decision.
6. Explain why a business is unlikely to accept an order that makes a negative contribution.
7. State two non-financial factors that a business would need to take into account before buying-in a product that it once made.
8. State three possible limiting factors in production.
9. Under what circumstances does marginal costing give a higher net profit than absorption costing?
10. State three limitations to marginal costing.

unit 52

Job, batch, contract and activity based costing

unit**objectives**

To understand:
- **job costing;**
- **batch costing;**
- **contract costing;**
- **activity based costing.**

Job costing

A business might use JOB COSTING if it produces 'one-off' products for its customers. The process involves calculating the cost of meeting a specific order. Businesses that use job costing include builders when constructing a house extension, engineering companies when making a special type of machine, or catering companies when providing a wedding banquet. Because every job is different, it is likely that each will require different amounts of labour, materials and other resources. Therefore it will be necessary to calculate the cost of each job separately.

Sometimes job costing is necessary so that a business can provide a quotation for a specific order or to put in a tender for the work. This is common in the construction industry. When a business prepares a quote for a job, it usually needs to:
- estimate the amount of labour and materials that will be needed;
- decide how much to allow for overheads (overhead absorption rates might be used);
- decide what to add on as a 'mark-up' for profit.

Each job is, in effect, treated as a cost centre. All of the costs involved in completing the job are calculated so that they can be recovered.

To illustrate how job costing might be used by a business, consider the example of Jack Higgins & Son, a small building company. Figure 52.1 shows a cost sheet that the company has prepared to give a price quotation to Mr and Mrs Anslow who want a house extension.

Figure 52.1 Cost sheet prepared by Jack Higgins & Son

JOB COST SHEET: Mr & Mrs Anslow - house extension

	£	£
Direct materials		
Timber	870	
Bricks	650	
Windows and doors	500	
Slates	800	
Sand and cement	150	
Other materials	910	
		3,880
Direct labour		
400 hours × £10		4,000
Other direct costs		
Equipment hire		400
Overheads		2,000
Total cost		10,280
Profit		
25% × 10,280		2,570
Price to be quoted		**12,850**

The cost sheet in Figure 52.1 shows a breakdown of the various estimated costs. The building materials are listed and total £3,880. The labour is charged at £10 per hour and the job is expected to take 400 labour hours. Therefore the total labour cost will be £4,000. To complete the extension, the company would need to hire a JCB to dig the foundations. This is expected to cost £400 and is shown as another direct cost. £2,000 is added to cover the overheads. This is based on an absorption rate of £5 per direct labour hour (ie £5 × 400 hours). Finally, the profit mark-up is added. For Jack Higgins & Son, this is 25% of the total cost. The price that the company will quote for the job is £12,850.

Job costing has a number of **advantages**.

- It helps businesses to set a price for individual jobs. Once they have worked out the cost of completing a job, they can add on a mark-up for profit.
- The job cost sheet provides a valuation for work-in-progress at the end of the financial year. Work-in-progress is a form of stock and must be valued in the accounts at the lower of cost or net realisable value. The job cost sheet provides the necessary cost information.
- Job cost sheets can be used to help provide customers with instant quotes if a new job is similar to an old one.
- Job cost sheets can provide a controlling mechanism. If a business records actual costs and compares them with the estimated costs, differences between the two can be investigated. For example, if labour costs are significantly higher than those estimated, it might mean that workers are being less productive than expected. This type of investigation is called **variance analysis** and is explained in unit 56.

QUESTION 1

Barry Melling is a sole trader who makes replacement windows. He has received an order from Heather Newton, a new customer. After discussing the design and other specifications with his customer, Barry will prepare a job cost sheet.

The cost of materials for the job is expected to be £2,400 for timber, £500 for glass and £100 for other materials. Barry expects that the job will take 80 hours and he charges £10 per hour for his labour. His overhead absorption rate is £5 per labour hour and he then adds a profit mark-up of 30% to overall costs.

(a) Prepare a job cost sheet for Barry Melling.
(b) What benefits might Barry Melling obtain by preparing a job cost sheet?

Batch costing

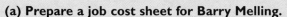

Many businesses produce output in batches. A batch is a specific number of identical units. For example, an engineering company might produce 500 identical brackets for a customer. Each bracket in the batch will be made using exactly the same resources and exactly the same production processes. BATCH COSTING involves calculating the cost of making a whole batch. It is similar to job costing because each batch is treated as a cost unit. To illustrate the method, consider Cains Products, a manufacturer of sheet metal parts. Following an order for 300 metal lockers, the following information is estimated.

- Materials will cost a total of £1,500.
- The direct labour cost of cutting is £12 per hour, folding £10 per hour, welding £20 per hour and finishing £5 per hour.
- To manufacture one locker will require 20 minutes of cutting, 30 minutes of folding, 30 minutes of welding and 1 hour of finishing. So, for example, cutting will cost one third (ie 20 minutes ÷ 60 minutes) of the £12 direct labour cost per hour.
- The overhead absorption rate is £6 per unit.
- 20% of total cost is added as a profit mark-up.

The cost of meeting this order is shown in Figure 52.2. This information can be used to calculate the average or unit cost. This is found by dividing the total batch cost, including profit, by the number of units in the batch. The cost of one locker in this case is £42 (£12,600 ÷300).

Figure 52.2 *Batch cost for Cains Products - order for 300 lockers*

BATCH COST: 300 metal lockers

		£	£
Materials			1,500
Labour			
Cutting	300 × 1/3hr × £12	1,200	
Folding	300 × 1/2hr × £10	1,500	
Welding	300 × 1/2hr × £20	3,000	
Finishing	300 × 1hr × £5	1,500	7,200
Direct costs			8,700
Overheads	300 × £6		1,800
Total cost			10,500
Profit	20% × 10,500		2,100
Total			**12,600**

QUESTION 2

Sandra Phillips and Tanya Boksic are partners in a business that designs and manufactures children's clothes. Most of their orders are for small batches, ranging from 10 to 100 garments. The direct labour costs in the business are:

- cutting - £10 per hour;
- sewing - £12 per hour;
- finishing - £6 per hour.

The overhead absorption rate is £2 per garment and the partners add a 40% profit mark-up to total costs. In December 2001, an order for 70 romper suits was received from a customer. The material costs per garment were expected to be £4.50. It was estimated that cutting would take 30 minutes, sewing 15 minutes and finishing 30 minutes per garment.

(a) Calculate the cost of producing the batch and add on the profit mark-up.
(b) What is the cost (plus profit) of producing one romper suit?

Contract costing

CONTRACT COSTING is a technique that is applied to long term projects such as civil engineering, shipbuilding or the installation of IT systems. The distinctive features of contract costing include some of the following.

- A contract job might take a long time to complete, perhaps several years.
- Contract work usually involves very large financial transactions.
- Payment might be made in instalments over the period of the contract.
- A percentage of the payment might be held back by the customer after the contract is completed. This is called **retention money**. It gives the customer time to assess whether the contract has been completed satisfactorily. If it has not, the money will not be paid until the contractor has remedied the defects.
- Most of the costs incurred in contract work are classified as direct. This is because contract work is often carried out on-site and all the costs incurred on that site will relate to that one job or contract. This means that items which are traditionally classed as indirect costs, such as telephone, supervisory expenses and electricity, are treated as direct costs.

Accounting for contract work Because contracts sometimes take a number of years to complete, they will span several accounting periods. Therefore special consideration has to be given to when profit is realised, ie recognised in the profit and loss account. Under normal circumstances, according to the realisation concept, profit should be realised when ownership of goods is passed to the customer. However, in the case of long-term contract work, if a contractor waits until the completion of contracts before profit is recognised, the profit and loss account will not give a true and fair indication of events. For example, in a year where no contracts were actually completed, a business would show a loss even though the long-term financial position of the business might be very profitable. The accounting standard SSAP9 *Stocks and work-in-progress* deals with this problem. It states the following.

- It is appropriate to recognise turnover and profit while contracts are in progress provided there is reasonable certainty that the contract will be completed for the sum agreed. The term **attributable profit** is used to describe that part of the overall profit that is recognised at a specific accounting date.

- Businesses should act in accordance with the concept of prudence when calculating the profit attributable to a particular year in the contract. For example, if in the early stages of a long-term contract the outcome is not known with reasonable certainty, no profit should be recognised. Nor should any retention money be classed as turnover until the customer has agreed that the work is complete.

- The calculation of profit must allow for increases in costs not recoverable under the terms of the contract. This might arise if, for example, faulty work has to be corrected after the contract is completed.

- If a loss is expected on the contract as a whole, all of the loss should be recognised as soon as it is foreseen. Under these circumstances, the loss should be written off against profit and loss.

Calculating attributable profit The amount of profit that is recognised in a particular year of a contract can be calculated in different ways. The method that is used depends on how far into the contract a business has progressed. For contracts that are less than 35% complete, it is usual not to anticipate any profit at all. This is because the outcome of a contract is not known with reasonable certainty. For contracts that have progressed between 35% and 85%, it is common practice to attribute $\frac{2}{3}$ or $\frac{3}{4}$ of the profit to date. Under these circumstances, assuming that $\frac{2}{3}$ is recognised, the attributable profit is calculated as follows.

$$\text{Attributable profit} = (\frac{2}{3} \times \text{ profit to date}) \times \frac{\text{payment received on account}}{\text{value of work certified}}$$

Where profit to date = value of work certified - cost of work certified (also known as cost of sales)

The value of **work certified** is determined by an architect at key stages in the completion of a contract. For example, when the foundations of a building have been laid, an architect might issue a certificate to certify the value of work done to date. The payment received on account is the money paid by the customer to the contractor for part-completion of the work.

If a contract has progressed beyond 85%, the attributable profit on a contract can be estimated with reasonable certainty. To calculate the profit in these circumstances, a number of methods are used. Two are shown below.

$$\text{Attributable profit} = \frac{\text{value of work certified}}{\text{contract price}} \times \text{estimated total profit}$$

$$\text{Attributable profit} = \frac{\text{payment received to date}}{\text{contract price}} \times \text{estimated total profit}$$

To illustrate how these methods are applied, consider the example of Watkins Construction. This is a building company with three contracts currently underway. Watkins Construction has a policy of attributing $\frac{2}{3}$ of any profit on work certified in the current year's accounts if work is between 35% and 85% complete. Some information regarding the contracts is given in Figure 52.3.

Figure 52.3 *Details of three contracts being undertaken by Watkins Construction*

	Contract 1	Contract 2	Contract 3
	£	£	£
Contract price	600,000	200,000	500,000
Cost to date	170,000	17,000	300,000
Estimated further costs	220,000	160,000	20,000
Work certified to date	120,000	-	250,000
Cost of work certified	84,000	-	200,000
Payment received on account	108,000	-	150,000
Profit attributed in previous years' accounts	10,000	-	40,000

To calculate the amount of profit attributable to the current year's accounts, the following steps are taken.

- First it is necessary to determine how far the contracts have progressed. This can be calculated by looking at the costs incurred to date in relation to the total expected costs of the contract. The total cost is made up of the cost incurred so far, plus the estimated further costs to completion.

$$\text{For Contract 1} = \frac{\text{cost to date}}{\text{total expected cost}} \times 100 = \frac{£170,000}{(£170,000 + £220,000)} \times 100 = 43.6\%$$

$$\text{For Contract 2} = \frac{£17,000}{(£17,000 + £160,000)} \times 100 = 9.6\%$$

$$\text{For Contract 3} = \frac{£300,000}{(£300,000 + £20,000)} \times 100 = 93.8\%$$

- Contract 1 is 43.6% complete (ie between 35% and 85%) so some of the profit can be recognised in the current year. The profit to date on Contract 1 is determined by first subtracting the cost of work certified from the value of work certified. It is £36,000 (£120,000 - £84,000). The attributable profit is given by:

$$\text{Attributable profit} = (\frac{2}{3} \times \text{profit to date}) \times \frac{\text{payment received on account}}{\text{value of work certified}}$$

$$= \frac{2}{3} \times £36,000 \times \frac{£108,000}{£120,000} = £21,600$$

The final step is to subtract the profit already attributed in the accounts. This is £10,000. Therefore the amount of profit attributable to the current accounts is £11,600 (£21,600 - £10,000).

- Since Contract 2 is only 9.6% complete, the outcome of the contract cannot be ascertained with any reasonable certainty. Therefore, in accordance with the concept of prudence, no profit from this contract will be attributable in the current accounts.
- Contract 3 is 93.8% complete. Under these circumstances the attributable profit is given by:

$$\text{Attributable profit} = \frac{\text{value of work certified}}{\text{contract price}} \times \text{estimate total profit (ie contract price less total costs)}$$

$$= \frac{£250,000}{£500,000} \times (£500,000 - [£300,000 + £20,000]) = £90,000$$

The amount of profit to be attributed to the current accounts is therefore £50,000, ie £90,000 less the £40,000 already attributed.

West London Construction Ltd specialises in small housing developments. At the current time, the company is working on three contracts (see Figure 52.4). These are based on three sites, one in Shepherds Bush, one in Paddington and the other in Brentford. When preparing its accounts, the company calculates the profit to be attributed in the following way:

When work is between 35% and 85% complete, profit $= (\frac{2}{3} \times \text{profit to date}) \times \dfrac{\text{payment received on account}}{\text{value of work certified}}$

When work is over 85% complete, profit $= \dfrac{\text{value of work certified}}{\text{contract price}} \times \text{estimated total profit}$

Figure 52.4 *Financial information relating to West London Construction's contracts*

	Shepherds Bush	Paddington	Brentford
	£	£	£
Contract price	500,000	200,000	1,000,000
Cost to date	350,000	20,000	400,000
Estimated further costs	40,000	120,000	350,000
Work certified to date	250,000	-	340,000
Cost of work certified	100,000	-	280,000
Payment received on account	200,000	-	170,000
Profit already attributed to accounts	18,000	-	10,000

(a) Determine the extent to which each of the contracts is complete.

(b) Calculate the profit attributable in the current accounts for each of the contracts.

(c) Explain why the calculations in (a) are necessary.

Contract accounts

When businesses operate a system of CONTRACT COSTING, they generally open a CONTRACT ACCOUNT. A separate account is opened for each contract. Examples of entries that are likely to be made in the contract account are shown in Figure 52.5.

Figure 52.5 *Examples of entries in a contract account*

Debit	Contract Account	Credit
Material costs		Materials removed from site
Labour costs		Net book value of plant and machinery
Net book value of plant and machinery on site		removed from site
Other site costs		Value of work certified
Head office costs (apportioned)		Cost of work not certified

Entries on the debit side of the contract account relate to the various costs incurred whilst the contract is in progress. Examples are material costs, labour costs, other site costs such as the leasing of equipment, any general overheads that have been apportioned and the net book value of plant and machinery on the site. Entries on the credit side include the value of materials or equipment that have been transferred from the site, perhaps to another site, and the value of the work certified.

When a contractor receives an architect's certificate for work completed, the customer is generally invoiced for a progress payment. The bookkeeping entries required for this transaction are:
- debit customer account;
- credit work certified account.

At the end of the trading year, it is necessary to bring down a number of debit balances on the contract account. These include:

- the cost of materials still on site;
- the net book value of plant and equipment on site;
- the cost of work not certified (balancing figure).

To illustrate how a business might use a contract account, consider the example of the Bingham Building Co. On 2 January 2000, the company began work on a two-year contract to build factory units on a Coventry industrial estate. At the end of the financial year, 31 December 2000, the value of materials on site was £3,200 and the value of plant was estimated at £80,000. An architect's certificate for work completed had been issued for £134,000 and Bingham received payment from the customer (less an agreed 10% retention fee). This payment amounted to £120,600. The following details were also provided for the year ended 31 December 2000.

Materials delivered to site	£50,000
Materials transferred to another site	£2,500
Site wages	£80,000
Sub contracting payments	£21,000
Architects fees	£2,800
Other direct expenses	£5,600
Apportioned overheads	£5,000
Plant used on site	£100,000
Cost of work not certified	£132,000

The contract account for Bingham Building Co is shown in Figure 52.6. The account is divided into three sections. The first section is used to calculate the cost of work certified. This is the balancing figure on the credit side of the account after all the appropriate costs have been entered on the debit side and the appropriate entries made on the credit side. For Bingham, the cost of work certified was £46,700.

Figure 52.6 *Contract account for the Bingham Building Co*

Dr	£	Contract Account	Cr	£
Materials delivered to site	50,000	Materials transferred off site		2,500
Site wages	80,000	Materials on site at 31.12.00 c/d		3,200
Sub contracting payments	21,000	Value of plant at 31.12.00 c/d		80,000
Architects fees	2,800	Cost of work not certified c/d		132,000
Other direct expenses	5,600	Cost of work certified		
Overheads apportioned	5,000	(ie cost of sales) c/d		46,700
Plant sent to site	100,000			
	264,400			264,400
Cost of work certified b/d	46,700	Architects certificate for work certified		134,000
Profit and loss (attributable profit)	52,380			
Profit not attributed c/d	34,920			
	134,000			134,000
Materials b/d	3,200	Profit not attributed b/d		34,920
Plant on site b/d	80,000			
Cost of work not certified b/d	132,000			

The second section shows the profit attributable to the current year's accounts. The company calculates the attributable profit in the following way.

$$\text{Attributable profit} = (\frac{2}{3} \times \text{profit to date}) \times \frac{\text{payment received}}{\text{value of work certified}}$$

$$= \frac{2}{3} \times (£134,000 - £46,700) \times \frac{£120,600}{£134,000}$$

$$= \frac{2}{3} \times £87,300 \times \frac{9}{10}$$

$$= £52,380$$

The attributable profit, £52,380, is debited to the second section of the contract account. The profit not attributable (ie $\frac{1}{3}$ of the profit to date) is also debited to the second section of the contract account. It amounts to £34,920 (£87,300 - £52,380). This section of the account balances because the value of the architect's certificate, on the credit side, must be equal to the profit on the contract to date (attributed profit and profit not taken) plus the cost of work certified, on the debit side.

The third section of the account shows the balances brought down for the next trading year. The debit balances include the materials on site left over from the current year, the value of plant still on site and the cost of work not yet certified. On the credit side of the account, the profit not yet attributed is shown.

Activity based costing

Traditional methods of costing involve apportioning overheads to cost centres and cost units. Direct costs tend to be greater than overhead costs and overheads are generally apportioned according to the number of direct labour hours or machinery hours used in production. However, in modern production techniques, overheads tend to make up a much bigger proportion of overall costs than in traditional manufacturing. For example, direct labour might only form a very small proportion of costs in a modern electronics factory. Overheads such as purchasing, handling materials, maintenance, programming, quality control and despatching form the bulk of the costs. As a result, ACTIVITY BASED COSTING (ABC) has been developed to apportion the overheads incurred in production more accurately. ABC charges overheads to products using COST POOLS and COST DRIVERS.

Figure 52.7 shows how a business organisation's activities might be divided into cost pools. A cost pool is a range of costs that are all linked to a specific activity such as purchasing, programming machinery or quality control. Costs in the purchasing cost pool might include the wages of staff in the purchasing department, the telephone calls made to suppliers and the maintenance contracts on the computers used by the purchasing staff. A cost driver is a specific action that results in a cost being incurred. For example, in purchasing, every time a purchase order is placed, costs are incurred. In this case, the cost driver is the processing of an order. Figure 52.7 shows cost drivers that relate to particular cost pools.

Figure 52.7 *Cost pools and cost drivers*

COST POOL	COST DRIVER
Purchasing	Number of purchase orders
Maintenance	Number of maintenance hours
Materials handling	Quantity of material handled
Material receipt	Number of batches received
Production planning	Number of production runs
Machine programming	Number of set-ups
Quality control	Number of inspections
Despatching	Number of despatches

Once cost pools and cost drivers have been established, it is necessary to calculate **cost driver rates** so that overheads can be charged to units of output. In general, cost driver rates are given by:

$$\text{Cost driver rate} \quad = \quad \frac{\text{Total cost of pool}}{\text{Cost drivers (number)}}$$

In the case of purchasing, for example, the cost driver rate might be the cost per order placed. This rate can be calculated using the formula below:

$$\text{Cost driver rate for purchasing} \quad = \frac{\text{Total purchasing costs}}{\text{Number of purchases}}$$

So, if total purchasing costs are £50,000 in a particular year and 2,000 orders are processed, the cost driver rate will be:

$$= \quad \frac{£50,000}{2,000} \quad = \quad £25 \text{ per order}$$

Advantages of activity based costing

- When overheads are apportioned according to the activities that generate them, as opposed to the number of direct labour or machine hours used in production, costing becomes more accurate.
- A company can identify its most profitable and least profitable products more easily.
- Managerial control might be more efficient if overheads are analysed and classified into cost drivers.
- A business might design new products which allow low cost drivers to be exploited.
- Budget setting and sensitivity analysis can be more accurate (see unit 51).
- ABC can be used by businesses that supply services in addition to those that manufacture products.

Disadvantages of activity based costing

- Obtaining the information required to calculate cost driver rates might be time consuming and expensive.
- In businesses where a simple standard product is produced, it might be more appropriate and easier to use more traditional methods of costing based on direct labour or machine hours.
- Choosing appropriate cost drivers might not be straightforward. For example, if it is decided that the cost driver for a purchasing department will be the number of orders placed, this will be misleading if some orders take much longer than others to process. It might also be difficult to identify precisely the costs associated with a particular cost driver.

key terms

Activity based costing (ABC) - a costing method that involves charging overheads to the activities that generate the cost.
Batch costing - a costing method that calculates the cost of producing a number of identical units for a customer.
Contract account - an account that records the costs of, and revenues from, a particular contract. It is used to find the cost of work certified.
Contract costing - a costing method that is used to calculate the cost of contract work.
Cost driver - a specific action that results in a cost being incurred.
Cost pool - a range of costs that are linked to a specific activity.
Job costing - a costing method that calculates the cost of meeting a specific customer order.

QUESTION 4

LBC is a building company in Ludlow, Shropshire. In January 2001, the company won a contract to build a new library. The contract was expected to take two years and, at the end of the first year, a contract account was drawn up. This is shown in Figure 52.7 and is incomplete. For the purpose of drawing up its accounts, LBC uses the following method to calculate the attributable profit.

$$\text{Attributable profit} = (\tfrac{2}{3} \times \text{profit to date}) \times \frac{\text{payment received on account}}{\text{value of work certified}}$$

Figure 52.8 *Contract account for LBC - library contract*

Dr	£	Cr	£
Materials delivered to site	35,500	Materials transferred off site	1,200
Site wages	41,000	Materials on site at 31.12.01 c/d	1,100
Sub contracting payments	5,000	Value of plant at 31.12.01 c/d	24,000
Architects fees	1,800	Cost of work not certified c/d	32,000
Other direct expenses	2,600	Cost of work certified	
Leasing charges	3,600	(ie cost of sales) c/d	?
Plant sent to site	30,000		
Overheads apportioned	4,000		
	123,500		123,500
Cost of work certified b/d	?	Architect's certificate	100,000
Profit and loss (attributable profit)	?		
Profit not attributed c/d	?		
	100,000		100,000

(a) Calculate the cost of work certified (ie cost of sales).

(b) Calculate the profit attributable to the 2001 accounts. The company received a payment of £90,000 when the architect's certificate was issued.

(c) What is the value of profit not taken into the 2001 accounts?

(d) Prepare the third section of the contract account.

summary questions

1. Give three examples of businesses that might use job costing.
2. What is meant by a batch in production?
3. Give three examples of contract work.
4. State four features of contract work.
5. Why might the realisation concept not be applicable for contract work?
6. State a formula that might be used for calculating attributable profit if a contract has progressed beyond 85%.
7. State four examples of debit entries on a contract account.
8. What is the balancing item on a contract account?
9. Explain the difference between cost drivers and cost pools.
10. State three advantages and three disadvantages of ABC.

UNIT ASSESSMENT   QUESTION 1

Helen Hardwick owns a catering company. She employs 2 full-time members of staff and several part-timers to help out with serving at events. The part-timers are paid £6 per hour. The company's latest order is to provide catering for a large dinner. The client requires a 5-course meal for 250 guests. After agreeing a menu with the client, Helen has started to plan the job. She estimates that 50 hours of labour will be required from part-time staff. Crockery and cutlery will have to be hired at a cost of £300. She also estimates the cost of food as follows:

meat and fish	£900;
fruit and vegetables	£450;
dairy produce	£300;
other foodstuffs	£100;
miscellaneous items	£250.

(a) Produce a job cost sheet that shows how much Helen will charge for the job. She calculates overheads at 50% of total food costs and adds a profit mark-up of 40% of total costs.

(b) Calculate the price per guest for the client.

UNIT ASSESSMENT   QUESTION 2

The Horrock's Construction Co. specialises in the maintenance and construction of bridges. In September 2000, the company won a three-year contract with the Highway Agency. Work began in January 2001. A £225,000 payment from the Agency was made at the end of 2001 for work certified by the architect (10% was held in retention). At the end of the year, the value of plant on site was £8,000 and the value of materials was £5,900. The following information is also provided for the year ended 31 December 2001.

Materials delivered to site	£60,000
Materials transferred to another site	£12,700
Plant sent to site	£20,000
Site wages	£150,000
Sub contracting payments	£21,000
Architects fees	£4,000
Other direct expenses	£21,600
Apportioned overheads	£20,000
Cost of work not certified	£50,000
Value of work certified	£250,000

For the purpose of drawing up its accounts, Horrock's uses the following method to calculate the attributable profit.

$$\text{Attributable profit} = (\tfrac{2}{3} \times \text{profit to date}) \times \frac{\text{payment received on account}}{\text{value of work certified}}$$

(a) Determine the cost of work certified by preparing and balancing the first section of the contract account for 2001.

(b) Calculate the profit attributable to the 2001 accounts and complete the second section of the contract account.

(c) Complete the third section of the contract account.

Labour costing and remuneration

unitobjectives

To understand:
- methods of remuneration;
- direct and indirect labour costs;
- how labour costs are recorded.

What is remuneration?

REMUNERATION is a payment for services rendered. In the context of labour, it is the pay and other FRINGE BENEFITS that employees receive from their employers. The weekly pay that is earned by manual and lower grade employees is generally called a **wage** and the monthly pay earned by other employees is generally called a **salary**. However, in recent years, the distinction between the two terms has become blurred and they are now often used interchangeably.

Fringe benefits vary from employee to employee. Lower paid employees tend to receive few benefits apart from a contribution towards their pension. In some cases they might also receive a uniform to wear at work and a subsidised canteen. Higher paid employees might receive additional 'perks' such as a company car, a clothing allowance and private health insurance, as well as a pension contribution.

Labour remuneration is important for businesses because it affects:
- the costs of production and therefore the cost of finished goods and services;
- the morale and efficiency of employees.

How are employees remunerated?

Methods of remuneration include:
- time rates, where people are paid according to the length of time they spend at work;
- piece rates, where people are paid according to the output they produce;
- bonus or incentive schemes, where people are rewarded for extra effort or contribution.

Systems of remuneration help to motivate employees, provide rewards that are linked to effort and assist in the recruitment and retainment of staff. Poor remuneration systems are likely to result in low morale, poor workmanship, resentment amongst workers, high staff turnover and absenteeism and recruitment difficulties.

The method of remuneration chosen by a business will depend to some extent on the nature of the work being performed and the particular industry involved.

Time rates When employees are paid according to the number of hours they spend at work, the method of payment is called a TIME RATE. For these employees, their wage is calculated by multiplying the number of hours worked by the hourly wage rate. Any hours worked above the agreed working week is called **overtime**, which is often paid at a higher rate.

The **advantages** of time rate systems of payment include:
- they provide a simple and easily understood method of calculating employees' pay;
- they are appropriate when the quality of the employees' output is more important than the quantity of items produced;
- they are appropriate when output cannot be measured and therefore there is no basis for payment by results.

The **disadvantages** of time rates are:
- they reward attendance but not work. Highly productive employees will be paid exactly the same as those who are less productive. This might create resentment amongst staff and demotivate the more efficient workers;
- there is little incentive for employees to improve their performance.

Annualised hours Some businesses have found that a time rate based on a set working week of 40 hours, for example, is too inflexible for their needs. There might be quiet periods of the year when employees have very little to do. At other times, employees might be working overtime to meet customer orders. To deal with irregular production levels, some businesses now pay employees to work for a fixed number of hours per year. This system is known as ANNUALISED HOURS. Employees might be expected to work longer days when the business is busy and perhaps take extended holidays when there is no work to do. Employees' pay is calculated according to a fixed working week of, say, 40 hours and is paid regardless of the actual number of hours worked.

The **advantages** of an annualised hours system are that:

- employers do not have to pay overtime when demand is high, and therefore labour costs are reduced;
- flexibility and efficiency are improved because employers can be certain that the workforce will be available to meet periods of high demand.

The **disadvantages** of the system are that:

- employees might resist the move towards more flexible working and the loss of overtime pay, and might therefore become resentful and demotivated;
- wage rates, and therefore production costs, might have to be raised in order to persuade the workforce to accept the new system.

QUESTION 1

Burton's Pies makes meat pies and other pastry products in its Norwich factory. The company employs 25 production staff who are paid an average of £5.40 per hour. The working week at Burton's Pies is 35 hours and employees receive three weeks annual holiday on full pay. During the winter months, the factory can be very busy and workers are often asked to work overtime. However, during summer, there is sometimes not enough work to keep the employees busy for a full week. When this happens, the factory closes early although the employees are still paid for 35 hours work per week. The overtime rate is 'time and a half', ie one and a half times the normal hourly rate. During the last financial year, the production staff each worked an average of 120 hours overtime.

In order to increase flexibility of the workforce, the managing director has proposed that a new annualised hours contract should be drawn up for production employees. The proposal is for an annual total of 1,820 hours to be worked at an hourly rate of £5.80 per hour. Instead of overtime payments, employees would be expected to work extra hours at busy periods and would be compensated by time off at quiet periods.

(a) Calculate the total annual labour costs of the production staff at Burton's Pies in the last financial year. Assume that it was a 52 week year.

(b) State an advantage and a disadvantage to Burton's Pies of remunerating staff using time rates.

(c) Outline the advantages and disadvantages to Burton's Pies of moving to the proposed system of annualised hours.

(d) What are the advantages and disadvantages of the annualised hours proposal to the employees?

Piece rates In a PIECE RATE system, workers are paid according to what they produce. It is sometimes called a **payment by results** system. Wages are calculated by multiplying the number of units produced by the rate of pay per unit. For example, a textile worker might be paid according to the number of collars that are stitched onto shirts.

The **advantages** of a piece rate system are:

- employees are given an incentive to be productive, so output is raised;
- productive workers are rewarded and inefficient workers are penalised;
- the system is relatively easy to administer as long as output can easily be monitored.

The **disadvantages** include:

- quality might suffer and there might be more wastage and accidents if employees rush their work to maximise their earnings;
- costs might increase if supervisors and inspectors are needed to monitor the quality of items produced;

- it is often difficult to establish a 'fair rate' in terms of how many items it is reasonable to expect a worker to produce in a given period of time;
- machine breakdowns or cuts in the supply of key components can cause employees to lose pay through no fault of their own. This tends to cause industrial unrest and even strikes;
- the system is unsuitable if the output of employees cannot be measured.

Bonus or incentive schemes BONUS or INCENTIVE SCHEMES are a means of encouraging greater productivity in workforces which are paid a time rate. Such a scheme might involve paying staff an hourly rate plus an additional sum, a bonus, if a target level of output is reached. The aim is to combine the advantages of the time rate system with the advantages of the piece rate system.

There are several different ways of administering bonus or incentive schemes.

- COMMISSION This is a form of payment that is made to sales staff. The salesperson's pay is linked to the value of the goods or services sold. In a minority of cases, the entire earnings of an employee could be commission. However, a more common system is for sales staff to be paid a guaranteed basic wage, plus a payment for commission. The commission is likely to be a fixed percentage of the value of sales made. So, for example, staff in a car showroom might be paid an annual basic wage of £15,000 plus 1% of the value of the cars that they individually sell.
- PROFIT RELATED PAY Some businesses reward their employees according to how much profit is made during the year. For example, a bonus that is related to profit might be paid at Christmas or at the end of the financial year. This payment does not depend upon individual performance but on the collective efforts of everyone in the business. It is therefore most appropriate in businesses where the whole staff work as a team. However, it might be demotivating for an individual who consistently outperforms the team.
- PERFORMANCE RELATED PAY (PRP) This type of pay scheme is growing in popularity, both in the public and the private sector. Financial institutions such as the major banks, manufacturers such as Cadbury's and Nissan, and public sector organisations such as the NHS and schools, all use performance related pay. The scheme often involves an annual review, or appraisal, of an individual's performance by a senior manager. This might take the form of comparing the individual's performance with agreed targets set in the previous appraisal. At the end of the review, employees are placed in a 'performance category' so that the size of their pay increase can be determined. The system has the advantage that it rewards efficiency. However, it is sometimes criticised on the grounds that it is often difficult to measure individual performance and that it relies on the subjective judgment of managers.

QUESTION 2

The Croydon Gazette employs four telephone sales staff to sell advertising space. All of the staff receive a basic monthly wage of £300 plus commission based on their monthly sales. The commission is 5% of the value of monthly sales. The table in Figure 53.1 shows the value of advertising space sold by each member of staff in November 2000.

Figure 53.1 *Croydon Gazette advertising sales for November 2000*

Week	B. Roberts £	L. Singh £	B. Comyn £	T. Southgate £
1	4,500	5,300	4,800	4,300
2	4,700	5,200	4,600	4,800
3	4,300	4,300	5,000	4,300
4	5,600	5,100	5,200	3,400

(a) Calculate the November 2000 earnings for each salesperson.
(b) Suggest two advantages of remunerating staff in this way.
(c) Explain why a payment by results system might not be appropriate for the production employees who print the newspaper.

Direct and indirect labour costs

When accountants calculate the amount of gross and net profit that a business makes, they must work out the direct and indirect costs of production. **Direct labour** costs are the wages of production workers who are directly involved in making a product or providing a service. For example, the wages paid to workers who assemble cars on an assembly line would be classed as direct labour costs. **Indirect labour** costs are the wages paid to non-productive workers in the production department, such as supervisors, and the wages and salaries paid to administration and sales staff. These indirect costs are known as **overheads**.

Cost behaviour is a term used to describe how labour costs vary with different levels of production. **Fixed costs** are those costs that do not change with different levels of output. The indirect labour costs of administration staff usually fall into this category. **Variable costs** are those costs that do vary with output. Examples would include the direct labour costs of production workers who are paid on piece rates.

Although it is often the case that indirect labour costs are fixed and direct labour costs are variable, there are many exceptions. For example, the wages of sales staff who earn commission are indirect costs yet they do vary with the sales output of a business. On the other hand, the wages of production workers who are paid on time rates are direct costs yet they are fixed. In the longer run, if output rises or falls so much that more or fewer production workers are employed, these direct costs will also change. Under these circumstances they might be classed as **semi-variable** costs.

Recording labour costs

Most businesses keep records of the amount of time that employees spend at work. This information is used for payroll preparation, particularly in the case of hourly paid workers. Cost accountants need this information so that they can calculate the cost of specific business activities. For example, a cost accountant will need to know how many hours each employee works on a particular job to determine the labour cost of meeting a specific order.

To record the amount of time that employees spend at work, some businesses use a time-recording clock. This stamps the time on a card when the card is inserted by employees as they arrive and depart from work. More sophisticated methods use electronic swipe cards. The information is used to calculate the hours worked each day, week or month. An alternative system is for employees to complete **timesheets** which show the hours worked each day or week.

In other businesses, employees are required to record the amount of time they spend on each job. For example, in a garage, mechanics might have to fill in a sheet that shows how long it takes them to service a particular car. These **job time bookings** can be done manually or by using a time-recording clock. In some cases, employees also have to record any **idle time**. This is the amount of time that they spend not working. It might occur if an employee cannot proceed with a task because of a machine breakdown or a shortage of parts. This information can be useful to managers in monitoring and improving efficiency.

An example of a timesheet is given in Figure 53.2. It shows the hours worked by Terry Smyth and the jobs he worked on during one week in September 2001. Terry works for Bathgate Engineering Ltd and he operates a computerised cutting machine. During the week, he worked on 7 different jobs. His working week is 37 hours and any time worked over this is paid at an overtime rate of time and a half.

At the end of each week, Terry's timesheet is signed by his supervisor to verify its accuracy. The timesheet is used by the personnel department to calculate Terry's weekly wage. His pay rate is £6 per hour so his gross wages (ie before deductions for tax and National Insurance) for the week were £339.00 (37 x £6 + 13 x £9.00).

Figure 53.2 *Time sheet for Terry Smyth*

BATHGATE ENGINEERING LTD

NAME Terry Smyth   WEEK ENDING   21.9.01

Job no.	Monday	Tuesday	Wednesday	Thursday	Friday	Saturday	Total
193	2 hours		1 hour				3 hours
197	6 hours	2 hours					8 hours
198	2 hours						2 hours
200		6 hours	8 hours				14 hours
207				1 hour		1 hour	2 hours
208				1.5 hours		3 hours	4.5 hours
210				7 hours	6.5 hours	1.5 hours	15 hours
Idle					1.5 hours		1.5 hours
TOTAL	10 hours	8 hours	9 hours	9.5 hours	8 hours	5.5 hours	50 hours

Signed: **T. Betts**   (Supervisor)

Normal time 37 hours
Overtime   13 hours

The time sheet is used by the company's cost accountant to apportion labour costs to different jobs in the factory. For example, Terry spent a total of 14 hours on job number 200. This means that a direct labour charge equivalent to 14 times the hourly rate would be apportioned to job number 200. In practice, it is likely that a **standard hourly rate** would be applied. This is a predetermined, nominal pay rate which is used to calculate costs of production. It avoids complications such as which job was done on overtime and which job was done on the 'normal' rate. The issue of standard hourly rates and standard costs is dealt with in unit 56.

summary questions

1. State two advantages of time rates.
2. State two disadvantages of time rates.
3. Explain how the annualised hours system of remuneration increases flexibility for employers.
4. Explain how piece rates might motivate workers.
5. Which category of employees might be paid commission at work?
6. State two advantages to employers of profit related pay.
7. State two features of performance related pay.
8. Give four examples of fringe benefits.
9. Explain the difference between direct and indirect labour.
10. Explain how time sheets might help cost accountants.

QUESTION 3

Bernadette Harrington is employed as a trainee solicitor for Brennan, Lawler and Watson. She works mainly on divorce cases and is paid a trainee's salary of £17,000 p.a. The partnership requires all staff involved in legal work to complete timesheets. The partnership calculates client's fees by multiplying the number of hours that staff work on each case by a set hourly rate. However, not all staff charge clients the same rate, it depends on seniority. Bernadette's rate is £20 per hour. A timesheet completed by Bernadette is shown in Figure 53.3.

Figure 53.3 *Time sheet for Bernadette Harrington*

BRENNAN, LAWLER AND WATSON

NAME Bernadette Harrington				WEEK ENDING W/E 23.6.01		
Client	Monday	Tuesday	Wednesday	Thursday	Friday	Total
T. Jones	1.5 hrs	2.5 hrs			1 hr	5 hrs
W. Forshaw			4 hrs			4 hrs
E. Curtis	3.5 hrs	4.5 hrs			1 hr	9 hrs
B. Evans	2 hrs					2 hrs
P. Norton				7 hrs		7 hrs
T. Westwood					5 hrs	5 hrs
F. Ponting			3 hrs			3 hrs
Total	7 hrs	7 hrs	7 hrs	7 hrs	7 hrs	35 hrs

Signed: **J. Brennan** (Partner)

(a) **Explain why the timesheet shown in Figure 53.3 is necessary when Bernadette is not paid by the hour.**
(b) **Assuming that Bernadette works an average of 35 hours per week for 48 weeks per year, calculate the difference between Bernadette's salary and the amount that clients would be charged over the year for Bernadette's time.**
(c) **Why do you think the timesheet is signed by a partner?**

key terms

Annualised hours - a payment system based on a fixed number of hours to be worked each year, but a flexible number of hours to be worked each day, week or month.
Bonus or incentive scheme - a payment system in which an extra payment made in recognition of the contribution a worker has made.
Commission - a payment system that involves paying staff according to the value of goods or services they sell.
Fringe benefit - a non-monetary form of remuneration, for example a company car or a subsidised canteen.
Performance related pay - a payment system that links a worker's efforts and achievements to pay.
Piece rate - a payment system in which employees are paid a set rate for every unit of output they produce.
Profit related pay - a payment system that involves linking part of a worker's pay to the profit made by the business.
Remunerution - the pay and other benefits that employees receive from their employer.
Time rate - a payment system in which employees are paid according to the amount of time they spend at work.

UNIT ASSESSMENT QUESTION 1

Atkinson's Ltd assembles electric motors for washing machines. The company employs 60 production workers who are paid £5.60 per hour. The working week is 35 hours and, at present, there is no system of overtime. In the last two years, demand for Atkinson's motors has increased. However, the company has struggled to meet some of the orders on time. The board of directors is considering two possible schemes to increase production.

- **Bonus scheme** At present, the average output in a 7 hour shift is 20 motors per person, ie 600 motors per shift. Under the proposed scheme, staff would each be offered a bonus payment of £25 per week if the average shift output throughout the week was raised to 660 motors.
- **Overtime payments** The company estimates that an average of 120 hours per week overtime would be sufficient to meet demand. The employees' trade union has indicated that employees would be prepared to work overtime at a rate of £9.60 per hour.

(a) Calculate the weekly wage bill if the bonus scheme was introduced and output was raised to 660 motors per shift.

(b) Calculate the weekly wage bill if the overtime scheme was introduced and 120 hours per week overtime was worked.

(c) What factors might influence the board of directors in choosing either of the schemes?

(d) From the employees' point of view, what are the advantages and disadvantages of the two schemes?

UNIT ASSESSMENT QUESTION 2

Alid Fabrics Ltd has a small factory in which jeans are manufactured. There are currently 20 machinists who are paid a piece rate of 60 pence per item produced. On average, each machinist can produce 7 items per hour working a 40 hour week. During the past year, a series of mistakes in the ordering department has meant that stocks of denim material have run out at crucial times. When this has happened, machinists have been sent home and have therefore lost pay. As a result, five of the more efficient machinists have left and obtained jobs in factories where workers are paid an hourly rate.

In order to prevent the loss of experienced staff, the owner of Alid Fabrics is considering changing from a piece rate system to an hourly rate of pay.

(a) Calculate the weekly earnings of a machinist who produces an average of (i) 5 items per hour, (ii) 7 items per hour and (iii) 9 items per hour under the piece rate system.

(b) John Siddall is a machinist who produces an average of 7 items per hour. If the company changes from a piece rate to a time rate system, what must be his hourly rate of pay if he is neither to gain nor lose?

(c) From Alid Fabrics' point of view, suggest an advantage and a disadvantage of moving from a piece rate to a time rate.

(d) Suggest how the disadvantages of moving to time rates might be overcome.

(e) From the machinists' point of view, what are the advantages and disadvantages of moving from a piece rate to a time rate?

Budgets and budgetary control

unit**objectives**

To understand:
- **the nature and purpose of budgets;**
- **how budgets are prepared;**
- **budgetary control.**

What is the purpose of budgets?

A BUDGET is a financial statement that sets out plans for a future accounting period, such as the next financial year. Businesses use budgets for a number of reasons.

Planning The process of preparing a budget forces managers to draw up plans of action. This approach to management is generally considered more effective than simply reacting to events as they occur. Planning helps managers clarify their aims, consider and evaluate alternative courses of action and choose the best course that is available. It also helps managers foresee future problems. As a result, solutions to the problems can be found in advance and the consequences of their impact can be reduced or avoided.

Coordination Budgeting helps to coordinate the activities of all departments. During the budget setting process, an overall plan will be produced. Managers will then prepare their departmental budgets to fit in with the overall plan. It is important that different areas of a business do not operate in isolation. For example, if a sales department plans a big promotion without consulting the production department, the result might be that orders will not be fulfilled.

Control Budgets provide a useful means of financial control and of evaluating performance. During and at the end of a budget period, a business is likely to compare actual income and expenditure with the budgeted amounts. The differences between actual and planned totals are called **variances** (see unit 56). A business is likely to investigate reasons for any significant variances and use the information to help improve future performance. The use of budgets to monitor performance is sometimes called **budgetary control**. It is explained in more detail later in the unit.

Communication Budgets are a means by which targets are communicated to and from managers and other employees. Departmental budgets show how the activity in each area of a business fits in with the overall plan.

Motivation It is sometimes claimed that budgeting improves motivation by setting managers clear targets and relating these targets to the overall goals of the business. In addition, budgeting can help motivation if a number of staff are involved in the process. By taking part in budget preparation, staff might gain a greater sense of 'ownership' and will therefore try harder to achieve the planned outcomes.

Types of budgets

Businesses produce a wide range of different budgets depending on their needs and circumstances. Small businesses might only prepare a **cash budget** showing payments and receipts. Larger businesses might produce complex **master budgets** that summarise the budgets for every department or 'functional area' within the organisation. The most commonly used budgets include the following.

- **The sales budget** This shows the value of sales that a business plans to make each month. It is an important budget because it influences all other budgets. For instance, if a business plans to increase sales, then it will have to produce more and make more purchases.
- **The (finished goods) stock budget** This shows the planned increase or decrease in stocks of finished goods. It is sometimes expressed in units of output rather than as a monetary value.
- **The production budget** This shows the planned output each month. The production budget

will generally be based on the sales budget. It sometimes incorporates the finished goods stock in order to show the quantity of goods available for sale.

- **The purchases budget** This shows the value of planned purchases of raw materials and components that are required in the production process.
- **The debtors and creditors budgets** These set out the planned totals owed by debtors and owed to creditors at the end of each month. The closing balances will be determined by the value of planned sales and purchases made on credit each month, together with the amounts received from customers and the amounts paid to suppliers.
- **The cash budget** This is sometimes called a **cash flow budget**, a **cash flow forecast** or a **cash flow projection**. It shows the planned flows of cash into and out of the business each month. It is described in more detail in unit 42.
- **The master budget** This includes the budgeted profit and loss account and the budgeted balance sheet. These are sometimes called **forecast final accounts**. They summarise the other budgets and are drawn up and presented in the same way as the final accounts. However, since they are for internal use only, they are not subject to the requirements of the Companies Acts. They are described in more detail in unit 55.

QUESTION 1

Figure 54.1 shows a sales budget for Kingham Ltd, a manufacturer of domestic refrigerators. The company makes four models and the planned monthly sales of each are shown in the budget for 2001.

Figure 54.1 *Sales budget for Kingham Ltd, 2001*

	Jan	Feb	Mar	Apr	May	Jun	Jul	Aug	Sep	Oct	Nov	Dec	Total
	£000	£000	£000	£000	£000	£000	£000	£000	£000	£000	£000	£000	£000
Kingham 1	100	100	80	80	80	60	60	60	40	40	0	0	700
Kingham 2	40	40	40	60	60	60	80	80	100	100	120	140	920
Deluxe	50	50	50	50	50	50	50	50	50	50	50	50	600
Family	65	65	65	70	70	70	75	75	75	80	80	80	870
Total	255	255	235	260	260	240	265	265	265	270	250	270	3,090

(a) Briefly describe and comment on the main features of the sales budget.
(b) How might the sales budget be of help to other departments at Kingham Ltd?
(c) State two other possible functions of the sales budget.

Preparation of budgets

In large businesses, the coordination, administration and monitoring of budgets is generally the responsibility of a **budget committee**. This committee of senior executives is usually assisted by a **budget officer** who prepares the cash and master budgets from the **functional budgets** drawn up by departmental managers. Figure 54.2 shows one possible approach to budget setting.

- The first stage in the budgeting process is to set the budget period and to establish the budgetary aims and objectives. The budget period can vary according to the needs of the business, but annual or monthly budgets are the most common. The aims of the business will generally be set by the board of directors or the owners and will be in line with long-term strategic objectives.
- The next stage is to identify the **limiting budget factor.** This is the key constraint that limits the activities of the business. In most cases, it is sales demand. This affects the level of sales and therefore, indirectly, the level of production. However, in some cases, the limiting factor might be the capacity of production machinery or the scarcity of raw materials. Such constraints are also called **key budget factors** or **principal budget factors**.
- A range of information must be gathered before budgets can be prepared. The information is often based on historical data. For example, the level of costs in one year might provide an accurate indicator of costs in the following year. In some cases, particular costs are known. For instance, when preparing the overheads budget, a business will know how much rent it will pay. However, some of the most important information relates to future sales levels, which are subject

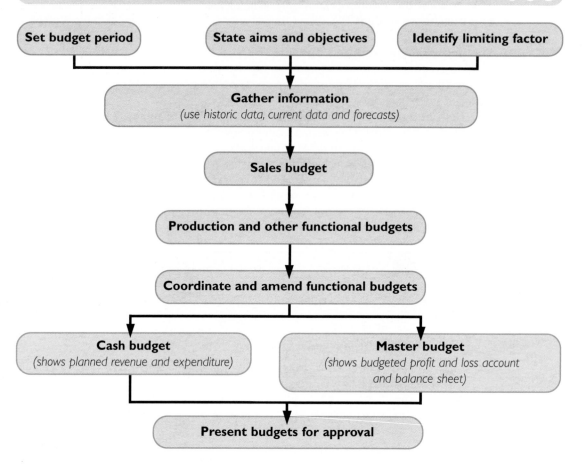

Figure 54.2 *Stages in the preparation of budgets*

to external factors and cannot be easily predicted. Methods of obtaining such information is discussed in the next section of the unit.

- The department faced with the limiting factor will be the first to prepare its budget. So, if the limiting budget factor is sales demand, it will be the sales department that produces the first budget.
- Once the sales budget has been agreed, the preparation of other budgets can follow. These will include the budgets for functional areas such as the production department and the purchasing department.
- The departmental budgets are likely to be reviewed by the budget officer or budget committee. It is important to check that departmental budgets are consistent with each other and with the overall budget.
- Once the functional budgets have been agreed, the cash budget and the master budget can be prepared. The cash budget will show the flows of cash into and out of the business. The master budget will show the forecast profit and loss account and the forecast balance sheet for the budget period.
- The final step in the process is to present the budgets to the budget committee. If approval is given, then no further preparation is necessary. However, after the budget is accepted it is usual for the budget committee to compare actual results with the budget plans. This process of review might cause the budget to be revised if, for example, there is a fall in consumer confidence or the price of raw materials rises.

Preparing a sales budget

A sales budget can be difficult to prepare because sales levels are affected by factors outside the control of the business. These factors include the state of the economy, the actions of competitors, interest rates, seasonal factors and changes in consumer tastes. However, some examples of ways in which future sales levels might be forecast are outlined on the next page.

- **Extrapolation** This method involves using historical sales data. Future sales levels are estimated by projecting past trends into the future. For example, if sales have been increasing by 5% per annum in the last 6 years, extrapolation would suggest that sales will also rise by 5% in the next year.
- **Market research** This involves questioning potential customers about their future buying intentions. However, market research can be unreliable if, for example, an unrepresentative sample of customers are questioned.
- **Sales force composite method** This relies on individual sales staff providing their own sales forecasts and then adding the totals. It is sometimes claimed that individual sales staff who deal with customers on a daily basis are in the best position to predict future demand.

To prepare a sales budget it is first necessary to estimate the volume of future sales and the prices that will be charged for each unit. Using this information, the planned sales revenue can be calculated. To illustrate how a sales budget might be prepared, consider Johnson's Caravans, a manufacturer of touring caravans. The company produces two different models, the Grand Tourer and the Family Tourer. The company bases its estimates of future sales by using historical data. Figure 54.3 shows the actual monthly sales of each model in 2001.

Figure 54.3 *Numbers of each caravan model sold in 2001*

	Jan	Feb	Mar	Apr	May	Jun	Jul	Aug	Sep	Oct	Nov	Dec	Total
	units	units	units	units	units	units	units	units	units	units	units	units	units
Grand Tourer	10	10	20	30	40	40	30	20	20	10	10	10	250
Family Tourer	20	20	20	40	40	50	50	40	20	20	20	10	350
Total	30	30	40	70	80	90	80	60	40	30	30	20	600

For 2002, Johnson's expected that its sales would rise by 10%. This was in line with past performance and is shown in Figure 54.4. Each sales figure is 10% higher than the 2001 figure. The sales budget for 2002 was prepared using this information together with the selling price. The Grand Tourer was priced at £18,000 and the Family Tourer was priced at £12,000. The sales budget is shown in Figure 54.5. It shows the planned monthly sales revenue and the annual total of £9,570,000.

Figure 54.4 *Number of caravans that Johnson's planned to sell in 2002*

	Jan	Feb	Mar	Apr	May	Jun	Jul	Aug	Sep	Oct	Nov	Dec	Total
	units	units	units	units	units	units	units	units	units	units	units	units	units
Grand Tourer	11	11	22	33	44	44	33	22	22	11	11	11	275
Family Tourer	22	22	22	44	44	55	55	44	22	22	22	11	385
Total	33	33	44	77	88	99	88	66	44	33	33	22	660

Figure 54.5 *Sales budget for Johnson's Caravans, 2002*

	Jan	Feb	Mar	Apr	May	Jun	Jul	Aug	Sep	Oct	Nov	Dec	Total
	£000	£000	£000	£000	£000	£000	£000	£000	£000	£000	£000	£000	£000
Grand Tourer	198	198	396	594	792	792	594	396	396	198	198	198	4,950
Family Tourer	264	264	264	528	528	660	660	528	264	264	264	132	4,620
Total	462	462	660	1,122	1,320	1,452	1,254	924	660	462	462	330	9,570

QUESTION 2

Montgomery Ltd makes plastic chairs. The company produces three styles (traditional, modern and stacking) and most are sold to schools, colleges, hospitals and offices. Although sales in 2001 were relatively stable, it was expected that new foreign competition would cause sales of the traditional and modern styles to fall by 10% in 2002. Sales of the stacking chair were expected to remain the same.

Figure 54.6 shows the 2001 sales for each of the three styles. The 2002 prices were: traditional £3.00; modern £4.00; and stacking £4.50.

Figure 54.6 *Sales of plastic chairs for Montgomery Ltd in 2001 (000s)*

	Jan	Feb	Mar	Apr	May	Jun	Jul	Aug	Sep	Oct	Nov	Dec	Total
	units (000)	units (000)	units (000)	units (000)	units (000)	units (000)	units (000)	units (000)	units (000)	units (000)	units (000)	units (000)	units (000)
Traditional	100	100	100	100	100	100	100	100	100	100	100	100	1,200
Modern	50	50	50	50	50	50	50	50	60	60	60	60	640
Stacking	40	40	40	40	30	30	30	30	20	20	20	20	360
Total	190	190	190	190	180	180	180	180	180	180	180	180	2,200

(a) **What information would the sales manager of Montgomery Ltd require in order to prepare the 2002 sales budget? Suggest possible sources for this information.**
(b) **Produce the 2002 sales budget for Montgomery Ltd.**
(c) **Calculate the budgeted change in sales revenue over the two years.**

Production and other functional budgets

Assuming that customer demand is the limiting budget factor, when a business has drawn up its sales budget, other budgets can then be prepared. For example, when a particular sales figure has been decided, it is possible to plan production and stock levels to meet this demand. Following on from this, a purchases budget, a creditors budget and a debtors budget can all be drawn up. To illustrate how these budgets are prepared, consider the example of Elizabeth Chan & Co. This is a new company that makes silk pyjamas. It started production last January and its sales budget for the year is shown in Figure 54.7. The price of each pair of pyjamas was set at £100.

Figure 54.7 *Elizabeth Chan & Co sales budget (in units and in financial terms)*

	Jan	Feb	Mar	Apr	May	Jun	Jul	Aug	Sep	Oct	Nov	Dec	Total
Pyjamas (units)	0	60	70	80	90	100	100	100	100	100	100	100	1,000
Sales (£)	0	6,000	7,000	8,000	9,000	10,000	10,000	10,000	10,000	10,000	10,000	10,000	100,000

The company's policies regarding stock, production levels and other issues are set out below.
- Sales are expected to be maintained at 100 units per month during the following year.
- The company plans to produce at such a level that sufficient stocks of finished goods for each month's sales are available at the end of the preceding month.
- A just-in-time production policy is used so that, each month, purchases are just sufficient to meet that month's production needs.
- The raw material costs are expected to be £50 per garment.
- All sales are on one month's credit.
- All purchases of raw materials are on one month's credit.

Production and finished goods stock budget In order to produce enough goods to meet demand, and to fulfil the company's policy on stock levels, the budget in Figure 54.8 was prepared. It is expressed in units of production. Note that each month's production was planned so that the stock of finished goods at the end of the month was sufficient to meet the following month's demand. So, for instance, production in January was 60 units and, because stocks were zero, this was just sufficient to meet the planned sales for February. The sales are taken from the sales budget in Figure 54.7.

Figure 54.8 *Production and finished goods stock budget*

	Jan	Feb	Mar	Apr	May	Jun	Jul	Aug	Sep	Oct	Nov	Dec	Total
	units	units	units	units	units	units	units	units	units	units	units	units	units
Opening stock	0	60	70	80	90	100	100	100	100	100	100	100	
Production	60	70	80	90	100	100	100	100	100	100	100	100	1,100
	60	130	150	170	190	200	200	200	200	200	200	200	
Less sales	0	60	70	80	90	100	100	100	100	100	100	100	1,000
Closing stock	60	70	80	90	100	100	100	100	100	100	100	100	

Purchases budget Once production levels were determined, it was possible to prepare the purchases budget in Figure 54.9. It is expressed in financial terms. For example, in January, purchases of raw materials for the production of 60 garments was required. At £50 per garment, this totalled £3,000. The total purchases for the year were planned to be £55,000. This includes purchases of £5,000 for the first month of the next year.

Figure 54.9 *Purchases budget*

	Jan	Feb	Mar	Apr	May	Jun	Jul	Aug	Sep	Oct	Nov	Dec	Total
	£	£	£	£	£	£	£	£	£	£	£	£	£
Purchases	3,000	3,500	4,000	4,500	5,000	5,000	5,000	5,000	5,000	5,000	5,000	5,000	55,000

Creditors budget When planned purchases have been calculated, it is possible to draw up a budget to show how much money is owed by the business at the end of each month. Elizabeth Chan & Co is given one month's credit by its suppliers. So, for example, purchases of £3,000 in January are not paid for until February. The budget is shown in Figure 54.10. Note that the total payments were £5,000 less than the total purchases because of the credit period granted by suppliers.

Figure 54.10 *Creditors budget*

	Jan	Feb	Mar	Apr	May	Jun	Jul	Aug	Sep	Oct	Nov	Dec	Total
	£	£	£	£	£	£	£	£	£	£	£	£	£
Opening bal.	0	3,000	3,500	4,000	4,500	5,000	5,000	5,000	5,000	5,000	5,000	5,000	
Purchases	3,000	3,500	4,000	4,500	5,000	5,000	5,000	5,000	5,000	5,000	5,000	5,000	55,000
	3,000	6,500	7,500	8,500	9,500	10,000	10,000	10,000	10,000	10,000	10,000	10,000	
Less payment	0	3,000	3,500	4,000	4,500	5,000	5,000	5,000	5,000	5,000	5,000	5,000	50,000
Closing bal.	3,000	3,500	4,000	4,500	5,000	5,000	5,000	5,000	5,000	5,000	5,000	5,000	

Debtors budget This budget is prepared using the sales budget. It shows how much is owed by customers to the business at the end of each month. The budget is shown in Figure 54.11. The company allows all its customers one month's credit and, in this example, there are no customers who pay by cash. Therefore all the sales and receipts are shown in the debtors budget. At the end of the year, total sales were £100,000 and total payments received were £90,000. The difference between the two figures is because £10,000 was outstanding from customers.

Figure 54.11 *Debtors budget*

	Jan	Feb	Mar	Apr	May	Jun	Jul	Aug	Sep	Oct	Nov	Dec	Total
	£	£	£	£	£	£	£	£	£	£	£	£	£
Opening bal.	0	0	6,000	7,000	8,000	9,000	10,000	10,000	10,000	10,000	10,000	10,000	
Sales	0	6,000	7,000	8,000	9,000	10,000	10,000	10,000	10,000	10,000	10,000	10,000	100,000
	0	6,000	13,000	15,000	17,000	19,000	20,000	20,000	20,000	20,000	20,000	20,000	
Less receipts	0	0	6,000	7,000	8,000	9,000	10,000	10,000	10,000	10,000	10,000	10,000	90,000
Closing bal.	0	6,000	7,000	8,000	9,000	10,000	10,000	10,000	10,000	10,000	10,000	10,000	

QUESTION 3

The Layton Dairy Co produces and sells yoghurt to health food shops. The company is successful and its sales have grown steadily over a number of years. Its 2002 sales budget is shown in Figure 54.12. The opening balance on its 2002 debtors budget was £11,000. The company allows its customers one month's credit. So, in January, £11,000 was received from these debtors.

Figure 54.12 *Layton Dairy Co sales budget, 2002*

	Jan	Feb	Mar	Apr	May	Jun	Jul	Aug	Sep	Oct	Nov	Dec	Total
	£000	£000	£000	£000	£000	£000	£000	£000	£000	£000	£000	£000	£000
	12	12	13	14	14	15	16	16	15	15	14	14	170

(a) Prepare the 2002 debtors budget.
(b) Explain why the debtors budget cannot be prepared until the sales budget is complete.
(c) Explain why the planned total of receipts is not the same as the planned total sales revenue.

Budgetary control

BUDGETARY CONTROL is a process by which financial control is exercised within a business. Managers of departments such as sales, purchasing and production are given responsibility for meeting their budgets. Then, throughout the budget period, the budgets are compared with actual performance to establish any differences or **variances**. The budgetary control process is summarised in Figure 54.13.

Figure 54.13 *Stages in budgetary control*

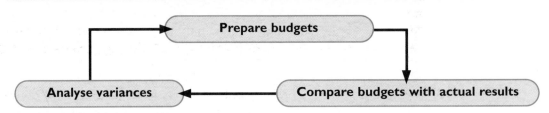

- The first stage in the process is to prepare the various budgets. The budgets will reflect the plans made by the business to achieve its aims and objectives. Individual budgets will be prepared in a coordinated way so that conflict and inconsistencies are avoided.
- During and at the end of the budget period comparisons are made between the income and expenditure outlined in the budgets and the actual results. Budgetary control will be more effective if budget data is collected and processed as quickly as possible. The size of the variances between budgeted values and actual results will reflect the success or failure of individual departments in achieving their objectives. The calculation and analysis of variances is explained in unit 56.
- Once the variances have been identified, the final stage in the process is to analyse why they have occurred and, if necessary, to take remedial action. This is the most important stage in the control process. Differences between actual and planned results will help to measure the performance of individual departments. For example, if the production department is unable to produce the planned output, this might be regarded as a failure. If managers can find reasons for the variances, they can make adjustments to help improve performance in the next budget period.

Benefits and limitations of budgetary control

In the UK, most large manufacturing businesses use some form of budgetary control. The benefits and limitations of this system of management are outlined on the next page.

Benefits of budgetary control

- It provides a means of controlling expenditure and therefore cash flow.
- It allows a business to review its activities and provides a warning when things are going wrong. Remedial action might then be possible.
- It helps to emphasise and clarify the responsibilities of managers.
- It helps coordination within a business and improves communication between departments.
- It provides clear targets for all staff and therefore improves the likelihood of achieving objectives.

Limitations of budgetary control

- It can lead to complacency if managers find it relatively easy to meet their budgets and there is no incentive to improve performance.
- It can be a wasteful exercise if the budgets are not carefully prepared and the actual performance is very different from the budgeted outcomes.
- It might lead to lost opportunities if budgets are too inflexible. For example, an opportunity to develop a new overseas market might be missed if the sales department's travel budget has been spent.
- It might lead to resentment among some staff if they have not been involved in the budget setting process. This can result in poor motivation and missed targets.

Behavioural aspects of budgeting

Budgets are prepared with the intention of affecting the attitudes and behaviour of managers. Depending on how well the budgeting process is carried out, studies show that budgets can either motivate or demotivate staff. Three factors have been identified which affect the extent to which budgets contribute to business success.

The tightness of budgets Should budgets be set 'tight' or 'loose'? A tight budget means that income and expenditure targets will be difficult to achieve. A loose budget means that targets will be much easier to achieve. Some studies have argued that the use of budgets will only improve performance if they are set at a particular degree of tightness. For example, a budget that is too loose will encourage inefficiency and a budget that is too tight will result in a disillusioned staff and poor performance. It is sometimes claimed that, to improve efficiency and motivation, budgets should be set just slightly tighter than expected by staff. An alternative approach is to use a system of **flexible budgets** in which a range of outcomes is given. Then, for example, at every level of possible sales, budget figures are adjusted accordingly.

The use of budgets How should budgets be used to evaluate staff performance? There are two broad approaches to performance evaluation, **budget-orientated** and **profit-orientated**. If evaluation is budget-orientated, staff performance is linked to whether targets outlined in budgets have been achieved. Although this approach can be successful, studies suggest that staff sometimes make decisions to meet budget targets even if this undermines the performance of the whole organisation. For example, in order to avoid overspending on a materials budget, a manager might order cheaper but inferior materials. This might help to meet the budget target, but could also result in customer dissatisfaction.

On the other hand, if evaluation is profit-orientated, a broader, long-term view might be taken by staff. It might not matter if some departments fail to meet their budget targets provided that the long-term profitability of the company improves. Such an approach is often more acceptable to staff and, arguably, better for the business. However, this policy requires senior managers to relinquish a measure of budgetary control and be prepared to trust junior staff to act responsibly.

Participation To what extent should staff participate in the preparation of budgets? Studies increasingly suggest that 'top-down budgeting' is inappropriate. This is where budgets are prepared by senior managers with little or no consultation with others. Budget targets are far more likely to be met if staff are involved in their preparation. Staff will also be better motivated if they have been given the opportunity to contribute. However, there is the danger that 'bottom-up budgeting' will result in budgets that are too loose. This is because staff who have control over their own budgets might be tempted to overstate costs and understate revenues so that the budget is more easily achieved.

summary questions

1. Explain the purpose of budgets.
2. What is a functional budget?
3. Give three examples of functional budgets.
4. What is the difference between a cash budget and the master budget?
5. What is the role of a budget committee?
6. Explain what is meant by a limiting factor in budgeting.
7. Under what circumstances might production rather than sales be a limiting factor?
8. State three ways in which future sales might be forecast.
9. State three benefits and three drawbacks of budgetary control.
10. Explain what is meant by the behavioural aspects of budgetary control.

UNIT ASSESSMENT — QUESTION 1

Harvester & Co manufactures health drinks. The marketing manager prepared a quarterly sales projection for 2001 as follows:

	Sales volume (units)
Quarter 1	40,000
Quarter 2	40,000
Quarter 3	40,000
Quarter 4	40,000

The sale price per bottle was 50p for the first quarter but, at the start of the second quarter, it was planned to raise the price to 60p per bottle for the rest of the year. The raw materials cost 20p per bottle during the first quarter but this was expected to rise at the start of the second quarter to 25p for the rest of the year.

Closing stocks of bottles at the end of each quarter (including the last quarter of 2000) were planned as being equivalent to 5% of the next quarter's sales. Purchases of raw materials during each quarter were planned so that the amount purchased was just sufficient to meet production needs.

Prepare the following budgets for 2001 showing the planned values for each quarter and the year in total.
(a) Sales budget (in monetary terms).
(b) Production and finished stock budget (in units).
(c) Purchases budget (in monetary terms).
(d) What additional information would be required in order to prepare (i) a debtors budget and (ii) a creditors budget?

UNIT ASSESSMENT QUESTION 2

Clare Hanson has bought a small jewellery shop. She will commence trading on 1 July and has acquired all the assets and liabilities of the business. The working capital of the business (ie its net current assets) as at 30 June is given below. It shows that debtors owed £400 and creditors are owed £3,500 on that date.

	£
Current assets	
Stock	4,000
Debtors	400
	4,400
Current liabilities	
Creditors	3,500
Net current assets	900

The debtors who owed money in June were expected to settle their debts in July. Clare expects that most of her customers will pay cash, but 10% of sales will be budgeted as credit sales with these customers being given one month's credit. The creditors who were owed money in June would be paid in August. Subsequently, Clare expected to be given two months' credit by her suppliers.

The budgeted sales and purchases for the first six months were as follows.

	Jul	Aug	Sep	Oct	Nov	Dec
	£	£	£	£	£	£
Sales	2,000	3,000	4,000	5,000	5,000	5,000
Purchases	2,000	1,000	1,500	1,500	1,500	1,500

Prepare the following budgets for the July - December period.
(a) Debtors budget.
(b) Creditors budget.
(c) Briefly explain why Clare should produce budgets for her new business.

key terms

Budget - a financial statement that outlines planned expenditure or revenue over a future time period.
Budgetary control - a process that involves making financial plans, calculating the differences or variance between planned values and actual values, and identifying reasons for the differences.

The cash budget and the master budget

unitobjectives

To understand:
- the purpose of a cash budget;
- the preparation of a cash budget;
- the preparation of a master budget.

The purpose of a cash budget

The final stage in the budgetary process, outlined in unit 54, is to prepare the CASH BUDGET and the MASTER BUDGET. The cash budget shows the planned flows of cash into and out of the business each month. The master budget contains the budgeted (or forecast) profit and loss account and balance sheet.

The cash budget is extremely important because a business cannot continue to operate if it runs out of cash. Workers will not work if their wages are not paid, utilities such as electricity and water will be cut off if bills are not settled and banks will call in loans if repayments are missed. Business owners and managers need to be aware of cash flow problems before they occur. This enables them to make preparations before a shortage of cash threatens the survival of the business. For example, if a business can see from its cash budget that it will run out of cash in six months' time, it can make arrangements to borrow money or raise some extra capital from the owners before the problem arises.

Preparing a cash budget

To illustrate how a cash budget is constructed, consider the example of Hudsons Flowers Ltd, a wholesaler of fresh flowers. The budget is prepared for a six month period and is based on the information contained in functional budgets, such as the sales budget and the purchases budget. The budget statement, shown in Figure 55.1, has three sections:
- cash inflows, or receipts;
- cash outflows, or payments;
- the net cash flow and cash balance.

Cash inflows/receipts Most of the cash flowing into the business results from the sale of goods to customers. However, other examples of cash inflows could include injections of new capital from the owners, money from bank loans, interest from bank deposits held by the business and proceeds from the sale of unwanted fixed assets.

It is usual to show the cash from credit sales separate from that of cash sales. The cash budget for Hudsons Flowers indicates that, in January, the business expects to receive £10,000 from cash sales and a further £33,000 from credit sales. Hudsons Flowers allows 30 days credit, so these credit sales will have been made in the December of the previous budget period. This information comes from the business's sales budget. Hudsons Flowers also expects to receive £3,000 cash from the sale of a van in January. Total receipts for January are expected to be £46,000.

Cash outflows/payments A number of expected cash payments are listed for Hudsons Flowers. For example, in January, the business expects to spend £24,000 on purchases of flowers from suppliers. Hudsons Flowers pays cash for all of its purchases in order to take advantage of cash discounts. Other examples of payments that are expected in January include wages of £3,500, rent of £2,000, taxation of £12,000 and other expenses of £4,000. The total expected cash outflow during January is £47,800. This information comes from different functional budgets. For example, the total for purchases comes from the purchases budget and the total for rent comes from the overheads budget. Non-cash expenses such as depreciation and bad debts are not entered. This is because they do not result in any movement of cash and therefore do not affect the closing cash balance.

Net cash flow The final section of the cash budget shows the net cash flow for each month, the opening cash balance and the closing cash balance. The net cash flow is calculated by subtracting payments from receipts. Figure 55.1 shows that, in January, the payments are greater than receipts, leading to a negative cash flow of -£1,800 (£46,000 - £47,800). Because the net cash flow is negative, it is shown in brackets. In March, however, receipts are greater than payments so net cash flow is positive (£67,000 - £40,800 = £26,200).

The opening cash balance for January is £1,500. This is equal to the closing balance in December of the previous budget period. It is added to the net cash flow to obtain the closing cash balance. Because the net cash flow in January is negative, -£1,800, and is greater than the the the opening balance, the closing balance is also negative, -£300. This amount then becomes the opening cash balance for February.

Figure 55.1 *A cash budget for Hudsons Flowers Ltd*

	Jan £	Feb £	Mar £	Apr £	May £	Jun £
Cash Budget for the six months ending 30.6						
Receipts						
Receipts from cash sales	10,000	23,000	16,000	10,000	10,000	10,000
Receipts from credit sales	33,000	34,000	51,000	42,000	31,000	31,000
Sale of delivery van	3,000					
Total cash receipts	46,000	57,000	67,000	52,000	41,000	41,000
Payments						
Purchases	24,000	34,000	29,000	23,000	23,000	23,000
Wages	3,500	3,500	3,500	3,500	3,500	3,500
Rent	2,000	2,000	2,000	2,000	2,000	2,000
Motor expenses	2,300	2,300	2,300	3,600	2,300	2,300
Insurance				1,200		
Tax	12,000					
New delivery van		18,000				
Other expenses	4,000	4,000	4,000	4,000	4,000	4,000
Total cash payments	47,800	63,800	40,800	37,300	34,800	34,800
Net cash inflow/(outflow)	(1,800)	(6,800)	26,200	14,700	6,200	6,200
Opening balance	1,500	(300)	(7,100)	19,100	33,800	40,000
Closing balance	(300)	(7,100)	19,100	33,800	40,000	46,200

Management action When a cash budget is prepared, it gives managers an indication of potential problems or opportunities that might arise. Figure 55.1 shows that, in the very short-term, Hudsons Flowers will have a cash deficit. If the company does not have sufficient reserves to cover this, it needs to take remedial action. For example, it might arrange a short term loan or overdraft from the bank, or it might make a special effort to reduce debtors by asking for early payment. Alternatively, it might ask its suppliers for a period of credit.

The cash budget shows that, within six months, Hudsons Flowers expects to move into a position of surplus on its cash flow. This money could be used, for instance, to earn interest for the company by placing it in a bank deposit account. The money could also be used to finance a sales drive by offering new and existing customers a longer period of credit.

Figure 55.1 only shows the expected cash flows in the short term. A cash budget for a year or more ahead can be used to help with long-term decision making. If, for example, a cash budget showed a likely cash deficit in the long term, owners and managers might consider closing the business, or refinancing it with new share capital. On the other hand, a long-term cash surplus could be used to expand or diversify the business, or to replace fixed assets.

QUESTION 1

Ribbleton Quarries plc extracts limestone and manufactures cement. Figure 55.2 shows an incomplete cash budget for a six month budget period in 2002.

Figure 55.2 *Cash budget for Ribbleton Quarries*

			Cash Budget for the six months ending 30.6.02			
	Jan	Feb	Mar	Apr	May	Jun
	£	£	£	£	£	£
Receipts						
Receipts from credit sales	70,000	80,000	100,000	120,000	100,000	110,000
Bank loan	20,000					
Total cash receipts	90,000	80,000	100,000	120,000	100,000	110,000
Payments						
Purchases	5,000	4,000	5,000	6,000	5,000	5,000
Wages	45,000	40,000	50,000	60,000	50,000	55,000
Administration	10,000	10,000	10,000	10,000	10,000	10,000
Plant maintenance	6,000	6,000	6,000	6,000	6,000	6,000
Insurance				23,000		
Fuel	3,000	2,500	3,500	4,000	3,500	4,000
New bulldozer	70,000					
Taxation			65,000			
Other expenses	2,000	4,000	3,000	5,000	2,000	2,000
Total cash payments	141,000	66,500	142,500	114,000	76,500	82,000

Net cash inflow/(outflow)
Opening balance
Closing balance

(a) **Complete the cash budget for Ribbleton Quarries. The closing cash balance in December 2001 was £2,300.**
(b) **Taking the role of the finance director, write a memo to the managing director that briefly outlines the cash position of the company and the possible options open to the company.**
(c) **Where might the information have come from to complete the receipts and payments sections of the cash budget?**

Budgeted profit and loss account

The master budget is made up of the budgeted profit and loss account and the budgeted balance sheet. They are sometimes called **forecast final accounts**. The budgeted profit and loss account is set out in exactly the same way as the profit and loss account that is published in the final accounts. The key difference is that the budgeted profit and loss account does not contain historical information. It contains data based on the forecasts in the functional budgets.

In order to illustrate how a budgeted profit and loss account is prepared, consider Moretti & Co, a wholesaler of herbal remedies to retailers in the UK. Some information regarding the company is provided in Figure 55.3. The balance sheet shows the position of the company as at 31 March 2002, and the forecast sales and purchases are given for the four month period immediately following 31 March.

Figure 55.3 *Balance sheet as at March 31 2002, sales and purchases forecasts and other information for Moretti & Co*

Moretti & Co
Balance Sheet as at 31.3.02

	£	£	£
Fixed assets			
Fixtures and fittings at cost		30,000	
Less depreciation		21,000	
Net book value			9,000
Current assets			
Stock	12,000		
Debtors	3,600		
Bank	2,400		
		18,000	
Less current liabilities			
Trade creditors		1,700	
Net current assets			16,300
Net assets			25,300
Capital and reserves			
Paid up capital			25,300

Forecast sales and purchases

	Apr	May	Jun	Jul
	£	£	£	£
Sales	3,700	4,000	4,500	5,000
Purchases	1,800	1,800	2,300	2,400

Additional information:

(i)   All sales and purchases are undertaken on 30 days credit. The actual sales and purchases for March were £3,600 and £1,700 respectively.

(ii) Annual rent of £10,000 is payable 6 months in advance and is due in April.

(iii) A casual worker is paid £200 per month.

(iv) The company has general expenses of £200 per month.

(v)   The owner plans to introduce £4,000 of capital in April to help pay for more stock and fund a new computer system.

(vi) A new computer system costing £3,000 will be purchased in May. Annual depreciation is charged at 10% of cost on all fixed assets.

(vii) The owner will make drawings of £800 per month for personal expenses.

(viii) The owner has estimated that the value of stock at the end of July will be £13,000.

- Before preparing the budgeted profit and loss account, the cash budget must be drawn up. This is shown in Figure 55.4. The top section shows the expected cash inflows from credit sales. The amount for April, £3,600, relates to the credit sales in March, as stated in the additional information provided. The amount for May is £3,700 which relates to the credit sales in April. There is also an expected cash inflow of £4,000 in April from capital introduced by the owner. The total cash receipts are shown for each month.

- The payments section includes cash paid to suppliers for credit purchases, plus all payments for expenses, payments for a new computer and drawings. The amount paid to suppliers in April is expected to be £1,700. This is for credit purchases made in March. The rent payment of £5,000 is half of the £10,000 annual amount. It is due in advance, in April. The payment of £3,000 for the computer is classed as capital expenditure and therefore would not be shown on the profit and loss account. However, it is shown in the cash budget because it represents a cash outflow. Similarly, drawings would not be shown on the profit and loss account, but are shown in the cash budget, again because they represent a cash outflow. The total expected payments are given for each month.

- In the bottom section of the cash budget, the closing cash balance for each month is calculated. The opening cash balance for April, £2,400, is taken from the bank balance in the balance sheet shown in Figure 55.3. Because, in this case, the net cash flow is negative, the closing balance for April is found by subtracting the net cash flow from the opening balance (£2,400 - £300). Therefore the closing balance is £2,100. This becomes the opening balance for May.

Figure 55.4 *A four month cash budget for Moretti & Co, 2002*

Cash Budget for the four months ending 31.7.02

	Apr £	May £	Jun £	Jul £
Receipts				
Cash from credit sales	3,600	3,700	4,000	4,500
Capital introduced	4,000			
Total cash receipts	7,600	3,700	4,000	4,500
Payments				
Purchases	1,700	1,800	1,800	2,300
Rent	5,000			
General expenses	200	200	200	200
Casual labour	200	200	200	200
Computer		3,000		
Drawings	800	800	800	800
Total cash payments	7,900	6,000	3,000	3,500
Net cash inflow/(outflow)	(300)	(2,300)	1,000	1,000
Opening balance	2,400	2,100	(200)	800
Closing balance	2,100	(200)	800	1,800

- The budgeted profit and loss account in Figure 55.5 starts with the trading account. It shows sales of £17,200 which is the sum of the forecast monthly sales shown in Figure 55.3 (£3,700 + £4,000 + £4,500 + £5,000). The cost of sales is calculated by adding the opening stock of £12,000 (from the balance sheet) to purchases £8,300, again from Figure 55.3 (£1,800 + £1,800 + £2,300 + £2,400) and then subtracting the closing stock, £13,000, which is provided in the additional information. This gives a total of £7,300 which is subtracted from sales to give a gross profit of £9,900.
- The list of expenses in the budgeted profit and loss account includes rent, casual labour, general expenses and depreciation. Although £5,000 rent is paid in April, only £3,333 of this is attributable to the four month budget period ($\frac{4}{6}$ x £5,000). This is because the rent is for a six month period. The four month totals for casual labour and general expenses are both £800. The charge for depreciation includes £1,000 for the fixtures and fittings ($\frac{4}{12}$ x 10% x £30,000), and £300 for the computer ($\frac{4}{12}$ x 10% x £3,000). This makes a total depreciation charge of £1,100. Depreciation does not appear in the cash budget because it is a non-cash expense. Although drawings are included as a cash outflow in the cash budget, they do not appear in the profit and loss account. This is because drawings are not a business expense. However, they are included in the balance sheet which is shown later in the unit.
- The forecast net profit is calculated by subtracting the total expenses, £6,033 from the gross profit, £9,900. This gives a total of £3,867.

Moretti & Co
Budgeted Profit and Loss Account for the 4 months ending 31.7.02

	£	£
Sales		17,200
Cost of sales		
Opening stock	12,000	
Add purchases	8,300	
	20,300	
Less closing stock	13,000	
		7,300
Gross profit		9,900
Less expenses		
Rent	3,333	
Casual labour	800	
General expenses	800	
Depreciation	1,100	
		6,033
Net profit		3,867

Budgeted balance sheet

The budgeted balance sheet shows the expected values of assets, liabilities and capital of a business at the end of a budget period. As with the profit and loss account, the key difference between a budgeted balance sheet and a balance sheet in the final accounts is the time period for which they are drawn. A budgeted balance sheet contains information that relates to future plans. A balance sheet in the final accounts contains actual values of assets, liabilities and capital on the day it is prepared.

To illustrate how a budgeted balance sheet is prepared, consider again the example of Moretti & Co. The company's balance sheet as at 31 March 2002 in Figure 55.3, the cash budget in Figure 55.4 and the budgeted profit and loss account in Figure 55.5 are all used in the preparation. The budgeted balance sheet for Moretti & Co as at 31.7.02 is shown in Figure 55.6.

Figure 55.6 *Budgeted balance sheet for Moretti & Co as at 31.7.02*

Moretti & Co
Budgeted Balance Sheet as at 31.7.02

	£	£	£
Fixed assets			
Fixtures and fittings at cost		33,000	
Less depreciation		22,100	
Net book value			10,900
Current assets			
Stock	13,000		
Debtors	5,000		
Prepayment	1,667		
Bank	1,800		
		21,467	
Less current liabilities			
Trade creditors		2,400	
Net current assets			19,067
Net assets			29,967
Capital and reserves			
Opening capital			25,300
Add capital introduced			4,000
Add net profit			3,867
			33,167
Less drawings			3,200
			29,967

QUESTION 2

Ivanovic Timber sells a wide range of timber to builders and retailers. All sales are made on 30 days credit and the business also receives 30 days credit from suppliers. Figure 55.7 shows the balance sheet as at 31.12.00 and a three month cash budget for Ivanovic Timber.

Figure 55.7 *Balance sheet as at 31.12.00 and a three month cash budget for Ivanovic Timber*

Ivanovic Timber
Balance Sheet as at 31.12.00

	£	£	£
Fixed assets			
Premises at cost		50,000	
Less depreciation		25,000	
Net book value			25,000
Machinery at cost		20,000	
Less depreciation		10,000	
Net book value			10,000
Lorry at cost		10,000	
Less depreciation		5,000	
Net book value			5,000
			40,000
Current assets			
Stock	38,000		
Debtors	23,700		
Cash at bank	2,600		
		64,300	
Less current liabilities			
Trade creditors		11,000	
Net current assets			53,300
Net assets			93,300
Capital and reserves			
Paid up capital			93,300

Cash Budget for the three months ending 31.3.2001

	Jan £	Feb £	Mar £
Receipts			
Cash from credit sales	23,700	25,700	30,100
Payments			
Purchases	11,000	12,000	15,000
Wages	4,000	4,000	4,200
Motor expenses	1,100	1,200	1,500
General expenses	2,500	3,500	2,500
Drawings	2,000	2,000	2,000
Electric saw		4,000	
Total cash payments	20,600	26,700	25,200
Net cash inflow/(outflow)	3,100	(1,000)	4,900
Opening balance	2,600	5,700	4,700
Closing balance	5,700	4,700	9,600

Additional information:
(i)   The forecast sales and purchases for March are £32,000 and £16,000 respectively.
(ii) Depreciation is charged at 10% of cost on all fixed assets.
(iii) The value of stock at the end of March is expected to be £43,500.

(a) Prepare a budgeted profit and loss account for Ivanovic Timber for the three month period ending 31 March 2001.

(b) (i) State two payments that appear in the cash budget but not in the budgeted profit and loss account. (ii) Explain why these payments do not appear in the profit and loss account.

(c) Ivanovic Timber is planning to purchase a new delivery lorry in April. It is expected to cost £15,000. Would you advise the company to pay for it from internal funds?

- The **value of fixed assets** on the budgeted balance sheet is different from the values as at 31 March 2002 for two reasons. The cost of assets rises to £33,000 from £30,000 because a new computer is purchased for £3,000. This is shown in the cash budget. It is also necessary to charge for four months **depreciation**. Annual depreciation is charged at 10% of cost. Therefore, including the new computer, the annual depreciation charge would be £3,300 (10% × £33,000). So, the charge for four months is £1,100 ($\frac{4}{12}$ × £3,300) and this is added to the previous total of £21,000. As a result of these adjustments, the budgeted net book value of fixed assets is £10,900.

- The **current assets** are listed at their expected values as at 31 July. **Stock** is expected to be worth £13,000 at the end of the budget period, according to the owner's valuation (see additional information at the end of Figure 55.3). **Debtors** are expected to rise to £5,000. This figure is given in the sales forecast for July, also in Figure 55.3. The expected **cash balance** at the end of the budget period is £1,800. This is taken from the cash budget in Figure 55.4. A **new current asset** is also shown. This relates to a **prepayment** of rent. The £5,000 to be paid in April for rent includes two months for the next budget period. So, £1,667 ($\frac{2}{6}$ × £5,000) is the prepayment. The total for current assets is shown as £21,467.

- Moretti & Co has only one current liability. It is the £2,400 owed to trade creditors shown in the forecast purchases for July in Figure 55.3.

- The value of **net current assets** is calculated by subtracting current liabilities from current assets. It is shown as £19,067 in the budgeted balance sheet. This is then added to fixed assets of £10,900 to give net assets of £29,967.

- The **capital and reserves section** of the budgeted balance sheet begins with the opening capital of £25,300. This is the same as the capital in the balance sheet in Figure 55.3. New capital of £4,000 (as detailed in the additional information) and the budgeted net profit shown in Figure 55.5 are added. Drawings of £3,200 (shown in the additional information) are then subtracted. This gives a forecast closing capital balance of £29,967, which is equal to the value of net assets.

QUESTION 3

Use the information relating to Ivanovic Timber in Question 2 to answer this question.

(a) Prepare a budgeted balance sheet for Ivanovic Timber as at 31 March, 2001.

(b) Briefly explain the key difference between a budgeted balance sheet and a balance sheet that is published in the final accounts.

summary questions

1. What is the main purpose of a cash budget?
2. Describe the three sections in a cash budget.
3. Give three examples of cash inflows in the cash budget.
4. Give four examples of cash outflows in a cash budget.
5. Explain why depreciation does not appear in a cash budget.
6. Explain how the closing balance is calculated in a cash budget.
7. State two examples of expenditure that would appear in the cash budget but not in the budgeted profit and loss account.
8. Explain where a bad debt provision would appear in a business's budgets.
9. Explain how a budgeted profit and loss account is different from a profit and loss account in the final accounts.
10. State two figures that would appear both in the budgeted balance sheet and the cash budget.

key terms

Cash budget - a statement that shows the expected cash position of a business at the end of each month. It records monthly inflows and outflows of cash.
Master budget - the budgeted (or forecast) profit and loss account and balance sheet.

UNIT ASSESSMENT QUESTION 1

Anna and Sam Buckley plan to open a new night club called Juice. They have found a disused warehouse in a city centre back street that is ideal for conversion. Anna and Sam's bank manager has asked that they prepare a cash budget, a budgeted profit and loss account and budgeted balance sheet for the first four months trading. Figure 55.8 shows a sales turnover and stock purchases forecast for the first four months.

Figure 55.8 *Sales turnover and stock purchases forecast for Juice*

	Dec	Jan	Feb	Mar
	£	£	£	£
Sales turnover	50,000	35,000	30,000	30,000
Purchases	45,000	15,000	10,000	15,000

Additional information:
(i)   All sales are for cash and all purchases are on 30 days credit.
(ii)   At the start of December, Anna and Sam will provide £100,000 capital for the business.
(iii) The bank will lend the business £50,000 as a long term loan in December.
(iv) The purchase price of the warehouse, including conversion costs, is £120,000 (to be paid in December).
(v)   Wages are expected to be £8,000, £7,000, £5,000 and £6,000 in December, January, February and March respectively.
(vi)   All fixtures, fittings and equipment will be leased for £4,000 per month.
(vii) Loan interest is £500 per month and loan repayments are £1,000 per month.
(viii) £2,000 will be spent on advertising in December and then £1,000 per month.
(ix)   Other expenses are expected to be £2,500 per month.
(x)   Anna and Sam plan to draw £1,000 per month from the business for personal use.
(xi)   The value of premises will be written off over 20 years using the straight line method of depreciation.
(xii) The value of stock at the end of March is expected to be £19,000.

(a) **Prepare a cash budget for Juice for the four month period.**
(b) **Prepare a budgeted profit and loss account for Juice for the four month period.**
(c) **Prepare a budgeted balance sheet for Juice as at 31 March.**
(d) **Anna and Sam's accountant suggests that their revenue forecasts are too optimistic. If they are lowered by £10,000 per month, what effect would this have on the (i) closing cash balance (ii) net profit and capital? Assume that all other figures remain the same.**

UNIT ASSESSMENT QUESTION 2

Price plc manufactures compact discs for the European market. Figure 55.9 shows Price's budgeted sales for a five month period ending 31 July 2002. The compact disc business is very seasonal and, apart from a small rise in early summer, the bulk of Price plc's sales occur in the three months before Christmas.

Figure 55.9 *Budgeted sales of Price plc*

	Mar £000	Apr £000	May £000	Jun £000	Jul £000
Sales	300	320	360	400	360

Additional information:

(i) Price plc expects that half its sales will be paid for in the month in which they are made and these customers will be given a 5% cash discount. The remainder, ie credit customers, are expected to pay in full during the following month.

(ii) Purchases are made so that the stock at the end of each month exactly equals the budgeted sales for the following month.

(iii) Half of the purchases are paid for in the month they are received. The company receives a 10% discount for this prompt payment. All other purchases are paid for in full during the following month.

(iv) General expenses, excluding depreciation, are £24,000 per month.

(v) The closing cash balance for the company at the end of March was £50,000.

(a) **Prepare a cash budget for Price plc for the three months ending 30 June 2002.**

(b) **Briefly describe the cash budget.**

(c) **What additional information would be useful when analysing the company's cash flow?**

unit 56 Standard costing and variance analysis

unitobjectives

To understand:
- the nature and purpose of standard costing;
- the nature of variance analysis;
- reconciliation statements;
- interrelationships between variances;
- advantages and limitations of standard costing.

The nature and purpose of standard costing

A STANDARD COST is a planned or 'target' cost of production. It is usually expressed in terms of the cost per unit of output. Standard costs are not the same as **budgeted costs** (see unit 54). Budgeted costs relate to a business as a whole, or to a department within a business. Standard costs relate to individual cost units. For example, the budgeted cost of a production department might be £100,000. This figure might be calculated on the basis of a planned output of 50,000 units and a standard cost of £2 per unit.

STANDARD COSTING is a management technique that involves comparing standard costs with actual costs. The difference between standard and actual costs is known as a VARIANCE. **Variance analysis** is used to examine the differences. When actual costs are significantly different from standard costs, it means that the production process is not going to plan. Identifying variances alerts managers to this problem, allowing them to take corrective action.

Types of standards

In addition to standard costs, which are expressed in monetary terms, businesses sometimes use other 'standard' measures. For example, a business might decide that a standard performance for labour is that it will take two hours for a worker to produce a unit of output. This might then be combined with a standard wage of £6.00 per hour to give a standard labour cost of £12.00 per unit.

When setting standards, managers need to be aware of two requirements. First, standards must provide a means of controlling production by establishing planned outcomes. Second, standards must have the effect of motivating staff rather than demotivating them. Two approaches to setting standards are outlined below.

Ideal standards One approach is to base standards on what can be achieved under the most favourable operating conditions. This involves setting standards on the assumption that all the resources used by a business will operate to their optimal efficiency. So, for example, it is assumed that:
- all machines will work non-stop without breaking down;
- all workers will work to their maximum efficiency, without taking unofficial breaks or time off work;
- all materials and services will be supplied on time, without any wastage.

This approach is sometimes criticised because such standards are unrealistic and not likely to be attainable. Staff might therefore become frustrated and demotivated. However, ideal standards can be used to identify the extent to which present performance falls short of the ideal. This might help management identify areas of particular weakness.

Attainable standards A more common approach is to base standards on what should be achieved if resources are used to their maximum efficiency, but also taking into account 'normal' levels of disruption and wastage. This approach accepts that machinery will need to be maintained and might sometimes break down. It also accepts that some materials and other resources will be wasted and that workers are likely to have some **idle time**, ie periods when they are not being productive. By setting standards that are demanding, yet realistic, employees are likely to be positive towards achieving targets that are set.

Increasingly, businesses are involving employees in setting standards. By consulting their workforce on the standards that are achievable, businesses believe that staff will have a greater sense of 'ownership'. They will therefore be better motivated in their work. On the other hand, workers who have standards imposed on them might become demotivated.

Setting cost standards

The process of setting standard costs is complex and might involve a large number of people over a lengthy period of time. The first step in the process is to gather relevant information. This can take a number of forms.

- The production department will provide information relating to the resources that are needed to make one unit of production. For example, it will know the quantity of materials and the number of machine and labour hours that are required.
- The human resources or personnel department will know the salaries and current wage rates that are paid to different grades of worker, and overtime, bonus and piecework rates.
- The purchasing department will be able to provide information about the cost of materials and other resources such as energy, insurance and advertising.
- Some businesses employ consultants to carry out a work study. This involves measuring the amount of time it takes an 'average' worker to perform tasks in the production process.

The information gathered by the business is then used to calculate the standard cost. This can be broken down into three components, the standard material cost, the standard labour cost and the standard overhead cost.

Standard material cost This is the cost of the direct materials that are used to make a standard unit. In this context, a standard unit consists of one item of production. It could be a car, a book, a shirt or a loaf of bread. In order to calculate the standard cost, it is first necessary to draw up a **standard product specification**. This is a list of the quantities of raw materials and components required per unit. The standard material cost is found by multiplying the quantities of materials and components by their prices. The purchasing department will estimate these prices by reference to current prices, expected price increases and, in some cases, to price discounts that might be available.

Standard labour cost This is the cost of direct labour required to make one unit of output. In order to calculate the cost, it is necessary to draw up a **standard operation sheet** which specifies the number of hours spent by different workers to produce one unit. The standard cost is then determined by multiplying the number of hours by the wage rates that are paid to workers. This calculation can become complex when different grades of workers, paid on different wage rates, are involved in the production process.

Standard overhead cost This is the cost of a business's overheads per unit of output. It can be calculated using overhead absorption rates (see unit 51). Two examples are given.

- If the basis of absorption is direct labour hours and if overheads are absorbed at a rate of £2.50 per direct labour hour, and 3 hours of direct labour are used to produce one unit, the standard overhead cost is £7.50 (3 × £2.50).
- If a cost unit overhead absorption rate is used, the standard overhead cost is calculated by dividing the total overheads by the total output for a given budget period. For example, if total overheads are £50,000 and budgeted output is 10,000, the standard overhead cost is £5.00 per unit (£50,000 ÷ 10,000).

In some cases, overheads might be divided into fixed overheads, that do not change with output such as factory rent, and variable overheads that do change with output such as commission earned by sales personnel. It is possible, under these circumstances, that different absorption rates might be used for fixed and variable overheads.

To illustrate how the standard cost for a unit of output might be calculated, consider Blakes Ltd, a specialist manufacturer of audio speakers. The following information relates to the production costs of one standard speaker unit.

	£	£
Direct materials		
Wood	1.20	
Fabric	1.80	
Wire	1.70	
Electronic components	7.50	
Other materials	2.80	
Standard material cost		15.00
Direct labour		
1.5 hours @ £6 per hour	9.00	
1.5 hours @ £10 per hour	15.00	
2.0 hours @ £5 per hour	10.00	
Standard labour cost		34.00
Overheads		
Total overhead cost	£28,000	
Budgeted production total	5,000	
Standard overhead cost (£28,000 ÷ 5,000)		5.60
Standard cost per unit		**54.60**

The standard cost per unit is the total of the standard material, standard labour and standard overhead costs. In this example it is £54.60. The standard material cost is calculated by adding together the cost of all the components that are required in the production of one unit. The standard labour cost is calculated by working out the number of hours that different grades of employees spend in making one unit and then multiplying this by the relevant wage rates. The standard overhead cost of £5.60 is calculated by dividing the total overhead cost by the budgeted output.

In some cases when calculating the standard cost, wastage of materials must be taken into account. To illustrate this, suppose in the example above that 20% of materials were wasted in the production process. Therefore, in order to manufacture one unit, more than £15 worth of materials must be purchased. To calculate how much must be purchased, the following method is used:

$$\text{Standard material cost (taking account of 20\% wastage)} = \text{cost of materials without wastage (£15)} \times \frac{100}{100 - 20}$$

$$= £15 \times 1.25 = £18.75$$

Note that the amount to be purchased is not simply 20% more than the amount needed, ie an extra £3. This is because the wastage is 20% of the total amount purchased. So, if £15 worth of materials are required to make one unit, £18.75 worth of materials must be purchased. It is 20% of this amount, ie £3.75, that is waste.

A similar calculation is required if an amount of idle time is to be built into the standard cost. Suppose that it takes 10 hours of labour to produce an item and the wage rate is £6 per hour. If an allowance for 20% idle time is incorporated, the standard labour cost will be:

$$\text{Standard labour cost (taking account of 20\% idle time)} = \text{cost of labour without idle time (10 × £6)} \times \frac{100}{100 - 20}$$

$$= £60 \times 1.25 = £75$$

So, in this case, the standard labour cost is £75. This is the cost of 10 labour hours at a wage rate of £6 per hour, assuming that 20% of the time will not be spent productively.

QUESTION 1

Fistral Ltd makes a single style of wet suit for sailboarders. Some cost information relating to the manufacture of one wet suit is given below. The company uses two systems of absorption costing. For its fixed overheads, the basis of absorption is direct labour hours at a rate of £5.00 per hour. For its variable overheads, the basis of absorption is the variable overhead cost per unit of budgeted output.

Direct materials	
Neoprene	£21.50
Glue and tape	£3.40
Other materials	£2.30
Direct labour	
2 hours @ £10.00	£20.00
Variable overheads	£10,000.00
Budgeted output	5,000

(a) Calculate the standard cost of a wet suit for Fistral Ltd.
(b) What is the standard labour cost if a 20% allowance for idle time is built into the calculation?
(c) What factors might Fistral Ltd take into account when setting its standard cost?

Variance analysis

Standard costing compares actual costs with standard costs. A **cost variance** exists if actual costs and standard costs are different. If actual performance is better than standard, there is said to be a **favourable cost variance** (F). For example, if the standard labour cost for a product is £36, but actually works out as £32, there is a favourable variance of £4 (£36 - £32). This means that costs are lower than expected. However, if actual performance is worse than standard, there is said to be an **adverse** (or unfavourable) **variance** (A). For example, if the standard material cost for a product is calculated as £26.50 but the actual cost is £27.90, there is an adverse variance of £1.40 (£27.90 - £26.50). This means that costs are higher than expected.

Figure 56.1 shows some examples of different variances that a business might calculate and analyse. The diagram shows that the overall **profit variance** is influenced by all the other variances. The profit variance is the difference between budgeted profit and actual profit. An important point to note in the diagram is that the profit variance depends not only on costs of production but also on sales revenue. Just as cost variances can be analysed, so can SALES VARIANCES. These are the differences between the budgeted sales revenue and the actual sales revenue. Both sales and profit variances are explained in more detail later in the unit.

Figure 56.1 *Variances within a business*

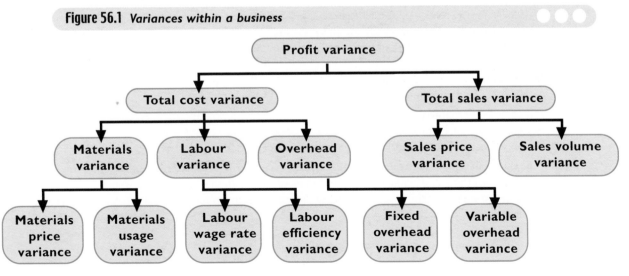

542

Materials variance

Figure 56.1 shows that the **total cost variance** is influenced by three cost variances. One of these is the materials variance. This is the difference between the standard materials cost and the actual materials cost. To illustrate how the materials variance is calculated, consider the example of Dawsons Ltd, a pet food manufacturer. One of the materials used by Dawsons to make pet food is cereal. Figure 56.2 shows the standard and actual price and usage of cereal for Dawsons in a particular budget period. According to the information, the standard materials cost for the budgeted period was £10,200. However, the actual cost was £9,790. This means that less was spent on cereal than was expected. The materials variance was therefore favourable and equal to £410 (£10,200 - £9,790).

Figure 56.2 *Cost and usage of cereal for Dawsons Ltd*

	Price (per kilo)	Usage (kilos)	Materials cost
Standard	£1.20	8,500	£10,200
Actual	£1.10	8,900	£9,790
Materials variance			**£410 (F)**

The favourable materials variance shown in Figure 56.2 is influenced by two 'sub-variances'. These relate to the price paid for the materials and the amount used.

Materials price variance The materials price variance is calculated by multiplying the difference between the actual and standard prices by the actual amount used. A favourable materials price variance arises if the actual price paid for materials is lower than the standard, ie planned price. An adverse materials price variance arises if the actual price of materials is more than the standard price. For Dawsons, the materials price variance is given by:

$$
\begin{aligned}
\text{Material price variance} &= \text{(standard price - actual price)} \times \text{actual usage} \\
&= (£1.20 - £1.10) \times 8,900 \\
&= £0.10 \times 8,900 \\
&= £890 \text{ (F)}
\end{aligned}
$$

The materials price variance for Dawson's is favourable because the actual price was 10p lower than the standard price. When multiplied by the actual amount used, the price paid for materials was £890 lower than expected.

Materials prices variances might occur for a number of reasons:
- materials might be purchased at special discount prices for a period;
- a new, lower priced supplier might be found;
- unexpected inflation might increase prices;
- a fall in the exchange rate might cause the price of imported materials to increase, or a rise in the exchange rate might cause import prices to decrease;
- a price war might break out between suppliers;
- a change might be made in the product specification, either raising or lowering the quality required;
- cheaper, inferior materials might be purchased.

If an adverse materials price variance occurs, it might be possible for a purchasing department to 'shop around' for less expensive sources. This could involve negotiating deals for bulk purchase discounts or looking abroad for lower priced imports.

Materials usage variance The materials usage variance is calculated by subtracting the actual amount from the standard amount of materials used and then multiplying by the standard price. Note that the difference is valued at the standard price and not the actual price. For Dawsons, the materials usage variance is given by:

$$
\begin{aligned}
\text{Materials usage variance} &= \text{(standard usage - actual usage)} \times \text{standard price} \\
&= (8,500 - 8,900) \times £1.20 \\
&= -400 \times £1.20 \\
&= £480 \text{ (A)}
\end{aligned}
$$

The materials usage variance for Dawsons is adverse because more materials were actually used than the standard amount. Materials usage variances might arise for a number of reasons:

- materials might be wasted due to careless work, or used more efficiently if staff are better trained;
- materials might be wasted because they are of poor quality, possibly as a result of a decision to buy cheaper materials;
- poor stock control or pilferage could cause materials to be lost;
- materials might be wasted due to a machine malfunction.

If the materials usage variance is adverse due to defective materials, managers might try to improve quality control systems in the purchasing department. If the problem arises in the production department, managers might be able to reduce wastage by better maintenance of machinery or better training of the workforce.

The materials variance for Dawsons in Figure 56.2 is shown as £410 (F). It is caused by the materials price variance which is favourable, £890, and the materials usage variance which is adverse, £480. In this case, the favourable price variance outweighs the adverse usage variance. The difference between the two gives the overall materials variance (£890 - £480).

QUESTION 2

Jacobelli's is a manufacturer of ice cream in Cornwall. The most important raw material is fresh cream, which is bought in large quantities from a wholesaler. Figure 56.3 shows the standard and actual prices paid for cream and the standard and actual usage over a particular budget period.

Figure 56.3 *Standard and actual prices and usage of cream for Jacobelli's*

	Price (per kilo)	Usage (kilos)
Standard	£3.80	10,500
Actual	£4.10	12,400

(a) For the budget period, calculate: (i) the materials price variance; (ii) the materials usage variance; (iii) the materials variance.
(b) Explain how the results might affect the business.
(c) State two possible reasons for the materials usage variance.

Labour variance

Figure 56.1 shows that a component of the total cost variance is the labour variance. This is the difference between the standard cost of labour and the actual cost. To illustrate how labour variances are calculated, consider again the example of Dawsons Ltd, the pet food manufacturer. Figure 56.4 shows the standard wage rate and actual wage rate and the standard number of labour hours and the actual number of labour hours for a particular budget period. The labour variance for Dawsons is £9,300 (A) (£108,300 - £99,000). This adverse variance means that the wage bill was higher than the budgeted amount.

Figure 56.4 *Standard and actual wage rates and labour hours for Dawsons Ltd*

	Wage rate	Labour hours	Wage bill
Standard	£5.50	18,000	£99,000
Actual	£5.70	19,000	£108,300
Labour variance			**£9,300 (A)**

The standard cost of labour can be divided into two sub-variances. These are the wage rate variance and the labour efficiency variance. In order to understand and explain the labour variance, the two sub-variances must be analysed.

Wage rate variance This is calculated by subtracting the actual wage rate from the standard wage rate and multiplying the difference by the actual number of hours worked. In the case of Dawsons, the wage rate variance is given by:

$$\begin{aligned}
\text{Wage rate variance} \quad &= \text{(standard wage rate - actual wage rate)} \times \text{actual hours} \\
&= (£5.50 - £5.70) \times 19,000 \\
&= -£0.20 \times 19,000 \\
&= £3,800 \ (A)
\end{aligned}$$

Dawsons' wage rate variance is adverse because the actual wage rate was higher than the standard wage rate. The factors that might affect the wage rate variance include:
- a pay rise caused by trade union pressure;
- a shortage of skilled labour;
- government legislation such as raising the minimum wage;
- the use of unskilled or trainee workers at lower rates of pay than standard.

Labour efficiency variance This is calculated by subtracting the actual number of hours worked from the standard number of hours and multiplying the difference by the standard wage rate. For Dawsons, the labour efficiency variance is given by:

$$\begin{aligned}
\text{Labour efficiency variance} &= \text{(standard hours - actual hours)} \times \text{standard wage rate} \\
&= (18,000 - 19,000) \times £5.50 \\
&= -1,000 \times £5.50 \\
&= £5,500 \ (A)
\end{aligned}$$

The labour efficiency variance is adverse for Dawsons because the actual number of hours worked was greater than the standard or budgeted number. The causes of labour efficiency variances include:
- greater or reduced reliability of machinery used by workers, perhaps caused by changes in maintenance procedures;
- improvements or reductions in the quality of raw materials and components;
- changes in the productivity of workers, possibly due to changes in the level of training provided;
- changes in working practices, such as teamworking, which might lead to improvements in worker motivation;
- loss of morale and motivation in the workforce, possibly caused by fears of job losses.

The labour variance for Dawsons is £9,300 (A). It is caused by the wage rate variance, £3,800 (A), and the labour efficiency variance, £5,500 (A). If managers decided that these variances were so large that action should be taken, they might consider a number of options. For example, they might automate the production process so that less skilled, lower paid workers could be used. An alternative policy could be to try and improve productivity by rewarding workers for suggestions on how output might be increased.

Overhead variance

The third component of the total cost variance in Figure 56.1 is the overhead variance. This is the difference between standard overheads and actual overheads. The **total overhead variance** is often divided into two sub-variances, the **variable overhead variance** and the **fixed overhead variance**.

Variable overhead variance This is the difference between the actual variable overhead and the standard variable overhead. To illustrate how the variable overhead variance is calculated, consider again the example of Dawsons, the pet food manufacturer. Figure 56.5 shows the standard variable overhead rate, the actual variable overhead rate, the standard number of production hours and the actual number of production hours for a budget period.

Figure 56.5 *Standard and actual variable overhead rates and production hours for Dawsons*

	Overhead rate	Production hours	Variable overhead
Standard	£5.00	4,000	£20,000
Actual	£5.50	4,200	£23,100
Variable overhead variance			**£3,100 (A)**

Dawsons' variable overhead variance is £3,100 (A). In this case, both the overhead rate and the number of production hours were higher than expected. The factors that might affect the variable overhead variance include:
- changes in the price of variable overheads such as fuel, cleaning materials, telephone charges and delivery costs;
- changes in the amount of variable overheads used;
- changes in the efficiency of staff providing overhead services;
- changes in the number of production hours, possibly caused by poor quality raw materials, so causing changes in the use of variable overheads such as fuel or servicing.

Fixed overhead variance This is the difference between the actual fixed overhead and the standard fixed overhead. Figure 56.6 again uses the example of Dawsons Ltd. It shows the standard fixed overhead rate, the actual fixed overhead rate, the standard number of production hours and the actual number of production hours for a budget period.

Figure 56.6 *Standard and actual fixed overhead rates and production hours for Dawsons*

	Overhead rate	Production hours	Fixed overheads
Standard	£10.00	4,000	£40,000
Actual	£8.00	4,000	£32,000
Fixed overhead variance			**£8,000 (F)**

The fixed overhead variance for Dawsons is £8,000 (F). This means that fixed overheads were lower than expected. In this case, the actual number of production hours was the same as the standard. However, the actual fixed overhead rate was lower than the standard rate.

QUESTION 3

Musgrove & Co makes optical instruments. At one time the company used mainly skilled workers but now much of the production is automated and handled by semi-skilled workers. However, some work is still carried out by skilled engineers. Figure 56.7 shows some information relating to wage rates and hours worked by production staff.

(a) Calculate the labour variance and suggest the effect this would have on profit for Musgrove & Co.
(b) Calculate (i) the wage rate variance; (ii) the labour efficiency variance, for both skilled and unskilled workers.
(c) Suggest reasons for the labour efficiency variance for semi-skilled workers.

Figure 56.7 *Standard and actual wage rates and hours worked by production staff at Musgrove & Co*

Skilled workers

	Wage rate	Labour hours
Standard	£10.00	5,000
Actual	£10.00	5,200

Semi-skilled workers

	Wage rate	Labour hours
Standard	£6.00	60,000
Actual	£6.20	56,000

The factors that might affect the fixed overhead variance include:
- changes in the price of fixed overheads such as rent, rates or insurance;
- changes in the efficiency of staff providing overhead services.

When faced with an adverse overhead variance, managers might try to reduce their costs. However, the price of overheads that are external to the business, such as insurance or rent, could be difficult to control. It might be easier to adjust those overheads that are internal to the business, such as cleaning and maintenance. But, if this policy is adopted, care must be taken that overall efficiency is not damaged. For instance, if it was decided to cut the number of hours spent maintaining machinery, the effect might be to cause more breakdowns and lost production time.

Total overhead variance This is the sum total of the variable and fixed overhead variances. In the case of Dawsons, it is £4,900 (F). It is calculated by adding the variable overhead variance, £3,100 (A) to the fixed overhead variance, £8,000 (F). Note that, in this example, the variable overhead variance is adverse and is therefore treated as a negative number.

Sales variance

A sales variance is the difference between budgeted sales revenue and actual sales revenue. If actual revenue is higher than budgeted revenue, there is said to be a **favourable variance**. However, if actual revenue is lower than budgeted revenue, there is said to be an **adverse variance**.

Figure 56.8 shows standard and actual prices and standard and actual sales volumes for cases of pet food for Dawsons. The actual sales revenue of £231,000 is higher than the budgeted sales revenue of £187,600. As a result, there is a favourable sales variance of £43,400.

Figure 56.8 *Standard and actual prices and sales volumes for cases of pet food*

	Price (per case)	Sales (cases)	Sales revenue
Standard	£6.70	28,000	£187,600
Actual	£6.60	35,000	£231,000
Sales variance			**£43,400 (F)**

The sales variance is dependent on two sub-variances, the sales price variance and the sales volume variance.

Sales price variance This is calculated by subtracting the standard price from the actual price and multiplying the difference by the actual number of sales. For Dawsons, the sales price variance is given by:

$$
\begin{aligned}
\text{Sales price variance} &= \text{(actual price - standard price)} \times \text{actual sales} \\
&= (£6.60 - £6.70) \times 35,000 \\
&= -£0.10 \times 35,000 \\
&= £3,500 \text{ (A)}
\end{aligned}
$$

The sales price variance is adverse because the actual price charged by Dawsons was lower than the standard price. Sales price variances might arise due to:
- unplanned sales in new markets at different prices, for example sales to a new export market at a lower price than charged in the home market;
- new competitors in the market causing prices to be lower, or rivals leaving the market allowing prices to be raised;
- discounts for bulk buying customers.

Sales volume variance This is calculated by subtracting the standard number of sales from the actual number of sales and multiplying the difference by the standard price. In the case of Dawsons, the sales volume variance is given by:

$$
\begin{aligned}
\text{Sales volume variance} &= \text{(actual sales - standard sales)} \times \text{standard price} \\
&= (35,000 - 28,000) \times £6.70 \\
&= 7,000 \times £6.70 \\
&= £46,900 \text{ (F)}
\end{aligned}
$$

The sales volume variance for Dawsons is favourable because the actual level of sales was higher than expected. Sales volume variances might be caused by:

- changes in the state of the economy, so causing a rise or fall in consumer demand;
- competitors' actions, for example a new advertising campaign;
- sudden changes in consumer tastes, perhaps caused by health 'scares';
- government policy, such as a change in VAT, income tax or interest rates;
- changes in the quality of the product;
- changes in marketing techniques, for example a new direct mail campaign to potential customers.

In the case of Dawsons, the £43,400 favourable sales variance is the result of the £3,500 adverse sales price variance combined with the £46,900 favourable sales volume variance, ie £46,900 - £3,500.

The analysis of sales variances is generally the responsibility of the sales and marketing department within a business. If an adverse variance occurs, a number of policies might be adopted. These include a greater effort in promoting the product, perhaps by advertising or by offering more generous incentives to sales staff. Sometimes a policy of price cuts can increase the sales volume so much that overall revenue increases. However, the success of such a policy depends to a large extent on the reaction of competitors and on the perception of consumers. So, for example, price cuts would not be successful if competitors immediately copied the policy, or if consumers felt that cheaper prices meant a lowering of quality.

QUESTION 4

The Harpenden Toy Company manufactures a range of children's toys. In January 2001, the company launched an imaginative new game called Gate Crash. The directors felt confident that the launch would be a huge success. Twelve months later, the following information was available.

(a) Calculate the: (i) sales price variance; (ii) sales volume variance; (iii) sales variance.

(b) Suggest possible causes for the variances calculated in (a).

(c) How might The Harpenden Toy Company respond to the variances?

Figure 56.9 *Prices and sales volumes for Gate Crash, 2001/2002*

	Price (per unit)	Sales volume (units)
Standard	£9.50	100,000
Actual	£4.50	90,000

Flexible budgets

The variances for Dawsons Ltd, outlined in the unit so far, are based on the assumption that the level of output and sales remained unchanged. However, when considering Dawsons' sales variances, the actual level of sales was 35,000 units as compared with the budgeted sales of 28,000 units. So, in order to compare 'like with like', the budget must be FLEXED to take account of the increase in sales. The process of **flexing** a budget involves adjusting the costs and revenue according to the level of activity actually achieved.

The first stage in producing a flexed budget is to adjust the figure for sales revenue. This is done by multiplying the actual number of sales by the standard price. In this case, the flexed budget revenue is £234,500 (£6.70 × 35,000).

The next stage is to adjust the costs of production. Figure 56.10 shows the flexed budget costs for Dawsons. The original standard costs are adjusted to take account of the rise in sales. This is done by multiplying the original standard usage by the actual number of sales (ie 35,000) and dividing by the original standard number of sales (ie 28,000). The flexed standard usage is then multiplied by the standard rate. Note that the fixed standard overheads of £40,000 remain unchanged because, by definition, they do not vary with the level of output.

Figure 56.10 *Flexed budget costs for Dawsons*

	Original standard		Flexed standard	Rate £	Cost £
Materials	8,500 kilos × (35,000÷28,000)	=	10,625	1.20	12,750
Labour	18,000 hrs × (35,000÷28,000)	=	22,500	5.50	123,750
Variable overheads	4,000 hrs × (35,000÷28,000)	=	5,000	5.00	25,000
Fixed overheads	£40,000				40,000
Total					201,500

The **profit variance** is the difference between the actual profit made by a business and the profit arising from the flexed budget. Figure 56.11 is a summary of the variances for Dawsons that have been previously outlined. It also shows the actual profit, £57,810, and flexed budget profit, £33,000, leading to the favourable profit variance of £24,810.

Figure 56.11 *Summary of variances for Dawsons*

	Flexed budget £	Actual £	Variance £
Sales	234,500	231,000	3,500 (A)
Costs			
Materials	12,750	9,790	2,960 (F)
Labour	123,750	108,300	15,450 (F)
Variable overheads	25,000	23,100	1,900 (F)
Fixed overheads	40,000	32,000	8,000 (F)
Total costs	201,500	173,190	28,310 (F)
Profit	33,000	57,810	24,810 (F)

Reconciliation statements

In the context of variance analysis, the purpose of a reconciliation statement is to explain why actual results are different from the standard or budgeted figures. Such statements can be prepared for profit, costs or sales. For example, a profit reconciliation statement will show why the actual profit for the year differs from the budgeted profit. In order to illustrate how to prepare a profit reconciliation statement, consider Phelps Ltd, a food processing company that produces bottled cooking oil. Figure 56.12 shows a summary of the flexed budget profit statement and the actual results for 2001.

Figure 56.12 *Budget profit statement and actual results*

	Budget £		Actual £	
Sales	540,000	(£0.30 × 1,800,000)	532,000	(£0.28 × 1,900,000)
Direct costs				
Corn	240,000	(3,000 tonnes × £80 per tonne)	248,000	(3,100 tonnes × £80 per tonne)
Other materials	16,000	(800 tonnes × £20 per tonne)	14,250	(750 tonnes × £19 per tonne)
Labour	186,000	(30,000 hours × £6.20 per hour)	185,600	(29,000 hours × £6.40 per hour)
Total direct costs	442,000		447,850	
Overheads	75,000		60,000	
Total costs	517,000		507,850	
Profit	23,000		24,150	

The first step in the preparation of the profit reconciliation statement is to calculate the variances. In this case, variances are calculated for the sales price, sales volume, material price, material usage, wage rate, labour efficiency and total overheads. They are shown below.

Sales price variance	= (£0.28 - £0.30) × 1,900,000	= £38,000 (A)
Sales volume variance	= (1,900,000 - 1,800,000) × £0.30	= £30,000 (F)
Material price variance (corn)	= (£80 - £80) × 3,100	= 0
Material price variance (other)	= (£20 - £19) × 750	= £750 (F)
Material usage variance (corn)	= (3,000 - 3,100) × £80	= £8,000 (A)
Material usage variance (other)	= (800 - 750) × £20	= £1,000 (F)
Wage rate variance	= (£6.20 - £6.40) × 29,000	= £5,800 (A)
Labour efficiency variance	= (30,000 - 29,000) × £6.20	= £6,200 (F)
Overhead variance	= (£75,000 - £60,000)	= £15,000 (F)

Figure 56.13 shows the reconciliation statement for Phelps Ltd. It includes the variances shown above that are calculated from the budgeted and actual figures in Figure 56.12.

Figure 56.13 *Profit reconciliation statement for Phelps Ltd*

	£	£	£
Budgeted profit			23,000
Sales variances	**Adverse**	**Favourable**	
Sales price	(38,000)		
Sales volume		30,000	(8,000)
Profit adjusted for sales variances			15,000
Cost variances			
Material price (corn)	0	0	
Material price (other)		750	
Material usage (corn)	(8,000)		
Material usage (other)		1,000	
Wage rate	(5,800)		
Labour efficiency		6,200	
Overhead		15,000	
	(13,800)	22,950	9,150
Actual profit			24,150

- The first entry in the profit reconciliation statement is the budgeted profit. According to Figure 56.12, this is £23,000.
- The budgeted profit is then adjusted for the sales variances. The adverse variances are listed in one column and the favourable variances in another. Note that the adverse variances are negative amounts and are shown in brackets. Overall there is an adverse sales variance of £8,000 which is subtracted from the budgeted profit to give a figure of £15,000.
- The cost variances are then listed in the appropriate columns and totalled. The overall cost variance is favourable at £9,150. It is calculated by subtracting the total adverse variances from the total favourable cost variances (£22,950 - £13,800). This figure is then added to the adjusted profit to obtain the actual profit for the year. This is shown in the statement as £24,150, which is £1,150 higher than the budgeted amount.

The completed reconciliation statement helps to identify the reasons for the differences between the budgeted profit and the actual profit. In the case of Phelps, the adverse sales price variance outweighed the favourable sales volume variance. This caused revenue and therefore profit to be £8,000 lower than expected. It is likely that Phelps' management would wish to investigate possible reasons for this.

An analysis of the cost variances shows that more corn was used than the standard amount and the wage rate was higher than the standard rate. Managers might decide to investigate the causes of these variances. However, labour efficiency, the price of corn and the material usage of other material variances were all favourable. Most significant of all, overheads were much lower than expected. As a result, costs were £9,150 less than the budgeted amount.

Interrelationships between variances

Figure 56.1 shows how different variances are linked. For example, if the total cost variance is adverse, this means that costs are higher than expected and profit will be lower than budgeted. There is a number of other interrelationships between variances.

- If wages rise unexpectedly during a budget period, this will result in an adverse wage rate variance. However, higher wages might raise labour productivity and therefore the labour efficiency variance might improve.
- If the purchasing department obtains cheaper materials and components, the materials price variance is likely to improve. However, the materials and components might be inferior and result in more materials being wasted. This could lead to a worsening of the materials usage variance.
- Purchasing cheaper, lower quality raw materials might have an effect on the sales volume variance if consumers buy fewer products.
- Reducing the amount spent on maintaining and lubricating machinery might improve the variable overhead variance. However, if the machines then break down and workers are idle, the labour efficiency variance will worsen.

The advantages of standard costing

There is a number of advantages of using standard costing techniques.

Management control By calculating variances, a business can identify areas of weakness and inefficient practice. For example, if a member of staff in the purchasing department buys materials from more expensive suppliers, this is likely to show up in the materials price variance. When analysing variances, some businesses use an approach called **management by exception**. It involves investigating variances only if they are exceptional. This allows some tolerance in the control system. Variances are considered acceptable provided they do not exceed certain limits. For example, a business might only investigate variances that are more than 5% different from the standard. This approach means that a business will not waste time investigating the cause of trivial variances.

Staff motivation If staff are consulted and given responsibility for meeting their own cost, volume and price targets, they might take more pride in their work and have increased job satisfaction when targets are met. Such an approach is called **responsibility accounting**. Some businesses reward staff financially if variances are favourable. This is also likely to increase motivation.

Business planning Predetermined standards can be used in budgets to calculate the quantity of resources needed in the next budget period. If standard costs are monitored and updated regularly, the accuracy of budgets will be improved.

Setting prices Standard costs represent the best estimate of what a product should cost to make. So, by using standard costs, estimates of costs for products and price quotations for orders are likely to be more reliable.

The limitations of standard costing

Surveys indicate that most medium to large sized manufacturing businesses in the UK use some form of standard costing. However, it is recognised that the system has some limitations.

Cost of implementation Standard costing requires a business to gather a large amount of information. This process can be time consuming and expensive. Also, since standard costs are regularly updated, this cost is ongoing.

'Modern' management Companies that adopt modern approaches to business management might find that standard costing is inappropriate. For example, if a technique such as Kaizen is adopted, where employees are expected to strive for continuous improvement, standards might become a barrier to innovation. This is because they might be regarded as a ceiling for employees' improvement efforts. Once the standard is reached, there is no incentive to make further improvements.

Unforeseen consequences Standard costing is likely to encourage staff to strive for favourable variances, even if this harms a business's overall objectives. For example, in order to achieve a favourable materials price variance, a member of the purchasing department might order some cheap, but inferior quality, materials. This might damage the reputation of the company and possibly lead to a fall in sales.

Service industries In some service sector businesses, staff performance indicators cannot be easily quantified and do not necessarily relate to costs. For example, in retailing, the quality of customer service provided by staff is very important but it is also very difficult to measure. Standard costing has little or no role to play in these circumstances.

key terms

Flexed budget - a budget that is adjusted according to the level of activity actually achieved.
Sales variance - the difference between budgeted and actual sales revenue
Standard cost - a planned or 'target' cost of production.
Standard costing - a system in which standard costs (and revenues) are compared with those that actually occur.
Variance - the difference between a standard or budgeted cost (or revenue) and the actual cost (or revenue).
Variance analysis - the process of calculating variances and attempting to identify their causes.

UNIT ASSESSMENT QUESTION 1

The Patio Co. manufactures and sells sets of patio furniture. The company has 3 regional sales offices and sales are mainly to garden centres. Sales staff are rewarded by a system that links bonuses to the sales variances. Fifty per cent of any favourable sales margin variance is shared between the sales staff in the region. Figure 56.14 shows the prices and sales volumes for 2001.

Figure 56.14 *Prices and sales volumes for the Patio Co.*

NORTHERN	Price (per unit)	Sales volume	Sales revenue
Standard	£100	80,000	£8m
Actual	£90	90,000	£8.1m
CENTRAL	**Price (per unit)**	**Sales volume**	**Sales revenue**
Standard	£100	80,000	£8m
Actual	£88	100,000	£8.8m
SOUTHERN	**Price (per unit)**	**Sales volume**	**Sales revenue**
Standard	£120	80,000	£9.6m
Actual	£120	78,000	£9.36m

(a) Calculate the (i) sales price variance; (ii) sales volume variance and (iii) sales variance for each region.
(b) Calculate the annual bonuses that each region would share amongst its staff for 2001.
(c) Outline the advantages to the Patio Co. of using standard costing.
(d) What would be the effect of the sales variance on the Patio Co's profit?

summary questions

1. Explain the purpose of standard costing.
2. Explain the difference between ideal and attainable standards.
3. Why might a work study be used in standard costing?
4. What is meant by an adverse variance?
5. What is a labour efficiency variance?
6. Which two sub-variances affect the materials variance.
7. What is the difference between the sales price variance and the sales volume variance?
8. State two possible causes of a favourable materials efficiency variance.
9. State two possible causes of an adverse sales variance.
10. Outline three advantages and three limitations of standard costing.

UNIT ASSESSMENT QUESTION 2

Quarry Hill is a wine producer in the south of England. The wine is sold in cases to wine merchants across the UK. The business is owned by the Rosenberg family and employs 4 full-time staff. Quarry Hill is profitable and owes much of its success in a very competitive market to careful cost control. Barry Rosenberg, the finance director, uses a system of standard costing. Figure 56.15 shows a range of information relating to standard and actual costs and revenues for the business in 2001.

Figure 56.15 *Standard and actual costs for Quarry Hill*

Sales	Price (per case)	Sales volume (cases)	Sales revenue
Standard	£30	10,000	£300,000
Actual	£32	9,500	£304,000

Grapes	Price (per tonne)	Usage (tonnes)	Materials cost
Standard	£200	500	£100,000
Actual	£180	520	£93,600

Bottles	Price (each)	Usage (units)	Materials cost
Standard	£0.07	120,000	£8,400
Actual	£0.07	114,000	£7,980

Labour	Wage rate	Hours worked	Wage bill
Standard	£6.00	7,000	£42,000
Actual	£6.00	7,200	£43,200

Fixed overheads	Standard	Actual
Rent and rates	£50,000	£50,000
Insurance	£3,000	£3,000
Other overheads	£21,000	£30,300
Total	£74,000	£83,300

(a) Calculate the flexed budget totals of (i) grapes usage; (ii) bottles usage; (iii) labour hours worked.

(b) Calculate the flexed budget totals of (i) sales revenue; (ii) materials costs (grapes and bottles); (iii) labour and (iv) overheads.

(c) Draw up profit statements for the flexed budget and actual results. Show the variances.

(d) Comment on the profit variance and suggest reasons for its size.

unit 57

Capital investment appraisal

unitobjectives

To understand:
- cash flows resulting from investment;
- payback;
- net present value;
- accounting rate of return;
- non-financial factors that influence investment decisions.

What is capital investment appraisal?

The evaluation of investment opportunities is called INVESTMENT APPRAISAL. This might involve deciding whether to make a particular investment, or choosing between a number of different investment opportunities. In this context, INVESTMENT (or capital expenditure) is expenditure on **fixed assets** such as plant, machinery, equipment, tools, property and vehicles. These assets are used by businesses to produce other goods and services. The term investment is sometimes also used to describe expenditure on research and development, staff retraining, promotional campaigns and the purchase of other businesses.

One of the features of investment is that businesses hope the expenditure will generate benefits in the long term, over a number of years. Often, large sums of money are invested. Another feature of investment is that there is a risk involved. For example, a supermarket chain might spend £10 million on building a new store. It will hope that revenue and profits will be generated over the next 10 to 20 years. However, factors such as competition from rivals, or a downturn in the economy, could result in losses and the closure of the store. It is this uncertainty that makes investment decisions so difficult.

Investment cash flows

When evaluating investment projects, it is usual to analyse the **net cash flow** resulting from the investment. Net cash flow is the difference between the cash inflow and the cash outflow. The cost of the investment is calculated and then set against the expected income to decide if the investment is likely to be worthwhile.

Figure 57.1 shows the expected cash flows from an engineering company's investment in a new computer numerically controlled (CNC) machine. According to Figure 57.1, the company will pay £250,000 for the machine. The amount is shown in brackets to indicate a negative cash flow. In year 1, the machine is expected to earn the company £130,000. However, operating costs of £25,000 are also expected to be incurred. Consequently, the net cash flow in year 1 is expected to be £105,000 (£130,000 - £25,000).

Figure 57.1 Cash flows from an investment in a CNC machine

	Initial cost £	Year 1 £	Year 2 £	Year 3 £	Year 4 £	Year 5 £	Total £
Cash outflow	(250,000)	(25,000)	(25,000)	(25,000)	(25,000)	(25,000)	(375,000)
Cash inflow		130,000	150,000	150,000	100,000	50,000	580,000
Net cash flow	(250,000)	105,000	125,000	125,000	75,000	25,000	205,000
Cumulative cash flow	(250,000)	(145,000)	(20,000)	105,000	180,000	205,000	205,000

The cumulative cash flow is also shown in Figure 57.1. This is a running total of cash flows for each year. It takes into account all cash flows to date. For example, at the end of year 5, the total cash outflow is £375,000 and the total cash inflow is £580,000. Therefore the cumulative cash flow is £205,000 (£580,000 - £375,000).

These cash flows form the basis of most investment appraisal. There are several different methods that can be used to evaluate investment projects. Each one uses a different criterion in its assessment.

Payback

The PAYBACK method of investment appraisal involves calculating the PAYBACK PERIOD. This is the amount of time it takes a business to recover the initial cost of an investment. For example, Betts & Co, a food processing company, is planning to buy a new packing machine. The machine is expected to have a productive life of 6 years and will cost £120,000. The expected net cash flows are shown in Figure 57.2.

Figure 57.2 *Expected net cash flows from a new machine*

	Initial cost	Year 1	Year 2	Year 3	Year 4	Year 5	Year 6
	£	£	£	£	£	£	£
Net cash flow	(120,000)	20,000	30,000	30,000	40,000	30,000	20,000
Cum. cash flow	(120,000)	(100,000)	(70,000)	(40,000)	0	30,000	50,000

In this case, the payback period is exactly 4 years. After 4 years, the net cash flow equals the £120,000 that the business paid for the machine (£20,000 + £30,000 + £30,000 + £40,000). The cumulative net cash flow after 4 years is therefore zero (£120,000 - £120,000). Figure 57.2 also shows that after 6 years, which is the expected life of the machine, the cumulative total net cash flow is £50,000.

When using the payback method to choose between different investment projects, the project with the shortest payback period will usually be selected. To illustrate this, consider the example of a business that is appraising three investment projects which all cost £50,000. The expected net cash flows and payback periods for each are shown in Figure 57.3.

Figure 57.3 *Expected net cash flows and payback periods for 3 investment projects*

Project	Initial cost	Year 1	Year 2	Year 3	Year 4	Year 5	Total cash flow	Payback period
	£	£	£	£	£	£	£	
A	(50,000)	10,000	20,000	20,000	30,000	10,000	40,000	3yrs
B	(50,000)	30,000	20,000	20,000	10,000	0	30,000	2yrs
C	(50,000)	10,000	10,000	20,000	30,000	30,000	50,000	3yrs 4mths

It is usual to show the payback period to the nearest month. In the case of project C, the payback period goes into the 4th year (after 3 years only £40,000 has been recovered). To calculate how many months of the 4th year are needed to recover the remaining cost (a further £10,000), the following calculation is made:

$$\text{Number of months} = \frac{\text{Cash required}}{\text{Net cash flow for year}} \times 12$$

$$= \frac{£10,000}{£30,000} \times 12$$

$$= 4 \text{ months}$$

Therefore the payback period for project C is 3 years and 4 months, as shown in Figure 57.3. According to the payback method of appraisal, project B would be selected because it has the shortest payback. Both project A and C take longer to pay back, at 3 years and 3 years 4 months respectively. Note that the total cash flow over the entire investment period is not taken into account when using this method. Indeed, project B has the lowest total net cash flow of the three projects.

Advantages of the payback method
- It is relatively simple to apply.
- This method is appropriate when technology changes rapidly, such as in computing. New, more efficient and more powerful computers emerge on the market very quickly. It is important to recover the cost of a computer before the new generation becomes available.
- Businesses might adopt this method if they have cash flow problems. This is because the chosen project will pay back the cash expenditure more quickly than the others.
- Because all investment projects are risky to some degree, the shorter the payback period, the less risk involved.

Disadvantages of the payback method
- Cash earned after the payback period is not taken into account in the investment decision.
- The overall profitability of investment projects is ignored. This is because the speed of repayment is the sole criterion used for selection.
- The timing of the cash flows within the payback period are ignored.

QUESTION

Qplex Ltd manufactures tyres for the motor industry. It operates from a factory in Coventry and supplies a number of large car manufacturers in the West Midlands. The directors of the company have recently decided to invest some money into a new, more flexible, moulding machine. Three suitable models have been identified. The cost and the expected cash flow from each model are shown in Figure 57.4.

Figure 57.4 *Cost and expected cash flow from 3 moulding machines*

Model	Initial cost	Expected net cash flow					
		Year 1	Year 2	Year 3	Year 4	Year 5	Total
	£	£	£	£	£	£	£
Mouldmaster	(150,000)	20,000	40,000	60,000	90,000	90,000	300,000
Fleximould	(110,000)	30,000	30,000	30,000	30,000	30,000	150,000
Supermould	(200,000)	100,000	100,000	50,000	20,000	10,000	280,000

(a) Calculate the payback period (to the nearest month) for each of the moulding machines.
(b) Which machine should Qplex Ltd purchase according to the payback method of appraisal?
(c) Explain two disadvantages to Qplex Ltd of using this method of investment appraisal.

Net present value

The NET PRESENT VALUE (NPV) method of investment appraisal considers the costs and benefits of an investment. It also takes into account the effect that **interest rates** and **time** have on the investment decision.

To understand the NPV method of appraisal, it is important to appreciate that money earned or paid in the future is worth less than it is today. To illustrate this, compare the value of £1,000 received today with the value of £1,000 received in one year's time. Suppose the £1,000 received today was deposited in a bank account with a rate of interest of 5%. At the end of one year it would be worth £1,050 (£1,000 + [£1,000 × 5%]). Therefore, £1,000 received today would be worth £50 more than £1,000 received in a year's time.

When calculating the NPV of an investment, all the costs and benefits are given at their PRESENT VALUE. This is the value of a sum of money available in the future, expressed in terms of what it is worth today. The following formula is used to calculate the present value of future cash flows:

$$\text{Present value of cash flow in year n} = \frac{\text{Actual cash flow in year n}}{(1 + r)^n}$$

where r is the rate of interest (expressed as a decimal rather than a percentage) and n is the year of the cash flow (ie the number of years into the future).

For example, what would be the present value of £1,000 received in 3 year's time, assuming the rate of interest is 5% (ie 0.05)? This is calculated as:

Present value of cash flow in year 3 $\quad = \quad \dfrac{£1,000}{(1 + 0.05)^3}$

$= \quad \dfrac{£1,000}{1.16} \quad$ (rounded to 2 decimal places)

$= \quad £862.07 \quad$ (rounded to nearest penny)

This shows that the £1,000 received in 3 years time is worth just £862.07 today. This value depends on two things:

- the rate of interest;
- the number of years in the future when the cash flow occurs.

To illustrate the difference that interest rates make, suppose that instead of 5% they were 20% (ie 0.2). The present value would then be £578.03. This is shown below.

Present value of cash flow in year 3 $\quad = \quad \dfrac{£1,000}{(1 + 0.2)^3}$

$= \quad \dfrac{£1,000}{1.73} \quad$ (rounded to 2 decimal places)

$= \quad £578.03 \quad$ (rounded to nearest penny)

To illustrate the difference that the length of time makes, suppose that instead of three years the length of time was five years. The present value would then be £781.25. This is shown below.

Present value of cash flow in year 5 $\quad = \quad \dfrac{£1,000}{(1 + 0.05)^5}$

$= \quad \dfrac{£1,000}{1.28} \quad$ (rounded to 2 decimal places)

$= \quad £781.25 \quad$ (rounded to nearest penny)

These calculations show that the present value of an investment falls if either the interest rate or the length of time increases. The opposite is also true. The present value rises if either the rate of interest or the length of time decreases.

To illustrate how the NPV method is used in investment appraisal, consider an investment project that costs £100,000 and earns revenue of £50,000 in year 1, £40,000 in year 2 and £35,000 in year 3. Assuming that the rate of interest remains at 5% throughout the period, the present value of this future income is:

Present value of cash flow $\quad = \quad \dfrac{£50,000}{(1 + 0.05)^1} \; + \; \dfrac{£40,000}{(1 + 0.05)^2} \; + \; \dfrac{£35,000}{(1 + 0.05)^3}$

$= \quad \dfrac{£50,000}{1.05} \; + \; \dfrac{£40,000}{1.1} \; + \; \dfrac{£35,000}{1.16} \quad$ (rounded to 2 decimal places)

$= \quad £47,619.05 \; + \; £36,363.64 \; + \; £30,172.41 \quad$ (rounded to nearest penny)

$= \quad £114,155 \qquad$ (rounded to the nearest pound)

Once the present value of future cash inflows has been calculated, it is possible to calculate the net present value of the investment project. This is given by:

NPV = Present value of future cash flows - initial outlay

For the project in the example above, the net present value is:

NPV = £114,155 - £100,000 = £14,155

In this example, the NPV is a positive amount, £14,155, and the business might therefore decide that it is worthwhile to go ahead with the project. However, the business might compare the NPV of this investment with that from different projects and decide to go ahead with the project that gives the highest NPV.

If the calculation had shown a negative NPV, this means that the money would have earned a higher return by depositing it in a bank and earning interest. Under these circumstances, it is unlikely that a business would go ahead with the investment.

Discounted cash flow

When future cash flows are adjusted to give their present value, the technique is known as DISCOUNTED CASH FLOW. Because it is difficult and time consuming to calculate present values, **discount tables** are often used. These apply **discount factors** to show the present value of £1 at the end of a given number of years at different rates of interest. Figure 57.5 shows an extract from a discount table. The discount factors are given for **discount rates** of 5%, 8%, 10%, and 15% over a period of 5 years.

Figure 57.5 *Discount factors for interest rates of 5%, 8%, 10% and 15% over 5 years*

Years ahead	5%	8%	10%	15%
1	0.952	0.926	0.909	0.870
2	0.907	0.857	0.826	0.756
3	0.864	0.794	0.751	0.658
4	0.823	0.735	0.683	0.572
5	0.784	0.681	0.621	0.497

To calculate the present value of the revenue from the investment in the earlier example, the following calculations are required:

Present value of cash in year 1 = 0.952 × £50,000   =   £47,600
Present value of cash in year 2 = 0.907 × £40,000   =   £36,280
Present value of cash in year 3 = 0.864 × £35,000   =   £30,240
Total present value of all cash   =   £114,120

This figure of £114,120 compares with the figure of £114,155 from the previous calculation. The difference is due to rounding and is generally ignored.

Advantages of NPV method
- The method takes into account interest rates and the timing of future cash flows.
- The returns from alternative investment projects can easily be compared.
- The **opportunity cost** of money is taken into account. In other words, the investment decision is based not simply on the net cash flow but on the interest 'foregone' by not depositing the money in a bank account.

Disadvantages of NPV method
- The method does not provide an accurate means of comparison if the initial outlay on projects is different. For example, a NPV of £50,000 on a £5,000,000 investment would generally be considered not as good as a NPV of £40,000 on a £200,000 investment, even though the NPV is higher.

QUESTION 2

Fashion Plus plc manufactures a range of up-market clothing. The company uses modern manufacturing techniques and is committed to investment as a means of keeping ahead of its competitors. In 2001, the company decided to purchase some new computerised sewing machines. A number of models were available but the production manager identified two that would be most suitable. The cost and estimated net cash flows for the two models are shown in Figure 57.6. Discount factors are also shown for 5 years at a rate of 5%.

Figure 57.6 *Cost and future net cash flows for two sewing machines*

Model	Initial cost	Expected net cash flow					
		Year 1	Year 2	Year 3	Year 4	Year 5	Total
	£	£	£	£	£	£	£
Burrel	(110,000)	35,000	35,000	35,000	30,000	25,000	160,000
Crawford	(140,000)	40,000	40,000	40,000	40,000	40,000	200,000

The present value of £1 at a 5% discount rate

	Year 1	Year 2	Year 3	Year 4	Year 5
	0.952	0.907	0.864	0.823	0.784

(a) Using the figures above, calculate the net present values for the two sewing machines.
(b) Based on your findings in (a) which machine should Fashion Plus purchase?
(c) Explain two disadvantages to Fashion Plus of using this method of investment appraisal.

- NPV is complex to calculate without a computer or discount tables.
- The future rate of interest is likely to vary in an unpredictable fashion. Therefore, a positive NPV over the medium term could become negative if volatile conditions exist.

Accounting rate of return (ARR)

The ACCOUNTING RATE OF RETURN (ARR) method of appraisal measures the average annual **profit** as a percentage of the average **investment** over the life of an investment. It is calculated using the formula:

$$\text{Accounting rate of return} = \frac{\text{average annual profit}}{\text{average investment}} \times 100$$

To illustrate this method of appraisal, consider the example of Crest Ltd, a manufacturer of kitchen implements. The company is considering buying a machine costing £150,000. The machine is expected to last for five years after which it will have a scrap value of zero. When the additional costs from operating the machine, including depreciation, are subtracted from the additional revenue earned, the following additional profits are estimated.

Year 1	Year 2	Year 3	Year 4	Year 5	Total
£30,000	£30,000	£50,000	£60,000	£30,000	£200,000

To calculate the accounting rate of return for the new machine, the following steps are taken.
- Subtract the cost of the machine from the total additional profit to obtain the overall profit. Using the information above, this gives a figure of £50,000 (£200,000 - £150,000).
- Calculate the average annual profit by dividing the total profit by the number of years the machine is expected to last. So, in this case, the average annual profit is £10,000 (£50,000 ÷ 5).
- Calculate the average investment over the life span of the machine. Assuming that the straight line method of depreciation is used, accountants use the following formula.

$$\text{Average investment} \quad = \quad \frac{\text{Cost of machine } + \text{ disposal or scrap value (if any)}}{2}$$

So, in this case because there is no scrap value, the average investment is £75,000 (£150,000 ÷ 2).

The ARR can now be calculated.

$$\text{Accounting rate of return} \quad = \quad \frac{\text{average annual profit}}{\text{average investment}} \times 100$$

$$= \quad \frac{£10,000}{£75,000} \quad \times \quad 100$$

$$= \quad 13.33\%$$

In order to decide whether the 13.33% return is acceptable, Crest Ltd will have to compare this figure with the return made by other parts of the business and with other possible investments. Some companies adopt a policy whereby investment projects must give a minimum return before they are considered. So, for example, if Crest had a minimum acceptable return of 15%, the company would decide not to purchase this machine.

Advantages of ARR method
- The profitability of an investment project is clearly identified rather than simply the cash flow.
- It is relatively easy to make comparisons between different types of investment projects.
- The method can be used to compare the return on a particular project with the return on capital employed (ROCE) within a business as a whole (see unit 44).

Disadvantages of ARR method
- The method does not take into account the timing of cash flows. This might cause problems for businesses that suffer from poor or irregular cash flow.
- It uses profit figures which include non-cash items such as depreciation and provision for bad debts. This can distort the calculation depending on how depreciation and other provisions are calculated.
- Problems can arise with averaging because it does not show whether a project is more or less profitable in its early or later stages.
- It ignores the 'time-value' of money, ie that money is worth more now than in the future.
- It does not take account of how long the investment will last, nor how long it will take for income to cover the initial outlay.

Non-financial factors that influence investment decisions

When making investment decisions, businesses might take into account a number of social, economic and other factors that are not directly related to the financial costs and benefits.

Impact on the workforce Investment decisions often affect the workforce of a business. For example, investment in automated machinery can lead to redundancies if the machines are used to replace workers. A business might decide to postpone or abandon such a project if it feels that the social consequences of redundancies and unemployment are too severe.

Another reason for abandoning the project might be that the redundancy payments for the sacked workers could be very expensive. If the consequences of an investment project are likely to lead to conflict with trade unions, a business might decide against going ahead. This will depend upon the strength of the trade union and the amount of disruption to the business that would occur if, for example, a strike occurred. Similarly, investment might be reconsidered by a business if it fears that its public image will suffer as a result of unemployment or industrial relations problems. For instance, if a business had spent many years building up a 'caring', friendly image, its reputation could be damaged if it announced that mass redundancies were necessary to increase its profits.

Some businesses try to lessen the impact of automation by retraining their employees into areas that will provide more secure employment. For instance, if a warehouse was automated, the redundant workers might be retrained as drivers or as security guards. However, such a policy involves training costs and a business will have to judge whether this is worthwhile.

QUESTION 3

Taylor & Cork plc supplies the motor vehicle industry with equipment. Although the industry is very competitive, Taylor and Cork has been able to survive because of its investment in new technology. The production department has requested a new welding machine which will help to improve the quality of its products. Two different models are currently available and details of their cost and the expected additional profits for the company are shown in Figure 57.7. In both cases, after five years the expected scrap value of the machines is zero.

Figure 57.7 *Costs and expected profitability from two machines*

Model	Cost	Expected net cash flow				
		Year 1	Year 2	Year 3	Year 4	Year 5
	£	£	£	£	£	£
Model 1	(100,000)	20,000	25,000	25,000	30,000	30,000
Model 2	(130,000)	35,000	35,000	30,000	30,000	30,000

(a) Calculate the accounting rate of return (ARR) for the two machines.
(b) Which machine would you recommend to Taylor and Cork? Explain your reasons.
(c) Outline two limitations of using the ARR method of appraisal in this case.

Corporate objectives The views that businesses take on investment decisions often reflect their overall objectives. For example, a business that is pursuing a policy of fast growth might prefer to invest by taking-over a rival business rather than developing a new research centre. Alternatively, a business that is trying to expand its market share might prefer to invest in a market research programme rather than replace its delivery vehicles.

Ethical considerations Many businesses strive to be 'good corporate citizens' and to be socially responsible when making decisions. They might adopt this policy because they believe it is the right thing to do, or because they believe it will improve their public image. For example, in order to win customer approval in the UK, a business might decide against building a new factory in a Third World country where the workforce is poorly paid. Alternatively, a business might decide to build a new manufacturing plant in a location that minimises environmental damage rather than build it in the cheapest location.

Business confidence Entrepreneurs and managers have to take a long-term view when making investment decisions. If they are optimistic and full of confidence, they are more likely to spend money on investment projects. If they are pessimistic, they are likely to postpone or abandon projects. Business confidence is influenced by a range of factors such as the success of previous investments, the levels of unemployment, inflation and consumer demand, the stock market and, in some countries, by the degree of political stability.

Sunk costs This is money that is spent on capital items but which cannot be recovered. For example, expenditure on a new railway tunnel is classed as a sunk cost. In order to use the tunnel, the railway company must build a new railway line which involves extra investment in track, signalling and rolling stock. Sometimes, businesses go ahead with investments simply because they have spent a large amount of money on sunk costs. However, it is much more sensible to regard the sunk cost as a 'past cost' and disregard it when making a decision. So, in the example relating to the railway tunnel, if the business is considering whether it is worthwhile going ahead with a new rail service through the tunnel, it should only consider the additional costs and revenue that will arise. It should disregard its previous investment expenditure on the sunk cost of the tunnel.

QUESTION 4

The new Wembley Stadium - news report, January 2002

The Football Association (FA) has been pondering over a very big investment decision for a number of years. In May 2000, Aston Villa and Chelsea were the last teams to play an FA Cup final at Wembley Stadium. Since then, the decision to rebuild Wembley Stadium, or relocate the national football stadium to Birmingham, or not to build one at all has attracted a great deal of media and public attention. It now seems likely that the FA has opted to build a 90,000 capacity stadium at the site of the old Wembley Stadium. The cost of this investment is still unclear. However, if demolition costs, construction costs, local infrastructure and other costs are taken into account, it could amount to around £1 billion. It is estimated that over £100 million has already been spent in clearing the site.

If a new stadium is built at Wembley, it will be a controversial decision. Supporters of the Wembley development argue that Wembley is steeped in history and that it is the 'home' of world football. They also say that Wembley's location in London is ideal for visitors from all over the country and from all over the world. However, opponents of the plan say that a similar stadium could be built in Birmingham for around £470 million. They also claim that a Birmingham site is more central for visiting fans, has better rail and road communications and, according to surveys, has the support of the majority of football fans in the country.

(a) If the FA goes ahead with the Wembley development, the payback period could be at least 20 years. Explain what this means and suggest why such a lengthy period could be a problem.
(b) What financial factors will the FA have taken into account when making the investment decision?
(c) What non-financial factors might also have been considered?

key terms

Accounting rate of return - a method of investment appraisal that measures the average annual profit as a percentage of the average investment over the life of a project.

Discounted cash flow (DCF) - a technique in which future cash flows are adjusted to give their present value.

Investment - expenditure on capital goods, fixed assets and items such as research and development.

Investment appraisal - the evaluation of investment projects to determine whether they should go ahead.

Net present value - a method of investment appraisal that considers all the costs and benefits of an investment and also takes into account the timing of those costs and benefits.

Payback - a method of investment appraisal that focuses on the amount of time it takes to recover the initial cost of an investment.

Payback period - the length of time that it takes to recover the initial cost of an investment.

Present value - the value of a sum of money available in the future, expressed in terms of what it is worth today.

summary questions

1. State two examples of investment that do not involve the purchase of capital goods.
2. Explain the difference between net cash flow and the flow of profits from an investment.
3. How is the payback period calculated?
4. What main disadvantage does the payback method of appraisal have compared with the net present value method?
5. How is a discount factor used?
6. What happens to the present value of money if interest rates rise?
7. If the present value of future income from an investment project is £345,000 and the cost is £309,000, what is the net present value?
8. What is the formula for calculating the accounting rate of return?
9. State two advantages of the accounting rate of return method of appraisal.
10. State three non-financial factors a business might take into account when making investment decisions.

UNIT ASSESSMENT QUESTION 1

Corbridge Carriers is a transport company in Northumberland. The business is expanding and, in order to meet demand, needs to acquire a new vehicle. The owner is considering two options. The first is to buy a new lorry for £60,000. The second option is to take-over a local rival, Prudhoe Transport. This company has been badly run and has built up large debts. It could be purchased for £40,000. The expected net cash flows from the two investments are shown in Figure 57.8. Both projects are expected to generate returns for a 6 year period. Figure 57.8 also shows discount factors for 6 years at 5%.

Figure 57.8 *Expected net cash flows from the two investment projects for Corbridge Carriers*

Investment	Expected net cash flow					
	Year 1	Year 2	Year 3	Year 4	Year 5	Year 6
	£	£	£	£	£	£
New lorry	10,000	13,000	15,000	15,000	14,000	14,000
Acquisition	5,000	10,000	15,000	20,000	20,000	20,000

The present value of £1 at a 5% discount rate

	Year 1	Year 2	Year 3	Year 4	Year 5	Year 6
	0.952	0.907	0.864	0.823	0.784	0.746

(a) **Using the figures above, calculate the net present value of each project.**
(b) **Calculate the payback period for each project.**
(c) **In which project should Corbridge Carriers invest according to your calculations in (a) and (b)? Explain your answer.**
(d) **What would be the impact on the net present value of the two projects if interest rates fell?**

UNIT ASSESSMENT QUESTION 2

Evert Valley Leisure Club is a private health club. It owns a fitness suite and golf course. The owners of the club are considering two quite different investment projects. They do not have sufficient funds for both projects.

- New equipment for the fitness suite (cost: £60,000).
- Sprinkler system for the golf course (cost: £80,000).

Figure 57.9 shows the expected additional profits for the two projects. It is expected that there will be no scrap value for the investments at the end of their lives.

Figure 57.9 *Expected additional profits for two investment projects*

Investment	Expected net cash flow						
	Year 1	Year 2	Year 3	Year 4	Year 5	Year 6	Year 7
	£	£	£	£	£	£	£
Fitness suite	13,000	13,000	13,000	13,000	13,000	13,000	-
Golf course	40,000	30,000	20,000	10,000	5,000	-	-

(a) Calculate the accounting rate of return (ARR) for the two projects.

(b) What factors are likely to influence the club in its investment decision?

(c) Under what circumstances might it be more appropriate for the club to use the payback method of appraisal?

unit 58 Examinations in business accounting

Examination presentation

In accounting examinations, students must ensure that their answers are presented in a style that is acceptable. This unit provides help and guidance in presenting work in a conventional format.

Memos and reports

Memos and reports are the main forms of written communication within business organisations. Memos are relatively short documents. The term memo is short for memorandum (the plural is memoranda). Reports are generally longer documents than memos. Both memos and reports have a layout that shows:

- to whom the communication is addressed;
- from whom it is sent;
- the date;
- the subject of the correspondence.

Memos These are documents used internally within an organisation. They are often written on pre-printed paper. Memos are generally used for short messages. Abbreviations can be used, but the language should be grammatically correct. A memo to a close colleague might use much less formal language than one sent to someone in a senior position.

Figure 58.1 *An example of a correct format for a memo*

JOHNSON WEBBING ● ——— Company name on pre-printed paper.

Memorandum ● ——— Often shortened to memo if hand written.

To:
From: ———— **Date:** ——— Memo head should always include: to, from and date.

Subject: ● ——— Re (short for regarding) is sometimes used instead of subject.

———— Signature is not necessary.

enc ● ——— Enclosure reference (ie is anything attached?)
cc ● ——— Copies to (ie the names or initials of anyone else who has been sent a copy).

Reports Like memos, reports tend to be for internal use in a business, although in certain cases, such as published annual reports, they are intended for external use. They have preset formats and are often complex with several headings and subheadings. They do not need to include the address of the organisation if they are going to be used internally. If the report is to be sent to 'important' people in the organisation then it will be formal, ie written in an impersonal style. This means that pronouns such as 'I', 'we', 'you', 'my', 'your', 'us' or 'our' should not be used.

Figure 58.2 *An example of the layout for a short formal report*

To: **Ref:**   *Initials or number for filing purposes.*

From: **Date:**

Subject: *This will be the title of the report.*

1.0   Terms of Reference
This is the introduction saying who asked for the report, why it is required and what is the deadline.

2.0   Procedure
This sets out how the information is to be gathered and what research methods will be used.

3.0   Findings
This gives the information that has been requested. If necessary it will be broken into sub-headings, each with its own reference, eg 3.1, or even broken down further, eg 3.2i or 3.2.2 or 3.2a.

4.0   Conclusions
Here a summary of the main findings is given. It is useful for people who do not wish to read the detailed findings.

5.0   Recommendations
These are your suggestions based on the findings. If you have not been asked to make any - do not use this heading.

For an informal report, people generally use fewer sub-headings. A possible format is given below.

Figure 58.3 *An example of an informal report layout*

From: **Ref:**

To: **Date:**

Subject:

1.0   Introduction

2.0   Findings

3.0   Summary

For both memos and reports, it is important to write clearly and concisely. A checklist of points to consider is given below.

Accurate: Is all the necessary information included and correct?
Concise: Is everything to the point and relevant?
Legible: Can the document be read easily?
Logical: Is the information presented in a sensible order?
Polite: Does the document display courtesy, tact and understanding?
Format: Is the material set out and ordered in a proper fashion using appropriate headings, indentation, text size and conventions?
Is the format appropriate to the audience and purpose?
Spelling, grammar and punctuation:
Are these checked and do they follow standard conventions?

Layout of final accounts

When setting out final accounts, the '3 Ws' are important. This means that the following should be included:

- **who?** - the name of the business;
- **what?** - the type of financial statement;
- **when?** - the date or period covered.

For example:

Coopers Ltd
Profit and Loss Account
for the year ended 30.11.01

or:

Bennett Ltd
Balance Sheet
as at 31.12.01

It is conventional to use the expression 'for the year ended ...' in the header of a profit and loss account and the expression 'as at ...' in the header of a balance sheet.

Where appropriate, subheadings, subtotals and columns should be used. So, for example, a subtotal of 'net current assets' might be shown in a balance sheet as a separate column with its own subheading.

Although examination candidates are not expected to produce accounts to the same standard as those published by plcs, it is important to present information in a clear fashion. This gives candidates the best chance of achieving maximum marks. Note that it is conventional to give figures to the nearest pound.

Calculations

When calculations are required, it is important to set out workings in full. This is because the 'own figure' (O/F) rule might apply. For example, suppose a question asks students to calculate the depreciation over a 3 month period on a computer that cost £3,000. The annual rate of depreciation is 10%. If a student simply writes the answer £100, calculated by calculator, this is incorrect and gains no marks.

But, if the student sets out the workings and states the method used:

$$10\% \text{ of } £3,000 \text{ for 3 months} \quad = \frac{10}{100} \times £3,000 \times \frac{1}{3} = £100$$

this is still incorrect. (The correct answer is £75.) However, it might gain a mark because the examiner can see that the student is applying the correct model/method even though he or she has multiplied by a third rather than by a quarter. If this is part of a longer question, all the subsequent answers might also be incorrect. However, students can still get credit as long as their answer is consistent and mathematically correct from that point on.

When dealing with ratios or formula, follow the '4Ss' routine:
- **state** the formula or model;
- **substitute** the data in the formula;
- **solve** the equation;
- **show** and clearly identify your workings. **Do not cross them out.**

Rounding Unless otherwise instructed, present final answers to 2 decimal places or to the nearest £. For example, suppose a question asks students to calculate the acid test ratio from some given figures. The answer should be set out as follows:

$$\text{Acid test ratio} = \frac{\text{current assets - stocks}}{\text{current liabilities}} = \frac{£698m - £415m}{£1,781m}$$

$$= \frac{£283m}{£1,781m} = 0.16 \text{ (expressed as a ratio, } 0.16 : 1 \text{)}$$

If you use a calculator to work this out, the answer is 0.1588994. The answer given is rounded to two decimal places.

Totals Totals and subtotals should be clearly indicated in accounts and other financial records. For example, the opening capital for a business could be shown as:

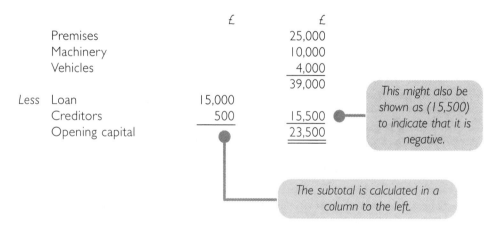

		£	£
	Premises		25,000
	Machinery		10,000
	Vehicles		4,000
			39,000
Less	Loan	15,000	
	Creditors	500	15,500
	Opening capital		23,500

This might also be shown as (15,500) to indicate that it is negative.

The subtotal is calculated in a column to the left.

Time management

In an examination, it is important that students work out how much time should be spent on each question. It is much better to leave a question unfinished rather than attempting to achieve a 'perfect' answer at the expense of other questions.

So, at the start of the examination, students should decide how much time should be allocated to each question and then stick rigidly to the timetable. If possible, some time should also be allocated to 'reading through' the answers. Then, if there is any time left, students should return to any unanswered questions.

In some examinations, students are given a choice in the questions to be answered and the order in which they can be attempted. It is always worthwhile spending a few minutes at the start of an examination in reading through the paper and planning which questions are to be answered, and in which order.

UNIT 1

1. Which of the following is not an example of a business transaction?
A The sale by a travel agent of a week's holiday to Ibiza.
B The purchase of fuel by a transport company.
C The gift of a new car from a business owner to her husband.
D The payment of rent to a landlord.

2. Why is it important for a business to record all business transactions?
A Because a company's financial circumstances are a matter of public interest.
B So that profit can be calculated and the owner can assess the business's performance.
C Because competitors might wish to check the accuracy of financial records.
D Because manual records are less accurate than computerised records.

3. Sales are transactions that involve:
A expenditure by a business on raw materials;
B payment of rent for business premises;
C receipt of money in the form of a government grant;
D receipt of money from customers for goods and services provided.

4. Purchases are transactions that involve:
A expenditure on goods intended for resale;
B expenditure on employee's wages;
C expenditure on business premises;
D payment of tax to the government.

5. Which type of information is not generally the concern of accountants?
A The amount of tax owed by a business.
B The likely cost of producing a new model of motor vehicle.
C The level of profit that a business has made in the past year.
D The length of time it takes for employees to commute to work.

6. Which of the following is normally the responsibility of a financial accountant?
A Calculating the cost of producing a new design.
B Controlling the budget of the marketing department.
C Deciding which type of production machinery should be purchased.
D Keeping proper accounting records of financial transactions.

7. A management accountant is generally most concerned with:
A minimising a business's tax bill;
B keeping accurate financial records;
C providing information that will be useful to managers;
D auditing and checking the accounts.

8. An auditor has the responsibility of:
A drawing up the final accounts of a business;
B communicating the level of profitability to a business's owners;
C checking that accounts are 'true and fair';
D commenting on the level of efficiency within a business.

9. Which of the following statements is incorrect?
A Suppliers are not stakeholders because they have no interest in how a business performs.
B Employees are stakeholders because they have a vested interest in their employer's business.
C The users of accounting information are both internal and external to a business.
D A stakeholder is not necessarily the owner of a business.

10. A purchases ledger clerk is not likely to deal with:
A customer accounts;
B supplier accounts;
C purchase transactions;
D the buying of raw materials.

UNIT 2

1. Bookkeeping is most likely to involve which of the following?
A Communicating accounting information to external users.
B Recording financial information in the books of prime entry.
C Preparing the final accounts for publication in an annual report.
D Analysing a rival business's balance sheet.

2. Which of the following is not a source document?
A A purchases day book.
B An invoice.
C A receipt.
D A paying-in slip.

3. Which of the following is a book of prime entry?
A A balance sheet.
B A cash book.
C A profit and loss account.
D A nominal ledger.

4. A sales day book is used for which of the following purposes?
A Recording transactions in which goods are purchased by a business.
B Recording payments into a bank account.
C Recording details of sales made to customers.
D Recording details of goods returned to suppliers.

5. The journal is not normally used for which of the following purposes?
A To record transfers between accounts.
B To record the correction of errors.
C To record details of less common transactions.
D To record details of credit sales.

6. The double entry system of bookkeeping is normally used in which of the following?
A Sales day book.
B Sales return day book.
C Sales ledger.
D Sales invoice.

7. A nominal ledger is different from a sales ledger because it:
A summarises financial information;
B is normally computerised;
C does not contain personal accounts;
D is a legal requirement to have a nominal ledger.

8. An impersonal account might contain which of the following?
A The details of a customer.
B The details of wage payments.
C The details of a supplier.
D The details of how much is owed by particular customers.

9. A trial balance might be prepared at which stage in the accounting process?
A Between the ledger accounts and the final accounts.
B Between the source documents and the books of prime entry.
C Between the books of prime entry and the ledger accounts.
D Between the profit and loss account and the balance sheet.

10. The profit and loss account shows:

A the value of resources owned by a business;

B the amount of money that a business has borrowed;

C the amount of money that owners have supplied to a business;

D the income and expenditure of a business.

UNIT 3

1. Which of the following is not a function of a source document?

A It provides documentary evidence that a transaction has taken place.

B It provides detailed information about a transaction.

C It can be used to clarify misunderstandings if a trading dispute occurs.

D It can be used as a summary of internal financial information.

2. Which of the following is not a source document?

A Quotation.

B Cash flow statement.

C Invoice.

D Remittance advice.

3. Which of the following is a source document?

A Order form.

B Requisition form.

C Application form.

D Profit and loss account.

4. Which of the following documents is used to tell a customer that a business is able to supply the goods that have been ordered?

A Quotation.

B Acknowledgement note.

C Delivery note.

D Goods received note.

5. Which of the following information is not likely to be included on a statement of account?

A A description of goods.

B The total amount owing.

C The address of the supplier.

D Payment details.

6. Which of the following documents is most central to the bookkeeping process?

A Quotation.

B Delivery note.

C Invoice.

D Goods received note.

7. Which of the following numbers is not likely to be contained on a delivery note?

A Supplier's telephone no.

B Customer's order no.

C Supplier's VAT reg. no.

D Customer's VAT reg. no.

8. Which of the following documents might be sent by a customer with a cheque for payment?

A Quotation.

B Debit note.

C Remittance note.

D Credit note.

9. Which of the following documents will be sent to a customer if faulty goods are returned?

A Credit note.

B Debit note.

C Invoice.

D Audit note.

10. Which of the following terms is not likely to appear on an invoice?

A Carriage paid.

B E & OE.

C VAT.

D Profit.

UNIT 4

1. Which of the following is the person or business on whom a cheque is drawn?

A Drawee.

B Drawer.

C Payee.

D Payer.

2. Which of the following is the payee on a cheque?

A The person who signs the cheque.

B The person or business who is receiving payment.

C The bank on whom the cheque is drawn.

D The cashier.

3. A cheque is a written order from the:

A drawer to a bank.

B drawer to a payee.

C bank to a payee.

D bank to a drawer.

4. The imprest amount in petty cash is:

A the amount of money left at the end of the period;

B the amount of money that is used during the period;

C the amount of money at the start of the period;

D the amount of money introduced at the end of the period.

5. Which of the following can be used to buy goods on credit?

A Debit card.

B Store card.

C Cheque card.

D Bank giro credit.

6. In which of the following cases is there an immediate transfer of funds from the purchaser's bank account to the vendor's bank account?

A A payment by cheque.

B A payment by cash.

C A payment by debit card.

D A payment by credit card.

7. A bank giro credit is most likely to be used in which of the following cases?

A When posting a cheque to pay a utility bill.

B When paying the bill at a supermarket checkout.

C When buying petrol using a credit card.

D When selling goods on a market stall.

8. Which of the following documents provides a record of transactions for a retailer?

A Direct debit mandate.

B Cheque stub.

C Receipt.

D Till roll.

9. Which of the following information is not likely to be printed on a receipt?

A Date of transaction.

B Name of seller.

C Value of transaction.

D Name of the customer.

10. Which of the following is the least secure form of payment from a retailer's point of view?

A   A cash payment.
B   A cheque unsupported by a cheque card.
C   A payment by debit card.
D   A cheque supported by a cheque card.

UNIT 5

1.   Which of the following is <u>not</u> an asset?

A   Trade creditor.
B   Trade debtor.
C   Cash at bank.
D   Machinery.

2.   Which of the following is <u>not</u> a liability?

A   Trade creditor.
B   Bank loan.
C   Bank overdraft.
D   Office equipment.

3.   The capital of the business is provided by which of the following?

A   Banks.
B   Owners.
C   Creditors.
D   Suppliers.

4.   If total assets = £14,500 and capital = £7,200, what is the value of liabilities?

A   £14,500.
B   £21,700.
C   £7,300.
D   £7,200.

5.   A business buys a new machine from a supplier on credit. What effect will this transaction have on the accounting equation?

A   Assets increase and capital falls.
B   Assets decrease and liabilities increase.
C   Assets increase and liabilities increase.
D   Assets increase and liabilities fall.

6.   A business buys a vehicle for cash. What effect will this transaction have on the accounting equation?

A   One asset falls and another asset rises.
B   Assets rise and liabilities rise.
C   Assets rise and liabilities fall.
D   Assets fall and liabilities rise.

7.   Any profit made by a business is added to which of the following in the balance sheet?

A   Assets.
B   Liabilities.
C   Capital.
D   None of these.

8.   Money taken from the business by the owner is called which of the following?

A   Capital.
B   Expenses.
C   Revenue.
D   Drawings.

9.   If total assets = £33,000, capital = £12,000, revenue = £43,000, expenses = £28,000 and drawings = £10,000.
What is the value of liabilities?

A   £33,000.
B   £12,000.
C   £15,000.
D   £16,000.

10. Profit can be defined as the difference between:

A   revenue and expenses;
B   revenue and liabilities;
C   capital and expenses;
D   drawings and expenses.

UNIT 6

1.   Which of the following is an example of capital expenditure?

A   Fuel costs.
B   Purchase of raw materials.
C   Purchase of a new vehicle.
D   The cost of heat and light.

2.   Which of the following is an example of revenue expenditure?

A   Purchase of a machine.
B   Stationery costs.
C   Building costs.
D   Purchase of a lorry.

3.   Spending on which of the following is <u>not</u> revenue expenditure?

A   Advertising.
B   Fixtures and fittings.
C   Bank charges.
D   Interest.

4.   Spending on which of the following is <u>not</u> capital expenditure?

A   Interest on a loan to fund the purchase of a factory.
B   Installation costs of a new computer system.
C   Building a factory extension.
D   The purchase of office furniture.

5.   Which of the following items of expenditure would be listed in the profit and loss account as an expense?

A   Rental charges for a photocopier.
B   Purchase of a CCTV camera for security.
C   Carriage charges for a new machine.
D   Architects fees for drawing plans for a new warehouse.

6.   If the £6,700 cost of a new vehicle is mistakenly entered in the profit and loss account, which of the following is correct?

A   Profit will be overstated by £6,700.
B   Profit will be understated by £6,700.
C   Expenses will be understated by £6,700.
D   Fixed assets will be overstated by £6,700.

7.   If a company purchases a drinks vending machine, which of the following assets should be entered in the balance sheet?

A   Vending machine.
B   Vending machine plus stock of soft drinks.
C   Vending machine, stock of soft drinks plus stock of paper cups.
D   None of the above.

8.   The following expenses were incurred when a business installed some new machinery:
Purchase cost: £150,000
Installation: £4,000
Annual insurance premium: £2,500
Carriage: £900
Fuel (oil): £400

What is the total capital expenditure?

A   £150,000.
B   £154,000.
C   £155,900.
D   £154,900.

9. Which of the following is capital revenue?
A The sale of stock by a retailer.
B The sale of tables by a furniture manufacturer.
C The sale of an oven by a restaurant.
D The sale of financial services by a bank.

10. If revenue expenditure is treated as capital expenditure by mistake, which of the following is true?
A Profit and fixed assets will be understated.
B Expenses and profit will be understated.
C Profit and fixed assets will be overstated.
D Revenue will be overstated.

UNIT 7 ● ● ●

1. Which of the following accounting concepts was defined as 'fundamental' in the Accounting Standards Committee's Statements of Standard Accounting Practice (SSAP 2)?
A Realisation concept.
B Historical cost concept.
C Money measurement concept.
D Going concern concept.

2. A business owner uses her car for both business and personal use. The total cost of running the car in a year is £800. According to her records she drove 15,000 miles for the business and 5,000 miles for her own use. According to the business entity concept how much of the cost should be attributed to the business?
A £800.
B £600.
C £200.
D None of the above.

3. According to the money measurement concept which of the following business assets could not be recorded in the balance sheet?
A Fixtures and fittings.
B Vehicles.
C Management expertise.
D Cash.

4. Which accounting concept states that a business should value its fixed assets according to the price it paid for them?
A Realisation.
B Historical cost.
C Materiality.
D Money measurement.

5. The net realisable value of an asset is best described as its:
A sale value;
B replacement value;
C historical value;
D value in contributing to profits.

6. Which of the following accounting concepts assumes that a business will continue to trade into the foreseeable future?
A Realisation.
B Going concern.
C Accruals.
D Matching.

7. Decide whether the following statements are true or false.

(i) According to the consistency concept, accountants should never change their methods.

(ii) A transaction is considered material if its omission would be misleading.
A (i) True; (ii) True.
B (i) True; (ii) False.
C (i) False; (ii) True.
D (i) False; (ii) False.

8. Which of the following concepts makes a distinction between the payment of cash and the receipt of goods?
A Matching.
B Consistency.
C Historical cost.
D Accruals.

9. Which of the following items of capital expenditure is likely to be treated as revenue expenditure according to the materiality concept?
A Van for £2,800.
B Bucket for £3.99.
C Computer for £2,000.
D Machinery for £3,100.

10. Which of the following accounting concepts states that costs should be allocated to the accounting period in which the revenue they help generate is recorded?
A Consistency.
B Materiality.
C Matching.
D Realisation.

UNIT 8 ● ● ●

1. Which of the following transactions relates to a change in liabilities?
A Sale of services to a customer.
B Purchase of raw materials by cash.
C Payment of wages.
D Receipt of a bank loan.

2. Which of the following transactions relates to a change in revenue?
A Introduction of capital.
B Withdrawal of capital.
C Payment of wages.
D Receipt of money for services provided.

3. Which of the following is not regarded as expenses?
A Wages.
B Rent.
C Sales revenue.
D Bank charges.

4. A business pays wages of £5,000. Which of the following sets of entries represent the correct way of recording this transaction?
A Debit bank account, credit wages account.
B Credit bank account, debit wages account.
C Debit wages account, debit bank account.
D Credit bank account, credit wages account.

5. Which of the following entries is correct if a business sells £500 of goods to a customer who pays by cheque?
A Debit bank account with £500.
B Debit sales account with £500.
C Credit bank account with £500.
D Credit purchases account with £500.

6. **Which of the following entries is correct if a business receives a loan of £2,000?**
A Debit loan account with £2,000.
B Credit bank account with £2,000.
C Credit capital account with £2,000.
D Credit loan account with £2,000.

7. **If a business pays £12,000 for a vehicle, which of the following entries is correct?**
A Debit bank account with £12,000.
B Debit vehicle account with £12,000.
C Credit capital account with £12,000.
D Credit vehicle account with £12,000.

8. **Which of the following information would not normally be recorded in a T account?**
A Folio.
B Date.
C Value of transaction.
D Name of the bookkeeper.

9. **A debit entry represents which of the following?**
A Receiving value.
B Giving value.
C An increase in the value of capital.
D An increase in liabilities.

10. **If there is an outflow of money from the cash account of a business, which of the following is correct?**
A The account has received value.
B There has been an increase in the value of assets.
C There has been a decrease in liabilities.
D The account has given value.

UNIT 9

1. **What is meant by the trade credit period?**
A The time between an entry being recorded in the sales day book and the ledger.
B The time between an invoice being issued and the agreed payment date.
C The time it takes for an invoice to reach a customer.
D The time between an invoice being issued and the date on which payment is received.

2. **Which of the following documents is used when recording information in the sales day book?**
A Receipt.
B Delivery note.
C Credit note.
D Sales invoice.

3. **Which of the following details are not entered in the sales day book?**
A Description of the goods sold.
B Date of transaction.
C Name of customer.
D Value of transaction.

4. **A business makes a credit sale for £400. This does not include VAT. How much VAT should be charged if the VAT rate is 17.5%?**
A £470.
B £70.
C £40.
D £400.

5. **A sales day book is best described as:**
A a book of prime entry;
B a ledger;
C a source document;
D a final account.

6. **Which of the following contains the accounts of individual debtors?**
A Sales account.
B Sales day book.
C Sales ledger.
D Nominal ledger.

7. **Which account in the nominal ledger is used to record credit sales?**
A Sales account.
B Customer account.
C Personal account.
D Nominal account.

8. **Which of the following is correct when transferring information from the sales day book to the sales ledger?**
A Credit customer account.
B Debit customer account.
C Credit sales account.
D Debit sales account.

9. **Which of the following is correct when transferring information from the sales day book to the nominal ledger?**
A Credit customer account.
B Debit customer account.
C Credit sales account.
D Debit sales account.

10. **What is a price reduction for early payment called?**
A Special offer.
B Credit discount.
C Cash discount.
D Trade discount.

UNIT 10

1. **In bookkeeping, a credit purchase refers to:**
A buying goods with a credit card;
B buying goods and paying immediately;
C spending on goods on which there is a discount;
D spending on goods that are paid for at a later date.

2. **Which of the following items of expenditure would not be regarded as purchases for a restaurant?**
A Potatoes.
B Cooking oil.
C Card for printing menus.
D Flour.

3. **An analysed purchases day book contains which of the following?**
A A debit and a credit side.
B Columns for recording different categories of expenditure.
C A column to record details from sales invoices.
D The description of goods bought on credit.

4. **Which of the following documents are used to record information in the purchases day book?**
A Bank statement.
B Purchase invoice.
C Sales invoice.
D Delivery note.

5. **Which of the following is an alternative name for a purchases day book?**
A Purchases account.
B Purchases ledger.
C Purchases journal.
D Purchase invoice.

6. Which types of accounts are contained in the purchases ledger?

A Customer accounts.
B Debtors accounts.
C Supplier accounts.
D Purchases account.

7. A folio is used for:

A tracing where purchase invoices are filed;
B checking the amount of VAT on a transaction;
C checking that a payment has been made;
D tracing the ledger page in which a transaction is recorded.

8. When transferring information from the purchases day book to the ledgers, which of the following entries is correct?

A Supplier accounts are credited.
B Supplier accounts are debited.
C Debtor accounts are credited.
D Debtor accounts are debited.

9. Which of the following accounts in the nominal ledger is debited when transferring information from the purchases day book?

A Sales account.
B Purchases account.
C Supplier accounts.
D Customer accounts.

10. When recording credit purchases, how are trade discounts treated?

A Debited to a trade discount account.
B Credited to a trade discount account.
C Credited to the purchases account.
D None of the above.

UNIT 11 ●●●

1. From a purchaser's point of view, which of the following describes goods sent back to a supplier?

A Sales returns.
B Goods inwards.
C Misposted.
D Returns outwards.

2. Which of the following is an alternative term for returns inwards?

A Sales returns.
B Purchases returns.
C Goods outwards.
D Inferior goods.

3. Which of the following is a source document when goods are returned?

A Sales ledger.
B Purchases returns day book.
C Returns inwards journal.
D Credit note.

4. Which of the following is a book of prime entry and is used by a business to record goods returned to a supplier?

A Purchases returns day book.
B Purchases ledger.
C Sales returns day book.
D Sales ledger.

5. In which of the following is the double entry system used?

A Purchases returns day book.
B Sales journal.
C Nominal ledger.
D Returns inwards day book.

6. Which of the following postings are used when transferring information from the returns inwards day book to the ledgers?

A Credit customer account and debit returns inwards account.
B Debit customer account and credit returns inwards account.
C Credit supplier account and debit returns outwards account.
D Debit supplier account and credit returns outwards account.

7. Which of the following postings are used when transferring information from the returns outwards day book to the ledgers?

A Credit customer account and debit returns outwards account.
B Debit supplier account and credit returns outwards account.
C Credit supplier account and debit returns outwards account.
D Debit customer account and credit returns outwards account.

8. Which of the following is not used when recording sales returns?

A Nominal ledger.
B Purchases ledger.
C Sales ledger.
D Returns inwards day book.

9. When a control account is used, which of the following is described as a memorandum account?

A Returns inwards account.
B Returns outwards account.
C Sales ledger control account.
D Customer account.

10. A credit entry in a customer account indicates which of the following?

A The customer has purchased some goods.
B The customer has returned some goods.
C The supplier is owed money by the customer.
D The supplier's assets have increased.

UNIT 12 ●●●

1. Which transactions are recorded in the cash book?

A Credit sales.
B Credit purchases.
C Payments and receipts.
D Sales and purchases returns.

2. Which of the following is recorded on the receipts side of the three column cash book?

A Discounts received.
B Discounts allowed.
C Payment to a supplier.
D Payment to the Inland Revenue.

3. A two column cash book normally does not contain a column for which of the following?

A Cheque payments.
B Cash receipts.
C Folios.
D Discounts received.

4. Which source document is not likely to be used when recording transactions in the cash book?

A Credit note.
B Cheque counterfoil.
C Receipt.
D Paying-in slip.

5. Debit entries in the cash book are:

A credited to the sales ledger or nominal ledger;
B credited to the purchases ledger or nominal ledger;
C debited to the sales ledger or nominal ledger;
D debited to the purchases ledger or nominal ledger.

6. Credit entries in the cash book are:

A credited to the sales ledger or nominal ledger;

B credited to the purchases ledger or nominal ledger;

C debited to the sales ledger or nominal ledger;

D debited to the purchases ledger or nominal ledger.

7. A cheque paid by a customer to settle a credit transaction is recorded in the cash book and which of the following?

A Purchases ledger.

B Sales ledger.

C Nominal ledger.

D Journal.

8. Where might a contra entry be used?

A In the nominal ledger to record discounts received.

B In the cash book to record a cash payment for goods.

C In the cash book to record a withdrawal of cash from the bank.

D In a customer account to record the settlement of a credit transaction.

9. A payment to a supplier for goods bought over the counter with cash is recorded in the cash book and which of the following?

A Purchases ledger.

B Sales ledger.

C Nominal ledger.

D Journal.

10. How is the total of discounts allowed recorded?

A Credited to the discounts allowed account.

B Debited to the discounts allowed account.

C Credited to the purchases account.

D Debited to the purchases account.

6. When transferring funds into the petty cash system from the bank, which of the following entries is made in the cash book?

A Bank account is debited.

B Bank account is credited.

C Cash account is debited.

D Cash account is credited.

7. Which of the following is not likely to be a sundry expense?

A £5 paid for stationery.

B £10 donation to a local charity.

C £1 for an office light bulb.

D £2 for plasters for first aid kit.

8. To which types of account in the ledgers are the payments in the petty cash book most likely to be posted?

A Customer accounts.

B Expenses accounts.

C Real accounts.

D Personal accounts.

9. The imprest amount is best described as:

A the cash float.

B the amount spent from petty cash.

C the amount transferred from the bank into petty cash.

D the amount paid to regular suppliers from petty cash.

10. The petty cash book is different from the cash book because:

A it has both a debit and a credit side;

B it only records cash transactions;

C it is both a book of prime entry and a ledger;

D it is in the form of a T account.

UNIT 13 ● ● ●

1. Which of the following payments is least likely to be entered in the petty cash book?

A £5 paid to a window cleaner.

B £3.90 paid to send a registered letter.

C £24 paid for petrol.

D £200 paid for new office furniture.

2. Which of the following source documents is used to record transactions in the petty cash book?

A Sales invoice.

B Purchase invoice.

C Receipt.

D Paying-in-slip.

3. Which of the following layouts of the petty cash book is most useful when classifying expenditure?

A Three column.

B Two column.

C One column.

D Analysed.

4. Which of the following is not normally entered in the petty cash book when recording transactions?

A Date.

B Petty cash voucher number.

C Folio.

D Name of payee.

5. A debit entry in the petty cash book is matched with a credit entry in which other book?

A Sales ledger.

B Purchases ledger.

C Nominal ledger.

D Cash book.

UNIT 14 ● ● ●

1. Which type of transaction is recorded in the journal?

A Return of faulty goods.

B Introduction of starting capital.

C Cash sale of goods.

D Cash purchase of raw materials.

2. Which of the following is not recorded in the journal?

A Opening entry.

B Purchase of a fixed asset.

C Error correction.

D Purchase of stock for resale.

3. The journal is an example of which type of book?

A Ledger.

B Cash book.

C Book of prime entry.

D Returns book.

4. Which of the following is an alternative name for the journal?

A Bought ledger.

B Sold day book.

C Journal proper.

D Purchases day book.

5. Which of the following is not a function of the journal?

A It is used to record cash payments and receipts.

B It is used to record credit purchases of assets.

C It provides a means of tracing non-routine transactions.

D It acts as a diary of events.

6. The purpose of the narrative in the journal is to:
A state the value of the transaction;
B describe the transaction;
C show which account is to be debited;
D show which account is to be credited;

7. The purpose of the folio in the journal is to provide:
A a cross-reference to ledger accounts;
B a cross-reference to source documents;
C a cross-reference to the purchase invoice;
D a cross reference to other day books.

8. When posting information from the journal to the ledgers, which of the following occurs?
A Debit entries are credited to accounts in the ledgers.
B Debit entries are debited to accounts in the ledgers.
C Credit entries are debited to accounts in the ledgers.
D None of the above.

9. The introduction of capital by an owner is recorded in the journal as:
A a debit in the bank account and a credit in the capital account;
B a credit in the bank account and a debit in the capital account;
C a debit in the bank account and a credit in the cash account;
D a credit in the capital account and a debit in the drawings account.

10. The purchase of a fixed asset on credit is posted from the journal to the ledgers as:
A a credit in the fixed asset account and a debit in the supplier account;
B a debit in the bank account and a credit in the purchases account;
C a credit in the bank account and a debit in the purchases account;
D a debit in the fixed asset account and a credit in the supplier account.

UNIT 15 ●●○

1. Which of the following is <u>not</u> a reason why accounts are balanced?
A To prepare a profit and loss account.
B To forecast future profits.
C To check the accuracy of the bookkeeping.
D To prepare a trial balance.

2. A debit balance on an account in the sales ledger suggests which of the following?
A A customer owes money to the business.
B Money is owed to a supplier.
C The balance is equal to the total value of sales.
D The account has been settled.

For questions 3 - 5 use the following account.

PURCHASES LEDGER

	Dr		M. Hatton	Cr	
		£			£
12.4	Bank	500	1.4	Balance b/d	350
16.4	Returns	100	11.4	Purchases	710

3. Which of the following will be the balance c/d?
A £350.
B £600.
C £460.
D £1,060.

4. Which of the following will be the total on both sides of the account?
A £600
B £1,200
C £1,060
D £460

5. Which of the following will be the balance b/d on 1 May?
A Credit balance of £460.
B Debit balance of £460.
C Credit balance of £350.
D Debit balance of £350.

6. Which accounts are balanced in the cash book?
A Cash account and sales account.
B Bank account and capital account.
C Bank account and cash account.
D Cash account and capital account.

7. Consider whether the following two statements are true or false.

(i) Accounts in the nominal ledger can have debit or credit balances.

(ii) Accounts in the sales ledger are not likely to have credit balances.

A (i) True (ii) True.
B (i) True (ii) False.
C (i) False (ii) True.
D (i) False (ii) False.

For questions 8 - 10 use the following account.

NOMINAL LEDGER

	Dr	Rent Account	Cr	
		£		£
1.5	Balance b/d	4,000		
2.5	Bank	1,000		

8. What will be the totals on either side of the account when it is balanced?
A £4,000.
B £0.
C £1,000.
D £5,000.

9. What will be the balance b/d on 1 June?
A Debit balance of £5,000.
B Credit balance of £5,000.
C Debit balance of £1,000.
D Credit balance of £4,000.

10. The account can best be described as an:
A asset account;
B expenses account;
C debtor account;
D revenue account.

UNIT 16 ●●●

1. Which of the following is <u>not</u> a debit entry in the trial balance?
A Purchases.
B Rent paid.
C Capital.
D Cash.

2. Which of the following is not a credit entry in the trial balance?
A Wages.
B Sales.
C Discounts received.
D Purchases returns.

3. Which of the following could be a debit or a credit entry in the trial balance?
A Bank account.
B Bad debts.
C Sales.
D Drawings.

4. The trial balance must balance because:
A the value of assets is equal to the value of liabilities;
B the value of income must be the same as the value of expenditure;
C all transactions are entered twice in the bookkeeping system;
D the value of debtors is equal to the value of creditors.

5. Which of the following tasks does not involve using the trial balance?
A Preparing a balance sheet.
B Preparing a cash flow forecast statement.
C Checking the arithmetic accuracy of the accounts.
D Preparing a profit and loss account.

6. Which of the following accounting errors would not be identified even if the trial balance were to balance?
A A transaction is debited to the right account but not credited to any account.
B A transaction is posted to the right accounts but for wrong amount.
C A transaction is recorded only on the credit side of the accounts.
D One of the accounts has been balanced incorrectly.

Questions 7 to 10 require the following answer list where students need to identify the appropriate error from the description.
A An error of commission.
B An error of principle.
C An error of omission.
D An error of original entry.
E Reversal of entries.

7. A transaction has been completely missed by the bookkeeper.

8. A transaction is recorded in the wrong type of account.

9. A transaction is posted to the right type of account but in the wrong name.

10. A transaction is entered correctly in the bookkeeping system but for the wrong amount.

UNIT 17

1. Which of the following is not a final account?
A Trading account.
B Capital account.
C Profit and loss account.
D Balance sheet.

2. Which of the following is subtracted from sales to give net sales in the trading account?
A Returns inwards.
B Returns outwards.
C Opening stock.
D Closing stock.

3. Decide whether the following two statements are true or false.
(i) Gross profit = sales - cost of sales.
(ii) Net profit = gross profit - cost of sales.
A (i) True; (ii) True.
B (i) True; (ii) False.
C (i) False; (ii) True.
D (i) False; (ii) False.

4. Decide whether the following statements are true or false.
(i) Non-operating income is subtracted from gross profit in the profit and loss account.
(ii) Overhead expenses are subtracted from gross profit to calculate net profit.
A (i) True; (ii) True.
B (i) True; (ii) False.
C (i) False; (ii) True.
D (i) False; (ii) False.

5. Which of the following is not generally considered a purpose of the profit and loss account?
A To measure business performance.
B To assess the ability to meet immediate payments.
C To measure business growth.
D To calculate tax owed.

6. Which of the following is not a current asset?
A Stocks.
B Cash at bank.
C Debtors.
D Creditors.

7. How is working capital calculated in the balance sheet?
A Current assets - fixed assets.
B Fixed assets - current assets.
C Current assets - current liabilities.
D Current assets + current liabilities.

8. Which of the following is not a fixed asset?
A Cash.
B Premises.
C Fixtures and fittings.
D Vehicles.

9. Which of the following is said to be a guide to the value of a business?
A Working capital.
B Fixed assets.
C Total assets.
D Net assets.

10. Decide whether the following two statements are true or false.
(i) When presenting the balance sheet the vertical format is now generally preferred to the horizontal format.
(ii) Capital employed = net assets.
A (i) True; (ii) True.
B (i) True; (ii) False.
C (i) False; (ii) True.
D (i) False; (ii) False.

UNIT 18   ○○○

1. Decide whether the following two statements are true or false.

(i) The trial balance is used to produce final accounts.

(ii) The trial balance is classed as one of the final accounts.

A (i) True; (ii) True.
B (i) True; (ii) False.
C (i) False; (ii) True.
D (i) False; (ii) False.

2. Decide whether the following two statements are true or false.

(i) Debit entries in the trial balance are all expenses.

(ii) Credit entries in the trial balance are either revenue, liabilities or capital.

A (i) True; (ii) True.
B (i) True; (ii) False.
C (i) False; (ii) True.
D (i) False; (ii) False.

Look at the trading account for T Smith before answering questions 3 - 6

T Smith
Trading Account
for the year ended 31.10.01

	£	£
Sales		98,520
**********	12,100	
**********	76,540	
	88,640	
Less **********	6,750	
Cost of sales		******
**********		16,630

For questions 3-6 choose one of the following answers.
A £16,630.
B £76,540.
C £6,750.
D £81,890.

3. What is the closing stock?

4. What is the cost of sales?

5. What is purchases?

6. What is the gross profit?

7. How is working capital calculated in the balance sheet?
A Fixed assets plus current assets.
B Current assets plus current liabilities.
C Current liabilities less current assets.
D Current assets less current liabilities.

8. Which of the following is true?
A Current assets equal current liabilities.
B Net assets equal capital employed.
C Fixed assets equal long term liabilities.
D Opening capital equals total assets.

9. The total of fixed assets for a business is £120,000, the total of working capital is £25,000 and the total of long term liabilities is £20,000. What is the total of net assets?
A £125,000.
B £145,000.
C £165,000.
D £140,000.

10. Decide whether the following two statements are true or false.

(i) The balance sheet is not part of the double entry system.

(ii) Net profit is added to opening capital in the balance sheet.

A (i) True; (ii) True.
B (i) True; (ii) False.
C (i) False; (ii) True.
D (i) False; (ii) False.

UNIT 19   ○○○

1. Which of the following would not normally require an adjustment to the trial balance?
A Prepayment.
B Bad debt.
C Depreciation.
D Goods returned.

2. What is the main purpose of making adjustments?
A To calculate the value of expenses for the year.
B To help produce accounts that show 'a true and fair view' of a firm's financial circumstances.
C To calculate the value of debtors and creditors at the end of the year.
D To calculate the value of profit for the year.

3. At the end of the trading year a business still owes a market research agency £340. What is this an example of?
A Accrued expense.
B Prepayment.
C Accrued revenue.
D Doubtful debt.

4. On 3.8.00 a business pays a quarterly gas bill for £450. The bill is for the period 1.5.00 to 31.7.00. If the year end for the business is 30.6.00 what is the value of the accrued expense?
A £450.
B £300.
C £150.
D £600.

5. A business pays six months rent on 1.8.00. The rent paid is £6,000. How much of this is prepaid if the year end for the business is 31.12.00?
A £1,000.
B £2,000.
C £3,000.
D £4,000.

6. Which of the following is an example of accrued revenue?
A Interest owed by a bank.
B Money owed to the Inland Revenue.
C Money owed by a customer.
D Money owed to a supplier.

7. Decide whether the following two statements are true or false.

(i) A prepayment of electricity is shown as a debit in the trial balance.

(ii) An accrued expense is shown as credit in the trial balance.

A (i) True (ii) True.
B (i) True (ii) False.
C (i) False (ii) True.
D (i) False (ii) False.

8. **Decide whether the following two statements are true or false.**

   (i) **A prepayment of an insurance premium will increase an expense for the year.**

   (ii) **An accrued expense will increase an expense for the year.**

A (i) True (ii) True.
B (i) True (ii) False.
C (i) False (ii) True.
D (i) False (ii) False.

Questions 9 and 10 relate to the account below.

Dr		£	Cr		£
2000			2000		
31.12	Balance c/d	312	2.7	Bank	312
31.12	Profit & loss	661	31.12	Balance b/d	312
			31.12	balance c/d (accrual)	349
		661			661
2001					
1.1	Balance b/d	349			

Rent Received Account

9. **The balance b/d of £349 is an example of which of the following?**
A Prepayment.
B Accrued expense.
C Accrued revenue.
D Stocks.

10. **What is the total rent actually received for the year.**
A £349.
B £661.
C £312.
D None of the above.

UNIT 20

1. **Selling goods on credit means that:**
A customers must pay immediately by cash;
B customers must pay by credit card;
C customers are allowed a period of trade credit;
D customers can decide when they pay their debts.

2. **Which of the following is a likely cause of a bad debt?**
A Efficient credit control.
B A rise in the number of customers paying by cash.
C A fall in the number of business failures.
D Insolvency of a customer.

3. **Consider whether the following statements are true or false.**

   (i) **Bad debts are treated as an expense in accounting.**

   (ii) **The bad debts account is in the nominal ledger.**
A (i) True (ii) True.
B (i) True (ii) False.
C (i) False (ii) True.
D (i) False (ii) False.

4. **Consider whether the following statements are true or false.**

   (i) **When accounting for a bad debt the customer account is debited with the amount of the bad debt.**

   (ii) **When accounting for a bad debt the bad debts account is debited with the amount of the bad debt.**
A (i) True (ii) True.
B (i) True (ii) False.
C (i) False (ii) True.
D (i) False (ii) False.

5. **A business has total debtors of £167,000. It makes a general provision for doubtful debts of 5% each year. Which of the following is the provision for doubtful debts?**
A £167,000.
B £83,500.
C £8,350.
D £835.

6. **Which of the following is most likely to require that a business increases its provision for doubtful debts?**
A The value of total debtors rises.
B The value of total debtors falls.
C Fewer bad debts occur because trading conditions improve.
D The trade credit period is shortened.

7. **Consider whether the following statements are true or false.**

   The bookkeeping entries required when creating a general provision for doubtful debts are:

   (i) **credit the provision for doubtful debts account;**

   (ii) **debit the profit and loss account.**
A (i) True (ii) True.
B (i) True (ii) False.
C (i) False (ii) True.
D (i) False (ii) False.

8. **Consider whether the following statements are true or false.**

   (i) **The recovery of a bad debt reduces profit.**

   (ii) **The bad debts recovered account is debited when a bad debt is recovered.**
A (i) True (ii) True.
B (i) True (ii) False.
C (i) False (ii) True.
D (i) False (ii) False.

9. **Which of the following factors might cause a business to refuse credit to a customer?**
A The customer can provide a positive reference from a credit agency.
B The customer is new and cannot provide references from other suppliers.
C The customer has a good track record of paying invoices on time.
D The customer operates in a fast expanding sector of the economy.

10. **Which of the following is not a way of evaluating the effectiveness of a credit control department?**
A Measure the total amount of bad debts as a proportion of outstanding debts.
B Calculate the average number of days it takes customers to pay.
C Calculate the proportion of cash customers to credit customers.
D Calculate the change in the proportion of bad debts.

UNIT 21 ● ● ●

1. Which of the following is <u>not</u> usually classed as a fixed asset?
A Land.
B Delivery vehicle.
C A stock of heating oil.
D An office desk.

2. Which of the following is classed as a tangible fixed asset?
A Leasehold property.
B Patent.
C Brand name.
D Goodwill.

3. Depreciation is best defined as which of the following?
A The fluctuation in the value of property.
B The measure of consumption of a fixed asset.
C The disposal value of a fixed asset.
D The difference between the purchase price and the historic cost of an asset.

4. Which of the following terms can mean the same as depreciation?
A Net book value.
B Capitalisation.
C Amortisation.
D Investment.

5. Which of the following is <u>not</u> normally classed as an intangible asset?
A Copyright on intellectual property.
B A logo.
C A trademark.
D Freehold property.

6. Which of the following is stated in the accounting standard FRS10 *Goodwill and intangible assets*?
A Internally generated goodwill should be omitted from the balance sheet.
B Purchased goodwill should be omitted from the balance sheet.
C Purchased goodwill should be classed as a tangible fixed asset.
D The value of goodwill should never be included on a balance sheet.

7. Which of the following is stated in the accounting standard SSAP 13 *Accounting for research and development*?
A The cost of research and development should both be capitalised.
B The cost of research and development should both be excluded from the balance sheet.
C The cost of research should be included on the balance sheet.
D The cost of development can be included on the balance sheet.

8. When the cost of an acquired brand name is amortised, it means that:
A the cost is written off in the profit and loss account;
B the cost is depreciated;
C the brand name is considered to have risen in value;
D the brand name is considered to have lost all its value.

9. An investment shown on a balance sheet might be which of the following?
A Shares in a subsidiary company.
B The value of a purchased brand name.
C The cost of acquiring a patent.
D The purchase price of new premises.

10. A fixed assets register might show all of the following <u>except</u>:
A the date on which a new computer was purchased;
B the date on which a patent was sold;
C the amount of depreciation on office furniture;
D the disposal price of a fork-lift truck.

UNIT 22 ● ● ●

1. Which of the following would <u>not</u> cause a fixed asset to depreciate?
A Decrease in the cost of new fixed assets.
B Wear and tear.
C Obsolescence.
D Inadequacy.

2. What is the annual depreciation charge for a machine costing £12,000 with a residual value of £2,000 and an expected life of 10 years, using the straight line method?
A £1,000.
B £2,000.
C £3,000.
D £10,000.

3. Which type of fixed asset is most likely to be depreciated using the reducing balance method?
A Assets that depreciation uniformly over time.
B Wasting assets.
C Vehicles.
D Fixtures and fittings.

4. Which of the following methods of calculating depreciation writes off most value in the early years?
A Straight line method.
B Sum-of-the-year's digits method.
C Depletion method.
D Revaluation method.

5. Which type of assets are likely to be depreciated using the revaluation method?
A Cars.
B Small hand tools.
C Office furniture.
D Mines and quarries.

6. Which of the following is one of the main advantages of the usage method for calculating depreciation?
A A larger charge is made in the early years.
B It is suitable for low cost fixed assets.
C The depreciation charge is linked more closely to the benefit produced by the asset.
D It is easy to calculate.

7. Which of the following depreciation methods is most appropriate for writing off the value of an oil well?
A Revaluation method.
B Reducing balance method.
C Depletion method.
D Usage method.

8. A business disposes of a vehicle for £34,500. The net book value is £39,100. What is the profit or loss on disposal?
A Profit of £4,600.
B Loss of £4,600.
C Profit of £34,500.
D Loss of £39,100.

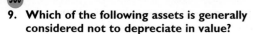

9. Which of the following assets is generally considered not to depreciate in value?

A   Vehicles.
B   Machinery.
C   Leasehold buildings.
D   Freehold land.

10. Which of the following assets are most likely to be revalued?

A   Office block.
B   Computer.
C   Car.
D   Furniture.

UNIT 23   ● ● ●

1.   In which account is depreciation usually recorded?

A   Depreciation charge account.
B   Provision for depreciation account.
C   Fixed asset account.
D   Bank account.

2.   The net book value of a fixed asset is the difference between which of the following?

A   Credit balance on the fixed asset account and debit balance on the provision for depreciation account.
B   Debit balance on the fixed asset account and the debit balance on the provision for depreciation account.
C   Credit balance on the fixed asset account and the credit balance on the provision for depreciation account.
D   Debit balance on the fixed asset account and the credit balance on the provision for depreciation account.

3.   The net book value of fixed assets is usually included in which of the following?

A   Profit and loss account.
B   Purchases ledger.
C   Balance sheet.
D   Nominal ledger.

4.   When will a business make a profit on the disposal of a fixed asset ?

A   When the sale proceeds are less than the provision for depreciation.
B   When the sale proceeds are less than the net book value.
C   When the sale proceeds equal the net book value.
D   When the sale proceeds are greater than the net book value.

5.   If a business makes a loss on disposal of a fixed asset, which of the following bookkeeping entries is correct?

A   The loss is credited to the fixed asset account.
B   The loss is debited to the fixed asset account.
C   The loss is credited to the disposal of fixed asset account.
D   The loss is debited to the disposal of fixed asset account.

6.   When selling a fixed asset, which of these bookkeeping entries is correct?

A   The disposal of fixed asset account is credited with the payment received.
B   The disposal of fixed asset account is debited with the payment received.
C   The fixed asset account is credited with the payment received.
D   The fixed asset account is debited with the payment received.

7.   Consider whether these two statements are true or false:

(i)   **When making a part-exchange, the provision for depreciation account is not affected.**

(ii) **A profit or loss cannot be made on disposal if there is a part-exchange transaction.**

A   (i) True   (ii) True.
B   (i) True   (ii) False.
C   (i) False (ii) True.
D   (i) False (ii) False.

8.   Which of the following is not required when calculating the net book value of a fixed asset?

A   Accumulated provision for depreciation up to the current year.
B   Replacement cost.
C   Historical cost.
D   The current year's depreciation charge.

9.   Which of the following statements is not true for the trial balance extract below?

	Trial Balance extract as at 31.12.00	
	Dr	**Cr**
	£	£
Tractor	27,000	
Provision for depreciation		10,000

A   The historical cost of the tractor is £27,000.
B   The historical cost of the tractor is £17,000.
C   The net book value of the tractor is £17,000.
D   If the tractor was sold for £15,000, a loss on disposal would be made.

10. Which of the following statements is not true for the disposal account below?

Dr	Disposal of Machine Account		**Cr**	
2000	£	2000		£
31.12 Machine	14,000	31.12 Provision for depreciation		8,000
		31.12 Bank		4,000
		31.12 Profit and loss		2,000
	14,000			14,000

A   A profit of £2,000 was made on disposal.
B   The historical cost of the machine was £14,000.
C   The net book value was £6,000.
D   The machine was sold for £4,000.

UNIT 24   ● ● ●

1.   A partly completed house on a building site is an example of which type of stock?

A   Raw materials and components.
B   Work-in-progress.
C   Goods for resale.
D   Finished goods.

2.   For a hotel, stocks of cleaning materials such as washing up liquid, furniture polish and disposable dusters, would be classified as which type of stock?

A   Work-in-progress.
B   Consumables.
C   Goods for resale.
D   Raw materials and components.

3. The closing stock value is required to calculate which of the following?
A Cost of sales.
B Fixed assets.
C Liabilities.
D Net profit.

4. A retailer buys goods from a supplier for £12,500. The supplier is also paid £200 for transporting the goods, and the goods are expected to sell for £17,000. How should the goods be valued for stock purposes?
A £12,500.
B £17,000.
C £17,200.
D £12,700.

5. If the FIFO method of stock valuation is used, the value of stock will reflect which of the following at the end of the year?
A The prices paid for stock at the beginning of the year.
B The prices paid for stock at the end of the year.
C None of the actual prices paid for stock
D The lowest price paid for stock

6. If the LIFO method of stock valuation is used, the value of stock will reflect which of the following at the end of the year?
A The prices paid for stock at the beginning of the year.
B The prices paid for stock at the end of the year.
C None of the actual prices paid for stock
D The lowest price paid for stock

7. If the AVCO method of stock valuation is used, the value of stock will reflect which of the following at the end of the year?
A The prices paid for stock at the beginning of the year.
B The prices paid for stock at the end of the year.
C A weighted average of the actual prices paid for stock.
D The lowest price paid for stock.

8. A business purchases 40,000 units of stock at 80p each, and then a further 20,000 units at £1.10 each. According to the AVCO method, the value of this stock is which of the following?
A 80p.
B £1.10.
C 90p.
D None of these.

9. Which of the following is a disadvantage of the FIFO method of stock valuation?
A It is more difficult to calculate than other methods.
B It is not acceptable to the Inland Revenue.
C The closing stock is valued at older prices.
D When prices are rising, stock is always valued at the highest prices.

10. A higher closing stock valuation will have which of the following effects on the accounts?
A Increase gross profit and lower current asset values.
B Increase gross profit and increase current asset values.
C Decrease gross profit and lower current asset values.
D Decrease gross profit and increase current asset values.

UNIT 25

● ● ●

1. If a cheque is unpresented, it can mean which of the following?
A It has not been paid into the bank by the payee.
B It has been dishonoured by the bank.
C It has been cleared by the bank.
D It has been stopped by the drawer.

2. A cheque is cleared at the moment when:
A it is received in payment for goods and services;
B money is transferred from the drawer's account to the payee's account;
C it appears on a bank statement;
D it is paid into a bank.

3. Which of the following is the person who signs a cheque?
A Payee.
B Drawer.
C Drawee.
D Clearer.

4. Which of the following is not a likely reason for a cheque to be dishonoured?
A There are insufficient funds to cover the cheque.
B The drawer has stopped the cheque.
C The payee has stopped the cheque.
D The cheque is unsigned.

5. During the process of bank reconciliation, a tick is made on the bank statement entries to show which of the following?
A The entry does not match an entry in the cash book.
B The entry is a direct debit.
C The balance has become overdrawn.
D The entry matches an entry in the cash book.

6. On a bank statement, a credit means which of the following?
A Money has been paid into the bank.
B Money has been credited to the cash book.
C Money has been paid out of the bank.
D There is a credit balance on the bank account.

7. The balance in the cash book for a business is £5,699, the value of unpresented cheques is £231 and uncleared lodgements is £432. What is the closing balance on the bank reconciliation statement?
A £5,699.
B £5,498.
C £5,900.
D £6,362.

8. Which of the following should be undertaken when preparing a bank reconciliation where the business is overdrawn at the bank?
A Add unpresented cheques and subtract uncleared lodgements.
B Add unpresented cheques and add uncleared lodgements.
C Subtract unpresented cheques and add uncleared lodgements.
D Subtract upresented cheques and subtract uncleared lodgements.

9. Which of the following is not generally a reason for preparing a bank reconciliation statement?
A Checking the accuracy of the bookkeeping in the cash book.
B Identifying dishonoured cheques.
C Improving profitability.
D Helping control cash flow.

10. Consider whether the following statements are true or false.

(i) When preparing a bank reconciliation statement, a business must always use the balance from the cash book as the opening balance.

(ii) When updating the cash book, direct debits and standing orders are always listed as receipts.
A (i) True (ii) True.
B (i) True (ii) False.
C (i) False (ii) True.
D (i) False (ii) False.

UNIT 26

1. What type of tax is VAT?
A Direct.
B Indirect.
C Income tax.
D Corporation tax.

2. Which of the following goods or services are zero rated for VAT?
A Alcohol.
B Insurance.
C Fresh food.
D Education.

3. Which of the following goods or services are exempt from VAT?
A Newspapers.
B Insurance.
C Medicines.
D Children's clothes.

4. A business sells £1,057.50 (including VAT) of goods to a customer. How much VAT is collected by the business?
A £1,057.50.
B £185.06.
C £900.00.
D £157.50.

5. A business buys £528.75 (including VAT) of goods from a supplier. What is the price of the goods excluding VAT?
A £528.75.
B £450.00.
C £78.75.
D £478.75.

6. Decide whether the following statements are true or false.

(i) When recording VAT on credit sales, the VAT account is credited with the amount of VAT charged to customers.

(ii) When recording VAT on credit sales, customer accounts are debited with the price of the transaction including VAT.

A (i) True (ii) True.
B (i) True (ii) False.
C (i) False (ii) True.
D (i) False (ii) False.

7. Decide whether the following statements are true or false.

(i) The VAT on returns outwards is debited to the VAT account.

(ii) The VAT on purchases is debited to the VAT account.

A (i) True (ii) True.
B (i) True (ii) False.
C (i) False (ii) True.
D (i) False (ii) False.

8. Decide whether the following statements are true or false.

(i) The VAT on cash sales is credited to the VAT account.

(ii) Wages are not charged with VAT.

A (i) True (ii) True.
B (i) True (ii) False.
C (i) False (ii) True.
D (i) False (ii) False.

9. Which of the following transactions would not be debited to the VAT account?
A VAT on purchases.
B VAT on returns inwards.
C VAT on expenses.
D VAT on sales of fixed assets.

10. When are VAT returns usually made?
A Weekly.
B Monthly.
C Quarterly.
D Annually.

UNIT 27

1. Decide whether the following two statements are true or false.

(i) A control account can be used to control an entire ledger or sections of a ledger.

(ii) Control accounts do not form part of the double entry system.

A (i) True (ii) True.
B (i) True (ii) False.
C (i) False (ii) True.
D (i) False (ii) False.

2. Decide whether the following statements are true or false.

(i) A control account is a total account.

(ii) Control accounts are kept in the nominal ledger.

A (i) True (ii) True.
B (i) True (ii) False.
C (i) False (ii) True.
D (i) False (ii) False.

3. Which of the following will not appear on the credit side of the sales ledger control account?
A Value of credit sales.
B Returns inwards.
C Bad debts written off.
D Cash payments made by customers.

4. Which of the following will appear on the debit side of the sales ledger control account?
A Discounts allowed.
B Discounts received.
C Dishonoured cheques.
D Cheque payments made by customers.

5. Which of the following entries will not appear on the debit side of the purchases ledger control account?
A The total of credit purchases.
B Discounts received.
C Returns outwards.
D Cheque payments made to suppliers.

6. Decide whether the following two statements are true or false.

(i) The total of bad debts written off in the sales ledger control account comes from the sales day book.

(ii) The total of returns inwards in the sales ledger control account comes from the journal.

A (i) True (ii) True.
B (i) True (ii) False.
C (i) False (ii) True.
D (i) False (ii) False.

7. Where will the information come from for the total of sales that is recorded in the sales ledger control account?

A Cash book.
B Sales day book.
C Journal.
D None of these.

8. Where will the information come from for the total of discounts received that is recorded in the purchases ledger control account?

A Cash book.
B Purchases day book.
C Bank statement.
D Journal.

9. Which of the following is not a purpose of a control account?

A To detect errors in the bookkeeping.
B To deter fraud.
C To determine the amount owed by individual customers.
D To help determine the totals of debtors and creditors more easily.

10. What does a debit balance on the purchases ledger control account show?

A The amount owed to suppliers.
B The amount owed by suppliers to the business.
C The amount owed to customers.
D The amount the business owes to customers.

UNIT 28

1. Decide whether the following two statements are true or false.

(i) An error will be detected in the bookkeeping system if the balance on the sales ledger control account is the same as the total of the debtors on the sales ledger.

(ii) An error will be detected in the bookkeeping system if the balance on the sales ledger control account is different from the total of the debtors on the sales ledger.

A (i) True (ii) True.
B (i) True (ii) False.
C (i) False (ii) True.
D (i) False (ii) False.

2. Decide whether the following two statements are true or false.

(i) All errors will affect both the control account and the individual accounts.

(ii) Casting errors will not be detected when using control accounts.

A (i) True (ii) True.
B (i) True (ii) False.
C (i) False (ii) True.
D (i) False (ii) False.

3. Which type of error will be detected when using control accounts?

A Errors of omission.
B Transposition errors.
C Errors of commission.
D Errors of original entry.

4. Decide whether the following two statements are true or false.

(i) A transaction not entered in a book of prime entry will also be omitted from both the control account and the individual account.

(ii) If a transaction is misposted from the prime record to the individual account, the control account is not affected.

A (i) True (ii) True.
B (i) True (ii) False.
C (i) False (ii) True.
D (i) False (ii) False.

5. Decide whether the following two statements are true or false.

(i) A transaction that is entered incorrectly in the book of prime entry will be repeated only in the control account.

(ii) The corrections of errors are usually recorded in the journal.

A (i) True (ii) True.
B (i) True (ii) False.
C (i) False (ii) True.
D (i) False (ii) False.

6. A bad debt for £1,900 was written off in the sales ledger but not entered in the journal. Which of the following is the appropriate correction?

A Debit the control account with £1,900 and add £1,900 to the debtors list.
B Credit the control account with £1,900 and add £1,900 to the debtors list.
C Debit the control account with £1,900 and subtract £1,900 from the debtors list.
D Credit the control account with £1,900.

7. A purchase for £9,900 was completely omitted from the records. Which of the following is the appropriate correction?

A The control account must be debited with £9,900.
B The control account must be credited with £9,900.
C The control account must be credited with £9,900 and the creditors list increased by £9,900.
D The control account must be debited with £9,900 and the creditors list increased by £9,900.

8. An amount of £1,200 was entered in the purchases day book when the correct value was £10,200. Which of the following is the appropriate correction?

A Credit the control account with £9,000 and add £9,000 to the list of creditors.
B Debit the control account with £9,000 and deduct £9,000 from the list of creditors.
C Credit the control account with £10,200.
D Credit the control account with £9,000.

UNIT 29

1. Which of the following does not appear as a column in the extended trial balance?

A Balance sheet.
B Profit and loss.
C Adjustments.
D The journal.

2. Which of the following is the first column of figures in the extended trial balance?

A Adjustments.
B Trial balance.
C Profit and loss.
D Balance sheet.

3. Decide whether the following two statements are true or false.

   (i) All adjustments have both a debit and a credit entry in the extended trial balance.

   (ii) All adjustments are extended both to the profit and loss column and the balance sheet column.

A (i) True (ii) True.
B (i) True (ii) False.
C (i) False (ii) True.
D (i) False (ii) False.

4. Decide whether the following two statements are true or false.

   (i) The closing stock appears as a debit entry in the profit and loss column and a credit entry in the balance sheet column.

   (ii) The purchases entry in the trial balance is extended to the credit side of the profit and loss column.

A (i) True (ii) True.
B (i) True (ii) False.
C (i) False (ii) True.
D (i) False (ii) False.

5. After all entries have been extended to the profit and loss column, the total of debit entries is £432,910 and the total of credit entries is £387,040. What does this mean?

A A net loss of £45,870 is made.
B A net profit of £45,870 is made.
C A net profit of £432,910 is made.
D A net loss of £432,910 is made.

Suppose the cost of a machine is £40,000 and the current book value is £28,000. For questions 6 - 8, choose one of the following answers.

A £40,000.
B £28,000.
C £12,000.
D £68,000.

6. Which figure represents the total provision for depreciation?

7. Which figure will appear as a debit balance in the balance sheet column?

8. Which figure will appear as credit balance in the balance sheet column?

Suppose the annual rent for a business has been recorded as £14,000. However, £2,000 of this represents a prepayment for the following year. For questions 9 and 10, choose one of the following answers.

A £14,000.
B £2,000.
C £12,000.
D £16,000.

9. Which figure will appear as a debit balance in the profit and loss column?

10. Which figure will appear as a prepayment in the balance sheet?

UNIT 30

1. Decide whether the following two statements are true or false.

   (i) A suspense account will always have a debit balance.

   (ii) A suspense account is a temporary account.

A (i) True (ii) True.
B (i) True (ii) False.
C (i) False (ii) True.
D (i) False (ii) False.

2. State whether the following two statements are true or false.

   (i) A suspense account is maintained in the nominal ledger.

   (ii) A suspense account will have a debit balance if the total of debits in the trial balance is greater than the total of credits.

A (i) True (ii) True.
B (i) True (ii) False.
C (i) False (ii) True.
D (i) False (ii) False.

3. If a debit balance on the suspense account is not cleared before the final accounts are produced, where will the balance be posted?

A On the debit side of the profit and loss account.
B On the credit side of the profit and loss account.
C As an asset in the balance sheet.
D As a liability in the balance sheet.

4. Which of the following errors will not cause a difference in the trial balance?

A An error of principle.
B The sales day book being overcast.
C The sales day book being undercast.
D A failure to complete the double entry.

5. Which of the following errors will not affect the suspense account?

A The sales day book being overcast.
B A failure to complete the double entry.
C A credit sale being posted to the wrong customer account.
D A transposition error in the purchases day book.

6. If the purchases day book has been undercast, what journal entries are required to correct the error?

A The purchases account is credited and the suspense account is debited.
B The suspense account is credited and the purchases account is debited.
C The suspense account is debited and the creditors account is credited.
D The creditors account is debited and the suspense account is credited.

7. If a cash sale is not entered in the sales account, what journal entries are needed to correct the error?

A The debtors control account should be debited and the suspense account credited.
B The suspense account should be debited and the debtors control account credited.
C The sales account should be debited and the suspense account credited.
D The suspense account should be debited and the sales account credited.

Questions 8 and 9 relate to the following suspense account.

Dr		Suspense Account		Cr
2001	£	2001		£
31.10 Difference per trial balance	12,390	5.11 Sales		11,500
5.11 Sundry expenses	1,090	5.11 Purchases		1,980
	13,480			13,480

8. Decide whether the following statements are true or false.

(i) The difference on the trial balance is £13,480.

(ii) The total of debits exceeds the total of credits by £12,390.

A (i) True (ii) True.
B (i) True (ii) False.
C (i) False (ii) True.
D (i) False (ii) False.

9. Decide whether the following statements are true or false.

(i) The total of sales is overstated by £11,500.

(ii) The total of sundry expenses is overstated by £1,090.

A (i) True (ii) True.
B (i) True (ii) False.
C (i) False (ii) True.
D (i) False (ii) False.

10. Which of the following would not generally be considered a help in minimising errors in the bookkeeping system?

A The use of ledgers.
B The use of computerised accounts.
C Checking statements from suppliers.
D The use of control accounts.

UNIT 31 ● ● ●

1. Which of the following is not a likely reason why a small business might have incomplete records?

A Cash-based businesses might decide they do not need to use all of the books associated with double entry.
B Some businesses might have lost records in a flood or a fire.
C The Inland Revenue only requires large businesses to keep accurate records.
D Some business owners do not have the resources to devote to systematic bookkeeping.

2. Which of the following information is least likely to be available if a business does not use double entry bookkeeping?

A Cash book.
B Ledger balances.
C Sales receipts.
D Invoices.

3. Decide whether the following two statements are true or false.

(i) A single entry bookkeeping system requires businesses to maintain a nominal ledger.

(ii) A single entry bookkeeping system relies on businesses recording payments and receipts in a cash book.

A (i) True (ii) True.
B (i) True (ii) False.
C (i) False (ii) True.
D (i) False (ii) False.

4. Which of the following equations can be used to calculate profit?

A Profit = opening capital - closing capital - capital introduced + drawings.
B Profit = closing capital - opening capital + capital introduced + drawings.
C Profit = closing capital - opening capital - capital introduced - drawings.
D Profit = closing capital - opening capital - capital introduced + drawings.

5. The following information is supplied by a business at the beginning of the year. Assets = £32,670 and liabilities = £12,310. Which of the following must be correct ?

A Profit = £20,360.
B Closing capital = £20,360.
C Opening capital = £20,360.
D Total capital = £44,980.

6. Decide whether the following two statements are true or false.

(i) A statement of affairs is used to calculate the total of sales and purchases.

(ii) It is impossible to produce a profit figure if records are incomplete.

A (i) True (ii) True.
B (i) True (ii) False.
C (i) False (ii) True.
D (i) False (ii) False.

7. Which of the following does a statement of affairs include?

A Assets and liabilities.
B Expenses.
C Drawings.
D Sales and purchases.

Look at the statement of affairs for C. Bryant to answer questions 8 and 9.

C. Bryant
Statement of Affairs
As at 31.12.01

	£	£
Fixed assets		
Lorry		18,000
Tools and equipment		4,500
		22,500
Current assets		
Stock	390	
Debtors	***	
Cash at bank	3,220	
Cash in hand	520	
		4,530
		27,030
Less current liabilities		
Trade creditors	3,290	
Other creditors	1,450	

A £4,740.
B £27,030.
C £400.
D £22,290.

8. What is the total of debtors?

9. What is the closing capital?

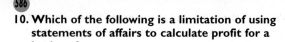

10. Which of the following is a limitation of using statements of affairs to calculate profit for a business?

A   The method can only be used to calculate gross profit.
B   The method depends crucially on the quality of information provided by the business.
C   The method only works if the total of sales is known.
D   The method can only be used if a cash book has been maintained.

UNIT 32   ● ● ●

1. Which of the following missing figures could a cash book summary help to determine?

A   Credit purchases.
B   Credit sales.
C   Opening capital.
D   Drawings.

2. Which of the following missing figures is <u>most</u> likely to be found by using a statement of affairs?

A   Opening capital.
B   Closing bank balance.
C   Drawings.
D   Total creditors.

3. Which of the following missing figures could a sales ledger control account help to determine?

A   Drawings.
B   Credit sales.
C   Credit purchases.
D   Expenses.

4. Which of the following would be useful in determining an amount of missing cash?

A   Cash book summary.
B   Statement of affairs.
C   Purchases ledger control account.
D   Gross profit margin.

5. What is the the gross profit margin if mark-up is 100%?

A   10%.
B   20%.
C   50%.
D   200%.

6. If a business has sales of £120,000, what is the gross profit if the gross profit margin is 40%?

A   £20,000.
B   £30,000.
C   £48,000.
D   £120,000.

7. Decide whether the following statements are true or false.

(i) Mark-up is a relationship between gross profit and cost of sales.

(ii) If opening capital is £0 closing capital must also be £0.

A   (i) True (ii) True.
B   (i) True (ii) False.
C   (i) False (ii) True.
D   (i) False (ii) False.

8. If the opening balance for creditors is £12,880, the closing balance for creditors is £13,420 and money paid to suppliers is £125,220, what is the total of purchases?

A   £138,100.
B   £138,640.
C   £125,760.
D   £124,680.

9. Decide whether the following statements are true or false.

(i) The value of missing stock can be determined by using a cash book summary.

(ii) Accounting ratios can be used to determine the amount of missing cash.

A   (i) True (ii) True.
B   (i) True (ii) False.
C   (i) False (ii) True.
D   (i) False (ii) False.

10. Decide whether the following two statements are true or false.

(i) A sales ledger control account can be used to determine the sales total.

(ii) It is not possible to determine both an amount of missing cash and cash drawings using a cash book summary.

A   (i) True (ii) True.
B   (i) True (ii) False.
C   (i) False (ii) True.
D   (i) False (ii) False.

UNIT 33   ● ● ●

1. Which of the following is an incorporated business organisation?

A   Private limited company.
B   Sole trader.
C   Partnership.
D   Friendly society.

2. Which of the following business organisations is most likely to be owned by a large number of shareholders?

A   Private limited company.
B   Sole trader.
C   Partnership.
D   Public limited company.

3. Which of the following is <u>not</u> a legal responsibility of a sole trader?

A   It must pay income tax and national insurance contributions.
B   It must comply with consumer legislation.
C   It must comply with the Companies Acts.
D   It must obtain a licence if alcohol is to be sold.

4. Which of the following business organisations have unlimited liability?

A   Sole trader.
B   Plc.
C   Ltd company.
D   Limited Liability Partnership.

5. Which of the following would <u>not</u> normally be found in a Deed of Partnership?

A   The amount of capital that each partner contributes.
B   How much control each partner has.
C   The amount of tax each partner must pay.
D   The rules for recruiting new partners.

6. Which of the following would <u>not</u> be found on a Memorandum of Association?

A   The number of shares to be issued.
B   The name of the company.
C   The scope of activities.
D   The rights of shareholders.

7. **Limited companies are owned by which of the following groups?**
A Shareholders.
B Directors.
C Employees.
D Customers.

8. **Which of the following documents is issued to the public in a stock market flotation?**
A Prospectus.
B Statutory Declaration.
C Certificate of Incorporation.
D Partnership Agreement.

9. **Which of the following is most likely to be an example of a non-profit making organisation?**
A Golf club.
B Public limited company.
C Ltd company.
D Partnership.

10. **Which of the following organisations is owned by its customers?**
A Plc.
B Charity.
C Unincorporated business.
D Mutual building society.

UNIT 34 ●●○

1. **Share capital that is never repaid by a business is best described by which of the following terms?**
A Irredeemable.
B Called-up.
C Authorised.
D Issued.

2. **Which of the following terms best describes the total amount of share capital that a company is allowed to raise?**
A Issued.
B Permanent.
C Ordinary.
D Authorised.

3. **Under what circumstances might an ordinary shareholder make a capital gain?**
A By selling shares at a lower price than they cost.
B By obtaining shares in a bonus issue.
C By receiving a fixed dividend.
D By selling shares at a higher price than they cost.

4. **Which of the following methods of issuing shares does not involve raising any more share capital?**
A Rights issue.
B Placing.
C Bonus issue.
D Public issue.

5. **Which of the following methods of issuing shares involves selling to the highest bidder?**
A Public issue.
B Sale by tender.
C Placing.
D Bonus issue.

6. **Which of the following is a likely reason for the directors of a private limited company to decide not to become a plc?**
A Fear of losing control.
B Shortage of capital.
C Desire for expansion.
D Desire for more publicity as a company.

7. **Which of the following is the most likely reason for a private investor to hold preference shares rather than ordinary shares?**
A To exercise control over the company.
B To have a relatively risk free investment.
C To maximise dividend payments when profits are high.
D To take advantage of rising stock market prices.

8. **The nominal value of a share is 50p and the share is issued at a price of £1.20. What is the share premium per share?**
A 50p.
B 170p.
C 70p.
D 120p.

9. **Decide whether the following statements are true or false.**

(i) **The bookkeeping entries required to record the receipt of cash from share applications is to debit the bank account and credit the application and allotment account.**

(ii) **The bookkeeping entries required to record the refunds made to unsuccessful applicants are to credit the bank account and debit the share premium account.**

A (i) True (ii) True.
B (i) True (ii) False.
C (i) False (ii) True.
D (i) False (ii) False.

10. **Decide whether the following statements are true or false.**

(i) **AIM is more highly regulated than the London Stock Exchange.**

(ii) **Changes in share prices might result from changes in a company's profitability.**

A (i) True (ii) True.
B (i) True (ii) False.
C (i) False (ii) True.
D (i) False (ii) False.

UNIT 35 ●●●

1. **Which of the following debentures is secured on specified assets?**
A Redeemable.
B Floating charge.
C Fixed charge.
D Naked.

2. **Which of the following debentures are issued without security?**
A Irredeemable.
B Naked.
C Convertible.
D Floating charge.

3. **Which of the following is not a long term source of finance?**
A Debenture.
B Bank overdraft.
C Mortgage.
D 10 year unsecured bank loan.

4. **Decide whether the following two statements are true or false.**

   (i) **Debenture holders are entitled to vote at a company's AGM.**

   (ii) **Mortgages provide a relatively expensive source of long term funding.**

A (i) True (ii) True.
B (i) True (ii) False.
C (i) False (ii) True.
D (i) False (ii) False.

5. **Funds for a hire purchase agreement are provided by which of the following?**
A Finance house.
B Venture capitalist.
C Business angel.
D Building Society.

6. **Which of the following is considered to be a flexible source of short term funding?**
A Bank overdraft.
B Dividends.
C Trade credit.
D Bank loan.

7. **Which of the following business locations is least likely to qualify for European Union funding?**
A Surrey.
B Cornwall.
C Inner Liverpool.
D South Yorkshire.

8. **Which of the following is not an internal source of funding?**
A Reduction in stock levels.
B Retained profit.
C Sale of assets.
D Debt factoring.

9. **Which of the following sources of funds would be most suitable when purchasing new premises?**
A Bank overdraft.
B Trade credit.
C Mortgage.
D Trade bill.

10. **Which of the following does not form part of a company's capital structure?**
A Long term loans.
B Short term loans.
C Dividend payments.
D Share capital.

UNIT 36

1. **Which of the following would not be recorded in the profit and loss appropriation account of a partnership?**
A Interest on partners' loans.
B Interest on partners' capital.
C Interest on drawings.
D Salaries.

2. **Decide whether the following statements are true or false.**

   (i) **The balance sheet for a partnership might contain a current account.**

   (ii) **The profit and loss appropriation account will show interest charged on partners' drawings.**

A (i) True (ii) True.
B (i) True (ii) False.
C (i) False (ii) True.
D (i) False (ii) False.

3. **In the absence of a Deed of Partnership, which of the following will not apply according to the Partnership Act?**
A Profits or losses are shared equally.
B Interest on partners' loans can be 5%.
C There are no salaries.
D Interest on partners' capital can be 5%.

4. **Which of the following will not be a debit on a partner's current account?**
A Interest on drawings.
B Interest on capital.
C Share of loss.
D Partner's drawings.

5. **Which of the following will not be a credit on a partner's current account?**
A Partner's salary.
B Interest on loans made to the business.
C Interest on capital.
D Interest on partner's drawings.

6. **What is the name given to a partner's account that contains all transactions between the business and a partner?**
A Fixed capital account.
B Rotating capital account.
C Fluctuating capital account.
D Undulating capital account.

7. **Louise Simpson, one of the partners in a solicitors practice, has an opening credit balance on her current account of £1,270. During the year she received a salary of £30,000, a share of profit of £12,500 and withdrew £41,200. What is the closing balance on her current account?**
A £2,570 credit.
B £84,970 debit.
C £1,270 credit.
D £24,970 debit.

8. **Decide whether the following statements are true or false.**

   (i) **A debit balance on a partner's current account means that the business owes money to the partner.**

   (ii) **A credit balance on a partner's fixed capital account means that the partner owes money to the business.**

A (i) True (ii) True.
B (i) True (ii) False.
C (i) False (ii) True.
D (i) False (ii) False.

9. **How are the salaries of partners treated in the profit and loss account?**
A As an expense when calculating net profit.
B As a cost of sales.
C As a deduction in the appropriation account after net profit is shared.
D As a deduction in the appropriation account before net profit is shared.

10. **The partners' capital is equal to which of the following.**
A Current assets.
B Net assets.
C Total assets.
D Total liabilities.

UNIT 37

1. **Which of the following would <u>not</u> result in a change in the ownership of a partnership?**
A   Retirement of a partner.
B   The revaluation of premises.
C   The death of a partner.
D   The introduction of a new partner.

2. **Which of the following terms best describes goodwill?**
A   Intangible asset.
B   Tangible asset.
C   Current asset.
D   Current liability.

3. **Decide whether the following two statements are true or false.**

   (i) An entry on the credit side of a revaluation account shows that an asset has fallen in value.

   (ii) An increase in a provision for bad debts will appear on the debit side of the revaluation account.
A   (i) True   (ii) True.
B   (i) True   (ii) False.
C   (i) False   (ii) True.
D   (i) False   (ii) False.

4. **Decide whether the following two statements are true or false.**

   (i) A downward revaluation of an asset will be recorded on the credit side of the revaluation account.

   (ii) If an asset has fallen in value it will be recorded on the debit side of the asset account.
A   (i) True   (ii) True.
B   (i) True   (ii) False.
C   (i) False   (ii) True.
D   (i) False   (ii) False.

5. **Which of the following bookkeeping entries is <u>not</u> required when a new partner is admitted?**
A   A goodwill account is debited with an agreed value for goodwill.
B   The original partners' capital accounts are credited with the value of goodwill according to the profit sharing ratios.
C   The new partner's capital account is debited with the amount that is paid into the business's bank account.
D   The goodwill account is closed by crediting the account with the agreed value of goodwill split between the original partners and the new partner.

Use the realisation account below to answer questions 6 to 8.

Dr		Realisation Account	Cr
	£		£
Premises	70,000	Premises	80,000
Vehicles	25,000	Vehicles	21,000
Computer	3,000	Computer (taken by Watson)	2,000
Debtors	4,200	Debtors	4,200
Bank - realisation expenses	2,000		
Profit on realisation			
Roberts (1/2)	1,500		
Watson (1/2)	1,500		
	107,200		107,200

6. **The disposal of the vehicles has resulted in which of the following?**
A   Profit of £4,000.
B   Loss of £4,000.
C   Total proceeds of £25,000.
D   Profit of £21,000.

7. **The disposal of the premises has resulted in which of the following?**
A   Loss of £10,000.
B   Loss of £80,000.
C   Profit of £10,000.
D   Profit of £80,000.

8. **What will happen to the £3,000 profit made on realisation?**
A   Credited to the partners' capital accounts.
B   Debited to the partners' capital accounts.
C   Credited to the partners' current accounts.
D   Credited to the bank account.

9. **State whether the following two statements are true or false.**

   (i) The bookkeeping entries for the death of a partner are basically the same as those for the retirement of a partner.

   (ii) Realisation and dissolution expenses will appear as a debit on the realisation account.
A   (i) True   (ii) True.
B   (i) True   (ii) False.
C   (i) False   (ii) True.
D   (i) False   (ii) False.

10. **State whether the following statements are true or false.**

   (i) The Garner v Murray rule does not apply if an alternative agreement is stated in the Deed of Partnership.

   (ii) A loss on the realisation account will appear on the credit side.
A   (i) True   (ii) True.
B   (i) True   (ii) False.
C   (i) False   (ii) True.
D   (i) False   (ii) False.

UNIT 38

1. **Which of the following is <u>not</u> an example of a selling and distribution expense?**
A   Sales person's salary.
B   Advertising.
C   Warehousing.
D   Interest.

2. **Which of the following would <u>not</u> be found in the appropriation account of a limited company?**
A   Proposed dividends.
B   Corporation tax.
C   Administration overheads.
D   Retained profit.

3. **Which of the following terms is used in the profit and loss account to describe the money received by a limited company from selling goods or services?**
A   Turnover.
B   Sales.
C   Revenue.
D   Profit.

4. **Which of the following is <u>not</u> an example of creditors: amounts falling due within one year?**
A   Taxation.
B   Trade creditors.
C   Bank overdraft.
D   Mortgage.

5. Which of the following is an example of non-operating income for a retailer?

A Discount received.

B Profit made on the sale of fixed assets.

C Cash payments made by customers.

D Turnover.

6. Which of the following terms is used to describe dividend income from shares owned by a limited company in a published profit and loss account?

A Other operating income.

B Other investment income.

C Other interest receivable and similar income.

D Revenue reserve.

7. Decide whether the following two statements are true or false.

(i) Share premium and revaluation are examples of revenue reserves.

(ii) Only capital reserves can be used to distributed to shareholders.

A (i) True (ii) True.

B (i) True (ii) False.

C (i) False (ii) True.

D (i) False (ii) False.

8. State whether the following two statements are true or false.

(i) According to the Companies Act, a large limited company must produce a profit and loss account, balance sheet, auditors' report and a directors' report.

(ii) The salaries paid to directors must be included in the accounts.

A (i) True (ii) True.

B (i) True (ii) False.

C (i) False (ii) True.

D (i) False (ii) False.

9. Which of the following stakeholders have a claim on the reserves of a limited company?

A Creditors.

B Shareholders.

C Bankers.

D Directors.

10. Which of the following is not included in shareholders funds?

A Issued share capital.

B Revaluation.

C Debenture.

D Share premium.

UNIT 39

1. Which of the following entries would not appear on the receipts side of the receipts and payments account for a non-profit organisation?

A Gross profit.

B Subscriptions.

C Donations.

D Proceeds from raffle.

2. Which of the following entries would not appear on the payments side of the receipts and payments account for a non-profit making organisation?

A Motor expenses.

B Committee expenses.

C Equipment.

D Interest received.

3. Decide whether the following two statements are true or false.

(i) Only revenue expenditure is recorded in the receipts and payments account.

(ii) Most non-profit making organisations elect a treasurer to oversee the accounts and produce financial statements.

A (i) True (ii) True.

B (i) True (ii) False.

C (i) False (ii) True.

D (i) False (ii) False.

4. Which of the following entries is not recorded as expenditure in an income and expenditure account?

A Motor expenses.

B Sundry expenses.

C Expenditure on fixed assets.

D Travelling expenses paid to a guest.

5. A sports club has an accumulated fund of £12,300. At the end of the financial year expenditure exceeds income by £1,800. What is the new balance on the accumulated fund?

A £14,100.

B £12,300.

C £10,500.

D £1,800.

6. Which of the following could be used to find the value of the accumulated fund?

A Trading account.

B Balance sheet.

C Receipts and payments account.

D Bank account.

7. A disadvantage of using an income and expenditure account in a non-profit making organisation is that:

A it does not show the depreciation of assets;

B it requires some knowledge of bookkeeping and accounting principles;

C it does not distinguish between revenue and capital expenditure;

D it cannot be used to prepare a balance sheet.

8. Decide whether the following statements are true or false.

(i) All donations should be treated as income in the year that they are received.

(ii) Clubs with no fixed assets cannot have an accumulated fund.

A (i) True (ii) True.

B (i) True (ii) False.

C (i) False (ii) True.

D (i) False (ii) False.

9. Decide whether the following statements are true or false.

(i) A non-profit making organisation is generally said to produce a surplus rather than a profit.

(ii) Subscriptions for life membership are not generally credited to the income and expenditure account in the year they are received.

A (i) True (ii) True.

B (i) True (ii) False.

C (i) False (ii) True.

D (i) False (ii) False.

10. Which of the following would <u>not</u> be produced by a non-profit making organisation?
A   Balance sheet.
B   Income and expenditure account.
C   Receipts and payments account.
D   Capital account.

UNIT 40 ● ● ●

1. Which of the following is <u>not</u> an example of indirect labour costs?
A   Maintenance staff wages.
B   Assembly line workers' wages.
C   Supervisors' salaries.
D   Factory cleaners' wages.

2. Which of the following is equal to prime cost?
A   Direct labour + indirect labour.
B   Direct materials + direct labour.
C   Overheads + direct costs.
D   Direct materials + direct labour + direct expenses.

3. Which of the following is <u>not</u> an example of a direct materials cost?
A   Raw materials.
B   Components.
C   Packaging.
D   Cleaning materials.

4. Which of the following would <u>not</u> appear in a manufacturing account?
A   Prime cost.
B   Direct labour.
C   Administrative costs.
D   Indirect expenses.

5. Where is the total production cost transferred to from the manufacturing account?
A   Trading account.
B   Profit and loss account.
C   Balance sheet.
D   Profit and loss appropriation account.

6. Which of the following is <u>not</u> used to calculate total production cost in the manufacturing account?
A   Stocks of finished goods.
B   Stocks of raw materials.
C   Work-in-progress.
D   Stocks of components.

7. Decide whether the following two statements are true or false.

(i) Selling and administration costs do not appear in the manufacturing account.

(ii) Indirect costs are the overheads incurred by a business.

A   (i) True (ii) True.
B   (i) True (ii) False.
C   (i) False (ii) True.
D   (i) False (ii) False.

8. Decide whether the following two statements are true or false.

(i) Factory profit is subtracted from trading profit in the profit and loss account.

(ii) When a transfer price is charged, stocks of finished goods in the warehouse will be overvalued.

A   (i) True (ii) True.
B   (i) True (ii) False.
C   (i) False (ii) True.
D   (i) False (ii) False.

9. Which of the following accounts is used to adjust stocks of finished goods when applying a transfer price?
A   Manufacturing account.
B   Provision for unrealised profit account.
C   Stock account.
D   Provision for depreciation account.

10. An <u>increase</u> in the provision for unrealised profit is:
A   added to net profit;
B   subtracted from net profit;
C   added to factory profit;
D   subtracted from factory profit.

UNIT 41 ● ● ●

1. Which of the following businesses is most likely to prepare departmental accounts?
A   Car manufacturer.
B   Bus company.
C   Power generator.
D   Supermarket.

2. Decide whether the following two statements are true or false.

(i) One of the reasons for producing departmental accounts is to analyse the assets and liabilities of each department.

(ii) Departmental accounts can be used to help calculate profit-related bonuses to departmental managers.

A   (i) True (ii) True.
B   (i) True (ii) False.
C   (i) False (ii) True.
D   (i) False (ii) False.

3. Decide whether the following statements are true or false.

(i) The gross profit margin is a better measure of departmental performance than the size of gross profit.

(ii) Analysed day books are likely to be used when recording transactions of departments.

A   (i) True (ii) True.
B   (i) True (ii) False.
C   (i) False (ii) True.
D   (i) False (ii) False.

4. Which of the following is used to calculate the gross profit margin?

A $\dfrac{\text{Gross profit}}{\text{Cost of sales}} \times 100$

B $\dfrac{\text{Sales}}{\text{Gross profit}} \times 100$

C $\dfrac{\text{Gross profit}}{\text{Stock}} \times 100$

D $\dfrac{\text{Gross profit}}{\text{Sales}} \times 100$

5. Decide whether the following two statements are true or false.

   (i) One of the main problems when producing departmental profit and loss accounts is deciding how to apportion direct costs.

   (ii) One arbitrary method used to apportion overheads is to apportion them in relation to each department's direct costs.

A (i) True (ii) True.
B (i) True (ii) False.
C (i) False (ii) True.
D (i) False (ii) False.

6. Which of the following costs would not need to be apportioned when producing departmental accounts?

A Office expenses.
B Purchases.
C Rates.
D Depreciation.

7. Which of the following overheads might be apportioned according to floor space?

A Depreciation.
B Rent.
C Office wages.
D Advertising.

8. A department has sales of £211,200, net profit of £26,400 and cost of sales of £69,800. What is the net profit margin?

A 33%.
B 37.8%.
C 12.5%.
D £26,400.

9. Which of the following accounts would not usually be produced for departments?

A Balance sheet.
B Trading account.
C Profit and loss account.
D None of these.

10. Decide whether these two statements are true or false.

   (i) If overheads are apportioned unfairly, it becomes difficult to compare departmental performances.

   (ii) The costs incurred in closing a poorly performing department might outweigh the benefits.

A (i) True (ii) True.
B (i) True (ii) False.
C (i) False (ii) True.
D (i) False (ii) False.

UNIT 42

1. Which of the following is the most liquid form of asset?

A Bank current account.
B Notes and coins.
C Bank deposit.
D Treasury Bill.

2. Decide whether the following statements are true or false.

   (i) Drawings will reduce profit and the amount of cash in the bank.

   (ii) The profit and loss account includes non-cash transactions.

A (i) True (ii) True.
B (i) True (ii) False.
C (i) False (ii) True.
D (i) False (ii) False.

3. Decide whether the following statements are true or false.

   (i) Capital expenditure will reduce the bank balance and result in a lower level of profit for the year.

   (ii) The repayment of a loan will reduce the level of profit.

A (i) True (ii) True.
B (i) True (ii) False.
C (i) False (ii) True.
D (i) False (ii) False.

4. Which of the following is not included in the reconciliation of operating profit to net cash flow from operating activities?

A Depreciation.
B Changes in creditors.
C Taxation paid.
D Changes in stock levels.

5. Which of the following is treated as a cash inflow when calculating the net cash flow from operating activities?

A Depreciation.
B Increase in stocks.
C Increase in debtors.
D Increase in creditors.

6. Which of the following is equivalent to the operating profit for a sole trader?

A Gross profit plus taxation and net interest.
B Net profit plus net interest.
C Retained profit plus dividends.
D Net profit less dividends.

7. A business makes an operating profit of £45,000. Depreciation is £5,000, stocks increase by £6,500, debtors increase by £2,000 and creditors increase by £2,700. What is the net cash flow from operating activities?

A £57,200.
B £44,200.
C £48,200.
D £61,200.

8. Which of the following would not appear on a cash flow statement?

A Depreciation.
B Taxation.
C Equity dividends.
D Loans repaid.

9. Which of the following would cause a cash inflow on a cash flow statement?

A Taxation paid.
B Drawings.
C Capital expenditure.
D Share issue.

10. Which of the following would <u>not</u> appear on the cash flow statement of a limited company?

A Equity dividends.

B Acquisitions and disposals.

C Drawings.

D Interest received.

UNIT 43

1. Which of the following groups would be most likely to use accounts for assessing the creditworthiness of a business?

A Government.

B Inland Revenue.

C Suppliers.

D Customers.

2. Which of the following has a legal right to be provided with a company's accounts?

A Competitors.

B Financial analysts.

C Employees.

D Registrar of Companies.

3. Decide whether the following statements are true or false.

(i) Inter-firm comparisons are particularly useful for potential investors.

(ii) Owners will be particularly interested in the 'bottom line'.

A (i) True (ii) True.

B (i) True (ii) False.

C (i) False (ii) True.

D (i) False (ii) False.

4. Which of the following is generally considered the best indicator of the size of a business?

A Turnover.

B Net profit.

C Gross profit.

D Retained profit.

5. The difference between gross profit and net profit represents which of the following?

A Cost of sales.

B Turnover.

C Overheads.

D Dividends.

6. A decrease in gross profit when turnover remains the same could be caused by which of the following?

A An increase in the cost of sales.

B A decrease in the cost of sales.

C An increase in selling price.

D A rise in overheads.

7. What effect will an increase in non-operating income have?

A Increase gross profit.

B Increase turnover.

C Increase net profit.

D Decrease retained profit.

8. Which of the following is the best indicator of the value of a business?

A Current assets - current liabilities.

B Working capital.

C Total assets.

D Net assets.

9. Under which of the following circumstances is a company said to be low geared?

A When loan capital equals share capital.

B When loan capital is greater than share capital.

C When loan capital is less than share capital.

D When loan capital is greater than fixed assets.

10. Which of the following is <u>not</u> shown on the balance sheet?

A Working capital.

B Net assets.

C Asset structure.

D Non-operating income.

UNIT 44

1. Which of the following is an activity ratio?

A Return on capital employed.

B Price earnings ratio.

C Asset turnover.

D Earnings per share.

2. Which of the following is a shareholders' ratio?

A Stock turnover.

B Gross profit margin.

C Return on net assets.

D Dividend yield.

3. Which of the following is a liquidity ratio?

A Current ratio.

B Debt collection period.

C Return on equity.

D Dividend cover.

4. If current assets = £24.6m, current liabilities = £18.6m and stocks = £7.86m, what is the acid test ratio?

A 0.9.

B 1.7.

C 1.3.

D £24.6m.

5. The current ratios for 4 companies are shown below. Which company has most money tied up in liquid resources?

A 1.2.

B 0.9.

C 4.3.

D 2.1.

6. Decide whether the following two statements are true or false.

(i) The gearing ratio is a useful indicator of a company's long-term indebtedness.

(ii) A company with a gearing ratio of 13% would generally be considered too highly geared.

A (i) True (ii) True.

B (i) True (ii) False.

C (i) False (ii) True.

D (i) False (ii) False.

7. Which of the following statements best describes the net profit ratio?

A It shows how well a company is controlling its overhead expenses.

B It shows how well a company is controlling its cost of sales.

C It shows how much profit will be paid to ordinary shareholders.

D It shows how efficiently a company's assets are being used.

8. **Which of the following ratios is generally expressed as a number of days?**
A Current ratio.
B Price earnings ratio.
C Debt collection period.
D Asset turnover.

9. **Which of the following stock turnovers is likely to represent that of a newspaper vendor?**
A 1 day.
B 364 days.
C 52 days.
D 7 days.

10. **The return on net assets is a version of which of the following ratios?**
A Gearing.
B Return on capital employed.
C Liquidity.
D Shareholder.

UNIT 45 ● ● ●

1. **Which of the following is a non-monetary factor that will affect the performance of a company?**
A Turnover.
B Cost of production.
C Motivation of the workforce.
D Interest payments.

2. **The effect of not including intangible fixed assets on a balance sheet is to:**
A overstate the value of current assets;
B overstate the value of working capital;
C understate the value of current assets;
D understate the total value of assets.

3. **Which of the following requires a subjective judgment?**
A Whether to record interest payments as a business expense.
B Whether to value stocks at the lower of cost or net realisable value.
C Whether to value assets at their historical cost or their current value.
D Whether to record a cash sale as an addition to revenue.

4. **The Financial Reporting Standard *Tangible fixed assets* allows companies some freedom of choice in which of the following areas?**
A The writing off of bad debts.
B The recognition of earnings.
C The valuation of stocks.
D The depreciation of assets.

5. **If a business chooses to capitalise its development expenditure, which of the following is likely to occur?**
A The current year's profit will be lower.
B The current year's profit will be higher.
C Future profits will be higher.
D Future depreciation charges will be lower.

6. **If a company changes its method of stock valuation so that the cost of sales is reduced, which of the following is likely to occur?**
A Profit will fall and the balance sheet will be unchanged.
B Profit will fall and the value of current assets will also fall.
C Profit will rise and the balance sheet will be unchanged.
D Profit will rise and the value of current assets will also rise.

7. **By selling a fixed asset for cash and then leasing it back, a company can achieve which of the following?**

A Lower its liquidity.
B Lower the value of total assets.
C Raise its liquidity.
D Lower the value of its current assets.

8. **Which of the following is not an external factor that affects business performance?**
A A fall in interest rates.
B A rise in the minimum wage.
C A rise in the productivity of the business's workforce.
D A fall in the exchange rate.

9. **Over a period of time, inflation causes which of the following?**
A A rise in the monetary value of property.
B A fall in the monetary value of property.
C A rise in the value of cash assets.
D A fall in the monetary value of stocks.

10. **The aim of the Accounting Standards Board can best be described as:**
A to protect the directors of companies from their shareholders;
B to make the accounting process faster and cheaper;
C to regulate government activity;
D to protect shareholders and investors from misleading information.

UNIT 46 ● ● ●

1. **Decide whether the following statements are true or false.**

   (i) Current legislation does not provide a legal framework for social accounts.

   (ii) There is no standard format for the presentation of social accounts.
A (i) True (ii) True.
B (i) True (ii) False.
C (i) False (ii) True.
D (i) False (ii) False.

2. **Which group of stakeholders has traditionally been the most important focus of attention when producing company accounts?**
A Employees.
B Suppliers.
C Customers.
D Shareholders.

3. **Which of the following is not likely to be a reason for a business adopting a more socially responsible stance?**
A Improved image.
B Motivate staff.
C Reduce energy costs.
D Reduce staff costs.

4. **Which of the following best describes ethical consumerism?**
A A desire always to buy the cheapest goods.
B A desire to obtain the best value for money.
C A desire to avoid products made by multinational companies.
D A desire to avoid goods made by companies engaged in armament production.

5. **Which of the following issues are not the subject of a legal requirement in company accounts?**
A Employment policy regarding disabled people.
B Charitable donations.
C Energy conservation.
D Political donations.

6. Which of the following could best be described as an ethical objective?

A Remove employment barriers for female employees.
B Increase the use of recycled paper.
C Increase dividends per share.
D Increase return on capital employed.

7. Which of the following methods might be used to gather information for social accounts?

A Social audit.
B Financial audit.
C Analysis of profit and loss account.
D Opinion survey.

8. Which of the following is <u>not</u> an essential criteria when selecting an indicator for social accounts?

A It must be specific.
B It must be measurable.
C It must be expressed in monetary terms.
D It must relate to the business.

9. Why might it be difficult for a company to reconcile its social, environmental and financial targets?

A Because environmental improvements can reduce profitability.
B Because some targets are more difficult to achieve than others.
C Because social targets always reduce profitability.
D Because companies are not required by law to produce social accounts.

10. Decide whether the following statements are true or false.

(i) A social audit involves calculating the financial loss that is made when a company fulfils its social responsibilities.

(ii) Social accounting involves gathering, analysing and presenting information to stakeholders about a firm's social performance.

A (i) True (ii) True.
B (i) True (ii) False.
C (i) False (ii) True.
D (i) False (ii) False.

UNIT 47 ● ● ○

No questions are set on this unit.

UNIT 48 ● ● ○

1. Cost accountants are mainly concerned with which of the following?

A Producing the final accounts.
B Overseeing the bookkeeping system.
C Reporting information on costs of production to managers.
D Ensuring that accounts are prepared in accordance with accounting standards.

2. Which of the following is an indirect cost?

A Business rates.
B Raw materials.
C Packaging.
D Components.

3. The wages paid to a machine operator are an example of which of the following costs?

A Indirect labour.
B Administration overheads.
C Direct labour.
D Direct materials.

4. Which of the following is <u>not</u> a fixed cost for a builder?

A Rent for builder's yard.
B Sand and cement.
C Business rates.
D Annual leasing charge for tools.

5. Which of the following is <u>not</u> a variable cost for a hospital?

A Dressings for wounds.
B Medicines and drugs.
C Staff costs paid to a nursing agency.
D Cost of refurbishing a ward.

6. A business incurs £30,000 of fixed costs and variable costs are £20 per unit. What is the total cost if 2,000 units are produced?

A £30,020.
B £32,000.
C £40,000.
D £70,000.

7. The marginal cost of production is equal to which of the following?

A Unit cost.
B Total fixed costs less total variable costs.
C The extra revenue gained by selling one extra item.
D The extra cost incurred in producing one extra item.

8. Which of the following costs can be classified as both an overhead and a fixed cost for a dairy farmer?

A Cattle food bought from an agricultural supplier.
B Depreciation on the milking parlour.
C Fuel for tractor that is used to cut hay.
D Wages for the farm worker who operates the milking parlour.

9. Which of the following costs is <u>least</u> likely to be a controllable cost for the production manager in an engineering company?

A Overtime pay of production workers.
B Telephone charges for the sales department.
C Raw materials used in production.
D Maintenance costs of machinery.

10. Consider whether the following statements are true or false.

(i) Total revenue is equal to cost price multiplied by the quantity produced.

(ii) Variable costs are always greater than fixed costs.

A (i) True (ii) True.
B (i) True (ii) False.
C (i) False (ii) True.
D (i) False (ii) False.

UNIT 49 ● ● ●

1. Contribution is best defined as which of the following?

A The difference between fixed cost and variable cost.
B The difference between price and variable cost.
C Total revenue less total cost.
D Total cost less variable cost.

2. If the contribution is £5 and the selling price is £10, what is the contribution margin?

A £5.
B £10.
C 50%.
D 150%.

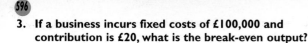

3. If a business incurs fixed costs of £100,000 and contribution is £20, what is the break-even output?

A £20.

B 20 units.

C 5,000 units.

D 20%.

4. If total cost (TC) = £4,000 + £200Q and total revenue (TR) = £250Q, where Q is the quantity sold, what is the break-even level of output?

A 80 units.

B 50 units.

C £50.

D 20 units.

5. If the break-even point is 200 units per week and the current level of sales is 500 units per week, what is the margin of safety expressed as a percentage?

A 100%.

B 80%.

C 60%.

D 40%.

6. What does a profit-volume chart show?

A Total revenue earned from sales.

B Total costs of production.

C Variable costs of production.

D The profit or loss made at different sales levels.

7. On a break-even chart, at points to the left of the break-even point, which of the following always occurs?

A A profit is made.

B Variable costs are greater than fixed costs.

C A loss is made.

D Total revenue is greater than total costs.

8. On a break-even chart, which of the following is least likely when the sales level is zero?

A Total revenue is zero.

B Variable costs are zero.

C The graph will show that a loss is made.

D Fixed costs are zero.

9. Which of the following is not a limitation of break-even analysis?

A The lines of total cost and total revenue are not likely to be linear in practice.

B Some output might remain unsold.

C The effect on profit of a change in sales cannot be shown.

D Fixed costs are sometimes stepped.

10. If a business sells more than one product, break-even analysis is made difficult because of which of the following?

A It is impossible to calculate the variable costs of production.

B The way that fixed costs are shared between the products affects the break-even point.

C Total revenue becomes less easy to calculate.

D Fixed costs are likely to fall.

UNIT 50 ●●●

1. Which of the following is most likely to be a service cost centre in a factory that produces motor vehicles?

A Machining.

B Maintenance.

C Assembly.

D Painting.

2. Which of the following cost centres in a manufacturing plant is least likely to be directly involved in producing cost units?

A Assembly.

B Packing.

C Finishing.

D Canteen.

3. Supervisory costs are most likely to be apportioned using which of the following bases?

A Floor area.

B Book value of assets.

C Number of staff employed.

D Direct material costs.

4. A business with two departments A and B pays rent of £20,000 per year. Department A has a floor area of 6,000m² and department B has a floor area of 4,000m². If the basis for apportionment is floor area, how much rent should be apportioned to department B?

A £20,000.

B £8,000.

C £10,000.

D £12,000.

5. Decide whether the following two statements are true or false.

(i) Overheads in service departments must be reapportioned to production departments.

(ii) All overheads must eventually be charged to cost units.

A (i) True (ii) True.

B (i) True (ii) False.

C (i) False (ii) True.

D (i) False (ii) False.

6. Decide whether the following two statements are true or false.

(i) Businesses should never apportion overheads in an equitable way.

(ii) Allocating overheads equally between cost centres is not always equitable.

A (i) True (ii) True.

B (i) True (ii) False.

C (i) False (ii) True.

D (i) False (ii) False.

7. Decide whether the following two statements are true or false.

(i) When service department overheads are reapportioned to production departments, the process is sometimes known as secondary apportionment.

(ii) Cost allocation involves charging certain overheads to a single cost centre.

A (i) True (ii) True.

B (i) True (ii) False.

C (i) False (ii) True.

D (i) False (ii) False.

8. If a production department is labour intensive, which of the following OARs is most appropriate?

A Machine hour OAR.

B Indirect labour OAR.

C Cost unit OAR.

D Direct labour OAR.

9. Under which circumstances will overheads be under absorbed?

A Actual overheads are lower than those predicted.
B Actual number of hours available are higher than those predicted.
C Actual overheads are equal to those predicted.
D Actual overheads are higher than those predicted.

10. What bookkeeping entries are needed to record over absorption?

A Debit overheads account and credit profit and loss account.
B Credit overheads account and debit profit and loss account.
C Credit overheads account and debit trading account.
D Debit overheads account and credit trading account.

UNIT 51

1. What is marginal cost if output rises from 10 units to 11 units and total cost rises from £4,000 to £4,500?

A £4,000.
B 1 unit.
C £500.
D £4,500.

2. Which of the following is not likely to be included as a marginal cost of production?

A Rent.
B Raw materials.
C Packaging.
D Power.

3. Marginal costing focuses on which of the following costs?

A Fixed costs.
B Indirect costs.
C Total costs.
D Variable costs.

4. A business receives a contribution of £19 from a unit of output that is sold for £65. What is the variable cost of that unit?

A £19.
B £84.
C £46.
D £65.

5. Marginal costing is also known as which of the following?

A Average costing.
B Absorption costing.
C Fixed costing.
D Direct costing.

6. Which of the following is not generally a factor that a business would consider when deciding whether to buy-in a product?

A Quality.
B Selling price to customers.
C Long term price guarantee.
D Satisfactory delivery time.

7. Decide whether the following two statements are true or false.

(i) When ranking products, a business should show a preference to those with the highest marginal cost.

(ii) When ranking products, a business will focus production on those with the lowest contribution.

A (i) True (ii) True.
B (i) True (ii) False.
C (i) False (ii) True.
D (i) False (ii) False.

8. A business decides to reduce the selling price of one of its products from £43 to £29. If the marginal cost is £28, which of the following will be true?

A Contribution per unit will rise by £1.
B Profit will fall by £29.
C Contribution will fall by £14.
D Marginal cost will rise by £1.

9. A business makes two products. Product A makes a contribution of £42 and uses 3 labour hours. Product B makes a contribution of £105 and uses 7 labour hours. Which of the following statements is correct?

A The contribution per labour hour for product B is £15.
B The contribution per labour hour is higher for product A.
C The profit made by product B is £105.
D If there is a shortage of labour, the business should concentrate production on product A.

10. Decide whether the following two statements are true or false.

(i) Marginal costing gives a higher profit figure if stocks decrease.

(ii) Absorption costing gives a lower profit figure if stocks increase.

A (i) True (ii) True.
B (i) True (ii) False.
C (i) False (ii) True.
D (i) False (ii) False.

UNIT 52

1. Which of the following businesses is least likely to use job costing?

A House building company.
B Boat builder.
C Oil refinery.
D A catering company.

2. Which of the following is not an advantage of job costing?

A It improves credit control.
B It helps to set an individual price for a job.
C The job cost sheets can be used to provide quotes.
D The estimated costs of a job can be compared with the actual costs to help detect reasons for differences.

3. Which of the following businesses is most likely to use batch costing?

A Dairy farmer.
B Clothes manufacturer.
C Hairdresser.
D Solicitor.

4. A business produces a batch of 400 standard products for a customer. Total labour costs are £300, material costs are £500 and overheads £400. What is the cost per unit?

A £1,200.
B £3.
C £4.
D £5.

5. Which of the following is not usually a feature of contract work?

A The job extends over a number of years.
B Payment is usually made in instalments.
C Some work is certified before the contract is completed.
D Most of the costs are classified as indirect.

6. Which of the following is not a debit on a contract account?

A Material costs.
B Materials transferred to another site.
C Labour costs.
D Apportioned overheads.

7. Which of the following is not a credit on a contract account?

A Value of work certified.
B Cost of work not certified.
C Plant removed from site.
D Direct site costs.

8. A business has completed 90% of a contract. The payment received on account is £300,000, the contract price is £400,000 and the estimated profit is £50,000. What amount would it be reasonable to attribute as profit?

A £37,500.
B £50,000.
C 2/3 × £50,000.
D 90% × £50,000.

9. Which of the following is not an example of a cost driver?

A Number of inspections.
B Number of batches received.
C Number of direct labour hours.
D Number of purchase orders.

10. Decide whether the following two statements are true or false.

(i) One of the advantages of activity based costing is that a business can more easily identify its most profitable products.

(ii) An example of a cost pool is all the costs associated with quality control.

A (i) True (ii) True.
B (i) True (ii) False.
C (i) False (ii) True.
D (i) False (ii) False.

UNIT 53

1. For an engineering company, which of the following staff would not be classified as direct labour?

A Receptionist.
B Welder.
C Lathe operator.
D Assembly worker.

2. Which of the following is not an example of indirect labour in a clothes manufacturing company?

A Maintenance worker.
B General manager.
C Machinist.
D Office worker.

3. Which of the following methods of remuneration involves paying staff according to the number of hours they spend at work?

A Bonus scheme.
B Time rate.
C Piece rate.
D Performance related pay.

4. Workers are sometimes paid extra if they work more hours than the set working week. What are these payments called?

A Bonus payments.
B Piece rates.
C Performance related pay.
D Overtime.

5. Which of the following is generally not an advantage of an annualised hours system for employers?

A Overtime is reduced.
B Efficiency is improved.
C Labour flexibility is increased.
D Hourly wage rates are reduced.

6. Which of the following is the least likely outcome of a piece rate system?

A Reduced quality.
B Reduced production.
C Increase in accidents.
D More wastage.

7. An insurance salesperson gets a basic wage of £100 per week and an extra £50 for each policy sold during the week. If 9 policies are sold in a particular week, what is the employee's remuneration?

A £100.
B £450.
C £550.
D None of these.

8. Which of the following is a disadvantage of performance related pay?

A It rewards incentive.
B It is based on the subjective judgment of the employee.
C It requires the performance of employees to be monitored.
D It is sometimes difficult to measure the performance of an individual employee.

9. Which of the following can be classed as both a direct cost and a variable cost in a manufacturing company?

A Overtime paid to a keyboard operator in the administration department.
B Overtime paid to an assembly line worker.
C Basic weekly pay of assembly line workers who are paid an hourly rate.
D Commission paid to the sales staff.

10. Which of the following is not a reason for recording labour costs?

A To calculate VAT on the finished product.
B To provide information for charging clients.
C To provide information for payroll preparation.
D To provide cost accountants with information to help them cost specific business activities.

UNIT 54

1. Decide whether the following two statements are true or false.

(i) Budgets are primarily concerned with past events.

(ii) Information in the sales budget might be based on historical data.

A (i) True (ii) True.
B (i) True (ii) False.
C (i) False (ii) True.
D (i) False (ii) False.

2. Which of the following is not usually the purpose of a budget?

A Recording accounting information.
B Controlling business activities.
C Planning future events.
D Coordinating activities.

---

3. Which of the following budgets is most likely to be prepared first?
A Cash budget.
B Purchases budget.
C Stock budget.
D Sales budget.

4. Which of the following is a component of the master budget?
A Debtors budget.
B Budgeted profit and loss account.
C Sales budget.
D Research and development budget.

5. Which of the following shows the planned flows of payments and receipts for a business?
A Sales budget.
B Cash budget.
C Budgeted balance sheet.
D Capital budget.

6. Which of the following is not required when producing a debtors budget?
A Sales budget.
B Estimated payments by credit customers.
C Budgeted payments to suppliers.
D Opening balance of the amount owed by customers.

7. Which of the following is not an example of a functional budget?
A Sales budget.
B Production budget.
C Cash budget.
D Purchases budget.

8. Under which circumstances is the level of production most likely to be the limiting budget factor?
A There is a fall in consumer demand.
B There is a shortage of skilled production workers.
C There is a rise in consumer demand.
D There is a rise in the retail price of the product.

9. Which of the following is not generally considered to be a benefit of budgetary control?
A It helps to control income and expenditure.
B It helps to increase profit margins.
C It provides clear targets for staff.
D It helps to emphasise and clarify managerial responsibilities.

10. Which of the following is most closely associated with the behavioural aspects of budgeting?
A Financial performance.
B Cash flow.
C Customer demand.
D Staff motivation.

UNIT 55 ●●●

1. What is the main purpose of a cash budget?
A To show the expected cash position at the end of each month in the budget period.
B To show the value of assets, liabilities and capital at the end of the budget period.
C To show shareholders how well the company is doing.
D To show a business where the profit comes from.

2. What does the top section of a cash budget show?
A Expected cash outflows.
B Expected profit.
C Expected cash inflows.
D Expected cash balance.

3. Which of the following is not a cash inflow in a cash budget?
A Cash sales.
B Cash from credit sales.
C Newly introduced capital.
D Profit.

4. The opening cash balance in a cash budget for a month is minus £12,000. In the same month, total cash receipts are expected to be £145,000 and total cash payments are expected to be £164,000. What will be the closing cash balance?
A -£12,000.
B £19,000.
C £7,000.
D -£31,000.

5. Which of the following would not be an example of a cash outflow in a cash budget?
A Tax refund from the Inland Revenue.
B Wages.
C VAT payment.
D Purchases.

6. Which of the following payments would appear in a cash budget but not in the budgeted profit and loss account?
A Payment of wages.
B Purchase of a new vehicle.
C Purchase of raw materials.
D Corporation tax payment.

7. Which of the following expenses would appear in the profit and loss account but not in the cash budget?
A Heat and light.
B Depreciation.
C Motor expenses.
D Accountancy fees.

8. Decide whether the following statements are true or false.

(i) A provision for bad debts will appear in the cash budget because it is an expense.

(ii) The value of closing stock will not appear in the cash budget.

A (i) True (ii) True.
B (i) True (ii) False.
C (i) False (ii) True.
D (i) False (ii) False.

9. Which of the following will appear in both the cash budget and the budgeted balance sheet at the end of the budget period?
A Cash balance.
B Trade creditors.
C Closing capital.
D Trade debtors.

10. The value of cash from credit sales in the cash budget is likely to be shown in which other budget?
A Production budget.
B Sales budget.
C Capital expenditure budget.
D Materials budget.

UNIT 56 ●●●

1. Which of the following best describes a standard cost?
A Estimated cost.
B Planned cost.
C Historical cost.
D Actual cost.

2. Which of the following terms is used to describe a standard that is only achieved in the most favourable conditions?

A Historical.
B Attainable.
C Basic.
D Ideal.

3. A business makes a profit of £456,000 and the budgeted profit is £432,000. What is the profit variance?

A £456,000 (F).
B £24,000 (A).
C £24,000 (F).
D £432,000 (F).

4. The standard cost for a material is £4 per unit and the actual cost is £4.20 per unit. The standard usage is 40,000 units and the actual usage is 35,000 units. What is the materials price variance?

A £7,000 (A).
B £7,000 (F).
C £8,000 (A).
D £8,000 (F).

5. Which of the following would not cause an adverse materials usage variance?

A Careless or sloppy work.
B New more efficient machinery.
C Pilferage.
D Purchasing inferior quality materials.

6. The standard wage for a business is £7 per hour and the actual wage paid is £7.50 per hour. The standard labour hours worked is 40,000 hours and the actual hours worked is 36,000 hours. What is the labour efficiency variance?

A £28,000 (A).
B £28,000 (F).
C £18,000 (A).
D £18,000 (F).

7. Which of the following would most likely cause an adverse wage rate variance?

A Shortages of labour.
B Improvements in the productivity of labour.
C A fall in the productivity of labour.
D A reduction in the minimum wage.

8. The standard price charged by a business is £100 and the actual price charged is £95. The standard sales volume is 2,000 units and the actual volume is 2,100 units. What is the sales variance?

A £10,000 (F).
B £10,000 (A).
C £10,500 (A).
D £500 (A).

9. Which of the following is least likely to cause a favourable sales variance?

A Rivals leaving the market.
B A rise in demand for the product.
C Investment in advertising and promotion.
D More competition in the market.

10. Which of the following variances are not likely to be linked?

A Profit and total cost.
B Total cost and wage rate.
C Materials usage and sales price.
D Overheads and profit.

UNIT 57

1. Which of the following types of spending is not usually classed as investment expenditure?

A Raw materials.
B Machinery.
C Vehicles.
D Take-over of rival company.

2. Which of the following is least likely to be a feature of investment?

A It is risky.
B Income is generated in the future.
C Initial outlay is usually high.
D Future cash flows are easily predictable.

3. Decide whether following statements are true or false.

(i) The payback period is the amount of time it takes to recover the initial cost of an investment project.

(ii) The payback method of appraisal is simpler to calculate than the net present value method.

A (i) True (ii) True.
B (i) True (ii) False.
C (i) False (ii) True.
D (i) False (ii) False.

4. A business invests £100,000 in a new machine. The net cash flow from the investment is a constant £40,000 per annum for 4 years. What is the payback period?

A £160,000.
B 2 years.
C 2 years 6 months.
D 4 years.

5. For which of the following types of investment would the payback method be most appropriate?

A Computer.
B Warehouse.
C Lorry.
D Office furniture.

6. Which of the following best describes the accounting rate of return?

A Initial cost as a percentage of average profits.
B Average annual profit as a percentage of average investment.
C Total profit as a percentage of total investment.
D Net cash flow as a percentage of average investment.

7. If a business invests £100,000 in a 4 year project which yields additional profit of £180,000 (excluding depreciation), what is the accounting rate of return?

A £180,000.
B 10%.
C 25%.
D 40%.

8. Decide whether the following statements are true or false.

(i) The accounting rate of return takes interest rates into account.

(ii) The accounting rate of return makes comparisons between alternative projects relatively easy.

A (i) True (ii) True.
B (i) True (ii) False.
C (i) False (ii) True.
D (i) False (ii) False.

9. **What is the present value of £20,000 to be received in 4 years time if the discount rate of interest is 10%?**

A £13,600.

B £20,000.

C 10%.

D £2,000.

10. **A sunk cost is best described as which of the following?**

A The total cost of an investment over its lifetime.

B The initial cost of an investment.

C A past, irrecoverable cost.

D A cost which should be an important consideration in investment appraisal.

UNIT 58 ● ● ●

No questions are set on this unit.

Answers to multiple choice questions

Unit 1
1C 2B 3D 4A 5D 6D 7C 8C 9A 10A

Unit 2
1B 2A 3B 4C 5D 6C 7C 8B 9A 10D

Unit 3
1D 2B 3A 4B 5A 6C 7D 8C 9A 10D

Unit 4
1B 2B 3A 4C 5B 6C 7A 8D 9D 10B

Unit 5
1A 2D 3B 4C 5C 6A 7C 8D 9D 10A

Unit 6
1C 2B 3B 4A 5A 6B 7A 8D 9C 10C

Unit 7
1D 2B 3C 4B 5A 6B 7C 8D 9B 10C

Unit 8
1D 2D 3C 4B 5A 6D 7B 8D 9A 10D

Unit 9
1B 2D 3A 4B 5A 6C 7A 8B 9C 10C

Unit 10
1D 2C 3B 4B 5C 6C 7D 8A 9B 10D

Unit 11
1D 2A 3D 4A 5C 6A 7B 8B 9D 10B

Unit 12
1C 2B 3D 4A 5A 6D 7B 8C 9C 10B

Unit 13
1D 2C 3D 4D 5D 6B 7A 8B 9A 10B

Unit 14
1B 2D 3C 4C 5A 6B 7A 8B 9A 10D

Unit 15
1B 2A 3C 4C 5A 6C 7A 8D 9A 10B

Unit 16
1C 2A 3A 4C 5B 6B 7C 8B 9A 10D

Unit 17
1B 2A 3B 4C 5B 6D 7C 8A 9D 10A

Unit 18
1B 2C 3C 4D 5B 6A 7D 8B 9A 10A

Unit 19
1D 2B 3A 4B 5A 6A 7A 8C 9C 10C

Unit 20
1C 2D 3A 4C 5C 6A 7A 8D 9B 10C

Unit 21
1C 2A 3B 3C 5D 6A 7D 8B 9A 10B

Unit 22
1A 2A 3C 3B 5B 6C 7C 8B 9D 10A

Unit 23
1B 2D 3C 3D 5C 6A 7B 8B 9B 10A

Unit 24
1B 2B 3A 3D 5B 6A 7C 8C 9D 10B

Unit 25
1A 2B 3B 3C 5D 6A 7B 8A 9C 10D

Unit 26
1B 2C 3B 3D 5B 6A 7C 8A 9D 10C

Unit 27
1B 2A 3A 3C 5A 6D 7B 8A 9C 10B

Unit 28
1C 2D 3B 3A 5C 6D 7C 8A

Unit 29
1D 2B 3A 4D 5A 6C 7A 8C 9C 10B

Unit 30
1C 2B 3C 4A 5C 6B 7D 8D 9A 10A

Unit 31
1C 2B 3C 4D 5C 6D 7A 8C 9D 10B

Unit 32
1D 2A 3B 4A 5C 6C 7B 8C 9D 10A

Unit 33
1A 2D 3C 4A 5C 6D 7A 8A 9A 10D

Unit 34
1A 2D 3D 4C 5B 6A 7B 8C 9B 10C

Unit 35
1C 2B 3B 4D 5A 6A 7A 8D 9C 10C

Unit 36
1A 2A 3D 4B 5D 6C 7A 8D 9D 10B

Unit 37
1B 2A 3C 4D 5C 6B 7C 8A 9A 10A

Unit 38
1D 2C 3A 4D 5B 6B 7D 8A 9B 10C

Unit 39
1A 2D 3C 4C 5C 6B 7B 8D 9A 10D

Unit 40
1B 2D 3D 4C 5A 6A 7A 8C 9B 10D

Unit 41
1D 2C 3A 4D 5C 6B 7B 8C 9A 10A

Unit 42
1B 2C 3D 4C 5D 6B 7B 8A 9D 10C

Unit 43
1C 2D 3A 4A 5C 6A 7C 8D 9C 10D

Unit 44
1C 2D 3A 4A 5C 6B 7A 8C 9A 10B

Unit 45
1C 2D 3C 4D 5B 6D 7C 8C 9A 10D

Unit 46
1A 2D 3D 4D 5C 6A 7D 8C 9A 10C

Unit 47
No questions are set on this unit.

Unit 48
1C 2A 3C 4B 5D 6D 7D 8B 9B 10D

Unit 49
1B 2C 3C 4A 5C 6D 7C 8D 9C 10B

Unit 50
1B 2D 3C 4B 5A 6C 7A 8D 9D 10A

Unit 51
1C 2A 3D 4C 5D 6B 7D 8C 9A 10B

Unit 52
1C 2A 3B 4B 5D 6B 7D 8A 9C 10A

Unit 53
1A 2C 3B 4D 5D 6B 7C 8D 9B 10A

Unit 54
1C 2A 3D 4B 5B 6C 7C 8B 9B 10D

Unit 55
1A 2C 3D 4D 5A 6B 7B 8C 9A 10B

Unit 56
1B 2D 3C 4A 5B 6B 7A 8D 9D 10C

Unit 57
1A 2D 3A 4C 5A 6B 7D 8C 9A 10C

Unit 58
No questions are set on this unit.

APPENDIX 2 — ANSWERS TO UNIT QUESTIONS

UNIT 1

QUESTION 1
(a) 1,4 and 5 Sales; 2 Wages; 3 Purchases.
(b) By totalling sales (£525); wages (£450); and purchases (£210).
(c) To calculate profit and tax owed.

QUESTION 2
(a) Management accountant.
(b) Cost control and decision making.

QUESTION 3
(a) 1. Pauline; 2. Ruth; 3. Ron; and 4. Beth.
(b) Overall responsibility, supervisor, decision making, member of senior management team, handling budget and staff management.
(c) Can judge managers by level of profitability.

UNIT ASSESSMENT QUESTION 1
(a) Maxine.
(b) Tariq (responsible for credit control), or Maxine (who might have failed to record the transaction).
(c) To keep records of transactions and provide financial information for management and owners.

UNIT ASSESSMENT QUESTION 2
(a) The owners.
(b) Employees, lenders, government, customers, suppliers.

UNIT 2

UNIT ASSESSMENT QUESTION 1
(a) 1. Personal; 2. Personal; 3. Impersonal; 4. Personal; 5. Impersonal.
(b) With source documents.
(c) To prove that the business transactions occurred.

UNIT ASSESSMENT QUESTION 2
(a) 1. Nominal ledger; 2. Purchases ledger; 3. Nominal ledger; 4. Sales ledger.
(b) The accountant's job is easier; less time is needed to produce the accounts and the charge will be lower.
(c) Profit calculation is likely to be wrong. Inaccurate tax assessment.

UNIT 3

QUESTION 1
(a) Information to be included in a letter: source documents provide information about a transaction, ensure that right goods are sent to the right place at the right time, provide evidence that a transaction has taken place, and provide a means of checking and settling trading disputes.

QUESTION 2
(a) Sefton Council.
(b) To invite tenders to supply a pier tram service and 'fit-out' the pier pavilion.
(c) Ensures competition between suppliers. Reduces resources spent on finding a supplier.

QUESTION 3
(a) Buyer is McClelland Ltd; seller is Delpoint Screenprint Company.
(b) To show McClelland how much it owes for the goods bought.
(c) (i) £318.43, (ii) Payment must be sent within 28 days of the invoice date.
(d) It is the official date of the transaction and tax point.

QUESTION 4
(a) To reduce the amount owed by Mary Tench.
(b) Goods have been returned because the item was faulty.
(c) Offset against a future purchase or subtracted from the current amount owing if other items have been ordered at the same time.
(d) If the customer has been undercharged or has underpaid.

UNIT ASSESSMENT QUESTION 1
(a) Quotation.
(b) To explain to a customer the terms under which goods or services can be supplied.
(c) £179.20 including VAT (£105.77 + £3.91 + £0.71 + £68.81).
(d) An invoice. There is no transportation of goods - so there would be no delivery note.
(e) To identify precisely the parts that are being bought.

UNIT ASSESSMENT QUESTION 2
(a) The completed invoice should include: the date; the order reference number; the address of the customer; the itemised goods supplied; the price including VAT.
(b) £465.30 (inc. VAT)
(c) Delivery note. It describes the goods being sent.
(d) To clarify what is being paid. To match the payment with the invoice.
(e) If a customer has underpaid.

(b) Assets: £20,130; capital: £10,940; liabilities: £9,190.

UNIT ASSESSMENT QUESTION I

(a) Assets (computer, software, furniture, car and money at bank). Liabilities (bank loan). Capital (money from parents).

(b) Assets = Capital + Liabilities
(£900 + £1,100 + £3,500 + £1,760 + Bank) = £5,000 + £3,000
£7,260 + Bank = £8,000
Bank = £8,000 - £7,260
Bank = £740
There is £740 in the bank for Adrian's business.

(c)

Adrian Stilgoe
Balance Sheet as at 31.10.00

	£
Assets	
Computer	900
Software	1,100
Furniture	1,760
Car	3,500
Cash	740
	8000
Less liabilities	
Bank loan	3,000
	5,000
Financed by	
Capital	5,000
	5,000

UNIT ASSESSMENT QUESTION 2

(a) Assets (£3,050) = Capital (£2,700) + Liabilities (£350)

(b)

Lorna Hignett
Balance Sheet as at 30.9.00

	£
Assets	
Van	2,400
Tools and equipment	350
Cash in hand/at bank	300
	3,050
Less liabilities	
Trade creditor	350
	2,700
Financed by	
Capital	2,700
	2,700

UNIT 4

QUESTION I

(a) (i) Great Barr Timber Ltd. (ii) The NorthWest Bank (iii) The Birmingham Post.
(b) Cheque not signed. Amount in words different from amount in writing.
(c) To keep a record of the payment.
(d) Only allow authorised signatories to sign cheques. Two people must sign.

QUESTION 2

(a) £158.50 (£200 - £41.50).
(b) A receipt. Take it to the petty cashier and complete a petty cash voucher.
(c) The amount of cash used by the business in a given period.

QUESTION 3

(a) Credit card.
(b) An Elite 1212 printer. In case of dispute, eg if the item is faulty.
(c) Proof of payment and date.

UNIT ASSESSMENT QUESTION I

(a) To provide a record of bank transactions and a means of checking.
(b) The bank account became overdrawn. Paula needs to know that she owes the bank money.
(c) The balance would be £491.89 (£589.89 - £98.00).
(d) The cheque has not been presented or cleared.

UNIT ASSESSMENT QUESTION 2

(a) Convenient, allows telephone transactions, provides free credit for short period, avoids Jeremy using his own money and reclaiming.
(b) Transactions are summarised on the credit card statement.
(c) Check the card signature against that on the voucher. Ask for extra ID.

UNIT 5

QUESTION I

(a) Two coaches, portakabin, yard, storage tank and the diesel fuel it contains, and the £439 in the bank.
(b) £10,900 (£500 + £10,400).
(c) £35,900 (£25,000 + £10,900).

QUESTION 2

(a) £297,100 = £260,500 + £36,600.
(b) £294,000 = £260,500 + £33,500.
(c) No change.

QUESTION 3

(a) Assets: £21,100); capital: £11,440; liabilities: £9,660). Both focus on assets, liabilities and capital.

(c) Assets (£3,050 + £350) = Capital (£2,700) + Liabilities (£350) + Revenue (£400) - Expenses (£50) - Drawings (£0)
So: £3,400 = £3,400

(d)

Lorna Hignett
Profit and Loss Account
for the month ended 31.10.00

	£
Revenue	400
Less	
Expenses	50
Profit	350

(e)

Lorna Hignett
Balance Sheet as at 31.10.00

	£
Assets	
Van	2,400
Tools and equipment	350
Cash in hand/at bank	650
	3,400
Less liabilities	
Trade creditor	350
	3,050
Financed by	
Capital	2,700
Profit	350
	3,050

UNIT 6

QUESTION 1
(a) Capital expenditure, eg the new laser printer and the upgrade to the dryer.
Revenue expenditure, eg staff wages, rent and phone bill, cleaning fluids and stationery.
(b) Capital expenditure: £460 (£210 + £250).
Revenue expenditure: £1,190 (£800 + £110 + £110 + £150 + £96 + £34).
(c) No because £460 is capital expenditure.

QUESTION 2
(a) Capital expenditure.
(b) Capital expenditure: £72,900 (£52,000 + £3,000 + £5,000 + £4,000 + £4,200 + £4,700);
Revenue expenditure: £6,100 (£3,200 + £2,900).

(c) Revenue expenditure.

QUESTION 3
(a) Capital expenditure: electronic till and installation of new fixtures and fittings.
Revenue expenditure: stock, wages, heat and light, repairs to heating system, interest and other operating expenses.

(b)

Lorraine Day
Profit and Loss Account
for the year ended 31.12.00

	£	£
Revenue		112,500
Less expenses		
Stock	65,400	
Wages	23,000	
Heat and light	760	
Repairs to heating	430	
Interest	960	
Other expenses	3,400	
		93,950
Profit		18,550

(c) Expenditure on the till and fixtures will be listed in the balance sheet under assets.

QUESTION 4
(a) Refrigerator should not be listed as an expense.
(b) Profit has been understated by £4,000 because expenses should be reduced by £4,000 from £95,600 to £91,600.
(c) The expenditure should be transferred to the balance sheet.

UNIT ASSESSMENT QUESTION 1
(a) In this case the value of capital expenditure includes all the costs associated with buying the computer system and getting it operational. These costs are:

Cost of computer	£1,900
Cost of printer	£450
Installation and testing	£200
Staff training	£500
Rewiring	£340
	£3,390

(b) Profit would be reduced by £299 because expenses rise; paper (£110) + insurance (£90) + maintenance (£99).
(c) Rent and staff wages.
(d) Revenue expenses would increase, so profit would fall.

UNIT ASSESSMENT QUESTION 2

(a) Revenue expenditure because the spending is for a repair.

(b) Annual profit will be reduced by £1,200.

(c) (i) Profit will fall by £4,000; (ii) Business assets will be understated by £4,000.

(d) Capital income because it is the sale of fixed assets.

UNIT 7

QUESTION 1

(a) Paul's financial affairs and those of his business must be kept separate.

(b) 75% (ie 30/40) of £2,400 = £1,800.

(c) Heat and light, telephone.

QUESTION 2

(a) Advantage: objective. Disadvantage: the warehouse asset is undervalued.

(b) Profit in money terms overstates the true position.

QUESTION 3

(a) Fixtures and fittings, display cabinets and electronic till.

(b) Classify expenditure under a certain amount as revenue expenditure.

QUESTION 4

(a) The price paid for them, ie their historic cost.

(b) Their second-hand/disposal value.

UNIT ASSESSMENT QUESTION 1

(a) 1. £500 rent should be recorded in the current year's accounts (1/12 × £6,000): matching concept. 2. £1,400: historical cost concept. 3. £2,300 revenue (£3,200 - £900) and £900 overpayment: accruals concept.

(b) Accounting concepts allow accountants to work according to common guidelines, allow comparisons to be made and reduce the scope for misleading information.

UNIT ASSESSMENT QUESTION 2

(a) £80,000 (£50,000 + £30,000) according to the historical cost, realisation and prudence concepts.

(b) The £600 should be entered as revenue.

(c) As a bad debt, recorded as an expense.

UNIT 8

QUESTION 1

(a)

Sales Account

Dr			Cr		
2000		£	2000		£
			11.1	Cash	150
			25.1	Cash	80

Cash Account

Dr			Cr		
2000		£	2000		£
11.1	Sales	150			
25.1	Sales	80			

(b) Debit - an entry on the left-hand side of the cash account because asset, ie cash, has increased. Credit - an entry on the right-hand side of the sales account because revenue has increased, ie income from repairing dinghy.

QUESTION 2

(a) 1: assets, capital; 2: assets (twice); 3: assets, expenses; 4: assets, revenue.

(b)

Bank Account

Dr			Cr		
2000		£	2000		£
3.6	Capital	20,000	5.6	Computer	2,700
9.6	Sales	1,000	6.6	Rent	500

Capital Account

Dr			Cr		
2000		£	2000		£
			3.6	Bank	20,000

Computer Account

Dr			Cr		
2000		£	2000		£
5.6	Bank	2,700			

Rent Account

Dr			Cr		
2000		£	2000		£
6.6	Bank	500			

Sales Account

Dr			Cr		
2000		£	2000		£
			9.6	Bank	1,000

UNIT ASSESSMENT QUESTION I

(a)

Capital Account

Dr		Cr	
2000	£	2000	£
		28.8 Bank	8,000

Office Equipment Account

Dr		Cr	
2000	£	2000	£
28.8 Bank	1,400		

Loan Account

Dr		Cr	
2000	£	2000	£
		29.8 Bank	4,000

Computer Account

Dr		Cr	
2000	£	2000	£
30.8 Bank	1,700		

Advertising Account

Dr		Cr	
2000	£	2000	£
1.9 Bank	900		

Stationery Account

Dr		Cr	
2000	£	2000	£
3.9 Bank	85		

Commission Account

Dr		Cr	
2000	£	2000	£
		7.9 Bank	500

(b) (i) Asset accounts: Office equipment and Computer. (ii) Expense accounts: Advertising and Stationery. (iii) Revenue account: Commission. (iv) Liability account: Loan account.

QUESTION 3

(a) (i and ii) 1. bank (value given), vehicles (value received); 2. bank (value given), repairs (value received); 3. bank (value given), purchases (value received); 4. cash (value received), sales (value given); 5. cash (value given), drawings (value received); 6. bank (value received), sales (value given); 7. bank (value given), wages (value received).

(b)

Bank Account

Dr		Cr	
2000	£	2000	£
25.5 Sales	1,340	22.5 Vehicles	4,000
		22.5 Repairs	400
		23.5 Purchases	11,700
		26.5 Wages	2,500

Cash Account

Dr		Cr	
2000	£	2000	£
24.5 Sales	85	25.5 Drawings	50

Vehicles Account

Dr		Cr	
2000	£	2000	
22.5 Bank	4,000		

Repairs Account

Dr		Cr	
2000	£	2000	£
22.5 Bank	400		

Purchases Account

Dr		Cr	
2000	£	2000	£
23.5 Bank	11,700		

Drawings Account

Dr		Cr	
2000	£	2000	
25.5 Cash	50		

Sales Account

Dr		Cr	
2000		2000	£
		24.5 Cash	85
		25.5 Bank	1,340

Wages Account

Dr		Cr	
2000	£	2000	
26.5 Bank	2,500		

UNIT ASSESSMENT QUESTION 2

(a) 1: assets, capital; 2 assets (twice); 3 assets, expenses; 4 assets, expenses; 5 assets, expenses.

(b)

Bank Account

Dr		Cr	
2000	£	2000	£
6.11 Capital	6,000	13.11 Machinery	3,200
		15.11 Leasing	200
		16.11 Purchases	700
		24.11 Wages	400

Capital Account

Dr		Cr	
	£	2000	£
		6.11 Bank	6,000

Machinery Account

Dr		Cr	
2000	£		£
13.11 Bank	3,200		

Leasing Account

Dr		Cr	
2000	£		£
15.11 Bank	200		

Purchases Account

Dr		Cr	
2000	£		£
16.11 Bank	700		

Wages Account

Dr		Cr	
2000	£		£
24.11 Bank	400		

UNIT 9

QUESTION 1

(a) and (b)

SALES DAY BOOK 2000 (page 102)

Date	Customer	Invoice no.	Total	VAT	Price
			£	£	£
18.9	T. Jones	01299	117.50	17.50	100.00
18.9	A. Thompson	01300	305.50	45.50	260.00
18.9	B. Reynolds	01301	246.75	36.75	210.00
18.9	M. Khan	01302	105.75	15.75	90.00
18.9	C. Button & Son	01303	141.00	21.00	120.00
18.9	L. Bennett	01304	58.75	8.75	50.00
18.9	A. Ng	01305	117.50	17.50	100.00
	Totals		1,092.75	162.75	930.00

(c) Avoids overfilling the ledgers.

QUESTION 2

(a)

SALES LEDGER

Bolton College (page 12)

Dr		Cr	
	£		£
31.10 Sales SDB197	310		

The Red Cow (page 34)

Dr		Cr	
	£		£
31.10 Sales SDB197	260		

B. Naughton (page 56)

Dr		Cr	
	£		£
31.10 Sales SDB197	150		

NOMINAL LEDGER

Sales Account (page 22)

Dr		Cr		
	£			£
		31.10	Credit sales SDB197	720

(b) Helps cross reference between ledgers and sales day book, and between sales day book and invoices.

UNIT ASSESSMENT QUESTION 1

(a)

SALES DAY BOOK 2000 (page 00)

Date	Customer	Invoice no.	Amount
			£
26.2	P. Collingwood	0428	15.50
26.2	Lizard Book Shop	0429	255.00
26.2	Transferred to Sales Account		270.50

(b)

SALES LEDGER

P. Collingwood

Dr		Cr	
	£		£
26.2 Sales	15.50		

Lizard Book Shop

Dr		Cr	
	£		£
26.2 Sales	255.00		

NOMINAL LEDGER

Sales Account

Dr		Cr	
	£		£
		26.2 Credit sales	270.50

(c) To encourage sales to trade customers.

UNIT 10

QUESTION 1
(a) and (b)

PURCHASES DAY BOOK 2000 (page 2)

Date	Supplier	Invoice no.	Total £	VAT £	Price £
3.1	Malden Electrics	1458	705.00	105.00	600.00
3.1	TLD Ltd	01332	646.25	96.25	550.00
3.1	ELCO	0231	1,645.00	245.00	1,400.00
3.1	Herrod Alarms	6241	3,760.00	560.00	3,200.00
3.1	Massey Wright & Co	0944	1,410.00	210.00	1,200.00
		Totals	8,166.25	1,216.25	6,950.00

QUESTION 2
(a) Purchase invoices.

(b)

PURCHASES LEDGER

Britten & Co (page 21)

Dr			Cr	
£				£
		25.2	Purchases PDB56	459

Lockworld (page 45)

Dr			Cr	
£				£
		25.2	Purchases PDB56	490

Keys & Co (page 34)

Dr			Cr	
£				£
		25.2	Purchases PDB56	90

NOMINAL LEDGER

Purchases Account (page 94)

Dr			Cr
£			£
25.2	Credit purchases PDB56	1,039	

UNIT ASSESSMENT QUESTION 2
(a)

SALES DAY BOOK 2000

Date	Customer	Invoice no.	Amount £
2.4	A. Killin	02488	1,200
2.4	The Welford Hotel	02489	760
2.4	B. Collins	02490	210
2.4	The Bulldog Inn	02491	320
2.4	W.Thomas	02492	540
2.4	Transferred to Sales Account		3,030

(b)

SALES LEDGER

A. Killin

Dr		Cr
£		£
2.4 Sales	1,200	

The Welford Hotel

Dr		Cr
£		£
2.4 Sales	760	

B. Collins

Dr		Cr
£		£
2.4 Sales	210	

The Bulldog Inn

Dr		Cr
£		£
2.4 Sales	320	

W.Thomas

Dr		Cr
£		£
2.4 Sales	540	

NOMINAL LEDGER

Sales Account

Dr		Cr	
£			£
		2.4 Credit sales	3,030

UNIT ASSESSMENT QUESTION 1

(a), (b) and (c)

PURCHASES DAY BOOK 2000 (page 200)

Date	Supplier	Invoice no.	Folio	Amount
				£
3.5	Betty Collins & Co	871	PL	460.00
10.5	Wilson Cotton	2339	PL	4,900.00
12.5	Jones Bros	4453	PL	650.00
22.5	Oldham Cotton Supplies	3321	PL	2,500.00
26.5	Birmingham Dyes	0911	PL	800.00
31.5	Transferred to Purchases Account		NL	9,310.00

PURCHASES LEDGER

Betty Collins & Co

Dr		Cr	
£		£	
		3.5 Purchases PDB200	460

Wilson Cotton

Dr		Cr	
£		£	
		10.5 Purchases PDB200	4,900

Jones Bros

Dr		Cr	
£		£	
		12.5 Purchases PDB200	650

Oldham Cotton Supplies

Dr		Cr	
£		£	
		22.5 Purchases PDB200	2,500

Birmingham Dyes

Dr		Cr	
£		£	
		26.5 Purchases PDB200	800

NOMINAL LEDGER

Purchases Account

Dr		Cr	
£		£	
31.5 Credit purchases PDB200	9,310		

(d) The more transactions, the more often will the totals be transferred.

UNIT ASSESSMENT QUESTION 2

(a)

PURCHASES LEDGER

Wade Food Supplies (page 32)

Dr		Cr	
£		£	
		8.6 Purchases PDB71	245

Winters Farm Products (page 34)

Dr		Cr	
£		£	
		9.6 Purchases PDB71	260

Manninghams (page 23)

Dr		Cr	
£		£	
		11.6 Purchases PDB71	100

S.A. Wholefood (page 28)

Dr		Cr	
£		£	
		11.6 Purchases PDB71	160

Lindemans Herbs (page 20)

Dr		Cr	
£		£	
		14.6 Purchases PDB71	210

NOMINAL LEDGER

Purchases Account

Dr		Cr	
£		£	
14.6 Credit purchases PDB71	975		

(b)

INVOICES

sales → SALES DAY BOOK → SALES LEDGER debit customer accounts

→ NOMINAL LEDGER credit sales account

purchase → PURCHASES DAY BOOK → PURCHASES LEDGER credit supplier accounts

→ NOMINAL LEDGER debit purchases account

Details from invoices are recorded in day books

Details from the day books are posted to ledger accounts using the double entry system

UNIT 11

QUESTION 1

(a)

RETURNS INWARDS DAY BOOK 2000   (page 40)

Date	Customer	Credit note no.	Folio	Amount
				£
28.9	The Hop Pole	57		120.00

(b) It reduces the amount owed by the customer.

QUESTION 2

(a)

SALES LEDGER

Sanjay's Balti House (page 34)

Dr		Cr		
£		£		
	3.6	Returns inwards	RIDB27	120

Bay of Bengal (page 12)

Dr		Cr		
£		£		
	6.6	Returns inwards	RIDB27	96

Gate of India (page 23)

Dr		Cr		
£		£		
	9.6	Returns inwards	RIDB27	56

NOMINAL LEDGER

Returns Inwards Account (page 18)

Dr			Cr
£			£
10.6	Returns	RIDB27	272

(b) The average number of credit notes issued per week or month. The time involved in making the entries.

QUESTION 3

(a) and (b)

RETURNS OUTWARDS DAY BOOK 2000

Date	Supplier	Credit note no.	Folio	Amount
				£
2.5	C. Bartlett	1200	PL	45
4.5	D. Perkins	0332	PL	120
6.5	C. Bartlett	1203	PL	45
7.5	C. Bartlett	1205	PL	90
7.5	D. Perkins	0335	PL	70
				370
7.5	Transferred to returns outwards account		NL	370

PURCHASES LEDGER

C. Bartlett

Dr			Cr	
£			£	
2.5	Returns outwards	RODB	45	
6.5	Returns outwards	RODB	45	
7.5	Returns outwards	RODB	90	

D. Perkins

Dr			Cr	
£			£	
4.5	Returns outwards	RODB	120	
7.5	Returns outwards	RODB	70	

NOMINAL LEDGER

Returns Outwards Account

Dr		Cr		
£		£		
		7.5	Returns RODB	370

UNIT ASSESSMENT QUESTION 1

(a) A. Maxwell - Sales Ledger; Rochdale Textiles - Purchases Ledger.
(b) Goods priced at £450 returned to Apex Promotional Products by a customer, A. Maxwell.
(c) £2,320 (£980 + £780 + £1,010 - £450).
(d) The entry has been posted from page 11 in the returns outwards day book.
(e) Repeated returns to the supplier.

UNIT ASSESSMENT QUESTION 2

(a) Reduce the amount owed by £600.

(b) and (c)

RETURNS OUTWARDS DAY BOOK 2000

Date	Supplier	Credit note no.	Folio	Amount
				£
4.8	Alvin Gem Supplies	046	PL	600.00
4.8	Transferred to Returns Outwards Account		NL	600.00

PURCHASES LEDGER

Dr		Alvin Gem Supplies		Cr
		£		£
4.8	Returns outwards RODB	600		

NOMINAL LEDGER

Dr		Returns Outwards Account		Cr
		£		£
			4.8	Returns RODB	600

UNIT 12

QUESTION 1

(a) Cheque counterfoil and cheque.

(b)

CASH BOOK

	Debit				Credit		
Date	Details	Cash	Bank	Date	Details	Cash	Bank
		£	£			£	£
12.4	Cleethorpes Motors		1,300	12.4	Ford Motors (012339)		2,850
12.4	Sales	120		12.4	Wages	1,200	
12.4	P. Linton		450	12.4	Insurance (012340)		350
				12.4	Advertising (012341)		280

QUESTION 2

(a)

SALES LEDGER

Dr		W. Simpkins (page 9)		Cr
		£		£
			12.8	Bank CB12	1,110

Dr		Bentham's (page 7)		Cr
		£		£
			15.8	Bank CB12	1,780

PURCHASES LEDGER

Dr		W. B. Jones (page 41)		Cr
		£		£
18.8	Bank CB12	3,450		

NOMINAL LEDGER

Dr		Rent Account (page 23)		Cr
		£		£
16.8	Bank CB12	1,000		

Dr		Motor Expenses Account (page 18)		Cr
		£		£
20.8	Cash CB12	26		

(b) The double entry is in the sales ledger:

(c) The double entry would be a credit in the sales account in the nominal ledger:

QUESTION 3

(a)

CASH BOOK (Dave Smith)

	Debit					Credit			
Date	Details	Discounts allowed	Cash	Bank	Date	Details	Discounts received	Cash	Bank
		£	£	£			£	£	£
5.12	Halesowen Carpets	25		475	6.12	P. Hunter (002220)	10		190
8.12	Cash		100		8.12	Bank			100

(b) A contra entry in the cash book is when there is a transfer between the cash and bank accounts. In this case, £100 was transferred from the bank account to the cash account.

UNIT ASSESSMENT QUESTION 1

(a) 5% to her customer; 10% from her supplier:

(b)

NOMINAL LEDGER

Dr	Discounts Allowed Account (page 21)		Cr
	£		£
18.3 Cash book CB102	25		

Dr	Discounts Received Account (page 22)		Cr
	£		£
		18.3 Cash book CB102	10

SALES LEDGER

Dr	A. McDonald (page 31)		Cr
	£		£
		13.3 Bank CB102	475
		13.3 Discount CB102	25

PURCHASES LEDGER

Dr	W. Willis (page 42)		Cr
	£		£
17.3 Bank CB102	90		
17.3 Discount CB102	10		

UNIT ASSESSMENT QUESTION 2

(a)

NOMINAL LEDGER

Dr	Motor Expenses Account (page 2)		Cr
	£		£
29.10 Cash CB41	54		

Dr	Discounts Allowed Account (page 3)		Cr
	£		£
30.10 Cash book CB41	120		

Dr	Discounts Received Account (page 4)		Cr
	£		£
		30.10 Cash book CB41	75

SALES LEDGER

Dr	Watkins Toys (page 16)		Cr
	£		£
		24.10 Bank CB41	380
		24.10 Discount CB41	20

Dr	Forest Cycles (page 23)		Cr
	£		£
		27.10 Bank CB41	1,900
		27.10 Discount CB41	100

PURCHASES LEDGER

Dr	Olton Racers (page 6)		Cr
	£		£
25.10 Bank CB41	760		
25.10 Discount CB41	40		

Dr	Smith & Son (page 51)		Cr
	£		£
28.10 Bank CB41	665		
28.10 Discount CB41	35		

(b) It is a cash payment for an expenses item.

UNIT 13

QUESTION 1

(a) and (b)

Debit					PETTY CASH BOOK					Credit		
Receipts	Folio	Date	Details	Voucher no.	Total payments	Petrol	Postage	Cleaning	Sundry expenses	Stationery	Folio	Ledger account
£					£	£	£	£	£	£		£
100.00	CB	12.6	Stamps	87	5.40		5.40					
		13.6	Petrol	88	48.00	48.00						
		14.6	Charity	89	5.00				5.00			
		14.6	Repairs	90	35.00				35.00			
		15.6	Envelopes	91	8.50					8.50		
100.00	CB	16.6	Cleaning materials	92	18.00			18.00				
		16.6			119.90	48.00	5.40	18.00	40.00	8.50		
200.00												

UNIT ASSESSMENT QUESTION 1

(a) It avoids posting every transaction to the ledgers.

(b) (i) and (ii)

PETTY CASH BOOK

Receipts £	Folio	Date	Details	Voucher no.	Total payments £	Travel expenses £	Cleaning £	Sundry expenses £	Stationery £	Folio	Ledger account £
100.00	CB	2.10	Post Office	43	3.50			3.50			
		3.10	Petrol	44	12.00	12.00					
		5.10	Stationery	45	32.80				32.80		
		10.10	Taxi	46	21.00	21.00					
		11.10	Window cleaner	47	13.00		13.00				
100.00	CB	12.10									
		13.10	Gardener	48	50.00			50.00			
		13.10	Cleaning materials	49	20.00		20.00				
					152.30	33.00	33.00	53.50	32.80		
200.00											

UNIT ASSESSMENT QUESTION 2

(a)

CASH BOOK (page 31)

Debit						Credit					
Date	Details	Folio	Cash £	Bank £			Date	Details	Folio	Cash £	Bank £
							10.7		PCB9		100
							14.7		PCB9		100

QUESTION 2

(a) (i) It is the amount of cash withdrawn from the bank and paid into the petty cash box.

(ii) It is a cash payment to a supplier of goods.

(b) and (c)

PETTY CASH BOOK (page 28)

Receipts £	Folio	Date	Details	Voucher no.	Total payments £	Travel expenses £	Cleaning £	Sundry expenses £	Stationery £	Folio	Ledger account £
300.00	CB7	12.3									
		14.3	Train fare	65	54.80	54.80					
		14.3	Pens, pencils	66	4.90				4.90		
		15.3	Taxi fare	67	11.00	11.00					
		16.3	B. Milton & Co	68	22.00					PL16	22.00
		17.3	Cleaning fluids	69	25.00		25.00				
		17.3	Padlock	70	12.50			12.50			
		17.3	Ink cartridge	71	13.80				13.80		
		17.3			144.00	65.80	25.00	12.50	18.70		22.00
300.00						NL19	NL8	NL21	NL32		
300.00											

NOMINAL LEDGER

Travel Expenses Account (page 19)

Dr			£	Cr	£
17.3	Petty cash PCB28		65.80		

Cleaning Account (page 8)

Dr			£	Cr	£
17.3	Petty cash PCB28		25.00		

Sundry Expenses Account (page 21)

Dr			£	Cr	£
17.3	Petty cash PCB28		12.50		

Stationery Account (page 32)

Dr			£	Cr	£
17.3	Petty cash PCB28		18.70		

PURCHASES LEDGER

B. Milton & Co (page 16)

Dr			£	Cr	£
17.3	Petty cash PCB28		22.00		

QUESTION 2

(a) Because it represents an increase in an asset.

(b)

CASH BOOK (page 1)

Debit						Credit					
Date	Details	Folio	Cash	Bank		Date	Details	Folio	Cash	Bank	
			£	£					£	£	
10.6	Capital	NL2		5,000							

NOMINAL LEDGER
Capital Account (page 2)

Dr				Cr		
						£
				10.6	Bank CB1	5,000

QUESTION 3

(a) and (b)

JOURNAL

Date	Details	Folio	Debit	Credit
			£	£
14.8	Cash	CB	2,000	
	Bank	CB	2,000	
	Capital	NL		4,000
	Assets and liabilities at the start of business			
15.8	Van	NL	1,350	
	Watford Van Sales	NL		1,350
	Purchase of van			

PETTY CASH BOOK (page 9)

Receipts	Folio	Date	Details	Voucher no.	Total payments	Motor expenses	Sundry expenses	Stationery	Folio	Ledger account
£					£	£	£	£		£
100.00	CB31	10.7	Envelopes	22	6.80			6.80		
		11.7	Petrol	23	25.00	25.00				
		11.7	Tea and coffee	24	8.50		8.50			
		12.7	Milk bill	25	18.30		18.30			
		13.7	Petrol	26	34.00	34.00				
100.00	CB31	14.7	T. Burton Ltd	27	23.50				PL6	23.50
		14.7	Meal with client	28	29.80		29.80			
					145.90	59.00	56.60	6.80		23.50
200.00						NLI2	NLI8	NLI7		

NOMINAL LEDGER
Motor Expenses Account (page 12)

Dr				Cr	
		£			£
14.7	Petty cash PCB9	59.00			

Sundry Expenses Account (page 18)

Dr				Cr	
		£			£
14.7	Petty cash PCB9	56.60			

Stationery Account (page 17)

Dr				Cr	
		£			£
14.7	Petty cash PCB9	6.80			

PURCHASES LEDGER
T. Burton Ltd (page 6)

Dr				Cr	
		£			£
14.7	Petty cash PCB 9	23.50			

UNIT 14

QUESTION 1

(a) Van purchase; error correction; loan repayment.

(b) Sale of signs - sales day book; purchase of goods - purchases day book; goods returned to supplier - returns outwards day book; cash sale - cash book.

QUESTION 1

(a)

SALES LEDGER

Roberts Gymnasium

Dr						Cr
	£					£
3.4	Sales	220	30.4	Bank		836
10.4	Sales	187				
16.4	Sales	199				
23.4	Sales	230				
		836				

Kendal Beauty Centre

Dr						Cr
	£					£
17.4	Sales	228	30.4	Bank		228

(b) When there is just one, equal entry on each side of the account, the only action required to balance the account is to double underline both sides.

QUESTION 2

(a)

SALES LEDGER

Benny Dodds

Dr						Cr
	£					£
1.7	Sales	280	18.7	Bank		500
4.7	Sales	230	28.7	Bank		450
9.7	Sales	389	31.7	Balance c/d		210
19.7	Sales	261				
		1,160				1,160
1.8	Balance b/d	210				

(b) It shows that the Tile Warehouse is owed £210 by Benny Dodds.

QUESTION 3

(a)

NOMINAL LEDGER

Property Repairs Account

Dr						Cr
	£					£
12.2	Bank	2,500	28.2	Balance c/d		2,500
1.3	Balance b/d	2,500				

(b) The narrative serves as a reminder of the transaction. It also helps trace source documents.
The folio entries show to which ledger accounts the details are posted.

UNIT ASSESSMENT QUESTION 1

(a)

JOURNAL

Date	Details	Folio	Debit	Credit
			£	£
23.3	Computer	NL	2,500	
	Kidlington Computers	NL		2,500
	Purchase of computer			
	model no DS99747			
27.3	T. Jackson	SL	350	
	P. Johnson	SL		350
	Correction of mispost			

(b) To correct an error and to show accurately who owed money.

UNIT ASSESSMENT QUESTION 2

(a)

CASH BOOK (page 12)

	Debit					Credit			
Date	Details	Folio	Cash	Bank	Date	Details	Folio	Cash	Bank
2001			£	£	2001			£	£
21.2	Loan account	NL28		3,000	21.2	Bank	CB12		3,000

NOMINAL LEDGER

Loan Account (page 28)

Dr				Cr
	£			£
		21.2	Bank CB12	3,000

Oven Account (page 10)

Dr				Cr
	£			£
2001				
25.2	Cooker Warehouse NL15	1,450		

Cooker Warehouse (page 15)

Dr				Cr
	£			£
		2001		
		25.2	Oven NL10	1,450

(b) The balances mean that Holgate Sports has £160 cash in hand and £143 in the bank.

UNIT ASSESSMENT QUESTION 1

(a)

PURCHASES LEDGER

Rode Heath Farm

Dr			£	Cr			£
13.6	Bank		1,000	1.6	Balance b/d		1,760
15.6	Purchases returns		180	6.6	Purchases		345
27.6	Bank		500	18.6	Purchases		480
30.6	Balance c/d		905				
			2,585				2,585
				1.7	Balance b/d		905

Prenton Farm

Dr			£	Cr			£
30.6	Bank		1,340	1.6	Balance b/d		1,340
30.6	Balance c/d		1,490	19.6	Purchases		1,490
			2,830				2,830
				1.7	Balance b/d		1,490

San Pedro Foods

Dr			£	Cr			£
17.6	Bank		2,000	1.6	Balance b/d		1,970
28.6	Bank		2,000	9.6	Purchases		1,870
30.6	Balance c/d		1,380	18.6	Purchases		1,540
			5,380				5,380
				1.7	Balance b/d		1,380

NOMINAL LEDGER

Telephone Account

Dr			£	Cr			£
1.6	Balance b/d		231	30.6	Balance c/d		509
23.6	Bank		278				
			509				509
1.7	Balance b/d		509				

Insurance Account

Dr			£	Cr			£
26.6	Bank		1,270	30.6	Balance c/d		1,270
1.7	Balance b/d		1,270				

3(a) continued

Sales Account

Dr			£	Cr			£
28.2	Balance c/d		3,520	1.2	Balance b/d		2,100
				14.2	Cash sales		990
				26.2	Credit sales		430
			3,520				3,520
				1.3	Balance b/d		3,520

Capital Account

Dr			£	Cr			£
28.2	Balance c/d		134,210	1.2	Balance b/d		132,210
				4.2	Bank		2,000
			134,210				134,210
				1.3	Balance b/d		134,210

(b) Property repairs account - £2,500 has been spent on property repairs. Sales account - the value of sales to date is £3,520. Capital account - the value of capital provided by Gerald and Ruby Armstrong is £134,210.

QUESTION 4

(a)

CASH BOOK

Debit					Credit				
Date	Details	Cash	Bank		Date	Details	Cash	Bank	
		£	£				£	£	
1.5	Balances b/d	120	320		1.5	T. Winters		320	
5.5	Sales	150			4.5	Eastern Electricity		145	
11.5	B. Gall		730		12.5	Soccer Supplies		250	
18.5	Terry Sports		520		16.5	Petty cash	200		
22.5	Sales	90			22.5	Royal Insurance		129	
28.5	B. Foster		510		23.5	Fullers Footwear		340	
31.5	T. Wells		488		31.5	Wages		1,000	
					31.5	Buttermead Sports		241	
					31.5	Balance c/d	160	143	
		360	2,568				360	2,568	
1.6	Balances b/d	160	143						

Loan Account

Dr			Cr	
	£			£
12.6 Bank	5,500	1.6	Balance b/d	5,500

(b) The balances will be used to produce a trial balance which helps check the bookkeeping and is an interim stage in producing the final accounts.

UNIT ASSESSMENT QUESTION 2

(a)

CASH BOOK

Debit

Date	Details	Cash £	Bank £
2.1	Balances b/d	150	3,490
3.1	Sales	230	650
4.1	L. Jones		258
4.1	Sales	165	440
5.1	National Rec.		1,800
7.1	Sales	120	750
		665	7,388
9.1	Balances b/d	319	3,688

Credit

Date	Details	Cash £	Bank £
3.1	Devon CC		890
4.1	CD Motors	124	320
4.1	Bensons		
6.1	Devon Cars	87	
6.1	Wages		2,490
6.1	Petty cash	135	
8.1	Balances c/d	319	3,688
		665	7,388

(b)

PETTY CASH BOOK

Receipts £	Date	Details	Voucher	Total £	Drawings £	Carriage £	Stationery £	Sundries £	Folio	Ledger £
200.00	2.1	Balance b/d								
	2.1	Paper	15	21.50			21.50			
	2.1	L. Miles	16	20.00	20.00					
	3.1	Coffee	17	2.70				2.70		
	3.1	Carriage	18	12.00		12.00				
	4.1	L. Miles	19	30.00	30.00					
	5.1	T. Peel	20	11.50					PL5	11.50
	6.1	Carriage	21	12.30		12.30				
	6.1	L. Miles	22	20.00	20.00					
	6.1	Milk	23	5.00				5.00		
				135.00	70.00	24.30	21.50	7.70		11.50
135.00	6.1	Cash								
	8.1	Balance c/d		200.00						
335.00				335.00						
200.00	9.1	Balance b/d								

(c) To check the book balances with actual balances and to produce a bank reconciliation statement.

UNIT 16

QUESTION 1

(a) Interest received: £141; total credits: £27,628.

(b) Interest received: £341; total credits and total debits: £27,828.

QUESTION 2

(a) and (b)

Bank Account

Dr				Cr	
		£			£
2.6	Capital	2,000	9.6	Machine	1,000
21.6	Sales	250	30.6	Purchases	100
			30.6	Balance c/d	1,150
		2,250			2,250
1.7	Balance b/d	1,150			

Capital Account

Dr				Cr	
		£			£
30.6	Balance c/d	2,000	2.6	Bank	2,000
		2,000			2,000
			1.7	Balance b/d	2,000

QUESTION 3

Castleford Bearings Ltd
Trial Balance as at 30.6.00

	Dr £	Cr £
Sales		5,466,891
Purchases	4,070,615	
Staff wages	981,990	
Directors' wages	400,000	
Factory overheads	127,098	
Bank charges	3,422	
Bank interest	24,870	
Machinery	300,000	
Sundry expenses	12,000	
Trade debtors	143,222	
Trade creditors		345,887
Bank deposit	23,561	
Bank loan		224,000
Capital		50,000
	6,086,778	6,086,778

Machine Account

Dr		£	Cr		£
9.6	Bank	1,000	30.6	Balance c/d	1,000
		1,000			1,000
1.7	Balance b/d	1,000			

Purchases Account

Dr		£	Cr		£
16.6	Trade creditor	200	30.6	Balance c/d	300
30.6	Bank	100			
		300			300
1.7	Balance b/d	300			

Trade Creditors Account

Dr		£	Cr		£
30.6	Balance c/d	200	16.6	Purchases	200
		200	1.7	Balance b/d	200
					200

Sales Account

Dr		£	Cr		£
30.6	Balance c/d	550	21.6	Bank	250
			25.6	Trade debtors	300
		550			550
			1.7	Balance b/d	550

Trade Debtors Account

Dr		£	Cr		£
25.6	Sales	300	30.6	Balance c/d	300
1.7	Balance b/d	300			

(c)

James Ashworth
Trial Balance as at 30.6.

	Dr £	Cr £
Bank	1,150	
Capital		2,000
Machine	1,000	
Purchases	300	
Trade creditors		200
Sales		550
Trade debtors	300	
	2,750	2,750

QUESTION 4

(a) Sales should be £98,321 and purchases should be £87,991.

(b) Errors might have arisen in extracting balances from ledgers. In the first case, there is a transposition error.

UNIT ASSESSMENT QUESTION 1

(a) and (b)

Bank Account

Dr		£	Cr		£
1.3	Capital	10,000	1.3	Rent	1,000
8.3	Sales	320	30.3	Leasing	200
30.3	Trade debtors	500	31.3	Balance c/d	9,620
		10,820			10,820
1.4	Balance b/d	9,620			

Purchases Account

Dr		£	Cr		£
3.3	Trade creditors	2,000	31.3	Balance c/d	2,450
20.3	Trade creditors	450			
		2,450			2,450
1.4	Balance b/d	2,450			

Trade Creditors Account

Dr	£	Cr	£
31.3 Balance c/d	2,450	3.3 Purchases	2,000
		20.3 Purchases	450
	2,450		2,450
		1.4 Balance b/d	2,450

Sales Account

Dr	£	Cr	£
31.3 Balance c/d	1,070	5.3 Trade debtors	190
		8.3 Bank	320
		14.3 Trade debtors	560
	1,070		1,070
		1.4 Balance b/d	1,070

Trade Debtors Account (Kent Taxis)

Dr	£	Cr	£
5.3 Sales	190	30.3 Bank	500
14.3 Sales	560	31.3 Balance c/d	250
	750		750
1.4 Balance b/d	250		

Capital Account

Dr	£	Cr	£
31.3 Balance c/d	10,000	1.3 Bank	10,000
	10,000		10,000
		1.4 Balance b/d	10,000

Rent Account

Dr	£	Cr	£
1.3 Bank	1,000	31.3 Balance c/d	1,000
1.4 Balance b/d	1,000		

Leasing Account

Dr	£	Cr	£
30.3 Bank	200	31.3 Balance c/d	200
1.4 Balance b/d	200		

(c)

Julian Arranovic and Barry Cairns
Trial Balance as at 31.3.01

	Dr £	Cr £
Bank	9,620	
Purchases	2,450	
Trade creditors		2,450
Sales		1,070
Trade debtors (Kent Taxis)	250	
Capital		10,000
Rent	1,000	
Leasing	200	
	13,520	13,520

(d) Error of omission; reversal of entries.

(e) The errors will not prevent the trial balance from balancing because they affect the debit and credit side by the same amounts.

(f) The first error will reduce sales (on the credit side) and bank (on the debit side) by £320. The second error will result in a reduced debit balance for purchases. It will fall by £900 to £1,550. The credit balance for trade creditors will also fall by £900 to £1,550. The effect of both errors on the trial balance will be to reduce the totals on the both sides of the trial balance to £12,300.

UNIT ASSESSMENT QUESTION 2

(a)

Slimwear Ltd
Trial Balance as at 31.1.00

	Dr £	Cr £
Sales		341,998
Purchases	223,900	
Purchase returns		21,001
Postage & packaging	23,776	
Advertising	65,990	
Wages	87,990	
Rent and rates	12,900	
Trade debtors	54,000	
Trade creditors		32,771
Interest paid	4,553	
Sundry expenses	2,991	
Bank overdraft		13,330
Bank loan		119,000
Director's salary	40,000	
Motor car	10,000	
Taxation paid	12,000	
Capital		10,000
	538,100	538,100

(b) Check additions; check that ledger balances are entered under the correct heading (Dr or Cr); check that all figures have been included; check for transposition if the difference is divisible by 9.

(c) (i) These errors are for exactly the same amounts (£1,000) on each side of the trial balance. Therefore the trial balance will still balance and the errors could go undetected.
(ii) The totals on both sides of the trial balance will rise by £1,000.

UNIT 17

QUESTION 1
(a) (i) £62,410 (ii) £65,510.
(b) (i) £60,430 (ii) £67,490.
(c) Because returns outwards represent goods sent back to the supplier, and so were never bought.

QUESTION 2
(a) (i) £67,300 (ii) £55,650.
(b) Net profit would fall by £430 because sales would fall by this amount.

QUESTION 3
(a) £267,280 (ii) £190,020 (£300,030 - £110,010).
(b) There is no entry under fixed assets for premises.
(c) £267,280.
(d) £57,790 (ie trade creditors plus loan).

UNIT ASSESSMENT QUESTION 1
(a)

Tom Brookes & Son
Trading Account for the year ended 31.12.01

	£	£	£
Sales			187,210
Opening stock		13,890	
Add purchases	96,340		
Carriage in	50		
Less returns outwards	610		
Net purchases		95,780	
Less closing stock		15,120	
Cost of sales			94,550
Gross profit			92,660

(b) £51,640 (£92,660 - £41,020).
(c) It is a means of assessing business performance, calculating tax, measuring growth and seeing how well overheads have been controlled.

UNIT ASSESSMENT QUESTION 2
(a) The business was worth approximately £78,490.
(b) Because drawings are higher than net profit.
(c)

Plantworld
Balance Sheet as at 31.8.01
(after new capital is introduced)

	£	£
Fixed assets		
Premises		120,000
Van		3,200
Equipment		2,100
		125,300
Current assets		
Stocks	4,200	
Debtors	12,800	
Cash at bank	4,550	
Cash in hand	250	
	21,800	
Less current liabilities		
Trade creditors	4,610	
Working capital		17,190
		142,490
Less long term liabilities		
Mortgage		56,000
Net assets		86,490
Financed by		
Opening capital		89,210
Add net profit		21,700
		110,910
Add new capital introduced		8,000
Less drawings		32,420
Capital employed		86,490

UNIT 18

QUESTION 1

(a)

Heather Davies
Trial Balance as at 31.12.01

	Debit	Credit	
	£	£	
Sales		110,050	Trading account
Purchases	72,990		Trading account
Opening stock	9,100		Trading account
Wages	6,300		Profit and loss
Telephone	430		Profit and loss
Motor expenses	590		Profit and loss
Light and heat	320		Profit and loss
Rates	670		Profit and loss
Sundry expenses	420		Profit and loss
Premises	46,000		
Fixtures and fittings	1,280		
Van	3,650		
Cash in hand	390		
Trade creditors		3,890	
Bank overdraft		430	
Capital		39,770	
Drawings	12,000		
	154,140	154,140	

Additional information: the value of closing stock on 31.12.01 was £10,320. *Trading account*

(b)

Heather Davies
Trading and Profit and Loss Account
for the year ended 31.12.01

	£	£
Sales		110,050
Opening stock	9,100	
Purchases	72,990	
	82,090	
Less closing stock	10,320	
Cost of sales		71,770
Gross profit		38,280
Less expenses		
Wages	6,300	
Telephone	430	
Motor expenses	590	
Light and heat	320	
Rates	670	
Sundry expenses	420	
		8,730
Net profit		29,550

QUESTION 2

(a)

Heather Davies
Trial Balance as at 31.12.01

	Debit	Credit	
	£	£	
Sales		110,050	
Purchases	72,990		
Opening stock	9,100		
Wages	6,300		
Telephone	430		
Motor expenses	590		
Light and heat	320		
Rates	670		
Sundry expenses	420		
Premises	46,000		Balance sheet (assets)
Fixtures and fittings	1,280		Balance sheet (assets)
Van	3,650		Balance sheet (assets)
Cash in hand	390		Balance sheet (assets)
Trade creditors		3,890	Balance sheet (liabilities)
Bank overdraft		430	Balance sheet (liabilities)
Capital		39,770	Balance sheet (capital)
Drawings	12,000		Balance sheet (drawings)
	154,140	154,140	

(b)

Heather Davies
Balance Sheet as at 31.12.01

	£	£
Fixed assets		
Premises		46,000
Fixtures and fittings		1,280
Van		3,650
		50,930
Current assets		
Stock	10,320	
Cash in hand	390	
	10,710	
Current liabilities		
Trade creditors	3,890	
Bank overdraft	430	
	4,320	
Working capital		6,390
Net assets		57,320
Financed by		
Opening capital		39,770
Add net profit		29,550
		69,320
Less drawings		12,000
Capital employed		57,320

(c) £57,320, ie the value of the business's net assets.

QUESTION 3

(a)

Dr Brenda Fortune
Trial Balance as at 31.12.01

	Debit	Credit	
	£	£	
Fees		132,800	Profit and loss
Secretarial fees	16,340		Profit and loss
Telephone	780		Profit and loss
Motor and travel expenses	4,200		Profit and loss
Lecture trip expenses	3,210		Profit and loss
Rates	890		Profit and loss
Insurance	1,290		Profit and loss
Subscriptions	410		Profit and loss
Light and heat	1,200		Profit and loss
Bank charges	210		Profit and loss
Freehold surgery and office	159,000		Balance sheet (assets)
Fixtures and fittings	11,910		Balance sheet (assets)
Motor vehicle	27,500		Balance sheet (assets)
Debtors	2,190		Balance sheet (assets)
Cash at bank	2,100		Balance sheet (assets)
Sundry creditors		1,270	Balance sheet (liabilities)
Mortgage		105,000	Balance sheet (liabilities)
Capital		21,040	Balance sheet (capital)
Drawings	28,880		Balance sheet (drawings)
	260,110	260,110	

(b)

Dr Brenda Fortune
Profit and Loss Account
for the year ended 31.12.01

	£	£
Fees		132,800
Less expenses		
Secretary's wages	16,340	
Telephone	780	
Motor and travel expenses	4,200	
Lecture trip expenses	3,210	
Rates	890	
Insurance	1,290	
Subscriptions	410	
Light and heat	1,200	
Bank charges	210	
		28,530
Net profit		104,270

UNIT ASSESSMENT QUESTION 1

(a)

Evans Fabrics
Trading and Profit and Loss Account
for the year ended 30.4.01

	£	£
Sales		181,400
Opening stock	25,610	
Purchases	121,020	
	146,630	
Less closing stock	28,560	
Cost of sales		118,070
Gross profit		63,330
Discounts received		2,410
		65,740
Less expenses		
Wages	21,890	
Motor expenses	4,120	
Heat and light	1,650	
Rent and rates	7,210	
Insurance	650	
Sundry expenses	2,190	
		37,710
Net profit		28,030

(c)

Dr Brenda Fortune
Balance Sheet as at 31.12.01

	£	£	£
Fixed assets			
Freehold property		159,000	
Fixtures and fittings		11,910	
Motor vehicle		27,500	
		198,410	
Current assets			
Debtors	2,190		
Cash at bank	2,100		
	4,290		
Current liabilities			
Sundry creditors	1,270		
Working capital		3,020	
		201,430	
Less long term liabilities			
Mortgage		105,000	
Net assets		96,430	
Financed by			
Opening capital		21,040	
Add net profit		104,270	
		125,310	
Less drawings		28,880	
Capital employed		96,430	

(b)

Evans Fabrics
Balance Sheet as at 30.4.01

	£	£
Fixed assets		
Fixtures and fittings		3,500
Motor vehicle		5,900
		9,400
Current assets		
Stock	28,560	
Cash at bank	2,530	
Cash in hand	670	
	31,760	
Current liabilities		
Trade creditors	15,070	
Working capital		16,690
Net assets		26,090
Financed by		
Opening capital		43,200
Add net profit		28,030
		71,230
Less drawings		45,140
Capital employed		26,090

(b)

Simon Parker
Balance Sheet as at 31.3.01

	£	£
Fixed assets		
Fixtures and fittings		1,870
Motor vehicle		18,600
Computer		2,600
		23,070
Current assets		
Debtors	2,840	
Cash at bank	3,100	
	5,940	
Current liabilities		
Sundry creditors	810	
Working capital		5,130
		28,200
Less long term liabilities		
Bank loan		3,500
Net assets		24,700
Financed by		
Opening capital		6,500
Add net profit		34,960
		41,460
Less drawings		16,760
Capital employed		24,700

UNIT ASSESSMENT QUESTION 2

(a)

Simon Parker
Profit and Loss Account
for the year ended 31.3.01

	£	£
Fees		42,810
Less expenses		
Rent	3,000	
Motor expenses	1,780	
Telephone	450	
Insurance	740	
Light and heat	680	
Rates	1,200	
		7,850
Net profit		34,960

UNIT 19

QUESTION 1

(a) The £3,500 that is owed to a regular supplier of goods; it is already accounted for.

(b) £600 (£300 for advertising, plus £300 for the electricity used in the current year).

(c) £2,300 (£1,800 rent, plus £500 bank interest for the 5 months of the current year).

(c) Because Simon Parker is a service provider; he does not buy raw materials or goods for resale. Therefore there are no cost of sales.

QUESTION 2

(a)

Telephone Account

Dr		£			Cr	£
2000				2000		
1.3	Bank	231		31.12	Balance c/d	752
6.6	Bank	310				
8.9	Bank	211				
		752				752
31.12	Balance b/d	752		31.12	Profit & loss	1,030
31.12	Balance c/d (accrual)	278				
		1,030				1,030
2001				2001		
1.1	Balance b/d	349		1.1	Balance b/d	278

(b)

Interest Received Account

Dr		£			Cr	£
2000				2000		
31.12	Balance c/d	312		2.7	Bank	312
		312				312
31.12	Profit & loss	661		31.12	Balance b/d	661
				31.12	Balance c/d (accrual)	349
		661				661
2001						
1.1	Balance b/d	349				

Muscles
Trial Balance as at 31.12.00 (extract)

	Dr £	Cr £
Telephone	1,030	
Telephone accrued		278
Interest received		661
Interest accrued	349	

(c)

QUESTION 3

(a) Rent prepayment: £1,000; insurance prepayment: £100.

(b)

Rent Account

Dr		£			Cr	£
2000				2000		
2.2	Bank	4,000		31.12	Balance c/d	13,000
2.5	Bank	3,000				
3.8	Bank	3,000				
1.11	Bank	3,000				
		13,000				13,000
31.12	Balance b/d	13,000		31.12	Profit & loss	12,000
				31.12	Balance c/d (prepayment)	1,000
		13,000				13,000
2001						
1.1	Balance b/d	1,000				

(c)

Insurance Account

Dr		£			Cr	£
2000				2000		
1.3	Bank	600		31.12	Balance c/d	600
						600
31.12	Balance b/d	600		31.12	Profit & loss	500
				31.12	Balance c/d (prepayment)	100
		600				600
2001						
1.1	Balance b/d	100				

UNIT ASSESSMENT QUESTION 1

(a) 3/12 (or 1/4) × £2,400 = £600.

(b) 2/3 × £180 = £120.

(c) Prepayment reduces total business rates expense to £1,800. Accrued expense raises total electricity expense to £660.

(d)

Stellios Panopoulos
Trial Balance as at 31.12.00 (extract)

	Dr £	Cr £
Rates	1,800	
Prepayment	600	
Electricity	660	
Electricity accrued		120

(e) A prepayment is an asset.

(f) An accrued expense is a liability.

UNIT ASSESSMENT QUESTION 2

(a)

Veterinary Fees Account

Dr			Cr	
	£	2001		£
2001		30.6 Profit & loss		4,630
30.6 Balance b/d	4,390			
30.6 Balance c/d (accrual)	240			
	4,630			4,630
		1.7 Balance b/d		240

(b)

Rent Received Account

Dr			Cr	
	£	2001		£
2001		30.6 Balance b/d		6,000
30.6 Profit & loss	7,200	30.6 Balance c/d (accrual)		1,200
	7,200			7,200
		1.7 Balance b/d		1,200

(c)

Equipment Leasing Account

Dr			Cr	
	£	2001		£
2001		30.6 Profit & loss		3,100
30.6 Balance b/d	2,500	30.6 Balance c/d (prepayment)		600
	3,100			3,100
1.7 Balance b/d	600			

(d)

Hallatrow Farm
Trial Balance as at 30.6.01 (extract)

	Dr	Cr
	£	£
Veterinary fees	4,630	
Vet fees accrued		240
Rent received		7,200
Rent accrued	1,200	
Equipment lease	2,500	
Lease prepayment	600	

UNIT 20

QUESTION 1

(a)

T. Walters

Dr			Cr	
	£			£
23.5 Sales	800	12.11 Bank		500
		31.12 Bad debts		300
	800			800

Gregsons

Dr			Cr	
	£			£
6.1 Sales	178	4.5 Bank		178
12.3 Sales	291	12.7 Bank		291
26.8 Sales	110	31.12 Bad debts		110
	579			579

(b)

Bad Debts Account

Dr			Cr	
	£			£
31.12 T.Walters	300	31.12 Profit and loss		410
31.12 Gregsons	110			
	410			410

(c) Profit is reduced by £410.

QUESTION 2

(a) It might be difficult and time consuming to identify specific doubtful debts.

(b) £375.

(c)

Profit and Loss Account

Dr		Cr
	£	£
31.5 Provision for doubtful debts	375	

Provision for Doubtful Debts

Dr		Cr	
	£	2000	
		31.5 Profit and loss	375

(d) Profit will fall by £375.

QUESTION 3

(a) £1,140 (ie 3% x £38,000).

(b) Increase of £240 (ie £1,140 - £900).

(c)

Dr		Provision for Doubtful Debts		Cr
2000	£	2000		£
31.12 Balance c/d	900	31.12 Profit and loss		900
		2001		
		1.1 Balance b/d		900
		31.12 Profit and loss		240
		(increase in provision)		

(d)

Dr		Profit and Loss Account	Cr
2001	£		£
31.12 Provision for doubtful debts	240		

UNIT ASSESSMENT QUESTION 1

(a)

Dr		Peter Collins		Cr
2000	£	2001		£
10.9 Sales	890	31.8 Bad debts		890

Dr		Fishmart		Cr
2000	£	2000		£
6.9 Sales	228	4.12 Bank		228
2001		2001		
12.1 Sales	333	12.4 Bank		333
26.5 Sales	120	31.8 Bad debts		120
	681			681

(b)

Dr		Bad Debts Account		Cr
2001	£	2001		£
31.8 Peter Collins	890	31.8 Profit and loss		1,010
31.8 Fishmart	120			
	1,010			1,010

(c)

Dr		Peter Collins		Cr
2001	£	2001		£
10.9 Sales	890	31.8 Bad debts		890
		21.11 Bank		890

Dr		Bad Debts Recovered Account		Cr
2001	£	2001		£
21.11 Bad debts recovered	890	21.11 Peter Collins		890

Dr		Bank Account		Cr
2001	£			£
21.11 Peter Collins	890			

UNIT ASSESSMENT QUESTION 2

(a) To calculate the provision for doubtful debts for Devon Plant Hire, it is necessary to determine the total amount owed in each time period.

AGED DEBTORS SCHEDULE

Account	Customer	Balance £	Current £	30+days £	60+days £	90+days £
EN11	Ensor	230.00	230.00			
BL16	Blacks	870.00	370.00	300.00	200.00	
ER29	Eric Jones	340.00				340.00
TA65	Taunton KVB	2,890.00	1,690.00	1,200.00		
LI57	Lister Bros	300.00		300.00		
VA49	VA Builders	2,800.00	1,200.00	1,200.00		400.00
WI10	Wilson	980.00	400.00	280.00	300.00	
		8,410.00	3,890.00	3,280.00	500.00	740.00

The next step is to multiply the total debt in each column by the estimated percentage of doubtful debts. These are then added to get the total. This is shown below.

Current	£3,890	× 1%	=	£38.90
31-60 days	£3,280	× 3%	=	£98.40
61-90 days	£500	× 5%	=	£25.00
90+ days	£740	× 10%	=	£74.00
Total provision for doubtful debts				**£236.30**

(b)

Dr		Profit and Loss Account	Cr
	£		£
31.12 Provision for doubtful debts	236.30		

Dr		Provision for Doubtful Debts		Cr
	£			£
		31.12 Profit and loss		236.30

(c) Past experience of real bad debts.

(c)

Year	Cost of fixtures £	Annual depreciation charge £	Accumulated depreciation £	Net book value £
1	20,000	4,000	4,000	16,000
2		4,000	8,000	12,000
3		4,000	12,000	8,000
4		4,000	16,000	4,000
5		4,000	20,000	0

(d) Wear and tear, obsolescence, inadequacy.

QUESTION 2
(a)

Year	Cost of vehicle £	Annual depreciation charge £	Accumulated depreciation £	Net book value £
1	12,000	4,800 (12,000 × 40%)	4,800	7,200
2		2,880 (7,200 × 40%)	7,680	4,320
3		1,728 (4,320 × 40%)	9,408	2,592
4		1,037 (2,592 × 40%)	10,445	1,555

(b) Reducing balance method gives a higher depreciation charge in early years. Straight line method gives the same depreciation charge every year. The reducing balance more accurately reflects the actual value of vehicles such as Jennifer's taxi.

QUESTION 3
(a)

Year	Cost of truck £	Annual depreciation charge £	Accumulated depreciation £	Net book value £
1	25,000	8,000 (24,000 × 5/15)	8,000	17,000
2		6,400 (24,000 × 4/15)	14,400	10,600
3		4,800 (24,000 × 3/15)	19,200	5,800
4		3,200 (24,000 × 2/15)	22,400	2,600
5		1,600 (24,000 × 1/15)	24,000	1,000

(d) The weights used by Devon Plant Hire take into account the greater likelihood of old debts becoming bad.

(e) Because the value of total debtors is likely to change.

(f) Risky customers will not obtain credit. More accurate records might be kept. More pressure might be applied on customers to pay.

UNIT 21

QUESTION 1
(a) Properties: £5,064m (£5,968m - £904m); fixtures, equipment, vehicles: £1,499m (£3,664 - £2,165m).

(b) Land, supermarket buildings, vehicles, fixtures, fixtures and fittings within the supermarkets.

(c) (i) They have physical substance. (ii) They will be used for more than 1 year.

QUESTION 2
(a) Tangible: physical, can be touched, eg BT's telephone lines, British Rail's trains and track. Intangible: non-physical eg mobile phone frequencies, information in databases.

(b) The value is determined by the price someone is willing to pay. In this case, the mobile phone licenses were sold for £20bn. It is possible that intangible assets owned by the BBC might be worth £4bn, but this could not be certain until the offer was made and accepted.

UNIT ASSESSMENT QUESTION 1
(a) £1.74bn (11.6% × £15bn).

(b) The famous brand names help retain customer loyalty.

(c) The value could fall sharply.

(d) Subsidiary companies that provide raw materials or produce the brands in different countries.

UNIT ASSESSMENT QUESTION 2
(a) It provides detailed information about each asset. Allows regular checks to identify any missing assets.

(b) Transit van - it has been sold and its sale price is shown.

(c) The £400,000 represents the value of intangible assets. Most or all of this will be goodwill.

(d) By generating more regular custom, by improving the image and reputation of the hotel by advertising, and by raising the standard of customer service.

UNIT 22

QUESTION 1
(a) £4,000 (£20,000 - £0)/5.

(b) 20% (£4,000/£20,000) × 100.

(b)

Year	Historical cost /revaluation £	Annual depreciation charge £	Net book value £
1995	140,000	5,600	134,400
1996	140,000	5,600	128,800
1997	140,000	5,600	123,200
1998	140,000	5,600	117,600
1999	140,000	5,600	112,000
2000	220,000	11,000	209,000
2001	220,000	11,000	198,000
2002	220,000	11,000	187,000
2003	220,000	11,000	176,000
2004	220,000	11,000	165,000

(c) Because they sometimes rise in value and the balance sheet should show a 'true and fair' view of the business's assets.

(d) The annual depreciation charge and the net book value of the tractor for two years is shown in the table below.

Year	Cost of tractor £	Annual depreciation charge £	Accumulated depreciation £	Net book value £
1	30,000	9,000 (30,000 × 30%)	9,000	21,000
2		6,300 (21,000 × 30%)	15,300	14,700

According to the table, the net book value of the tractor is currently £14,700.

(e) Milking equipment, plough, other vehicles.

UNIT 23

QUESTION 1

(a) £1,200 (30% × £4,000).

(b) Profit: £900 (£11,500 - £10,600).

(c) Net book value at the end of year 2: £15,400 (£25,000 - (2 × £4,800)). Loss on disposal: £3,900 (£11,500 - £15,400).

(d) The straight line method results in a loss because the net book value of the truck is higher in the early years.

UNIT ASSESSMENT QUESTION 1

(a) The annual depreciation charge and the net book value for one of the lorries is shown for three years in the table below.

Year	Cost of lorry £	Annual depreciation charge £	Accumulated depreciation £	Net book value £
1	40,000	16,000 (40,000 × 40%)	16,000	24,000
2		9,600 (24,000 × 40%)	25,600	14,400
3		5,760 (14,400 × 40%)	31,360	8,640

According to the information in the table, the net book value of the two year old lorries is £14,400 each. The book value of the three year old lorry is £8,640.

(b) The annual depreciation charge and the net book value of the van is shown for three years in the table below.

Year	Cost of van £	Annual depreciation charge £	Accumulated depreciation £	Net book value £
1	20,000	8,000 (20,000 × 40%)	8,000	12,000
2		4,800 (12,000 × 40%)	12,800	7,200
3		2,880 (7,200 × 40%)	15,680	4,320

According to the table, the current book value of the van is £4,320.

(c) Profit: £180 (£4,500 - £4,320).

(d) Annual depreciation charge: £100 ((£2,200 - £200)/20).

(e) Vehicles and furniture depreciate at different rates.

UNIT ASSESSMENT QUESTION 2

(a) (i) £5,600 ((£140,000 - £0)/25). (ii) £11,000 ((£220,000 - £0)/20).

(b)

Dr	Sewing Machine Account		Cr
	£		£
2000			
1.1 Bank	4,000		

Dr	Provision for Depreciation (Sewing Machine) Account		Cr
	£		£
		2000	
		31.12 Profit and loss	1,200

(c)

Dr	Sewing Machine Account		Cr
	£		£
2000		2000	
1.1 Bank	4,000	31.12 Balance c/d	4,000
2001			
1.1 Balance b/d	4,000		

Dr	Provision for Depreciation (Sewing Machine) Account		Cr
	£		£
2000		2000	
31.12 Balance c/d	1,200	31.12 Profit and loss	1,200
		2001	
		1.1 Balance b/d	1,200

QUESTION 2

(a)

Dr	Furniture and Fittings Account		Cr
	£		£
2000		2000	
1.2 Bank	9,200	31.12 Balance c/d	9,200
2001		2001	
1.1 Balance b/d	9,200	31.12 Balance c/d	9,200
2002			
1.1 Balance b/d	9,200		

Dr	Provision for Depreciation (Furniture and Fittings) Account		Cr
	£		£
2000		2000	
31.12 Balance c/d	920	31.12 Profit and loss	920
2001		2001	
31.12 Balance c/d	1,840	1.1 Balance b/d	920
		31.12 Profit and loss	920
			1,840
		2002	
		1.1 Balance b/d	1,840

Dr	Taxi Account		Cr
	£		£
2000		2000	
1.8 Bank	15,000	31.12 Balance c/d	15,000
2001		2001	
1.1 Balance b/d	15,000	31.12 Balance c/d	15,000
2002			
1.1 Balance b/d	15,000		

Dr	Provision for Depreciation (Taxi) Account		Cr
	£		£
2000		2000	
31.12 Balance c/d	3,000	31.12 Profit and loss	3,000
2001		2001	
31.12 Balance c/d	7,800	1.1 Balance b/d	3,000
		31.12 Profit and loss	4,800
			7,800
		2002	
		1.1 Balance b/d	7,800

(b)

Wasim Ahmed
Balance Sheet (extract) as at 31.12.01

	Historical cost	Depreciation to date	Net book value
Fixed asset	£	£	£
Furniture and fittings	9,200	1,840	7,360
Taxi	15,000	7,800	7,200

QUESTION 3

(a) Net book value on 31.12.2000 was £3,000 less accumulated depreciation (£2,000 + £500) = £500. So profit was £100 (£600 - £500).

(b)

Dr	Machine Account		Cr
	£		£
2000		2000	
1.1 Balance b/d	3,000	31.12 Disposal of machine	3,000

Dr	Provision for Depreciation (Machine) Account		Cr
	£		£
2000		2000	
31.12 Disposal of machine	2,500	1.1 Balance b/d	2,000
		31.12 Profit and loss	500
	2,500		2,500

3(b) continued

Disposal of Machine Account

Dr		£	Cr		£
2000			2000		
31.12	Machine	3,000	31.12	Provision for depreciation	2,500
31.12	Profit and loss	100	31.12	Bank	600
		3,100			3,100

UNIT ASSESSMENT QUESTION 1

(a) At 31.12.00 depreciation charge: £1,600; net book value: £2,400. At 31.12.01 accumulated depreciation charge: £2,560; net book value: £1,440.

(b) £840 loss (£600 - £1,440).

(c)

Computer Account

Dr		£	Cr		£
2000			2000		
1.1	Bank	4,000	31.12	Balance c/d	4,000

Dr   Provision for Depreciation (Computer) Account   Cr

		£			£
2000			2000		
31.12	Balance c/d	1,600	31.12	Profit and loss	1,600

Computer Account

Dr		£	Cr		£
2000			2000		
1.1	Balance b/d	4,000	31.12	Balance c/d	4,000
2001			2001		
1.1	Balance b/d	4,000	31.12	Disposal of computer	4,000

Dr   Provision for Depreciation (Computer) Account   Cr

		£			£
2000			2000		
31.12	Balance c/d	1,600	31.12	Profit and loss	1,600
2001			2001		
31.12	Disposal of computer	2,560	1.1	Balance b/d	1,600
			31.12	Profit and loss	960
		2,560			2,560

(d)

Disposal of Computer Account

Dr		£	Cr		£
2001			2001		
31.12	Computer	4,000	31.12	Provision for depreciation	2,560
			31.12	Bank	600
			31.12	Profit and loss	840
		4,000			4,000

UNIT ASSESSMENT QUESTION 2

(a)

Cutting Machine Account

Dr		£	Cr		£
2001			2001		
1.1	Balance b/d	32,000	31.12	Disposal of cutting machine	32,000
31.12	Disposal of cutting machine	5,000	31.12	Balance c/d	45,000
31.12	Bank	40,000			
		45,000			45,000

Provision for Depreciation (Cutting Machine) Account

Dr		£	Cr		£
2001			2001		
31.12	Disposal of cutting machine (part-exchange)	24,000	1.1	Balance b/d	16,000
			31.12	Profit and loss	8,000
		24,000			24,000

Dr   Disposal of Cutting Machine Account   Cr

		£			£
2001			2001		
31.12	Cutting machine	32,000	31.12	Provision for depreciation	24,000
			31.12	Cutting machine	5,000
			31.12	Profit and loss	3,000
		32,000			32,000

(b)

Extended Trial Balance as at 31.12.00 (extract)

	Ledger balances		Adjustments	
	Dr £	Cr £	Dr £	Cr £
Cutting machine - at cost	32,000			
Depreciation charge for the year			8,000	
Provision for depreciation		8,000		8,000

UNIT 24

QUESTION 1

(a) Goods for resale.

(b) All of the cars owned by Steve Westwood's business should be valued at cost except for one. The NRV (£1,500) of the Fiat Brava is £400 lower than cost (£1,900). Therefore, the value of closing stock for Steve Westwood's business is £14,200 (£14,600 - £400). This values all cars at cost except for the Fiat Brava which is valued at NRV.

(c) £14,200.

(d) Raises it by £100, assuming that the car can be repaired and sold for more than £2,400.

QUESTION 2

(a) (i) According to the calculations below, when the FIFO method of stock valuation is applied, the value of closing stock for Sorensen Mills is £2,400.

Date	Stock received			Stock issued			Stock valuation			
	Qty tonnes	Price £	Value £	Qty tonnes	Price £	Value £	Qty tonnes	Price £	Value £	Total £
3.4	20	100	2,000				20	100	2,000	2,000
10.4	40	110	4,400				20	100	2,000	6,400
							40	110	4,400	
12.4				20	100	2,000	20	110	2,200	2,200
				20	110	2,200				
18.4	40	120	4,800				20	110	2,200	7,000
							40	120	4,800	
29.4				20	110	2,200	20	120	2,400	2,400
				20	120	2,400				

(ii) According to the calculations below, when the LIFO method of stock valuation is applied, the value of closing stock for Sorensen Mills is £2,000.

Date	Stock received			Stock issued			Stock valuation			
	Qty tonnes	Price £	Value £	Qty tonnes	Price £	Value £	Qty tonnes	Price £	Value £	Total £
3.4	20	100	2,000				20	100	2,000	2,000
10.4	40	110	4,400				20	100	2,000	6,400
							40	110	4,400	
12.4				40	110	4,400	20	100	2,000	2,000
18.4	40	120	4,800				20	100	2,000	6,800
							40	120	4,800	
29.4				40	120	4,800	20	100	2,000	2,000

(b) FIFO - the stock is perishable.

QUESTION 3

(a) According to the calculations below, when the AVCO method of valuation is applied, the

Date	Stock received			Stock issued	Average cost	Stock valuation	
	Qty	Price £	Value £	Qty	£	Qty	Value £
Jan	200	20	4,000		20.00	200	4,000
Feb				150	20.00	50	1,000
March	200	30	6,000		28.00	250	7,000
April				200	28.00	50	1,400
May	200	24	4,800		24.80	250	6,200
June				150	24.80	100	2,480

value of closing stock for Mark Peters' business is £2,480.

(b) Advantages: logical, evens out price fluctuations, close to last purchase price, conforms to SSAP9 and acceptable to Inland Revenue.

Disadvantages: complex calculation, does not reflect any actual price paid nor the replacement price.

UNIT ASSESSMENT QUESTION 1

(a) £19,300.

(b) Because stock groups must be valued separately not collectively.

(c) (i) Profit is lower by £1,000; (ii) Current assets are lower by £1,000.

UNIT ASSESSMENT QUESTION 2

(a) (i) The value of closing stock for Luton Taxis is £6,000 if the FIFO method is used.

Date	Stock received Qty litres	Price £	Value £	Stock issued Qty litres	Price £	Value £	Stock valuation Qty litres	Price £	Value £	Total £
June	10,000	0.70	7,000				10,000	0.70	7,000	7,000
June				7,000	0.70	4,900	3,000	0.70	2,100	2,100
July	10,000	0.75	7,500				3,000	0.70	2,100	
							10,000	0.75	7,500	9,600
July				3,000	0.70	2,100				
				5,000	0.75	3,750	5,000	0.75	3,750	3,750
Aug	15,000	0.80	12,000				5,000	0.75	3,750	
							15,000	0.80	12,000	15,750
Aug				5,000	0.75	3,750				
				10,000	0.80	8,000	5,000	0.80	4,000	4,000
Sept	15,000	0.75	11,250				5,000	0.80	4,000	
							15,000	0.75	11,250	15,250
Sept				5,000	0.80	4,000				
				7,000	0.75	5,250	8,000	0.75	6,000	6,000

(ii) The value of closing stock for Luton Taxis is £6,080 when the AVCO method of stock valuation is used (figures are rounded to the nearest pence).

Date	Stock received Qty litres	Price £	Value £	Stock issued Qty litres	Average cost £	Stock valuation Qty litres	Value £
June	10,000	0.70	7,000		0.70	10,000	7,000
June				7,000	0.70	3,000	2,100
July	10,000	0.75	7,500		0.74	13,000	9,620
July				8,000	0.74	5,000	3,700
Aug	15,000	0.80	12,000		0.79	20,000	15,800
Aug				15,000	0.79	5,000	3,950
Sept	15,000	0.75	11,250		0.76	20,000	15,200
Sept				12,000	0.76	8,000	6,080

(b) FIFO method gives lower profit.

(c) Disadvantages: selling price of products might not reflect the most up to date costs; when prices are rising, FIFO values stock at its latest and often highest prices.

UNIT 25

QUESTION 1

(a) £1,210.

(b) Payee has not yet paid them into the bank. The cheques have not yet been cleared by the bank.

QUESTION 2

(a) £3,360.

(b) Businesses will not normally know the precise amount of bank charges until they are picked up from the bank statement.

QUESTION 3

(a) and (b)

NorthWest
Current account
Mancini's Restaurant

17 Church Street
Cheltenham
GL14 9TB

Sheet No. 66

STATEMENT DATE 31.03.01

Account No. 01366201

Date	Payment details	Payments	Receipts	Balance (£)
1 Mar	Balance b/f from sheet no. 65			✓540.70
7 March	Cheque 000441	✓56.10		284.60
	Cheque 000443	✓200.00		1,584.50
12 March	Credit 000012		✓1,299.90	1,494.50
17 March	Direct debit AA Subscription	90.00		1,149.50
22 March	Cheque 000444	✓345.00		1,082.00
24 March	Bank charges	67.50		501.05
25 March	Cheque 000445	✓580.95		501.05
31 March	Balance c/f to sheet no. 67			

CASH BOOK

	Debit				Credit	
Date	Details	Bank	Date	Details		Bank
2001		£	2001			£
1.3	Balance b/d	✓540.70	2.3	Squires Supplies 000441		✓56.10
9.3	Sales	✓1,299.90	2.3	Robertson's 000442		209.00
			2.3	Telecom Connect 000443		✓200.00
			16.3	Brown Meats 000444		✓345.00
			20.3	Wages (C. Raffo) 000445		✓580.95
			31.3	AA subscription (17.3)		90.00
			31.3	Bank charges (24.3)		67.50
			31.3	Balance c/d		292.05
		1840.60				1840.60

(c)

Mancini's
Bank Reconciliation Statement as at 31 March 2001

	£
Balance at bank as per cash book	292.05
Add unpresented cheque 000442	209.00
	501.05
Less uncleared lodgement	0.00
Balance as per bank statement	501.05

UNIT ASSESSMENT QUESTION I

(a)

Data Plus
Bank Reconciliation Statement as at 31 August 2001

		£
Balance at bank as per cash book		1,900.30
Add unpresented cheques		
000991	43.90	
000995	1,528.00	
000999	269.07	
		1,840.97
		3,741.27
Less uncleared lodgement		670.00
Balance as per bank statement		3,071.27

(b)

Data Plus
Bank Reconciliation Statement as at 31 August 2001

		£
Balance as per bank statement		3,071.27
Add uncleared lodgement		670.00
		3,741.27
Less unpresented cheques		
000991	43.90	
000995	1,528.00	
000999	269.07	
		1,840.97
Balance at bank as per cash book		1,900.30

(c) It is important for Rachel to know exactly how much money the business has to spend. If the balance in the cash book is incorrect, Rachel might spend more money than the business can afford.

UNIT ASSESSMENT QUESTION 2

(a)

CASH BOOK

	Debit			Credit	
Date	Details	Bank	Date	Details	Bank
2001		£	2001		£
1.2	Balance b/d	221.90	1.2	Edinburgh DC 000431	125.00
5.2	Sales	590.00	6.2	T. McDonald 000432	23.60
11.2	Sales	670.60	7.2	B. McDowd 000433	120.00
18.2	Sales	561.00	8.2	Tesco 000434	12.50
26.2	Sales	680.00	25.2	Wages 000435	1,000.00
			28.2	DLR Insurance (12.2)	45.00
			28.2	Bank charges (16.2)	34.50
			28.2	Stamford BS (25.2)	450.00
			28.2	Balance c/d	912.90
		2,723.50			2,723.50

(b)

Juniors
Bank Reconciliation Statement as at 31 February 2001

	£
Balance at bank as per cash book	912.90
Add unpresented cheque 000433	120.00
	1,032.90
Less uncleared lodgement	680.00
Balance as per bank statement	352.90

(c) To: check the accuracy of the records in the cash book; identify dishonoured cheques; check on fraud and embezzlement; identify bank errors and help avoid cash flow problems.

(b)

SALES LEDGER

Swansea Catering (page 32)

Dr					Cr
					£
4.4	Sales	SDB103			376.00

Bunters (page 6)

Dr					Cr
					£
9.4	Sales	SDB103			658.00

Jones Bros (page 21)

Dr					Cr
					£
13.4	Sales	SDB103			223.25

NOMINAL LEDGER

Sales Account (page 12)

Dr					Cr
					£
			14.4	Credit sales SDB103	1,070.00

VAT Account (page 37)

Dr					Cr
					£
			14.4	SDB103	187.25

(c) Premier Packaging owes £187.25 of VAT to the Customs and Excise.

QUESTION 3

(a)

PURCHASES LEDGER

Welford Paper (page 43)

Dr					Cr
					£
			2.3	Purchases PDB53	376.00

T. Watkins & Co (page 40)

Dr					Cr
					£
			9.3	Purchases PDB53	188.00

Algo Logistics (page 3)

Dr					Cr
					£
			14.3	Purchases PDB53	235.00

UNIT 26

QUESTION 1

(a) (i) £13,440; (ii) £21,980; (iii) £8,540.

(b) £14.

(c) £650.

QUESTION 2

(a) Total price: £1,070.00; total VAT: £187.25; total amount: £1,257.25.

3(a) continued

NOMINAL LEDGER
Purchases Account (page 21)

Dr	£	Cr	£
14.3 Credit purchases PDB53	680.00		

VAT Account (page 41)

Dr	£	Cr	£
14.3 PDB53	119.00		

(b) £119.00 VAT is owed by Oxford Books.
(c) Oxford Books can reclaim VAT input tax even though books are zero rated.

QUESTION 4

(a)

CASH BOOK

	Debit					Credit			
Date	Details	VAT £	Cash £	Bank £	Date	Details	VAT £	Cash £	Bank £
1.9	Balance b/d			230.00	3.9	Tractor parts	28.00		188.00
6.9	Sales	17.50	96.00		7.9	Robinson Seeds			493.50
11.9	Preston GC			587.50	10.9	L.E.P.	17.50		117.50
21.9	Sales	140.00		940.00	17.9	V. Jones			564.00
25.9	T. Cook		117.50	869.50	21.9	Wages			600.00
					30.9	Balance c/d		213.50	664.00
		157.50	213.50	2,627.00			45.50	213.50	2,627.00
1.10	Balance b/d		213.50	664.00					

(b)

NOMINAL LEDGER
VAT Account

Dr	£	Cr	£
30.9 Cash book	45.50	30.9 Cash book	157.50

(c) The receipt from Preston GC does not show any VAT because this transaction might have gone through the sales ledger. The payment to Robinson Seeds might have gone through the purchases ledger, or Robinson Seeds might not be registered for VAT.

UNIT ASSESSMENT QUESTION 1

(a) (i)

SALES LEDGER
Brighton Seaport (page 23)

Dr	£	Cr	£
3.8 Sales	7,520		

Benson's Skis (page 18)

Dr	£	Cr	£
6.8 Sales	10,340		

T Gordon (page 9)

Dr	£	Cr	£
8.8 Sales	5,405		

NOMINAL LEDGER
Sales Account (page 25)

Dr	£	Cr	£
		9.8 Credit sales	19,800

VAT Account (page 39)

Dr	£	Cr	£
		9.8 SDB	3,465

(ii)

SALES LEDGER
Brighton Seaport (page 23)

Dr	£	Cr	£
3.8 Sales	7,520	9.8 Returns inwards	940

T. Gordon (page 9)

Dr	£	Cr	£
8.8 Sales	5,405	12.8 Returns inwards	235

NOMINAL LEDGER
Returns Inwards Account (page 27)

Dr	£	Cr	£
9.8 RIDB	1,000		

VAT Account (page 39)

Dr	£	Cr	£
9.8 RIDB	175		

(b) (i) £506.38. (ii) The VAT account would be debited with £506.38.
(c) Examples could be insurance, banking, leasing of property or postal services.

UNIT ASSESSMENT QUESTION 2

(a) (i) £21,630 (17.5% × £123,600). (ii) £10,902.50 (17.5% × (£45,500 + £16,800)) (no VAT on wages).
(b) (i) £10,727.50 (£21,630 - £10,902.50).
(c) Turnover was below VAT threshold.

UNIT 27

QUESTION 1

(a)

Sales Ledger Control Account

Dr		Cr	
	£		£
1.10 Balances b/d	10,200	31.10 Bank	33,600
31.10 Credit sales	36,000	31.10 Balance c/d	12,600
	46,200		46,200
1.11 Balances b/d	12,600		

(b) The customer accounts are memorandum accounts and are therefore not part of the double entry system.

QUESTION 2

(a)

Sales Ledger Control Account

Dr		Cr	
	£		£
1.9 Balances b/d	5,700	1.9 Balances b/d	350
30.9 Sales	35,680	30.9 Bank	32,360
30.9 Balances c/d	170	30.9 Cash	4,300
		30.9 Returns inwards	1,350
		30.9 Balances c/d	3,190
	41,550		41,550
1.10 Balances b/d	3,190	1.10 Balances b/d	170

(b) (i) Sales day book; (ii) Returns inwards day book; (iii) Cash book.
(c) Overpayment by customers or returned goods after payment.

QUESTION 3

(a)

Purchases Ledger Control Account

Dr		Cr	
	£		£
31.7 Bank	222,000	1.7 Balances b/d	37,450
31.7 Returns outwards	12,900	31.7 Purchases	231,600
31.7 Discounts received	6,770	31.7 Balances c/d	560
31.7 Balances c/d	27,940		
	269,610		269,610
1.8 Balances b/d	560	1.8 Balances b/d	27,940

(b) (i) Returns outwards day book; (ii) Cash book; (iii) Cash book.
(c) Money (£560) owed to Hendon Paper by suppliers.

QUESTION 4

(a) and (b)

SALES LEDGER

Elmdon Copper

Dr		Cr	
	£		£
15.4 Credit sales	1,560	30.4 Contra Purchases ledger	1,560

PURCHASES LEDGER

Elmdon Copper

Dr		Cr	
	£		£
30.4 Contra Sales ledger	1,560	2.4 Purchases	2,600
30.4 Balance c/d	1,040		
	2,600		2,600
		1.5 Balance b/d	1,040

(c) Creditor.

UNIT ASSESSMENT QUESTION 1

(a)

Purchases Ledger Control Account

Dr		Cr	
	£		£
1.10 Balances b/d	320	1.10 Balances b/d	5,600
31.10 Bank	33,010	31.10 Purchases	35,650
31.10 Returns outwards	900		
31.10 Contra Sales ledger	500		
31.10 Discount received	600		
31.10 Balances c/d	5,920		
	41,250		41,250
		1.5 Balances b/d	5,920

(b) A different member of staff could be made responsible for maintaining the control account. Therefore, one person's fraudulent entry would be detected by the other.
(c) Celia Dobrolowski has bought goods from T. Bosworth and settled some of the account by selling £500 of goods back to T. Bosworth.

UNIT ASSESSMENT QUESTION 2

(a)

Sales Ledger Control Account

Dr		£			£
1.8	Balances b/d	27,400	1.8	Balances b/d	800
31.8	Sales	101,000	31.8	Bank	102,000
31.8	Dishonoured cheques	3,900	31.8	Contra Purchases ledger	2,000
			31.8	Bad debts written off	4,600
			31.8	Returns inwards	1,400
			31.8	Discounts allowed	500
			31.8	Balances c/d	21,000
		132,300			132,300
1.9	Balances b/d	21,000			
1.9	Balances b/d	2,010			

(b)

Purchases Ledger Control Account

Dr		£			£
31.8	Cash	1,100	1.8	Balances b/d	14,610
31.8	Bank	56,100	31.8	Purchases	51,090
31.8	Returns outwards	1,200			
31.8	Discount received	1,750			
31.8	Contra Sales ledger	2,000			
31.10	Balances c/d	3,550			
		65,700			65,700
			1.9	Balances b/d	3,550

(c) Memorandum accounts provide back-up information and details of individual customers and suppliers. They are not part of the double entry system.

UNIT 28

QUESTION 1

(a)

Sales Ledger Control Account

Dr		£			£
1.9	Balances b/d	8,390	30.9	Bank	52,500
30.9	Sales	45,790	30.9	Returns	700
30.9	Dishonoured cheques	1,500	30.9	Bad debts written off	470
			30.9	Balances c/d	2,010
		55,680			55,680
1.10	Balances b/d	2,010			

(b) The balance on the control account (£2,010) is not the same as the total of debit balances (£3,010). Therefore, at least one error has been made.

QUESTION 2

(a)

Sales Ledger Control Account

Dr		£			£
30.4	Balances b/d	11,800	30.4	Balance c/d	16,500
30.4	Adjustment to sales (omission)	3,400			
30.4	Adjustment to sales (omitted from day book)	1,300			
		16,500			16,500
30.4	Balances b/d	16,500			

(c)

Calculation of revised debtors balance

	£	£
Amount of debtors before adjustment		£14,000
Add		
Further debit - A Watkins		£3,400
		£17,400
Deduct		
Transposition (£2,100 - £1,200)		£900
Balance as per control account		£16,500

QUESTION 3

(a) Error 1: Credit control account with £2,100. Add £2,100 to creditors list.
Error 2: Credit control account with £1,000. No effect on individual account.
Error 3: Control account not affected. Add £90 to creditors list.

(b)

Purchases Ledger Control Account

Dr		£			£
28.2	Balances c/d	26,860	28.2	Balances b/d	23,760
			28.2	Adjustment to purchases (omission)	2,100
			28.2	Adjustment to discounts received (omission)	1,000
		26,860			26,860
			28.2	Balances b/d	26,860

(c)

Calculation of revised creditors balance

	£
Amount of creditors before adjustment	£24,670
Add	
Omitted purchase	£2,100
Transposition error	£90
Balance as per control account	£26,860

UNIT ASSESSMENT QUESTION 1

(a)

Dr		**Sales Ledger Control Account**		**Cr**
	£			£
31.3 Balances b/d (Balancing figure)	15,220	31.3 Adjustment to bank (cashbook undercast)		2,000
31.3 Adjustment for missing invoice	1,670	31.3 Bad debt written off		300
		31.3 Balances c/d		14,590
	16,890			16,890
1.4 Balances b/d	14,590			

(b)

Calculation of revised debtors balance

	£
Amount of debtors before adjustment	£13,020
Add	
Omitted sale	£1,670
	£14,690
Deduct	
Omitted discount allowed	£100
Balance as per control account	£14,590

UNIT ASSESSMENT QUESTION 2

(a) Error 1: Credit control account with £1,000. No effect on individual account.

Error 2: Credit control account with £650. No effect on individual account.

Error 3: No effect on control account. Add £1,800 to list of creditors.

Error 4: Credit control account with £2,000. Add £2,000 to list of creditors.

Error 5: Debit control account with £3,600. Deduct £3,600 from creditors list.

(b)

Dr	**Purchases Ledger Control Account**		**Cr**
	£		£
31.7 Adjustment for returns outward	3,600	31.7 Balances b/d	32,190
31.7 Balances c/d	32,240	31.7 Purchases (undercast)	1,000
		31.7 Correct contra entry (recorded twice)	650
		31.7 Returns disallowed	2,000
	35,840		35,840
		1.8 Balances b/d	32,240

(c)

Calculation of revised creditors balance

	£
Amount of creditors before adjustment	£32,040
Add	
Omitted balances	£1,800
Returns disallowed	£2,000
	£35,840
Deduct	
To record returns outwards	£3,600
Balance as per control account	£32,240

UNIT 29

QUESTION 1
(a) and (b)

The Worcester Wool Company
Extended trial balance as at 31.7.01

Details	Trial Balance Dr £	Trial Balance Cr £	Adjustments Dr £	Adjustments Cr £
Sales		219,300		
Opening stock	12,390			
Purchases	143,980			
Wages	43,750			
Rent and rates	15,600			350
Motor expenses	5,340			
Electricity	2,420			
Telephone	750			
Bank charges	560		310	
Sundry expenses	4,320			
Machinery	24,000			
Provision for depreciation - machinery		15,000		3,000
Motor vehicles	41,500			
Provision for depreciation - motor vehicles		20,000		4,000
Debtors	3,270			
Cash at bank	6,260			
Trade creditors		2,300		
Capital		74,320		
Drawings	26,780			
Closing stock - P & L				14,320
Closing stock - Bal. sheet			14,320	
Depreciation: machinery			3,000	
Depreciation: motor vehicles			4,000	
Prepayment			350	
Accrual				310
	330,920	330,920	21,980	21,980

QUESTION 2
(a) (b) (c) (d)

Plymouth Furniture Supplies
Extended trial balance as at 31.3.01

Details	Trial Balance Dr £	Trial Balance Cr £	Adjustments Dr £	Adjustments Cr £	Profit and loss Dr £	Profit and loss Cr £	Balance sheet Dr £	Balance sheet Cr £
Sales		211,110				211,110		
Opening stock	31,900				31,900			
Purchases	121,190				121,190			
Carriage	1,100				1,100			
Wages	31,000				31,000			
Rent and rates	23,150				23,150			
Light and heat	2,440				2,440			
Motor expenses	2,230				2,230			
Insurance	1,220				1,220			
Advertising	2,210				2,210			
Motor vehicles	15,000						15,000	
Provision for depreciation - motor vehicles		6,000		3,000				9,000
Fixtures and fittings	3,500						3,500	
Provision for depreciation - fixtures and fittings		1,050		350				1,400
Trade debtors	4,100						4,100	
Cash in hand	760						760	
VAT		2,440						2,440
Trade creditors		7,010						7,010
Bank overdraft		1,900						1,900
Capital		45,040						45,040
Drawings	34,750						34,750	
Closing stock - P & L				35,330		35,330		
Closing stock - Bal. sheet			35,330				35,330	
Depreciation: vehicles			3,000		3,000			
Depreciation: fixtures			350		350			
Accountancy fees - expense			2,000		2,000			
Accruals				2,000				2,000
Net profit					24,650			24,650
	274,550	274,550	40,680	40,680	246,440	246,440	93,440	93,440

QUESTION 3

(a) (b) (c) (d)

Marco Bellini
Extended trial balance as at 31.12.01

Details	Trial Balance Dr £	Cr £	Adjustments Dr £	Cr £	Profit and loss Dr £	Cr £	Balance sheet Dr £	Cr £
Sales		81,310				81,310		
Opening stock	13,250				13,250			
Purchases	46,730				46,730			
Motor expenses	1,380				1,380			
Rent and rates	8,590			400	8,190			
Light and heat	1,560		240		1,800			
Telephone	520				520			
Bank interest	180				180			
Van	4,300						4,300	
Provision for depreciation - van		2,500		500				3,000
Fixtures and fittings	3,000						3,000	
Provision for depreciation - fixtures and fittings		1,500		300				1,800
Trade debtors	320						320	
Cash at bank	780						780	
Cash in hand	310						310	
Trade creditors		2,310						2,310
Capital		5,000						5,000
Drawings	11,700						11,700	
Closing stock - P & L				15,300		15,300		
Closing stock - Bal. sheet			15,300				15,300	
Depreciation: van			500		500			
Depreciation: fixtures			300		300			
Accrual				240				240
Prepayment			400				400	
Net profit					23,760			23,760
	92,620	92,620	16,740	16,740	96,610	96,610	36,110	36,110

(e)

Trading and Profit and Loss Account
for the year ended 31.12.01

	£	£
Sales		81,310
Opening stock	13,250	
Purchases	46,730	
	59,980	
Less closing stock	15,300	
Cost of sales		44,680
Gross profit		36,630
Less expenses		
Motor expenses	1,380	
Telephone	520	
Rent and rates	8,190	
Interest	180	
Light and heat	1,800	
Depreciation	800	
		12,870
Net profit		23,760

UNIT ASSESSMENT QUESTION 1

(a)

Damien McGill
Extended trial balance as at 31.1.01

Details	Trial Balance Dr £	Trial Balance Cr £	Adjustments Dr £	Adjustments Cr £	Profit and loss Dr £	Profit and loss Cr £	Balance sheet Dr £	Balance sheet Cr £
Sales		98,450				98,450		
Opening stock	14,360				14,360			
Purchases	34,210				34,210			
Rent	6,000				6,000			
Casual labour	6,100		200		6,300			
Motor expenses	1,440				1,440			
Telephone	340				340			
Sundry expenses	2,130				2,130			
Vehicle	15,000						15,000	
Provision for depreciation- vehicle		6,000		2,000				8,000
Fixtures and fittings	13,500						13,500	
Provision for depreciation- fixtures and fittings		8,100		1,350				9,450
Trade debtors	3,210						3,210	
Cash at bank	2,340						2,340	
Trade creditors		2,110						2,110
Capital		12,340						12,340
Drawings	28,370						28,370	
Closing stock - P & L				12,220		12,220		
Closing stock - Bal. sheet			12,220				12,220	
Depreciation: vehicle			2,000		2,000			
Depreciation: fixtures			1,350		1,350			
Accrual				200				
Accountancy fees - expense			1,300		1,300			
Accrual				1,300				200
Net profit					41,240			1,300
	127,000	127,000	17,070	17,070	110,670	110,670	74,640	41,240
								74,640

Marco Bellini
Balance Sheet as at 31.12.01

	£	£	£
Fixed assets			
Van at cost	4,300		
Less depreciation	3,000	1,300	
Fixtures and fittings at cost	3,000		
Less depreciation	1,800	1,200	
			2,500
Current assets			
Stock	15,300		
Debtors	320		
Prepayments	400		
Cash at bank	780		
Cash in hand	310		
		17,110	
Current liabilities			
Trade creditors	2,310		
Accruals	240		
		2,550	
Net current assets			14,560
Net assets			17,060
Financed by			
Capital			
Opening capital			5,000
Add net profit			23,760
			28,760
Less drawings			11,700
Capital employed			17,060

644

(b)

Damien McGill
Trading and Profit and Loss Account
for the year ended 31.1.01

	£	£
Sales		98,450
Opening stock	14,360	
Purchases	34,210	
	48,570	
Less closing stock	12,220	
Cost of sales		36,350
Gross profit		62,100
Less expenses		
Casual labour	6,300	
Motor expenses	1,440	
Telephone	340	
Rent	6,000	
Depreciation	3,350	
Accountancy fees	1,300	
Sundry expenses	2,130	
		20,860
Net profit		41,240

Damien McGill
Balance Sheet as at 31.1.01

	£	£	£
Fixed assets			
Vehicle at cost		15,000	
Less depreciation		8,000	7,000
Fixtures and fittings at cost		13,500	
Less depreciation		9,450	4,050
			11,050
Current assets			
Stock		12,220	
Debtors		3,210	
Cash at bank		2,340	
		17,770	
Current liabilities			
Trade creditors	2,110		
Accruals	1,500		
		3,610	
Net current assets			14,160
Net assets			25,210
Financed by			
Capital			
Opening capital			12,340
Add net profit			41,240
			53,580
Less drawings			28,370
Capital employed			25,210

UNIT ASSESSMENT QUESTION 2

(a)

Jean Watkinson
Trading and Profit and Loss Account
for the year ended 31.12.01

	£	£
Sales		32,680
Opening stock	640	
Purchases	20,660	
	21,300	
Less closing stock	1,060	
Cost of sales		20,240
Gross profit		12,440
Less expenses		
Casual labour	2,200	
Telephone	300	
Rent	4,800	
Depreciation	950	
Insurance	560	
Interest	760	
Sundry expenses	3,220	
		12,790
Net profit (loss)		(350)

(b)

Jean Watkinson
Extended trial balance as at 31.12.01

Details	Trial Balance Dr £	Trial Balance Cr £	Adjustments Dr £	Adjustments Cr £	Profit and loss Dr £	Profit and loss Cr £	Balance sheet Dr £	Balance sheet Cr £
Sales		32,680				32,680		
Opening stock	640				640			
Purchases	21,010			350	20,660			
Rent	5,000			200	4,800			
Casual labour	2,200				2,200			
Insurance	560				560			
Interest	760				760			
Telephone	230		70		300			
Sundry expenses	3,220				3,220			
Equipment	9,500						9,500	
Provision for depreciation-equipment		4,750		950				5,700
Cash in hand	440						440	
Trade creditors		1,260						1,260
Bank overdraft		1,210						1,210
Capital		9,700						9,700
Drawings	6,040		350				6,390	
Closing stock - P & L				1,060		1,060		
Closing stock - Bal. sheet			1,060				1,060	
Depreciation: equipment			950		950			
Prepayment			200				200	
Accrual				70				70
Net profit/loss						350	350	
	49,600	49,600	2,630	2,630	34,090	34,090	17,940	17,940

Note that the loss of £350 is entered as a credit in the profit and loss column and as a debit in the balance sheet column.

2(b) continued

Jean Watkinson
Balance Sheet as at 31.12.01

	£	£	£
Fixed assets			
Equipment at cost		9,500	
Less depreciation		5,700	
			3,800
Current assets			
Stock		1,060	
Prepayment		200	
Cash in hand		440	
		1,700	
Current liabilities			
Trade creditors	1,260		
Accruals	70		
Bank overdraft	1,210		
		2,540	
Net current assets			(840)
Net assets			2,960
Financed by			
Capital			
Opening capital			9,700
Deduct net loss			(350)
			9,350
Less drawings			6,390
Capital employed			2,960

(c) No, the business made a loss.

QUESTION 2

(a)

JOURNAL

Date	Details	Folio	Debit	Credit
			£	£
2001				
4.11	Purchases		100	
	Suspense			100
	Correction of casting error			
4.11	Drawings		680	
	Suspense			680
	Correction of error, completion of double entry			

(b)

Garden World
Trial Balance as at 31.10.01

	Debit	Credit
	£	£
Sales		151,520
Opening stock	12,410	
Purchases	84,420	
Wages	32,180	
Motor expenses	2,060	
Rates and insurance	3,280	
Heat and light	1,450	
Sundry expenses	650	
Van	13,400	
Provision for depreciation - van		6,000
Fixtures and fittings	3,500	
Provision for depreciation - fixtures and fittings		1,400
Cash at bank	2,270	
Cash in hand	670	
Trade creditors		3,740
Capital		13,180
Drawings	19,550	
	175,840	175,840

UNIT 30

QUESTION 1

(a) £950 credit balance.

(b)

Suspense Account

Dr			Cr
£	2001		£
	31.3	Difference per trial balance	950

(c) As a liability in the balance sheet.

QUESTION 3

(a)

JOURNAL

Date	Details	Folio	Debit £	Credit £
2002				
14.1	Suspense		1,000	
	Purchases			1,000
	Correction of casting error			
14.1	Suspense		90	
	Motor expenses			90
	Correction of transposition error			

(b)

	£
Net profit (before adjustment)	45,310
Add	
Purchases overcast	1,000
Transposition error	90
Adjusted net profit	46,400

QUESTION 4

(a)

JOURNAL

Date	Details	Folio	Debit £	Credit £
2001				
3.6	Suspense		580	
	P. Hendry			580
	Correction of misposting error			
3.6	Purchases		3,000	
	Suspense			3,000
	Correction of casting error			
3.6	A. Larkin		340	
	Sales			340
	Correction of omission error			
3.6	Telephone		310	
	Suspense			310
	Correction of error, completion of double entry			

(b)

Dr		Suspense Account		Cr

2001		£	2001		£
31.5	Difference per trial balance	2,730	3.6	Purchases	3,000
3.6	P. Hendry	580	3.6	Telephone	310
		3,310			3,310

(c) Error I does not affect net profit.

(c)

Dr		Suspense Account		Cr
2001	£	**2001**		£
31.3 Difference per trial balance	5,330	1.4	Creditors	210
1.4 Purchases	300	1.4	Bank	5,100
		1.4	Heat and light	320
	5,630			5,630

(d)

Errol Drakes
Trial Balance as at 1.4.01

	Debit	Credit
	£	£
Sales		172,020
Interest received		540
Opening stock	6,320	
Purchases	91,660	
Wages	49,450	
Motor expenses	2,100	
Insurance	210	
Advertising	650	
Telephone	430	
Heat and light	1,180	
Sundry expenses	2,560	
Motor vehicle	21,000	
Provision for depreciation - motor vehicle		8,000
Cash at bank	2,550	
Trade creditors		4,090
Capital		23,290
Drawings	29,830	
	207,940	207,940

(e) None, the balance sheet is affected because the error affects trade creditors.

(d)

	£	£
Net profit (before adjustment)		54,330
Add		
Sales understated		340
		54,670
Less		
Purchases understated	3,000	
Telephone expenses	310	
		3,310
Adjusted net profit		51,360

UNIT ASSESSMENT QUESTION 1

(a) Debit balance of £5,330.

(b)

JOURNAL

Date	Details	Folio	Debit	Credit
2001			£	£
1.4	Creditors		210	
	Suspense			210
	Correction of error, completion of double entry			
1.4	Bank		5,100	
	Suspense			5,100
	Correction of misposting error			
1.4	Heat and light		320	
	Suspense			320
	Correction of error, completion of double entry			
1.4	Suspense		300	
	Purchases			300
	Correction of casting error			

UNIT ASSESSMENT QUESTION 2

(a)

JOURNAL

Date	Details	Folio	Debit	Credit
			£	£
2001				
7.8	Sales			400
	Suspense		400	
	Correction of casting error			
7.8	Telephone			145
	Sundry expenses		145	
	Correction of misposting error			
7.8	Rates			90
	Suspense		90	
	Correction of transposition error			
7.8	Purchases			430
	A. Wilson		430	
	Correction of omission error			
7.8	Drawings			200
	Suspense		200	
	Correction of error, completion of double entry			
7.8	Suspense			460
	Sales		460	
	Correction of error, completion of double entry			

(b)

Suspense Account

Dr				Cr		
2001		£		2001		£
31.7	Difference per trial balance	230		7.8	Sales	400
7.8	Sales	460		7.8	Rates	90
				7.8	Drawings	200
		690				690

(c)

	£	£
Net profit (before adjustment)		24,020
Add		
Sales understated		460
		24,480
Less		
Sales overstated	400	
Transposition	90	
Purchases understated	430	
		920
Adjusted net profit		23,560

UNIT 31

QUESTION 1

(a) Shelly has not kept a full double entry record of her business transactions. She can only supply a limited amount of information to her accountant. Thus, her records are incomplete.

(b) Cash book, drawings, sales and expenses.

(c) Accountancy fees might be lower. An accurate tax assessment will be possible.

QUESTION 2

(a) Opening capital = £26,440, closing capital = £30,210.

(b) Profit = £18,270.

(c) Profit would be overstated by £350.

QUESTION 3

(a) and (b)

Gary Manning
Statement of Affairs

	As at 31.8.01		As at 1.9.00	
	£	£	£	£
Fixed assets				
Motor vehicle		6,500		8,000
Tools and equipment		8,100		5,400
		14,600		13,400
Current assets				
Stock	5,890		4,430	
Debtors	2,600		2,270	
Prepayments	1,000		800	
Cash at bank	3,920		2,290	
		13,410		9,790
		28,010		23,190
Less current liabilities				
Trade creditors		4,380		3,430
Net assets		23,630		19,760
Financed by				
Capital		23,630		19,760

(c) £23,370.

UNIT ASSESSMENT QUESTION 1

(a) and (b)

Elizabeth Baker
Statement of Affairs

	As at 31.10.02		As at 1.11.01	
	£	£	£	£
Fixed assets				
Motor car		4,500		5,000
Computer		1,600		2,000
Books and equipment		1,250		1,500
		7,350		8,500
Current assets				
Prepayments	400		350	
Cash at bank	2,430		670	
Cash in hand	120		150	
		2,950		1,170
		10,300		9,670
Less long term liabilities				
Bank loan		3,000		5,000
Net assets		7,300		4,670
Financed by				
Capital		7,300		4,670

(c) £8,130.

(d) (i)

Elizabeth Baker
Statement of Affairs

As at 31.10.02

	£	£
Fixed assets		
Motor car	4,500	
Computer	1,600	
Books and equipment	1,250	
		7,350
Current assets		
Prepayments	400	
Cash at bank	2,430	
Cash in hand	120	
		2,950
		10,300
Less current liabilities		
Owed to garage	320	
Less long term liabilities		
Bank loan	3,000	
		3,320
Net assets		**6,980**
Financed by		
Capital		6,980

(ii) £8,310.

(e) Depends on accuracy of information. Elizabeth forgot about two transactions that affected the amount of profit. A complete trading and profit and loss account cannot be produced.

UNIT ASSESSMENT QUESTION 2
(a) and (b)

Gordon Poole
Statement of Affairs

	As at 31.12.01			As at 1.1.01	
	£	£		£	£
Fixed assets					
Van		6,500			8,000
Tools and equipment		3,400			1,500
		9,800			9,500
Current assets					
Stock	710			430	
Cash at bank	-			1,010	
Cash in hand	610			350	
		1,320			1,790
		11,120			11,290
Less current liabilities					
Trade creditors	1,340			1,290	
Other creditors	600			450	
Income prepaid	200			-	
Bank overdraft	340			-	
		2,480			1,740
Net assets		8,640			9,550
Financed by					
Capital		8,640			9,550

(c) £13,590.

(d) Reduce profit by £300.

UNIT 32

QUESTION 1
(a)

CASH BOOK

Debit				Credit			
Date	Details	Cash	Bank	Date	Details	Cash	Bank
2001		£	£	2001		£	£
1.1	Balances b/d	210	920		Payments to creditors	1,110	8,190
	Cash sales	3,410			Expenses		2,830
	Receipts from debtors		20,000		Drawings	1,990	530
				31.12	Balances c/d	520	9,370
		3,620	20,920			3,620	20,920

(b) (i) £1,990 (ii) £9,370.
(c) Bank statements and cheque stubs.

QUESTION 2
(a)

Sales Ledger Control Account

Dr	£		Cr	£
1.1 Balances b/d	12,880		Receipts from debtors	213,210
Sales	**211,720**	31.12	Balances c/d	11,390
	224,600			224,600

(b) Sales will increase by £890 to £212,610.

QUESTION 3
(a)

Kim Williams
Trading Account

	£	£
Sales		120,000
Opening stock	15,340	
Purchases	74,110	
	89,450	
Closing stock	17,450	
Cost of sales		72,000
Gross profit (40% × £120,000)		48,000

(b) 66.6% or 2/3.

QUESTION 4
(a)

Clive Cox
Statement of Affairs
as at 1.1.01

	£	£
Fixed assets		
Premises		56,000
Current assets		
Stock	2,360	
Debtors	2,300	
Cash at bank	2,440	
Cash in hand	1,660	
	8,760	
		64,760
Less long term liabilities		
Mortgage		20,000
Capital		**44,760**

(b)

CASH BOOK

	Debit				Credit	
Date	**Details**	**Cash**	**Bank**	**Date**	**Details**	**Cash**	**Bank**
		£	£			£	£
2001				2001			
1.1	Balances b/d	1,660	2,440		Payments to creditors		34,070
	Cash sales	12,310			Expenses	3,290	3,200
	Receipts from debtors		54,700		Interest		1,300
					Wages		14,000
					Drawings	8,250	
				31.12	Balances c/d	2,430	4,570
		13,970	57,140			13,970	57,140

(c)

Sales Ledger Control Account

Dr	£		Cr	£
1.1 Balances b/d	2,300		Cheques received	54,700
Credit sales	**55,690**	31.12	Balances c/d	3,290
	57,990			57,990

So, overall sales were £68,000 (credit sales £55,690 plus cash sales £12,310).

(d)

Clive Cox
Trading and Profit and Loss Account
for the year ended 31.12.01

	£	£
Sales		68,000
Opening stock	2,360	
Purchases	34,070	
	36,430	
Less closing stock	2,110	
Cost of sales		34,320
Gross profit		33,680
Less expenses		
Wages (£14,000 + £240)	14,240	
General expenses	6,490	
Interest	1,300	
Depreciation	4,000	
		26,030
Net profit		7,650

UNIT ASSESSMENT QUESTION 1

(a)

Helen Wallace
Statement of Affairs
as at 1.8.00

	£	£	£
Fixed assets			
Vehicle			7,000
Current assets			
Stock		5,160	
Cash at bank		1,220	
Cash in hand		810	
			7,190
			14,190
Less current liabilities			
Trade creditors			2,460
			11,730
Capital			

(b)

CASH BOOK

	Debit					Credit		
Date	Details	Cash	Bank		Date	Details	Cash	Bank
		£	£				£	£
2000					2000			
1.8	Balances b/d	810	1,220			Payments to creditors		63,000
	Cash sales	126,000				General expenses	1,720	4,110
	Cash (contra)		93,070			Heat and light		3,220
						Wages	17,200	
						Drawings	10,400	
						Bank (contra)	93,070	
					2001	Lease		15,000
					31.7	**Missing cash**	**3,400**	
						Balances c/d	1,020	**8,960**
		126,810	94,290				126,810	94,290

(e)

Clive Cox
Balance Sheet as at 31.12.01

	£	£
Fixed assets		
Premises	56,000	
Less depreciation	4,000	52,000
Current assets		
Stock	2,110	
Debtors	3,290	
Cash at bank	4,570	
Cash in hand	2,430	
	12,400	
Current liabilities		
Accrual (wages)	240	
Net current assets		12,160
		64,160
Less long term liabilities		
Mortgage		20,000
Net assets		44,160
Financed by		
Capital		
Opening capital		44,760
Add net profit		7,650
		52,410
Less drawings		8,250
Capital employed		44,160

(c)

Dr	Purchases Ledger Control Account			Cr
	£	2000		£
2000 Payments	63,000	1.8	Balances b/d	2,460
2001			Purchases	**63,680**
31.7 Balances c/d	3,140			
	66,140			66,140

(d)

Helen Wallace
Trading and Profit and Loss Account
for the year ended 31.7.01

	£	£
Sales		126,000
Opening stock	5,160	
Purchases	63,680	
	68,840	
Less closing stock	6,220	
Cost of sales		62,620
Gross profit		63,380
Less expenses		
Wages	17,200	
General expenses	5,830	
Lease	15,000	
Heat and light (£3,220 + £310)	3,530	
Missing cash	**3,400**	
Depreciation	1,000	
		45,960
Net profit		17,420

(e)

Helen Wallace
Balance Sheet as at 31.12.01

	£	£	£
Fixed assets			
Vehicle		7,000	
Less depreciation		1,000	6,000
Current assets			
Stock		6,220	
Cash at bank		8,960	
Cash in hand		1,020	
		16,200	
Current liabilities			
Trade creditors	3,140		
Accrual (heat and light)	310	3,450	
Net current assets			12,750
Net assets			18,750
Financed by			
Capital			
Opening capital			11,730
Add net profit			17,420
			29,150
Less drawings			10,400
Capital employed			18,750

UNIT ASSESSMENT QUESTION 2

(a)

Dr	Purchases Ledger Control Account			Cr
	£	2001		£
2000 Payments	65,620	1.3	Balances b/d	0
2001			Purchases	**77,930**
28.2 Balances c/d	12,310			
	77,930			77,930

(b) £2,330.

(c)

CASH BOOK

	Debit				Credit	
Date	Details	Cash	Date	Details		Cash
2001		£	2001			£
1.3	Balance b/d	0		Bank		71,670
	Sales	93,000		Sundry expenses		2,100
				Drawings		**16,450**
			2002			
			28.2	Balance c/d		2,780
		93,000				93,000

(d)

Sara Jarvis
Trading and Profit and Loss Account
for the year ended 28.2.02

	£	£
Sales		93,000
Opening stock	0	
Purchases	77,930	
	77,930	
Less closing stock		
(£10,500 + £2,330)	12,830	
Cost of sales		65,100
Gross profit		27,900
Less expenses		
Rent (£13,000 - £1,000)	12,200	
Heat and light	1,800	
Stolen stock	2,330	
Interest	780	
Sundry expenses	3,220	
Depreciation	1,000	21,130
Net profit		6,770

(e)

Sara Jarvis
Balance Sheet as at 28.2.02

	£	£	£
Fixed assets			
Fixtures and fittings		9,000	
Less depreciation		1,000	8,000
Current assets			
Stock		10,500	
Prepayment		1,000	
Cash in hand		2,780	
		14,280	
Current liabilities			
Trade creditors	12,310		
Bank overdraft	4,650		
		16,960	
Net current assets			(2,680)
			5,320
Long term liabilities			
Bank loan			5,000
Net assets			320
Financed by			
Capital			
Opening capital			10,000
Add net profit			6,770
			16,770
Less drawings			16,450
Capital employed			320

UNIT 33

QUESTION 1

(a) Liabilities = Assets - Capital = £29,160 - £20,000 = £9,160.

(b) When the business closed and the assets were disposed of, there was not enough money to pay back the creditors. Beryl would have to use £1,160 of her personal wealth to pay off the business creditors.

(c) Advantages: to set up the business without following any legal process, to keep all the profits if the business was successful and to be independent.
Disadvantages: can be very hard work and it can be lonely and difficult having sole responsibility. If the business fails, it is the owner's own money that is at risk.

QUESTION 2

(a) None on the original capital. Tom will receive £150 (£3,000 × 5%) interest each year on his extra contribution.

(b) Advantages: More capital is raised, partners can specialise, partners can share the burden of running the business.

(c) A Deed of Partnership can avoid disputes if partners fall out or disagree on their verbal agreement.

QUESTION 3

(a) To raise more capital, to gain the financial protection that limited liability provides.

(b) Simon retained 52% of the shares so he remained in complete control.

(c) Preparing and submitting the Memorandum of Association and the Articles of Association to the Registrar of Companies.

(d) If Simon and Julie do not want to, or cannot afford to buy Helen's stake, a suitable new owner must be found.

QUESTION 4

(a) The large amount of money that is raised and the free publicity.

(b) If an outsider can buy 51% of the shares, they will take control. Cost of flotation.

UNIT ASSESSMENT QUESTION 1

(a) To raise more capital, to share responsibility, to gain outside expertise.

(b) To clarify the rights of partners and to establish the aims of the business.

(c) The amount of capital each partner has contributed; the rate of interest, if any, to be paid on capital; how profits or losses should be shared; the procedure for winding up the partnership; partners' salaries; how much control each partner has; rules for recruiting new partners.

(d) Having to share the profits, possible future disagreements on the running of the business.

UNIT ASSESSMENT QUESTION 2

(a) (i) The money they got from the flotation. (ii) Carphone raised £185 million to finance investment.

(b) Possible loss of control by the founder; unstable share price, large expense involved in the flotation, time and effort spent in flotation rather than running the company.

UNIT 34

QUESTION 1

(a) Preference dividend: £400; ordinary share dividend: £530.

(b) Depends on the size of profit and directors' policy.

(c) Advantages: priority in dividend payment and return of capital. Disadvantages: size of dividend is limited and (probably) no voting rights.

QUESTION 2

(a) New shares issued at a discount to existing shareholders.

(b) (i) £1,335 (ii) £252.50.

(c) Relatively cheap and administratively easy.

QUESTION 3

(a) 5p.

(b) £60 million.

(c) £1.45.

QUESTION 4

(a)

Bank Account

Dr	£	Cr	£
Application and allotment	11,125,000	Application and allotment	1,125,000
Application and allotment	10,000,000	Balance c/d	30,000,000
Call	10,000,000		
	31,125,000		31,125,000
Balance b/d	30,000,000		

Application and Allotment Account

Dr	£	Cr	£
Bank (refunds to investors)	1,125,000	Bank (application money)	11,125,000
Ordinary share capital	10,000,000	Bank (balance on allotment)	10,000,000
Share premium	10,000,000		
	21,125,000		21,125,000

Ordinary Share Capital Account

Dr	£	Cr	£
Balance c/d	20,000,000	Application and allotment	10,000,000
		Call	10,000,000
	20,000,000		20,000,000
		Balance b/d	20,000,000

Call Account

Dr	£	Cr	£
Ordinary share capital	10,000,000	Bank	10,000,000

Share Premium Account

Dr	£	Cr	£
Balance c/d	10,000,000	Application and allotment	10,000,000
		Balance b/d	10,000,000

(b) £30m.

(c) Current assets would increase by £30m. In the Financed by section, £20m would be added to ordinary share capital and £10m would be put in the share premium reserve.

QUESTION 1

(a) Specialists that provide business capital.

(b) Unable to raise finance elsewhere.

(c) Share profit and influence control.

QUESTION 2

(a) (i) Requires combine harvester urgently and does not have funds to buy outright. (ii) No responsibility for maintenance and repairs. Up to date equipment and machinery.

(b) Revenue expenditure - so treated as an expense in profit and loss account.

QUESTION 3

(a) Bank overdraft - only pay interest on amount outstanding. Interest rate often higher than bank loan. Bank loan is less flexible, with a fixed term.

(b) Lower interest rate, certainty of interest payments.

(c) A debt factor gives an injection of short term finance, but will charge a fee and could cause impression of a cash flow problem. Berwick Rugs might prefer to maintain its own debt control system so, instead, might raise a bank loan. It will compare the interest charged on the loan with the cost of factoring.

QUESTION 4

(a) MFI raises less from long term funds and relies more on short term funding. Both raise approximately 60% from shareholders.

(b) Kewill Systems.

(c) The value of fixed assets is approximately the same as long term funding. Current assets might be considered low.

UNIT ASSESSMENT QUESTION 1

(a) Avoids expensive investment.

(b) Company was loss making.

(c) Falling share price made a successful share issue unlikely. Large losses would make institutions unwilling to lend.

UNIT ASSESSMENT QUESTION 1

(a) (i) Shares sold directly to selected investors and institutions. (ii) Shares sold to an issuing house who then make the issue to the general public.

(b) Cheaper and less regulation.

(c) To earn a dividend and also make a capital gain.

UNIT ASSESSMENT QUESTION 2

(a)

Dr	Bank Account		Cr
	£		£
Application and allotment	20,562,500	Application and allotment	562,500
Application and allotment	20,000,000	Balance c/d	80,000,000
Call	40,000,000		
	80,562,500		80,562,500
Balance b/d	80,000,000		

Dr	Application and Allotment Account		Cr
	£		£
Bank (refunds to investors)	562,500	Bank (application money)	20,562,500
Ordinary share capital	40,000,000	Bank (balance on allotment)	20,000,000
	40,562,500		40,562,500

Dr	Ordinary Share Capital Account		Cr
	£		£
Balance c/d	80,000,000	Application and allotment	40,000,000
		Call	40,000,000
	80,000,000		80,000,000
		Balance b/d	80,000,000

Dr	Call Account		Cr
	£		£
Ordinary share capital	40,000,000	Bank	40,000,000

(b) £41,600,000.

(c) To ensure success of issue and retain shareholder loyalty.

(d) Current assets would increase by £44m (20m shares × £2.20). Ordinary share capital would increase by £20m (20m shares × £1 nominal value). Share premium reserve would increase by £24m (20m shares × £1.20).

(e) A rights issue is a method of raising extra capital from existing shareholders. Current assets, capital and reserves all increase on the balance sheet. A bonus issue does not raise any new capital but it transfers reserves to ordinary shareholders. Current assets are unaffected and the only difference on the balance sheet is a transfer from reserves to ordinary shareholders' capital.

QUESTION 1

(a)

Wilson and Patel

Profit and Loss Appropriation Account for the year ended 31.12.00

	£	£
Net profit b/d		83,000
Less interest on capital:		
Wilson	750	
Patel	250	
		1,000
		82,000
Less salaries:		
Wilson	30,000	
Patel	40,000	
		70,000
		12,000
Share of remaining profit:		
Wilson (50%)	6,000	
Patel (50%)	6,000	
		12,000

(b)

Wilson and Patel

Profit and Loss Appropriation Account for the year ended 31.12.01

	£	£
Net profit b/d		58,000
Less interest on capital:		
Wilson	750	
Patel	250	
		1,000
		57,000
Less salaries:		
Wilson	30,000	
Patel	40,000	
		70,000
		(13,000)
Share of remaining profit (loss):		
Wilson (50%)	(6,500)	
Patel (50%)	(6,500)	
		(13,000)

UNIT ASSESSMENT QUESTION 2

(a)

MEMO

From: A. Student   Date: 22 June
To: Angela and Graham Pinkerton   Subject: Sources of finance

A combination of sources might provide the necessary funds without having to resort to a venture capitalist.

1. Internal sources:
- Use some of the cash that has built up from retained profits.
- Retain extra profits by reducing or cutting your dividend payments.
- Use a debt factor to raise cash.
- Reduce the stock level.
- Sell any unwanted assets, or arrange a sale and leaseback of any property owned outright.

2. External short term sources:
- Bank loan or overdraft might be appropriate for some of the short term funding requirements.
- Hire purchase arrangement for equipment or vehicles.

3. External long term sources:
- Issue new shares, either by using your own resources (if available), or by approaching family/friends to see if they are willing to contribute.
- Raise a loan or mortgage from a financial institution. But, as the company is already highly geared, potential lenders will be unwilling to provide extra funds without some form of extra security.
- A flotation of shares to the public to become a plc is a theoretical option but is not practical in this case. The cost of flotation might be greater than the funds required.

(b) Fear of sharing profit and losing some control.
(c) Pinkerton was already quite highly geared. Might not want to, or be able to, borrow any more.

(c) Expense in profit and loss account (**not** the profit and loss appropriation account).

QUESTION 2

(a)

Date	Sarah Abbot interest	Christine Cox interest	Matthew Cairns interest
	£	£	£
1.1.00	300.00 (12/12 × 10% × 3,000)	200.00 (12/12 × 10% × 2,000)	
1.3.00	275.00 (10/12 × 10% × 3,300)	166.67 (10/12 × 10% × 2,000)	208.33 (10/12 × 10% × 2,500)
1.5.00	200.00 (8/12 × 10% × 3,000)	133.33 (8/12 × 10% × 2,000)	
1.7.00	200.00 (6/12 × 10% × 4,000)	100.00 (6/12 × 10% × 2,000)	
1.9.00	133.33 (4/12 × 10% × 4,000)	66.67 (4/12 × 10% × 2,000)	83.33 (4/12 × 10% × 2,500)
1.11.00	66.67 (2/12 × 10% × 4,000)	33.33 (2/12 × 10% × 2,000)	
Total 1,175		**700**	**292 (rounded to nearest £)**

(b)

Abbott, Cox and Cairns

Profit and Loss Appropriation Account for the year ended 31.12.00

	£	£
Net profit b/d		78,000
Add interest on drawings:		
Abbott	1,175	
Cox	700	
Cairns	292	2,167
		80,167
Less interest on capital:		
Abbott	600	
Cox	600	
Cairns	1,200	2,400
		77,767
Less salaries:		
Abbott	25,000	
Cox	25,000	
Cairns	5,000	55,000
		22,767
Share of profit:		
Abbot (40%)	9,107	
Cox (40%)	9,107	
Cairns (20%)	4,553	22,767

QUESTION 3

(a) and (b)

Partners' Fixed Capital Accounts

Dr		Tillett	Hopkins				Cr Tillett	Hopkins
		£	£				£	£
2001				2001				
31.12 Balances c/d		7,000	7,000	1.1	Balances b/d		7,000	7,000
				2002				
				1.1	Balances b/d		7,000	7,000

Partners' Current Accounts

Dr		Tillett	Hopkins				Cr Tillett	Hopkins
		£	£				£	£
2001				2001				
31.12 Drawings		30,500	16,000	1.1	Balances b/d		2,300	3,800
31.12 Balances c/d		13,500	17,500	31.12	Salaries		26,000	14,000
				31.12	Profit		15,700	15,700
		44,000	33,500				44,000	33,500
				2002				
				1.1	Balances b/d		13,500	17,500

The current account balances both increased because drawings were not as high as the salaries and shared profits.

QUESTION 4

(a)

Lee and Wong

Balance Sheet extract as at 31.7.01

			£	£
Financed by				
Capital accounts				
Lee			12,000	
Wong			12,000	
				24,000
Current accounts		Lee	Wong	
		£	£	
Opening balance		4,100	200	
Add				
Salary		25,000	25,000	
Share of profit		8,160	5,440	
		37,260	30,640	
Less				
Drawings		25,000	28,600	
Closing balance		12,260	2,040	14,300
Capital account				38,300

(b) £38,300.

UNIT ASSESSMENT QUESTION 1

(a)

Willis and Daly
Profit and Loss Appropriation Account for the year ended 31.12.01

	£	£
Net profit b/d		(24,600)
Share of profit (loss):		
Willis (50%)	(12,300)	
Daly (50%)	(12,300)	
		(24,600)

(b)

Dr Partners' Fixed Capital Accounts **Cr**

		Willis £	Daly £			Willis £	Daly £
2001				2001			
31.12	Balances c/d	20,000	25,000	1.1	Balances b/d	20,000	25,000
				2002			
				1.1	Balances b/d	20,000	25,000

Dr Partners' Current Accounts **Cr**

		Willis £	Daly £			Willis £	Daly £
2001				2001			
31.12	Loss	12,300	12,300	1.1	Balances b/d	12,300	14,300
31.12	Drawings	14,000	11,500	31.12	Balances c/d	14,000	9,500
		26,300	23,800			26,300	23,800
2002							
1.1	Balances b/d	14,000	9,500				

(c)

Willis and Daly
Profit and Loss Appropriation Account for the year ended 31.12.01

	£	£
Net profit b/d		(24,600)
Less salary:		
Willis	20,000	
Daly	10,000	
		30,000
		(54,600)
Share of profit (loss):		
Willis (50%)	(27,300)	
Daly (50%)	(27,300)	
		(54,600)

UNIT ASSESSMENT QUESTION 2

(a)

Davies and Bishop
Profit and Loss Account for the year ended 31.1.01

	£	£
Fees		406,600
Opening stock	5,300	
Add purchases	76,200	
	81,500	
Less closing stock	6,300	
Cost of sales		75,200
Gross profit		331,400
Less expenses		
Wages and salaries	112,600	
Leasing	24,000	
Motor expenses	53,500	
Office expenses	12,400	
Insurance (£3,200 + £500)	3,700	
Other overheads	3,900	
Depreciation	8,500	
		218,600
Net profit		112,800
Less interest on capital:		
Davies	1,000	
Bishop	500	
		1,500
		111,300
Less salaries:		
Davies	33,000	
Bishop	30,000	
		63,000
		48,300
Share of profit:		
Davies	36,225	
Bishop	12,075	
		48,300

UNIT 37

QUESTION 1

(a) Average profit (£38,200) × 4 = £152,800.

(b) Goodwill (£152,800) + Net assets (£18,800) = £171,600.

(c) Expected future profits - depends on the nature of the business, the relationship with customers and the state of the economy.

QUESTION 2

(a)

Goodwill Account

Dr		Cr	
	£		£
Value divided:		Value divided:	
Fox (1/2)	30,000	Fox (1/3)	20,000
Ball (1/2)	30,000	Ball (1/3)	20,000
		Benni (1/3)	20,000
	60,000		60,000

Partners' Capital Accounts

Dr	Fox	Ball	Benni	Cr	Fox	Ball	Benni
	£	£	£		£	£	£
Goodwill written off	20,000	20,000	20,000	Balances b/d	25,000 25,000		
Balances c/d	35,000	35,000	30,000	Goodwill created	30,000 30,000		
				Bank		55,000	50,000
	55,000	55,000	50,000		55,000	55,000	50,000
				Balances b/d	35,000 35,000	30,000	

(b) John Fox: £35,000; Gillian Ball: £35,000; Ricardo Benni: £30,000.

(c) It is not standard accounting practice to show goodwill on the balance sheet unless it has been purchased. Goodwill is generally written off at the earliest opportunity.

QUESTION 3

(a)

Revaluation Account

Dr		Cr	
	£		£
Computer	2,100	Premises	112,000
Provision for bad debt	1,500		
Capital:			
Peters (50%)	54,200		
Moss (50%)	54,200		
	112,000		112,000

(c) Recognition of Helen's seniority and larger contribution of capital.

(b)

Davies and Bishop
Balance Sheet as at 31.1.01

	£	£
Fixed assets		
Equipment	45,000	
less depreciation	25,000	20,000
Vehicles	32,000	
less depreciation	17,500	14,500
		34,500
Current assets		
Stocks	6,300	
Debtors	42,700	
Bank	9,500	
	58,500	
Current liabilities		
Trade creditors	3,400	
Accrual	500	3,900
Net current assets		54,600
Net assets		**89,100**

Financed by		
Capital accounts		
Davies	20,000	
Bishop	10,000	30,000

Current accounts	Davies	Bishop
	£	£
Opening balance	(400)	3,900
Add		
Salary	33,000	30,000
Interest on capital	1,000	500
Share of profit	36,225	12,075
	69,825	46,475
Less		
Drawings	31,800	25,400
	38,025	21,075
Capital employed	**59,100**	
		89,100

QUESTION 4

(a)

Dr		Goodwill Account		Cr	
	£				£
Value divided:			Value divided:		
Done (1/3)	30,000		Done (1/4)		22,500
Bryce(1/3)	30,000		Bryce (1/4)		22,500
Wallace (1/3)	30,000		Wallace (1/2)		45,000
	90,000				90,000

Partners' Capital Accounts

Dr	Done	Bryce	Wallace		Cr	Done	Bryce	Wallace
	£	£	£			£	£	£
Goodwill written off	22,500	22,500	45,000	Balances b/d		10,000	15,000	15,000
Balances c/d	17,500	22,500	-	Goodwill created		30,000	30,000	30,000
	40,000	45,000	45,000			40,000	45,000	45,000
				Balances b/d		17,500	22,500	-

(b) Alastair Wallace has compensated Kate Done and Angus Bryce for their loss of goodwill. In effect Alastair has paid Kate and Angus £7,500 each for a share of their goodwill.

(c) Goodwill is not usually shown on a balance sheet.

UNIT ASSESSMENT QUESTION 1

(a)

Dr		Realisation Account		Cr	
	£				£
Premises	64,000		Premises		84,000
Fixtures and fittings	4,300		Fixtures and fittings		1,000
Computer	1,500		Computer (taken by Hart)		1,000
Debtors	3,200		Debtors		2,900
Bank - realisation expenses	1,200				
Profit on realisation					
Hart (1/2)	7,350				
Brown (1/2)	7,350				
	88,900				88,900

(b) £14,700. This is the balance on the realisation account.

(b)

Peters, Moss and Cherry
Balance Sheet as at 1.5.01

	£	£
Fixed assets		
Premises		190,000
Fixtures and fittings		18,000
Equipment		6,500
Computer		200
		214,700
Current assets		
Debtors and prepayments	5,700	
Bank	29,200	
	34,900	
Less current liabilities		
Trade creditors	5,300	
Net current assets		29,600
		244,300
Less long term liabilities		
Mortgage		60,000
Net assets		184,300

Financed by

Capital accounts		£
Peters		79,200
Moss		79,200
Cherry		25,000
		183,400

Current accounts	Peters	Moss	Cherry
	£	£	£
Opening balance	1,500	2,100	-
Add			
Share of profit	26,200	26,200	-
	27,700	28,300	-
Less			
Drawings	27,600	27,500	-
	100	800	-
			900

Capital employed		184,300

(c)

Bank Account

Dr	£		Cr	£
Balance b/d	5,200		Trade creditors	4,000
Realisation: Assets sold			Mortgage	30,000
Premises	84,000		Realisation expenses	1,200
Debtors and prepayments	2,900		Capital accounts:	
Fixtures and fittings	1,000		Hart	32,150
			Brown	25,750
	93,100			93,100

Partners' Capital Accounts

Dr	Hart £	Brown £		Cr	Hart £	Brown £
Realisation (computer)	1,000			Balances b/d	20,000	20,000
Current account		1,600		Current account		5,800
Bank to close	32,150	25,750		Profit on realisation	7,350	7,350
	33,150	27,350			33,150	27,350

UNIT ASSESSMENT QUESTION 2

(a) (i)

Goodwill Account

Dr	£		Cr	£
Value divided:			Value divided:	
Hussain (1/3)	30,000		Hussain (1/2)	45,000
Munton (1/3)	30,000		Rose (1/2)	45,000
Rose (1/3)	30,000			
	90,000			90,000

(ii)

Revaluation Account

Dr	£		Cr	£
Fixtures and fittings	400		Premises	37,000
Capital accounts:				
Hussain	12,200			
Munton	12,200			
Rose	12,200			
	37,000			37,000

(iii)

Partners' Capital Accounts

Dr	Hussain £	Munton £	Rose £		Cr	Hussain £	Munton £	Rose £
Goodwill written off	45,000		45,000		Balances b/d	40,000	40,000	40,000
Loan a/c - Munton		82,200			Goodwill created	30,000	30,000	30,000
Balances c/d	37,200		37,200		Revaluation	12,200	12,200	12,200
	82,200	82,200	82,200			82,200	82,200	82,200
					Balances b/d	37,200		37,200

(iv)

Loan Account - Karen Munton

Dr	£		Cr	£
Balance c/d	84,100		Capital a/c - transfer	82,200
			Current a/c - transfer	1,900
	84,100			84,100
			Balance b/d	84,100

(v)

Premises Account

Dr	£		Cr	£
Balance b/d	83,000		Balance c/d	120,000
Revaluation	37,000			
	120,000			120,000
Balance b/d	120,000			

QUESTION 1

(a)

Weston Toys Ltd
Trading and Profit and Loss account
for the year ended 30.11.01

	£000s	£000s	£000s
Turnover			12,432
Cost of sales			5,332
Gross profit			7,100
Less expenses			
Selling and distribution:			
Salespersons' salaries	210		
Distribution	312		
Other selling expenses	448	970	
Administration:			
Office expenses	1,237		
Directors' remuneration	560		
Other admin. expenses	732		
Depreciation	176	2,705	3,675
			3,425
Interest paid			153
Profit before taxation			3,272
Taxation			800
Profit after taxation			2,472
Dividends proposed			1,000
Retained profit for the year			1,472
Retained profit b/f			6,920
Retained profit c/f			8,392

(b) £8,392,000.

(c) As a precaution and to help fund investment.

(b)

Hussain and Rose
Balance Sheet as at 1.1.02

	£	£
Fixed assets		
Premises		120,000
Van		7,000
Fixtures and fittings		4,800
		131,800
Current assets		
Stock	18,400	
Debtors	5,300	
Bank	27,400	
	51,100	
Less current liabilities		
Trade creditors	16,600	
Net current assets		34,500
		166,300
Less long term liabilities		
Loan - Munton		84,100
Net assets		82,200
Financed by		
Capital accounts		
Hussain	37,200	
Rose	37,200	
		74,400
Current accounts		
Hussain	3,100	
Rose	4,700	
		7,800
Capital employed		82,200

QUESTION 2

(a)

Heyford plc
Balance Sheet extract as at 30.6.01

	£000	£000
Capital and reserves		
Authorised share capital		
25,000,000 ordinary shares of 50p each	12,500	
Issued and fully paid up		
10,000,000 ordinary shares of 50p each	5,000	
Share premium account	6,000	
Revaluation reserve	12,400	
Profit and loss account	20,629	
Shareholders' funds	44,029	

(b) £44,029,000.

(c) They are both capital reserves and are therefore non-distributable.

QUESTION 3

(a) (i) £10,506,000 (ii) £7,434,000.

(b) Office salaries, depreciation, auditors' fees, motor expenses, stationery, insurance.

(c) Large increase in turnover (approx 44%), significant increase in profit before tax (approx 15%) but smaller increase in profit after tax (approx 7%).

(a)

Robson's Locks Ltd
Profit and Loss Account
for the year ended 31.12.01

	£	£
Gross profit		672,100
Selling and distribution:		
Advertising and marketing	21,900	
Administration:		
Office wages and salaries	166,300	
Directors' salaries	102,300	
Motor expenses	43,100	
Bad debt	2,400	
General expenses	32,400	
Depreciation	10,000	
		378,400
		293,700
Interest (1,500 paid + 1,500 owing)		3,000
Profit before taxation		290,700
Taxation		50,000
Profit after taxation		240,700
Dividends proposed		60,000
Retained profit for the year		180,700
Retained profit b/f		563,800
Retained profit c/f		744,500

UNIT ASSESSMENT QUESTION 2

(a)

Somerfield plc
Balance Sheet as at 29.4.00

	£m
Fixed assets	
Tangible assets	960.3
Investments	4.4
	964.7
Current assets	
Stock	372.6
Debtors	145.4
Short term investments	3.9
Cash at bank and in hand	238.3
	760.2
Creditors:	
amounts falling due within one year	(655.5)
Net current assets	104.7
Total assets less current liabilities	1,069.4
Creditors:	
amounts falling due after more than one year	(328.8)
Provisions for liabilities and charges	(24.8)
Net assets	715.8
Capital and reserves	
Called-up share capital	49.4
Share premium account	32.8
Revaluation reserve	82.4
Other reserves	335.3
Profit and loss account	215.9
Shareholders' funds	715.8

(b)

Robson's Locks Ltd
Balance Sheet as at 31.12.01

	£	£	£
Fixed assets			
Tangible assets			
Factory			1,300,000
Motor vehicles	41,800		
Less depreciation	24,000		17,800
Plant and equipment	65,000		
Less depreciation	42,000		23,000
			1,340,800
Current assets			
Stock		43,000	
Debtors		27,400	
Cash at bank		16,300	
		86,700	
Creditors: amounts falling due within one year			
Creditors	21,500		
Accrual	1,500		
Taxation	50,000		
Dividends proposed	60,000		
		(46,300)	
Net current assets			1,294,500
Creditors: amounts falling due after more than one year			
Debentures 6%			(50,000)
Net assets			1,244,500
Capital and reserves			
Authorised and issued share capital			
500,000 ordinary shares of £1 each			500,000
Profit and loss account			744,500
Shareholders' funds			1,244,500

(b) Land, property, fixtures and fittings, vehicles.
(c) An exceptional item is a transaction that falls within the ordinary activities of the company but is of an exceptional magnitude. For Somerfield, an example is the restructuring cost of £100 million.
(d) Short term investments are financial assets that are not likely to be held for more than one year. When listed under fixed assets, investments are likely to be held for more than one year.

UNIT 39

QUESTION 1

(a)

Wheatsheaf Rambling Club
Receipts and Payments Account for the year ended 31.12.01

Receipts	£	Payments	£
Balance b/d	260	Coach hire	1,660
Subscriptions received	980	Advertising	340
Coach fares	780	Maps	280
Proceeds from jumble sales	920	First aid kits	240
Proceeds from T-shirts	110	Stationery	190
Sponsorship	200	Miscellaneous expenses	220
		Balance c/d	320
	3,250		3,250
Balance b/d	320		

(b) £320.

(c) To show members of the Rambling Club where money has come from, where it has gone to and how much is left at the end of the year.

QUESTION 2

(a)

Werndene Tennis Club
Income and Expenditure Account for the year ended 31.3.01

	£
Income	
Subscriptions (2,100 received + 140 owing - 230 prepaid)	2,010
Net proceeds from summer ball	3,130
Net proceeds from presentation dinner	2,100
Net proceeds from summer fete	450
	7,690
Expenditure	
Affiliation to county tennis association	400
Heat and light	270
Groundsman's wages (680 + 50)	730
General expenses	380
Depreciation (1,000 + 500 + 300)	1,800
	3,580
Surplus of income over expenditure	4,110

(b) Transactions such as accruals, prepayments and depreciation can be shown. It also provides information for a balance sheet.

QUESTION 3

(a)

Hampton Rowing Club
Balance Sheet as at 31.5.01

	£	£
Fixed assets		
Boats and equipment	22,700	
Less depreciation	3,500	19,200
Current assets		
Debtors (subscriptions owing)	300	
Prepayments	400	
Cash at bank and in hand	4,560	
	5,260	
Current liabilities		
Accrual	130	
Working capital		5,130
		24,330
Long term liabilities		
Loan (member)		(5,000)
Net assets		19,330
Financed by		
Accumulated fund		18,800
Surplus of income over expenditure for the year		530
		19,330

UNIT ASSESSMENT QUESTION 1

(a)

Glenroyd Rugby Club
Bar Trading Account for the year ended 31.12.01

	£	£
Sales		32,100
Less cost of sales		
Opening stock	2,360	
Purchases (11,780 + 450)	12,230	
	14,590	
Closing stock	3,100	
		11,490
Gross profit		20,610
Less wages to bar steward		14,000
Profit on bar		6,610

(b) Members will know the value of assets and liabilities, and therefore net assets of the club.

(b)

Glenroyd Rugby Club
Income and Expenditure Account for the year ended 31.12.01

	£	£
Income		
Subscriptions		6,375
Profit on bar		6,610
Net proceeds from presentation		1,190
Donations		850
Sponsorship		500
		15,525
Expenditure		
Travelling expenses	1,500	
Committee expenses	560	
Heat and light (650 + 150)	800	
Groundstaff wages	3,600	
Rugby kit	5,200	
Water rates	720	
Stationery	120	
Sundry expenses	1,670	
Depreciation	4,200	
		18,370
Deficit of income over expenditure		(2,845)

(c) Accumulated fund = £28,560 - £2,845 = £25,715.

UNIT ASSESSMENT QUESTION 2

(a) Net assets (as at 1.1.01) = total assets (£6,550) - total liabilities (£190) = £6,360. This is therefore the value of the accumulated fund.

(b)

Knighton History Society
Income and Expenditure Account for the year ended 31.12.01

	£	£
Income		
Subscriptions		670
Fares from visits		1,200
Net proceeds from Xmas raffle		810
		2,680
Expenditure		
Expenses to guest speakers	430	
Motor expenses (760 +50 - 100)	710	
Rent	260	
Fees for film hire (240 - 60 + 80)	260	
Sundry expenses	130	
Depreciation	900	
		2,690
Deficit of income over expenditure		(10)

(c)

Knighton History Society
Balance Sheet as at 31.12.01

	£	£
Fixed assets		
Minibus	4,300	
Less depreciation	600	3,700
Books	2,030	
Less depreciation	200	1,830
Film projector	350	
Less depreciation	50	300
Camera	400	
Less depreciation	50	350
		6,180
Current assets		
Prepayments	100	
Cash at bank and in hand	380	
	480	
Current liabilities		
Accruals - film	80	
Book supplier	230	
	310	
Working capital		170
Net assets		6,350
Financed by		
Accumulated fund		6,360
Deficit of income over expenditure for the year		(10)
		6,350

(see next page)

2(c) continued Note that the historical value of books, ie before depreciation, was £2,030. This figure is calculated as follows:

	£
Value of books as at 1.1.01	1,200
Add purchases	730
Add money owing to book supplier as at 31.12.01	230
	2,160
Less money owing to book supplier as at 1.1.01	130
	2,030

(b) The value of partly completed goods should not be transferred to the trading account because they are not ready or available to sell.

UNIT 40

QUESTION 1

(a) (i) Clay, (ii) pottery worker; (iii) electricity for pottery kiln.

(b) The direct costs are directly related to the manufacture of individual items of pottery. The indirect production costs cannot be directly related, for example, insurance on the factory and depreciation on the kilns.

QUESTION 2

(a)

Cartwright Holdings Ltd
Manufacturing Account for the year ended 31.3.01

	£000	£000
Direct materials		
Stock at 1.4.00	1,769	
Purchases	12,001	
	13,770	
Less stock at 31.3.01	1,988	
		11,782
Direct labour		15,332
Other direct expenses		4,880
Prime cost		31,994
Add production overheads		
Indirect materials	7,443	
Indirect labour	4,009	
Indirect expenses	2,773	
		14,225
		46,219
Add work-in-progress at 1.4.00		2,122
		48,341
Less work-in-progress at 31.3.01		2,431
Production cost		45,910
(Cost of goods transferred to trading account)		

QUESTION 3

(a)

Celtic Plastics Ltd
Manufacturing Account for the year ended 31.7.01

	£000	£000
Direct materials		
Stock at 1.8.00	169	
Purchases	2,331	
	2,500	
Less stock at 31.7.01	188	
		2,312
Direct labour		1,911
Direct expenses		199
Prime cost		4,422
Add production overheads		
Indirect materials	1,222	
Indirect labour	987	
Indirect expenses	1,852	
		4,061
		8,483
Add work-in-progress at 1.8.00		340
		8,823
Less work-in-progress at 31.7.01		401
Production cost		8,422
Sales		9,156
Less cost of sales		
Stocks of finished goods (1.8.00)	421	
Production cost	8,422	
	8,843	
Less stocks of finished goods (31.7.01)	459	
		8,384
Gross profit		772
Less selling and distribution expenses	768	
Administration expenses	889	
		1,657
		(885)
Less interest paid		100
Net profit/(loss)		(985)

(b)

Celtic Plastics Ltd
Balance Sheet (extract)
as at 31.7.01

	£000
Current assets	
Direct materials	188
Work-in-progress	401
Finished goods	459
	1,048

QUESTION 4

(a)

Anslow Furnishings Ltd
Manufacturing, Trading and Profit and Loss Account
for the year ended 31.1.01

	£	
Prime cost		184,200
Overheads		65,800
Production cost		250,000
Factory profit (40%)		100,000
Production cost		350,000
Sales		540,100
Less cost of sales		
Opening stock	41,000	
Production cost	350,000	
	391,000	
Less closing stock	43,200	
Cost of goods sold		347,800
Gross profit		192,300
Less selling costs	78,000	
Administration costs	56,000	
		134,000
Trading profit		58,300
Factory profit		100,000
Net profit		158,300

UNIT ASSESSMENT QUESTION 1

(a)

Quentin Carmichael Ltd
Manufacturing Account

	for the year ended 31.12.00			for the year ended 31.12.01		
	£	£	£	£	£	£
Direct materials						
Opening stock		24,000			25,600	
Purchases (120,000 + 340,200)		460,200		(124,000 + 342,100)	466,100	
		484,200			491,700	
Less closing stock		25,600			27,800	
			458,600			463,900
Direct labour			451,000			377,800
Direct expenses			146,200			144,500
Prime cost			1,055,800			986,200
Add production overheads						
Indirect materials		45,600			43,800	
Indirect labour (67,000 + 54,000)		121,000		(61,000 + 48,000)	109,000	
Indirect expenses (100,000 + 78,500)		178,500		(100,000 + 81,200)	181,200	
			345,100			334,000
			1,400,900			1,320,200
Add opening work-in-progress			38,000			41,000
			1,438,900			1,361,200
Less closing work-in-progress			41,000			45,000
Production cost			1,397,900			1,316,200
(Cost of goods transferred to trading account)						

(b) Production costs have been cut by £80,700. Most of this has been cut from direct labour.

(b) One factor is the amount of profit made in manufacturing compared with trading. In this example, based on the assumption of a 40% notional charge for factory profit, the company makes almost twice the profit in manufacturing than it does in trading.

Closing stock of finished goods: £80,000 × 25/125 = £16,000

(b) Based on the assumption of a 25% notional charge for factory profit, manufacturing contributes just over one third of net profits.

UNIT 41

QUESTION 1

(a) To compare departmental performance and to reward departmental managers on the basis of departmental performance.

(b) Factors outside their control might affect profit. For example, managers might not be in control of pricing and profit margins.

QUESTION 2

(a)

	Bedroom £	Dining room £	Suites £	Total £
Sales	236,800	155,400	733,900	1,126,100
Opening stock	24,100	21,900	53,900	99,900
Purchases	132,900	111,100	363,500	607,500
	157,000	133,000	417,400	707,400
Closing stock	23,800	22,700	54,000	100,500
Cost of sales	133,200	110,300	363,400	606,900
Gross profit	103,600	45,100	370,500	519,200

(b) £519,200.

(c) (i) Bedroom: 43.75%; dining room: 29.02%; suites: 50.48%. (ii) The dining room department has the lowest margin, well below the bedroom department and the suites which is the best performing department.

QUESTION 3

(a)

	Food hall £	Electrical goods £	Sports and leisure wear £	Total £
Gross profit	221,400	150,900	99,000	583,300
Manager's salary	24,000	29,000	27,000	80,000
Heat and light	20,000	10,000	10,000	40,000
Depreciation	10,000	5,000	5,000	20,000
Advertising	15,000	15,000	15,000	45,000
Total overheads	69,000	59,000	57,000	185,000
Net profit	152,400	91,900	42,000	398,300

UNIT ASSESSMENT QUESTION 2

(a)

Boswell, Burns & Co
Manufacturing, Trading and Profit and Loss Account
for the year ended 31.12.01

	£	£
Direct materials		
Opening stock	30,000	
Purchases	351,000	
	381,000	
Less closing stock	32,000	
		349,000
Direct labour		511,000
Direct expenses		110,000
Prime cost		970,000
Add production overheads		
Indirect materials	28,000	
Indirect labour	98,000	
Indirect expenses	52,000	
		178,000
		1,148,000
Add work-in-progress at 1.1.01		54,000
		1,202,000
Less work-in-progress at 31.12.01		60,000
Production cost		1,142,000
Factory profit at 25%		285,500
Production cost of goods completed (including factory profit)		1,427,500
Sales		2,520,000
Less cost of sales		
Opening stocks of finished goods	70,000	
Production cost (including factory profit)	1,427,500	
	1,497,500	
Less closing stocks of finished goods	80,000	
		1,417,500
Gross profit		1,102,500
Less selling and distribution expenses	290,000	
Administration expenses	341,000	
		631,000
Trading profit		471,500
Factory profit	285,500	
Less provision for unrealised profit*	2,000	
		283,500
Net profit		755,000

* Opening stock of finished goods: £70,000 × 25/125 = £14,000

(b) Gross margins: food hall: 33.34%; electrical goods: 27.79%; sports and leisure wear: 46.91%.
The gross margin of the sports and leisure wear department is by far the highest. It might therefore benefit the business to expand this department. However, the way that overheads are apportioned would also have to be taken into account.

UNIT ASSESSMENT QUESTION 1

(a)

	Shoes and accessories £	Lingerie £	Evening wear £	Casual wear £	Total £
Sales	127,400	106,500	231,000	163,900	628,800
Opening stock	12,500	14,300	27,500	16,400	70,700
Purchases	46,300	43,200	117,000	102,000	308,500
	58,800	57,500	144,500	118,400	379,200
Closing stock	13,900	15,300	26,400	19,800	75,400
Cost of sales	44,900	42,200	118,100	98,600	303,800
Gross profit	82,500	64,300	112,900	65,300	325,000
Less overheads					
Wages	60,000	40,000	60,000	80,000	240,000
Rent and rates	10,000	10,000	10,000	20,000	50,000
Heat and light	4,000	4,000	4,000	8,000	20,000
Other expenses	3,000	3,000	3,000	3,000	12,000
Total	77,000	57,000	77,000	111,000	322,000
Net profit/(loss)	5,500	7,300	35,900	(45,700)	3,000

(b) Yes, the £45,700 loss almost wipes out the entire profit made by the other departments.
(c) Apportionment of overheads, size of gross profit, attraction to customers, closure costs and alternative resource use.

UNIT ASSESSMENT QUESTION 2

(a) (b) and (c)

	Dudley £	Gornal £	Sedgley £	Oldbury £	Walsall £	Total £
Sales	65,000	69,000	86,700	43,100	121,900	385,700
Opening stock	1,200	1,500	1,300	1,100	2,700	7,800
Purchases	32,100	36,400	43,800	17,500	64,000	193,800
	33,300	37,900	45,100	18,600	66,700	201,600
Closing stock	1,300	1,600	1,200	1,300	3,000	8,400
Cost of sales	32,000	36,300	43,900	17,300	63,700	193,200
Gross profit	33,000	32,700	42,800	25,800	58,200	192,500
Overheads	6,400	7,500	8,500	5,300	21,000	48,700
Manager's salary	15,000	15,000	15,000	15,000	15,000	75,000
Office expenses	9,000	9,000	9,000	9,000	9,000	45,000
	30,400	31,500	32,500	29,300	45,000	168,700
Net profit/(loss)	2,600	1,200	10,300	(3,500)	13,200	23,800
Salary bonus	260	120	1,030	0	1,320	
Net profit margin (rounded)	4.00%	1.74%	11.88%		10.83%	

(d) It is an incentive to earn high profits, but it does not necessarily reflect the highest profit margins. In this case, the manager with the highest net profit, ie Walsall, does not achieve as high a profit margin as Sedgley.

UNIT 42

QUESTION 1

	Effect on profit	on cash
1 Bought a new delivery van for cash.	none	decrease
2 Repaid a short term bank loan.	none	decrease
3 Issued new shares for cash.	none	increase
4 Received cash from a trade debtor.	none	increase
5 Made a large sale on credit.	increase	none
6 Increased provision for depreciation on its buildings.	decrease	none
7 Sold a surplus fork lift truck for cash.	none	increase
8 Arranged a long term bank loan.	none	increase

QUESTION 2

(a)

	£
Operating profit	11,500,000
Depreciation	1,600,000
Decrease in stock	300,000
Increase in debtors	(1,100,000)
Decrease in creditors	(600,000)
Net cash flow from operating activities	**11,700,000**

(b) Depreciation is a non-cash transaction. It is treated as an expense but does not result in any cash flow from the business. Therefore it must be added to profit.

QUESTION 3

(a) £60,400 (£51,100 + £9,300).

(b)

	£
Operating profit	60,400
Depreciation	2,500
Increase in stock	(7,900)
Decrease in debtors	1,100
Decrease in creditors	(800)
Net cash flow from operating activities	**55,300**

(c)

Jason Simmons
Cash Flow Statement for the year ended 31.12.01

	£
Net cash flow from operating activities	55,300
Returns on investments and servicing of finance	
Net interest paid (net profit £51,100 - operating profit £60,400)	(9,300)
Taxation	-
Capital expenditure and financial investment	-
Acquisitions and disposals	-
Equity dividends	
Drawings	(56,400)
Cash inflow before use of liquid resources and financing	(10,400)
Financing	
Bank loan	5,000
Decrease in cash in the period	(5,400)

(d)

Cash in hand (£1,200) and owed to bank (£18,700) (31.12.00)	(£17,500)
Net cash outflow	(£5,400)
Cash in hand (£500) and owed to bank (£23,400) (31.12.01)	(£22,900)

(e) (i) The amount of cash in the business fell by £5,400. The bank overdraft increased by £4,700 and the amount of cash decreased by £700.

(ii) Increase in stock and increase in drawings. Drawings were greater than the net cash flow from operating activities.

UNIT ASSESSMENT QUESTION 1

(a) Net cash flow from operating activities is the amount of cash generated from trading. It includes the operating profit and the cash flow resulting from non-cash transactions, and changes in the value of stock, debtors and creditors. The loss or gain on the disposal of any fixed assets is also taken into account. The increase in cash, which is calculated in the cash flow statement, includes not only the movements resulting from trading activities, but also those resulting from other transactions such as interest and taxation payments. It also includes cash flows resulting from funding transactions such as loans.

(b) Decrease in stock, £6,000 bank loan and, to a lesser extent, decrease in debtors and increase in creditors.

UNIT ASSESSMENT QUESTION 2

(a) £54,400 (Change in profit and loss account (£88,600 - £71,500) + Taxation owed £11,000 + Dividends proposed £10,000 + Net interest paid £16,300).

(b)

	£
Operating profit	54,400
Depreciation	80,000
Decrease in stock	7,600
Increase in debtors	(2,000)
Increase in creditors	2,000
Net cash flow from operating activities	**142,000**

Note that in this answer, the change in creditors **excludes** the bank overdraft. This is because money in the business's bank account is classed as cash and therefore forms part of the actual cash flow. The decrease in cash (£21,300) shown in part (c) of this question is equal to the reduction in the cash and bank balances of the business (from plus £12,700 to an overdraft of £8,600). Tax and dividends are also excluded.

QUESTION 3

(a) Increased sales volume and/or rising prices - supported by the large increase in selling and distribution expenses from £140,000 to £240,000.

(b) Net profit was significantly lower than gross profit, due to high selling and distribution and administration costs and high interest payments.

(c) The increase in interest payments from £90,000 to £165,000 suggests that debt increased significantly.

QUESTION 4

(a) The value of plant and equipment increased by £4.6m (ignoring depreciation). Funding appears to have come from cash at bank and non-payment of dividends. There was no increase in loans (debentures) or share capital.

(b) Net assets increased from £16.3m to £18.1m, therefore the value of the business could be said to have increased by this amount. However, this excludes the value of intangible assets. The revaluation reserve increased from £0.8m to £1.2m, possibly reflecting a rise in value of the business's premises.

(c) Working capital in 2001 was £2.9m. It had fallen significantly over the two years but current assets were still 1.55 times the value of current liabilities.

(d) No change in gearing - loan capital (£3m) and share capital (£8m) do not change.

UNIT ASSESSMENT QUESTION 1

(a) Matthews - best profit, property included and scope for more profit if bad debts are eliminated. Wignall - cheapest of the two, has potential because it has been run down and still makes a profit. Buyers could reduce the wage bill by supplying their own labour.

(b) There is no 'interest paid' in the profit and loss account for either business, suggesting that there are no outstanding debts.

(c) Balance sheet information such as the value of assets and value of liabilities. Also the condition of assets, value of goodwill and knowledge of competition. Accounts from several years would reveal more than just one year's.

UNIT ASSESSMENT QUESTION 2

(a) Increase in gross profit, increase in turnover, increase in net profit, increase in retained profit, increase in fixed assets, increase in current assets, increase in working capital, increase in net assets, no increase in long term debt.

(b) (i) Improving trading position, improving working capital, sufficient liquid assets, some fixed assets which might be used as security. (ii) High gearing and therefore high burden of interest payments (loan capital £75,000 is higher than share capital £40,000).
The improvement in 2001 could be a temporary improvement and the 2000 figures could be a truer indication of the company's longer term performance. Insufficient information is provided and more year's accounts are therefore needed.

(c)

Scottish Fabrics Ltd
Cash Flow Statement for the year ended 31.12.01

	£
Net cash flow from operating activities	142,000
Returns on investments and servicing of finance	
Net interest paid	(16,300)
Taxation	
Tax paid	(25,000)
Capital expenditure and financial investment	
Purchase of plant and equipment	(550,000)
Receipts from sale of equipment	100,000
Acquisitions and disposals	
Sale of investments	10,000
Equity dividends	
Dividends paid	(12,000)
Cash inflow before use of liquid resources and financing	(351,300)
Financing	
Bank loan	100,000
Increase in mortgage	30,000
Share issue	200,000
Decrease in cash in the period	(21,300)

(d) Spending on plant and equipment was not fully covered by new financing. High interest payments.

UNIT 43

QUESTION 1

(a) To calculate Carol's tax liability.

(b) (i) No, net profit has increased by only 15.3%. (ii) To complete her tax self-assessment form. To compare business income with other possible sources of income such as earnings from employment.

(c) If Carol applies for a loan for her business.

QUESTION 2

(a) Quest's performance appears superior for two reasons. It generates about the same profit as Millstone from a much lower turnover. Carter's profit has fallen over the time period and is much lower than Quest's.

(b) The companies are not identical. They are involved in slightly different construction activities, eg Millstone does contract work for the government. Also, Millstone is a much bigger company than Quest with nearly double the turnover and Carter's is slightly smaller.

(c) Abnormal years can be identified and ignored. Trends can be detected.

UNIT 44

QUESTION 1

(a) (i) 2000 = 23.53%; 2001 = 20.41% (ii) 2000 = 5.88%; 2001 = 7.09%

(b) The fall in the gross margin from 23.53% to 20.41% would be expected as a result of Jenny reducing prices. The increase in net margin from 5.88% to 7.09% would also be expected as a result of Jenny cutting overheads.

(c) (i) ROCE = 4.38%. (ii) By comparison with current interest rates. More could be earned from a bank deposit account which carries no risk.

QUESTION 2

(a) (i) 1999 = 94 days; 2000 = 81 days; 2001 = 70 days.

(ii) Yes - the debt collection period has fallen from 94 days to 70 days. Customers settled their debts more quickly. The cash position also improved.

(b) (i) 2000 = 50 days; 2001 = 80 days (ii) Stock turnover slowed down. This might be because customers found alternative suppliers as a result of the pressure to speed up payment.

QUESTION 3

(a) (i) 2001 = 1.35:1 ; 2000 = 1.40:1; 1999 = 1.94:1; 1998 = 2.00:1.

(ii) 2001 = 1.29:1; 2000 = 1.17:1; 1999 = 1.02:1; 1998 = 1.04:1.

(b) The current ratio fell but the acid test improved. Applying the more rigorous acid test, the liquidity of Brockhurst improved. The company had much less money tied up unproductively in stocks, but had more money in the bank.

QUESTION 4

(a) (i) 2001 = 11.67; 2000 = 13.33 (ii) 2001 = 10p; 2000 = 12p

(iii) 2001 = 2.04%; 2000 = 2.31%.

(b) In all cases the ratios show a deterioration in performance. Therefore it might be time to sell.

(c) Other helpful information might include the current national economic circumstances, the performance of other companies in the same industry, information for more years, information relating to gearing, liquidity and efficiency.

UNIT ASSESSMENT QUESTION 1

(a) (i) 2001 = 1.06:1; 2000 = 1.68:1 (ii) 2001 = 0.64:1; 2000 = 0.74:1 (iii) 2001 = 49.63%; 2000 = 48.3% (iv) 2001 = 1.5 times; 2000 = 11.2 times.

(b) Probably not - there was a serious decline in working capital according to current and acid test ratios. The interest cover fell dramatically due to a fall in profit. Although gearing was not especially high, there was a significant amount of loan capital.

(c) (i) 2001 = 78 days; 2000 = 43 days.

(ii) Debt collection period increased significantly. This confirms problems with debt collection.

UNIT ASSESSMENT QUESTION 2

(a) Assuming that growth is an investment objective, CanCo should have been chosen. This is because there was consistent growth in ROCE and dividend yield. The p/e ratio also suggests that there was a lot of confidence in the company. AK Foods was successful and stable but did not appear to have growth potential.

(b) (i)

	ROCE	Div. Yield	P/E ratio
A K Foods	12.20%	1.86%	16.69
CanCo	14.54%	2.30%	23.0

(ii) No - the new information reinforces the decision. CanCo continues to grow and A K Foods remains stable.

(c) Figures for 5 years help to detect trends. The stability of AK Foods, and the growth of Can Co, could not be detected with 1 or 2 year's figures.

UNIT 45

QUESTION 1

(a) To boost its share price, to attract investment, exaggerate its position to its rivals.

(b) By reducing depreciation charges, overheads will fall and profits will rise.

UNIT ASSESSMENT QUESTION 1

(a) The companies have different locations and different capital structures. They are also in slightly different lines of business.

(b) Because external factors such as consumer confidence can vary significantly over time.

(c) Route 1 owns its vehicles and therefore incurs no leasing charges. Its customers are more concentrated regionally so costs might be lower. It might be able to charge higher prices to customers in London and the South East. It might have more efficient managers and better motivated employees. However, it will incur higher interest charges because of its loan capital.

UNIT ASSESSMENT QUESTION 2

(a) To raise the share price, so reducing the risk of a takeover bid. To put the business's finances in a more favourable light to attract new share or loan capital.

(b) Capitalising development spending would reduce overheads. Recognising earnings at an earlier stage would increase current turnover. Both would increase profits. The sale of assets would not increase profits, unless they were sold for more than their net book value. However, the leasing charge would reduce profits.

(c) The value of fixed assets would fall and the value of current assets (cash) would rise. If some of the cash was used to pay creditors, current liabilities would fall. The liquid ratio would rise.

(d) The Companies Act and the ASB lay down rules on presentation and content so analysis is made easier. Companies have to declare changes in accounting policy and any breaches of standards.

UNIT 46

QUESTION 1

(a) Shareholders will benefit from a fall in fuel costs which will increase profitability; UK population will benefit from less pollution from car exhausts, and possibly fewer road accidents if mileage is reduced; world population will benefit from fewer greenhouse gases.

(b) Laing might believe it is the socially responsible thing to do. It might believe that the company's image will improve and this will attract more customers.

UNIT ASSESSMENT QUESTION 1

(a) Employees will suffer fewer deaths and injuries; shareholders will benefit from reduction in energy costs; community groups and people who receive help from charities will benefit from charitable donations.

(b) Families of employees will benefit if there are fewer injuries. Health care costs for the local community will also be reduced. Suppliers of energy might suffer from loss of sales but there will be less pollution if less energy is used. Greenhouse gas emissions will be less, as will emissions from power stations. Charitable giving might have spin-off effects on the local community and economy. Recipients of the charity will spend the money, so raising demand for other goods and services.

UNIT ASSESSMENT QUESTION 2

(a) Shareholders will be interested in the financial results, particularly the dividend per share that they receive. The increase in gross profit margin and the fall in gearing might raise demand for the company's shares, so increasing the value of the shares.

(b) Shareholders might benefit if overall sales increase, but suffer if development costs are high or if sales are less than expected. Customers will benefit from increased choice and, possibly, from more competitive prices. Competitors might suffer from loss of sales. Prospective employees will gain employment and income, and this will benefit the whole of the local economy, as long as other shops do not go out of business. Suppliers will benefit from increased sales to the company. Builders and local contractors will benefit if they are employed to build the new shop. The local community might benefit via the increased business taxes that will be paid to the council. Depending on the style, location and design of the new store, the city might improve its visual attractiveness. Shoppers from elsewhere might be attracted to the city, so benefiting other shops and services.

(c) Customers could be surveyed in terms of their satisfaction with the service they receive. Employee satisfaction could be measured by opinion survey, or by measuring absenteeism or turnover rates. Supplier satisfaction could be assessed by opinion survey, or by calculating the average length of time that bills are outstanding. The impact on the local community could be measured by the amount of money given to charity, or by the amount of sponsorship given to local events.

UNIT 47

UNIT ASSESSMENT QUESTION 1

(a) Systems become out of date and must be replaced or upgraded. Technology is expensive.

Staff have to be trained and retrained. Computers are vulnerable to infection from viruses.

(b) Selective access to information. Protection from viruses. Protection from computer hackers.

(c) Accounts can be produced instantly. Information will be up to date. Comparisons can be made between countries because information for each country will be presented in a standard format.

UNIT ASSESSMENT QUESTION 2

In a report format:

Advantages

- Long term bookkeeping and accounting costs will be reduced.
- Computerised systems are user friendly, no computer knowledge is necessary.
- Large amounts of data on new customers can be stored, manipulated and retrieved easily.
- Credit control may be improved.
- Payroll can be undertaken 'in-house', therefore cost savings will be made.
- Accounts and reports can be generated on a regular basis which can be used by Mary to help decision making.

Disadvantages

- High initial cost.
- There might be teething problems.
- Staff will have to be trained.
- Some staff might resist the system because they are concerned about job security.
- If the business continues to expand, the system might not be able to cope in the future. Therefore it will have to be upgraded or replaced.

UNIT 48

QUESTION 1

(a) £163,000 (raw materials £53,000 plus production staff wages £110,000).

(b) £148,000 (admin wages £56,000 + production overheads £16,000 + admin expenses £42,000 + selling overheads £34,000).

(c) £311,000 (£163,000 + £148,000).

QUESTION 2

(a)

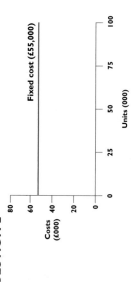

(b) (i) £55,000; (ii) £55,000.

(c) Fixed costs might rise because the business will be at full capacity. More fixed costs, eg new machines or extra workers, would have to be incurred to raise output.

QUESTION 3

(a) Glass, wood, glue, screws and packaging.

(b)

Output (units)	Fixed cost £	Variable cost £	Total cost £
0	5,000	0	5,000
5	5,000	500	5,500
10	5,000	1,000	6,000
15	5,000	1,500	6,500
20	5,000	2,000	7,000
25	5,000	2,500	7,500
30	5,000	3,000	8,000
35	5,000	3,500	8,500
40	5,000	4,000	9,000

(c) £350 (£7,000/20).

(d) Fixed costs would rise by £400 at every level of output.

(e) Delivery vehicle running costs will be variable, insurance, MOT, road fund licence will be fixed.

QUESTION 4

(a) £188 (£20 + [240 × £0.2] + [240 × £0.3] + [240 × £0.2]).

(b) 70p.

UNIT ASSESSMENT QUESTION 1

(a) Fuel, oil, maintenance, tyres and brake pads.

(b) (i) £23,900 ([52 × £150] + £400 + £1,700 + £14,000); (ii) £26,000 (52 × 1000 × £0.5); (iii) £49,900 (£23,900 + £26,000).

(c) 50p.

(d) £54,600 (52 × 1,000 × £1.05), assuming no holidays.

(e) Fall by £2,000 (4 × 1,000 × £0.5).

UNIT ASSESSMENT QUESTION 2

(a) Direct costs are those that can be identified with either of the components, for example the metal used in manufacturing. Indirect costs are those that cannot be associated with a particular component, for example the rent.

(b) X12: £6,000 ([3 × £500] + [1,000 × £1.20] + [1,000 × £2.30] + [1,000 × £1.00]); C33: £6,800 ([3 × £600] + [1,000 × £1.50] + [1,000 × £2.00] + [1,000 × £1.50]).

(c) £14,900 (£6,000 + £6,800 + [3 × £500] + [3 × £150]).

(d) They are direct costs because each machine is associated with a particular component. They are fixed costs because they will not change according to the number of units produced.

QUESTION 1

(a) £15 (£24 - £9).

(b)

	£
Selling price (SP)	24
Less variable cost (VC)	9
Equals contribution per book	15
Multiplied by number of books	6,000
Equals total contribution	90,000
Less fixed cost	90,000
Equals profit	0

Break-even point = 6,000 (fixed cost of £90,000/contribution per unit of £15).

(c) £90,000 (£15 × 6,000).

(d) 4,000 books (TR = 24Q, TC = £60,000 + 9Q).

QUESTION 2

(a) (i) 400 sets, (ii) £5,000, (iii) £10,000, (iv) £15,000, (v) £30,000.

(b) (i) 200 sets, (ii) 33.3% ([200/600] × 100).

QUESTION 3

(a) TC = £600 + £2Q and TR = £3Q.

(b) 600 meals.

(c) (d) (e) Break-even is 600 meals so margin of safety is 600 to 1,000 meals, (ie 400 meals).

(f) £400.

UNIT ASSESSMENT QUESTION 1

(a)

	£
Selling price (SP)	5
Less variable cost (VC)	3
Equals contribution per unit	2
Multiplied by number of units	20,000
Equals total contribution	40,000
Less fixed cost	40,000
Equals profit	0

Break-even point = 20,000 (fixed cost of £40,000/contribution per unit of £2).

(b) (c) Margin of safety: 20,000 to 35,000 units, (ie 15,000 units).

(d) £30,000.

(e) 30,000 units.

UNIT ASSESSMENT QUESTION 2

(a) (i) 80 cases, (ii) £4,000.

(b) (i) £1,000 loss, (ii) £1,000 profit.

(c) (i) £50 (£8,000/160), (ii) £12.50 (£2,000/160), (iii) £25 (£4,000/160), (iv) £12.50 (£2,000/160), (v) 80 cases (160 - 80).

(d) (i) £25 (£50 - £25), (ii) £4,000 (£25 × 160).

(e) The memo should have the following layout and should have a sentence or two expanding each point made.

MEMO

To: Wine Shop manager
From: Owner

Date: 20 June
Subject: Break-even analysis

Advantages of using break-even analysis:
- has a visual impact and is easy to understand if a chart is used;
- shows the margin of safety and what happens to profit if sales levels change;
- allows different possibilities regarding price and costs to be explored.

Disadvantages of using break-even analysis:
- data might be uncertain or based on estimates;
- costs cannot always be divided into fixed and variable;
- cost and revenue relationships might not be linear;
- multi-product businesses are difficult to analyse because fixed costs are shared;
- some production might remain unsold.

UNIT 50

QUESTION 1

(a) Rent, rates and electricity will be more equitably apportioned using floor space. Administration will be more equitably apportioned using the number of staff. These are appropriate methods because they give a good indication of how the overheads are actually incurred. For example, rent is related to the floor area used. Administration (of wages, for example) is related to the number of employees.

(b)

	Food hall	Women's wear	Men's wear	Electrical	Toys	Total
	£	£	£	£	£	£
Rent and rates	80,000	40,000	20,000	40,000	20,000	200,000
Electricity	40,000	20,000	10,000	20,000	10,000	100,000
Administration	60,000	40,000	20,000	30,000	50,000	200,000
Total	180,000	100,000	50,000	90,000	80,000	500,000

QUESTION 2

(a) and (b)

	Planning	Moulding	Finishing	Stores	Maintenance	Total
	£	£	£	£	£	£
Overheads	200,000	500,000	100,000	50,000	150,000	1,000,000
Stores reapportioned	4,167	16,667	25,000	(50,000)	4,167	
Sub-total	204,167	525,000	116,667	-	154,167	1,000,000
Maintenance reapp.	30,833	77,083	46,250	-	(154,167)	
Total	235,000	602,083	162,917	-	-	1,000,000

Figures are rounded to the nearest pound.

(c) All overheads must be apportioned to production cost centres so that they can be charged to cost units.

QUESTION 3

(a) Cutting: £3.75 per machine hour; Welding: £9 per direct labour hour; Finishing: £5 per direct labour hour.

(b) £7,525, ie $100 \times ([3 \times 3.75] + [6 \times 9] + [2 \times 5])$.

(c) Because the cutting department is capital intensive.

UNIT ASSESSMENT QUESTION 1

(a)

	Artwork	Typesetting	Graphics	Printing	Distribution	Total
	£	£	£	£	£	£
Direct labour	280,000	224,000	322,000	350,000	224,000	1,400,000
Other direct costs	15,000	17,000	8,000	6,000	4,000	50,000
Overheads:						
Heat and light	10,000	10,000	10,000	20,000	30,000	80,000
Administration	104,000	83,200	119,600	130,000	83,200	520,000
Cleaning etc.	12,500	12,500	12,500	25,000	37,500	100,000
Depreciation	60,000	120,000	40,000	30,000	50,000	300,000
Total	481,500	466,700	512,100	561,000	428,700	2,450,000

Bases for apportionment: Heat and light: floor area; Administration: direct labour costs; Cleaning and maintenance: floor area; Depreciation: book value of assets.
Figures are rounded to the nearest pound.

(b) Because full or total costs include both direct and indirect costs.

UNIT ASSESSMENT QUESTION 2

(a)

	Cell 1	Cell 2	Cell 3	Canteen	Total
	£	£	£	£	£
Apportioned overheads	600,000	300,000	250,000	50,000	1,200,000
Canteen overheads reapportioned	31,250	12,500	6,250	(50,000)	-
Total	631,250	312,500	256,250		1,200,000

Basis for reapportionment: number of employees.

(b)

Cell 1: $\text{OAR} = \dfrac{£631,250}{200,000} = £3.16$ per direct labour hour.

Cell 2: $\text{OAR} = \dfrac{£312,500}{200,000} = £1.56$ per direct labour hour.

Cell 3: $\text{OAR} = \dfrac{£256,250}{100,000} = £2.56$ per machine hour.

(c) For a single cost unit in Cell 1:

	Arctic		Moorlander		Trekker	
	£	£	£	£	£	£
Selling price		60.00		40.00		30.00
Material cost (pair)	8.00		7.00		4.00	
Labour hours (pair)	21.00		14.00		10.50	
Machine hours (pair)	20.00		15.00		12.50	
Total variable cost		49.00		36.00		27.00
(a) Contribution per pair		11.00		4.00		3.00
Number of machine hours per pair		4		3		2.5
(b) Contribution per machine hour		£2.75		£1.33		£1.20
Ranked order		1st		2nd		3rd
Monthly demand		5,000		10,000		20,000
Hours available	55,000					
Hours needed to meet demand		20,000		30,000		50,000
Hours allocated		20,000		30,000		5,000
(c) Production		5,000		10,000		2,000
Contribution per pair		£11		£4		£3
Contribution		£55,000		£40,000		£6,000
Total contribution £101,000						
Less fixed cost £36,000						
(d) Profit £65,000						

UNIT ASSESSMENT QUESTION 1

(a)

Products	Oval		Majestic		Fen	
	£	£	£	£	£	£
Price		8,000		6,000		12,000
Materials	2,500		2,000		3,000	
Direct labour	3,000		2,500		5,000	
Variable overheads	1,000		1,000		1,500	
Total variable cost		6,500		5,500		9,500
Contribution		1,500		500		2,500

(b) Withdraw the Majestic because it makes the smallest contribution.

(c) £600 (£300 + £200 + £100) because this covers variable costs.

(d) Yes, as long as fixed overheads were paid for by conservatory production. Any price above £600 would make a positive contribution. The greenhouse production might be worthwhile if it keeps employees busy during otherwise quiet periods.

Total cost = Direct labour + materials + overheads
= (10 × £10) + £25 + (10 × £3.16)
= £100 + £25 + £31.60
= £156.60

So, total cost of order = 1,000 × £156.60 = £156,600.

(d) For a single cost unit in Cell 3:

Total cost = (5 × £10) + £45 + (5 × £2.56)
= £107.80

So, total cost of order = 2,000 × £107.80 = £215,600.

UNIT 51

QUESTION 1

(a) £135 (£80 + £20 + £25 + £10).

(b) £2,500 (£160 × 100) - (£135 × 100).

(c) They would remain the same as long as the company has spare capacity.

QUESTION 2

(a)

	£
Selling price (SP)	85
Less variable cost (VC)	55
Equals contribution per unit	30
Multiplied by number of units	11,000
Equals total contribution	330,000
Less fixed cost	120,000
Equals profit/(loss)	210,000

(b) £5,000 (contribution per unit [£65 - £55] × number of units [500]).

(c) Yes because the contribution is positive.

(d) The amount of spare capacity in January, the response from established customers, the likelihood of more orders from the new customer.

QUESTION 3

(a) £550.

(b) Continue to buy-in. Buying-in cost is £510 (3,000 × £0.17).

(c) Better quality control. Less vulnerable to disruption in supply.

QUESTION 4

(a) (b) (c) and (d)

UNIT ASSESSMENT QUESTION 2

(a)

Boxit Ltd
Profit Statement for 2000 and 2001

	2000		2001	
	£(000s)	£(000s)	£(000s)	£(000s)
Sales (£3 × number of units sold)		300		390
Opening stock	-		40	
Add variable production cost (£2 × 120,000)	240		240	
Less closing stock (£2 × number of items)	40		20	
Cost of sales	200		260	
Contribution (sales - cost of sales)		100		130
Less manufacturing fixed costs		60		60
Gross profit		40		70
Less other fixed costs		30		30
Net profit		10		40

(b)

Boxit Ltd
Profit Statement for 2000 and 2001

	2000	2001
	£(000s)	£(000s)
Sales (£3 × number of units sold)	300	390
Opening stock	-	50
Add production cost (VC + manufacturing FC)	300	300
Less closing stock (£2.50 × number of units)	50	25
Cost of sales	250	325
Gross profit	50	65
Less other fixed costs	30	30
Net profit	20	35

(c) In 2000, absorption costing gives the higher net profit (because stocks increase). In 2001, marginal costing gives the higher net profit (because stocks decrease).

UNIT 52

QUESTION 1

(a)

	£	£
Direct materials		
Timber	2,400	
Glass	500	
Other materials	100	
		3,000
Direct labour		
80 hours × £10		800
Overheads		
80 hours × £5		400
Total		4,200
Profit 30% × £4,200		1,260
Price		£5,460

(b) It helps to determine prices, to provide information for a work-in-progress valuation, to give fast quotes for similar future jobs and to help in cost control.

QUESTION 2

(a)

		£	£
Direct materials	70 × £4.50		315
Direct labour			
Cutting	70 × 1/2 × £10	350	
Sewing	70 × 1/4 × £12	210	
Finishing	70 × 1/2 × £6	210	
			770
Direct costs			1,085
Overheads	70 × £2		140
Total cost			**1,225**
Profit	40% × £1,225		490
Total			1,715

(d) £24.50 (£1,715/70).

QUESTION 3

(a) Shepherds Bush: 89.7%; Paddington: 14.3%; Brentford: 53.3%.

(b)

Shepherds Bush: Attributable profit $= \dfrac{£250,000}{£500,000} \times (£500,000 - [£350,000 + £40,000])$

$= £55,000$ less profit already attributed $(£18,000) = £37,000$

Paddington: nil.

Brentford: Attributable profit $= \frac{2}{3} \times (£340,000 - £280,000) \times \frac{£170,000}{£340,000} = £20,000 - £10,000 = £10,000.$

(c) The concept of prudence states that profits should not be recognised until it is reasonably certain that the contract is partly or nearly finished.

QUESTION 4

(a) £65,200.

(b) £20,880 $(= \frac{2}{3} \times [£100,000 - £65,200] \times \frac{£90,000}{£100,000}).$

(c) £13,920 $(= £100,000 - (£65,200 + £20,880)).$

(d)

Dr		Contract Account		Cr
	£			£
Materials b/d	1,100	Profit not taken b/d		13,920
Plant on site b/d	24,000			
Cost of work not certified b/d	32,000			

UNIT ASSESSMENT QUESTION 1

(a)

JOB COST SHEET: dinner for 250

	£	£
Direct materials		
Meat and fish	900	
Fruit and vegetables	450	
Dairy produce	300	
Other foodstuffs	100	
Miscellaneous items	250	
		2,000
Direct labour		
50 hours × £6		300
Other direct costs		
Crockery and cutlery hire		300
Overheads		
50% × £2,000		1,000
Total cost		3,600
Profit		
40% × 3,600		1,440
Price to be quoted		**5,040**

(b)
£20.16

UNIT ASSESSMENT QUESTION 2

(a) (b) and (c)

Dr		Contract Account		Cr
	£			£
Materials delivered to site	60,000	Materials transferred off site		12,700
Site wages	150,000	Materials on site at 31.12.01 c/d		5,900
Sub contracting payments	21,000	Value of plant at 31.12.01 c/d		8,000
Architects fees	4,000	Cost of work not certified c/d		50,000
Other direct expenses	21,600	Cost of work certified		
Overheads apportioned	20,000	(ie cost of sales) c/d		220,000
Plant sent to site	20,000			
	296,600			296,600
Cost of work certified b/d	220,000	Architect's certificate for work certified		250,000
Profit and loss (attributable profit)	18,000			
Profit not attributed c/d	12,000			
	250,000			250,000
Materials b/d	5,900	Profit not attributed b/d		12,000
Plant on site b/d	8,000			
Cost of work not certified b/d	50,000			

Attributable profit $= \frac{2}{3} \times (£250,000 - £220,000) \times \frac{£225,000}{£250,000} = £18,000$

UNIT 53

QUESTION 1

(a) £270,000 (basic pay £245,700 + overtime £24,300).

(b) Advantage: simple to administer. Disadvantage: no incentive for employees to increase productivity.

(c) Advantages: total wage bill of production staff falls from £270,000 to £263,900, and increased flexibility of workforce means that employees will be available to work extra hours at busy periods. Disadvantages: the basic hourly rate is increased, so if there are no busy periods, total wages might be higher than otherwise.

(d) Advantages: higher basic rate, higher guaranteed income and early finishes in the summer. Disadvantages: lose freedom to choose whether to work overtime, longer hours of work in busy periods.

QUESTION 2

(a) B. Roberts £1,255 L. Singh £1,295 B. Comyn £1,280 T. Southgate £1,140.

(b) Most of the earnings are linked to revenue and therefore costs are only incurred if revenue is generated. Earnings are related to performance and this might serve to motivate staff.

(c) The newspaper is likely to have a circulation that is relatively stable from day to day. Therefore it would be a waste of money for the company to give incentives to production workers to print more newspapers than necessary. Also, the company might not wish the workers to rush the job because the print quality of the newspaper is more important than the quantity produced.

QUESTION 3

(a) To calculate the fee charged to each client.

(b) £16,600 (annual fees £33,600 - salary £17,000).

(c) To check that the timesheet of the trainee is completed accurately. This might help to avoid overcharging or undercharging clients if errors were made.

UNIT ASSESSMENT QUESTION I

(a) (i) £13,260 (basic wage £11,760 [60 × 35 × £5.60] + bonus £1,500 [£25 × 60]).

(b) £12,912 (basic wage £11,760 [60 × 35 × £5.60] + overtime £1,152 [£9.60 × 120]).

(c) The overtime scheme raises direct labour costs less than the bonus scheme. But, if overtime was worked, the factory would be open longer and this would raise indirect costs such as administration overheads. The overtime scheme gives employees no incentive to raise output and they might even slow production in order to earn more overtime.

(d) The bonus scheme gives the possibility of earning higher wages yet working no extra hours. However, individual workers would be reliant on their colleagues and others in the company in meeting the extra production. An inefficient or unwilling worker, or a breakdown in component supplies could cost everyone their bonus. The overtime scheme is not dependent on raising output during the 'normal' working day so might be less stressful. However, to earn the extra money, longer hours must be worked.

UNIT ASSESSMENT QUESTION 2

(a) (i) £120, (ii) £168, (iii) 216.

(b) £4.20.

(c) Advantage: improves staff morale and retention. Disadvantage: removes incentive to maintain production levels.

(d) Introduce a bonus or incentive scheme that rewards employees who reach a set production target.

(e) Advantages: guaranteed earnings even during production breakdowns, also less pressure to produce items quickly. Disadvantages: lower earnings for the most productive staff, also unfair if there is a big gap between the most and least efficient.

UNIT 54

QUESTION I

(a) The sales budget shows the monthly and annual total planned sales revenue for the company, split between the four models. Sales of Kingham I are expected to fall from £100,000 in January to zero by November whereas sales of Kingham 2 are expected to rise from £40,000 per month in January to £140,000 in December. Sales of the Deluxe model are expected to be steady at £50,000 per month. Sales of the Family model are expected to rise slightly from £65,000 in January to £80,000 in December. Overall, monthly sales revenue is expected to rise from £255,000 in January to £270,000 in December, giving an annual total of £3,090,000.

(b) It helps in the planning and coordination of all other activities. For example, it shows how much must be produced and held in stock. Following on from this, it shows how many resources must be purchased. The debtors and creditors budgets can also be prepared, so enabling cash flows to be planned.

(c) It might act as a motivation for the sales force and it helps communication between departments.

QUESTION 2

(a) Expected sales figures (from historic data, from sales force predictions, from market research) and the selling price of each product (internally from within the company).

(b)

	Jan	Feb	Mar	Apr	May	Jun	Jul	Aug	Sep	Oct	Nov	Dec	Total
	£000	£000	£000	£000	£000	£000	£000	£000	£000	£000	£000	£000	£000
Traditional	270	270	270	270	270	270	270	270	270	270	270	270	3,240
Modern	180	180	180	180	180	180	180	180	216	216	216	216	2,304
Stacking	180	180	180	180	135	135	135	135	90	90	90	90	1,620
Total	630	630	630	630	585	585	585	585	576	576	576	576	7,164

	Traditional	Modern	Stacking
2001 sales	£3,600,000	£2,560,000	£1,620,000
2002 sales	£3,240,000	£2,304,000	£1,620,000
Change	-£360,000	-£256,000	£0

(c) Fall of £616,000 (£360,000 + £256,000).

QUESTION 3

(a)

	Jan	Feb	Mar	Apr	May	Jun	Jul	Aug	Sep	Oct	Nov	Dec	Total
	£000	£000	£000	£000	£000	£000	£000	£000	£000	£000	£000	£000	£000
Opening bal.	11	12	12	13	13	14	15	16	16	15	15	14	
Sales	12	12	13	14	14	15	16	15	14	15	14	14	170
Less receipts	11	12	12	13	13	14	15	16	15	15	15	14	167
Closing bal.	12	12	13	14	14	15	16	16	15	15	14	14	

(b) The debtors budget is dependent on the sales budget because planned credit sales must be known before it is possible to work out how much will be owed by customers.

(c) Because customers are given one month's credit, receipts are, in this case, less than sales.

UNIT ASSESSMENT QUESTION I

(a)

	Q1	Q2	Q3	Q4	Total
	£000	£000	£000	£000	£000
Sales revenue	20	24	24	24	92

(b)

	Q1 units (000)	Q2 units (000)	Q3 units (000)	Q4 units (000)	Total units (000)
Opening stock	2	2	2	2	
Production	40	40	40	40	160
	42	42	42	42	
Less sales	40	40	40	40	160
Closing stock	2	2	2	2	

(c)

	Q1 £000	Q2 £000	Q3 £000	Q4 £000	Total £000
Purchases	8	10	10	10	38

(d) (i) The proportion of customers who buy on credit and the amount of credit they receive.
(ii) The proportion of purchases made on credit and the period of credit given by suppliers.

UNIT ASSESSMENT QUESTION 2

(a)

	Jul £	Aug £	Sep £	Oct £	Nov £	Dec £
Opening bal.	400	200	300	400	500	500
Credit sales	200	300	400	500	500	500
	600	500	700	900	1,000	1,000
Less receipts	400	200	300	400	500	500
Closing bal.	200	300	400	500	500	500

(b)

	Jul £	Aug £	Sep £	Oct £	Nov £	Dec £
Opening bal.	3,500	5,500	3,000	2,500	3,000	3,000
Purchases	2,000	1,000	1,500	1,500	1,500	1,500
	5,500	6,500	4,500	4,000	4,500	4,500
Less payment	0	3,500	2,000	1,000	1,500	1,500
Closing bal.	5,500	3,000	2,500	3,000	3,000	3,000

(c) To help with planning, budgetary control and also monitoring the performance of the business.

QUESTION 1

(a)

	Jan £	Feb £	Mar £	Apr £	May £	Jun £
Net cash inflow/(outflow)	(51,000)	13,500	(42,500)	6,000	23,500	28,000
Opening balance	2,300	(48,700)	(35,200)	(77,700)	(71,700)	(48,200)
Closing balance	(48,700)	(35,200)	(77,700)	(71,700)	(48,200)	(20,200)

(b)

● For four months out of the six, the company had a positive cash flow, but this is not sufficient to bring about a positive cash balance in any month.

● Two negative cash flows are due to the acquisition of an asset (the bulldozer), in January, and the payment of tax in March.

● The bank loan of £20,000 in January might not be sufficient in the short-term to finance the new bulldozer.

● If the problem seems to be short-term, a bank overdraft might be a sensible option. This assumes that the trend of rising cash inflows at the end of the period continues.

● It might also be possible to 'chase' debtors and slow down payments to creditors.

● If the problem seems to be long-term, new capital might have to be raised.

● Alternatively, it might be advisable to consider closing down all or part of the business.

(c) From functional budgets such as the sales budget, purchases budget and overheads budget.

QUESTION 2

(a)

Ivanovic Timber
Budgeted Profit and Loss Account
for the 3 months ending 31.3.01

	£	£
Sales		87,800
Cost of sales		
Opening stock	38,000	
Add purchases	43,000	
	81,000	
Less closing stock	43,500	
		37,500
Gross profit		50,300
Less expenses		
Wages	12,200	
Motor expenses	3,800	
General expenses	8,500	
Depreciation	2,100	
		26,600
Net profit		23,700

Note: depreciation is calculated by adding the value of fixed assets £84,000 (£50,000 premises + £20,000 machinery + £10,000 lorry + £4,000 saw), then multiplying by 10% for the annual depreciation (£8,400) and multiplying by 3/12 to give the depreciation for 3 months.

(b) (i) Electric saw and drawings. (ii) Electric saw is capital expenditure and drawings is not a business expense.

(c) No, the closing cash balance in March is only £9,600.

QUESTION 3

Ivanovic Timber
Budgeted Balance Sheet as at 31.3.01

	£	£
Fixed assets		
Premises at cost	50,000	
Less depreciation	26,250	
Net book value		23,750
Machinery at cost	24,000	
Less depreciation	10,600	
Net book value		13,400
Lorry at cost	10,000	
Less depreciation	5,250	
Net book value		4,750
		41,900
Current assets		
Stock	43,500	
Debtors	32,000	
Bank	9,600	
	85,100	
Less current liabilities		
Trade creditors	16,000	
Net current assets		69,100
Net assets		111,000
Capital and reserves		
Opening capital		93,300
Add net profit		23,700
		117,000
Less drawings		6,000
		111,000

(b) A budgeted balance sheet shows the financial plans of a business and is produced from forecasts. A balance sheet that is published in the final accounts contains actual figures from a particular date in the past.

UNIT ASSESSMENT QUESTION 1

(a)

Juice
Cash Budget for the four months ending 31.3

	Dec £	Jan £	Feb £	Mar £
Receipts				
Sales	50,000	35,000	30,000	30,000
Capital	100,000			
Bank loan	50,000			
Total cash receipts	200,000	35,000	30,000	30,000
Payments				
Purchases	0	45,000	15,000	10,000
Wages	8,000	7,000	5,000	6,000
Leasing	4,000	4,000	4,000	4,000
Advertising	2,000	1,000	1,000	1,000
Loan interest	500	500	500	500
Loan repayments	1,000	1,000	1,000	1,000
Other expenses	2,500	2,500	2,500	2,500
Drawings	1,000	1,000	1,000	1,000
Warehouse	120,000			
Total cash payments	139,000	62,000	30,000	26,000
Net cash inflow/(outflow)	61,000	(27,000)	0	4,000
Opening balance	0	61,000	34,000	34,000
Closing balance	61,000	34,000	34,000	38,000

(b)

Juice
Budgeted Profit and Loss Account for the 4 months ending 31.3

	£	£
Sales		145,000
Cost of sales		
Opening stock	0	
Add purchases	85,000	
	85,000	
Less closing stock	19,000	
		66,000
Gross profit		79,000
Less expenses		
Wages	26,000	
Leasing	16,000	
Interest	2,000	
Advertising	5,000	
Other expenses	10,000	
Depreciation	2,000	
		61,000
Net profit		18,000

(see next page)

1 (a) continued

Note: annual depreciation of premises is £120,000/20 (years) = £6,000. So, for 4 months it is £6,000/3 = £2,000.

(c)

Juice
Budgeted Balance Sheet as at 31.3

	£	£	£
Fixed assets			
Premises at cost		120,000	
Less depreciation		2,000	
Net book value			118,000
Current assets			
Stock	19,000		
Cash	38,000		
		57,000	
Less current liabilities			
Trade creditors		15,000	
Net current assets			42,000
Less long term liabilities			
Bank loan			46,000
Net assets			114,000
Capital and reserves			
Opening capital			100,000
Add net profit			18,000
			118,000
Less drawings			4,000
			114,000

Note: original bank loan of £50,000 is reduced by 4 monthly repayments of £1,000.

(d) (i) Closing cash balance would be (minus) £2,000; (ii) net profit would be (minus) £22,000; (iii) closing capital would be £74,000.

UNIT ASSESSMENT QUESTION 2

(a)

Price plc
Cash Budget for the three months ending 30.6.02

	Apr £000	May £000	Jun £000
Receipts			
Cash sales	152	171	190
Credit sales	150	160	180
Total sales	302	331	370
Payments			
Cash purchases	162	180	162
Credit purchases	160	180	200
Expenses	24	24	24
Total payments	346	384	386
Net cash inflow/(outflow)	(44)	(53)	(16)
Opening balance	50	6	(47)
Closing balance	6	(47)	(63)

(b) There is a negative cash flow for all 3 months, however there is an improvement in June (-£16,000) compared with May (-£53,000). The negative cash flow causes the cash balance to worsen from a positive opening balance of £50,000 in April to a negative closing balance of -£63,000 in June.

(c) It would be useful to know the cash budget for the full year. In particular, whether there is a sufficient positive cash flow in the 3 months leading up to Christmas to cover the negative cash flow in April - June. It would also be useful to know of any plans for expenditure on fixed assets during the year.

UNIT 56

QUESTION 1

(a) Standard cost = £59.20 (direct materials £27.20 + direct labour £20.00 + variable overhead cost £2.00 [£10,000/5,000] + fixed overhead cost £10.00 [2 hours × direct labour overhead absorption rate £5.00]).

(b) £25 ([2 × 10] × 100/[100 - 20]).

(c) The likely idle time and wasted materials. The effect on the motivation of the workforce and the desire to set targets that are challenging yet attainable.

QUESTION 2

(a) (i) Materials price variance = £3,720 (A) (£0.30 × 12,400); (ii) Materials usage variance = £7,220 (A) (1,900 × £3.80); (iii) Materials variance = £10,940 (A) (£39,900 - £50,840).

(b) Cost of sales will be higher so profit will be lower unless other costs can be reduced or sales revenue increased.

(c) Poor quality raw materials, eg some cream might be 'off', faulty machinery causing materials to be wasted, unskilled or inexperienced staff causing mistakes in production.

QUESTION 3

(a) Labour variance = £10,800 (F) ([£360,000 - £347,200] + [£50,000 - £52,000]). This would reduce costs and therefore raise profit for Musgrove & Co.

(b) (i) Wage rate variance (skilled) = 0; wage rate variance (semi-skilled) = £11,200 (A) (£0.20 × 56,000); (ii) labour efficiency variance (skilled) = £2,000 (A) (200 × £10); labour efficiency variance (semi-skilled) = £24,000 (F) (4,000 × £6).

(c) Improved labour productivity, new working practices, better equipment or training.

QUESTION 4

(a) (i) Sales price variance = £450,000 (A) (£5 × 90,000); (ii) sales volume variance = £95,000 (A) (10,000 × £9.50); (iii) sales variance = £545,000 (A) (£405,000 - £950,000).

(b) Despite price cutting, sales were lower than expected. This might be due to intense competition by a rival, or a misjudgment of consumer tastes.

(c) Analyse the causes, perhaps by market research. Withdraw the product or relaunch in a different way.

UNIT ASSESSMENT QUESTION I

(a)

	North	Central	South
(i) Price variance	£0.9m (A) (£10 × 90,000)	£1.2m (A) (£12 × 100,000)	0
(ii) Volume variance	£1m (F) (10,000 × £100)	£2m (F) (20,000 × £100)	£0.24m (A) (2,000 × £120)
(iii) Sales variance	£0.1m (F) (£8.1m - £8m)	£0.8m (F) (£8.8m - £8m)	£0.24m (A) (£9.36m - £9.6m)
(b) Sales bonus	£50,000	£0.4m	0

(c) The Patio Co will benefit because the standard costing system is designed to motivate staff. They will strive to sell more because they receive bonuses based on favourable variances.

(d) Profit will increase by £0.66m assuming that costs remain unchanged.

UNIT ASSESSMENT QUESTION 2

(a) Grapes usage = 475 tonnes (500 tonnes × 9,500/10,000); bottles usage = 114,000 units (120,000 units × 9,500/10,000); labour hours worked = 6,650 hrs (7,000 hrs × 9,500/10,000).

(b) Sales revenue = £285,000 (500 tonnes × £30 × 9,500); (ii) grapes cost = £95,000 (£200 × 475); bottles cost = £7,980 (£0.07 × 114,000); (iii) labour = £39,900 (£6 × 6,650); overheads = £74,000 (fixed).

(c)

	Flexed budget	Actual	Variance
	£	£	£
Sales	285,000	304,000	19,000 (F)
Costs			
Grapes	95,000	93,600	1,400 (F)
Bottles	7,980	7,980	0
Labour	39,900	43,200	3,300 (A)
Overheads	74,000	83,300	9,300 (A)
Total costs	216,880	228,080	11,200 (A)
Profit	**68,120**	**75,920**	**7,800 (F)**

(d) The profit variance is £7,800 (F) (£75,920 - £68,120). Although there was a rise in overheads and a fall in labour efficiency, these were outweighed by a fall in the price paid for grapes and a rise in the sales price.

UNIT 57

QUESTION I

(a) Mouldmaster: 3 years 4 months ; Fleximould: 3 years 8 months; Supermould: 2 years.

(b) Supermould because it has the shortest payback period.

(c) The cash earned after the payback period is not taken into account in the investment decision. (In the long run, Mouldmaster gives the biggest net cash inflow.) The profitability of investment projects is ignored. This is because the speed of repayment is the only criteria used for selection.

QUESTION 2

(a)

	Burrel			Crawford		
	Cost/net cash flow	Discount factor 5%	Present value	Cost/net cash flow	Discount factor 5%	Present value
	£		£	£		£
Initial cost	(110,000)		(110,000)	(140,000)		(140,000)
Year 1	35,000	0.952	33,320	40,000	0.952	38,080
Year 2	35,000	0.907	31,745	40,000	0.907	36,280
Year 3	35,000	0.864	30,240	40,000	0.864	34,560
Year 4	30,000	0.823	24,690	40,000	0.823	32,920
Year 5	25,000	0.784	19,600	40,000	0.784	31,360
Total present value			139,595			173,200
NPV			**29,595**			**33,200**

(b) The Crawford machine has the highest NPV.

(c) Interest rates might change in future years. The different initial costs are not taken into account and the Burrel has a shorter payback period.

QUESTION 3

(a) Model 1: 12% (([£6,000/£50,000] × 100); model 2: 9.23% (([£6,000/£65,000] × 100).

(b) Model I because it earns a higher rate of profit over its lifetime.

(c) ARR does not show the timing of profits and, in this case, model 2 earns higher profits in its early years. Profitability is not the same as cash flow and might be distorted by the calculation of non-cash provisions such as depreciation.

QUESTION 4

(a) The payback period is the time it will take for net revenues to match the initial investment. In the very long term, the risks associated with an investment rises. For example, tastes might change, the FA might decide to use other venues, running costs might rise and traffic congestion might become so severe that public access is restricted.

(b) Factors include the initial cost of the project, which seems difficult to calculate, the interest rates over the period and the opportunity cost of the money, the operating costs and the likely revenues.

(c) Non-financial factors include the possible public reaction - particularly outside London, long term confidence in football and public support for visiting 'live' games, possible alternative uses for the venue - perhaps for other sports. The sunk costs already spent should not be a factor.

UNIT ASSESSMENT QUESTION 1

(a)

	New lorry			Acquisition		
	Cost/ net cash flow	Discount factor	Present value	Cost/ net cash flow	Discount factor	Present value
	£	5%	£	£	5%	£
Initial cost	(60,000)		(60,000)	(40,000)		(40,000)
Year 1	10,000	0.952	9,520	5,000	0.952	4,760
Year 2	13,000	0.907	11,791	10,000	0.907	9,070
Year 3	15,000	0.864	12,960	15,000	0.864	12,960
Year 4	15,000	0.823	12,345	20,000	0.823	16,460
Year 5	14,000	0.784	10,976	20,000	0.784	15,680
Year 6	14,000	0.746	10,444	20,000	0.746	14,920
Total present value			68,036			73,850
NPV			**8,036**			**33,850**

(b) New lorry: 4 yrs 6 months; acquisition: 3 yrs 6 months.

(c) Corbridge should acquire Prudhoe Transport because there is both a higher NPV and a shorter payback period.

(d) NPV will be higher because the present value of the income will be higher.

UNIT ASSESSMENT QUESTION 2

(a) Fitness suite: 10% (([£3,000/£30,000] × 100); golf course: 12.5% (([£5,000/£40,000] × 100).

(b) Financial considerations include the initial cost, the expected profitability, the timing of the receipts and the opportunity cost. Non-financial considerations include likely trends in consumer demand, corporate objectives in terms of which part of the business wish to develop and possible impact on the club's workforce.

(c) If the club has difficulty in raising the finance and it is important to repay the investment quickly, the payback method is more appropriate.

Index
· · · · ·